DREAMWORLDS OF RACE

Dreamworlds of Race

EMPIRE AND THE UTOPIAN DESTINY OF ANGLO-AMERICA

DUNCAN BELL

PRINCETON UNIVERSITY PRESS

PRINCETON & OXFORD

Published by Princeton University Press
41 William Street, Princeton, New Jersey 08540
6 Oxford Street, Woodstock, Oxfordshire OX20 1TR

press.princeton.edu

All Rights Reserved

Library of Congress Control Number: 2020943856
ISBN 9780691194011
ISBN (e-book) 9780691208671

British Library Cataloging-in-Publication Data is available

Editorial: Ben Tate and Josh Drake
Production Editorial: Nathan Carr
Jacket/Cover Credit: Fred T. Jane, from George Griffith's *The Angel of Revolution* (1893). Courtesy of the British Library.
Production: Danielle Amatucci
Publicity: Alyssa Sanford and Katie Lewis
Copyeditor: Hank Southgate

This book has been composed in Arno

Printed on acid-free paper. ∞

Printed in the United States of America

10　9　8　7　6　5　4　3　2　1

For Sarah

One dream of the earliest poets has never quite faded from the minds of men. Foretold by prophet and seer; vaguely described in popular myth; lying far back in some ideal past, or yet to be realized in the distant future by the triumph of religion or the gift of the higher powers, somewhere past or to come is a golden age, a wide community of men in all that is highest and best, free from the common ills of life, under the protection of some beneficent owner,—a world state, may we say, whose "officers shall be peace, and her exactors righteousness." This is a dream that has visited the poet in his moment of inspiration, or the common man under the stimulus of contrasted evils, or prophet and priest through the sight of faith; but can we venture to say of our own age that, first of all generations, it has begun to look forward, at least in some half-conscious way, to such a conclusion of time no longer as a dream of the imagination merely, but as the vision of a possibility, from the standing-ground of facts and sustained with reasons? The unity of mankind, the smallness of the earth, the swiftness of communication, and the growth of world-wide interests,—these things are certainly making familiar to our thoughts the fact that the necessary conditions of this result already exist.

GEORGE BURTON ADAMS,
"A CENTURY OF ANGLO-SAXON EXPANSION" (1897)

The contents of our dreams, imaginings, hopes, fantasies, and inventions should not be mistaken for elements of our waking world. Nevertheless in another sense dreams, desirous projections, utopian hopes are a part of our reality. That we have the ones we have is a fact about us. They do not come from nowhere.

RAYMOND GUESS, *REALITY AND ITS DREAMS* (2016)

CONTENTS

ACKNOWLEDGMENTS

I AM INDEBTED to the many people who have helped me with this book, in ways both large and small, over the last few years. David Armitage, Sarah Fine, Joel Isaac, Duncan Kelly, Jeanne Morefield, Srdjan Vucetic, Peter Mandler, Andrew Preston, Or Rosenboim, and Casper Sylvest have been incisive interlocutors during my time working on the ever-elusive Angloworld. This book has benefited enormously from my ongoing discussions with them. The following people helped in a variety of ways, whether reading draft material, offering excellent advice, or providing valuable information: Tarak Barkawi, Jens Bartelson, Alison Bashford, Ori Beck, Jamie Belich, Marina Bilbija, Jessica Blatt, Alex Bremner, Chris Brooke, Stewart Brown, Jude Browne, Robert Burroughs, Peter Cain, Martin Ceadel, Greg Claeys, Sarah Cole, Tommy Curry, Hannah Dawson, Daniel Deudney, Sean Fleming, Michael Freeden, Katrina Forrester, Andrew Gamble, Gary Gerstle, Adom Getachew, Nicholas Guyatt, Ian Hall, Ian Hesketh, Ian Hunter, Andrew Hurrell, Simon James, Charles Jones, Stuart Jones, Ira Katznelson, Zaheer Kazmi, Mike Kenny, Krishan Kumar, Alexander Livingston, Emma Mackinnon, Karuna Mantena, Mark Mazower, Dilip Menon, Charles Mills, Sam Moyn, Jess Nevins, Marc-William Palen, Patrick Parrinder, Susan Pedersen, Clare Pettit, Jennifer Pitts, Adam Roberts, Simon Schaffer, Malcolm Schofield, Jim Secord, David Sedley, Robbie Shilliam, Brendan Simms, Quentin Skinner, Philip Steer, Marc Stears, Gareth Stedman Jones, Anders Stephanson, John A. Thompson, Richard Tuck, James Tully, Mathias Thaler, Caroline Vout, Mark Walters, Stephen Wertheim, Bernardo Zacka, Ayse Zarakol, and Marcus Zunino. I am very grateful to all of them. Eliza Garnsey, David Kennerley, Marietta van der Tol, Hannah Woods, and Alexander Wong provided invaluable research assistance. Once again, it has been a pleasure to work with Princeton University Press. Ben Tate has been a generous and patient editor. The anonymous reviewers (including Reviewer 2!) provided extremely helpful comments. Hank Southgate was an exemplary copyeditor.

Several institutions helped to sustain my research for the book. Colleagues in the Department of Politics and International Studies (POLIS) at Cambridge have provided an extremely collegial environment to pursue research at the interface of political theory, intellectual history, and international relations. Christ's College, Cambridge, remains a beautiful and inspiring place to work. I am very grateful to the Leverhulme Trust for its vital financial support. Thanks also to Sebastian Conrad and Andreas Eckert for inviting me to spend a very stimulating period as a visiting fellow at the Research School for Global Intellectual History (Freie Universität Berlin and Humboldt-Universität zu Berlin). I am grateful to audiences at research seminars and conference (too numerous to list) where parts of this project have been presented over the last few years. The research would have been impossible without the expertise and generous assistance of librarians in Cambridge, Edinburgh, Keele, London, Manchester, Oxford, Urbana-Champaign, New York, and Washington.

Some of the material included in this book has been published elsewhere, in one form or another. Parts of chapter 3 can be found in the following articles: "Pragmatism and Prophecy: H. G. Wells and the Metaphysics of Socialism," *American Political Science Review*, 112/2 (2018); "Pragmatic Utopianism and Race: H. G. Wells as Social Scientist," *Modern Intellectual History*, 16/3 (2019); "Founding the World State: H. G. Wells on Empire and the English-Speaking Peoples," *International Studies Quarterly*, 62/4 (2018). Earlier (and much shorter) versions of chapters 5 and 6 were published as "Before the Democratic Peace: Racial Utopianism, Empire, and the Abolition of War," *European Journal of International Relations*, 20/3 (2014); "Beyond the Sovereign State: Isopolitan Citizenship, Race, and Anglo-American Union," *Political Studies*, 62/2 (2014). Thanks to the publishers and editors for permission to use this material.

This book is dedicated to Sarah Fine, with all my love.

DREAMWORLDS OF RACE

1

Introduction

DREAMWORLDS OF RACE

Axes of the Angloworld

The late nineteenth century was a time of social dreaming in Britain and the United States. Thousands of novels, songs, poems, and sermons flowed from printing presses, reshaping the sense of the possible. Speculative fiction proselytizing concrete programs for remaking the world jostled with political commentary articulating fantastical visions of the future. New conceptions of society, of cultural life, and of humanity itself proliferated.[1] Political imaginaries as well as literary genres were refashioned. The implications of emerging scientific knowledge and innovative technologies stood at the heart of this intellectual ferment.

The burst of utopianism at once reflected and helped to constitute debates over the future of global order. It found powerful expression in dreams of imperial and racial union. Encompassing the British settler empire and the United States, the Angloworld was a popular source and subject of utopian desire. Coalescing during the early nineteenth century, by the late Victorian age it formed a "politically divided but culturally and economically united intercontinental system."[2] The ambition to forge political unity animated various groups during the closing decades of the century. Imagining a vast

---

1. Michael Robertson, *The Last Utopians* (Princeton, 2018); Matthew Beaumont, *Utopia Ltd*, 2nd ed. (Edinburgh, 2009); Kenneth Roemer, "Paradise Transformed" in Gregory Claeys (ed.), *The Cambridge Companion to Utopian Literature* (Cambridge, 2010), 79–106; Gregory Claeys, "The Reshaping of the Utopian Genre in Britain, c.1870–1900" in Claeys (ed.), *Late Victorian Utopianism* (London, 2009), I, ix–xxx.

2. James Belich, *Replenishing the Earth* (Oxford, 2009), 9. Belich coined the term "Angloworld." Noting the Anglophone "propensity to gigantism" and "elephantiasis" (9, 14), he argues that the great "Anglo divergence"—the growing economic gap between the Angloworld and the

Angloworld political community, these efforts were driven by a fissile mix of anxiety and hope—anxiety that unless action was taken, and taken soon, the Angloworld would fragment, fatally undermining its transformative potential and condemning the British Empire to inevitable decline; hope, that the resulting combination would dominate and lead humanity. Though emanating principally from Britain, Angloworld advocacy was at once transatlantic and transcolonial in scope, drawing contributors from all the lands its proponents aimed to amalgamate. It assumed two principal forms. One focused on the consolidation of Britain and its remaining settler colonies in Canada, Australia, New Zealand, and (more ambivalently) southern Africa. Flowering in the 1880s, and echoing through the twentieth century and into the present, this debate unfolded under the sign of "imperial federation."[3] The other main axis focused on relations between Britain and the United States. This was the discourse of *Anglo-America*. These distinct but overlapping projects were often seen as compatible, although there was much disagreement over which should be prioritized and how they might be coordinated. They could also conflict. Some of the leading acolytes of Anglo-America recommended the dissolution of the British Empire, and showed little interest in the claims of the remaining settler colonies, while many imperial federalists regarded the United States as a threat to British primacy.

This book explores some of the most ambitious ideas about the unification of Anglo-America, concentrating on the years between 1880 and the First World War. During that tumultuous period, numerous members of the intellectual elite on both sides of the Atlantic—scholars, journalists, novelists, preachers, and politicians—encouraged closer cooperation, even political integration, between the two powers. Such arguments fused hard-headed geopolitical and economic reasoning with bombastic declarations about racial destiny, grounded in a fervent belief in the superiority of the "Anglo-Saxon race" or "English-speaking peoples." They were often framed in utopian terms: yoking together Britain and the United States would inaugurate an era of perpetual peace and global justice. Or so it was maintained. But while Anglo-American unionists concurred about the world-historical significance of the race, they diverged significantly over the constitutional form the emergent community should assume, the best political strategies to pursue, the value of

---

rest of the planet—was produced by a conjuncture of four revolutions, the French, American, Industrial, and Settler.

3. Duncan Bell, *The Idea of Greater Britain* (Princeton, 2007); Duncan Bell and Srdjan Vucetic, "Brexit, CANZUK, and the Legacy of Empire," *British Journal of Politics and International Relations*, 21/2 (2019), 367–82.

imperialism, and the ultimate ends of union. The object of competing claims and fantasies, the racial dreamworld was fractured, contested, and unstable.

Dreamworlds of Race can be read both as a stand-alone monograph and as the third volume of a loose trilogy dedicated to analyzing the metropolitan settler imaginary. In *The Idea of Greater Britain*, I dissected the discourse of imperial federation.[4] *Reordering the World* expanded my account of imperial ideology, stressing the intricate entanglement of liberal political thought and settler colonialism. *Dreamworlds of Race* turns to the other main axis of Anglo-world debate. Diplomatic and political historians have written extensively about the "rapprochement" between Britain and the United States, often divining in it the roots of the "special relationship" that did so much to shape twentieth-century geopolitics.[5] Cultural historians and literary scholars have probed the transatlantic intellectual worlds of the fin de siècle, mapping flows of people, images, and texts, as well as the lines of influence connecting writers and artists on either side of the ocean.[6] An impressive body of writing has tracked the wide circulation of ideas about domestic social and political reform.[7] Scholars of International Relations return incessantly to the era, attempting to explain the dynamics of "hegemonic transition," as one great power relinquished predominance to another without sparking war between them.[8] Work on the political thought of Anglo-America is rarer. Ideas of interimperial cooperation have drawn some attention, as has the ideology of Anglo-Saxonism and the recurrent use of British exemplars by American

---

4. On other aspects of the British settler empire, see Cecilia Morgan, *Building Better Britains?* (Toronto, 2016); Gary Magee and Andrew Thompson, *Empire and Globalisation* (Cambridge, 2010); Alan Lester and Fae Dussart, *Colonization and the Origins of Humanitarian Governance* (Cambridge, 2014).

5. Bradley Perkins, *The Great Rapprochement* (London, 1968); Iestyn Adams, *Brothers across the Ocean* (London, 2005); Kathleen Burk, *Old World, New World* (London, 2009), ch. 6.

6. Genevieve Abravanel, *Americanizing Britain* (Oxford, 2012); Christopher Mulvey, *Transatlantic Manners* (Cambridge, 1990); Paul Giles, *Atlantic Republic* (Oxford, 2009), chs. 3–6; Brook Miller, *America and the British Imaginary in Turn-of-the-Twentieth-Century Literature* (Basingstoke, 2010).

7. Leslie Butler, *Critical Americans* (Chapel Hill, 2009); Murney Gerlach, *British Liberalism and the United States* (Basingstoke, 2001); Daniel Rodgers, *Atlantic Crossings* (Cambridge, MA, 1998); James Kloppenberg, *Uncertain Victory* (Oxford, 1986); Marc Stears, *Progressives, Pluralists and the Problems of the State* (Oxford, 2002). For Australian-American circuits of influence, see Marilyn Lake, *Progressive New World* (Cambridge, MA, 2019).

8. Recent examples include Srdjan Vucetic, *The Anglosphere* (Stanford, 2011), ch. 2; Charles Kupchan, *How Enemies Become Friends* (Princeton, NJ, 2010), ch. 3; Kori Schake, *Safe Passage* (Cambridge, MA, 2017).

imperialists.[9] Yet the intellectual currents, concerns, and frameworks that un-derpinned and structured arguments for union remain poorly understood. My aim is not to provide a comprehensive account of the unification debate or pinpoint its impact on specific government policies or decisions. Rather I seek to analyze the boldest arguments about Anglo-America, the dreams that mo-tivated and shaped them, and the discourses in which they were embedded, with the intention of illuminating a pivotal moment in both the intellectual history of world order and the development of modern utopian thought. In particular, I want to suggest that they can be read productively as expressing a potent form of *racial utopianism.*

Four extraordinary individuals stand at the center of the book: Andrew Carnegie, Cecil J. Rhodes, W. T. Stead, and H. G. Wells. I focus on this quartet because they were the most high-profile and influential advocates of Anglo-American integration. Moreover, they constituted a loose network, bound to varying degrees by personal ties, professional connections, and a shared belief in racial destiny. One of the richest men in the world, Carnegie promoted the "reunion" of Britain and the United States tirelessly for over three decades, believing that the "English-speaking peoples," if combined politically, could serve as the engine of global industrial progress. Rhodes was the most promi-nent imperialist of the age, a man at once vilified as a megalomaniacal jingo and celebrated as a world-making colossus. Fulminating against the incompe-tence of the late eighteenth-century British statesmen who had driven the United States from the imperial embrace, he dreamt of a future Anglo-Saxon polity that adopted the American constitution as a model. Wells was renowned for both his speculative fiction and social prophecy. He predicted that Britain and the United States would fuse together during the twentieth century, creat-ing a "New Republic" that would dominate an unruly planet and lay the foun-dations of a universal world-state. The American political scientist and editor Albert Shaw anointed Stead "the man who above all others proclaimed the gospel of a world redeemed through the prevailing influence of the English-speaking race."[10] The most famous journalist in the British Empire, as well as a best-selling author in the United States, he believed that providence would deliver "one vast federated unity," an "English-speaking United States of the

9. Stuart Anderson, *Race and Rapprochement* (Rutherford, NJ, 1981); Paul Kramer, "Empires, Exceptions, and Anglo-Saxons," *Journal of American History*, 88/4 (2002), 1315–53; Patrick Kirk-wood, "'Lord Cromer's Shadow,'" *Journal of World History*, 27/1 (2016), 1–26; Stephen Tuffnell, "Anglo-American Inter-Imperialism," *Britain and the World*, 7/2 (2014), 174–95; Frank Schum-acher, "Lessons of Empire" in Ursula Lehmkuhl and Gustav Schmidt (eds.), *From Enmity to Friendship* (Augsburg, 2005), 71–98.

10. Albert Shaw, review of Frederic Whyte, *The Life of W. T. Stead, American Historical Review,* 32/1 (1926), 113.

World," to redeem humanity.[11] A friend and collaborator of both Rhodes and Carnegie, and a man who helped to launch Wells on his astonishing literary career, Stead utilized his editorial talents to spread the gospel of racial destiny through the media networks of the Angloworld. All four of them argued that Anglo-American union would inaugurate an era of perpetual peace. In the following chapters, they are joined by, and put into dialogue with, a large cast drawn from the intellectual and political elites on both sides of the Atlantic.

To capture the contours of the discourse, I mix fine-grained analysis of individual writers with more expansive discussions of themes and concepts. The former allows me to delve into the intellectual development and commitments of some of the key unionists, tracing the evolution of their thinking, its subtleties, confusions, targets, and sources. The latter allows me to locate unionist arguments in wider patterns of social and political thought, identifying the genealogy of some of the core ideas and the ways that the champions of Anglo-America intervened in and reshaped political debate. The first half of *Dreamworlds of Race* anatomizes the visions of Carnegie, Stead, Rhodes, and Wells. In chapter 2, I examine Carnegie's shifting ideas about union from the 1880s until the outbreak of war in 1914, reading them in the context of debates about war and peace, international law and empire, theology and race. Chapter 3 turns to Stead and Rhodes. I analyze the theological basis of Stead's account of the "English-speaking peoples," explore how he thought about the relationship between Anglo-America, imperial federation, and European union, and unpack his resolute belief that journalism was an ideal vehicle for proselyting racial union. I contend that Rhodes's ambiguous proposals for Anglo-America were developed in dialogue with Stead, who subsequently used his editorial platform to craft a public image of Rhodes as a fierce unionist. Chapter 4 offers a new interpretation of Wells's political thought, arguing that he should be read as a philosophical pragmatist. When combined with an abiding belief in the explanatory power of evolutionary theory, his philosophical commitments shaped his views about race, nation, and state, as well his conception of the "English-speaking peoples." At the turn of the century, Wells both predicted and embraced the future "synthetic" fusion of Britain and the United States, though he later argued that the United States was not yet ready to participate in such an ambitious state-building project.

The second half of the book analyzes some of the key themes that ran through Anglo-racial discourse. Chapter 5 argues that late Victorian science fiction was a pivotal site for the articulation of racial utopianism. Focusing on literary imaginings of future war, I discuss general trends in the popular

---

11. Stead has even been called (with some exaggeration) "the most important journalist of all time": Tristram Hunt, "Foreword," W. Sydney Robinson, *Muckraker* (London, 2012), xi.

transatlantic genre and read a variety of notable texts as paradigmatic expressions of the racial dreamworld. In Chapter 6, I track how ideas about citizenship and patriotism were recoded in debates over Anglo-America. Advocates of union often promoted a regime of "isopolitan" (or common) citizenship that would bind all the members of the Angloworld, and argued for the importance of "race patriotism," a fractal mode of political belonging that encompassed the totality of the "English race." I also discuss how unionists sought to build a globe-spanning racial community by crafting new historical narratives, symbols, and rituals. Chapter 7 turns to ideas about war and its supersession, delineating the assorted ways that empire and the Angloworld were presented as agents of global peace and order. As faith in the pacific character of democracy faded, it became increasingly common to suggest that Anglo-America could underwrite global stability, even perpetual peace. This was the dream of racial Pax. The conclusion examines two forms of writing that challenge the historical and conceptual assumptions of racial unionism. Staging a transhistorical encounter, I turn first to late twentieth-century neo-Victorian speculative fiction, investigating how the British-American relationship is recast in counterfactual historical narratives. I finish by discussing how fin-de-siècle Afro-modern thinkers, in particular the American sociologist and historian W. E. B. Du Bois and the Jamaican pan-Africanist T. E. S. Scholes, rebutted or reoriented claims about civilization, racial supremacy, and progressive historical development.

In the remainder of this introductory chapter, I sketch the (geo)political context in which the debates occurred, consider the self-consciously visionary character of many unionist claims as well as the conceptual elusiveness of racial categorization, and explore the centrality of communications technology in imagining the destiny of Anglo-America.

The Shape of Things to Come: Empire, War, Racial Union

I believe that the twentieth century is par excellence "The Anglo-Saxon Century," in which the English-speaking peoples may lead and predominate the world.[12]

(JOHN DOS PASSOS)

The transition from a world of empires to a world of states has often been presented, whether implicitly or explicitly, as a largely seamless, perhaps even

---

12. John Dos Passos, *The Anglo-Saxon Century and the Unification of the English-speaking People*, 2nd ed. (New York, 1903), vii. Dos Passos, a leading Republican lawyer in New York, was father of the famous novelist.

inevitable, movement from one form of political order to another. Yet it was contested bitterly throughout the decades in which it unfolded. During the mid-twentieth century, as Or Rosenboim shows, a loose network of thinkers in Europe and the United States—Raymond Aron, Friedrich Hayek, Owen Lattimore, Jacques Maritain, David Mitrany, Lionel Robbins, and Barbara Wootton, among others—elaborated contrasting political visions for the postwar years. A revitalized nation-state, European federalism, developmental accounts of empire, international federations, a world-state: all these and more were canvased.[13] From the interwar period and through the era of decolonization, as Adom Getachew shows, a global network of anticolonial thinkers—Nnamdi Azikiwe, Du Bois, Michael Manley, Kwame Nkrumah, Julius Nyerere, George Padmore, and Eric Williams, among others—sought to combine arguments for political self-determination with ambitious plans for reformatting the international system, moving beyond a restrictive view of the nation "to insist that the achievement of this ideal required juridical, political, and economic institutions in the international realm that would secure nondomination."[14] Their favored projects included the institutionalization of a right to self-determination at the United Nations, the establishment of regional federations, and ideas for a New International Economic Order to replace the systemic capitalist exploitation of the Global South.

The organizing principles of sociopolitical life were also in flux as the nineteenth century drew to a close. The future spatial configuration of politics was deeply uncertain, provoking widespread debate and a stream of creative speculation about the contours of the world to come. Imperial and regional federations, the rapid multiplication of nation-states, even a universal polity, were considered feasible options. So too were massive associations built around racial or linguistic identity. Pan-Africanism, Pan-Asianism, Pan-Islamism, Pan-Latinism, and Pan-Slavism all flowered in the shadow of geopolitical uncertainty, as thinkers throughout the world imagined new sources and modalities of political affiliation, legitimacy, and belonging.[15] Expressions of transnational whiteness, Anglo-Saxonism foremost among them, were among

13. Or Rosenboim, *The Emergence of Globalism* (Princeton, NJ, 2017).

14. Adom Getachew, *Worldmaking after Empire* (Princeton, NJ, 2019), 2. For a critique of the linear narrative that moves from the nation-state to cosmopolitan extraterritoriality, see Robbie Shilliam, "What about Marcus Garvey?," *Review of International Studies*, 32/3 (2006), 379–400.

15. Musab Younis, "'United by Blood,'" *Nations and Nationalism*, 23/3 (2017), 484–504; Sebastian Conrad and Dominic Sachsenmaier (eds.), *Competing Visions of World Order* (Basingstoke, 2007); Cemil Aydin, *The Politics of Anti-Westernism in Asia* (New York, 2007). See also the discussion of poststate visions in Daniel Deudney, *Bounding Power* (Princeton, NJ, 2007), pt. III.

the most prominent of numerous attempts to rethink the norms, values, and territorial patterns of global order. The Prophets of "the religion of whiteness," as Du Bois once called it, galvanized efforts to institutionalize racial supremacy within and beyond the borders of Europe and the Angloworld.[16]

The debate over Anglo-America bloomed in the final two decades of the nineteenth century and continued until the First World War. It was overdetermined, with multiple tributaries feeding the stream. Many British observers felt anxious about the power and prestige of the imperial state in a world apparently fated for domination by massive omnicompetent polities. Germany was emerging as a military and industrial giant, while France sought to reclaim its previous status, principally by challenging British imperial supremacy in Africa. On the eastern flank of the continent, Russia posed a threat to the empire in Asia. Far larger than Britain, and with an economy that was already pulling ahead, the United States looked set to assume its long-heralded role as a great power.[17] The twentieth century would be an American one. Britain was in danger of ceding both its global preeminence, and the leadership of the English-speaking world, to its colonial offspring. *Translatio imperii* would accompany geopolitical demotion.

I use the term "unionist" in a broad sense, to refer to those who sought to coordinate or integrate Britain and the United States, and to do so principally on the basis of their shared racial identity. Arguments for union drew on a variety of intellectual trends, precedents, and exemplars. The development of new transport and communications systems was an essential ingredient. Instantiating the very thing it celebrated, debate over Anglo-America was catalyzed and reproduced by powerful infrastructural technologies that facilitated the rapid transatlantic circulation of information, commodities, and people. Articles, pamphlets, books, speeches, telegrams, poems, novels, sermons, and a flood of personal correspondence—all flowed throughout Anglo-America, spreading information, sparking debate, provoking excitement, endorsement, and rejection. Moreover, as I discuss later in this chapter, interpretations of those same technologies, above all the electrical telegraph, led to a reassessment of the size and form of viable political communities. This recoding of space was amplified by widespread interest in the political technology of

16. The phrase is from W. E. B. Du Bois, "The Souls of White Folk" (1910), in *Writings by W. E. B. Du Bois in Periodicals Edited by Others*, ed. Herbert Aptheker (New York, 1982), II, 26.

17. For recent analyses of American Empire, see A. G. Hopkins, *American Empire* (Princeton, NJ, 2018); Daniel Immerwahr, *How to Hide an Empire* (New York, 2019); Greg Grandin, *The End of the Myth* (New York, 2019). For comparisons between the British and American empires, see Kathleen Burk, *The Lion and the Eagle* (London, 2018); Julian Go, *Patterns of Empire* (Cambridge, 2011).

federalism. It was, Ernest Barker wrote later, the "note of the hour."[18] Federal structures offered a way to reconcile vast geographical expanse, political dynamism, and individual liberty, allowing the rescaling of polities.[19] The United States in particular, but also Canada, Australia (from 1901), and South Africa (from 1910), demonstrated to many that it was an ideal form of political organization for consolidating the Angloworld.[20] Just as many imperial federalists were drawn to the idea, so too were some of the most ambitious devotees of Anglo-America. Moreover, a slew of racial theories, grounded in a confused admixture of philological speculation, evolutionary argumentation, and folk assumptions about hierarchy and difference, underwrote the belief that the scattered population of the Angloworld constituted a single superior people.

British observers had long been fascinated by the United States, often viewing it with a toxic mixture of arrogance and disdain that served to fuel Anglophobia.[21] In *Democracy in America*, Tocqueville had written that "nothing can be more virulent than the hatred which exists between the Americans of the United States and the English."[22] The tone and the terms of engagement shifted dramatically during the late Victorian years, as the American economy boomed, its universities and cultural life thrived, and its elites came into ever closer contact—through business, travel, intermarriage, and intellectual exchange—with those in the British world.[23] "English travellers and writers

---

18. Ernest Barker, *Political Thought in England, 1848–1914* (London, 1915), 181. See also Henry Sidgwick, *The Development of European Polity*, ed. Eleanor Sidgwick (London, 1903), 439.

19. For some prominent examples, see Charles Dilke, *Problems of Greater Britain* (London, 1890), I, 97; Sidgwick, *Development of European Polity*, 439; J. A. Hobson, *Imperialism*, ed. Philip Siegelman (1902; Ann Arbor, 1997), 350.

20. Bell, *Greater Britain*, ch. 4. For contemporary discussions of the meaning and efficacy of federation in the Angloworld, see Arthur Poley, *The Federal Systems of the United States and the British Empire* (Boston, 1913); H. A. L. Fisher, *Political Unions* (Oxford, 1911); Hugh Egerton, *Federations and Unions within the British Empire* (Oxford, 1911). Members of the Round Table movement, formed in 1909, and dedicated principally to imperial federation, drew much inspiration from the American experiment, especially as filtered through F. S. Oliver, *Alexander Hamilton* (London, 1906). See John Fair, "F. S. Oliver, Alexander Hamilton, and the 'American Plan' for Resolving Britain's Constitutional Crises, 1903–1921," *Twentieth Century British History*, 10/1 (1999), 1–26. On the Round Table and the United States, see Priscilla Roberts, "World War I and Anglo-American Relations," *Round Table*, 95/383 (2006), 113–39.

21. Christine DeVine (ed.), *Nineteenth-Century British Travelers in the New World* (Farnham, 2013); Mulvey, *Transatlantic Manners*; Burk, *Old World, New World*, ch. 4.

22. Alexis de Tocqueville, *Democracy in America*, ed. Henry Reeve (London, 1839), I, 426.

23. Hugh Tulloch, "Changing British Attitudes towards the United States in the 1880s," *Historical Journal*, 20/4 (1977), 825–40; Robert Frankel, *Observing America* (Madison, 2007); David

used no doubt formerly to assume airs of supercilious condescension which must have been offensive to Americans," James Bryce admitted in 1896. "But those airs were dropped twenty or thirty years ago, and the travellers who return now return full of gratitude for the kindness they have received and full of admiration for the marvellous progress they have witnessed."[24] Given American suspicion of "entangling alliances," and sensitive to the virulent strain of Anglophobia coursing through public debate, British race unionists recognized that they faced a formidable task. Their response was to insist either that union was inevitable due to a combination of deep racial connections and prevailing economic, political, and technological trends, or that the governments in London and Washington had to act swiftly and decisively because transatlantic integration was in their national interests.[25] They found some ready allies in the United States, including historians such as George Burton Adams and James Hosmer, who drew sustenance from Teutonic interpretations of transatlantic racial development, theologians such as Josiah Strong and Lyman Abbott, who preached a form of racial providentialism, and British emigrants seeking to (re)unify their two homelands, Carnegie among them. Most American unionists favoured increased co-operation with Britain rather than full political integration.

The "vortex of militarism," as Carnegie termed it, bolstered unionist discourse.[26] Impetus was provided by three geopolitical crises: the Venezuela border dispute (1895–96), the onset of the Spanish-American War (1898), and the British war in South Africa (1899–1902). The Venezuelan crisis briefly set Britain and the United States on a diplomatic collision course, generating a fresh wave of Anglophobia in the United States and a spirited response from those horrified at the prospect of an Angloworld civil war. It spurred efforts to establish cooperation on a firmer footing: campaigning groups were formed, transatlantic networks assembled, impassioned speeches delivered, articles, pamphlets, and books published. In February 1896, the "Anglo-American Union" was launched in London to agitate for an arbitration treaty between

---

Seed, "The Land of the Future," *European Journal of American Studies*, 11/2 (2016), 1–24. On marriage patterns, see Burk, *Old World, New World*, ch. 7; Dana Cooper, *Informal Ambassadors* (Kent, OH, 2014).

24. James Bryce, "British Feeling on the Venezuela Question," *North American Review*, 162/471 (1896), 150.

25. On Anglophobia, see Edward Crapol, *America for Americans* (Westport, CT, 1973); Stephen Tuffnell, "'Uncle Sam Is to Be Sacrificed,'" *American Nineteenth Century History*, 12/1 (2011), 77–99.

26. Andrew Carnegie, *The Autobiography of Andrew Carnegie* (1920; London, 2006), 308.

the two countries.[27] By the outbreak of the First World War, it was flanked by a series of other organizations, including the Anglo-American Committee (1898), the Anglo-American League (1898), the Atlantic Union (1901), and the Pilgrims Society (1902). A rich institutional ecology fostered personal connections and built a sense of solidarity between members of the transatlantic elite. It played an important role in the fabrication and dissemination of unionist projects.

The two imperial wars proved more divisive for unionists. Many Britons welcomed American efforts to carve out an extra-continental empire in Asia, assuming their fair share of Kipling's "White Man's Burden."[28] Embracing a form of inter-imperialism, they anticipated a joint mission to force open new markets and "civilise" swathes of the earth. Talk of a formal military alliance was rife. But other observers recoiled in horror. One of the most powerful ripostes came from Benjamin Harrison, the former President. "Are not the continuous good and close relations of the two great English-speaking nations— for which I pray—rather imperiled than promoted by this foolish talk of gratitude and of an alliance, which is often made to take on the appearance of a threat, or at least a prophecy, of an Anglo-Saxon 'paramountcy?'" The danger of racial exceptionalism loomed:

> If the nations are to be friends, if they are to live together in amity and work together in their foreign policies, must it not be upon a basis that does not repel but invites the participation of all other nations, in every project for the development and peace of the world—and not upon the pernicious and futile project of an Anglo-Saxon world? The moral quality of public acts must be taken account of; greed of territory and thoughts of political paramountcies enforced by the sword must be eliminated.[29]

While many racial unionists welcomed the conflict, others worried that American imperialism threatened rather than cemented authentic integration. Carnegie, for example, became one of its foremost critics. The violence in

---

27. The General Council of the organization included fourteen former Liberal Ministers and thirty-nine MPs: Thomas Boyle, "The Venezuela Crisis and the Liberal Opposition, 1895–6," *Journal of Modern History*, 50/3 (1978), 1205.

28. Though written in 1898, it was only published in 1899: Rudyard Kipling, "The White Man's Burden," *McClure's Magazine*, 12 (1899), 290–91; Patrick Brantlinger, 'Kipling's "'The White Man's Burden' and Its Afterlives," *English Literature in Transition, 1880–1920*, 50/2 (2007), 172–91.

29. Benjamin Harrison, "Musings upon Current Topics, II," *North American Review*, 172/532 (1901), 354, 358. See also Harrison, "The Status of Annexed Territory and of Its Free Civilized Inhabitants," *North American Review*, 172/530 (1901), 1–22.

South Africa likewise triggered a burst of affirmation and critique. In Britain, a cacophonous debate raged over the legitimacy and conduct of the war, with race unionists found on both sides. Stead and Rhodes railed against each other, with the former emerging as one of the most vociferous opponents of a war that the latter had helped to foment. In the United States, the neutral stance adopted by the Republican administration was lambasted by those who sided with the Boers against British aggression.[30] Even as the wars spurred support for rapprochement, they highlighted the political obstacles confronting unionism. Nevertheless, the general political trajectory was clear. While the Edwardian years were punctuated by a succession of fraught episodes—a second Venezuelan crisis in 1902–3, the rumbling Alaskan boundary dispute, tensions in the Caribbean, even squabbles over the 1908 Olympic Games—relations between Britain and the United States were far better than they had been a generation before. The foundations for deeper cooperation had been laid.

Racial unionism was a broad church, encompassing a variety of different positions. Its scope, as well as its indistinctness, was expressed in a resolution passed at the inaugural London meeting of the Anglo-American Committee in July 1898:

> Considering that the peoples of the British Empire and of the United States of America are closely allied in blood, inherit the same literature and laws, hold the same principles of self-government, recognize the same ideals of freedom and humanity in the guidance of their national policy, and are drawn together by strong common interests in many parts of the world, this meeting is of the opinion that every effort should be made in the interests of civilization and peace to secure the most cordial and constant cooperation between the two countries.[31]

Eliciting numerous expressions of support in the British and American press, the declaration contained some of the key themes—and ambiguities—that pervaded the discourse.[32] Multiple vectors of identity were posited: racial,

---

30. For the range of responses, see Kramer, "Empires, Exceptions, and Anglo-Saxons," 1341–44; Stuart Anderson, "Racial Anglo-Saxonism and American Response to the Boer War," *Diplomatic History*, 2/3 (1978), 219–36; Keith Wilson (ed.), *The International Impact of the Boer War* (Durham, 2001); Richard Mulanax, *The Boer War in American Politics and Diplomacy* (Lanham, 1994); Willard Gatewood, *Black Americans and the White Man's Burden, 1898–1903* (Urbana-Champaign, 1975).

31. Dos Passos, *Anglo-Saxon Century*, 57.

32. The meeting occurred on 13 July 1898. For coverage, see *New York Times* (15 July 1898); *San Francisco Call* (14 July 1898); *Los Angeles Herald* (14 July 1898); and Anglo-American

linguistic, historical, legal, moral, and political. A harmonious combination of sentiment and shared interests was asserted. The urgency of the situation and the need for collective action was postulated, as was the universal significance of the endeavor. And the document was intentionally vague about the form union might assume. Like the imperial federalists, Anglo-American unionists were divided sharply over the best arrangements to seek.[33] Three basic accounts can be discerned, each encompassing various strands. While all unionists accepted as an article of faith the fundamental unity and world-historical destiny of the race, they differed over the extent of institutionalization required. At one end of the spectrum were *maximalists* who propounded some kind of formal political (re)unification, typically either confederal or federal. They hoped to go much further than the Anglo-American Committee resolution presaged. This stance was adopted by all of my main protagonists. Wells hailed the emergence of a New Republic, while Rhodes imagined a day when the capital city of Anglo-America would alternate between London and Washington. During the 1880s and 1890s, Carnegie called for both the federation and the confederation of Britain and the United States, before switching gears to argue that Britain should be subsumed into an expanding United States. Following a similar trajectory, Stead championed the relentless "Americanization" of the world, moving from advocacy of confederation to the full absorption of Britain within an American-dominated "United States of the English-speaking World."[34] At the other end of the spectrum, *minimalists* rejected the need for any substantial institutional engineering, trusting the underlying motive power of racial kinship to bind Anglo-America. At most, they were willing to countenance an arbitration treaty, designed to eliminate the possibility of internecine violence and cement geopolitical cooperation. Arrayed between the two poles could be found various proposals for institutionalizing union short of full political integration. The two most popular were an alliance, usually centered on a defensive or offensive treaty, and the

---

Committee, *An American Response to Expressions of English Sympathy* (New York, 1899). The latter includes membership lists for the American and British branches of the Committee.

33. On the variety of imperial federal plans, see Bell, *Greater Britain*; Ged Martin, "Empire Federalism and Imperial Parliamentary Union, 1820–1870," *Historical Journal*, 16/1 (1973), 65–92; Seymour Cheng, *Schemes for the Federation of the British Empire* (New York, 1931).

34. H. G. Wells, *Anticipations of the Reaction of Mechanical and Scientific Progress upon Human Life and Thought* (1901; Mineola, 1999); Cecil J. Rhodes, *The Last Will and Testament of Cecil J. Rhodes*, ed. W. T. Stead (London, 1902); Andrew Carnegie, *The Reunion of Britain and America* (Edinburgh, 1893); Carnegie, *A Rectorial Address Delivered to the Students in the University of St. Andrews* (Edinburgh, 1902); William T. Stead, *The Americanization of the World* (London, 1902).

establishment of a system of common ("isopolitan") citizenship. Proposals for the former were especially popular in the wake of 1898. I return to the latter in chapter 6.

An intellectual history of Anglo-America could be written about the leading political actors in London and Washington. It would encompass a remarkable group of politicians, including William Gladstone, Lord Salisbury, Theodore Roosevelt, Woodrow Wilson, John Hay, Joseph Chamberlain, and Arthur Balfour. While an illuminating exercise, it would look rather different from the story that I chart. True believers in racial kinship, they all endorsed minimalist proposals—chiefly international arbitration and closer diplomatic cooperation—despite rhetorical flourishes that suggested more ambitious commitments. This is hardly surprising given their political roles. Roosevelt is exemplary. Embedded in a dense transatlantic network of correspondents and friends, he was keen to consolidate relations between what he regarded as the two main homes of the most "civilised" race on earth.[35] "It must always be kept in mind," he wrote in *The Naval War of 1812*, "that the Americans and the British are two substantially similar branches of the great English race, which both before and after their separation have assimilated and made Englishmen of many other peoples."[36] Underpinning his Anglophilia was a Lamarckian account of acquired racial characteristics that posited dynamic action— manifested in part as imperialism—as necessary to maintain the vigorous, manly qualities of the "English race." His multivolume *The Winning of the West*, published in 1889, opened with a famous chapter on "the spread of the English-speaking peoples" that tracked the historical continuities between Britons and Americans, and heralded their epochal role. "During the past three centuries," he boasted, "the spread of the English-speaking peoples over the world's waste spaces has been not only the most striking feature in the world's history, but also the event of all others most far-reaching in its effects and its importance." Constituting a single race, they now held "in their hands the fate of the coming

35. On Roosevelt's positive attitude to Britain, see William Tilchin, *Theodore Roosevelt and the British Empire* (London, 1997). Tilchin argues that until 1905 Roosevelt's positivity was accompanied by some ambivalence, but that afterwards his support was unqualified. See also David Burton, "Theodore Roosevelt and His English Correspondents," *Transactions of the American Philosophical Society*, 63/2 (1973), 3–70.

36. Theodore Roosevelt, *The Naval War of 1812* (1882; New York, 1900), I, 59. On Roosevelt's racialized vision of political order, see Thomas Dyer, *Theodore Roosevelt and the Idea of Race* (Baton Rouge, 1980); Michael Patrick Cullinane, "Imperial 'Character'" in Hans Krabbendam and John Thompson (eds.), *America's Transatlantic Turn* (Basingstoke, 2012), 31–47. On its intersection with his nationalism, see Gary Gerstle, "Theodore Roosevelt and the Divided Character of American Nationalism," *Journal of American History*, 86/3 (1999), 1280–307.

years."[37] Yet even as Roosevelt gushed about racial destiny, and pursued Anglo-American cooperation intently when in office, his ardent nationalism militated against projects for political integration.

Chamberlain and Balfour were the senior British politicians most closely associated with Anglo-America, but like Roosevelt their proposals rarely went beyond encomiums to the glory of kinship and support for cooperation or an arbitration body. Proclaiming that Americans and Britons were "all of the same race and blood," Chamberlain argued in Toronto in 1887 that the mighty "Anglo-Saxons" were "infallibly destined to be the predominant force in the future history and civilisation of the world."[38] This racial vision at once motivated his support for the "great dream" of imperial federation and his passionate support of Anglo-American rapprochment.[39] Extolling American imperialism, in May 1898 he floated the idea of an "alliance," though he meant close cooperation rather than any formal institutional connection.[40] A few months later, he invoked George Washington's farewell address to argue that Britain and the United States were better off without entangling alliances, while avowing that the two countries should collaborate to civilize "the Tropics."[41] Balfour likewise hymned the glory of racial unity without committing to political integration. "I am nothing if not an apostle of the English-speaking world."[42] A supporter of an Anglo-American arbitration treaty, he summarized his position in an address to the Pilgrims Society in 1905.

> There has grown up a sense of solidarity, a sense of common origin, and common objects, which, despite certain temporary and negligible fluctuations, leaves us to contemplate a time, not far distant, when, without engagements, without treatises, without any formal declaration, there will arise between this country and the United States that community of feeling which is more powerful than any diplomatic instrument, and which will make all men who speak the English language, in whatever part of the world

37. Theodore Roosevelt, *The Winning of the West* (New York, 1889), I, 17, 21.

38. Joseph Chamberlain, "The Mild Sovereignty of the Queen" (30 December 1887), in Chamberlain, *Foreign and Colonial Speeches* (London, 1897), 6.

39. Joseph Chamberlain, "The True Conception of Empire" (31 March 1897), in Chamberlain, *Foreign and Colonial Speeches*, 241–48; Bell, *Greater Britain*, 56–58.

40. Joseph Chamberlain, "Recent Developments of Policy in the United States," *Scribner's Magazine*, 24 (1898), 674–82; Joseph Garvin and Julian Amery (eds.), *The Life of Joseph Chamberlain* (London, 1932), III, 301–2. On the confusion precipitated by his use of the term "alliance," see Samuel Jeyes, *Mr. Chamberlain, His Life and Public Career* (London, 1903), 420–22. See also Peter Marsh, *Joseph Chamberlain* (New Haven, CT, 1994), 436, 438–39, 479.

41. Chamberlain, "Recent Developments," 676.

42. Blanche Dugdale, *Arthur James Balfour* (London, 1936), II, 401.

they dwell, feel they do indeed belong to a community which transcends national limits, and in whose fortunes perhaps the greatest interests of civilisation are bound up.[43]

Many unionists saw bold institutional solutions as either unrealistic (even if desirable) or as impediments to authentic racial union. Charles Dilke, the eminent liberal politician, discerned scant support in the United States for a "startling" departure from its isolationist tradition, but he reiterated the argument he had made originally in *Greater Britain*, that the countries formed the "two chief sections of our race." "Common action will . . . be increasingly probable," he concluded, "but of permanent alliance there is as yet no sign."[44] Racial utopianism was not restricted to institutional maximalists, however, for many of those who spurned formal reunification still invested race with transformative potential. The American theologian Lyman Abbott is a case in point. "[B]y the mere fact of their cooperation," Britain and the United States, "embodying the energy, the enterprise, and the conscience of the Anglo-Saxon race," would be "[i]nvincible against enemies, illimitable in influence, at once inspiring and restraining each other." Acting in concert, they could "produce a result in human history which would surpass all that present imagination can conceive or present hope anticipate."[45] Institutional minimalism could underpin utopian dreams of racial destiny.

Those skeptical about the necessity or viability of institutional change in the present were often open to unification in the future. They counseled patience, fearing that premature action would endanger fragile support for integration. History should be left to run its course. "There is no need to talk of any formal conventions or declarations," wrote the distinguished legal scholar Sir Frederick Pollock. "If the spirit is there, the letter can be provided when the

43. Arthur Balfour, Speech to the Pilgrims Society, 1905, in Balfour, *The Mind of Arthur James Balfour*, ed. Wilfrid Short (New York, 1918), 3–4. On the society and its role in Anglo-American relations, see Stephen Bowman, *The Pilgrims Society and Public Diplomacy, 1895–1945* (Edinburgh, 2018). For Balfour's support of an arbitration treaty, see his 1911 Guildhall speech (5–6). For a valuable account of his ideas about race and Anglo-American policy, see Jason Tomes, *Balfour and Foreign Policy* (Cambridge, 1997), chs. 2–4, 7. I return to his view on race and patriotism in chapter 6.

44. Charles Dilke, "An Anglo-American Alliance," *Pall Mall Magazine*, 16/65 (1898), 37, 38. On the profound political differences between the two powers, as well as their shared interests, see Dilke, "America and England in the East," *North American Review*, 169/515 (1899), 558–63. For his earlier argument, see Dilke, *Greater Britain*, 2 vols. (London, 1868).

45. Lyman Abbott, "The Basis of an Anglo-American Understanding," *North American Review*, 166/498 (1898), 521. I return to Abbott in chapter 2.

time calls for it."[46] This cautious position was encapsulated the following year by the historian J. Stanley Little. Any alliance "would have to come about by gradual processes, as I believe it is coming about." Neither an imperial federation nor Anglo-American unification "could be arranged on lines which give to the structure that symmetry and homogeneity on which the makers of paper constitutions dream." The "impatient doctrinaires" were hopelessly misguided if they thought that the "Anglo-Saxons" would accept drastic reforms to their constitutions.[47] The maximalists, in contrast, wagered that the time was ripe for substantial change.

It was often unclear where the boundaries of a future polity would be drawn. Although Wells's argument implied the unification of the whole Angloworld, he wrote almost exclusively about Britain and the United States, rarely mentioning the settler colonies. Stead promulgated both imperial federation and Anglo-American union, but from the 1890s onward the latter was his clear priority. Rhodes's vision encompassed the United States and the British Empire, while Carnegie favored the dissolution of the empire, focusing his attention on securing the union of Britain and the United States. Nor was theoretical precision a virtue of unionist discourse. The novelist and historian Walter Besant exemplified both the grandiose ambition and the argumentative slipperiness of unionist projects. Enumerating the territories occupied or administered by the "Anglo-Saxons," he yearned for "one United Federation of States," the "greatest, the richest, the most powerful empire, republic or state that history has ever recorded."[48] The six "nations"—Australia, Britain, the United States, Canada, New Zealand, and South Africa—should "form a firm alliance, offensive and defensive," controlling a navy that would outmatch all possible competitors. They would constitute "a great federation of our race, an immense federation, free, law-abiding, peaceful," yet nevertheless ready to fight if threatened.[49] A year later, Besant hailed the glorious future of the "United Federation of the English-Speaking States." Adamant that the "Congress" of this magnificent polity would not infringe legislatively on the sovereignty of its constituent units, that none would have authority over any other, he said little about how to reconcile autonomy with a functioning federal structure, the specificity of constitutional arrangements, or how state, nation,

46. Frederick Pollock, "The Monroe Doctrine," *Nineteenth Century and After*, 52/308 (1902), 553. Pollock was Secretary of the Anglo-American League.

47. J. Stanley Little, *Progress of British Empire in the Century* (London, 1903), 103.

48. Walter Besant, "The Future of the Anglo-Saxon Race," *North American Review*, 163/477 (1896), 133–34, 137. On Besant, see Simon Eliot, "'His Generation Read His Stories,'" *Publishing History*, 21/1 (1987), 25–67.

49. Besant, "Future of the Anglo-Saxon Race," 143.

republic, and empire should be differentiated conceptually.[50] What he lacked as a political theorist, Besant made up for as a eulogist. "I can see no limit to the boundary or power that will be possessed by such a Federation. It will be a power exerted altogether in the interests of peace."[51] Unionist advocacy was characterized by a mixture of conceptual ambiguity and grandiose claims about racial destiny.

Anglotopia: Racial Futurism and the Power of Dreams

> This may all seem Utopian, but we have had many prophetic voices, more than fulfilled, which were at the time of their inspired utterance much wilder than anything herein suggested. It may be all a dream but I am a dreamer of dreams. So be it. But if it be true that he who always dreams accomplishes nothing, so also is it none the less true that he who never dreams is equally barren of achievement.[52]
>
> (ANDREW CARNEGIE)

Utopias are engines of world-making, a nowhere that signals the possible future instantiation of a somewhere. A diagnostic probe of the present as well as a call to act, their imaginative power is generated by the simultaneous identification of pathology and the elaboration of a hypothetical resolution. Through imagining and meditating on potential futures, utopianism can motivate action by inspiring people to realize their desires. As Jay Winter observes, it has been "the core, the driving force of many social and political movements."[53] The projected site and form of utopia has morphed over time. Reinhart Koselleck argues that classical utopias, including those of More and Plato, were "spatialzed"—located in historically contemporaneous yet alien places. Absent from such accounts, he averred, was the "temporal dimension of utopia as a site of the future."[54] As the finite world was mapped and conquered

50. Walter Besant, *The Rise of the Empire* (London, 1897), 121–22.

51. Besant was a key figure behind the creation of the "Atlantic Union," a transatlantic association formed in 1901 to promote cooperation between the "English-speaking peoples." See here Besant, *Autobiography of Walter Besant* (New York, 1902), ch. 16; Besant, "Object of Atlantic Union," *New York Times*, 4 June 1900. He served as the Treasurer of the Union.

52. Carnegie, *Reunion*, 31.

53. Jay Winter, *Dreams of Peace and Freedom* (New Haven, CT, 2006), 2.

54. Reinhart Koselleck, "The Temporalization of Utopia," in *The Practice of Conceptual History*, trans. Todd Samuel Presener et al. (Stanford, 2002), 86. On the literary imagination of unattainable "atopic" zones—spaces that cannot be made into places due to their practical inaccessibility— up to 1850, see Siobhan Carroll, *An Empire of Air and Water* (Philadelphia, 2015). She discusses

by the Europeans, room for the imaginative projection of such places was gradually exhausted. Utopia was increasingly transposed into the future. During the long nineteenth century, it was "temporalized," representing "the metamorphosis of utopia into the philosophy of history."[55] Utopias came to be seen as potentially realizeable through collective action.

Utopian desire pervaded late nineteenth-century intellectual life. More utopian tales were written in the three decades following the publication of Edward Bellamy's *Looking Backward, 2000–1887* (1888) than in the previous several centuries combined.[56] They were consumed ravenously across the Angloworld.[57] "[S]ocial dreams are once more rife," declared the British journalist G. W. Foote in 1886.[58] The value of such thinking was widely acknowledged. Defending Bellamy against his detractors, the radical political economist J. A. Hobson wrote,

> Just as there is a sense in which history is stranger than fiction, so there is a sense in which fiction is truer than history; that is to say, the constructive imagination of man is able so to order outward and inward events of life that deep essential truths shine forth more clearly than in the grosser and more complicated order of "real" life which is not designed primarily for their disclosure.[59]

Well-designed ideal societies were not "opposed to the present real society," he argued, but instead constituted a "furtherance and completion of that reality" by conjoining the "strong and permanent" features of a given sociopolitical order with invented yet plausible modifications.[60] Utopian thinking was a legitimate, even necessary, dimension of political thought and activism.

Observing the appearance of "so many prophets and so many prophecies," G. K. Chesterton recognized the distinctiveness of the times. In *The Napoleon of Notting Hill*, his cutting satire on the genre, he observed that wherever one

---

polar regions, the oceans, the upper atmosphere, and subterranean spaces: "[s]paces that the empire could not successfully colonize were spaces that literature alone might claim" (9).

55. Koselleck, "Temporalization," 86.

56. Robertson, *Last Utopians*, 4.

57. Kenneth Roemer, *The Obsolete Necessity* (Kent, 1976); Claeys, "Reshaping of the Utopian Genre."

58. G. W. Foote, "Social Dreams," *Progress*, 6 (1886), 190. Foote was a well-known advocate of secularism.

59. J. A. Hobson, "Edward Bellamy and the Utopian Romance," *The Humanitarian*, 13 (1898), 179. The publication of *Looking Backward*, he suggested, was "one of the most important literary events of the century" (179).

60. Hobson, "Edward Bellamy," 179.

looked there were "clever men" plotting the future of humanity, "all quite clear, all quite keen-sighted and ruthless, and all quite different."[61] There was Wells, "who thought that science would take charge of the future," and Edward Carpenter, who yearned for a return to the virtuous simplicity of Nature. There was Tolstoy and a band of "humanitarians" ceaselessly preaching the creed of universalism and peace on earth, even as another vocal group were predicting the opposite, that the "lines of kinship would become narrower and sterner." Rhodes loomed large among them, a man "who thought that the one thing of the future was the British Empire, and that there would be a gulf between those who were of the Empire and those who were not, . . . similar to the gulf between man and the lower animals." Stead, meanwhile, "thought that England would in the twentieth century be united to America."[62] Although he missed the substantive convergence between Rhodes, Stead, and Wells, Chesterton saw clearly the interweaving of utopian visions of society and projects for world order. While fantasies of the future were expressed in different idioms and genres, they were a product of the same febrile milieu and they expressed many of the same anxieties and hopes.

Advocacy of Anglo-America was shot through with the imagery and language of dreams. Proud to call himself a "dreamer of dreams," Carnegie declared racial union the grandest of them all.[63] Rhodes once observed that "[i]t is the dreamers that move the world," and he was only too happy to sport the badge, an estimate shared by many of his devotees, who acclaimed him as a visionary genius.[64] Stead routinely assumed the mantle of social prophet, even purporting to act as an agent of providence, while Wells quickly established a reputation as one of the most important speculative thinkers of the age. Critics of the idea also recognized its utopian dimensions. The eminent positivist Frederic Harrison observed in 1906 that

> [T]his dream of welding into one the whole English-speaking people is a dangerous and retrograde Utopia, full of mischief and false pride of race. It is a subtler and more sinister form of Jingoism. We all need to have our national faults and weaknesses corrected by friendship with those of different ideals and without our special temptations. The English race is already

61. G. K. Chesterton, *The Napoleon of Notting Hill* (London, 1904), 14–15. For a critique of "prophets" and "political astrologers," see J. L. Hammond, "Colonial and Foreign Policy" in F. W. Hirst, Gilbert Murray, and Hammond, *Liberalism and the Empire* (London, 1900), 161–62.

62. Chesterton, *Napoleon of Notting Hill*, 15, 17, 18.

63. Carnegie, *Reunion*, 31.

64. Rhodes, conversation with Lady Warwick, quoted in Robert Rotberg, *The Founder* (Oxford, 1988), 670.

too domineering, ambitious, and self-centred. Combination with America would stimulate our vices, our difficulties—and our rivals.[65]

Those utilizing the language of dreams did not regard projects for Anglo-American unification as hopelessly unrealistic—indeed, they claimed that racial union was either a feasible political ambition, given appropriate political will, or that it was inevitable. They regarded dreaming, with Hobson, as an essential feature of reality—not antithetical to it. The invocation of dreams was simultaneously an acknowledgment and a celebration of the power of the imagination to remake sociopolitical order. To motivate and direct action, and to build support for significant change, it was necessary to escape the constraints imposed by present circumstances and conventional styles of thinking. While not all unionists were utopian, it is hard to make sense of much of the discourse, or comprehend its more radical expressions, without recognizing the self-consciously visionary ideas and hopes that pulsed through it. Seeking to confront or defuse economic, political, and social anxieties through establishing novel forms of association, racial utopians placed the latest technoscientific discoveries at the heart of their projects, seeing in them the material and symbolic means through which their grand aims could be achieved. By reading debates over Anglo-America in the context of fin-de-siècle utopianism, I seek to recover their transformative ambition and locate them in the wider cultural matrix that both produced them and rendered their claims intelligible.

Political commentary on Anglo-America also borrowed heavily from the repertoire of tropes, images, figures, and rhetorical gestures that characterized other forms of utopian writing. Poetry and speculative fiction were invoked routinely to communicate the grandeur and the glory of racial destiny. The most common literary reference point had been penned by Tennyson, an unmatched imperial dream weaver. Often cited as inspiration and guide, a passage in his numinous 1835 poem "Locksley Hall" captured attention.

Saw the Vision of the world, and all the wonder that would be;
Saw the heavens fill with commerce, argosies of magic sails,
Pilots of the purple twilight dropping down with costly bales;

---

65. Frederic Harrison, *The Positivist Review* (1906), cited in *Review of Reviews*, 202 (October 1906), 397. Hereafter this journal is cited as *RoR*. Pointing to the universalism of Comte, Stead retorted, "To oppose the reunion of the English-speaking race is hardly the line which we ought to expect from those who believe in the unity of mankind. What is more natural than that those who seek the larger unity should wish to secure as a stepping-stone thither the union of all those who speak the same language, read the same literature, and are on the same plane of civilisation?" Stead, *RoR*, 202 (October 1906), 397.

Heard the heavens fill with shouting, and there rain'd a ghastly dew
From the nations' airy navies grappling in the central blue;
Far along the world-wide whisper of the south-wind rushing warm,
With the standards of the peoples plunging thro' the thunder-storm;
Till the war-drum throbb'd no longer, and the battle-flags were furl'd
In the Parliament of man, the Federation of the world.[66]

Furnishing unionists with evocative imagery, a sense of cultural anchorage, and a claim on intellectual authority, this passage was elusive enough to be yoked to competing ends. It was cited frequently, especially by those who envisaged Anglo-American union as an initial step on the road to far grander forms of political association. We shall encounter it repeatedly in the following pages. Tennyson was not the only writer of fiction to be conscripted—as I discuss in chapter 6, Shakespeare, Milton, Kipling, Lowell, and the King James Bible were all called upon for support. Nor was the traffic one way. Novels and short stories were written to present idealized visions of imperial order and racial supremacy, run thought experiments about alternative geopolitical systems, and imagine future sociopolitical trajectories. Speculative literature was regarded as an effective medium of political thought and persuasion. Science fiction (as I discuss in chapter 5) proved an especially fruitful genre for racial utopianism. The "impulse to look ahead is universal," Stephen Kern observes, "but the quantity of science fiction in this period and its success in the marketplace suggest that this generation was especially eager to do it."[67] The future exerted a hypnotically powerful attraction. The line between fictional extrapolation, political manifesto, and social analysis was blurred, even dissolved, in a genre-straddling Anglo-America intertext.

"Utopia" is a term loaded with conflicting meanings.[68] It is worth drawing a distinction between two modes, one anthropic, the other programmatic. The former views utopianism as a ubiquitous aspect of the human condition. From this perspective, most human practices contain fugitive traces of utopia, for it

66. Alfred Tennyson, "Locksley Hall," in *Poems of Tennyson* (Oxford, 1910), 166. It also inspired the title of Paul Kennedy's history of the United Nations: *The Parliament of Man* (New York, 2006).

67. Stephen Kern, *The Culture of Time and Space, 1880–1918* (Cambridge, MA, 1983), 98.

68. For discussion of the concepts, see Frederic Jameson, *Archaeologies of the Future* (London, 2007); Ruth Levitas, *The Concept of Utopia* (Syracuse, NY, 1990); Frank Manuel and Fritzie Manuel, *Utopian Thought in the Western World* (Cambridge, 1979); Philip Wegner, *Imaginary Communities* (Berkeley, 2002); Lyman Tower Sargent, "The Three Faces of Utopianism Revisited," *Utopian Studies*, 5/1 (1994), 1–37; Gregory Claeys, "News from Somewhere," *History*, 98/330 (2013), 145–73.

is nothing less than a longing for an improved world. It is human, all too human. The most influential elaboration of this conception can be found in the writings of Ernst Bloch.[69] In his ornate dialectical account, written to salvage Marxism from the shadow of Marx, utopianism is expressed in a spectacular array of phenomena, including religion, architecture, art, fairy tales, and poetry, as well as social and political philosophies. "So far does utopia extend, so vigorously does this raw material spread to all human activities, so essentially must every anthropology and science of the world contain it."[70] In a less metaphysically freighted sense, utopia can be defined simply as "the envisioning of a transformed, better world."[71] On such accounts, the utopian impulse can be harnessed to a wide range of political goals, including deeply reactionary ones. Most advocacy of empire, and of Angloworld union, was an expression of anthropic utopian desire: it projected a vision of a supposedly better world—one more "civilised," one more in tune with the dictates of destiny, one that upholds the purported superiority of one political community or form of life over others—onto the drama of history. The problem with this picture (at least in its cruder renderings) is that it is too all-encompassing: the category of utopia is stretched so thinly that it loses distinctiveness and analytical purchase.

The programmatic form is more restricted. On this account, I argue, a political project can be considered utopian if, and only if, it invokes or prescribes the radical transformation, transcendence, or elimination of one or more pervasive practices, structures, or ordering principles that shape human collective life. This includes poverty, socioeconomic inequality, organized violence, political authority, the biochemical composition of the environment, and the ontological constitution of human beings, including death itself. Utopianism of this kind is predicated on a fundamental change in the order of things. It encompasses a spectrum of ambition, from positions that seek to address only

69. Ernst Bloch, *The Principle of Hope*, 3 vols. (1938–47; Cambridge, MA, 1986). For commentary, see Vincent Geoghegan, *Ernst Bloch* (London, 1996). For a similar definition see Ruth Levitas, "The Imaginary Reconstitution of Society" in Tom Moylan and Raffaella Baccolini (eds.), *Utopia-Method-Vision* (Oxford, 2007), 53–54.

70. Bloch, *Principle of Hope*, I, 624. For Bloch, most instantiations of utopianism are "abstract" in form; what differentiates Marxism—contra Marx—is its focus on "concrete" utopias.

71. Robertson, *Last Utopians*, 6. Note that my distinction does not map onto Jay Winter's conceptualization of "major" and "minor" utopias; his is chiefly an argument about ambition, not different modalities of the utopian imagination: Winter, *Dreams of Peace and Freedom*, ch. 1.

one of those phenomena through to more totalizing visions that aim to transcend several of them.

Gregory Claeys is right to argue that late Victorian utopianism was shaped chiefly by the intersection of socialist ideas and Darwinism.[72] The most popular topic of speculation was the "social question," triggered by the widespread poverty and despair that accompanied the voracious expansion of industrial capitalism.[73] But the dream of perpetual peace also suffused utopian visions. Even those texts read principally as answers to the social question charted an escape from a world of organized violence. In *Looking Backward*, Bellamy's regimented socialist state is presented as an agent of global peace. "The great nations of Europe as well as Australia, Mexico, and parts of South America," Dr Leete informs Julian West, "are now organized industrially like the United States, which was the pioneer of the evolution." The "advanced" parts of the world solve the problem of war through socioeconomic coordination and building international institutions, while the "backward" zones were developed and incorporated in a new civilizing mission.

> The peaceful relations of these nations are assured by a loose form of federal union of world-wide extent. An international council regulates the mutual intercourse and commerce of the members of the union and their joint policy toward the more backward races, which are gradually being educated up to civilized institutions. Complete autonomy within its own limits is enjoyed by every nation.[74]

In *News from Nowhere*, William Morris imagined a bucolic socialist world at peace, while in Wells's "modern utopia" the emergence of a functioning world-state ensures that the "peace of the world is established forever." They disagreed, though, over the question of transition, of how to escape from the current world and build a future one. In contrast to Bellamy, both of the British writers suggested that revolution and war were necessary.[75] As I explore at

---

72. Claeys, "Reshaping of the Utopian Genre." For a contemporary account of the genre, tying utopianism to socialism, see Moritz Kaufmann, *Utopias, or Schemes of Social Improvement, from Thomas More to Karl Marx* (London, 1879). On the large number of dystopian texts produced at the time, see Gregory Claeys, *Dystopia* (Oxford, 2017), ch. 5.

73. For a fascinating discussion, placing it in the context of other nineteenth-century questions, see Holly Case, *The Age of Questions* (Princeton, NJ, 2018).

74. Bellamy, *Looking Backward*, 82.

75. William Morris, *News from Nowhere and Other Writings*, ed. Clive Wilmer (London, 1993), ch. 17; H. G. Wells, *A Modern Utopia*, ed. Gregory Claeys (1905; London, 2005), 36 and ch. 8. Thomas More's utopians were not pacifists. While they regarded war as an "activity fit only for beasts," and saw no glory in military victory, they did not reject it entirely. More listed a

various points in the following chapters, disagreement over transition, and in particular whether it would require violence, ran through the discourse of Anglo-America. This is a fundamental challenge for any kind of utopian political thought.

Anglo-America was often figured as a programmatic utopian space. Although some prophetic writing on the subject discussed the abolition of poverty and the reduction of socioeconomic inequality, the primary utopian aim (shared by my main protagonists) was perpetual peace. Unification would, in the words of Carnegie, "end the murder of men by men." Mastering the flux of the modern world, Anglo-America was imagined as a racial-political order capable of bringing peace to a violent planet. The human condition could be reconfigured, bringing once distant peoples into close communion with one another and eradicating the age-old scourge of war. This was the *Anglotopian* dream. It represented the divinization of the political, a theological master-narrative infused with ideas about destiny and providence. It was also, and equally, an expression of technological fetishism, the belief in the transformative powers of the machine that pervaded the era.

Biocultural Assemblage: A Note on Race

[J]ust now, the world is in a sort of delirium about race and the racial struggle.[76]

(H. G. WELLS)

Providing an authoritative rationale for manifold forms of exclusion, oppression, and violence, race was often viewed as the basic ontological category of society and politics. It offered an interpretive grid to categorize and evaluate peoples, underwriting what Paul Gilroy refers to as the "raciological ordering of the world," and it was manifested in a range of legal, political, and social structures, a "racial nomos."[77] Claims about race played a fundamental, though often ambiguous, role in the Anglo-American dreamworld. All the main

---

set of legitimate reasons for embarking on war, including self-defence, aiding allies against invasion, and the liberation of oppressed peoples. Thomas More, *Utopia*, ed. George Logan and Robert Adams (1516; Cambridge, 1988), 87–95.

76. Wells, *Modern Utopia*, 218.

77. Paul Gilroy, *Against Race* (Cambridge, MA, 2002), 6; Gilroy, *Postcolonial Melancholia* (New York, 2006), 39. For a variety of theoretical accounts of race/racism, see Naomi Zack (ed.), *The Oxford Handbook of the Philosophy of Race* (Oxford, 2016); Duncan Bell (ed.), *Empire, Race and Global Justice* (Cambridge, 2019).

protagonists of this book insisted on its centrality, though they—as with so many of their contemporaries—diverged over its meaning and implications.

The prevailing historical view is that race/racism is largely an invention of Western modernity, emerging simultaneously (and not coincidentally) with the Spanish conquest of the Americas, although some scholars seek to locate its protoforms in the ancient world.[78] The racial order was transcontinental in reach from the outset, and subsequent centuries of imperialism both spread and consolidated it. By the nineteenth century it was an insidious feature of the Western political imaginary. But identifying the precise meanings of the term during the Victorian and Edwardian years is a thankless task. Racial thinking formed a shape-shifting amalgam of theories, vocabularies, practices, assumptions, and desires, and it both intersected and competed with other ways of conceptualizing human groups, most notably civilization and nationality.[79] Folk racial classifications vied with elaborate theoretical accounts, themselves divided along numerous dimensions. A phalanx of historians, including Henry Maine, E. A. Freeman, James Bryce, and Herbert Baxter Adams, claimed that over the centuries the Teutonic people had migrated from the forest clearings of Germany into Britain and onward to the United States, in a grand westward sweep of racial destiny.[80] Though most popular in the mid-Victorian years, this style of thinking resonated powerfully in the Anglo-American discourse (I return to it in chapter 2). Others drew from the expanding catalogue of evolutionary theories to ground claims about racial development in the authoritative idiom of biological science. Lamarckian views about inherited characteristics jostled and overlapped with multifarious

78. George Fredrickson, *Racism* (Princeton, NJ, 2002); Francisco Bethencourt, *Racisms* (Princeton, NJ, 2013). On the debate about precursors, see Miriam Eliav-Feldon, Benjamin Isaac, and Joseph Ziegler (eds.), *The Origins of Racism in the West* (Cambridge, 2009).

79. On alternative ways of conceptualizing groups, see Peter Mandler, *The English National Character* (New Haven, CT, 2006), chs. 3–5. For British debates over race, see Douglas Lorimer, *Science, Race Relations and Resistance* (Manchester, 2013); Sadiah Qureshi, *Peoples on Parade* (Chicago, 2011); Paul Rich, *Race and Empire in British Politics* (Cambridge, 1990), chs. 1–3; Patrick Brantlinger, *Taming Cannibals* (Ithaca, NY, 2011).

80. Oded Steinberg, *Race, Nation, History* (Philadelphia, 2019); Mandler, *English National Character*, 72–105; John Burrow, Stefan Collini, and Donald Winch, *That Noble Science of Politics* (Cambridge, 1983), 219–26; Duncan Bell, *Reordering the World* (Princeton, NJ, 2016), ch. 13. For a sweeping survey of racial ideas, written by a prominent critic, see Franklin Hankins, "Race as a Factor in Political Theory" in Charles Merriam and Harry Elmer Barnes (eds.), *A History of Political Theories, Recent Times* (New York, 1924), 508–48. Hankins stressed the pervasive confusion between "race" and "nationality" in scholarly and popular discourse.

readings of Darwin.[81] Many thinkers blended evolutionary and philological arguments in an unstable racial bricolage, while yet others bypassed scholarly strategies of racial identification, relying on assertion and appeals to vernacular notions of hierarchy and difference. Nascent scholarly disciplines, including anthropology, history, and political science, incubated and helped to legitimate racial discourses.[82]

Scholars often distinguish biological and cultural conceptions of race. An implicit normative evaluation underpins the distinction: due to their essentialism, biological accounts are viewed as more problematic than the purportedly fluid culturalist variants. Yet while this binary highlights the elusive character of racial vocabulary—the fact that it was often used synonymously with nationality or civilization—it obscures some important aspects of fin-de-siècle discourse. Conceptions of racial variability were almost always delimited by what Du Bois, speaking at the inaugural Pan-African Conference in 1900, famously termed the "colour line."[83] Debates over mutability almost always took place within the horizon of whiteness. Even as the nature and number of "races" continued to vex scholars, the existence of a color line was widely accepted. The liberal philosopher and sociologist L. T. Hobhouse was recycling a commonplace when in 1911 he wrote that "much of the future of the modern state, particularly of my own country, must depend on the relation of the white to the colored and non-European races."[84] Race demarcated boundaries of identification, conflict, and solidarity within and between states and empires. Despite widespread disagreement over its definition, history, and entailments, as well as its ethico-political valence, both unionists and their critics almost invariably employed race as a core category of analysis. Privileging it as an

81. Piers Hale, *Political Descent* (Chicago, 2014), chs. 3–7; John Burrow, *Evolution and Society* (Cambridge, 1966); Efram Sera-Shriar (ed.), *Historicizing Humans* (Pittsburgh, 2018).

82. Jessica Blatt, *Race and the Making of American Political Science* (Philadelphia, 2018); Robert Vitalis, *White World Order, Black Power Politics* (Ithaca, NY, 2015), pts. I–II; Sandra Den Otter, "The Origins of a Historical Political Science in Late Victorian and Edwardian Britain" in Robert Adcock, Mark Bevir, and Shannon Stimson (eds.), *Modern Political Science* (Princeton, NJ, 2007), 66–96; Peter Novick, *That Noble Dream* (Cambridge, 1988), 21–108; George W. Stocking, *Race, Culture, and Evolution* (New York, 1968); Lee Baker, *From Savage to Negro* (Berkeley, 1998).

83. W. E. B. Du Bois, "To the Nations of the World" (1900), W. E. B. Du Bois papers (MS 312), Special Collections and University Archives, University of Massachusetts Amherst Libraries. On the event, see Marika Sherwood, *The Origins of Pan-Africanism* (Abingdon, 2010); Hakim Adi, *Pan-Africanism* (London, 2018), 19–22. I return to it, and to Du Bois, in the conclusion.

84. Leonard T. Hobhouse, *Social Evolution and Political Theory* (London, 1911), 144.

ontological category was a potent form of what Mark Jerng terms "racial worldmaking," the "narrative and interpretive strategies that embed race into our knowledge and expectations of the world."[85] Such practices organize the perceptual field so that race is regarded, explicitly or implicitly, as a fundamental organizing principle. Centering race in a narrative or explanatory scheme has the cognitive effect of constructing "new ways of seeing, new objects of attention, and new ways of connecting diverse experiences such that one cannot frame the world without instituting racial difference in its composition."[86]

Race was typically figured as a *biocultural assemblage*, a hybrid compound of "cultural" and "biological" claims about human evolutionary history, individual and collective character, comportment, mental capacity, and physiognomy.[87] The racial identity of Anglo-America was most commonly described as "Anglo-Saxon." The term was usually employed to designate a human collectivity defined by a vague admixture of mythology, historical experience, shared values, institutions, language, religious commitments, and cultural symbolism, all circumscribed (but not fully specified) by whiteness.[88] Individual thinkers diverged chiefly over how they ranked and configured the various elements. Political liberty, free enterprise, a shared literary and religious heritage, the English language: all could be assigned priority. Lawyers tended to stress the centrality of the common law. Pollock asserted that neither biological descent nor "material interest" could adequately explain the rapprochement between Britain and America. "Beyond the facts of speech and kindred, deeper than all our occasions of difference, is the common stock of traditions and institutions, the ideal of political and intellectual freedom which was framed in England by centuries of toil and conflict, and has gone round the world with the law happily called by a name neither distinctively English or American—our Common Law."[89] For James Bryce, the law was a cherished

85. Mark C. Jerng, *Racial Worldmaking* (New York, 2017), 31.

86. Jerng, *Racial Worldmaking*, 34.

87. Note that I use "biocultural assemblage" as a descriptive category intended to capture a prominent way that race was conceptualized at the time, not a normative concept for how we *should* think about it today.

88. For the long and shifting history of ideas about Anglo-Saxons, see Allen Frantzen and John Niles (eds.), *Anglo-Saxonism and the Construction of Social Identity* (Gainesville, 1997); Reginald Horsman, *Race and Manifest Destiny*. For a rare exception, suggesting that "Africans" can become Anglo-Saxon, see Frederick William Chapman, "The Changed Significance of 'Anglo-Saxon,'" *Education*, 20 (1900), 368–69. For accounts of Anglo-Saxonism and rapprochement, see Anderson, *Race and Rapprochement*; Vucetic, *Anglosphere*, ch. 2.

89. Pollock, "Monroe Doctrine," 552.

"common possession" of Britain and the United States, and in no other domain, he argued in 1907, "does the substantial identity of the two branches of
the old stock appear so much as in the doctrine and practice of the law, for the
fact that many new racial elements have gone to the making of the American
people causes in this sphere very little difference."[90] As we shall see in chapter 6, A. V. Dicey adopted a similar argument to promote a system of common citizenship between Britain and the United States.[91] But the color line
delimited the space in which variability could be expressed. Not all whites
were Anglo-Saxon, but all Anglo-Saxons were white. The fusion of biological
and cultural arguments created an unstable compound that helped structure
the political imagination. Late Victorian whiteness was, as Bill Schwarz puts
it, an "entire, fantasized discursive complex."[92]

The character of the "Anglo-Saxons," and the reasons for their economic
and political domination, attracted interest from a variety of continental European observers. Some of this work was translated into English, feeding the
very debates it sought to comprehend. The most popular—for obvious
reasons—was the French social reformer Edmond Demolins's extended hymn
to *Anglo-Saxon Superiority*, an elevated status that he attributed to their "particularistic formation," wherein the "individual is made to prevail over the
community."[93] This was a variation on the self-congratulatory theme that Britain, alone among the European powers, properly understood and enshrined
individual liberty. Not everyone was convinced. In the early twentieth century,
Karl Peters, a German politician, writer, and zealous imperialist, declared that
Britain was showing signs of degeneration, although he finished his analysis
by commending the "immense civilizatory work performed by the Anglo-
Saxon race on our planet." He predicted the future integration of the British
Empire and possible union with the United States. "And if the Anglo-Saxon
world firmly resolves organisationally to consolidate itself over this planet into

90. James Bryce, "The Influence of National Character and Historical Environment on the
Development of the Common Law," *Journal of the Society of Comparative Legislation*, 8/2 (1907),
203, 216.

91. A. V. Dicey, "A Common Citizenship for the English Race," *Contemporary Review*, 71
(1897), 457–76.

92. Bill Schwarz, *The White Man's World* (Oxford, 2011), 20.

93. Edmond Demolins, *Anglo-Saxon Superiority*, trans. Louis Bert Lavigne (London, 1898),
xiii. A more sober analysis can be found in Gaston Boutmy, *The English People*, trans. E. English
(London, 1904). For a more critical account of British imperialism, see Victor Bérard, *British
Imperialism and Commercial Supremacy*, trans. H. W. Foskett (London, 1906). He took aim in
particular at Chamberlain. See, in general, Emile Chabal, "The Rise of the Anglo-Saxon," *French
Politics, Culture & Society*, 31/1 (2013), 24–46.

a great federal state, it is difficult to see what power could prevent it from doing so."[94] For Peters, the only viable response was a German-led European union.

Advocacy of transnational whiteness, and Anglo-Saxonism in particular, was popular across the Angloworld. In Canada, claims about shared racial identity underpinned support for both imperial federation and (far less commonly) incorporation within the United States.[95] In 1901, the Immigration Restriction Act came into force in Australia, giving legal expression to the "White Australia" policy that persisted until the 1970s.[96] Both "global in its power and personal in its meaning, the basis of geo-political alliances and a subjective sense of self," the transnational ideology of white supremacism infused political culture in the United States and the British Empire.[97] People excluded from the embrace of whiteness were largely absent from the unionist discourse, except when they were figured as a problem or threat. African-Americans rarely appeared in fantasies of a future Anglo-racial polity, their supposed inferiority and political subordination accepted as a given. The indigenous populations of North America and the Pacific were assumed to be either irrelevant—due to their relatively small numbers—or heading for eventual extinction, and thus not worth sustained discussion.[98] As Sinclair Kennedy put it in his 1914 tract *The Pan-Angles*, "The aborigines of the United States and Canada, of New Zealand and Australia, are now problems of the past, solved according to nature's rule of the survival of the fittest."[99]

The "Anglo-Saxon" variant of whiteness was popular but contested. Some critics highlighted terminological imprecision. Dismissing the idea as historically illiterate, Freeman preferred to talk of the Teutons, or the "English

94. Karl Peters, *England and the English* (London, 1904), 358, 386. His account of the empire drew heavily on Seeley's *Expansion of England*. On Peters, see Arne Perras, *Carl Peters and German Imperialism, 1856–1918* (Oxford, 2004).

95. Damien-Claude Bélanger, *Prejudice and Pride* (Toronto, 2011); Aaron Boyes, "Towards the 'Federated States of North America,'" (PhD diss., University of Ottawa, 2016); Edward Kohn, *This Kindred People* (Montreal, 2004). On Australia, see Marilyn Lake, "British World or New World?," *History Australia*, 10/3 (2013), 36–50.

96. Marilyn Lake and Henry Reynolds, *Drawing the Global Colour Line* (Cambridge, 2008), ch. 6.

97. Lake and Reynolds, *Colour Line*, 3. On conceptions of "whiteness" in an Angloworld context, see Anderson, *Race and Rapprochement*; Kramer, "Empires, Exceptions, and Anglo-Saxons"; Schwarz, *White Man's World*, chs. 1–3. On hierarchies within whiteness, see Thomas Guglielmo, *White on Arrival* (Oxford, 2000).

98. On the latter discourse, see Patrick Brantlinger, *Dark Vanishings* (Ithaca, NY, 2003).

99. Sinclair Kennedy, *The Pan-Angles* (London, 1914), 27.

race."[100] This line was followed by his American disciples, including John Fiske, a best-selling philosopher and historian, who regarded its application to Britain, let alone the United States, as "absurd and misleading." Lamenting the "loose and slovenly way" that it was employed in political debate, he too favored "English race."[101] The British liberal historian J. L. Hammond charged that "the word escaped ridicule by evading definition."[102] It "might pass muster" as a "pseudo-scientific" designation for the populations of parts of the British Isles, but it was foolish to stretch it to encompass the United States and the settler world. Others mocked the vacuity of the claims made in its name. "There are some people," the idealist philosopher David Ritchie admonished, "who seem to think that an unlimited supply of what we call the Anglo-Saxon race is the best remedy for all the evils of the world," but the history of British imperialism demonstrated that "the unlimited Anglo-Saxon" was not "an altogether unmitigated blessing."[103] It was frequently pointed out that the population of the United States could not be reduced to common racial origin or characteristics. "There is no fundamental reason rooted in human nature by virtue of a community of blood and religion why Americans as a nation should regard England with instinctive sympathy and friendship," wrote the American journalist Mayo Hazeltine at the height of the Venezuela crisis.[104] Shared identity was an illusion.

Others rejected claims about the political salience of racial affinity. Paul Reinsch, a prominent American political scientist based at the University of Wisconsin, expressed his skepticism in *World Politics*, published in 1900. He interpreted the thawing of Anglo-American relations as a product of growing recognition of shared interests, and the allure of world-ordering joint action, rather than racial solidarity. The change in orientation, in other words, "may be ascribed to their belief that these two powers can without let or hindrance order the government of the world according to their own convenience." Racial consciousness lacked the power to ground strong political ties. "Race is scarcely a sufficient bond for the unity of a single national state, much less an

100. Edward A. Freeman, *Lectures to American Audiences* (Philadelphia, 1882), 38–67.

101. John Fiske, *American Political Ideas Viewed from the Standpoint of Universal History* (London, 1885), 95, 97.

102. Hammond, "Colonial and Foreign Policy," 186. For further skepticism about racial purity, see Graham Wallas, *Human Nature and Politics* (London, 1908), 280–81.

103. David George Ritchie, *Darwinism and Politics* (London, 1889), 96. Though as I explore in chapter 7, Ritchie later advocated a form of imperial peace.

104. Mayo Hazeltine, "The United States and Great Britain," *North American Review*, 162/474 (1896), 597.

international alliance of many such states."[105] While significant, it was not determinate. Other variables had to be included in any explanation of rapprochement.

Du Bois argued that an obsessive belief in the superiority of "whiteness" had taken hold on both sides of the Atlantic. Public opinion was dominated by a creed proclaiming the "present civilization of Europe and America" as "the greatest the world has ever seen," and attributed this greatness "to the white Germanic peoples." The implication drawn by those professing such a view was clear: "these races have a divine right to rule the world in such way as they think best."[106] Yet the assertion of Teutonic racial superiority was based on a false historical premise. "We print in the opening chapters of our children's histories theories of the origin and destiny of races over which the gravest of us must smile," he continued. "[W]e assume, for instance, elaborate theories of an 'Aryan' type of political institution, and then discover in the pits of the South African Basutos as perfect an agora or tungemot as ever existed among Greeks or Germans."[107] Understood in a sufficiently capacious manner, the historical record undercut rather than proved claims about Teutonic historical greatness and contemporary supremacy. Scholes also challenged the ideological scaffolding of racial supremacy, adapting (like Du Bois) the popular Afrocentric argument that it was the black Africans of ancient Egypt, rather than the derivative Greeks or Romans, who stood at the very foundation of Western civilization.[108] In the conclusion to this book I return to their arguments about time and history.

Unionists adduced a variety of responses to their critics. One—perhaps the most common—was simply to ignore them, viewing Anglo-Saxon supremacy as self-evident. Another was to gloss over the demographic differences,

---

105. Paul S. Reinsch, *World Politics at the End of the Nineteenth Century* (New York, 1900), 358. On Reinsch and his role in the history of international thought, see Brian Schmidt, "Paul S. Reinsch and the Study of Imperialism and Internationalism" in David Long and Schmidt (eds.), *Imperialism and Internationalism in the Discipline of International Relations* (Albany, NY, 2005), 43–69; John M. Hobson, *The Eurocentric Conception of World Politics* (Cambridge, 2012), 25, 121–23.

106. W. E. B. Du Bois, "The Future of the Negro Race in America" (1904), in *Writings*, I, 189–90. The essay was published originally in the January 1904 edition of *The East and the West*, a London periodical.

107. W. E. B. Du Bois, "The Laboratory in Sociology at Atlanta University" (1903), in *Writings*, I, 158. This essay originally appeared in *Annals of the American Academy of Political and Social Science* (May 1903).

108. T. E. S. Scholes, *The British Empire and Alliances* (London, 1900), 277–78. On this form of "vindicationist" historiography, see Wilson Moses, *Afrotopia* (Cambridge, 1998).

insisting that the majority of whites, as well as the norms and values shaping society, could be classified accurately as Anglo-Saxon. William Croswell Doane, Episcopal Bishop of Albany, argued that the racial profile of Anglo-America was constituted by shared language, values, and institutions, not biological descent.

> It is quite true that, if the census of descent were taken as the test, the sons or descendants of Englishmen by no means make up the majority of American citizens. But there is descent other than that of birth and a lineage beside that of blood. The unity of language, literature, and law between England and America is a threefold cord that cannot be broken. To have our English Bible, our English Shakespeare, our English Blackstone all absolutely American in reverence and influence outweighs, outvotes and overwhelms all questions of racial compositeness.[109]

In 1898, Abbott acknowledged that the United States was, strictly speaking, neither a Christian nor an Anglo-Saxon country. "It is not officially Christian," he intoned, "if thereby is meant a nation which gives political or financial advantage to one religion over another," and nor was it Anglo-Saxon "if thereby is meant a nation which sets itself to confer political power upon one race over another," but the key point was that although it was "officially neither," it was "practically both."[110] The dominant culture was white, Anglo-Saxon, and Protestant.

Other unionists adopted a different conceptual framework. Some invoked the "English race," while others referred to the "English-speaking peoples," a formulation that was especially popular among those who dismissed the plausibility of Anglo-Saxonist contentions or worried that they might inadvertently disrupt arguments for racial commonality and destiny.[111] Roosevelt used both "English race" and "English-speaking peoples" instead of "Anglo-Saxons" in order to signal the capacity of European immigrants to transmute into upstanding white American citizens. Wells, as I discuss in chapter 4, thought Anglo-Saxonism lacked scientific credibility—the racial "delirium,"

---

109. William C. Doane, "Patriotism," *North American Review*, 166 (1898), 318.

110. Abbott, "Basis of an Anglo-American Understanding," 519.

111. I discuss Wells's views in Duncan Bell, "Pragmatic Utopianism and Race," *Modern Intellectual History*, 16/3 (2019), 863–95. On the genealogy of "English-speaking peoples," and the role played by Wells in popularizing it, see Peter Clarke, "The English-Speaking Peoples before Churchill," *Britain and the World*, 4/2 (2011), 199–231. On Gladstone's usage, see F. H. Herrick, "Gladstone and the Concept of the 'English-Speaking Peoples,'" *Journal of British Studies*, 12/1 (1972), 150–56. Cf. William E. Gladstone, "Kin beyond Sea," *North American Review*, 127/264 (1878), 179–212.

he charged, was legitimated by a "vast edifice of sham science."[112] Although both sometimes employed "Anglo-Saxon," Carnegie and Stead also preferred "English-speaking peoples." The archaeologist Charles Waldstein argued that the notion of "Anglo-Saxon" racial identity was both misleading and dangerous: "it opens the door to that most baneful and pernicious of modern national diseases, namely, Ethnological Chauvinism." He was adamant that Britain and the United States shared enough features to constitute "one nationality," and he advocated "a great English-speaking Brotherhood."[113] Yet such arguments were hard to distinguish from those of the Anglo-Saxonists, and the putatively discrete vocabularies often blurred together or were used interchangeably. Nor did their adherents (with the partial exception of Wells) challenge the color line. Rather than indicating a postracial vision of community, the category of "English-speaking peoples" invoked an alternative conception of the racial polity.

An important implication of the biocultural understanding of race was that all whites could in principle be transmuted into Anglo-Saxons through a combination of acculturation and work on the self. This belief was woven through Anglo-American discourse. "Anglo-Saxon America is constantly engaged in absorbing," marveled Besant. A teeming mass of European immigrants arrived each year. "They land: they scatter over the country: in a few years, like those who are American born, they bear the stamp of the English law and speak the English language."[114] John Dos Passos, a Portuguese immigrant to the United States, expounded this view in *The Anglo-Saxon Century and the Unification of the English-speaking People*, a book whose very title illustrates the conceptual fluidity of the discourse. "[W]e are of the same family," he wrote: "we speak the same language; we have the same literature; we are governed substantially by the same political institutions; we possess similar laws, customs, and general modes of legal procedure." He also stressed shared religious belief, increasing levels of intermarriage, and "innumerable similarities" in habits, hobbies, love of sport, and drama.[115] Evincing that the Anglo community was constantly reenergized by European immigration, he added that the "foreign

112. Wells, *Modern Utopia*, 224.

113. Charles Waldstein, "The English-speaking Brotherhood," *North American Review*, 167 (1898), 225, 230, 238. On the English as a diaspora, see Tanja Bueltmann, David Gleeson, and Donald MacRaild, "Invisible Diaspora?," *Journal of American Ethnic History*, 33/4 (2014), 5–30; Tanja Bueltmann and Donald MacRaild, "Globalizing St George," *Journal of Global History*, 7/1 (2012), 79–105; David Haglund, *The US "Culture Wars" and the Anglo-American Special Relationship* (New York, 2019).

114. Besant, "Future of the Anglo-Saxon Race," 129.

115. Dos Passos, *Anglo-Saxon Century*, 141.

element" almost invariably "disappears, almost like magic, in the bosom of American nationality."[116] But this argument did not—and could not—apply to Asian immigrants, African-Americans, or the indigenous population. As throughout the unionist discourse, the color line held firm.

Cyborg Imperium: Racial Informatics, Infrastructural Space

> It is no mere platitude that we have reached the threshold of a new age. Democracy, nationality, socialism, the constitution of the modern State, the standing of the Churches—all have come within the attraction of forces hitherto unknown. Science applied to material arts has stimulated production, facilitated transport, multiplied and shortened the channels of communication, made gold as mobile as quicksilver. In different words, the habitable globe has undergone consolidation that only half a century ago would have seemed a miracle.[117]
>
> (JOHN MORLEY)

Technoscientific capacity was interpreted as both cause and effect of global hierarchy. It supposedly demonstrated the inherent superiority of European (and especially Anglo) powers even as it provided them with the practical means to maintain it.[118] Moreover, the ability to dominate nature was believed to endow the Anglo-Saxons with a moral mission to govern those incapable of generating such Promethean feats. It also heralded the creation of new forms of political association. Shattering existing conceptions of time and space, new communications and transport technologies precipitated the cognitive transformation necessary to imagine Anglo-America as a unified community. In *The Idea of Greater Britain*, I argued that late Victorian visions of the settler colonial world were predicated on this altered spatiotemporal consciousness.[119] A politically integrated Anglo-America was likewise inconceivable without a dense communications infrastructure to weave it together.

116. Dos Passos, *Anglo-Saxon Century*, 101, 104.

117. John Morley, "Democracy and Reaction" (1904), *Critical Miscellanies* (London, 1908), IV, 291.

118. This connection between technology and legitimacy was a common view in Euro-American imperial discourse: Michael Adas, *Machines as the Measure of Men* (Ithaca, NY, 1999); Adas, *Dominance by Design* (Cambridge, MA, 2006). On the importance of technology for imperial expansion, see Daniel Headrick, *The Tools of Empire* (Oxford, 1981); Headrick, *Power over Peoples* (Princeton, NJ, 2010).

119. Bell, *Greater Britain*, ch. 3.

Seeking to ride the wave of interest in sociopolitical prophecy inspired by the success of Bellamy's *Looking Backward*, John Macnie, a Scottish emigrant to the United States writing under the pseudonym "Ismar Thiusen," responded with *Looking Forward*, a relabeled variant of *The Diothas; or, A Far Look Ahead*, his 1883 novel of life in the ninety-sixth century.[120] Although unimpressed by the tale, Stead agreed with Macnie that the electrical current was transforming the human condition. "We have yet to open our eyes to the extent to which Electricity has re-energised the world," he opined. "What the revival of learning was to the Renaissance, what the discovery of the New World was to the Elizabethans, what the steamship was to the century of Revolution, the application of electricity is to the New Generation."[121] It had "annihilated time and abolished space," reanimated the "ideal of human brotherhood," and it was the "destined agent" to bring peace to the earth.[122] He was far from alone in dreaming an electrical future.

Expressions of wonder and awe about new technological systems—the infrastructural sublime—were common in social and political commentary in the closing decades of the century. Wells was acutely sensitive to the changes unfolding around him. "[M]odern mechanism," he argued in *Anticipations*, had initiated an "absolute release from the fixed conditions about which human affairs circled," while *A Modern Utopia* declared that "[t]here appears no limit to the invasion of life by the machine."[123] Some went as far as suggesting that humanity had become inseparable from its technological artifacts. In "The Book of the Machines," published in 1872 as part of his dystopian novel *Erewhon*, Samuel Butler wrote that "Man's very soul is due to the machines; it is a machine-made thing: he thinks as he thinks, feels as he feels, through the work that machines have wrought upon him, and their existence is quite as much a sine qua non for his, as his for theirs."[124] The coevolution of technology and humanity had created a new form of subjectivity. Even those who did not follow Butler into a posthuman world recognized that the machinic interpenetration of society had reconstituted forms of life and expanded the possibilities of political order.

120. John Macnie, *The Diothas; or, A Far Look Ahead* (New York, 1883). Macnie spent most of his career as a professor of languages at the University of North Dakota.

121. W. T. Stead, "Looking Forward," *RoR*, 1 (March 1890), 230. On Victorian "electrical futures," see Iwan Rhys Morus, "No Mere Dream," *Centaurus*, 57/3 (2015), 173–91; Graeme Gooday, "Electrical Futures Past," *Endeavour*, 29/4 (2005), 150–55.

122. W. T. Stead, *RoR*, 1 (March 1890), 230.

123. Wells, *Anticipations*, 44; Wells, *Modern Utopia*, 71.

124. Samuel Butler, *Erewhon*, ed. Peter Mudford (1872; London, 1970), 207. See also Anna Neill, "The Made Man and the 'Minor' Novel," *Victorian Studies*, 60/1 (2017), 53–73.

Blending material innovation with epistemic justification, the telegraph was central to this shift in consciousness. After a false start in 1858, an Atlantic cable was layed successfully in 1866, linking Britain, Canada, and the United States. Australia was plugged into the network in 1871, with New Zealand following five years later. Allowing peoples dispersed across space to interact near-simultaneously, it reshaped the terms of human interaction, fabricated trans-versal publics, and consolidated a thick sense of sociopolitical identity. Bryce proclaimed that "[n]o such means of gathering, diffusing, and concentrating public opinion, of quickening its formation and strengthening its action, had ever been dreamt of before our own time."[125] Francis de Winton, President of the Geographical Section of the British Association for the Advancement of Science, hymned this "extraordinary condition of contactiveness."[126] What had once been thought possible only in spatially restricted societies was now viable on a planetary scale. Benedict Anderson argued that one of the prin-cipal facilitating conditions of nationalism was the emergence of "empty homogenous time." A product (in part) of the technological infrastructure of print capitalism, this sense of temporality allowed a cohesive national community to be imagined as a single unity moving through history. "[I]n the mind of each lives the image of their communion."[127] Until the second half of the nineteenth century, this conception of political community was physically limited by the modest reach and speed of communications tech-nologies, but the ocean-going steamship and the submarine telegraph recast the geographical bases of social identification.[128]

The new technology prompted, as is so often the case, a range of novel conceptual and linguistic changes. Telegraphic imagery served as a fecund resource for rethinking existing phenomena, while other discourses in the human and natural sciences supplied concepts, metaphors, and analogies to make sense of emergent technological possibilities. Political thinkers, cultural

---

125. James Bryce, "An Age of Discontent," *Contemporary Review*, 59 (1891), 19. For further discussion of instantaneity, see Carolyn Marvin, *When Old Technologies Were New* (Oxford, 1988).

126. Frances W. De Winton, "Address," *Proceedings of the Royal Geographical Society*, 11 (1889), 621.

127. Benedict Anderson, *Imagined Communities*, new ed. (London, 2006), 24–26, 6. On the continuing value of Anderson's cognitive approach to communal identify formation, see Max Bergholz, "Thinking the Nation," *American Historical Review*, 123/2 (2018), 518–28. Lake and Reynolds, *Drawing the Global Color Line*, criticize Anderson for normalizing the nation as the imagined community of modernity, effacing other forms of trans- or supranational affiliations, including race (6).

128. Bell, *Reordering the World*, ch. 7.

commentators, and scientists alike drew on the language of the nervous system to describe the nature and functioning of the telegraph, just as telegraphic imagery fed into scientific work on the human body.[129] The nervous system metaphor was fused with older organic images of the political community to provide a new account of the body politic: it was animated, controlled, and disciplined by the circulation of electrical pulses carrying information. The electrical dream pervaded Anglo-American discourse. Forming part of a cohesive information order, the "English race" was envisioned as a globally extended community bound and ordered by electricity. Obsessed with the political implications of communications technology, Carnegie asserted that immense expanses of water "no longer constitute barriers between nations." Spanning oceans and continents, forcing all into an intimate embrace, the chief agent of change was the telegraph.

> Without this agency it might well be doubted whether one central authority could act for all the scattered parts, but when events and problems as they arise, and the discussions upon them at the centre, can be instantly known at the extremities, and become everywhere the subject of contemporaneous debate and consideration, thus permitting the centre to influence the extremities and the extremities to respond to the centre, the pulse beat of the entire nation can be constantly felt by the government and all the people. No matter where the capital may be, it must still be omnipresent and in touch with all parts of the confederacy. Time is therefore no longer to be taken into account at all, and distance means but little when all can instantly hear everything that transpires.[130]

This technological wonder was the "most important factor in rendering political union possible, and I venture to say inevitable."[131] People distributed throughout the English-speaking world now occupied the same temporal plane—the image of their communion was vastly magnified by thousands of miles of copper wire girding the planet. They moved together through empty homogenous time. Stretched across thousands of miles, this newly constituted people could be imagined in the singular, an intricate synthesis of bodies, machinic infrastructure, and electrical current.

---

129. Laura Otis, *Networking* (Ann Arbor, 2011); Otis, "The Other End of the Wire," *Configurations*, 9/2 (2001), 191; Iwan Rhys Morus, "'The Nervous System of Britain,'" *British Journal for the History of Science*, 33/4 (2000), 455–75. On organic imagery, see also Katie-Louise Thomas, "Racial Alliance and Postal Networks in Conan Doyle's 'A Study in Scarlet,'" *Journal of Colonialism and Colonial History*, 2/1 (2001), 9–23.

130. Carnegie, *Reunion*, 12.

131. Carnegie, *Reunion*, 12.

The problem with the Victorian telegraph-as-nervous-system metaphor is that it either effaces or naturalizes the infrastructure necessary to sustain the information order. It effaces it insofar as it presents an image of a disembodied flow of data, abstracted from its material substrate. It naturalizes it insofar as it recodes as blood and flesh an infrastructural complex built with copper, steel, wood, and gutta-percha. The telegraphic network was no dematerialized stream of data, nor was it an organic whole: it was a formidably complicated translocal fusion of humans and machines. It provided fin-de-siècle racial unionists with a technological assemblage that knit together the far reaches of the "Anglo-Saxon" race. This was a cyborg vision of racial order.

The cyborg can be defined, Andrew Pickering writes, as a "part-human, part machine actor in which the two parts are constitutively coupled with one another."[132] The figure has been conceptualized in assorted ways.[133] For some, notably Donna Haraway, cyborgs are historically specific creations of post–World War II technoculture.[134] Others have expanded the historical compass of the idea. Allison Muri, for example, identifies early Enlightenment automata as cyborg beings.[135] A stronger claim can be made for the Victorian era. The boundaries between humanity and machinery were increasingly called into question, and a series of thinkers—including Charles Babbage, Harriet Martineau, and Karl Marx—invoked an evolving "human-machine complex."[136] The Victorians, Herbert Sussman argues, were "preoccupied with the mechanical/ organic problematic raised by the unprecedented self-acting machines of the

132. Andrew Pickering, "Cyborg History and the WWII Regime," *Perspectives on Science*, 3/1 (1995), 3. I expand on this argument in Bell, "Cyborg Imperium, c.1900" in Anne Chapman and Natalie Hume (eds.), *Coding and Representation from the Nineteenth Century to the Present* (London, forth.).

133. See especially Donna Haraway, "A Cyborg Manifesto" in Haraway, *Simians, Cyborgs, and Women* (London, 1991), 149–81; N. Katherine Hayles, *How We Became Posthuman* (Chicago, 1999); Chris Hables Gray, Heidi J. Figueroa, and Steven Menor (eds.), *The Cyborg Handbook* (London, 1995).

134. Haraway, *Simians, Cyborgs, and Women*, 1. Hayles argues persuasively that the cyborg is not a useful figure for comprehending human-machine sociotechnical systems in the internet age: "Unfinished Work," *Theory Culture Society*, 23/7 (2006), 159–66.

135. Allison Muri, *The Enlightenment Cyborg* (Toronto, 2007). For a challenge to this usage, see Koen Vermeir, "RoboCop Dissected," *Technology and Culture*, 49/4 (2008), 1036–44. On the long-standing ascription of agency to nonhumans, see Jessica Riskin (ed.), *Genesis Redux* (Chicago, 2007); Riskin, *The Restless Clock* (Chicago, 2016).

136. Tamara Ketabgian, *The Lives of Machines* (Ann Arbor, 2011); Otis, *Networking*. For a useful overview of the Victorian celebration of technoscience, see Herbert Sussman, *Victorian Technology* (Westport, 2009).

textile mills as well as the Babbage engines," wondrous machines that "transformed the meaning of 'computer' from a human being who calculated to a machine that thinks."[137] The image and ethos of technology permeated cultural consciousness, literary speculation, and social and political thought.

We can distinguish two conceptions of the cyborg, one *integrative*, the other *additive*. The additive model construes technology as prosthesis, a means of augmenting extant human capacities by harnessing the body in a complex technological array. Hence the new factory machines or computing devices of the early Victorian era can be seen as forming part of a cyborg system alongside their human operators. On such a view, many nineteenth-century systems—including global capitalism itself—display cyborg features. Arguably, though, this account is too broad, and misses something specific about cyborgs: the material interpenetration of technology and organism. In Pickering's felicitous phrase, cyborgs are "constitutively coupled." In the additive account, the pregiven body remains intact, albeit augmented in some sense, whether physical, cognitive, or both. The integrationist conception, by contrast, necessitates the transformation (maybe destruction) of the existent body, its meshing with technological artifacts to create a new entity.

A political order can be imagined as cyborg in at least two ways. First, as an entity populated by cyborg beings. Read in an additive sense, numerous representations of Anglo-America fit this description, perhaps most obviously those found in the ambitious science fiction portrayals of racial unity I discuss in chapter 5.[138] The technological marvels depicted in such texts, whether new weapons systems, communications devices, or modes of transport, are external to the body, not integrated into it. Technology serves as a powerful prosthetic extension, without requiring the machinic reconstitution of the human body. An alternative is where a (political) community is figured as a cyborg. This can be discerned in the Anglo-American discourse. The cyborg was produced by melding an organic conception of political community, a body politic, with the image of the telegraph-as-nervous-system. It allowed instantaneous communication across the different parts of the whole. Simultaneity conjured up the empty homogenous time that allowed Anglo-America (and the Angloworld as a whole) to be imagined as a single political community. In unionist discourse, the race was often construed as an agent—as doing,

---

137. Herbert Sussman, "Machine Dreams," *Victorian Literature and Culture*, 28/1 (2000), 202. On the cultural impact of the telegraph, see Caroline Arscott and Claire Pettit (eds.), *Victorians Decoded* (London, 2016).

138. Some work has explored the idea of individual Victorians as (Harawayian) cyborgs. On Harriet Martineau as a "chimera," see Abigail Mann and Kathleen Rogers, "Objects and Objectivity," *Prose Studies*, 33/3 (2011), 241–56.

thinking, feeling, and acting. Some of the more radical unionists, notably Wells, implied that the "nervous system" and "brain" of the race constituted a form of distributed intelligence and decision-making. In principle, there were no limits to the spatial dispersal of the race. Indeed, some speculative texts imagined a future cyborg imperium stretched across the cosmos, as the "Anglo-Saxons" set out to conquer the stars.[139] The interweaving of technological apparatus and humans portended a rethinking of the meaning of race. In addition to claims about its variable cultural content and physiological boundaries, Anglo-Saxondom (or the English-speaking people) depended upon, and was structured by, a sophisticated material infrastructure. Rather than seeing technology as separable from race—an exogenous product of Anglo-Saxon genius capable of being utilized for instrumental purposes—it was figured as an integral element of it. Race had been thoroughly technologized. The racial dreamworld was unintelligible without this conceptual reconfiguration.

139. See, for example, William Cole, *The Struggle for Empire 2236* (1900), in *Political Future Fiction*, ed. R. Bleiler (London, 2013), I, 133–99. I discuss this book in chapter 5.

2

The Dreamer of Dreams

ANDREW CARNEGIE AND THE REUNION OF THE RACE

Born a subject of the Monarchy, adopted a citizen of the Republic, how could it be otherwise than that I should love both lands and long to do whatever in me lay to bring their people to share that love for each other![1]

(ANDREW CARNEGIE)

Introduction

From the 1880s until his death in 1919, Andrew Carnegie proselytized the union of Britain and the United States. At his Scottish castle, Skibo, he flew a flag with the Union Jack embossed on one side and the Stars and Stripes on the other, a symbolic representation of both his dual identity and his dream of an Anglo future.[2] Carnegie saw himself as embodying the Anglo-American relationship, an Archimedean envoy translating Britain and the United States to each other and facilitating their reunification. The "Federation of English-speaking peoples," his first biographer recorded, is "the political project which is dearer to Mr Carnegie than any other."[3] This new polity, Carnegie claimed, would usher in an era of global peace and justice. The political millennium was within reach.

It is unsurprising that Carnegie was a fervent believer in the power of dreams. Born in poverty in Dunfermline, Scotland, his family emigrated to the

---

1. Andrew Carnegie, *Triumphant Democracy* (New York, 1886), v.

2. For mentions of the flag, see Andrew Carnegie, "Americanism versus Imperialism," *North American Review*, 168/506 (1899), 5–6; Speech in Ottawa, 28 April 1906, Box 252, 9, Carnegie papers; Carnegie, notes for a speech at the Presentation of the Freedom of Glasgow, 10 September 1909, Box 251, 6, Carnegie papers.

3. Barnard Alderson, *Andrew Carnegie* (New York, 1902), 105.

United States in 1848, and at the age of thirteen he started work in a cotton mill in Pittsburgh. By his thirtieth birthday, he was a multimillionaire.[4] He continued to accumulate wealth at an astonishing rate, first in the booming railway industry and then in steel, ending the century as one of the wealthiest individuals in the world. A man of endless contradictions, Carnegie proclaimed himself a humble friend of the workers while triggering some of the fiercest labor disputes in American history—most infamously at Homestead, where twelve of his employees were killed.[5] As he drove down wages in his steel plants, he distributed immense sums of money to a plethora of philanthropic endeavors throughout the English-speaking world, reveling in a reputation for generosity. And as he campaigned tirelessly for the peace movements in Britain and the United States, he chased steel orders to build ships for the US Navy. Keen to carve out a role in the republic of letters, and craving recognition as a serious thinker, Carnegie cultivated an extraordinary network of intellectuals and politicians on both sides of the Atlantic. A fluent and versatile author, his fame and wealth guaranteed a wide readership. Foremost among his obsessions was the reunification of Britain and the United States. Stead, a friend and confidant, praised him as the "leading exponent of the idea."[6] This chapter explores Carnegie's shifting racial dreamworld. The next section outlines his account of historical change, the value of social dreaming, and his early ideas about racial reunion. I then discuss some of the most popular historical narratives deployed by unionists, including Carnegie, to ground their claims about Anglo-America, focusing especially on Teutonist visions of racial development. The following sections analyze some of the responses prompted by Carnegie's writing, the connections he drew between war, empire, and reunion, and a range of theological arguments about racial destiny.

Anglo-America and the Logic of Historical Progress

Carnegie embraced the utopian character of his beloved project. "The dream, in which no one perhaps indulges more than the writer, of the union of the English-speaking race, even that entrancing dream must be recognized as only a dream," he wrote in 1893.[7] But in a democratic twist of Shelley's boast that poets are the unacknowledged legislators of the world, Carnegie insisted that

---

4. The best account of his life is David Nasaw, *Andrew Carnegie* (London, 2006).

5. Paul Kahan, *The Homestead Strike* (London, 2014). For his own self-serving account, see *Autobiography of Andrew Carnegie*, ch. 17.

6. Stead, *Americanization*, 407.

7. Carnegie, *Reunion*, 8.

dreams were both the prerogative and the privilege of the engaged citizen. In the career of the "statesman," marked by incremental adjustment and pragmatic decision-making, social dreaming was a vice not a virtue, a danger not a duty. "When a statesman has in his keeping the position and interests of his country," Carnegie maintained, "all speculation as to the future fruition of ideas of what should be or what will one day rule the world . . . must be resolutely dismissed." His task was to engage the present, not to speculate about the future.[8] Facing no such constraints, the private citizen was ideally placed to scan the horizon, searching for the veiled patterns of historical development. They could and should dream of better worlds. "I am a dreamer of dreams. So be it." Dreaming was a necessary spur and guide to action. "And if it be a dream, it is a dream nobler than most realities. If it is never to be realised, none the less it should be realised, and shame to those who come after us if it be not. I believe it will be, for all progress is on its side."[9]

Carnegie's adamantine confidence that progress would deliver racial reunion was derived from (or rationalized by) his interpretation of Herbert Spencer's philosophy of history. A man prone to credulous hero-worship, Carnegie elevated Spencer, along with Matthew Arnold, to his pantheon of intellectual gods, frequently describing himself as a "disciple" of the "master."[10] As he once wrote to Spencer, "To be able to call him [Matthew Arnold] and you as friends is my greatest privilege."[11] Carnegie first met Spencer in the early 1880s, and thereafter cultivated his friendship and cited him regularly as a source of inspiration—the cantankerous philosopher was "the greatest thinker of the age."[12] Carnegie's belief in the inviolability of Spencer's system underwrote what his friend John Morley, the liberal historian and politician, once referred to as his "invincible optimism."[13] Sounding much like John Stuart Mill's cherished memory of his first encounter with Bentham's writings, Carnegie recalled that after reading Spencer (and Darwin) as a young man, "I remember that light came as in a flood and all was clear. Not only had I got rid

8. Carnegie, "Americanism versus Imperialism," 8.

9. Carnegie, *Reunion*, 31.

10. Carnegie, *Autobiography*, chs. 22 and 25; Nasaw, *Andrew Carnegie*, ch. 12. See also his draft Rectorial Address, St Andrews, 1902, Box 251, 12; Carnegie to Stead, 1 February 1901, Fol 81, Carnegie papers. For Spencer's more cautious account of their first meeting, see Herbert Spencer, *An Autobiography* (New York, 1904), II, 396–97.

11. Carnegie to Spencer, 1 May 1897, Fol 41; see also Carnegie to Spencer, 10 October 1900, Fol 78, Carnegie papers.

12. Andrew Carnegie, *Round the World* (New York, 1884), 23.

13. John Morley, *Recollections* (London, 1917), II, 111. For the temperamental contrast between Morley and Carnegie, see Carnegie, *Autobiography*, 277–78.

of theology and the supernatural, but I had found the truth of evolution."[14] That Spencerian truth, at least as digested by Carnegie, was that humanity was by nature progressive and perfectible. "The endless progress of the [human] race is assured now that evolution has come with its message and shed light where before there was darkness."[15] "Man," Carnegie opined, "was not created with an instinct for his own degradation, but from the lower he has risen to the higher forms. Nor is there any conceivable end to his march to perfection." Dreams that might seem impossible "may prove easy of getting." Attaining Tennyson's Parliament of Man was "only a question of time in the mind of the evolutionist who sees no bounds to the advance of man in the line of brotherhood."[16] Carnegie once mused that human immortality was a possibility—inexorable sociotechnical progress would likely result in the supersession of death itself.[17]

This Panglossian rendering of Spencer's evolutionary social theory was encapsulated in a pithy motto that Carnegie had inscribed above his desk and that recurred throughout his writing: "All is well since all grows better." Perhaps revealing more than he intended, he concluded that this was his "true source of comfort."[18] Although it is questionable how much of Spencer's labyrinthine theoretical system Carnegie understood, he shared the naturalism, agnosticism, radical individualism, and belief in the progressive character of evolutionary development, enunciated by his favorite philosopher. Carnegie's account of historical change—a kind of naturalized secular theodicy—sustained his boundless optimism, moralized his rapacious capital accumulation, and guaranteed the realization of his political desires. "Utopian as the dream may seem," he declared, "I place on record my belief that it is one day to become a reality."[19]

Incessant travel around the world served only to confirm Carnegie's sanguine forecast. "The parts fit into one symmetrical whole," he noted in his

14. Carnegie, *Autobiography*, 291. Cf. John Stuart Mill, *Autobiography, Collected Works of John Stuart Mill*, ed. John Robson (Toronto, 1981), I, 68: "I now had opinions; a creed, a doctrine, a philosophy; in one (and the best) sense of the word, a religion." Mill was another of Carnegie's heroes.

15. Carnegie, *Round the World*, 204.

16. Andrew Carnegie, "Imperial Federation," *Nineteenth Century*, 30 (1891), 503.

17. Carnegie, *Autobiography*, 292.

18. Carnegie, *Autobiography*, 291. On its place above his desk, see his letter to David Jayne Hill, 27 August 1906, Fol 132, Carnegie papers. For skepticism about his grasp of the intricacies of Spencer's thought, see John White, "Andrew Carnegie and Herbert Spencer," *Journal of American Studies*, 13/1 (1979), 57–71.

19. Carnegie, *Reunion*, 3.

autobiography, "and you see humanity wherever it is placed working out a destiny tending to one definite end."[20] Although he never specified in any detail what form that end would assume, we can infer that it was a harmonious industrial republican order, lead wisely and beneficently by the politically integrated members of the "English-speaking race." Carnegie was quick to draw a moral lesson from his sweeping observations on historical destiny. "Humanity is an organism, inherently rejecting all that is deleterious, that is, wrong, and absorbing after trial what is beneficial, that is, right."[21] Unwittingly, he committed the "naturalistic fallacy"—the idea that the (moral) good can be derived from empirical properties of the world—that the philosopher G. E. Moore would soon make famous in his evisceration of Spencer's ethical naturalism.[22]

Dreams served a premonitory function, delineating the shape of future sociopolitical orders and identifying apposite ways of accelerating (or retarding) their emergence. They were anticipatory interventions in the flow of time. Admitting that his unionist project might seem a hopeless fantasy, Carnegie oscillated between claiming that it was probable or inevitable. In both cases he implicitly distinguished two modalities of utopian optimism, one admirable, the other deserving of contempt. The former identified visions of a perfected future that could be derived from a hard-headed analysis of social evolution. It aligned with the coordinates of historical development. Anglo-America was one such utopia. The latter promised something it could never deliver, conjuring up images of future worlds that failed to conform to the teleological trajectory of history. It was untimely. Hence in some of his other writings, notably the popular "Gospel of Wealth," Carnegie dismissed political movements that aimed to transform the socioeconomic foundations of capitalism. Rapid human progress was only possible in societies that encouraged fierce competition, and the aim of responsible politics (and philanthropy) was the "reconciliation" of rich and poor, not the abolition of inequality. Anarchist and socialist calls to eliminate private property were "not evolution, but revolution," necessitating a fundamental change in human nature, "a work of eons, even if it were good to change it, which we cannot know."[23] Carnegie was

---

20. Carnegie, *Autobiography*, 180. The theme of universal progress runs through Carnegie, *Round the World*.

21. Carnegie, *Autobiography*, 291.

22. George Edward Moore, *Principia Ethica* (Cambridge, 1903), 58.

23. Andrew Carnegie, "The Gospel of Wealth" (1889), reprinted in Carnegie, *Autobiography*, 327. For a further attack on socialism, see Carnegie, *Problems of Today* (New York, 1908). By then Carnegie defined himself (in the American context) as a "Progressive," and supported limited state intervention to address wealth inequality (121–39).

convinced that his dream of racial reunion was compatible with both human nature and the evolutionary dynamics of free-market capitalism.

Although his proposal for reunifying Britain and the United States only gained widespread attention during the 1890s, Carnegie had been pursuing the idea for at least a decade beforehand. During the 1880s he frequently yoked Anglo-American reunion to the cause of radical reform in British politics, making the creation of the former wholly dependent on the success of the latter. A descendent of Chartist agitators—and a self-professed Radical liberal until his dying days—Carnegie's most elaborate critique of British politics can be found in *Triumphant Democracy*, published in 1886.[24] Both a paean to his adopted country and a jeremiad aimed at his original homeland, it articulated a simple message: to achieve future success, Britain needed to mimic its off-spring across the Atlantic. Republican government was Carnegie's "fetish," and he was "an ardent worshipper at its shrine."[25] Although their political institutions and social systems differed greatly, the two populations, he argued, constituted a single "race."[26] Yet even as the immense potential of the race was being unleashed in an egalitarian democratic polity on one side of the Atlantic, it was hamstrung by obsolete feudal structures on the other. Institutional variation was reflected in contrasting rates of economic growth. In order to demonstrate the intrinsic superiority of republicanism, Carnegie set out to explain the massive burst in American productivity between 1830 and 1880. He posited three variables: "the ethnic character of the people, the topographical and climatic conditions under which they developed, and the influence of political institutions founded upon the equality of the citizen."[27] While all played a significant role, he concluded that political institutions made the greatest difference. Diagnosing the monarchy as the main impediment to British socioeconomic development, Carnegie called for the abolition of hereditary privilege and a written constitution. "The Republic honors her children at birth with equality; the Monarchy stamps hers with the brand of inferiority."[28] The autobiographical trace in this judgment was patent. The

24. Carnegie, *Triumphant Democracy*. See also his earlier attacks on British governing institutions: Andrew Carnegie, "As Others See Us," *Fortnightly Review*, 31/182 (1882), 157–65; Carnegie, "Democracy in England," *North American Review*, 142/350 (1886), 74–80. For a useful analysis of the text, see A. S. Eisenstadt, *Carnegie's Model Republic* (Albany, 2007).

25. Alderson, *Andrew Carnegie*, 94.

26. Carnegie, *Triumphant Democracy*, 16.

27. Carnegie, *Triumphant Democracy*, 11.

28. Carnegie, *Triumphant Democracy*, 498.

reception of *Triumphant Democracy* was largely predictable: while lambasted in Britain, it received a much more favorable response in the United States.[29]

This analysis of British institutions informed Carnegie's early advocacy of reunion. In an address delivered to the Liberal Association in Glasgow in 1887, for example, he called for the adoption of a written constitution modeled on the American template, predicting that eventually all of the English-speaking peoples would be governed by republican institutions. Reunion could be enacted only after that transformation had occurred.

> How long will it take after that assimilation is perfected before we have a Federal Council that will forever render it impossible that the blood of English-speaking man can be shed by English-speaking man (*Loud cheers*). Where lies your greatest hopes that your own race, the dominant power of the world, shall coalesce and form a union against which nothing on earth shall stand? (*Loud cheers*). In the assimilation of your institutions. There lies the point.[30]

Three years later, at an event in Dundee, he argued that "there is only one way you can make a step towards the unification and consolidation of the English-speaking race, and that is by bringing this little island into line with the progeny which she has established throughout the world. Monarchy is too small a tail to wag so big a dog as republicanism." The center of political gravity had shifted; the future was being forged in the United States. Britain needed to adapt to the American example or retreat into obscurity. Instituting an elected President, he continued, would be the "first step" in the "great mission of the English-speaking race" to enforce disarmament and spread peace. Further ahead, under a distant but perceptible horizon, a still grander apparition could be glimpsed, and he concluded both addresses with a peroration invoking the words of Tennyson. "Beyond this stretches the noble dream of the poet, and I believe it is salutary to dwell upon these dreams—dreams that should become realities. . . . After the English race become united we have 'the Parliament of man, the Federation of the world.'"[31] The reunification of the English-speaking peoples would herald the future unity of humanity.

---

29. On its reception, see Eisenstadt, *Carnegie's Model Republic*, chs. 5 and 6; Nasaw, *Andrew Carnegie*, 275–76. It sold seventeen thousand copies in the first few months (*Carnegie's Model Republic*, 8).

30. Andrew Carnegie, "Home Rule in America: A Political Address," St. Andrew's Hall, Glasgow, 13 September 1887, published as a pamphlet by the Glasgow Junior Liberal Association, Edinburgh, 1887 (Box 250, Carnegie papers), 52.

31. Andrew Carnegie, "Some Facts about the American Republic," 1 September 1890, reprinted in the *Dundee Advertiser*, 4 September 1890, 14 (Box 250, Carnegie papers); Carnegie,

During the 1890s, we can discern a subtle but important shift in Carnegie's argument. Decoupling political reform and racial (re)union, he recast domestic change as an inevitable outcome of future historical development rather than a precondition for initiating a process of integration. This allowed him to short-circuit his previous model of transition, suggesting that the first important steps to reunion could be taken prior to the comprehensive diffusion of republicanism throughout the Angloworld. This shift was welcomed by Stead, who had discussed it at length with his friend. "He is even prepared to abandon the extreme Republican doctrinaire view," Stead wrote in the *Review of Reviews* in June 1898, "and will no longer prescribe the abolition of Monarchy, House of Lords, Established Church, and Indian Empire, as a condition precedent to Reunion." Instead, Carnegie supported a version of "home rule all round" that allowed for considerable local institutional autonomy.[32]

Promotion of Anglo-American union and imperial federation were often conjoined, the two projects viewed as either complementary (and thus capable of being pursued simultaneously) or parts of a historical sequence leading to the eventual unification of all the English-speaking people (in which case it made sense to prioritize one of them). Carnegie rejected both approaches. In *Triumphant Democracy*, he lambasted imperial federation as both undesirable and unworkable, suggesting instead that in the future Britain and its settler colonies should form a "league of peace" between independent political communities.[33] Returning to the issue five years later, he once again advocated the dissolution of the settler colonial system. Canada remained "only nominally" part of the British empire, "a wayward child, unjust and tyrannical to her mother because bursting into manhood." A similar dynamic was shaping the destiny of Australia.[34] Adopting a common metaphor, he suggested that both would soon leave the household to seek their own (republican) fortune. Although Carnegie agreed with the imperial federalists about the civilizational superiority of the "English-speaking peoples" and the importance of building massive political associations to harness it, he regarded attempts to unite the British settler colonies and the "mother country" as absurd. Economically illiterate, politically hopeless, and based on a fatal misunderstanding of the

---

"Home Rule in America," 52, 53. The phrase—which I discussed in the book's introduction—is from Tennyson's "Locksley Hall" (1842).

32. W. T. Stead, *RoR*, 17 (June 1898), 612; Stead, *Americanization*, 411–12.

33. Carnegie, *Triumphant Democracy*, 77–78.

34. Andrew Carnegie, "The Venezuelan Question," *North American Review*, 162/471 (1896), 131–32.

colonial order, such plans were "mistaken, impractical, and pernicious."[35] Extending the familial metaphor, Carnegie argued for independence.

> It is of the utmost importance that the people of Britain should promptly realise her true relation to her colonies, which is just this: she is the motherland, and no nation has ever been blessed with a family so numerous, enterprising, and creditable. The only part open to her is to play the mother, as her children grow beyond the need of her fostering care, to endeavour to inculcate in them the ambition to go forth and manage themselves.[36]

Above all, imperial federation was a gratuitous distraction from the more important task of securing Anglo-American union. The Imperial Federation League, he maintained, was "a body, whose effort is to combine only the minority of the English-speaking race in a solid phalanx, leaving out the majority."[37] While motivated by admirable sentiments, its supporters failed to grasp the real source of British greatness. The choice was *between* imperial federation and Anglo-American union. Dismantling the colonial empire was a precondition for racial concord and stronger Anglo-American relations. Carnegie was likewise scathing of Chamberlain's plan for imperial tariff reform, which he regarded as an impediment to true racial union. "I am as you are a Race Imperialist," he wrote to Stead in 1903, "and this scheme thwarts that ideal."[38]

An equally pressing concern was the virulent strain of Anglophobia infecting American political culture. "This is all very unfortunate," Carnegie warned in 1890, "but a period cannot be fixed when this feeling against England will cease to affect the Young American." He identified the main cause as a deformation of collective psychology, grounded in intrafamilial envy and *ressentiment*.

> The relation between the old and the new lands has never, until now, been such as to furnish a good foundation for genuine friendship and increasing regard. The position of affairs between the two branches of the English-speaking race is just this: an eldest son has made a great success since he left his father's roof, and it is difficult for an energetic and pugnacious old gentleman to realize that the son has attained his majority, and has become a man resembling his parent in no quality more than in being determined

---

35. Carnegie, "Imperial Federation," 502. His position was criticized strongly by the prominent Canadian federalist George Parkin: *Imperial Federation* (London, 1892), ch. 11.

36. Carnegie, "Imperial Federation," 499.

37. Carnegie, "Imperial Federation," 496.

38. Carnegie to Stead, (?? 1903), Fol 99, Carnegie papers.

to make his own way in the world, and work out his destiny after his own fashion, feeling that destiny to be something so grand that the world has never seen the like.[39]

Despite the prevalence of intraracial animosity, Carnegie was unfailingly hopeful. Like other unionists, he had to address how such a radical change could be instigated. There were two main responses. A minority contended that it had to be driven from below, emanating from shifts in popular belief that the governing elite could then harness. Others, including Rhodes, Stead, and Wells, argued that it could only be fomented by enlightened leaders, a political avant-garde whose task it was to cajole the ignorant masses. Forming a clerisy, they would act in concert—either openly or in secret—to channel public opinion. Carnegie adopted the vanguardist position. "We must not expect the idea to win its way at first," he confided to Stead, "except with the finest and most intuitive minds: none the less, it is sure to come."[40]

While Carnegie promoted Anglo-American reunion throughout the 1880s, and concluded his attack on imperial federation in 1891 by making the case for "the unity of our race, and through that . . . the mastery of the world, for the good of the world," it was his essay "A Look Ahead" that generated the most attention.[41] Written as a new concluding chapter for the second edition of *Triumphant Democracy*, it was also published as a pamphlet, and as an article in the June 1893 volume of the *North American Review*.[42] 1893 was a propitious moment to divine the contours of the future. At a lecture in Chicago, the historian Frederick Jackson Turner outlined his "frontier thesis," warning that the closing of the American West threatened to dissipate the creative dynamism that had shaped the United States.[43] Stagnation and stupor beckoned, leading

39. Andrew Carnegie et al., "Do Americans Really Hate England?," *North American Review*, 150/403 (1890), 753, 758.

40. Carnegie to Stead, 11 August 1893, Fol 21, Carnegie papers.

41. Carnegie, "Imperial Federation," 502. He suggested, as a first step, commissions "charged with creating a system of weights, measures, and coins, of port dues patents, and other matters of similar character which are of common interest," and an arbitration "council" that could form the nucleus of a future "Supreme Court" of the English-speaking peoples (505–6).

42. The major difference between the two editions of *Triumphant Democracy* was the excision of the "General Reflections" from the first edition and its replacement with "A Look Ahead."

43. Frederick Jackson Turner, "The Significance of the Frontier in American History" (1893), in J. M. Faragher (ed.), *Rereading Frederick Jackson Turner* (New Haven, CT, 1998), 31–60. On Turner and the intellectual legacy of the thesis, see Kerwin Lee Klein, *Frontiers of Historical Imagination* (Berkeley, 1997). On the trope of the frontier in British and American fiction, see David Trotter, *The English Novel in History, 1895–1920* (Oxford, 1993), 144–51.

some of Turner's readers to propose imperial expansion as a natural extension of the frontier and a remedy to the dangers of spatial confinement.[44] The social gospel theologian Josiah Strong released *The New Era, or, The Coming Kingdom*, its title speaking to the eschatological perfectionism he envisaged as both the duty and the destiny of the Anglo-Saxons.[45] It was also the year that C. H. Pearson published *National Life and Character*. Penned by a radical liberal historian and politician based in Australia, it challenged triumphalist views of white racial destiny, imagining a future world dominated by bitter geo-racial competition, especially with the Chinese, and warning that the dominant powers may be "elbowed and hustled and perhaps even thrust aside."[46] This was a pessimistic counterview to the unabashed confidence pulsing through utopian visions of Anglo-Saxonism.

Unburdened by the anxiety driving many of his contemporaries into print, Carnegie veered between historical prediction and political advocacy, backing the creation of a "British American Union." Once people understood its manifold benefits, the idea would be "hailed with enthusiasm" on both sides of the Atlantic.[47] Reunion was economically rational. Unlike the chimera of imperial federation, it would help to secure free trade—a somewhat ironic line from a man who had made a fortune behind the steep tariff walls sheltering the American steel market.[48] Moreover, it would create a polity so vast that no other state would be willing or able to challenge it militarily. Portending an escape from the logic of interstate competition, peace and justice on earth was within reach.[49] A choice had to be made. Failure to act appropriately would see Britain demoted to "comparative insignificance" in a world dominated by the United States. Both global preeminence and intraracial leadership would be lost forever to its colonial heir. But if it was yoked to the United States,

44. William Appleman Williams, "The Frontier Thesis and American Foreign Policy," *Pacific Historical Review*, 24/4 (1955), 379–95.

45. Josiah Strong, *The New Era, or the Coming Kingdom* (New York, 1893).

46. Charles Pearson, *National Life and Character* (London, 1893), 85. For a useful discussion, see Lake and Reynolds, *Drawing the Global Colour Line*, chs. 3–4; John Tregenza, *Professor of Democracy* (Cambridge, 1968). Equally widely discussed, Benjamin Kidd's triumphalist *Social Evolution* (London, 1894) was often read as a riposte to Pearson's pessimism. Kidd argued that as the most "efficient" race, Anglo-Saxons would dominate the earth.

47. Carnegie, *Reunion*, 18.

48. In his attack on imperial federation, Carnegie endorsed the argument for infant industry protection made by John Stuart Mill and Alfred Marshall: Carnegie, "Imperial Federation," 493.

49. Carnegie, *Reunion*, 13. On the dream of peace, see also Carnegie, "Imperial Federation," 504–6, and my discussion in chapter 7.

Britain could retain a pivotal role in shaping human destiny. The politicians in London could either fight the tide of history or ride it.

Carnegie outlined a cyborg account of Anglo-America. The telegraph had rendered arguments from distance obsolete. Distributed across Britain, Canada, and the United States, the population of Anglo-America was bound tightly by racial origin and electrical current. Information flowed, opinions were formed, and debate unfolded on the same temporal plane. Instantaneity consolidated a singular sense of peoplehood: "the pulse beat of the entire nation can be constantly felt by the government and all the people." This infrastructural marvel was the "most important factor in rendering political union possible, and I venture to say inevitable."[50] Here, as elsewhere, a powerful strain of technological determinism ran through Carnegie's writing. "All that tends to the brotherhood of man tends to promote it. The tendency of the age is towards consolidation."[51] This historical development was morally sanctified: all is well since all grows better.

A biocultural conception of race lay at the heart of his argument. Carnegie insisted that the English-speaking peoples formed a single racial unit, and that this justified—even demanded—the effort to unite them politically. Kinship and racial solidarity were more basic, more fundamental, than the juridical architecture of states. Figured as both cause and effect, race was the main determinant of historical progress and a vital feature of the current distribution of talent and political virtue. The territorial divisions supervening on race obscured the existence of a deeper and more profound unity. He maintained that "in race—and there is a great deal in race—the American remains three-fourths purely British," and this fact fundamentally shaped the character of the American polity, rendering it suitable for reunion with the British empire-state.[52] Unlike many Anglo-Saxonists, he was a frequent critic of racial bigotry. At the height of nativist racism in the United States, when immigrant communities from East Asia and Eastern Europe were being subjected to vicious attacks, Carnegie praised immigrants and rejected calls for legislative discrimination.[53]

While nearly all Anglo-American enthusiasts emphasized the constitutive role of shared language in molding Anglo-Saxon identity, Carnegie aimed to

---

50. Carnegie, *Reunion*, 12.

51. Carnegie, *Reunion*, 31–32.

52. Carnegie, *Reunion*, 9.

53. Nasaw, *Andrew Carnegie*, 662. But he was no radical egalitarian. For his views about the integration of African-Americans, see Andrew Carnegie, *The Negro in America* (Inverness, 1907). Heaping praise on Booker T. Washington, he nevertheless supported limits to the franchise based on educational qualifications. For Carnegie, African-Americans did not constitute an equal part of the polity.

transform the vocabulary of English into a technology of political association. He helped lead the campaign to simplify the spelling of American English, aiming to rationalize the orthography of the language, a cause that attracted numerous supporters, including Theodore Roosevelt, Mark Twain, and—as we shall see—Stead and Wells.[54] Carnegie hoped that simplified spelling would consolidate a sense of Anglo-American unity. "Our language," he declared in 1906 when announcing funding for the Simplified Spelling Board, "is likely to prevail in the world, and we may hope it is to become finally the universal language, the most potent of all instruments for drawing the race together, insuring peace and advancing civilization."[55] He offered two distinct arguments, both of which pointed to the "noble purposes and high destiny" of the language and its speakers. The first was that simplified spelling would increase the efficiency of intraracial social interaction, eliminating one of the main sources of discord and confusion, the second that as the English-speakers enacted their historical destiny to govern the globe, an easily intelligible version of the language would be accessible to the polyglot masses who would come under their benign leadership. "The foreigner has the greatest difficulty in acquiring it because of its spelling," he warned.[56] There was an irony here, as the Simplified Spelling Board had been established by Columbia literature professor Brander Matthews, who had made his name arguing in *Americanisms and Briticisms* for a literary secession from British-English, and the celebration of a home-grown American idiom. "We know now that the mother-tongue is a heritage and not a loan. It is ours to use as we needs must."[57] Carnegie, by contrast, thought that a simplified language would lubricate racial reunion rather than buttress national independence. Refiguring the language was yet another means of achieving Anglo-American supremacy.

Carnegie's vision of an Anglo-future was chiefly confined to the northern hemisphere. Australia and New Zealand were excluded from the "reunited state," at least initially. Despite announcing the obsolescence of time and space, he insisted that the settler outposts were too far away for proper incorporation. Moreover, they were insufficiently populated or prosperous. Britain, the United

54. Jonathan Zimmerman, "Simplified Spelling and the Cult of Efficiency in the 'Progressive' Era," *Journal of the Gilded Age and the Progressive Era*, 9/3 (2010), 366–94; Nasaw, *Andrew Carnegie*, 664.

55. "Mr Carnegie Defends Spelling Reform Plan," *New York Times*, 25 March 1906, 4. Bankrolled by Carnegie, the Simplified Spelling Board was established in 1906 to push for change. His death led to the demise of the movement. See also Christine Ogren, "Complexities of Efficiency Reform," *History of Education*, 57/3 (2017), 333–68.

56. "Mr Carnegie Defends Spelling Reform Plan."

57. Brander Matthews, *Americanisms and Briticisms* (New York, 1892), 5.

States, and Canada boasted 108 million people between them, whereas all the other English-speaking communities could barely muster 5 million.[58] Spatial and demographic realities determined the ideal shape of the union. Adopting an argument common among American thinkers, Carnegie argued that Canada should be absorbed by the United States.[59] He thus envisaged a sequence enacted in four distinct steps. Britain would first grant independence to Australia, New Zealand, and Canada, before the United States swallowed its northern neighbor, whereupon the new American colossus would join with Britain to form "an indissoluble union of indestructible states."[60] Finally, the new English-speaking Atlantic polity would divest itself of its remaining imperial possessions throughout the world.

As befits a dream, Carnegie's political vision was often vague. In particular, he was neither clear nor consistent about the kind of political association he wanted. Throughout the 1880s and 1890s, he referred to a possible Anglo-American "federation."[61] In September 1891, though, he suggested that "each branch must manage its own household, and that there may be an alliance, but not a confederation."[62] But when transatlantic alliances were widely discussed in 1898, Carnegie rejected the idea.[63] In "A Look Ahead," he called for a "common British-American citizenship," which (as I discuss in chapter 6) did not require the creation of a supervenient armature of legal and political institutions, but his choice of vocabulary often implied something much more institutionally ambitious than common citizenship, a defensive alliance, or even confederation, as he repeatedly called for a "reunited state" and suggested that it necessitated a legislature granting full representation to the constituent polities.[64] But "state" hardly seems an appropriate designation for a polity in which the parts retained a significant degree of autonomy, such that neither "the old land or the new binds itself to support the other in all its designs, either at home or abroad."[65] He implied that in the future state sovereignty

---

58. Carnegie, *Reunion*, 28.

59. Carnegie, "Imperial Federation," 503. On Canadian Anglo-Saxonism, see Kohn, *This Kindred People*, while for debates over annexation, see Bélanger, *Prejudice and Pride*, ch. 7.

60. Carnegie, *Reunion*, 12, 28.

61. Carnegie, "Home Rule in America," 52; Carnegie, *Reunion*, 27; Carnegie to Stead, 11 August 1893, Fol 21, Carnegie papers.

62. Carnegie to Stead, 9 September 1891, Fol 12, Carnegie papers.

63. Carnegie, "Americanism versus Imperialism," 5–6.

64. Carnegie, *Reunion*, 10, 32, 22.

65. Carnegie, *Reunion*, 6. For contemporary conceptions of statehood, see Duncan Bell, "The Victorian Idea of a Global State" in Bell (ed.), *Victorian Visions of Global Order* (Cambridge, 2007), 159–85; James Meadowcroft, *Conceptualising the State* (Oxford, 1995).

would be maintained, writing that "[s]ome day . . . delegates from the three now separated branches will meet in London and readily agree upon and report for approval and ratification a basis for the restoration of an indissoluble union of indestructible states."[66] The proposed constitutional relationship between Britain and the United States was ambiguous. In "A Look Ahead," he declared that in the representative structure of any new union, Britain would remain "first among equals," but he failed to provide any details or address the compatibility of his argument about historical priority with his account of American predominance.[67] Given his belief in the future superiority of the United States, he seems to have meant that this primacy was honorific, Britain playing Greece to America's Rome.

The True Philosophy of History: Methodological Racialism and the Germanic Element

Carnegie's argument incorporated two principal claims about the origins, evolution, and character of Anglo-America. The first was that the majority of the American population was "essentially British."[68] The second was that the British were the latest instantiation of an ancient Teutonic race. "The Briton of to-day is himself composed in large measure of the Germanic element, and German, Briton, and American are all of the Teutonic race."[69] Despite the substantial impact of other European settlers, the Teutons shaped American society and politics. "The amount of blood other than Anglo-Saxon or Germanic which has entered into the American is almost too trifling to deserve notice, and has been absorbed without changing him in any fundamental trait."[70]

Racial dreamworlds were underwritten by the revision of established historical narratives. Methodological nationalism was supplanted by methodological racialism. Unionists emphasized deep Anglo-American connections over surface variation, historical continuity over rupture, identity over difference. This typically involved remapping key historical episodes, and especially the American War of Independence and Civil War. The variables posited to explain them, the normative frameworks used to judge them, their social and political implications: all were reworked to narrate a more positive account of

66. Carnegie, *Reunion*, 31.

67. Carnegie, *Reunion*, 23.

68. Carnegie, *Triumphant Democracy*, 16.

69. Carnegie, *Reunion*, 11.

70. Carnegie, *Reunion*, 9.

Anglo-American history. The Revolution was presented either as a tragedy for the race or (more commonly) as a "necessary condition" for successful racial development and possible future union.[71] Rather than traitors or terrorists, the Revolutionaries were celebrated.[72] The commonality of political and legal institutions was reiterated. It was often claimed, for example, that the British Monarchy and the American Presidency were variations on a common theme. Dicey spoke of the "English constitutional Monarchy and the English Federal Republic."[73] This was combined with an assault on the perceived sources of Anglophobia, which was presented either as an expression of unfortunate (and rectifiable) historical ignorance or the work of malign interest groups. An out-dated school curriculum was blamed for inculcating anti-British feeling in the young. All had to be challenged.

Feted on both sides of the Atlantic, Bryce was arguably the leading Anglo-American intellectual.[74] "[A] man who has touched life at every point—jurist, historian, professor, cabinet minister, diplomatist," as G. P. Gooch marveled, it was his self-defined task to strengthen Anglo-American relations, a mission that culminated in a successful stint as British Ambassador in Washington (1907–13).[75] Bryce's work was often cited in unionist accounts, though he lacked the utopian impulse that animated many of them, and his own proposals for unifying people of "Anglo-American stock" were relatively modest.[76] He supported an arbitration treaty between Britain and the United States

71. Adams, "Century of Anglo-Saxon Expansion," 531. As I discuss in chapter 3, Rhodes articulated the former position. Nimrod Tal has shown how scholars in the following period reimagined the Civil War to reinforce Anglo-American relations: Tal, "Putting Out the 'Embers of This Resentment,'" *Journal of the Civil War Era*, 8/1 (2014), 87–110. This reorientation was well underway among popular writers and publicists in the late nineteenth century.

72. Edward A. Freeman, "George Washington, the Expander of England" in Freeman, *Greater Greece and Greater Britain* (London, 1886), 66, 89, 69–70; Edwin Mead, "The United States as a World Power," *Advocate of Peace*, 75/3 (1913), 58.

73. Dicey, "Common Citizenship for the English Race," 468. "The institutions of America are in their spirit little else than a gigantic development of the ideas which lie at the basis of the political and legal institutions of England": Dicey, *Introduction to the Study of the Law of the Constitution*, 8th ed. (London, 1915), 135.

74. On his role in transatlantic intellectual life, see Butler, *Critical Americans*; Gerlach, *British Liberalism and the United States*.

75. G. P. Gooch, review of *The Hindrances of Good Citizenship*, *International Journal of Ethics*, 21/1 (1910), 111.

76. The phrase is from James Bryce, "Some Reflections on the State of Cuba," *North American Review*, 174/545 (1902), 454.

and (as I discuss in chapter 6) endorsed isopolitan citizenship.[77] While he did not draw explicitly on Bryce's work, Carnegie was a regular correspondent and often praised him for facilitating Anglo-American friendship. He was delighted with Bryce's appointment to Washington: "no one can doubt," Carnegie wrote to him, that "your career is to unite in stronger bonds than ever the two branches of our race."[78]

Published to great acclaim in 1888, Bryce's *The American Commonwealth* sold over two hundred thousand copies in the United Stated by the outbreak of the First World War.[79] Much of it was occupied with a detailed portrait of American laws and political institutions, but Lord Acton astutely recognized that it conveyed "a strongly marked and personal philosophy of American history."[80] It was conceived in part as a counterpoint to Tocqueville's sweeping proclamations about American social and political identity.[81] Bryce found many faults with the work of his esteemed predecessor, including a failure to discern the profound impact of British ideas and historical experience on the American constitution. Unlike the French revolution, "the spirit of 1787 was an English spirit, and therefore a conservative spirit."[82] It was only possible to comprehend American institutions by locating them in historical time. Bryce identified both a proximate and a deep context. The former was eighteenth-century constitutional debate: the revolutionaries had learnt much from Blackstone and the arch-Anglophile Montesquieu.[83] Bryce maintained that American institutions were largely modified variants of British ones, with the Presidency a "reduced and improved copy of the English king."[84] The deeper context was the history of Teutonic self-government, stretching back

77. Bryce, "British Feeling on the Venezuelan Question," 145–53; Bryce, "Arbitration with Great Britain," *Advocate of Peace*, 66/4 (1904), 64–65.

78. Carnegie to Bryce, 21 February 1907, MS Bryce U.S.A., Fol 16–17. See also Carnegie to Bryce, 28 December 1905, Bryce papers, MS Bryce U.S.A., Fol 13–14.

79. Hugh Tulloch, *James Bryce's American Commonwealth* (London, 1988). On his views, see also Edmund Ions, *James Bryce and American Democracy, 1870–1922* (London, 1968); Prochaska, *Eminent Victorians*, ch. 5.

80. John Emerich Edward Dalberg, Lord Acton, review of Bryce, *American Commonwealth*, *English Historical Review*, 4/14 (1889), 389.

81. James Bryce, "The Predictions of Hamilton and de Tocqueville," *Johns Hopkins Studies in Historical and Political Science*, 5th ser. 9 (1887), 5–57.

82. James Bryce, *The American Commonwealth* (London, 1888), I, 408.

83. Bryce, *American Commonwealth*, I, 34–36.

84. Bryce, *American Commonwealth*, I, 49. His work was influential on scholars of the United States. See for example, Charles Ellis Stevens, *Sources of the Constitution of the United States* (New York, 1894).

through England to the Germanic tribes. "There is much that is as old as Magna Charta." Expressive products of racial deep time, New England town meetings could trace their origins back centuries. The manifest success of the American Constitution was due to the "political genius, ripened by long experience, of the Anglo-Saxon race."[85]

Bryce discerned various faults in American institutions and mores. The system promoted mediocre statesmen, a governing elite too blasé about the rise of plutocracy, and rigidifying parties—and machine politicians—that threatened to derail the gains made over the previous century.[86] There were too many elections; the House was full of demagogues (though the Senate impressed him); the President had too much patronage to disburse: all these complaints and more were rehearsed at length. But Bryce's investigation exuded cautious optimism about the power of democracy and the future of the American state. What continued to bind the "Anglo-American stock" together was a shared racial inheritance embodied above all in the common law, which Bryce regarded as both a principal cause of Anglo-American progress and a manifestation of racial "genius."[87] He was far less optimistic about the color line. African-Americans, he complained in 1891, had been granted citizenship despite being "confessedly unfit for the suffrage." They were "naturally inferior to the whites—inferior in intelligence, in tenacity, in courage, in the power of organization and cohesion." He concluded that educational qualifications should be introduced to limit their access to political life.[88] Bryce's optimism was premised on entrenched white supremacy.

Teutonists usually imagined the dominant population groups in Britain and the United States as national threads of an overarching Germanic-Teutonic race that was itself descended from a primitive Aryan ur-race.[89] (Anglo-Saxons

85. Bryce, *American Commonwealth*, I, 35, 34. For the broader context, see John Burrow, "Some British Views on the United States Constitution" in R. C. Simmons (ed.), *The United States Constitution* (Manchester, 1989), 116–38.

86. For a comparative analysis of parties, see James Bryce, "Political Organisation in the United States and England," *North American Review*, 156/434 (1893), 105–18.

87. Bryce, *American Commonwealth*, I, 345. See also Bryce, "Influence of National Character," 203–16.

88. James Bryce, "Thoughts on the Negro Problem," *North American Review*, 153/421 (1891), 647, 654, 655–56. A version of this article was added as one of four new chapters included in the third edition of *The American Commonwealth* in 1895. In the conclusion, I discuss Scholes's critique of Bryce's views on African-Americans.

89. Henry Maine, *Ancient Law* (London, 1861); Edward Freeman, *Comparative Politics* (London, 1873). For discussion, see Steinberg, *Race, Nation, History*; John Burrow, *A Liberal Descent* (Cambridge, 1981).

were presented as the dominant modern branch of the Teutons.) As William Stubbs put it, the English were "a people of German descent in the main constituents of blood, character, and language, but most especially . . . in the possession of the elements of primitive civilisation and the common germs of German institutions."[90] An influential group of American historians picked up the Teutonic baton from the British, enacting the spatiotemporal dynamic they claimed to divine in the historical record. John Burgess, Herbert Baxter Adams, Andrew White, and Albert Bushnell Hart, among others, set out to chart the various manifestations of Teutonism in American institutions and norms.[91] They narrated a triumphal story of the westward movement of the race, culminating in the creation of the United States, that proved fertile soil for many advocates of Anglo-America. By the late 1890s, Teutonism was no longer at the cutting edge of historical scholarship, but popularizers such as Fiske and Hosmer kept it alive for the wider public, and unionists were only too happy to invoke it to support their case. There were notable geographical variations in how historians emplotted the history of the race. New England Brahmin Anglo-Saxonists, including Fiske and Hosmer, saw their home region as the very epicenter of the race, the point where it had reached its highest historical expression. Those from outside the area, notably Roosevelt, often considered the New England population as effete and lacking in the manly qualities necessary to develop further. They saw the future being forged in expansion on the Western frontier, an argument that Frederick Turner Johnson made his own.[92] For racial unionists, the similarities were more politically salient than the differences.

While Bryce was a key figure in transatlantic intellectual life, the work of his friend Freeman exerted an even greater influence on racial unionists. Resonating widely in the United States, his writings were more historically elaborate than those of Bryce, as well as grander in their claims about racial destiny.[93] Though Teutonism had been pioneered by scholars such as Henry Maine and Max Müller, Freeman tied it much more explicitly to the celebration of a

90. William Stubbs, *The Constitutional History of England* (London, 1874), I, 2.

91. Robert Adcock, *Liberalism and the Emergence of American Political Science* (Oxford, 2014), ch. 5; E. N. Saveth, *American Historians and European Immigrants, 1875–1925* (New York, 1948), chs. 1–2; Dorothy Ross, *The Origins of American Social Science* (Cambridge, 1992).

92. On this geographical variation, see Bluford Adams, "World Conquerors or a Dying People?," *Journal of the Gilded Age and Progressive Era*, 8/2 (2009), 189–215. Alongside Roosevelt, Adams cites Frederic Remington and Owen Wister. For fears of Anglo-Saxon decay, see Gail Bederman, *Manliness and Civilization* (Chicago, 1995), 185–87.

93. There was some irony here, for Freeman's knowledge of American history was modest: James Bryce, "Edward Augustus Freeman," *English Historical Review*, 7/27 (1892), 504.

transatlantic racial formation. Emphasizing the deep and abiding identity of the two countries, he Americanized the discourse. "To me most certainly the United States did not seem like a foreign country; it was simply England with a difference."[94] This empirical observation was rooted in a set of methodological and theoretical claims about how to understand historical development. He contended that a "true philosophy of history" required knowledge of the institutional similarities connecting descendants of the Aryan ur-race that were instantiated in "forms of government," including modern states, monarchical systems, and representative assemblies.[95] This enterprise, which he named "comparative politics," was predicated on an account of racial descent, the Aryans spawning assorted lineal descendants, the most significant of which were the Greeks, Romans, and Teutons.[96] All either had been or were the "rulers and the teachers of the world."[97] The Teutons were now the foremost race in the world, with the English their dominant branch. Their liberty-loving character flowered wherever they settled, including the United States, that "newer and vaster England beyond the Oceans."[98]

Freeman vested his hopes in the newer England, "brethren in a higher brotherhood, born of one ancient stock, speaking one ancient tongue, sharer under different forms of one ancient freedom."[99] He aimed to rouse Americans to accept the grand meaning of the racial community. "The feeling of unity between the two severed branches is really present in the American breast, but it needs something special to wake it up."[100] His call was heeded. The project of "comparative politics" played a formative role in the development of the academic human sciences in North America.[101] The main site of his influence was the famed "seminary" established at Johns Hopkins University by Herbert Baxter Adams to train students in "historical and political science." Alongside Bluntschli and Maine, Freeman was its guiding light, his pithy motto "history is past politics and politics are present history" adorning the

94. Edward A. Freeman, *Some Impressions of the United States* (London, 1883), 10.

95. Freeman, *Comparative Politics*, Lectures III–V. On Freeman and "democratic Teutonism," see Mandler, *English National Character*, 86–105.

96. Freeman, *Comparative Politics*, 33, 19. Maine declared Freeman's lectures on the topic the most interesting he had ever heard: Maine to Freeman, 22 December 1873, Freeman papers, John Rylands Library, University of Manchester, EAF/1/7.

97. Freeman, *Comparative Politics*, 38.

98. Freeman, *Comparative Politics*, 221–22.

99. Freeman, *Lectures*, 10.

100. Freeman, *Impressions*, 19. For context, see Jon Conlin, "The Consolations of Amero-Teutonism" in Conlin and Alex Bremner (eds.), *Making History* (Oxford, 2015), 101–18.

101. Adcock, *Liberalism and the Emergence of American Political Science*, ch. 5.

wall of the library and the front page of the house journal.[102] Freeman contributed an article, arguing that local institutions in the United States were expressions of the Teutonic branch of the "Aryan family."[103] Unlike his mentor, Adams praised the ambition of federal race unification, though he regarded the prospect as unlikely. "England and the United States will probably never be federated together in that magnificent imperial system which some people in your country are now advocating; but they will always remain one in blood and thought and speech, which are better ties than politics."[104] Kinship would have to suffice.

The imprint of Freeman's work can be seen in Carnegie's racial dreamworld. *Triumphant Democracy* listed the historian as among the elect of "really able" Britons, and quoted him on the robustness of American political institutions.[105] In "A Look Ahead," Carnegie reproduced a passage from Freeman's American lectures to make the argument that patriotism should encompass both the race and the nation.[106] He wasn't the only unionist to draw heavily from the Teutonist well. In *The Anglo-Saxon Century and the Unification of the English-speaking People*, John Dos Passos used Freeman and Bryce, among others, to elaborate his account of common citizenship and racial union.[107] "In the formation of the Constitution of the United States the theory and spirit, substance and form, of the political institutions of England were most strikingly followed."[108] A decade later, Sinclair Kennedy was still pushing a Teutonist line to justify the political unification of the "Pan-Angles."[109]

Few did more to spread the Teutonist gospel than Fiske. An itinerant philosopher and historian, he was arguably the most widely read American historical writer of his generation.[110] Fiske fused Spencerian evolutionism and Teutonist historical narrative to produce a sweeping synthetic account of the

---

102. Adams to Freeman, 10 July 1883, Freeman papers, EAF/1/7.

103. Adams to Freeman, 12 January 1885, 9 June 1882 and 25 December 1882, Freeman papers, EAF/1/7; Edward A. Freeman, "An Introduction to American Institutional History," *Johns Hopkins University Studies in Historical and Political Science*, 1/1 (1882), 13.

104. Adams to Freeman, 5 September 1884, Freeman papers, EAF/1/7.

105. Carnegie, *Triumphant Democracy*, 343, 347–48.

106. Carnegie, *Reunion*, 22. The passage is from Freeman, *Lectures*, 198: "He is no Englishman at heart, he has no true feeling of the abiding tie of kindred, who deems that the glory and greatness of the child (Republic) is other than part of the glory and greatness of the parent."

107. Dos Passos, *Anglo-Saxon Century*, 113–14, 188, 213.

108. Dos Passos, *Anglo-Saxon Century*, 124.

109. Kennedy, *Pan-Angles*, 4, 47.

110. Milton Berman, *John Fiske* (Cambridge, MA, 1961); Michael D. Clark, "The Empire of the Dead and the Empire of the Living," *American Studies*, 38/3 (1997), 91–107; Adams, "World

racial past, present, and future. His early philosophical work outlined a "cosmic theism," positing a god immanent in nature and history, working through humanity to bring eventual peace, cooperation, and justice to the earth.[111] The "English race" was the chosen vehicle for attaining the political millennium. Fiske's most ambitious account of racial development is found in *American Political Ideas Viewed from the Standpoint of Universal History*. Originally delivered as a series of lectures in London, the book was published in 1885. He argued that the English colonization of America was, due to its monumental consequences, "unquestionably the most prodigious event in the political annals of mankind."[112] In the famous final lecture, "Manifest Destiny," he predicted that

> the work which the English race began when it colonized North America is destined to go on until every land on the earth's surface that is not already the seat of an old civilization shall become English in its language, in its political habits and traditions, and to a predominant extent in the blood of its people. The day is at hand when four-fifths of the human race will trace its pedigree to English forefathers, as four-fifths of the white people in the United States trace their pedigree to-day.[113]

Fiske regarded the theory and practice of federalism as the culmination of the Teutonic genius for self-government. Its proliferation would come to shape human destiny, for it "contains within itself the seeds of permanent peace between nations; and to this glorious end I believe it will come in the fullness of time." Federalism was both the true source of American greatness and the political mechanism through which the "English race" would dominate and pacify the earth. The end result would be a world federation, the realization of Tennyson's "Parliament of Man."[114]

In *Triumphant Democracy*, Carnegie described *American Political Ideas* as an "excellent little book," and quoted from it a long passage about the quality

---

Conquerors?," 202–6; Lewis Saum, "John Fiske and the West," *Huntington Library Quarterly*, 48/1 (1985), 47–68.

111. John Fiske, *Outlines of Cosmic Philosophy* (Boston, 1874). For Fiske as philosopher, see Bruce Kuklick, *The Rise of American Philosophy* (New Haven, CT, 1977), 80.

112. Fiske, *American Political Ideas*, 117.

113. Fiske, *American Political Ideas*, 135. He argued that Stubbs and Freeman were correct to identify the Teutonic origins of English institutions (116). Andrew McFarland Davis noted that J. R. Green's *A Short History of the English People* also influenced Fiske (672): "John Fiske," *Proceedings of the American Academy of Arts and Sciences*, 37/23 (1902), 665–72.

114. Fiske, *American Political Ideas*, 126–27, 144.

of democratic life in New England.[115] Fiske continued to outline the case for the westward evolution of the race in books such as *The Critical Period of American History* (1888) and *The Beginnings of New England* (1889).[116] Freeman served as the principal inspiration for his historical writings. "No student of political development in our time," Fiske opined, "has made more effective use of the comparative method," and none had done as much to establish the continuities in transatlantic racial history.[117] In 1892, Fiske dedicated *The Discovery of America* to Freeman, saluting him as a "scholar who inherits the gift of Midas, and turns into gold whatever subject he touches."[118] Freeman regarded his American disciple as a faithful expositor of his historical theories, a worthy advocate of the racial creed to the fortunate inhabitants of the newer England.[119] "Truly you preach exactly the same doctrine as I do," he applauded Fiske after reading *American Political Ideas*.[120]

Hosmer tied his historical account of Anglo-Saxonism to a vision of future racial reunion. In 1890, he published *A Short History of Anglo-Saxon Freedom*, a book that synthesized much of the existing Teutonist literature and utilized it to argue for common identity and shared destiny.[121] Accepting the outlines of Hosmer's narrative, the eminent Harvard scholar A. L. Lowell thought that he had exaggerated the impact of British ideas on American institutions and the role of the American revolution in shaping British politics. "Scholars have long been telling us that the real stream of our social and political forces is to be traced through the whole course of English history to a tiny spring that flowed out of the darkness of German forests," he observed. While the idea could be pushed too far, and too enthusiastically, "in the main it is sound." Praising Hosmer's historical analysis as "impartial," Lowell was unwilling to follow his speculative imaginings. "[H]is enthusiasm for the race has a tendency to run

115. Carnegie, *Triumphant Democracy*, 73–74.

116. On the germ theory, see especially John Fiske, *The Critical Period of American History, 1783–1789* (Boston: Houghton Mifflin, 1888), ch. 5.

117. John Fiske, "Edward Augustus Freeman" in Fiske, *A Century of Science and Other Essays* (Boston, 1899), 268.

118. John Fiske, *The Discovery of America*, 2 vols. (Boston, 1892). Fiske's historical work was also utilized in Kennedy, *Pan-Angles*, 8–9, 180.

119. Freeman to Fiske, 9 August 1889, John Spencer Clark, *The Life and Letters of John Fiske* (Boston, 1917), 414.

120. Freeman to Fiske, 10 November 1889, *Life and Letters*, 415. Fearful of the damage that immigration posed to racial purity, Fiske served as Honorary President of the Immigration Restriction League.

121. James K. Hosmer, *A Short History of Anglo-Saxon Freedom* (New York, 1890).

away with his judgment, and his visions for the future might well strike a stranger to the blood as a trifle fanciful."[122]

In 1898, Hosmer advocated the federation of the Anglo-Saxon polities. He embedded this project in a sweeping teleological narrative of racial development, tracing an arc from the colonial era to a future reunion. A condition of "dependence" had defined the early relationship between the British state and the American colonies, but as the latter grew in strength, the demand for "independence" intensified. He argued that its realization through revolution was justified, though it was a tragedy that blood had been spilt, producing "a hatred which rankles yet."[123] Subsequently the United States had blossomed as an autonomous power, its potential clear for all to see, but "the wise and benevolent look forward to Tennyson's 'Parliament of man, the federation of the world.'" Anglo-America was the best vehicle for achieving it. Now was the time to inaugurate an era of racial "interdependence." Technoscientific progress underwrote reunion: "Through steam and electricity, time and space are annihilated. The seas no longer divide, but unite." While he suggested that an arbitration body was a wise first step, Hosmer dreamt of a yet grander future. "What is to hinder a further extension of the federal principle?" The United States should fuse with Britain and its settler colonies to constitute "a vaster United States," an epic project that was no "unreasonable or Utopian anticipation."[124] But that is exactly what it was.

Contesting Carnegie

"A Look Ahead" elicited numerous replies. Carnegie was inundated with letters endorsing his case. His friend Swire Smith, a British industrialist and senior Liberal Party organizer, praised the "attractive and statesmanlike . . . dream that all thoughtful and patriotic men and women of our race must often have cherished," while Hyde Clarke, philologist and engineer, argued contrary to Carnegie's intentions that union would allow Britain and the United States to carve up the Pacific between them. Thomas Wright, President of the Scotch-Irish Historical Society of America, suggested that an "Inter-national Congress" of the race should be convened at London, New York, or Montreal to

122. Lowell, review, Hosmer, *Annals of the American Academy of Political and Social Science*, 1/1 (1891), 494.

123. James K. Hosmer, "The American Evolution," *Atlantic Monthly*, 82 (July 1898), 31. Hosmer's article was cited by other unionists: Dos Passos, *Anglo-Saxon Century*, 224–25; W. T. Stead, *RoR*, 28 (August 1898), 191–92.

124. Hosmer, "American Evolution," 31, 32. On Hosmer, see Adams, "World Conquerors?," 206–9.

discuss the issue.[125] More significantly, Carnegie's arguments were dissected across the media networks of his beloved English-speaking world, with the most substantial rejoinders appearing in the *North American Review*.

First into print was Goldwin Smith, once Regius Professor of History at Oxford and by then the most prominent public intellectual in Canada.[126] Welcoming the sentiment for union, he was unconvinced about the viability of Carnegie's institutional proposals. He opened by acknowledging a thaw in relations between the two countries and a lessening of American Anglophobia. This augured well for the future. "A moral reunion of the race, with a common pride in its common history and a consciousness of the part which collectively it has played and may yet play in the development of humanity," he mused, "seems not very far from realization."[127] But political union did not necessarily follow—indeed it was "surely inconceivable." Too many questions remained unanswered. "Supposing such a union possible, what definite object would it have? Where would its centre be? Who would direct its policy?"[128] Smith pinpointed the constitutional slipperiness of Carnegie's analysis. He shared Carnegie's dismissal of imperial federation, accusing its proponents of mistaking an admirable sentiment of harmony with the need for supranational organization. For Smith, the most likely future scenario was neither imperial nor racial federation, but the absorption of Canada within the United States and a general "moral" union of independent English-speaking communities. Despite their differences, the two men concurred on many points, not least the imperative of Canadian incorporation. A couple of years later, Carnegie lauded Smith as "the only subject of Great Britain, as far as I know, who has probed the English-American Question to the bottom," surmising that it was

125. Swire to Carnegie, 22 July 1894, Fol 26; Clarke to Carnegie, 15 June 1893, Fol 21; Wright to Carnegie, 29 May 1894, Fol 25, Carnegie papers.

126. On Smith, see Bell, *Greater Britain*, ch. 7; Elisabeth Wallace, *Goldwin Smith, Victorian Liberal* (Toronto, 1957); Paul Phillips, *The Controversialist* (Westport, 2002).

127. Goldwin Smith, "Anglo-Saxon Union," *North American Review*, 157/441 (1893), 172. For his skepticism about imperial federation, see Smith, "The Expansion of England," *Contemporary Review*, 45 (1884), 524–40. Elsewhere Smith had acknowledged the significance of the flood of utopian writing. Observing, in a critical discussion of Bellamy, that just "as the rainbow in the spray of Niagara marks a cataract in the river, the appearance of utopias has marked a cataract in the stream of history," he discerned a new historical inflection point. Smith, "Prophets of Unrest," *The Forum*, 14/8 (1889), 600. He was, though, unpersuaded by the value of utopian writing. "Finality is the trap into which all utopians fall" (614).

128. Smith, "Anglo-Saxon Union," 172.

"truly, as you think, the presence of Britain upon this continent which prevents an alliance."[129]

A few months later, Arthur Silva White, a Scottish geographer and dedicated imperial federalist, espoused a limited Anglo-American alliance.[130] His was one of several responses calling for the creation of a military partnership, binding Britain and the United States through a new treaty. Like many of his fellow imperial unionists, White envisaged the project for Anglo-American rapprochement as complementary to the unification of the British settler empire. He contended that the welfare of the United States was bound to the British Empire, because American economic dynamism was dependent on the Royal Navy's command of the sea.[131] Given their joint interests in global stability and commerce, he recommended a defensive alliance sufficiently flexible to accommodate national differences but binding them together for a common purpose. It would only be actuated in specific circumstances. The agreement would postulate that

> Great Britain shall become an ally of the United States in the event of any European power or powers declaring war against the latter. On the other hand, the United States shall guarantee friendly neutrality in the event of Great Britain becoming involved in a war with one or more of the European powers concerning issues that in no way concern the pacific interests of the United States; and, under such circumstances, the United States shall render to Great Britain every assistance, positive and negative, allowed to neutrals.[132]

He thus envisaged a weak bond, allowing scope for each party to decide whether particular conflicts were in their own interest. But that was not the

---

129. Carnegie to Smith, 6 February 1896, Fol 36, Carnegie papers. Carnegie subsidized Smith's activities on behalf of Canadian-American union. In a letter to Smith (4 May 1896, Fol 37), he enclosed a check for $1,500 to "promote the cause." He also financed the National Continental Union League. Carnegie had endorsed Smith's views on Canadian incorporation in "Imperial Federation," 504.

130. Arthur Silva White, "An Anglo-American Alliance," *North American Review*, 158/449 (1894), 484–93. White was Secretary of the Scottish Geographical Society and a prolific writer on imperial affairs. See especially White (ed.), *Britannic Confederation* (London, 1892); White, "British Unity," *Scottish Geographical Magazine*, 12 (1896), 391–414; and, for his views on geography, White, "The Position of Geography in the Cycle of the Sciences," *Geographical Journal*, 2/2 (1893), 178–79. On his intellectual milieu, see Morag Bell, "Edinburgh and Empire," *Scottish Geographical Magazine*, 111/3 (1995), 139–49.

131. White, "Anglo-American Alliance," 488.

132. White, "Anglo-American Alliance," 492–93.

end of the story. "Some of us," he avowed, "look with hope for a confederation of all English-speaking countries," though such a union would have to be the "simplest and most flexible kind," namely a *Kriegsverein*, "or combination for mutual defence in time of war." It would ideally link all of the English-speaking communities, including the United States. "[W]hat is impossible now," he maintained, "may become possible enough at a future date."[133] White thought that an Anglo-American alliance and a "Britannic Confederation" might one day be converted into a single racial polity.

Alive to the utopian dimensions of Carnegie's dream, George Sydenham Clarke, a British army officer and politician, perceptively located the unionist argument within the currents of social prophecy circulating at the time.[134] "It is an inevitable tendency of our age to seek solace in dreams." The world was undergoing a profound transition, "the breaking up of old faiths, the oppressive sense of an existence ruled by inexorable law, the increasing subordination of men and matter to mere machinery political or technical." Unfettered speculation about the future flourished in response to this tumult. "[W]hether we linger over an anticipatory retrospect with Mr. Bellamy, indulge in 'a look ahead' with Mr. Carnegie, or—far less profitably—attempt to peer across the 'Borderland' with Mr. Stead, the same human craving supplies the impulse and explains the fascination." Such responses met a felt need to create order amid chaos, but they came at a significant cost—detachment from empirical reality and the conflation of theory with practice, principle with pragmatism. "To teach to the age the mere conditions of the problem seems," to those seers, "almost sufficient to secure the great object." Dreaming substituted for the hard work of political mobilization and legislative change. Moreover, Carnegie's argument was marked by a false sense of certainty. "What better form can our day-dreams assume than the portrayal of the ultimate and certain triumph?" Carnegie's "dreamland," as Clarke termed it, was at once alluring and

133. White, "Anglo-American Alliance," 491. This claim provoked a fierce rebuttal from Benjamin Trueblood, a leading American pacifist: "A Proposed Anglo-American War Alliance," *Advocate of Peace*, 56/5 (1894), 101–4. Trueblood later advocated a world state: *The Federation of the World* (Boston, 1899).

134. Commissioned in the Royal Engineers, Clarke served as Secretary to the Colonial Defence Committee (1885–92), for which he was knighted. He was subsequently appointed Governor of Victoria (1901–3) and Bombay (1907–13), after which he was elevated to the peerage as Baron Sydenham of Combe. Originally a liberal—and still one when he wrote this article—he later moved sharply to the right; during the 1920s and '30s he was an anti-Semitic conspiracy theorist and fascist. See John Gooch, "Sir George Clarke's Career at the Committee of Imperial Defence, 1904–1907," *Historical Journal*, 18/3 (1975), 555–69; Markku Ruotsila, "Lord Sydenham of Combe's World Jewish Conspiracy," *Patterns of Prejudice*, 34/3 (2000), 47–64.

profoundly implausible.[135] Carnegie might have replied that while some utopian projects were doomed to fail, others, including his own, were both feasible and desirable. The two modalities of dreaming were separated by how
closely they tracked the progressive direction of historical change.

Even as he praised the spirit of Carnegie's "dazzling essay," Clarke criticized
him for underplaying the significance of nationalism, and especially the development of the United States into a proud independent country. Formal reunion was out of the question. Despite growing recognition of kinship and
common interests, insuperable barriers remained. "Into dreamland, however,
no traveller can lead another; our visions are our own. To me, mountains loom
where Mr. Carnegie sees only the light mists of morning."[136]

> In Mr. Carnegie's vision, the British empire, parcelled off apparently into
> separate States, is bodily incorporated with the Union, thus changing a
> form of government which has been the growth of centuries, abandoning
> at one stroke the position of a sovereign state held for nearly a thousand
> years, and claiming henceforth only a minority representation in a new
> national parliament which might vote away the old flag.[137]

While theoretically possible, this act of constitutional transubstantiation was
politically unworkable. (It was also probably more radical than Carnegie actually intended at the time.) In particular, Clarke argued that Carnegie had failed
to grasp the popularity of the British monarchy and the benefits of imperial
occupation in India. Civilizing the subcontinent would take hundreds of years
and until that distant moment arrived, "peace, law, order, and defence against
external aggression" could only be secured by the British. He admonished
Carnegie for failing to learn an important lesson from the masters of the utopian genre. "Most wisely Mr. Bellamy forbore to explain how his social revolution was brought about," and as such his grand vision was less vulnerable to
objections about how best to realize it. "The dream of an Anglo-American
commonwealth, fascinating as it is, and promising unimaginable good to the
world, fades away, under Mr. Carnegie's treatment, into the dim mists of the
far future." It was undone by a premature discussion of constitutional means,
when it should have concentrated on the magnificent (racial) ends it sought

---

135. George Sydenham Clarke, "A Naval Union with Great Britain," *North American Review*,
158/448 (1894), 353.

136. Clarke, "Naval Union," 353.

137. Clarke, "Naval Union," 357. For the ideological context of debates over naval power, see
Bernard Semmel, *Liberalism and Naval Strategy* (London, 1986); Dirk Bönker, *Militarism in a
Global Age* (Ithaca, NY, 2012); Gabriela Frei, *Great Britain, International Law, and the Evolution
of Maritime Strategic Thought, 1865–1914* (Oxford, 2020).

to institute. Vagueness had its virtues. Instead of reunion Clarke proposed a naval league, a limited defensive alliance that "could in truth dictate, at will, peace throughout the sea highways of the world."[138] Drawing on the influential writings of the American historian and strategist Alfred Thayer Mahan, he painted a picture of a global system regulated by the navies of the English-speaking powers, "two nations, but only one race." He ended on a speculative note worthy of the utopianism he decried. "Putting aside all interference with established institutions, I firmly believe that a real federation, in the higher sense, may be attained. Then, as the twin stars brought hope to the mariner of old, so will the glorious flags of America and Great Britain promise abiding peace throughout the oceans and seas of the world."[139] Carnegie wrote privately to Clarke, praising his advocacy of naval cooperation while glossing over their deeper disagreements. "We strive for the same aims and have the same hope."[140]

Mahan was an intellectual celebrity on both sides of the Atlantic, chiefly due to the reception of *The Influence of Sea Power upon History, 1660–1783*, which had been published to great acclaim in 1890. In 1894, *The Times* declared him the "new Copernicus," his work revolutionizing the study of naval power while offering a penetrating account of the sources of British national success.[141] A staunch Anglophile, Mahan had long been interested in strengthening Anglo-American relations, although he was unconvinced by maximalist plans for reunification. Rapprochement with Britain was best achieved incrementally, through naval cooperation rather than treaty, let alone constitutional integration. The two countries had to pursue their own interests. In 1890 he had argued that the United States needed to "look outwards," and that one of its primary interests was to build a close relationship with Britain. While dismissing the possibility of formal union, he suggested that "a cordial recognition of the similarity of character and ideas will give birth to sympathy, which in turn will facilitate a cooperation beneficial to both; for, if sentimentality is weak, sentiment is strong."[142] A couple of years later he informed Clarke that working together "would be the highest statesmanship—for in political traditions as well as by blood we are kin, the rest alien." Yet, he continued, "[t]o reach this happy state then is needed first, an appeal to reason, or, as they say

138. Clarke, "Naval Union," 357, 359, 362.

139. Clarke, "Naval Union," 365. He also suggested an Anglo-American arbitration council (365).

140. Carnegie to Clarke, 27 April 1894, Carnegie papers.

141. Robert Seager, *Alfred Thayer Mahan* (Annapolis, 1977), 295.

142. Alfred T. Mahan, "The United States Looking Outward," *Atlantic Monthly*, 66 (December 1890), 821.

now, 'enlightened self-interest.' I trust that upon recognition of the facts, sentiments of affection may follow."[143] Mahan thus switched the causal arrow ubiquitous in debates at the time, arguing that affect followed interests, not
vice-versa.

In the pages of the *North American Review*, Mahan engaged in a debate over
Carnegie's proposals with Charles Beresford, an Admiral and Tory MP. Carnegie's dream, he suggested, was "rational but premature."[144] He welcomed the
underlying ambition motivating demands for reunion, but thought political
conditions ruled it out. Intriguingly, Mahan admitted in correspondence with
Clarke that he could not accentuate the similarities between their respective
positions in print because of the way that the government "looks on the expressing of political opinion." He had little time for Carnegie, describing him
as a man who "is nowhere—and vaporous."[145] In his exchange with Beresford,
Mahan distinguished two types of association: kinship and alliance. Kinship
was organic and resilient, while alliances were fragile and prone to dissolution.
Since relations between the United States and Britain were defined by the
former, attempting to reinforce them by establishing the latter would undermine the original intention. "When, if ever, an Anglo-American alliance, naval
or other, does come, may it be rather as a yielding to irresistible popular impulse, than as a scheme, however ingeniously wrought, imposed by the adroit-
ness of statesmen."[146] Unlike Carnegie, that is, Mahan thought that any major
change had to originate with a shift in public opinion, not from the machina-
tions of the political elite. Moreover, unlike Carnegie Mahan was skeptical
about the value of international law. He welcomed evidence that "a common
tongue and common descent are making themselves felt, and breaking down
the barriers of estrangement which have too long separated men of the same

143. Mahan to Clarke, 5 November 1892, Reel 2, Mahan papers.

144. Alfred T. Mahan and Charles Beresford, "Possibilities of an Anglo-American Reunion,"
North American Review, 159/456 (1894), 555. On Mahan, see Jon Tetsuro Sumida, *Inventing
Grand Strategy and Teaching Command* (Baltimore, 1997); Warren Zimmermann, *First Great
Triumph* (New York, 2002), ch. 3; David Milne, *Worldmaking* (New York, 2015), ch. 1.

145. Mahan to Clarke, 29 July 1894, Reel 2, Mahan papers. Mahan used a similar phrase in a
letter to James Thursfed (7 June 1894), *The Letters and Papers of Alfred Thayer Mahan*, ed. Robert
Seager and Doris Maguire (Annapolis, 1975), II, 283. Mahan was a vigorous opponent of arbitration treatises, which might partially explain his animosity to Carnegie. He worried that they
unjustly circumscribed the scope of state action and prioritized peace over justice. Alfred T.
Mahan, "The Peace Conference and the Moral Aspect of War," *North American Review*, 169/515
(1899), 433–47. Roosevelt, like Mahan, was scathing about Carnegie in private, though he tried
to cultivate him at various points: Nasaw, *Andrew Carnegie*, 675.

146. Mahan, "Anglo-American Reunion," 560.

blood," but insisted that no new political or legal mechanisms were necessary. The two countries shared a heritage defined by individual freedom and the rule of law. Equally important was their common strategic orientation, with both dependent on the sea: they required powerful navies rather than large and politically dangerous armies.[147] He cautioned restraint. "I would avoid all premature striving for alliance, an artificial and possibly even an irritating method of reaching the desired end." Instead, he argued, "I would dwell continually upon those undeniable points of resemblance in natural characteristics, and in surrounding conditions, which testify to common origin and predict a common destiny." The peoples of Britain and America were far from ready to accept reunion, and pushing too hard would harm relations between them. "There are things that cannot be forced, processes which cannot be hurried."[148] Rapprochement should be left to take its course.

Beresford challenged Carnegie's argument and offered an alternative plan. Admitting the "easy possibility of confederation between two races similar in character, ideas, and sentiments," he rejected aspects of Carnegie's economic analysis and (like Clarke) his denigration of empire and monarchy. India had always been ruled by the sword, and if the British withdrew, the result would not be self-government but a return to religious warfare, social stagnation, and political turmoil.[149] The empire ensured peace and stability. Beresford also recognized the value—and the utopian ambition—of Carnegie's proposal.

> Mr. Carnegie describes his views on the question of reunion as a dream, and he says it is a dream nobler than most realities—in which I entirely agree. Whether his views be accepted or not, his object is a glorious one, and he deserves the generous thanks of both great nations for stating the theory that reunion would be for the benefit of each. Were it possible for his happy dream to be converted into a reality, the English-speaking nations could control the future of the world, insure perpetual peace and prosperity, and maybe advance the advent of the millennium.[150]

Criticizing Clarke's plan for prematurely including too much detail, Silva White's for lacking ambition, while rebuffing Mahan's objections to legal instruments, Beresford advocated a full defensive alliance between the two empire-states, aimed at guaranteeing "the protection of those commercial properties in which both countries are equally interested."[151] Perhaps

---

147. Mahan, "Anglo-American Reunion," 551–52, 553.
148. Mahan, "Anglo-American Reunion," 554, 555.
149. Beresford, "Anglo-American Reunion," 567.
150. Beresford, "Anglo-American Reunion," 570.
151. Beresford, "Anglo-American Reunion," 572–73.

ironically, given their relatively cautious attitudes, both Mahan and Beresford were to play a further part in the racial utopian intertext, for as I show in chapter 5, idealized simulacra of the sailors were granted starring roles in some of the speculative fiction written during the late 1890s.

Writing in the *Review of Reviews*, Stead welcomed "A Look Ahead" as a "very remarkable" essay, deserving of "even more attention than it has already received." He was only too happy to embrace Carnegie's dream of the "organic political union" of the English-speaking peoples. Like Carnegie, Stead saw the idea as both visionary and practical: "events are tending in this direction." He agreed with Carnegie about the revolutionary potential of technology, the economic imperative for Britain to seek reunion, and that large states expanded the imaginative horizon of citizens. But Stead also claimed that his friend was mistaken to think that political institutions needed to be harmonized across the English-speaking lands, and that as such Britain needed to abolish the monarchy and hereditary aristocracy. "[I]t is perfectly possible," Stead argued, "to have a union between Britain and America which would enable us to cultivate those institutions as a harmless little peculiarity of our own." In making such sweeping claims, Carnegie was "walking more by faith than sight."[152] But the faith—the willingness to dream—was vital. Stead was more critical of the assorted ripostes to Carnegie, each of which he discussed in the *Review* as they were published. He deplored the overly narrow focus on naval alliances as a vehicle for reunion.[153] Carnegie was right to aim higher, to dream more ambitious dreams.

Though not the first manifesto for reunion, "A Look Ahead" caught the attention of some of the leading political commentators of the day, sparking a lively transatlantic debate. We see in the essay, and the responses to it, a snapshot of the discourse, with positions ranging from full-blown political integration, through politico-military alliances of one kind or another, to reliance on existing racial kinship as the basis for close cooperation. This spectrum largely defined the discursive boundaries of the unionist project for the following two decades.

The Vortex of Militarism: Empire, Race, International Law

Throughout the 1890s (and beyond), Carnegie offered his services to Presidents, Prime Ministers, Kaisers, and Tsars. Much as Jeremy Bentham had once bombarded the leaders of states with unsolicited constitutional plans, so Carnegie took it upon himself to submit advice about how best to avoid conflict.

152. W. T. Stead, *RoR*, 8 (July 1893), 22, 23.
153. W. T. Stead, *RoR*, 10 (December 1894), 572.

Unlike Bentham, though, Carnegie had regular access to the highest echelons of power in London and Washington—he was hard to ignore. He sought to convince leading politicians, as well as the wider public, of the need for radical change and the creation of new institutions for realizing it. Fearing the "vortex of militarism" endangering international stability, he disbursed his vast wealth to underwrite the peace movements on both sides of the Atlantic.[154] His advocacy of international peace was an integral part of his vision of Anglo-America.

By the turn of the twentieth century, both the British and American peace movements were dominated by a moderate form of legalism that emphasized the codification of international law and the practice of arbitration.[155] In 1902, Herbert Samuel, a British liberal writer and politician, observed that "[n]ot long ago it was the fashion to ridicule international arbitration as visionary. . . . But in spite of ridicule it has won its way into the field of practical politics."[156] A product of the rapid expansion of international law in the second half of the nineteenth century, arbitration blended Christian missionary zeal, pragmatic diplomatic reasoning, and claims about civilizational superiority. It appealed to many Americans because they viewed it through the prism of the Constitution, with the resolution of intrastate conflicts guaranteed by an authoritative legal process. Like its British proponents, they could boast that arbitration was a product of the legal genius of the Anglo-Saxons. Yet advocates of the idea did not sing from the same hymn sheet: arbitration came in more or less ambitious guises.

We can distinguish *regulatory* and *revisionary* models. Viewing arbitration as a relatively narrow legal instrument, the former sought to limit violence in the international system. A conservative conception of legal regulation, it presupposed the existence of both sovereign states and war as institutions of global order. The eminent lawyer John Westlake claimed that it signaled a retreat from grandly ambitious constitutional projects. No longer "under the spell" of thinkers like Saint Pierre, Bentham, or Kant, his contemporaries had "turned from sketching imaginary international governments to the more practical . . . task of promoting international arbitration."[157] In legal textbooks,

---

154. For the phrase, see Carnegie, *Autobiography*, 308, 314.

155. David Patterson, *Towards a Warless World* (Bloomington, 1976); Martin Ceadel, *Semi-Detached Idealists* (Oxford, 2000); Cecilie Reid, "Peace and Law," *Peace & Change*, 29/3 (2004), 521–48; Stephen Wertheim, "The League of Nations," *Journal of Global History*, 7/2 (2012), 210–32.

156. Herbert Samuel, *Liberalism* (London, 1902), 361.

157. John Westlake, "International Arbitration," *International Journal of Ethics*, 7/1 (1896), 2. He supported an Anglo-American Treaty (14, 18). For other contemporary analyses of the idea,

arbitration was almost invariably located in discussion of the laws of war, signaling that it was part of the system of organized violence, not an alternative to it.[158] The state had captured the dream of peace. "By the start of the twentieth century," Mark Mazower observes, "international law was the preeminent example of a once utopian internationalist creed harnessed and tamed by states themselves."[159] But a much more ambitious account of the nature and purpose of arbitration can also be discerned. Mixing revisionist ambition with visionary intent, the revisionary form regarded arbitration as an initial step on the road to geopolitical transformation. It was figured as an integral part of grander political projects, an institutional mechanism to catalyze or accelerate systemic change, principally through serving as the foundation for new supranational institutions or megapolities. Thus the economist H. Stanley Jevons welcomed the 1907 Hague conference as "the institution which will be shaped step by step into a worldwide federal government."[160] It was this type of arbitration that was promoted doggedly by Carnegie and Stead.

Many peace advocates, Carnegie among them, regarded an arbitration treaty between Britain and the United States as essential.[161] He had long promulgated Anglo-American arbitration, supporting the unsuccessful campaign to secure a treaty in 1887 and 1888.[162] During the 1890s, he repeatedly conjoined it with racial reunion. Carnegie made the connection clear in a memorandum he wrote to Gladstone—another of his heroes—in 1893. "Should Mr. G add this treaty of peace between Britain and America," Carnegie averred,

---

see Robert Finlay, "International Arbitration," *North American Review*, 179/576 (1904), 659–70; J. A. Hobson, "The Ethics of Internationalism," *International Journal of Ethics*, 17/1 (1906), 22–23; Eleanor Lord, "International Arbitration," *Annals of the American Academy of Political and Social Science*, 2 (1892), 39–55.

158. On the placement of such discussions, and for an account of continental European arbitration debates, see Kristina Lovric-Pernak, "Aim: Peace—Sanction: War" in Thomas Hippler and Milos Vec (eds.), *Paradoxes of Peace in Nineteenth-Century Europe* (Oxford, 2015), 67.

159. Mark Mazower, *Governing the World* (London, 2012), 67.

160. H. Stanley Jevons, "The Development of an International Parliament," *Contemporary Review*, 92 (1907), 323.

161. On the campaign for an Anglo-American arbitration treaty, see Patterson, *Towards a Warless World*, 18–29.

162. David Patterson, "Andrew Carnegie's Quest for World Peace," *Proceedings of the American Philosophical Society*, 114/5 (1970), 372; Paul Laity, *The British Peace Movement, 1870–1914* (Oxford, 2001), 109–13; Nasaw, *Andrew Carnegie*, 300, 311. For some early criticisms of militarism, see Andrew Carnegie, *An American Four in Hand in Britain* (New York, 1883), 14–16; Carnegie, *Round the World*, 14–15, 110. In recognition of his efforts, Carnegie was appointed by President Harrison as a delegate to the Pan-American Conference in 1892, which was concerned with inter-American arbitration.

"he will have laid the foundation for the coming re-union of the parts which should never have been separated." Historians in the years to come would look favorably on the accomplishment, characterizing it as an epoch-defining moment. "In the future history of the steps by which the race finally abolished the greatest stain upon humanity, the murder of man by man under the name of war, this treaty of peace would always find prominent place."[163]

The Venezuela crisis galvanized supporters of arbitration. The British claim that Guayana Esequiba formed part of British Guyana had long been rejected by the Venezuelans. After the dispute had dragged on for decades, Venezuela called on the United States to intercede, charging that the British were undermining the Monroe Doctrine by trespassing in Washington's backyard. They found a receptive audience among expansionist Americans. Henry Cabot Lodge put the point forcefully in June 1895: "[t]he supremacy of the Monroe doctrine should be established and at once—peaceably if we can, forcibly if we must."[164] The following month, Secretary of State Olney sent a letter to Lord Salisbury, the British Prime Minister, declaring that "today the United States is practically sovereign on this continent, and its fiat is law upon the subjects to which it confines its interposition."[165] Since the vital interests of the United States were at stake, London must accede to Washington's demand for arbitration. Miscalculating the anger of the Cleveland administration, the British government responded sluggishly, with Salisbury taking four months to flatly reject Olney's demands.[166] Patriotic fervor swept sections of the American political elite and media, as Cleveland sent a letter to Congress stating that he planned to establish a commission to investigate the territorial claims. The British were startled by American bellicosity. Bryce observed that

163. Carnegie to Gladstone, 27 July 1893, Fol 21; see also Carnegie to Benjamin Harrison, 25 January 1892, Fol 13; Carnegie to Arthur Balfour, 9 August 1901, Fol 84; Carnegie to the Duke of Devonshire, 22 December 1895, Fol 35, Carnegie papers. On the friendship between Carnegie and Gladstone, see Carnegie, *Autobiography*, ch. 24; H. C. G. Matthew, *Gladstone, 1809–1898* (Oxford, 1997), 569, 621–22; Nasaw, *Andrew Carnegie*, chs. 13–14.

164. Henry C. Lodge, "England, Venezuela, and the Monroe Doctrine," *North American Review*, 160/463 (1895), 658. See also Jay Sexton, *The Monroe Doctrine* (New York, 2012), 202–11; George Herring, *From Colony to Superpower* (Oxford, 2008), 307–8.

165. Olney to Thomas Bayard, 20 July 1895, cited in Herring, *From Colony to Superpower*, 307. This document has come to be known as the Olney interpretation of Manifest Destiny.

166. On British underestimation of American resolve, see Paul Gibb, "Unmasterly Inactivity?," *Diplomacy & Statecraft*, 16/1 (2005), 23–55. See also R. A. Humphrey, "Anglo-American Rivalries and the Venezuela Crisis of 1895," *Transactions of the Royal Historical Society*, 17 (1967), 131–64; A. E. Campbell, *Great Britain and the United States, 1895–1903* (London, 1960), ch. 2.

"[n]obody had the least idea that your Government considered the matter to be one of immediate and primary importance to America, justifying an ultimatum. That the Monroe Doctrine could be deemed involved had not occurred to our minds."[167] With little enthusiasm for conflict, the British quietly accepted arbitration and the issue fizzled out almost as quickly as it had flared.[168] But it left a mark.

Carnegie sought to interpose himself between the two sides. Furious with the British for their initial failure to arbitrate, he later suggested that it constituted a just cause for war against his original homeland.[169] In particular Carnegie blamed the Venezuela imbroglio (and much else besides) on Salisbury. "He, and he alone, is responsible for all the trouble."[170] Yet ever the optimist, Carnegie saw the crisis as an opportunity, a propitious moment to sign an arbitration treaty.[171] As he lectured a Scottish audience in October 1896, such an instrument would "render the murder of English-speaking men by English-speaking men in war impossible," because between them Britain and the United States "hold sway over every English-speaking community upon the face of the earth," and "those of us who do not owe allegiance to the one, owe it to the other."[172] Intraracial peace was a necessary foundation for the "English-speaking men" to embark on their mission to pacify the world.

Bryce argued that the crisis might stimulate mutual recognition of close kinship and shared interests, hastening the creation of a permanent system of Anglo-American arbitration.[173] Morley concurred with this diagnosis.[174] Besant proposed the creation of a Court of Arbitration: "The mere existence of

167. Bryce, "British Feeling on the Venezuela Question," 146.

168. An agreement was signed between Washington and London in November 1896, establishing a tribunal to adjudicate the claims. It reached its final decision in 1899, awarding Britain 90 percent of the territory.

169. Carnegie to Stead, 4 October 1900, Fol 78, Carnegie papers.

170. Carnegie to Morley, 27 January 1896, Fol 36, Carnegie papers. British liberals were more supportive of arbitration than Salisbury, who had never been keen: Boyle, "Venezuela Crisis and the Liberal Opposition, 1895–6."

171. Carnegie, "Venezuelan Question," 144. See also Carnegie, "Americanism versus Imperialism," 1–13.

172. Speech to open school in Dunfermline, October 1896, Box 251, Carnegie papers, 14–15.

173. Bryce, "Venezuela Question," 152. See also Bryce to Roosevelt, 1 January 1896, in Herbert A. L. Fisher, *James Bryce* (London, 1927), I, 318–19, and, in support of arbitration, Bryce to Stead, 10 January 1896, F. Whyte, *Life of W. T. Stead* (London, 1925), II, 79.

174. John Morley, "Arbitration with America," *Nineteenth Century*, 40 (1896), 320–37. Carnegie wrote to congratulate him on the essay: 1 August 1896, Fol 38, Carnegie papers.

such a Board will prevent cases from arising, while the knowledge that there can never be war between the two nations will at once alter the tone of the press in every Anglo Saxon country to that of permanent alliance."[175] The effort soon stalled, as the Olney-Pauncefote Treaty, which made it compulsory for certain Anglo-American disputes to be settled by arbitration, was rejected by the United States Senate. Despite constant setbacks, Carnegie never lost faith in the ameliorative power of arbitration, or its role as the potential institutional catalyst for Anglo-American union. Speaking at the memorial service for Gladstone in 1902, he declared that the supreme achievement of the "first citizen of the world" had been the *Alabama* arbitration and his support for the principle during the Venezuela crisis.[176]

Carnegie also sought to explain British policy to an American audience. In order to understand what was happening in Venezuela, he contended, it was necessary to recognize that "land hunger" was one of the chief characteristics of the English-speaking race. "It is a root passion, some of us think a prerogative, of our race to acquire territory."[177] Despite its professed anticolonialism, the United States was as guilty as Britain; the main difference was that American expansion had occurred within continental bounds, whereas the British had to venture overseas to acquire new territory. This accident of geography should not obscure the underlying similarity—the will to empire. Venezuela was a manifestation of both the checkered history of imperialism and of the inner drive of "the race," but in Carnegie's eyes this did not excuse British intransigence: "This is certainly one of the most flagrant exercises of brute force against a weak power which can be adduced to illustrate the propensity of the English-speaking race to absorb as much of the land of the world as it possibly can."[178]

American expansionists relished the opportunity to eject the Spanish empire from the Western hemisphere, and a revolt in Cuba provided a fortuitous opportunity to act. After a mysterious explosion sank the USS *Maine* in Havana harbor in February 1898, and against the backdrop of feverish jingoism, William McKinley declared war on Spain in April. The conflict soon spread to the Pacific, as the US Navy routed the Spanish fleet and occupied Manila. By the close of the year, the United States had seized Cuba, Guam, Puerto Rico,

175. Besant, "Future of the Anglo-Saxon Race," 143.

176. Carnegie at Hawarden, 14 October 1902, recorded in *Three Busy Weeks*, ed. S. Cunningham (Dunfermline, 1902), 82–83, Box 251 AC. See also Carnegie's 1905 Rectorial Address at St. Andrews, where he called on the assembled students to dedicate themselves to peace through arbitration: *A League of Peace* (Boston, 1906).

177. Carnegie, "Venezuelan Question," 131.

178. Carnegie, "Venezuelan Question," 135.

and Wake Island, and had established a precarious foothold in the Philippines. The following year saw the start of a vicious guerrilla campaign against Filipinos fighting for their independence. Anti-imperialist Leagues sprang up around the country. Divides ran deep, with politicians, intellectuals, and religious leaders pitted against each other.[179] The feminist movement was split, some seeing it as their duty to support the war, others that it was yet another expression of violent masculinity.[180]

Fierce debate over the justice of American imperialism raged among African-Americans. Cuba was frequently presented as a racially egalitarian paradise, and the ideal of an independent black republic appealed to many of those suffering the depredations of racial domination.[181] A handful of committed expansionists—including Edward E. Cooper, editor of *The Colored American*—argued that military action against Spain was in the interest of both the United States and of its black citizens.[182] It would serve as a sign and symbol of African-American patriotism, smoothing the path to social and political recognition. Others rejected the idea that an unjust regime could fight a just war, maintaining that the United States should address its own gross failings before turning its attention to others. The debate continued through 1898 and into the early years of the new century, though support for American expansionism dropped away, as black soldiers were maligned, even physically abused, and explicit racist arguments were mobilized to justify imperial conquest in the Caribbean and the Pacific.[183] The popularity of Kipling's "White Man's Burden" crystallized the deep disquiet felt by many African-Americans.[184] In contrast to the broad spectrum of views circulating prior to

179. For an acute analysis of justificatory arguments, see Anders Stephanson, *Manifest Destiny* (New York, 1995), ch. 4. For detailed accounts, see Fabian Hilfrich, *Debating American Exceptionalism* (Basingstoke, 2012); Robert Beisner, *Twelve against Empire* (New York, 1968); Michael Patrick Cullinane, *Liberty and American Anti-Imperialism* (Basingstoke, 2012); David Mayers, *Dissenting Voices in America's Rise to Power* (Cambridge, 2007), ch. 8.

180. Allison Sneider, *Suffragists in an Imperial Age* (Oxford, 2008), ch. 4; Kristin Hoganson, *Fighting for American Manhood* (New Haven, CT, 1998).

181. Gatewood, *Black Americans*, chs. 2–3.

182. Gatewood, *Black Americans*, 156, 253–54.

183. Gatewood, *Black Americans*, chs. 4–7. For a useful selection of primary sources, see George Marks (ed.), *The Black Press Views American Imperialism (1898–1900)* (New York, 1971). On African-American literary responses to American expansion, see John Cullen Gruesser, *The Empire Abroad and the Empire at Home* (Athens, 2012). On the contested reception of Kipling's poem, see Gretchen Murphy, *Shadowing the White Man's Burden* (New York, 2010), pt. I.

184. Though written in 1898, the poem was only published in 1899. It appeared in multiple outlets (e.g., *The Times, 4 February 1899; New York Tribune, 5 February 1899; McClure's Magazine,*

the conflict in Cuba, there was widespread—if never exhaustive—opposition to war in the Philippines.[185]

Most Anglo-race unionists were imperialists of one stripe or another, envisaging that closer relations between Britain and the United States would result—or even be driven by—a shared interest in governing their respective empires. Many supported collaboration in an inter-imperial mission to carve up the world for new markets in the name of civilization. Both Clarke and Beresford saluted the policy shift. "In the year now past," Clark wrote in 1899, "another vital question of supreme importance for good or evil presented itself for decision, and again . . . the true path has been chosen," although he concluded that there was still no viable case for a formal alliance.[186] Beresford was likewise supportive, contending that due to their historically unprecedented character, the United States and Britain could escape the fate of all previous empires. History taught a vital lesson:

> The great weakness of the nationalities which have been engulfed by the irresistible march of time has been the despotism which underlay their governments, the corruption which sapped their liberties, the luxury and indolence which ate into their vitality, and the remarkable fact that they became worn out and vicious, while the countries they had conquered, and the dependencies they had absorbed, at last broke away, imbued deeply with the vices and but few of the original virtues of the sovereign state.[187]

The Anglo-Saxons had worked out a way to circumvent the logic of decline and fall. In an act of racial alchemy, the United States transmuted white immigrants into members of the dominant racial order. "In a very few years, a generation at the outside, the new-comers are more Anglo-Saxon than the original stock, more keenly patriotic and more ready to resent any attack on the liberties of their chosen homeland."[188] Because it absorbed and assimilated peoples so effectively, it "will long postpone any decadence such as has

---

February 1899). For its reception history, see Brantlinger, "Kipling's 'The White Man's Burden' and Its Afterlives," 172–91.

185. Gatewood, *Black Americans*, ch. 10.

186. George Sydenham Clarke, "Imperial Responsibilities a National Gain," *North American Review*, 168/507 (1899), 132.

187. Charles Beresford, "The Future of the Anglo-Saxon Race," *North American Review*, 171/529 (1900), 803.

188. Beresford, "Anglo-Saxon Race," 804. Beresford supported the Open Door policy in China, and argued for maintaining the integrity of the Chinese empire under British leadership, with American cooperation: Beresford, "China and the Great Powers," *North American Review*, 168/510 (1899), 53–58; Beresford, *The Break-up of China* (New York, 1899).

befallen its predecessors."[189] The remarkable ability of the English-speaking world to escape political declension was a common refrain among imperial unionists, convinced that the British settler empire, unique in all history, had escaped the cycle of expansion and decay through granting self-government to its constituent parts.[190] It was also a popular theme among Anglo-American unionists. Insisting that they had always shared a common language and a glorious racial inheritance, Beresford nevertheless discerned a shift in Anglo-American relations, a growing recognition that the two countries "have a common duty to perform, a common office to fulfil, among the nations of the world," though he stopped short of endorsing an alliance. He ended on a prophetic note: "we may look confidently forward to its future and hope and pray that there is something, after all, in the visionaries' prophecy that through that race 'all the nations of the world shall be blessed.'"[191]

Mahan stuck to his earlier line. In 1898, as momentum for war against Spain gathered, he outlined his views on the timing of rapprochement to one of his numerous British military correspondents. "I am satisfied myself that the tendency is for our two countries to draw together, but the process is inevitably slow, and particularly with a huge, and as yet not homogenous, body politic as ours here. It takes a long time for a sentiment to permeate the mass."[192] It was best, for the moment at least, to rely on a sense of kinship to do the work. Much was at stake, he had written the previous year, for "in the unity of heart among the English-speaking races lies the hope of humanity in the doubtful days ahead."[193] Although he never advocated a full-blown union with the British Empire, Mahan increasingly came to see the benefits of close collaboration between a British imperial federation and the United States. In 1901, for example, he argued that imperial prestige had been augmented, not undercut, by the war in South Africa, and he offered staunch support for the federation

189. Beresford, "Anglo-Saxon Race," 804.

190. Bell, *Greater Britain*, ch. 8; Bell, "Empire" in Mark Bevir (ed.), *Historicism in the Victorian Human Sciences* (Cambridge, 2017), 211–36.

191. Beresford, "Anglo-Saxon Race," 809, 810. The quotation is from Genesis 22:18. In a talk in New York, Charles Beresford criticized Chamberlain's call for an "alliance" as premature: *New York Times*, 19 May 1898. As I noted in the introduction, Chamberlain's suggestion was less bold than it appeared.

192. Mahan to Col. Sterling, 4 March 1898, Reel 2, Mahan papers. Stead welcomed the publication of Mahan's *The Interest of America in Sea Power* in *RoR*, 27 (January 1898): "Captain Mahan throughout his book argues in favour of a reunion of the two great portions of the English-speaking race. But it must be a union of sentiment and mutual interest. And not one of political ties" (85).

193. Alfred T. Mahan, "A Twentieth Century Outlook," *Harper's*, 95/508 (1897), 531.

of the settler colonial system, "the importance of which to me is undeniable."[194] His account was as much epistemic as geostrategic. Mahan believed that British imperial experience, in Egypt above all, offered important lessons for American rule in the Philippines, while the American experience of federal union provided a valuable model for the British to emulate.[195] Such knowledge furnished a sound basis for future political developments. These two vast federal polities would cooperate closely in the coming century. In "language, law, and political traditions," he observed, "there is fundamental identity."[196] Mahan also retained his intense dislike of Carnegie and what he represented. Writing rote to a British naval officer in 1909, he confided that "The Peace and Arbitration people—above all Andrew Carnegie—get on my nerves."[197]

Carnegie demurred from the embrace of imperialism. He had frequently condemned British rule in India, arguing that it was a major economic and moral drain on the home country, as well as a source of great injustice to Indians.[198] He was appalled at the prospect of the United States mimicking Britain. Conflict threatened to undermine the democratic values and institutions that made America great.

> It has hitherto been the glorious mission of the Republic to establish upon secure foundations Triumphant Democracy, and the world now understands government of the people for the people and by the people. Tires the Republic so soon of its mission that it must, perforce, discard it to undertake the impossible task of establishing Triumphant Despotism, the rule of the foreigner over the people, and must the millions of the Philippines who have been asserting their God-given right to govern themselves, be the

194. Alfred T. Mahan, "The Influence of the South African War upon the Prestige of the British Empire," *National Review* (1901), in Mahan, *Retrospect & Prospect* (Boston, 1902), 57–88; Mahan, "Imperial Federation," *National Review* (1902), in Mahan, *Retrospect & Prospect*, 109.

195. Mahan, "Imperial Federation," 96–98. He imagined a full federal state, ruling over a scattered empire. The editor of the *National Review*, Leo Maxse, informed Mahan about the impact of his intervention, noting, for example, that *The Times* had led with the imperial federation essay, and that Joseph Chamberlain had drawn on it in a speech. Maxse to Mahan, 2 May 1903 and 29 May 1903, Reel 6, Mahan papers.

196. Mahan, "Imperial Federation," 134. He continued, "and in blood also, though to some extent differentiated in each by foreign admixture" (134). For criticism of his position, see "Captain Mahan on Imperial Federation," *The Nation*, 74 (1902), 400–401.

197. Mahan to Bouverie Clark, 23 July 1909, *Letters and Papers*, III, 308. He often linked Stead and Carnegie as key figures in the peace movement that he sought to oppose. See, for example, Mahan to Leopold Maxse, 5 March 1907, *Letters and Papers*, III, 207. For Mahan, Stead's saving grace was that he supported a large navy: Mahan, letter, *New York Times*, 24 May 1912, 10.

198. For his views on India, see Carnegie, *Reunion*, 23–24.

first victims of Americans, whose proudest boast is that they conquered independence for themselves?"[199]

He continued in this vein when the fighting erupted, counterposing a republican vision of "Americanism" against a degraded militaristic "Imperialism," and demanding that Cuba and the Philippine be granted independence. He adduced various reasons—military, economic, and moral—for rejecting the war. All were common currency in the anti-imperial movement. Possession of a territorial empire in Asia would expose the United States to grave military threats for which it was wholly unprepared; it offered no commercial benefits and threatened to divert or drain the sources of American wealth; moreover, it exposed the United States to the corrupting dynamics that beset all imperial powers, undermining public morality.[200] True republican government was incompatible with empire. As he scolded his readers in 1902, "We are engaged in work which requires suppression of American ideas hitherto held sacred."[201]

Carnegie drew on a venerable tradition of republican anti-imperialism, asserting that the very existence of the American political order was endangered by foreign aggression. According to republicans, Quentin Skinner argues, "[y]ou can hope to retain your individual freedom from dependence on the will of others if and only if you live as an active citizen of a state that is fully self-governing, and is consequently neither dominating nor dominated."[202] Carnegie adopted a similar line, skeptical of both the capacity of the United States (and Britain) to effectively govern other peoples, and warning of the moral and political dangers that followed from attempts to crush self-government abroad. After visiting India in the early 1880s, he wrote that "[i]f America can learn one lesson from England, it is the folly of conquest, where

199. Andrew Carnegie, "Distant Possessions," *North American Review*, 167/501 (1898), 244–45. For further discussion of the negative lesson taught by British imperial history, see also Carnegie's comments in Adlai Stevenson et al., "Bryan or McKinley?," *North American Review*, 171/527 (1900), 496–97. Carnegie was elected Vice President of the Anti-Imperialist League.

200. Andrew Carnegie, "Americanism versus Imperialism," *North American Review*, 168/506 (1899), 1–13; Carnegie, "Americanism versus Imperialism: II," 362. For typical economic justifications of the war, see Charles Conant, "The Economic Basis of Imperialism," *North American Review*, 167/502 (1898), 326–40; James Fernald, *The Imperial Republic* (New York, 1898). On debate over the war, see Cullinane, *Liberty and American Anti-Imperialism*; E. Berkeley Tompkins, *Anti-Imperialism in the United States* (Philadelphia, 1970); Beisner, *Twelve against Empire*.

201. Andrew Carnegie, "The Opportunity of the United States," *North American Review*, 174/546 (1902), 611.

202. Quentin Skinner, "On the Slogans of Republican Political Theory," *European Journal of Political Theory*, 9/1 (2010), 100. For further discussion, see Bell, *Reordering the World*, ch. 4.

conquest involves the government of an alien race."[203] He rejected the civilizing mission so dear to many liberal thinkers and politicians, now as then.
"Speaking broadly, I do not believe that it is in the power of England—and of
course much less of any other country—to confer upon another race benefits
which are not more than cancelled by the evil which usually follows from her
interference."[204]

The danger of shameful hypocrisy loomed. "The American idea of the
rights of man and of the right of self-government is not false. It is true. All
communities, however low they may be in the scale, have the germ of self-
government."[205] This was a conventional liberal internationalist claim an-
chored in a racialized vision of global order: all peoples possessed an immanent capacity for self-government, though it was considerably better developed
in some than others. The states of the North Atlantic were paradigmatic examples. Below them were arrayed the rest of the peoples of the world. Global
hierarchy was thus equated, in part, with governing capacity, defined in terms
derived solely from Western experience. This picture was at once universalist
and highly stratified, offering hope of future equality while simultaneously
reproducing patterns of inequality in the present. But whereas many liberals
thought that civilizing modes of imperialism were justified in such a world,
Carnegie rejected the attempt to accelerate the growth of self-government in
"backward" zones, arguing that peoples should be left to develop at their own
pace. Since Carnegie believed that "all is well since all grows better," and
because he defined improvement as the spread of democratic industrial capitalism, he was convinced that historical evolution would guarantee convergence on a single model of political-economic order. He was a modernization
theorist *avant la lettre*.

Carnegie also worried that the war threatened his dream of Anglo-American
union. He feared that it would be used as a convenient reason to forge a formal
military alliance, encouraging his two beloved countries to engage in destructive inter-imperial cooperation.

> The author of "A Look Ahead" . . . is not likely to be suspected of hostility
> to the coming together of the English-speaking race. It has been my dream,
> and it is one of the movements that lie closest to my heart. For many years
> the United Flag has floated from my summer home in my native land, the
> Stars and Stripes and the Union Jack sewn together—the first of that kind
> of flag ever seen. That flag will continue to fly there and the winds to blow

203. Carnegie, *Round the World*, 228 (on British rule in India, see also 284–93).
204. Carnegie, *Round the World*, 293.
205. Carnegie, "Opportunity of the United States," 611.

the two from side to side in loving embrace. But I do not favor a formal alliance. . . . On the contrary, I rely upon the "alliance of hearts," which happily exists to-day. Alliances of fighting power form and dissolve with the questions which arise from time to time. The patriotism of race lies deeper and is not disturbed by waves upon the surface.[206]

Despite the tribulations, Carnegie's belief in the viability of his dream remained intact. Reflecting on "A Look Ahead" in 1898, he wrote that "five years after these words were penned I have nothing to add to or deduct from them, on the contrary, I am as confident as ever of the coming fulfilment of that prediction."[207]

The British war in South Africa provoked similar horror in Carnegie, and he allied himself with the British "pro-Boers."[208] As with the Spanish-American war, he argued that the conflict was both unjust and a significant barrier to racial reunion. "No nation has a right to attack and endeavour to suppress a people so capable of self government as the Dutch and force its own supremacy, although in a minority."[209] The attempt to do so would invariably end in failure, because the desire for political independence was too strong to suppress permanently. Peaceful cooperation was a wiser course of action. Carnegie channeled money to the antiwar cause, including Stead's strident campaign.[210] He sought to place the conflict and its key actors in historical context, hoping that an appeal to posterity would spur action in the present. The most honored men in British history, "the true guides who pointed out the path their country should follow and denounced its errors," were those who had counseled against illegitimate wars: Burke and Chatham, Bright and Cobden. It was those who rushed to war, the jingoes, that history would judge dimly.

> The same fate awaits those who have precipitated war against the South African Republics, upon the pretence that they were concerned to make it easier for Britons there to abandon citizenship and become Afrikaners. Not these men, but Campbell-Bannerman, Harcourt, Morley, Courtney, Sir

206. Carnegie, "Americanism versus Imperialism," 5–6.

207. Andrew Carnegie, "Anglo-American Alliance: A Look Today," 1898, Box 251, Carnegie papers.

208. Andrew Carnegie, "The South African Question," *North American Review*, 169/517 (1899), 798–804.

209. Carnegie, "South African Question," 803. See also Carnegie to Rosebery, 23 November 1901.

210. In January 1900, for example, Stead wrote to Carnegie, thanking him for providing £1000 to help with the distribution of antiwar pamphlets: Stead to Carnegie, 12 January 1900, Fol 72, Carnegie papers.

Edward Clarke and their colleagues are soon to be held in esteem, and extolled as the true patriots who protested against the wrong.[211]

The war, Carnegie told Stead, threatened the "fall of the English-speaking race."[212] But ever the incorrigible optimist, he discerned grounds for hope. Despite the manifest injustice of the imperial wars, they demonstrated that the two powers shared both a history and a destiny. He made this clear in a speech in Ottawa in 1901, arguing that those who deplored the war could nevertheless find some comfort in the fact that Britain and America were now closer than they had been since the years before the Revolution. "It seems that the horoscope of the future shows common dangers likely to draw us closer and closer in the bonds of a Common Race."[213]

There were significant limits to Carnegie's professed "anti-imperialism." He supported the annexation of Hawaii on the grounds of strategic necessity, and while he opposed the initial occupation of Cuba, he later suggested that it too should be annexed.[214] Above all, he was a committed advocate of settler colonialism. British liberal thinkers often regarded settlement as a preferable model of empire to the conquest and alien rule associated with India. The colonies were imagined as spaces of political freedom for the white "civilised" settlers, unburdened from the moral and political dangers unleashed by despotic governance.[215] Carnegie accepted this self-serving account without qualification. While accepting that conventional forms of imperialism were motivated by avarice and caused endless problems for both the imperial power and those subjugated by it, he argued that settler colonialism was premised on the grant of self-government to the colonists. "It is in Colonies, not in Dependencies, that Britain has done good work."[216] In the colonies, he boasted,

---

211. Carnegie, "Bryan or McKinley?," 496–97. For later criticisms, see also Carnegie, Speech in Toronto, 27 April 1906, Box 252, Carnegie papers.

212. Carnegie to Stead, 22 August 1900.

213. Carnegie, Response to a toast, Canada, 1901, Box 251, Carnegie papers.

214. Carnegie, "Distant Possessions," 242–43.

215. Bell, *Reordering the World*, ch. 2. For further discussion of different kinds of imperialism, see James Tully, "Lineages of Contemporary Imperialism" in Duncan Kelly (ed.), *Lineages of Empire* (Oxford, 2009), 3–31. On how anti-imperial arguments have often been used to legitimate imperialism, see Ian Tyrrell and Jay Sexton (eds.), *Empire's Twin* (Ithaca, NY, 2015).

216. Carnegie, "Americanism vs. Imperialism: II," 370. Spencer was happy to endorse settler colonialism, as long as it was conducted by private initiative, not state action: Herbert Spencer, "The Proper Sphere of Government" (1843), in *The Man Versus the State* (Indianapolis, 1982), 224. Like Carnegie, he was a fierce critic of other forms of imperialism: Spencer, "Imperialism and Slavery" in Spencer, *Facts and Comments* (New York, 1902), 157–71.

we establish and reproduce our own race. Thus Britain has peopled Canada and Australia with English-speaking people, who have naturally adopted our ideas of self-government. That the world has benefited thereby goes without saying; that Britain has done a great work as the mother of nations is becoming more and more appreciated the more the student learns of worldwide affairs. No nation that ever existed has done so much for the progress of the world as the little islands in the North Sea, known as Britain.[217]

For Carnegie, British imperialism encompassed two countervailing trends. One of them, found in India and more recently Africa, was marked by shame and futility, and resulted in the accumulation of worthless—even dangerous— foreign possessions. "Beaconsfield was right," he admonished Stead in 1898: "the Colonies are useless, or worse, to Britain."[218] The Raj, in particular, was a threat to British prosperity and moral leadership. "The most grievous burden which Britain has upon her shoulders is that of India, for there it is impossible for our race to grow."[219] The other was a story of progressive transformation, the occupation and cultivation of territories that benefited Britain and the world. He characterized the latter as part of the beneficent teleology of evolution, "the fittest driving out the least fit; the best supplanting the inferior." Carnegie thought the same dynamic had been replicated in the violent settling of the American West. Land was necessary to spread civilization, and as such it was "right and proper that the nomadic Indian should give place to the settled husbandman in the prairies of the West," just as it was acceptable that "the Maori should fade away, and give place to the intelligent, industrious citizen, a member of our race."[220] Carnegie's use of passive language is telling. The indigenous populations were to "fade away"—not driven from their lands, quarantined, or killed by settlers—as part of a predetermined and progressive historical pattern. This was an example of the idea that the supposedly backward peoples of the world were fated to extinction.[221] Colonial elimitavism, based on violent dispossession, was recoded as an inexorable evolutionary process. Human agency, and thus moral responsibility, was effaced.

217. Carnegie, "Distant Possessions," 240.

218. Carnegie to Stead, 17 January 1898, Fol 48, Carnegie papers. The context of Disraeli's famous comment is explored in Peter J. Cain, "Radicalism, Gladstone, and the Liberal Critique of Disraelian 'Imperialism,'" in Duncan Bell (ed.), *Victorian Visions of Global Order* (Cambridge, 2007), 215–38.

219. Carnegie, "Distant Possessions," 240.

220. Carnegie, "Venezuela Question," 133.

221. Brantlinger, *Dark Vanishings*.

Racial Providence: The Political Theology of Unity

Theological arguments were deployed routinely to bolster racial supremacy. "God has chosen one race above all others because that race is the fittest to perform his work," wrote Montana preacher Martin Streator. "Those who attempt to thwart this manifest destiny of the Anglo-Saxon race do so to their own confusion and ruin."[222] Some of the most prominent religious thinkers in the United States argued that Anglo-American cooperation, even union, could serve as a temporal instrument of God's will, the chosen vessel for bringing about the millennium, for spreading civilization to the barbarians and evangelizing a heathen world.[223] Nicholas Guyatt delineates three forms of providentialism in American history. Historical providentialism posits that God anointed certain peoples, races, or nations to play a special role in history. Judicial providentialism claims that certain peoples, races, or nations are punished or rewarded according to their moral value. Finally, apocalyptic providentialism suggests that the book of Revelation offers a guide for understanding the dynamics of the contemporary world.[224] Both historical and juridical providentialism coursed through debates over Anglo-America.

Josiah Strong is a case in point. A Congregationalist minister and leading advocate of the reformist social gospel, he gained national attention with the publication of *Our Country* in 1885.[225] It contained a famous chapter on "The Anglo-Saxons and the World's Future," which predicted that the Anglo-Saxons were destined to bring civilization to the dark earth.[226] God's anointed people,

222. Martin Lyman Streator, *The Anglo-American Alliance in Prophecy, or the Promises to the Fathers* (London, 1900), 128. Streator argued that a worldwide Anglo-Saxon alliance had been foretold by the Hebrew prophets. See Annette Stott, "A Material Response to Spiritual Crisis," *Journal of the American Academy of Religion*, 87/1 (2019), 225–59.

223. Andrew Preston, *Sword of the Spirit, Shield of Faith* (New York, 2012), pt. III; Stephanson, *Manifest Destiny*.

224. Nicholas Guyatt, *Providence and the Invention of the United States, 1607–1876* (Cambridge, 2007).

225. Josiah Strong, *Our Country* (New York, 1885). It had sold 176,000 copies by the time of his death in 1916. Strong was General Secretary of the Evangelical Alliance (1886–98), and thereafter he led the League for Social Service.

226. For contrasting accounts of Strong's imperialism and nationalism, see Dorothea Muller, "Josiah Strong and American Nationalism," *Journal of American History*, 53/3 (1966), 487–503; James E. Reed, "American Foreign Policy, the Politics of Missions, and Josiah Strong, 1890–1900," *Church History*, 41/2 (1972), 230–45; Wendy Edwards, "Forging an Ideology for American Missions" in Wilbert Shenk (ed.), *North American Foreign Missions, 1810–1914* (Grand Rapids, MI, 2004), 163–91. Muller is persuasive in arguing that *Our Country* was read more as a call for

they were equipped to lead human progress because of their ardent commitment to fusing "pure spiritual Christianity" with civil liberty. Through missionary work, trade, commercial exchange, and colonial settlement, they were "divinely commissioned" to disseminate institutions and ideas, until, "in a very true and important sense," they had "Anglo-Saxonized mankind."[227] As the most fully realized instantiation of this blessed race, "the principal seat of his power, the center of his life and influence," the United States had an obligation to evangelize the world, converting it to a state of perfection.[228] A prophecy about the inevitable course of history rather than a call for immediate political action, Strong's message resonated more widely during the 1890s than in the decade it was published.

In *Our Country*, Britain was figured as the past to America's future, a land that had once incubated ideals that had subsequently been realized more comprehensively across the Atlantic. Having discharged its duty, Britain was destined to fall behind its offspring. But during the 1890s Strong assigned an important supporting role to Britain. In *The New Era, or the Coming Kingdom*, published in 1893, he once again celebrated the world-historical role of the Anglo-Saxons, arguing that they were "especially commissioned to prepare the way for the full coming of God's kingdom on earth."[229] Unfolding within states and on a global scale, the two main tendencies of the age—the cumulative product of all history—were the simultaneous growth of individualism and social organization. Whereas they had often been in tension, under modern conditions they were rightly seen as "correlative principles," and were best embodied in the Anglo-Saxon race. Combining the religiosity of the Hebrews, the individualistic spirit of freedom of the Greeks, and the technological mastery and genius for sociopolitical organization of the Romans, the Anglo-Saxons synthesized and then extended the inheritance of the great ancient civilizations. As time and space were transformed, so this new era of civilization—spread in part by colonial expansion—would become truly global. Never short of superlatives, Strong enumerated the sources of Anglo-Saxon superiority: they possessed the greatest religion, the most developed moral sense, the most effective humanitarian impulse, the most sophisticated

---

domestic reform than imperial expansion, but her attempt to save Strong from charges of belligerence are unpersuasive.

227. Strong, *Our Country*, 161, 178. He notes (160) that the argument parallels John Fiske's, "Manifest Destiny," *Harper's Magazine* 70 (March 1885), 578–89. On the messianic belief that America was destined to bring order to the world, see Ernest Tuveson, *Redeemer Nation* (Chicago, 1968); Stephanson, *Manifest Destiny*.

228. Strong, *Our Country*, 165.

229. Josiah Strong, *The New Era, or the Coming Kingdom* (New York, 1893), 69.

intellectual production, the wisest statesmanship, and the best institutions: "a balance of rights and duties, a union of liberty and law." They were the "race" most able to adapt to changing circumstances, marshaling the world toward perfection.[230] Although he still claimed that the United States had superseded Britain, as the Romans had the Greeks, he pointed to the British model of settler colonialism as one of the great engines of global Christian progress. "She has conquered these lands by giving to them her sons and daughters, her free institutions, her noble civilization. England might be sunk in the sea and these vast areas would remain her glory, loyal to the essential principles which she has given them."[231]

Chastened by the failure of his campaign for American intervention against the Armenian massacres in the mid-1890s, Strong came to see that the United States could not act unilaterally, and that close cooperation with the British Empire—and the world-wide Anglo-Saxon race—was essential to fulfill God's promise.[232] It was the institutional precondition for realizing the prophecy outlined in *Our Country*. The necessity of cooperation was reinforced by the growing interdependence of the planet, driven in large part by the communications revolution. "It is as if the earth had been, in two or three generations, reduced to a much smaller scale and set spinning on its axis at a far greater speed."[233] Here too he saw providence operating through the Anglo-Saxons. After all, he argued, "man's triumph over nature and his control of the physical conditions of life" was chiefly a product of Anglo-Saxon technoscience.[234] By 1900, Strong was committed to an imperial mission for the United States, drawing on Mahan among others to defend the annexation of Hawaii and Cuba, and the occupation of the Philippines. "[I]t is to be hoped," he announced, "that the day is not far distant when Great Britain and the United States will join hands in the defence of justice and liberty the world over."[235]

230. Strong, *New Era*, 59.

231. Strong, *New Era*, 68.

232. Reed, "American Foreign Policy." Reed argues that Strong switched from political isolationism to a form of Christian imperial-internationalism during the mid-1890s. For context, see Ann Marie Wilson, "In the Name of God, Civilization, and Humanity," *Le Mouvement Social*, 227 (2009), 27–44.

233. Strong, *New Era*, 2. See also Strong, *Our Country*, 13; Strong, *New Era*, 45; Strong, "Tendencies toward the Unity of the World," *Advocate of Peace*, 65/10 (1903), 178–79.

234. Strong, *New Era*, 65.

235. Josiah Strong, *Expansion under New World Conditions* (New York, 1900), 299 (and on Mahan's influence, 10, 156, 196). Strong was personally introduced to Mahan by Roosevelt. On Strong's growing pessimism about the prospects of Western civilization, see Paul Meyer, "The Fear of Cultural Decline," *Church History*, 42/3 (1973), 396–405.

The real tendency of the world involves the full coming of democracy and the completion of the organization of industry. We are entered upon the final stage of industrial development, which is the organization of a world industry. This world-tendency involves also the complete development of a world-life, a world-conscience. And all these involve ultimate international arbitration.[236]

Despite his providential vision of the Anglo-Saxons and his support for global British-American collaboration, Strong said little about the political institutions necessary for securing heaven on earth.

Abbott offered another high-profile religious defense of racial unity. He made his name by elaborating an evolutionary brand of Christianity, arguing that evolution demonstrated that Christianity was the most advanced religion and that the Christian nations—the United States above all—had built the most progressive civilization.[237] Led by the Anglo-Saxons, historical development would eventuate in universal peace as humanity came to incarnate the divine.[238] During the late 1890s he, like Strong, embraced America's new role as a "world nation" ready to take its place alongside Britain. Rather than breaking free of the gravitational pull exerted by the old colonial overlord, he saw this as an opportunity to renegotiate relations between the two, harnessing their combined power to a mission of earthly redemption. He contended that the United States and the British empire-state embodied a set of superior values—democratic, Christian, capitalist—and because they were ordained to shape the destiny of the world, it was necessary to "unite the New World with the Old" through trade, communications systems, and an arbitration tribunal. This would serve as an initial step to a "more formal alliance—civic, commercial, and industrial, rather than naval or military—and yet an alliance that will make us, for the purposes of our international life, one people, though not politically one nation."[239] The details of this entity—a people but not a nation—were vague, though its task was clear. Acting as one, the Anglo-Saxons

---

236. Josiah Strong, "Promoting Arbitration," *Advocate of Peace*, 60/9 (1898), 212–13.

237. Abbott was editor of *Outlook*, the leading Protestant periodical of the time (with a circulation of over one hundred thousand), and pastor of the famed Plymouth Congregational Church in Brooklyn, where he had succeeded Henry Ward Beecher. See Ira Brown, *Lyman Abbott, Christian Evolutionist* (Cambridge, MA, 1953). Carnegie praised Abbott in his *Autobiography*, 246, though without going into detail.

238. See especially Lyman Abbott, *The Evolution of Christianity* (Boston, 1892).

239. Abbott, "Basis of an Anglo-American Understanding," 516. On Abbott's justification of the war with Spain, see Benjamin Wetzel, "Onward Christian Soldiers," *Journal of Church and State*, 54/3 (2011), 406–25.

would bring a great "moral advantage to the world."[240] Returning to the subject a few years later, he praised the British Empire as a force for good in the world and welcomed the "informal and unphrased" alliance with Britain that had emerged from the convulsions of 1898. But he asserted that the United States remained in the vanguard of history, and was a step further along the road to instantiating and embodying the ultimate federal unification of the planet. The Anglo-Saxons, led by the Americans, would act in concert to realize this glorious dream by spreading civilization to those lacking its fruits. "Without these three elements, law, commerce, and education, no community is civilized or prosperous, no community has liberty or justice. It is the function of the Anglo-Saxon race to confer these gifts of civilization . . . on the uncivilised peoples of the world."[241]

Carnegie was horrified at the use of religious arguments to legitimate imperialism. He praised church leaders who spoke out against the violence, including the Episcopal Bishop of New York, H. C. Potter. Acknowledging the lure of a racial alliance "from a purely selfish standpoint," while rejecting it for that very reason, Potter endorsed a form of international government (based around a system of arbitration).[242] At the outset of war in 1898, Carnegie warned,

> There remains to-day, as the one vital element of imperialism, the contention that Providence has opened for the American people a new and larger destiny, which imposes heavy burdens indeed upon them, but from which they cannot shrink without evading holy duty; that it has become their sacred task to undertake the civilization of a backward people committed to their charge. A foundling has been left at their door, which it is their duty to adopt, educate and govern. In a word, it is "Humanity," "Duty," "Destiny," which call upon us again for sacrifice.[243]

This posture struck Carnegie as absurd. It was based on ignorance about the formidable difficulty of governing other "races" and a fundamental misunderstanding of moral duty. He drew an intriguing comparison between the opposition to imperialism widespread in the American South—among a people used to governing iniquitously—and those (presumably clustered in the

---

240. Abbott, "Basis of an Anglo-American Understanding," 519.

241. Lyman Abbot, *The Rights of Man* (Boston, 1902), 259, 272.

242. Henry Codman Potter, "National Bigness or Greatness: Which?," *North American Review*, 168/509 (1899), 443. On Potter, see Harriett Kayser, *Bishop Potter, the People's Friend* (New York, 1910). Cf. Carnegie, "Americanism versus Imperialism, II," 364, where he also lists Henry van Dyke, Theodore Cuyler, and Charles Parkhurst as staunch religious anti-imperialists.

243. Carnegie, "Americanism versus Imperialism: II," 363.

North East) who lacked such knowledge. There was a direct correlation, he argued, between enacting domination and rejecting imperial fervor. "This ignorance is truly as great as their belief implies. Their lack of knowledge is at fault, but the greater this lack the clearer is it that they can be credited with absolute sincerity, and with those very dangerous things when possessed without knowledge, 'good intentions.'"[244] In political life, good intentions untempered by pragmatic understanding were profoundly dangerous.

Carnegie branded William Croswell Doane, Bishop of Albany, the most egregious offender.[245] What seemed to worry him most about the theological strain of imperial justification was its apparent popular legitimacy; the "pulpit," he warned, generated most of the "remaining vitality" of the imperial cause. This derived from the altruistic vision of empire professed by the churchmen.[246] Rather than prioritizing strategic necessity, economic gain, or even American greatness, they stressed the benefits for those subjected to it. Accepting their sincerity, Carnegie admonished their naiveté. "In the Bishop's words," he observed, "we see some reason for the charge sometimes made against ecclesiastics, viz., that, their attention being chiefly fixed upon the other world, they seldom shine as advisers upon affairs pertaining to this."[247] He concluded with an affirmation of his own progressivist faith, contending that wherever he traveled in the world he found "universal laws everywhere working to higher and higher standards of national life," and that "[a]ll the world steadily improves." This modernist Panglossianism was directed against those who sought to hasten the perfection of humanity on earth, which only history—as a manifestation of social evolution—could guarantee. "Only impatient men, destitute of genuine faith in the divine government throughout all the world, doubt that all goes well."[248] He sometimes appealed to providence, even if only to reject the claims made on its behalf by the Christian imperialists.

> The religious school of Imperialists intend doing for the Filipinos what is best for them, no doubt; but, when we crush in any people its longing for independence, we take away with one hand a more powerful means of civilization than all which it is possible for us to bestow with the other. There is implanted in the breast of every human community the sacred germ of

244. Carnegie, "Americanism versus Imperialism: II," 364.

245. Carnegie, "Americanism versus Imperialism: II," 365.

246. Carnegie, "Americanism versus Imperialism: II," 364, 365. See also "Bishop Doane on the War," *New York Times*, 16 November 1898, 6.

247. Carnegie, "Americanism versus Imperialism: II," 365.

248. Carnegie, "Americanism versus Imperialism: II," 366.

self-government, as the most potent means of Providence for raising them in the scale of being.[249]

This rhetorical gesture did not accurately reflect Carnegie's idiosyncratic religious commitments. His conception of history and politics had little room for a divine creator. A proud agnostic, he lost his faith after reading Spencer and Darwin: "I had a philosophy at last. The words of Christ, 'The Kingdom of Heaven is within you,' had a new meaning for me. Not in the past or in the future, but now and here is Heaven within us." The conclusion he drew from this epiphany was simple: "All our duties lie in this world and in the present, and trying impatiently to peer in what lies beyond is as vain as fruitless."[250] In true Spencerian fashion, the supernatural was relegated to the realm of the unknowable, where it could be safely ignored. Dismissing revealed religion and church institutions alike, Carnegie sometimes claimed to be religious in a wider sense. Citing the authority of Benjamin Franklin, he once stated that there was "one truth I see. . . . 'The highest worship of God is service to Man.'"[251] As we shall see in the next chapter, this duty-based vision of human service brought him within the orbit of Stead's conception of faith. On occasion, God infiltrated Carnegie's private mental life. Among his papers can be found an undated document that recounts a dream in which God imbued him with the Solon-like power to end the "murder of men by men." In it, he recounted, "I become Peacemaker of the world,—the curse of centuries lifted at a single stroke."[252]

The irony was that Carnegie's own dreamworld was not as far removed from the theological vision of racial unity as he imagined. Unwittingly, he ended up substituting one kind of providentialism with another. Carnegie shared with the religious providentialists a teleological view of history that cast the Anglo-Saxons as agents of progress and regarded human perfectibility as achievable. They differed chiefly over the relevant mechanism of change. While Carnegie

249. Carnegie, "Americanism versus Imperialism: II," 370.

250. Carnegie, *Autobiography*, 179. For a more extended discussion of religion, see his proposed St. Andrews Rectorial Address, 1902, Box 251, Carnegie papers, LOC. He ended up speaking on a different topic. The address was later published as "Confession of Religious Faith," *Miscellaneous Writings of Andrew Carnegie*, ed. Burton Hendrick (New York, 1933), II. On his earlier engagement with religion, and in particular the Swedenborgians, see Carnegie, *Autobiography*, 24–25, 48–49.

251. Carnegie, *Autobiography*, 292. Franklin's own religious views are notoriously hard to pin down. Joseph Waligore, "The Christian Deist Writings of Benjamin Franklin," *Pennsylvania Magazine of History and Biography*, 140/1 (2016), 7–29.

252. Carnegie, Untitled document, 18 January 1907, Box 246, 2–3.

denied the role of an omniscient creator in history, he allocated Spencerian evolution an analogous function, as both engine of transformation and source of moral judgment. Both styles of argument issued in racial theodicies where suffering was framed in terms of the ultimate triumph of good.

Onward and Upward: And Some Day All under One Government

Carnegie sold his business empire in 1901, dedicating himself fully to public life and philanthropy. He focused in particular on the pursuit of interstate peace, traveling incessantly, writing frequently, and distributing money generously, to support the cause. This frenetic activity culminated in December 1910 when he established the Carnegie Endowment for International Peace, still going strong today, with a gift of ten million dollars.[253] He never lost his belief in human perfectibility or his ardent desire to see the consolidation of the "two branches of our race."[254] But during the early years of the new century, a second major shift occurred in Carnegie's account of racial union. Whereas his prior shift, during the 1890s, had concerned sequencing, and especially the political preconditions necessary for union, the latter change was about the form of polity he envisaged. Although Carnegie had never articulated precisely his desired model of union, it was clear enough during the 1880s and 1890s that he had in mind an association of rough parity between the United States and Britain. Although the Americans would be the larger partner, neither side would dominate the other. During the Edwardian years Carnegie shifted to a model in which the United States incorporated Britain.

Carnegie was adamant that the British were losing the battle for industrial supremacy. To avoid slow and painful decline, it was essential to act. He used his Rectorial Address at St. Andrews in 1902 to outline the economic case, arguing that despite its role catalyzing the Industrial Revolution, Britain was likely to fall ever-further behind the United States, as was the rest of Europe.

253. *New York Times*, 15 December 1910; "Mr. Carnegie's Greatest Gift," *The Nation*, 91 (1910), 597. In 1903 he had paid for the building of the "Temple of Peace" in The Hague, home to the Permanent Court of Arbitration. For an overview of his peace activism, see Patterson, "Andrew Carnegie's Quest for World Peace," 371–83. On the intersection of Carnegie's "scientific" philanthropy and his pacifism, see Peter Weber, "The Pacifism of Andrew Carnegie and Edwin Ginn," *Global Society*, 29/4 (2015), 530–50.

254. The quote is from Andrew Carnegie, *Speech by Andrew Carnegie at the Annual Meeting of the Peace Society in the Guildhall, London, May 24th, 1910* (London, 1910), 3. See also Carnegie, *A Rectorial Address Delivered to the Students in the University of Aberdeen, 6th June, 1912* (New York, 1912), 19–20.

Yet all was not lost, for "supremacy remains in the family." Race, he asserted, "still holds," and "Macbeth's fate is not Britain's. The sceptre of material supremacy has been wrenched by no unlineal hand. It is her eldest son, the rightful heir, who wears the crown, and he can never forget, nor cease to be proud, of the Mother to whom he owes so much."[255] With Europe likely to federate at some point in the future, Carnegie asked the assembled students what course Britain should adopt. An imperial federation could not match the economic power of either. Alternatively, Britain might unite with the Europeans, go it alone, or join with the United States and Canada. Although he did not fully endorse any of these options in the address, his choice of language—"[t]he English-speaking race thus becoming again as it was before . . . one and inseparable"—pointed clearly to his preferred outcome.[256] He made the explicit case for it frequently during the Edwardian years.

The future of Britain lay *within* an American Union. "Britain has no possible destiny worthy of her except with her Children in America, that is certain," he averred in 1904.[257] The country was too small to prosper in the emerging world of industrial giants. "The day of small nations is passing. Their incorporation with larger areas is to be hailed by lovers of progress," although it was essential to protect local traditions where possible.[258] The distant colonies were already following American institutional and legislative precedents, barring plural voting, furnishing more extensive political rights, adopting federal governance structures, and rejecting state religion.[259] The gravitational pull of the United States was simply too overwhelming to resist, and rather than attempting to federate the British Empire, the colonies could act first to trigger racial union.

255. Andrew Carnegie, *A Rectorial Address Delivered to the Students in the University of St. Andrews, 22nd October, 1902* (Edinburgh, 1902), 10. Carnegie's friend, Andrew Dickinson White, onetime President of Cornell, was impressed by the Address, which he attended. "It was deeply original," he wrote, and "prepared with skill and delivered with force." Carnegie "soon had the audience completely on his side": *The Autobiography of Andrew Dickinson White*, (London, 1905), II, 210.

256. Carnegie, *Rectorial Address* (1902), 49, 48. Carnegie's hero, Spencer, recognized that "at the present rate of progress" the United States would soon be the most powerful country in the world (*Autobiography*, II, 402). However, he was very critical of its condition; see, for example, Spencer, "Re-Barbarization" in Spencer, *Facts and Comments* (New York, 1902), 172–89, which (among other things) attacked the loss of freedom in American political life.

257. Carnegie to W. Reid, 29 September 1904, Fol 107, Carnegie papers. See also Nasaw, *Andrew Carnegie*, 626.

258. Andrew Carnegie, *Drifting Together* (New York, 1904), 10.

259. Andrew Carnegie, *Britain and Her Offspring* (London, 1911).

Carnegie argued repeatedly that the absorption of Canada into the United States was the most probable initial step. As he wrote to Balfour in 1903, "I believe that through Canada, the Union of Britain and America will finally come—Not for 100 years perhaps, or more, but the day is coming when this island will have to choose between becoming part of a large European Empire or an American Empire composed of her own children, that it to say, the English-speaking Race and language makes race."[260] Canadians and Americans, he argued in 1904, were "indistinguishable from one another," and when combined with their geographical proximity, this made the mechanics of union straightforward. "Nothing is surer in the near future than that they must unite. It would be criminal for them to stand apart."[261] His argument continued to resonate. Writing in the *Westminster Review* in 1905, the British author Edwyn Anthony described "A Look Ahead" as "that most remarkable and epoch-making essay." Praising Carnegie's "keen philosophical mind," he welcomed the vision of racial reunion, "a truly grand conception, the realisation of which would benefit the human race beyond any other political event within the bounds of probability."[262] In a speech delivered in Toronto in April 1906, Carnegie returned to his ultimate dream. "It matters little to me," he observed, "where one of my race is born or under what flag he marches, Union Jack or Stars and Stripes," because "I regard our race as whole": "It was once. So I see clearly it is again to become in due course." This vast political community would be headquartered in Washington.[263] Carnegie's argument elicited strong resistance in Canada, and in July that year he wrote to *The Times* to defend himself.

> I do not think that either Canada or America in the future is to need the support of the mother, but I do believe that someday the mother will find an alliance or union with her children across the Atlantic her refuge and her strength. During the life of many living, three hundred millions of English-speaking people, members of one race, are to dwell there. Britain, with say fifty millions and alien in Europe, will turn to and probably merge with them and they with each other, and then our race will fulfil its destiny, which is decisively to influence world affairs for the good of the world.[264]

260. Carnegie to Balfour, 1903 [n.d.]. The letter was unsent. See also Carnegie to Hay, 20 July 1904, Fol 106, Carnegie papers; and especially, Carnegie, *Drifting Together*.

261. Carnegie, *Drifting Together*. It was originally published in the *London Express*.

262. Edwyn Anthony, "Mr Andrew Carnegie and the Re-union of the English-speaking Race," *Westminster Review*, 163/6 (1905), 636–37.

263. Carnegie, Speech in Toronto, 27 April 1906, Box 252, 8–9, 10, Carnegie papers.

264. Carnegie, letter to *The Times*, 13 July 1906, Fol 131, Carnegie papers.

Carnegie's relentless peace advocacy and his racial dreamworld were interwoven. He argued that nationalism and international competition were slowing down the march of progress, and it was essential to eliminate them in order to unleash the full potential of humanity. When Carnegie returned to St. Andrews to give his second Rectorial Address in 1905, he chose arbitration as his main topic. Still professing adherence to a Spencerian view of progress—"all grows better"—he labeled war the "foulest blot that has ever disgraced the earth."[265] Arbitration was the best hope of ending the abomination. Carnegie was optimistic, perceiving in the legal developments of the previous few years that the "civilized world at last moves steadily to the reign of peace through arbitration."[266] He called for a treaty ensuring unrestricted arbitration between the United States and Britain, countries that could regain their joint crown as leaders of international progress after the disastrous wars in southern Africa and the Philippines.[267] In the years before the First World War, much of his writing and public speaking was dedicated to the cause of arbitration and in particular to advocacy of a "League of Peace"—a group of the great powers acting in concert to maintain peace in the system—led by the "English-speaking race."[268] Arbitration was at once the best mechanism for ameliorating international conflict, for demonstrating the moral leadership of the English-speaking peoples, and for catalyzing the reunification of the United States and Britain.

The fin-de-siècle imperial wars had not dented his adamantine belief in human perfectibility. "[P]rogress, development, is the law of man's being," and there was "no limit to man's upward ascent," he wrote in 1909.[269] Carnegie remained confident about the future, at least until the outbreak of the First World War. Historical evolution was still doing its magnificent work, he wrote to Stead in February 1911, and race reunion was all but inevitable: "It's coming

---

265. Carnegie, *Rectorial Address* (1905), 4. On the connection between peace and progress, see also Carnegie, "The Moral Issue Involved in War," *Advocate of Peace*, 73/2 (1911), 34–36; Carnegie, "War as the Mother of Valor and Civilization," *Advocate of Peace*, 72/4 (1910), 82–83.

266. Carnegie, *Rectorial Address* (1905), 10.

267. Carnegie, *Rectorial Address* (1905), 29.

268. On the League of Peace, see Carnegie, *Rectorial Address* (1905); Carnegie to Theodore Roosevelt, 27 August 1906, Fol 132, Carnegie papers; Carnegie to John Morley, 5 September 1906; Carnegie, *The Wrong Path* (New York, 1909); Carnegie, *Address to the Fourth American Peace Congress, St. Louis, May 1913* (New York, 1913). Such arguments were not uncommon—see, for another example, Robert Stein, "Anglo-French-German Alliance," *Advocate of Peace*, 67/7 (1905), 147–51.

269. Andrew Carnegie, "The Wrong Path," *Advocate of Peace*, 71/5 (1909), 103.

someday."[270] He insisted that there was widespread support for union among the British governing elite. A few months later, he told Stead of a recent meeting with Lord Rosebery, "the Orator of the Empire." Rosebery was willing, Carnegie claimed, "to have the capital of the United English-speaking race midway which is Washington, 3000 miles from Britain and an equal distance from the Pacific Coast. And some day all under one Government." It was for such reasons, he continued, that "I hold to my prophecy in the last chapter of *Triumphant Democracy*."[271] The dream of racial union would be realized, industrial capitalism would remake the world, and humanity would be at peace.

270. Carnegie to Stead, 21 February 1911, STED 1/16, Stead papers.
271. Carnegie to Stead, 26 June 1911, STED 1/16, Stead papers.

3

Americanizing the World

W. T. STEAD AND CECIL J. RHODES

The Briton . . . should cheerfully acquiesce in the decree of Destiny, and stand in betimes with the conquering American. The philosophy of common sense teaches us that, seeing we can never again be the first, standing alone, we should lose no time in uniting our fortunes with those who have passed us in the race. Has the time not come when we should make a resolute effort to realize the unity of the English-speaking race.[1]

(W. T. STEAD)

Introduction

William Thomas Stead was the most famous casualty of the *Titanic*. Impulsive, eccentric, and divisive, he channeled the "nonconformist conscience" into a potent style of moral crusading that transformed British journalism, helping to set the terms of national political debate from the 1870s onward.[2] He agitated for Anglo-American union throughout his adult life, deploying all of his remarkable editorial ingenuity, and his wide network of friends and collaborators, to further the cause. In the aftermath of the disaster, G. K. Chesterton observed that Stead had "toiled like a Titan for that Anglo-American

1. Stead, *Americanization*, 5–6.
2. Laurel Brake et al. (eds.), *W. T. Stead* (Chicago, 2013); Joel Weiner, *The Americanization of the British Press, 1830s–1914* (Basingstoke, 2011); Helena Goodwyn, "A 'New' Journalist," *Journal of Victorian Culture*, 23/3 (2018), 405–20. We still lack an authoritative general biography of Stead. A series of essays by J. O. Baylen are vital; I cite several in the following pages. The most comprehensive volume is Frederick Whyte, *The Life of W. T. Stead*, 2 vols. (London, 1925). Stewart J. Brown, *W. T. Stead* (Oxford, 2019), is excellent on his theological views. Robinson, *Muckraker*, is a readable popular account.

combination of which the ship that has gone down may well be called the emblem." He was not alone in noting the grim symbolism of Stead's death. The journalist J. L. Garvin wrote that "[h]is grave is where he might have chosen it, midway between England and America, under the full steam of their inter-course; and I cannot but think that his death was in accordance with his view of things."[3] Chesterton finished his peroration with a forecast: "His death may well become a legend."[4] Yet the legend failed to materialize, and Stead's name faded from public consciousness. In the mid-1920s, Albert Shaw, American scholar, journalist, and colleague of Stead, lamented the dimin-ished reputation of a "man of genius" who, "above all others," had campaigned for racial union.[5]

Born into an evangelical Calvinist family in 1849, Stead was appointed edi-tor of the *Northern Echo* at the prodigious age of twenty-one. The desire for a "huge earth-shadowing Confederation" encompassing Britain and the United States was a leitmotif of his early writings.[6] In 1879, he confided in his diary that "the Anglo-Saxon idea has gained possession of my brain."[7] Stead came to the attention of Gladstone and other liberal luminaries through his fervent support for muscular intervention over the "Bulgarian atrocities" in the mid-1870s.[8] In 1880, he moved to London, working as Morley's deputy at the *Pall Mall Gazette*, before taking the helm in 1883. He used his editorial platform to launch a series of influential campaigns. In 1890, he founded a new journal, the *Review of Reviews*, which he edited until his death. From the outset, it was a vehicle for propagating his obsessions. A committed liberal, Stead supported the suffragettes, Irish Home Rule, social reform, and the peace movement. An ardent imperialist and an indefatigable celebrant of the "English-speaking

---

3. J. L. Garvin, *RoR* (May 1912), cited in Whyte, *Life*, II, 315.

4. G. K. Chesterton, "The Great Shipwreck as Analogy," *Illustrated London News*, 11 May 1912, in Chesterton, *Collected Works* (San Francisco, 1988), XXIX, 291.

5. Albert Shaw, review of Whyte, *Life*, *American Historical Review*, 32/1 (1926), 113. Other assessments a decade or so after his death include "A Modern Knight-Errant," *Saturday Review*, 12 December 1925, 405; Herbert Horwill, "W. T. Stead," *The Nation*, 17 March 1926, 292; Robert Morss Lovett, "A Nonconformist Journalist," *New Republic*, 16 December 1925, 115.

6. *Northern Echo*, 1 January 1873, cited in Goodwyn, "'New' Journalist," 1. A year before he had written to John Coplestone, the then editor, asking, "Could you not do something in the way of producing union among our scattered English family?": Whyte, *Life*, I, 24.

7. Stead, 5 July 1874, excerpted in J. W. Robertson Scott, *The Life and Death of a Newspaper* (London, 1952), 101.

8. Whyte, *Life*, I, 45–57; Stéphanie Prévost, "W. T. Stead and the Eastern Question (1875–1911)," *19: Interdisciplinary Studies in the Long Nineteenth Century*, 16 (2013). Richard Shannon, *Gladstone and the Bulgarian Agitation 1876* (London, 1963), stresses the importance of Stead.

race," he worked closely with Rhodes and Carnegie. He served as both sounding board and cheerleader for Rhodes, who in turn was heavily influenced by Stead's thinking about global racial order. Stead and Carnegie discussed union regularly for over two decades. "If I ever wanted a missionary militant for the British American Union," Carnegie informed his friend in 1903, "you are the man—I know no other fit for the propaganda."[9]

Proclaiming the newspaper the "uncrowned king of an educated democracy," a formidable weapon for holding politicians accountable to the demos, Stead regarded journalism as a communicative technology to elevate and purify society.[10] To achieve this, he sought to revolutionize both medium and message, transforming the visual presentation of newsprint while utilizing fresh journalistic methods, from investigative campaigns to interviews with prominent public figures. Stead's influence almost matched his ambition. The editor of *The Nation*, H. M. Massingham, once opined that "from the Bulgarian atrocities to the Boer War, there has been no pen which in England wielded an ascendency comparable with Stead's."[11] Combining access to the highest reaches of power with an extensive readership, he was in a position to enlighten, enflame, and occasionally direct, public debate. "He exercised . . . an enormous influence on the masses," the journalist E. T. Raymond observed. "He could make an author; he could almost unmake a statesman."[12] Stead's innovations, often imported from the United States, were acclaimed and reviled in equal measure, with his most (in)famous exploit, "The Maiden Tribute of Modern Babylon"—an exposé of child prostitution in London during which he arranged the sale of a teenage girl—landing him both a prison sentence and considerable fame.[13] Journalism was the means to a higher end. Shaw put it well: "Although journalism supplied the agency through which he sought to influence public opinion, Stead was always the political and moral crusader rather than the vendor of news, the interpreter of events, or the mere supporter of party policies."[14] His most ambitious crusade was to "constitute

9. Carnegie to Stead, 30 May 1903, Fol 94, Carnegie papers.

10. W. T. Stead, "Government by Journalism," *Contemporary Review*, 49 (1886), 664. See also Stead, "The Future of Journalism," *Contemporary Review*, 50 (1886), 663–79.

11. Massingham, *The Nation*, April 1912, cited in Whyte, *Life*, I, 308.

12. E. T. Raymond, "W. T. Stead" in Raymond, *Portraits of the Nineties* (London, 1921), 179.

13. Judith Walkowitz, *City of Dreadful Delight* (Chicago, 1992), chs. 3–4; Cecily Devereux, "'The Maiden Tribute' and the Rise of the White Slave in the Nineteenth Century," *Victorian Review*, 26/2 (2000), 1–23.

14. Shaw, review of Whyte, *Life*, 113.

one vast federated unity the English-speaking United States of the World," centered on the fusion of Britain and the United States.[15]

This chapter explores how Stead and Rhodes imagined the future of the "English-speaking peoples." I open with an analysis of Stead's views on utopia and religion, before tracing his early political endeavors. I also show how he utilized the *Review of Reviews* to advocate a series of interconnected policies during the 1890s, including international arbitration, imperial consolidation, and increased naval spending, all of which were bound up with his dream of Anglo-America. I then turn to Stead's proposals for a federal racial union, focusing in particular on his arguments in *The Americanization of the World*, his most elaborate account of the dream. The remainder of the chapter discusses Rhodes's conception of empire, race, and Anglo-America, as well as his fantasy of a secret society to proselytize the cause of the "English race." While Rhodes was clearly an advocate of racial union, I argue that the character of his vision, as well as its public presentation, was shaped by Stead.

English-Speaking Man and the Economy of the Universe

Morley once described Stead as a zealous "believer in dreams and inspirations."[16] He recognized, even celebrated, the motive power of the imagination and the necessity of utopian speculation. Chesterton satirized him as one of the "prophets of the twentieth century," famed for dreaming that Britain and the United States would be united, while George Sydenham-Clarke characterized him as a utopian, and mocked his "attempt to peer across the 'Borderland,'" a reference to Stead's obsession with spiritualism, the belief that it was possible to commune with the dead.[17] Popular in the late nineteenth century, spiritualism attracted reputable scholars as well as an army of cranks.[18] In 1893, Stead founded a journal, *The Borderland*, to promulgate the idea. Convinced of his ability to converse with spirits, he imagined himself as the reincarnation of his early hero Oliver Cromwell, ran a salon for purported

---

15. Stead, *Americanization*, 397.

16. Wilfrid Blunt recorded the conversation in his diary in 1884: Whyte, *Life*, I, 80. On Stead as a visionary, see also Sidney Whitman, "W. T. Stead" in Whitman, *Things I Remember* (New York, 1916), 236–37.

17. Chesteron, *Napoleon of Notting Hill*, 15, 18; Sydenham-Clarke, "Naval Union with Great Britain," 353.

18. Ruth Brandon, *The Spiritualists* (New York, 1983); Nicola Brown, Carolyn Burdett, and Pamela Thurschwell (eds.), *The Victorian Supernatural* (Cambridge, 2004).

clairvoyants, and promoted his own telepathic powers.[19] He even claimed to have conducted an "interview" with Gladstone from beyond the grave. Following his death, assorted spiritualists maintained that Stead continued to communicate with them.[20] Even as he sought to traverse the boundary between life and death, his political utopianism resided elsewhere. He argued in 1896 that the English-speaking race had a "world mission" to accomplish, and the "supreme thing for the English-speaking man is to recognize his place in what may be called the economy of the universe."[21] Stead's self-appointed task was to reveal and disseminate this providential truth. In order to do so, he assumed the mantle of prophet.

Stead took a keen interest in the utopian literature of the time. While acknowledging the astonishing success of Bellamy's *Looking Backward*, he thought it "without any particular literary merit," and rejected the centralized militaristic "nationalism" it professed.[22] Elsewhere he recommended Eugen Richter's popular dystopian novel *Pictures of the Socialistic Future*, which warned darkly against the manifold dangers of collectivism.[23] He was more sympathetic to William Morris, praising him as a "man of genius" whose "dreams are often wiser than other people's waking thoughts," though Stead was unpersuaded by the rustic socialist vision pictured in *News from Nowhere*, that "prophet-seer's vision of a social millennium."[24] Stead wrote numerous fictional texts, each a vessel for his moral crusading. *From the Old World to the New*, for example, narrates a trip to the Chicago World's Fair, a plot that allowed Stead to compare the dynamism of the United States with the torpor of

---

19. W. T. Stead, *How I Know That the Dead Return* (Boston, 1909). See also Sarah Crofton, "'Julia Says,'" *19: Interdisciplinary Studies in the Long Nineteenth Century*, 16 (2013); Roger Luckhurst, *The Invention of Telepathy, 1870–1901* (Oxford, 2002), ch. 3.

20. "Gladstone's Ghost Talks with Stead," *New York Times*, 1 November 1909, 4. His spiritualism is discussed sympathetically in Estelle Stead, *My Father, Personal & Spiritual Reminisces* (London, 1913). For his supposed postdeath communication, see James Coates (ed.), *Has W. T. Stead Returned?* (London, 1913). One Major General Sir Alfred Turner later claimed to have communed with Stead's spirit: "Introduction" in Edith K. Harper, *Stead, the Man* (London, 1918), viii. Harper was a fellow spiritualist.

21. W. T. Stead, *RoR*, 13 (February 1896), 102.

22. Stead, *Americanization*, 289; Stead, *RoR*, 1 (March 1890), 230–41; Stead, *RoR*, 2 (July 1890), 53.

23. W. T. Stead, *RoR*, 7 (April 1893), 433–34. Eugen Richter, *Pictures of the Socialistic Future*, trans. Henry Wright (London, 1893). Richter was a leading German liberal politician.

24. Stead to Shaw, 15 April 1891, in Whyte, *Life*, I, 323. The title used in the *RoR* review (3 [May 1891], 509–13) was "A Poet's Vision of a Socialist Millennium."

his home country, while enumerating the virtues of reunion.[25] Published a decade later, *In Our Midst* was the story of an archetypal English explorer, Francis Tressider, who discovers a matriarchal utopian community, descended from Greece, located deep in the Congo. Stead used it to lambast aspects of British society, especially poverty and the mistreatment of women.[26] These stilted fictional exercises demonstrate both Stead's lack of talent as a novelist and his recognition of the communicative importance of mixed media. Stoking the imagination was essential for galvanizing social and political change. Affect had to be harnessed to the cause. Poetry too had a role to play, and throughout his writings on the Angloworld Stead invoked Tennyson, Shakespeare, Milton, Lowell, and Kipling. He once recommended that Kipling should pen "the song of the whole English-speaking race," a unionist catechism to be recited in schools.[27] Even as Stead disdained Bellamy's prose and projects, he welcomed his success as "evidence of the fact that the imagination of our race is once more awake." Such an awakening was a necessary condition for creating a new Anglotopian order.

Stead admitted that his plan to reunite the race would be dismissed as a grandiloquent "dream," but he insisted, as Carnegie had, that he was working with the grain of history, identifying tendencies of sociopolitical development rather than conjuring up impossible futures. Whereas Spencer's evolutionary architectonic underwrote Carnegie's proclamations, Stead relied on a Christian notion of divine providence, of the almighty communicating his message through the elect of history. His political vision was inseparable from his idiosyncratic religious beliefs.[28] Following an epiphany in jail, the strict Calvinism of his upbringing morphed into a "highly personal faith of sacrifice for

25. W. T. Stead, *From the Old World to the New* (London, 1893). The novel is discussed briefly in Seed, "Land of the Future," 8–9.

26. W. T. Stead, *In Our Midst* (London, 1903). See the discussion in Stephen Donovan, "Congo Utopia," *English Studies in Africa*, 59/1 (2016), 63–75. For Donovan, the novel, while not without interest, "rests upon a ragbag of racist clichés" (72).

27. W. T. Stead, *RoR*, 7 (April 1893), 507. This was prompted by his admiration of Kipling's poem "The Song of the English," written for the opening of the Imperial Institute. See also *RoR*, 3 (January 1891), 66, where Stead makes a similar point about Kipling's poem "A Lay of Imperial Unity," published in volume I of the *Proceedings of the Royal Colonial Institute*.

28. On his religious views, see especially Stewart Brown, "W. T. Stead and the Civic Church, 1886–1895," *Journal of Ecclesiastical History*, 66/2 (2015), 320–39; Brown, "W. T. Stead, the 'New Journalism,' and the 'New Church' in Late Victorian and Edwardian Britain" in Stewart Brown, Frances Knight, and John Morgan-Guy (eds.), *Religion, Identity, and Conflict in Britain* (Abingdon, 2013), 213–32; Brown, *W. T. Stead*.

others."[29] Stead accentuated the importance of individual character and action. Rather than holding a specific set of beliefs, he maintained that authentically religious persons were best defined by how they acted in the world. "The true religion is that which makes men most like Christ."[30] This ecumenical commitment, accessible to people of all conventional faiths and of none, was summarized in "The Gospel According to the *Pall Mall Gazette*," a document written to encapsulate the editorial agenda of the journal: "The man who acts as Christ would do under the same circumstance is the true believer, though all his dogmas be heretical and his mind in a state of blind agnosticism." This principle issued in a simple practical maxim: "To take trouble to do good to others."[31]

From the mid-1880s onward, Stead sought to build a nonsectarian "Church of the Future," open to all those dedicated to social improvement. He maintained that religiosity, properly understood, was singular not plural: there existed a basic set of ethical precepts capable of uniting people otherwise divided by sectarianism. "All earnest men have at bottom but one creed, but one ideal, but one duty in life," he wrote in 1886: "To spend our little life so that we may leave the great world better than we found it, that is the chief end of all good men."[32] Drawing inspiration from various sources, including the theosophist and socialist Annie Besant, William and Catherine Booth of the Salvation Army, and Cardinal Manning, the Catholic Archbishop of Westminster—all friends of his—Stead sought to reorient religion away from doctrinal disputation and toward a commitment to social amelioration. He equated this with the politics of Christian socialism, assigning individual initiative, civil society, and the state crucial roles in enacting change. "The work of the Civic Church," he intoned in 1893, "is to establish the kingdom of heaven here among men— in other words to reconstitute human society, to regenerate the state, and inspire it with an aspiration after a divine ideal."[33] The enlightened journalist had a key role in this endeavor. At once a "missionary and an apostle," they could divine God's will and preach it to the masses using the latest techniques

29. Brown, "W. T. Stead, the 'New Journalism,' and the 'New Church,'" 219.

30. W. T. Stead, *The Pope and the New Era* (1890), cited in Brown, "W. T. Stead and the Civic Church," 324.

31. W. T. Stead, "The Gospel According to the *Pall Mall Gazette*," reproduced in Whyte, *The Life of W. T. Stead*, II, 321.

32. [Stead] "A Church 'Exceeding Broad,'" *Pall Mall Gazette*, 10 June 1886, cited in Brown, "W. T. Stead and the Civic Church," 324. As Brown notes, Stead's idea struck many Christians, including nonconformists, as rather *too* broad.

33. W. T. Stead, "The Civic Church" (1893), in J. H. Barrows (ed.), *The World's Parliament of Religions* (London, 1893), II, 1209.

of the trade. "We have to write afresh the only bible which millions read."[34] His friend John Clifford, a prominent Baptist social reformer, captured this theological conception of journalistic practice. "To me," Clifford wrote, "he was as a prophet who had come straight out of the Old Testament into our modern storm-swept life," viewing the press as "a sword to cut down the foes of righteousness, a platform from which to hearten and inspire the armies of the Lord, a pulpit from which to preach his crusades, a desk at which he could expound his policy for making a new heaven and a new earth."[35] Stead sought to rebuild the city of God on terrestrial ground.

During the years when his fame and influence were at a peak—the two decades leading up to the war in South Africa—Stead assigned the "English-speaking peoples" an essential role in this providential plan, viewing them as God's temporal instrument for the redemption of humanity. "For clearly as the ultimate destiny of our planet is manifested in the progressive conquest of the globe by the English-speaking race," he wrote in the *Review of Reviews* in 1891, so it was also clear that they "possess the secret of the salvation of the world."[36] They were the elect of history, a people anointed to bring peace and justice to the earth. Religious belief had long been one of the main sources of his fascination with the United States. Stead had been fed a rich diet of American theological writing in his youth, and it left a lasting impression. He contended that a series of American religious trends—from revivalism through spiritualism and Temperance to the Christian Endeavor movement—had exerted a profound influence in Britain, and the frequent traffic between American churches and British nonconformity cemented ties between the two countries.[37] These contacts furnished a deep and abiding foundation for political union. Prone to megalomania, Stead often claimed that God was working directly through him to bring about the racial millennium. He was the chosen person among the chosen people. Outlining his ambitions for the *Review of Reviews* in his diary in 1891, he wrote, "I now see that I am called to found for the Nineteenth Century a city of God which will be to the age of the printing press and the steam engine what the Catholic Church was to the Europe of the 10th Century."[38] Here was a racial utopian vision to match anything proclaimed by the theologians of the American social gospel movement. The main

34. Stead, "Government by Journalism," 663–64.

35. John Clifford, *American Review of Reviews*, June 1912, 698.

36. W. T. Stead, *RoR*, 3 (April 1891), 353. See also Stead, "To All English-Speaking Folk," *RoR*, 1 (January 1890), 17.

37. Stead, *Americanization*, 262–75, 264.

38. W. T. Stead, unpublished memo (1891), Scott, *Life and Death of a Newspaper*, 152.

difference was that Stead regarded the editorial seat, not the pulpit, as the main vehicle for preaching the creed.

Another source of inspiration was James Russell Lowell, romantic poet, statesman, and minister in London between 1880 and 1885, "the greatest of contemporary Americans." Stead hailed Lowell as an unmatched "prophet of English-speaking Unity," the person most responsible for helping to heal the wounds opened by George the Third: "Let it be for us who come after him to carry on the good work to its full completion."[39] Stead claimed that Lowell had shaped his views on journalism and public duty, encouraging him to believe in the power of dreams. Replying to an article Stead had published in the *Pall Mall Gazette* sketching "a permanent tribunal which would form the first substantial nexus between the Empire and the Republic," Lowell apparently replied that "[i]t is a beautiful dream, but it's none the worse for that. Almost all the best things that we have in the world to-day began by being dreams."[40] For Stead, this was stirring confirmation of a theme that the great man had set in verse.

> And if it be a dream
> Such visions are of morning
>   There is no vague forewarning;
>   The dreams which nations dream come true,
> And shape the world anew.[41]

Stead saw himself as a dream-weaver, his sacred task to help the members of the transcontinental English-speaking "nation" recognize and embrace their destiny to remake the world.

---

39. W. T. Stead, "James Russell Lowell," *RoR*, 4 (August 1891), 235, 244–45. Sir George Grey made a similar claim: "The Federation of the English-speaking People," *Contemporary Review*, 66 (1894), 194–95. Stead observed that Lowell's best-known speech on the topic was an 1888 address to the Society of Authors. It was republished in Lowell, *American Ideas for English Readers* (London, 1902), 63–79. In the speech, Lowell welcomed efforts to strengthen the "good feeling" (65) between the two countries, and argued that London should be seen "as the centre of the races that speak English" (77), but he did not push further. Lowell's early biographers had little to say on the topic of Anglo-American union: Horace Elisha Scudder, *James Russell Lowell*, 2 vols. (Boston, 1901); Edward Everett Hale, *James Russell Lowell* (Boston, 1899). See, however, "Arbitrator," "Two Nations, One People," *American Advocate of Peace and Arbitration*, 53/7 (1891), 197. For his success as Minister, see Ferris Greenslet, *James Russell Lowell, His Life and Work* (Boston, 1905), 195–212.

40. W. T. Stead, *RoR*, 4 (August 1891), 244. See also Stead, *Americanization*, 16.

41. The passage is (perhaps ironically) from Lowell's "Ode to France" (1848). On Lowell and his milieu, see Butler, *Critical Americans*. See also Goodwyn, "'New' Journalist," 8–9.

To Carnegie, Stead was "My Dear Erratic Genius," a man of great brilliance and little common sense, tenacious but too quick to jump into quixotic campaigns or dubious business ventures.[42] They became friends and collaborators after corresponding about racial union in 1891.[43] Both saw Anglo-American union, international arbitration, and support for the transatlantic peace movement as bound together by the preordained role of the "English-speaking peoples." As I noted in the previous chapter, Stead publicized and commended Carnegie's writings in the *Review of Reviews*.[44] He welcomed "A Look Ahead" as a "very remarkable" intervention in the debate, though he disagreed sharply with Carnegie's view that union required the harmonization of political institutions.[45] He also waded into the controversy over the brutal labor dispute at Homestead, offering a stout defense of Carnegie's innocence.[46] Although they agreed on the necessity and value of union, the two men diverged over the form it might assume and whether the new polity should pursue an imperial policy. Unlike Carnegie, Stead was a staunch imperialist. Sketching out his "political creed" in 1877, the young journalist was convinced that the "English race . . . has a worldwide mission to civilise, colonise, Christianise, conquer, police the world and fill it with an English-speaking law-abiding Xian [*sic*] race."[47] One of Stead's most high-profile journalistic campaigns sought to mobilize public and political support to send General Charles Gordon to suppress the "Mahdi" revolt in Sudan in 1884, and then to relieve him when his forces were surrounded in Khartoum.[48] Stead was a friend,

42. Carnegie to Stead, 22 December 1897, Fol 47, Carnegie papers.

43. Carnegie wrote to Stead on 9 September 1891, to draw his attention to Carnegie's *Nineteenth Century* article "upon Race alliance" ("Imperial Federation"). Stead had already written to Carnegie about the article, as Carnegie notes in a subsequent letter (10 September 1891).

44. For examples, see W. T. Stead, *RoR*, 2 (July 1890), 34 (praising Carnegie's essay, "Do Americans Hate England?"); Stead, *RoR*, 4 (August 1891), 263 (disagreeing "heartily" with his critique of imperial federation); Stead, *RoR*, 8 (August 1893), 264 (criticizing his views on abolishing the monarchy in a future union).

45. W. T. Stead, *RoR*, 8 (July 1893), 23. Carnegie had long recognized their differences, and welcomed the cooling of Stead's republican ardor, by teasing him as a "man who talks to ghosts, or what is worse, allows ghosts to talk to him." Carnegie to Stead, 30 December 1897, STED 1/16, Stead papers.

46. W. T. Stead, *RoR*, 6 (July 1892), 109; Stead, *RoR*, 6 (September 1892), 233; Stead, *RoR*, 6 (October 1892), 354. Carnegie had written to Stead to defend his conduct: Carnegie to Stead, 11 August 1892, STED 1/16, Stead papers.

47. Stead, diary entry, 6 July 1877, reproduced in Robertson, *Life and Death*, 109.

48. Whyte, *Life*, I, 117–43.

mentor, and confidant of some of the leading imperialists of the age, including Rhodes and Milner.[49]

Stead utilized the *Pall Mall Gazette* and the *Review of Reviews* to promote the "imperialism of responsibility," his own cherished variant of liberal imperialism. In 1901, he gave one of the clearest accounts of his position, arguing that the imperialism of responsibility—"an Imperialism plus common sense and the Ten Commandments"—was antithetical to both "Little-Englandism," a selfish and barren creed, and Jingoism, the illegitimate expansionism of "pride and avarice."[50] This was a theological gloss on a conventional account of liberal civilizing imperialism, the justificatory argument elaborated most pithily by John Stuart Mill in *On Liberty*: "[d]espotism is a legitimate mode of government in dealing with barbarians, provided the end be their improvement, and the means justified by actually effecting that end."[51] Maintaining that liberal states have a right (even a duty) to spread "civilization" to the purportedly noncivilized peoples of the world, the advocates of liberal civilizing imperialism insisted that empire was legitimate only if it was primarily intended to benefit those subjected to it. British occupation of India and Africa, argued Stead, "can only be justified by the exercise of our authority in order to minimise the evils of native anarchy, on the one hand, and of the impact of civilization upon savagery on the other." Empire, properly understood, was a self-dissolving enterprise.

> Everywhere authority imposed by force, especially by foreign force, upon unwilling populations, is an evil in itself, only to be tolerated because for the time it staves off still greater evils. The object of all such arbitrary dominion must be to render its existence as speedily as possible unnecessary by educating and elevating the subject races to full control of their own destinies, the government of their own lands.[52]

Stead was also a passionate supporter of Home Rule, which he viewed less as a narrow policy proposal for resolving the Irish question than as a general political principle that balanced autonomy and unity. It could be adapted for

---

49. On Stead's influence on Milner, who had once served as his assistant, see J. Lee Thompson, *A Wider Patriotism* (London, 2007); Walter Nimcocks, *Milner's Young Men* (Durham, NC, 1968), 9–10, 14–15.

50. W. T. Stead, "The Great Pacifist," *Australian Review of Reviews*, 8 (August 1912), 610. This document (by then updated) was only published posthumously.

51. John Stuart Mill, *On Liberty* (1859), in *The Collected Works of John Stuart Mill*, ed. John Robson (Toronto, 1977), XVIII, 224. On forms of liberal imperialism, see Bell, *Reordering the World*.

52. Stead, "The Gospel According to the *Pall Mall Gazette*," 324.

use in various circumstances. This simultaneously aligned him with a key plank in Gladstone's legislative agenda while offering a constitutional template for the political unification of the British colonial empire and the English-speaking peoples. It underwrote his vociferous promotion of imperial federation. Converted to the cause in the 1870s, Stead's views crystallized during the following decade, as the movement to consolidate the empire burst onto the national political scene. Bewitched by J. R. Seeley's *The Expansion of England*, the most popular expression of the federalist cause, he crowed that the English had long been engaged in the glorious task of building up "New Englands beyond the Sea, the peopling of waste and savage continents with men of our speech and lineage," and that this legacy presented his contemporaries with a monumental task: "the knitting of the world-sundered members of the English realm into one fraternal union."[53] Veering between modest plans for constitutional realignment and a thoroughgoing federal vision, Stead used the *Pall Mall Gazette* and the *Review of Reviews* to showcase diverse unionist projects. In 1885, he proposed the creation of a Colonial Council, an advisory body composed of representatives from the colonies, as a first step to deeper integration.[54] A few years later, he reiterated his call for colonial representation, "pending the inevitable evolution of a true Imperial Senate."[55] While the former was a relatively limited proposal, the latter entailed a full-blown state. He even recommended that Seeley be placed in charge of a training college to instill the virtues of Greater Britain.[56] While Carnegie dismissed imperial federation as well-intentioned but absurd, Stead thought that it was compatible with Anglo-American union. They were part of the same world-making project.

Stead also backed the political unification of Europe. "The great object of England in the counsels of the Continent should be the establishment of the

---

53. W. T. Stead, "The Old and the New," *Pall Mall Gazette*, 1 January 1884, 1. Support for the idea came from Lord Rosebery (Rosebery to Stead, 10 January 1885, STED 1/60, Stead papers). Seeley is praised in Stead, "Old and the New," 1. See also Stead, "The English beyond the Sea," *Pall Mall Gazette*, 4 October 1884, 1; Whyte, *Life*, I, 99. Morley, on the other hand, was a trenchant critic of Seeley: "The Expansion of England," *Macmillan's Magazine*, 49 (1884), 241–58. For further discussion, see Simon Potter, "W. T. Stead, Imperial Federation, and the South African War" in Brake et al. (eds.), *W. T. Stead*, 115–32.

54. W. T. Stead, "Programme 1885," *Pall Mall Gazette*, 1 January 1885, 1. He immediately followed this up by republishing a plan developed by Earl Grey, the former Secretary of State for the Colonies, and seeking to generate a debate among leading political figures. See Earl Grey, "How Shall We Retain the Colonies?," *Nineteenth Century*, 5 (1879), 935–54; Whyte, *Life*, I, 106–7.

55. Stead, "To All English-Speaking Folk," 16.

56. Whyte, *Life*, II, 209–10. On Seeley's political theology of empire, see Bell, *Reordering the World*, ch. 11.

United States of Europe," he wrote in his early political catechism. He proposed the creation of a European Senate, controlling the military forces of the continent.[57] The "Gospel of the *Pall Mall Gazette*" provided further detail. Continental Europe was beset by violent conflict, and riven with commercial antagonisms, because it was a geographically restricted space divided into numerous sovereign polities. To secure peace and prosperity, it was necessary to eliminate the underlying source of competition, uniting the peoples of Europe in an overarching political structure. As with his vision of empire and the Angloworld, this was a variant of "home rule all round," an attempt to combine centralization with autonomy. The "special role of English statesmanship" was to hasten the "establishment of the Federated United States of Europe," an "organic whole, instead of being, as at present, a more or less anarchic amorphous congeries of States."[58] His most sustained articulation of the case was found in *The United States of Europe on the Eve of the Parliament of Peace*, published in 1899. The manifold success of the United States, he claimed, proved that European federation was practicable.[59] Early in his career Stead thought that regional or racial federations were a viable substitute for a universal world order. "If we cannot have a Parliament of Man and a Federation of the World," he had argued as a young man, "we ought at least to have a Parliament of Anglo-Saxondom and the federation of the English-speaking and English-ruled realms."[60] As he grew older, he came to see them as institutional stepping stones, forming part of an unfolding historical sequence that would terminate in the "Federation of the World" that Tennyson had hymned.

Across the course of his long career, then, Stead advocated three modalities of federation: imperial, Anglo-American, and European. While it was not unusual to yoke the first two together, it was much rarer to also emphasize the third. The weight Stead placed on each model changed over time, though he maintained support for all of them across nearly half a century of frenetic writing and political campaigning. During the 1880s, he focused principally on imperial federation, with Anglo-American union moving to the fore in the following decade and a half. Subsequent years saw European federation assuming ever-growing importance, though it never displaced his Anglotopian dream. He regarded all three as potential steps on the road to global cooperation, even a "World State."[61] Despite some shifts in institutional emphasis,

57. Stead, diary entry, 6 July 1877, 109.

58. Stead, "Gospel According to the *Pall Mall Gazette*," 327.

59. W. T. Stead, *The United States of Europe on the Eve of the Parliament of Peace* (London, 1899).

60. Stead, diary entry, 6 July 1877.

61. See, for example, Stead, "Great Pacifist," 619–20.

through his long and tumultuous career Stead remained convinced that the English-speaking peoples were destined for world-historical greatness.

He espoused a paradigmatic view of race as biocultural assemblage. In Stead's writings, it was defined less by biological inheritance or physiological similarity than by shared habitus, memory, and above all, language. Racial purity was an illusion. "There is no such thing as a common race even in England, let alone in the United States," he asserted. "We are all conglomerates, with endlessly varying constituents." Indeed, the greatness of the "English" race resulted in part from its "composite" nature.[62] Like Wells, Stead worried about the "race mania" that had "bitten a great number of political people," and in 1905 he praised the firebrand novelist for criticizing the idea of "the innate superiority of the white race, and especially of the Anglo-Saxon race." This was a fallacious argument that was sadly "used or abused as the justification for every species of injustice and abomination."[63] Rather than turning to biology, Stead emphasized the role of language in constituting political communities. The "great unifier of peoples," he wrote in 1891, "[l]anguage is the simplest and most conspicuous indication of nationality."[64] It bound the nation together, allowing its members to communicate with ease while acting as a carrier of historical memory and cultural value. This was reflected in Stead's choice of terminology. Although he used the term "Anglo-Saxon" freely as a young man, during the closing decade of the century he rejected it, preferring to talk of the "English-speaking race." Stead praised Lowell for coining the phrase, making him "the author of the only title by which the unity of the race can be described."[65] He canvased other options, searching for a designation capable of adequately capturing the object. "I say Anglo-American," he wrote in the *Review of Reviews* in June 1898, "for the convenience of nomenclature, for it is at least better than Anglo-Saxon, which excludes the Celts," but a new vocabulary was required: "the right term must be much wider."[66]

The adoption of English as a global language promised to resolve conflict and eliminate unruly plurality—it was a potent technology of human universality. In 1894, he contended that the

62. Stead, *Americanization*, 148–49, 147.

63. W. T. Stead, *RoR*, 31 (May 1905), 540.

64. W. T. Stead, *RoR*, 3 (May 1891), 419. I discuss Wells's critique of "race mania" in the next chapter.

65. Stead, "James Russell Lowell," 244–45. Stead also claimed (not wholly accurately) that he never used the term "Anglo-Saxon": Whyte, *Life*, II, 34.

66. W. T. Stead, *RoR*, 27 (June 1898), 602.

extension of the English language alone, as the inheritance of a multitude to which every generation gives vast increase, provides in itself the machinery for a further levelling down of international distinctions. The commanding influence of a common speech in harmonising all forms of thought and feeling can hardly be over-estimated, and vast regions of the earth are now welded into an intellectual unit by this engine alone.[67]

Like Carnegie, Stead supported the campaign to rationalize English spelling, maintaining that it was essential to harmonize the language, which was "more and more the universal currency of human thought."[68] He feared that if the British rejected the abridged orthography developed in the United States, a linguistic chasm would open up in the racial community, accentuating a damaging sense of difference.[69] Later he warned that if Americans unilaterally adopted the spelling reforms promoted by Roosevelt's Simplified Spelling Board, it would be a "catastrophe" for the dream of racial reunion. It was a "new Declaration of Independence, a subtler and more deadly revolt than that which broke up the Empire in the eighteenth century."[70] Linguistic unity was a necessary (though insufficient) condition of political unity.

Neither his celebration of British and American racial mixing, nor his stress on linguistic competence, transcended the color line. Although Stead rejected contemporary racial theory, his writings were studded with derogatory comments about other "races." He adhered to a conventional hierarchical vision of world order, declaring it the duty of advanced powers to civilize the "semi-civilised or wholly savage races."[71] This was the central task of the "imperialism of responsibility." In writing of the moral imperative for the United States to translate the Monroe doctrine into a formal imperial policy, he declared that the "whole of South and Central America have to be saved from their present more or less half-bred conditions and converted into English-speaking Republics."[72] He was explicit about the preeminence of whiteness. "The real kernel and nucleus" of Britain and the United States, "is to be found in their white citizens."[73] His was a utopian vision of global white supremacy.

67. W. T. Stead, *RoR*, 10 (June 1894), 3–4.

68. W. T. Stead, *RoR*, 15 (January 1897), 338.

69. Stead, *Americanization*, 301–3.

70. W. T. Stead, *RoR*, 34 (September 1906), 234. This Declaration of linguistic Independence was close to what Brander Matthews had in mind in his advocacy of simplified spelling (see the discussion in chapter 2).

71. W. T. Stead, *RoR*, 1 (January 1890), 17.

72. W. T. Stead, *RoR*, 3 (February 1891), 109.

73. Stead, *Americanization*, 28.

The Great Social Nexus: Global Governance by Journalism

The transoceanic circulation of printed materials, and especially newspapers, books, and periodicals, constituted a spatially extended imperial commons, a shared though heavily stratified space of information exchange and affective resonance.[74] Stead was a key node in this discursive network, though he also sought to extend it beyond the boundaries of the empire to encompass the United States. In 1890, he stepped down from the *Pall Mall Gazette* and founded a new journal, the *Review of Reviews*. Alive to the power of the media in building the imagined community of the English-speaking peoples, he envisaged it as a platform for disseminating the gospel of racial union.[75] Interspersing excerpted articles from the periodical press with his own wide-ranging commentary on world affairs, Stead hoped to educate, entertain, and persuade readers. His ambitions were not modest. "It will be father confessor, spiritual director, moral teacher, political conscience," he wrote in his diary in 1891. "It will be the great social nexus. It will be the mother of mankind."[76] An extension of his earlier boast about the elevated purpose of the press, it was an audacious experiment in global governance by journalism.

Stead opened the first edition of the *Review of Reviews* with an encomium addressed "To All English-Speaking Folk." He outlined the editorial agenda he was to pursue over the subsequent years. All of his obsessions were on display: responsible imperialism, Irish Home Rule, imperial federation, European integration, and the need for a new civic faith. Anglo-American unity was given a starring role. "Among all the agencies for the shaping of the future of the human race," he proclaimed, "none seem so potent now and still more hereafter as the English-speaking man. Already he begins to dominate the world."[77] The *Review of Reviews* would adopt "a deep and almost awestruck regard" for the "immense vocation" of the race. "Faith in 'God's Englishmen,'" Stead boomed, citing a famous phrase from John Milton, "will be our inspiring principle."[78] Racial union was a priority for his new Church. The

74. Antoinette Burton and Isabel Hofmeyr, "The Spine of Empire?" in Burton and Hofmeyr (eds.), *Ten Books That Shaped the British Empire* (Durham, NC, 2014), 1–28.

75. On the fortunes of the *Review* and Stead's role, see Joseph Baylen, "W. T. Stead as Publisher and Editor of the *Review of Reviews*," *Victorian Periodicals Review*, 12/2 (1979), 70–83.

76. Unpublished memo (18901), Robertson, *Life and Death*, 152.

77. Stead, "To All English-Speaking Folk," 15. He reiterated this point in a "Character Sketch" of the explorer Henry Morton Stanley: "unity of the English-speaking race is the key-note of the policy of the *Review of Reviews*": "Mr. H. M. Stanley," *RoR*, 1 (January 1890), 24.

78. Stead, "To All English-Speaking Folk," 15. The phrase is drawn from Milton's *Paradise Lost*, Bk. II.

English-speaking peoples had a "providential mission" to fulfill, while a revival of civic faith, "a quickening of life in the political sphere, the inspiring of men and women with the conception of what may be done towards the salvation of the world," was essential to bind and improve the people.[79] Stead fused theology and racial utopianism to powerful effect.

In order to facilitate this missionary work, Stead established an offshoot in the United States, the *American Review of Reviews*, founded in 1891, and the *Australasian Review of Reviews*, which appeared the following year. He was initially optimistic about their ability to serve the unionist cause. Once circulation had risen, he informed Rhodes in May 1891, "we shall have something like a solid foothold for our REVIEW in both hemispheres of the English-speaking world."[80] The *American Review of Reviews* was edited by Shaw, a progressive Republican, leading figure in the transatlantic social gospel movement, and noted scholar of municipal politics (he served as the second President of the American Political Science Association).[81] Though scathing about the extant British Empire, which he viewed as an instrument of despotism, Shaw endorsed the ideal of imperial federation, "an empire consisting of self-governing Britishers, in which each individual one of 'God's Englishmen' would have rights as extensive as any of his fellows," and where "each autonomous group would be as influential, in the proportion of its numbers, as any other."[82] But Shaw was no disciple of Stead, and refused to follow his monomaniacal line. "After a year or two," he wrote later, "the English *Review of Reviews* became rather the organ of Mr. Stead's personal views and active interests than the impartial exponent of world discussion."[83] He was unafraid to diverge from Stead's editorial admonitions. After Shaw criticized Britain during the

79. Stead, "To All English-Speaking Folk," 17. He reprinted the article the following year, announcing it as "our Confession of Faith": *RoR*, 3 (January 1891), 1.

80. Stead to Rhodes, 21 May 1891, Rhodes House Library, Cecil Rhodes papers, MSS Afr.s.228C28. Stead sent Rhodes a copy: "You will see that they have made you the Frontispiece."

81. Lloyd Graybar, *Albert Shaw of the Review of Reviews* (Lexington, 1974); Adcock, *Liberalism and the Emergence of American Political Science*, 150–55. At its peak, the circulation of the American edition reached 205,000. On the transatlantic social gospel, see Rodgers, *Atlantic Crossings*, 132–33; Helena Goodwyn, "Margaret Harkness, W. T. Stead, and the Transatlantic Social Gospel Network" in Lisa Robertson and Flore Janssen (eds.), *Margaret Harkness* (Manchester, forth).

82. Albert Shaw, "An American View of Home Rule and Federation," *Contemporary Review*, 62 (1892), 311–12. Stead welcomed the article (without accepting all its claims): *RoR*, 6 (September 1892), 247. See also Stead, *Americanization*, 415–16.

83. Shaw, review of Whyte, *Life*, 114.

Venezuela crisis of 1895–96, Stead complained that the journal was supposed to be "a pulpit from which to preach the Anglo-American alliance. I left you to keep the keys of my pulpit, and now you have shut me out of it."[84] His attempt to forge a transatlantic journalistic partnership to glorify the English-speaking peoples and their potential union had foundered.

"To All English-Speaking Folk" provoked a response from Arthur Conan Doyle, a writer Stead had championed at the *Pall Mall Gazette*. Professing "admiration and enthusiasm," Conan Doyle continued that "[i]t is a grand mission to find some sort of a voice and expression for all the dumb strength which lies in noble England. Milton's phrase must be enlarged, however. With 'God's Anglo-Saxons' lie the future of the earth."[85] When Stead proposed the creation of an association to promote Anglo-American unity in 1898, he approached Conan Doyle for an endorsement. The writer was only too happy to oblige, declaring that his earlier dedication was to "the greatest cause in the world." At the time, he continued, he had been asked what he meant. "No one would ask now. That shows how the idea has become familiarised." This was as true in the United States as in Britain. "In America three years ago I did not meet a single man who had thought about the matter. They seem to be thinking of it very much now."[86]

Verging on reverent devotion, Stead's early admiration of the United States was based on extensive reading and flights of hyperactive imagination rather than personal experience. He did not cross the Atlantic until 1893. Aimed at drumming up support for his idea of a civic church, his trip to Chicago was chastening, and prompted a revaluation of American society and its promise, although (perhaps surprisingly) it failed to dampen his passion for Anglo-American union. Horrified by the moral squalor and social deprivation he witnessed, as well as the abject complacency of the church and city administration, he embarked—in characteristic Steadean fashion—on a whirlwind "crusade" to mend a broken world. "I came to America to see what Mr. Carnegie described as the Triumph of Democracy," he observed. "I found instead the Evolution of Plutocracy."[87] His campaign for civic regeneration through the fusion of faith and municipal socialism drew huge

84. Stead to Shaw, 14 July 1897, cited in Graybar, *Albert Shaw*, 56.

85. Conan Doyle to Stead, ?? January 1891, STED 1/22, Stead papers

86. Conan Doyle to Stead, 30 May 1898, STED 1/22, Stead papers. In the same letter, he also modified his earlier racial classification: "But let it be Anglo-Celtic and not Anglo-Saxon re-union, please." Stead and Doyle later engaged in heated public polemic over the war in South Africa, which Stead bitterly opposed and Doyle supported. On the idea, see W. T. Stead, "The Anglo-American Association," *RoR*, 18 (July 1898), 77–82.

87. W. T. Stead, *If Christ Came to Chicago!* (London, 1894), 349.

crowds and achieved considerable success. The book he wrote about it, *If Christ Came to Chicago!*, sold three hundred thousand copies, becoming a best-seller on both sides of the Atlantic.[88] He preached ecumenical action. "The true religion," he reiterated, "is that which makes men most like Christ."[89] The poverty and corruption of the city had to be addressed. In an 1897 trip to New York, he tried (and failed) to repeat his earlier success.[90] Shaw distanced himself from Stead's hyperbolic attack on American institutions, arguing later that the campaign, though successful locally, damaged Stead's reputation in the United States and blunted the force of his wider sociopolitical message.[91]

A prominent though controversial figure in the British peace movement, Stead campaigned tirelessly for the regulation of international conflict.[92] Like Carnegie, he had long regarded an Anglo-American arbitration treaty as necessary for both limiting interstate war and securing racial union. The "Gospel of the *Pall Mall Gazette*" promoted a "High Court of Arbitration" as the first step in the "inevitable destiny" of the two countries to "coalesce."[93] Stead continued his mission in the *Review of Reviews*, making grand claims about the revisionary value of arbitration. In 1891 he argued that the creation of a permanent tribunal would "reconstitute the unity of the English-speaking race."[94] He was one of the first to warn of the brewing animosity in the United States over the Venezuela crisis. Shaw was appalled at British behavior, and the *American Review of Reviews* championed Washington's position. Stead was apoplectic, complaining bitterly to Bryce,

> Dr Shaw seems to have made up his mind to go to the Devil in his own way. . . . Anything more deplorable from the point of view of international good feeling, or anything more treacherous from the point of view of the

88. Stead, *If Christ Came to Chicago!* For the sales figures, see Joseph Baylen, "A Victorian's 'Crusade' in Chicago, 1893–94," *Journal of American History*, 51/3 (1964), 418–34. On the trip, see also Gary Love Smith, "When Stead Came to Chicago," *American Presbyterians*, 68/3 (1990), 193–205; Frankel, *Observing America*, ch. 1.

89. Stead, *If Christ Came to Chicago!*, 334.

90. W. T. Stead, *Satan's Invisible World Displayed* (London, 1898).

91. See the discussion in Frankel, *Observing America*, 32–33.

92. On Stead's role in the transatlantic peace movement, see Laity, *British Peace Movement*, 128–30, 157–58; Ceadel, *Semi-Detached Idealists*, 118–19, 151–58; Patterson, *Towards a Warless World*, 96–98.

93. Stead, "Gospel According to the *Pall Mall Gazette*," 323.

94. Stead, *RoR*, 3 (February 1891), 108. He reiterated this argument in *Americanization*, 323. Other examples of advocacy include *RoR*, 5 (May 1892), 438; *RoR*, 8 (August 1893), 263.

understanding on which he was engaged to edit the REVIEW in an admitted partnership, could not be imagined. It is not merely treason to the Unity of the Race, but it is a breach of trust, amounting to flagrant dishonesty. It is too bad to have created a Magazine for the express purpose of promoting Anglo-American Union, and then to find that your editor and partner is using that magazine for the express purpose of inflaming American hostility against England.[95]

Fiercely critical of the American line, and in particular of President Cleveland's intransigence, Stead sought to defuse the confrontation—"this miserable frontier squabble about swamp-lands." If allowed to fester, there was the possibility of "civil war" among the English-speaking people.[96] In *Always Arbitrate before You Fight! An Appeal to English-Speaking Folk*, published at the height of the crisis, he was adamant that "we want no foreigners to come between us, interfering in our family differences," and he argued that a bilateral treaty would facilitate "Anglo-American union by way of arbitration."[97] The crisis presented an opportunity to promote both arbitration and racial reunion.[98] Stead's conception of arbitration was much narrower than that of many of his contemporaries, including Carnegie. Most proponents argued for a system in which signatories had a legal obligation to refer all international disputes to mediation. Stead dismissed this as unrealistic, arguing that states would insist on retaining some decision-making autonomy. The idea was doomed to fail. He endorsed a weaker model, in which states voluntarily agreed to arbitration in the majority of cases, but retained freedom of action where they considered that core national interests (or "honour") were at stake. While many peace activists and international lawyers regarded arbitration as a panacea for the ills of the international system, Stead conceived of it as a fallible breaking mechanism, albeit a vitally important one. Despite the limited character of the arbitration model he endorsed, Stead still regarded it as an essential step on the road to grander integrationist projects.

---

95. Stead to Bryce, 1 June 1897, MS 140, Fol 115, Bryce papers. On the Bryce-Stead connection, see Whyte, *Life*, II, 78–80. For Bryce's support, see Bryce to Stead, 3 March 1898, STED 1/11, Stead papers.

96. W. T. Stead, *RoR*, 13 (January 1896), 26; Stead, *RoR*, 13 (December 1896), 507.

97. W. T. Stead, *Always Arbitrate before You Fight* (London, 1896). See also Stead, "Great Pacifist."

98. W. T. Stead, "Jingoism in America," *Contemporary Review*, 68 (1895), 334–47; Stead, "Character Sketch: President Cleveland," *RoR*, 18 (January 1896), 17–33; Stead, "To All English-Speaking Folk," 99–101. See also, Stead, *RoR*, 13 (March 1896), 260–66.

One of the most outspoken critics of British imperial policy in southern Africa, Stead used the *Review of Reviews* to ventilate his arguments throughout the 1890s and into the new century. In 1896, he castigated the "Jameson Raid," encouraged by Rhodes, while the final year of the century saw him launch relentless attacks on the unfolding war.[99] This placed great strain on some of his key friendships, though it reinforced his connection with Carnegie. While Stead thought the conflict unjust for many reasons, one of the most important was that it threatened the future unity of the English-speaking race.[100] As he complained to Carnegie in January 1900, "In this country we are rapidly awakening to the realisation of the fact that we have made the biggest blunder of the century, and the reign of Victoria is setting in blood, and we shall be lucky if we escape a break-up of the Empire, and the reduction of Great Britain to the status of a minor power."[101] Stead founded the Stop the War Committee in 1900 and the journal *War against War in South Africa*, as well as penning a series of increasingly graphic and polemical pamphlets.[102] Chastened by the war, he admitted that his avid support for imperialism, and for Rhodes in particular, had "contributed not a little to swell the tide of Jingoism which of late has carried everything before it" and stoked the flames of the conflict he sought to quench. Rather than disavowing his earlier passions, he deflected criticism by suggesting, in a plangent apologia, that his "disciples" had failed to heed his true message, leaving "unassimilated the moral considerations which were the indispensable corrective." His followers had mistaken jingoism for responsible imperialism and the "highly ideal" vision of empire adumbrated by Rhodes. "My only consolation in meditating upon this disastrous misapplication of my teaching," he moaned, "is that this has been the fate of nearly all those who have laboured for the moral improvement of their kind."[103] Stead saw himself as the sorcerer's apprentice, summoning spirits that escaped his control.

99. Joseph Baylen, "W. T. Stead's *History of the Mystery* and the Jameson Raid," *Journal of British Studies*, 4/1 (1964), 104–32.

100. Deborah Mutch, "'Are We Christians?'" in Brake, *W. T. Stead*, 133–48; Potter, "W. T. Stead"; Joseph Baylen, "W. T. Stead and the Irony of Idealism," *Canadian Historical Review*, 40/4 (1959), 304–14. Another important reason was his intense hatred of Joseph Chamberlain.

101. Stead to Carnegie, 6 January 1900, Fol 72, Carnegie papers. Despite his fierce opposition to the war, some still regarded him as complicit because of his previous support for Rhodesian imperialism: A. J. Wilson, *An Open Letter to Mr W. T. Stead on His Friendship for Cecil J. Rhodes* (London, 1902).

102. See, for example, W. T. Stead, *Shall I Slay My Brother Boer?* (London, 1899).

103. Stead, "Great Pacifist," 613. See also Stead, *RoR*, 21 (January 1900), 442.

A Kind of Human Flux: Stead's Racial Utopia

Would not the gain of the establishment of a Federal Parliament of the English-speaking race on American soil more than compensate us for any loss of what may be described as the parochial prestige of the insular Briton?[104]

We can read Stead's *The Americanization of the World*, the annual supplement to the *Review of Reviews* in 1902, as a prophet-seers vision of the political millennium. Characterized by John Lukacs as "the most direct and eloquent proposition of a union of the English-speaking nations" and (with rather less plausibility) as capturing "what people were thinking" at the time, it offered an extended meditation on the subject.[105] Throughout the text, Stead hymned the capacity of the politically united "English-speaking race" to bring peace, justice, and liberty to the earth.

From Baudelaire to the Frankfurt School and beyond, Americanization has typically been construed in negative terms, but for Stead it was an overwhelmingly positive phenomenon, characterized by the diffusion of a multifarious compound of American technology, literature, journalism, sport, and religion, all underwritten by astonishing economic power.[106] This inexorable force was remaking the world in the image of the United States. The process had been happening to Britain for decades. "Turn where we may," Stead had written in 1893, "we find evidence of the Americanisation of British institutions."[107] It was now unrolling across the world. This was no accident, Stead boasted, for the English-speaking peoples were the most advanced in human history. His evidence for this claim was principally technoscientific: they had mastered railways, steamships, telephones, telegraphs, and electricity, brushing aside competitors and establishing an unassailable lead over other peoples.[108] Material development was an expression of moral superiority. The English-speaking race also possessed superior values—especially those derived from Christian teaching—and political institutions. The combination was unprecedented and ordained them with both the power and duty to govern the world. Yet like so many of his contemporaries, Stead also observed a growing intraracial disparity, as the United States rapidly pulled ahead, usurping the

104. Stead, *Americanization*, 401.

105. John Lukacs, *A New Republic* (New Haven, CT, 2004), 207.

106. Stead, *Americanization*, pt. III. For other interpretations of American development, see Alan Lessoff, "Progress before Modernization," *American Nineteenth Century History*, 1/2 (2000), 69–96.

107. W. T. Stead, *RoR*, 8 (July 1893), 4.

108. Stead, *Americanization*, 9.

British claim to imperium. It "cannot be disputed," he opined, that race leadership now belonged to the United States. Stead followed the example of Carnegie in trying to explain American dynamism. While the steel magnate emphasized geography, population, and republican institutions, Stead isolated three distinct "secrets of American success": education, productive power, and democracy.[109] The United States possessed the best educated population, the most vibrant economy, and the most democratic political system in the world. And just as Carnegie had done, Stead inferred radical implications for the future of Britain from the shift in the balance of Anglo-American power.

The British Empire was also being Americanized. Such tendencies were already visible in Ireland and South Africa, with Stead even foreseeing the eventual secession of the former and its absorption into the United States.[110] British power was dissipating in the Caribbean. Different as they were, New Zealand and Australia were following a similar pattern, their political systems already more closely aligned with the Republic than with the "mother-country."[111] He was of two minds about Canada. Drawing in part on Carnegie, he argued that the colony might be the first to "throw in her lot" with the Americans.[112] Here he was reprising an argument that he had made throughout the 1890s, that Canada was the "pivot upon which will turn the future relations of the two great branches of the English-speaking family."[113] On the other hand, he thought that the Americanization of Canada was relatively limited, asserting that most Canadians remained loyal British subjects and rejected the idea of fusing with the United States.[114] Looking beyond the British Empire, Stead discerned further Americanization. While countries in Central or South America had largely escaped interference from Washington, in the future they would all be de facto subjects of the "suzerainty of Uncle Sam," even as they remained "nominally sovereign."[115] Although critical of the

---

109. Stead, *Americanization*, 4, 384ff.

110. Stead, *Americanization*, 39, 43–50. Here he cited Shaw, "American View."

111. Stead, *Americanization*, 127–40. Stead was no admirer of Australians: "A self-indulgent and undisciplined race which is suddenly called upon to cope with the delicate and dangerous problems of international policy is certain to be wilful, impulsive, impetuous, not to say reckless in the pursuit of its ideals" (136).

112. Stead, *Americanization*, 83.

113. W. T. Stead, *RoR*, 3/15 (1891), 214.

114. Stead, *Americanization*, 96, 113–15. This contrasted with the experience of J. A. Hobson, who only four years later diagnosed the thorough "Americanization" of the colony. Hobson, *Canada To-day* (London, 1906), ch. 12. This finally killed off Hobson's support for imperial federation: Bell, *Reordering the World*, ch. 14.

115. Stead, *Americanization*, 241.

war in the Philippines, Stead welcomed increasing American interest in the Pacific. Noting that the Americans had largely ignored Africa, he predicted that it too would soon fall under their benign influence, with African-Americans leading the way. "Not until Booker Washington and his like create an educated race of American blacks will the Americanization of Africa really begin." The Ottoman empire, long the target of Steadean moral opprobrium, was subject to increasing American influence, which would dissolve the carapace of imperial rule. Western Europe was the main bastion of opposition to Americanization, but it would eventually succumb to the magnetic power of American ideas and values. "The idea of a European solidarity of interest as against the United States is a vain dream."[116] Stead welcomed this vast expansion of America's global influence.

The apex of the "English-speaking race" was the modern white American man, "that richest ingot of humanity." Americans, he continued, had found themselves "free to face all the problems of the universe without any of the restraints of prejudices, traditions or old-established institutions which encumber the nations of the Old World." No mere transplanted Englishmen, they were something new—and better. "Being themselves an amalgam of many nations, they constitute a kind of human flux, which enables the diverse elements of hostile nationalities to form a harmonious whole."[117] Again he stressed the composite nature of the race. The greatest thing that Americans had done was to create a "smelting pot" capable of forging unity from disparate immigrant groups. "We are all conglomerates, with endlessly varying constituents, but we have at least a common language." Americanization had both domestic and global dimensions. It was simultaneously a process whereby European immigrants could be poured into an American mold and a medium for the export of ideas and institutions. Distributed throughout the world, the English-speaking race constituted a single *nation*, possessing a common language, history, type of government, culture, and religion, as well as shared interests.[118] The differences between the populations of Britain and the United States were synthesized in a higher unity. "It is in its essence moral, emotional, and intellectual," the strength of the state found in the "voluntary association of free, self-governing citizens." Though both the originary English and their American offspring were composite, there were strict limits

---

116. Stead, *Americanization*, 198, 181.

117. Stead, *Americanization*, 147, 232–33, 307.

118. Stead, *Americanization*, 149. He cited Charles Waldstein's definition of nationality. Although he didn't provide a reference, it is almost certainly "The English-speaking Brotherhood," *North American Review*, 167/501 (1898), 229. Stead had earlier praised Waldstein's critique of the idea of Anglo-Saxonism: *RoR*, 18 (September 1898), 260–61.

to Stead's account of hybridity. Whiteness bounded the syncretizing tendencies of the race. After all, the ingredients were "French Huguenots, German emigrants, fugitive Jews, Dutchmen and Spaniards," not African-Americans, East Asians, Indians, or Latin Americans. "The hundreds of millions of dusky subjects in Hindostan," he argued, "add nothing to the intrinsic strength of the British people." They were the subjects, not the agents, of Kipling's "White Man's Burden." If anything, they served to distort the nature of the true empire of the future: white citizens were, after all, the "real kernel" of the English-speaking peoples.[119]

Stead presented a stark choice: the British could meekly accept the unabated rise of the United States and the subsequent dissolution of their empire, retrogressing to an "English-speaking Belgium," or they could control their destiny by merging the Empire into "the United States of the English-speaking World," forming an integral element of the "greatest of all World-Powers," dominant in the arts of war and peace, and capable of "wielding irresistible influence in all parts of this planet."[120] The main political tendency of the previous half century had been the political unification of peoples who spoke a common language, with Germany and Italy the shining examples. It made sense to follow the same pattern. "All this means one thing and one thing only," he cautioned. "It is we who are going to be Americanized; the advance will have to be made on our side; it is idle to hope, and it is not at all to be desired, that the Americans will attempt to meet us half way by saddling themselves with institutions which many of us are longing earnestly to get rid of." Contrary to the dreams of the more speculative imperial federalists, Stead insisted that it was foolish to imagine the United States being reabsorbed into the British Empire. Since the "hegemony of the race" had already moved from London to Washington, it was essential to federate "the Empire and the Republic," while recognizing that the "fundamental feature of the Re-united States would become American, not British."[121] Wary of outlining an elaborate constitutional plan or a detailed account of political transition, he characterized his task as reading the tides of history. "I only seek to discuss tendencies, to estimate forces, and to forecast the probable course of the natural evolution of the existing factors," he remarked.[122] Conveniently, those tendencies and forces all pointed in one direction: the reunification of the United States and Britain under American leadership.

119. Stead, *Americanization*, 28.
120. Stead, *Americanization*, 396.
121. Stead, *Americanization*, 13, 23, 15.
122. Stead, *Americanization*, 17.

Although the future belonged to the United States, the true source of racial greatness originated in Britain. Stead put the point in his own distinctive terms, suggesting that the American was to the Briton as Christianity was to Judaism, both a foundation and a recurrent source of disquiet. "The philosopher recognizes that the world-mission of the Jews was only fulfilled through the Nazarene whom they crucified; and so in years to come the philosophical historian may record that the mission of the English fulfilled itself through the American." The Americanization of the world was the "Anglicizing of it at one remove." Indeed, the comparison was "dangerously exact," for many Americans displayed the same "unfilial ingratitude" that Christians so often directed at Jews.[123] Elsewhere in the book he substituted a causal claim about religion for a metaphor derived from it. Montesquieu, he argued, had been the "godfather" of the American Constitution, but it was "Puritan principles of free democracy," exported aboard the *Mayflower*, that had prepared the founders of the Republic for their monumental task. Americanization was thus the "spirit of Old England reincarnate in the body of Uncle Sam." As the "creation of the Americans is the greatest achievement of our race," he counseled, "there is no reason to resent the part the Americans are playing in fashioning the world in their image, which, after all, is substantially the image of ourselves."[124] At once deeply complacent and attuned to the shifting balance of power, this echoed—albeit with a theological twist—a famous claim made by Charles Dilke in *Greater Britain*, nearly thirty years before. "Through America," he had written, "England is speaking to the world."[125] Given the origins of Americanization, Stead continued, it would be churlish for the British to either resent or seek to halt the intraracial transfer of power. They should embrace the germinal role that they had played in bringing about the political millennium.

The constitutional details of Stead's argument were unclear. He was adamant that any future polity must protect the autonomy of its constituent units. This had been his main worry about Carnegie's "A Look Ahead." It is a "condition *sine qua non*," Stead argued, that the members of the federation would retain "freedom of national self-government" as well as "unrestricted sovereignty" except in policy domains reserved for the "central

123. Stead, *Americanization*, 3, 4.

124. Stead, *Americanization*, 26, 2.

125. Dilke, *Greater Britain*, I, 226. Stead played a central role in hounding Dilke from office over an adultery case, thus ending the career of a potential ally in the cause of consolidating the "English-speaking race." David Nicholls, *The Lost Prime Minister* (London, 1995), chs. 11–13. For Stead, the only redeeming feature of Dilke's career was the publication of *Greater Britain* (1868): W. T. Stead, "Character Sketch: Sir Charles Dilke," *RoR*, 6 (August 1892), 127–41.

authority."[126] Despite this self-conscious commitment, he also claimed that the American constitution provided the template for his vision. Stead adopted this view on both principled and pragmatic grounds. He worried about the difficulty of persuading the respective publics of the Empire and the Republic to merge. His answer, in part at least, was that although the American constitutional model would shape the institutional architecture of the federal polity, British traditions and customs would be protected. This implied that autonomy was limited to the realm of cultural practices, not political sovereignty. Any plan necessitating the rejection of the monarchy would be "fatal" to the cause, and he envisaged it retaining a limited role as a "distinctly local institution." He proposed a vast "English" polity, covering oceans and continents, and tasked with the amelioration—indeed perfection—of the world. It would be federal in form, have a written constitution, an elected head of state, no hereditary titles, and no state religion.[127] Britain would play a subordinate role.

> So far was I from indulging in any of the vainglory of nationalism of the Jingoistic type, that I have repeatedly declared that to secure the re-union of the English-speaking race I would willingly merge the independent existence of the British Empire in the American Republic, if that union could be brought about in no other way.[128]

Stead accepted that intermediate steps were necessary, and he sketched some ideas about how to cultivate the "sentiment of race unity" and create transitional institutions and practices.[129] Skeptical of "entangling" alliances, whether defensive or offensive, he nevertheless observed (following Silva White) that there were more flexible forms available, and some such connection might be a first step to a deeper union.[130] Like Dicey, he suggested establishing an intraracial zone of "common citizenship," a theme I return to in chapter 6.[131] These initial steps would allow for the erection of new political institutions.

Receiving a mixed reception, Stead catalogued various reactions to the book in the pages of the *Review of Reviews*.[132] He was gratified by the praise heaped on his utopian dream in the *Methodist Times*. "Words can hardly

---

126. Stead, *Americanization*, 419.

127. Stead, *Americanization*, 414, 20.

128. Stead, "Great Pacifist," 610.

129. Stead, *Americanization*, 319.

130. Stead, *Americanization*, 427–29. For discussion of White's plan, see chapter 2. He had made a similar point in 1898: *RoR*, 17 (May 1898), 454–58.

131. Stead, *Americanization*, 420. Cf. Dicey, "Common Citizenship for the English Race," 467–76.

132. Some British reviews are discussed in *RoR*, 25 (February 1902), 211–13.

express the benefits to us and to the human race that would follow so blessed a consummation as the reunion of the English-speaking world," wrote the Reverend Hugh Price Hughes, an influential Wesleyan reformer and journalist. "It would be the death-blow of war, and would inaugurate the millennium of peace, freedom and universal prosperity." It would also help to consolidate Protestantism, heralding an opportunity to reach "the entire human race as no religion on earth has ever yet had."[133] The most common response was to hail the sentiment of racial concord while rejecting maximalist proposals for unification. Stead's dream was too radical for many Anglo-unionists to stomach.[134] In *The Anglo-Saxon Century and the Unification of the English-speaking People*, Dos Passos offered an alternative.[135] Father of a famous son, and a prominent Republican lawyer with close ties to Roosevelt, he claimed that the Spanish-American war had forced people throughout the Atlantic world to recognize the importance of the issue. "Here was a new and undreamed-of combination."[136] Like Stead, he argued that one of the main purposes of reunification was to civilize a barbarian world. "The unification of the English and American people in the glorious mission of civilisation and peace is the next great preordained step in their national life."[137] But his own account of union was more modest. Dos Passos rejected alliances and full federation alike, the former because they were "dangerous," the latter because neither the British nor the Americans would be willing to surrender their "national individuality."[138] He dismissed Stead's advocacy of merging the two powers "into one nation" as "absolutely impracticable."[139] It would force a choice between monarchy and republicanism, a choice that neither country would accept (and that Stead himself had rejected). Dos Passos proposed a treaty that

133. W. T. Stead, *RoR*, 25 (February 1902), 212. Hughes, a liberal Welsh clergyman and famed orator, was one of the leading Methodists of the day. He founded and edited the *Methodist Times*, and established the West London Methodist Mission. See Christopher Oldstone-Moore, *Hugh Price Hughes* (Cardiff, 1999).

134. For discussion of the American reception, see W. T. Stead, *RoR*, 25 (March 1902), 316–17.

135. Dos Passos, *Anglo-Saxon Century*. For a positive review, focusing on its practicality, see [S. W. E.], *Yale Law Journal*, 13/2 (1903), 105–6. For an attempt to contrast the work of father and son, see Gayle Rogers, "Restaging the Disaster," *Journal of Modern Literature*, 36/2 (2013), 61–79.

136. Dos Passos, *Anglo-Saxon Century*, 49, 51.

137. Dos Passos, *Anglo-Saxon Century*, 96.

138. Dos Passos, *Anglo-Saxon Century*, 152, 155. Here he cited Freeman's critique of imperial federation.

139. Dos Passos, *Anglo-Saxon Century*, 94.

would regulate "their relations towards each other, but not to foreign nations," though the exact meaning of this prescription was unclear. This "conservative method" furnished a "practical means" for the creation of a permanent "union between the English-American peoples." More specifically, he envisaged the absorption of Canada into the United States, the establishment of common citizenship, free trade, a unified currency, and an arbitration tribunal.[140]

Stead, like Carnegie, was convinced that there was widespread support for union among the British political elite, though few dared voice it publicly. This was especially true of supporters of imperial federation, most of whom were open to ideas about supranational institutions, (con)federal structures, and constitutional innovation. "[P]rivately," he confided, "no one who moves in political and journalistic circles can ignore the fact that many of the strongest Imperialists are heart and soul in favour of seeing the British Empire and the American Republic merged into the English-speaking United States of the World."[141] Stead cited Balfour, long an admirer of the United States and another friend of his, to bolster the argument. He recalled that at the height of the Venezuelan agitation in 1896 Balfour had addressed a crowd in Manchester. He had outlined a counterfactual history of the late eighteenth and early nineteenth centuries in which judicious statesmanship prevented the Revolution, leaving the British Empire intact. "We may be taxed with being idealists and dreamers in this matter," Balfour warned, but "I would rather be an idealist and a dreamer, and I look forward with confidence to the time when our ideals will have become real and our dreams will be embodied in actual political fact." Without dreaming, progress was impossible. "[C]ircumstances will tend in that direction in which we look."[142] This sounded remarkably like Carnegie's prognostications on the use-value of social dreaming. Stead was only too happy to concur.

Stead and Carnegie disagreed over the potential imperial role of Anglo-America. Calling for the dissolution of the British Empire, Carnegie rejected an imperial mission for his beloved "Re-United States," while Stead oscillated between a largely pacific vision and one in which imperialism was a privileged technology of global transformation. Extremely critical of jingoism, he stressed the power of moral exemplarity. "It should be no ambition of ours to dominate

140. Dos Passos, *Anglo-Saxon Century*, 156ff. I return to Dos Passos's argument in chapter 6.

141. Stead, *Americanization*, 404.

142. Stead, *Americanization*, 16. The passage can be found in Balfour, *Mind of Arthur James Balfour*, 2. See also W. T. Stead, "Character Sketch: Arthur Balfour," *RoR*, 4 (November 1891), 457–69, which stressed his desire for reuniting the race. For Balfour's combination of visionary rhetoric and modest institutional proposals, see my discussion in the book's introduction.

the world save by the influence of ideas and the force of our example." Stead excoriated the arrogance of those who believed the English-speaking peoples should act as a divine global policeman. "The temptation to believe that we are the Vicegerent of the Almighty, charged with the thunderbolt of Heaven, for the punishment of evildoers," he thundered, "is one of the subtle temptations by which the Evil one lures well-meaning people to embark upon a course of policy which soon becomes indistinguishable from buccaneering pure and simple."[143] Yet there was a clear tension between this warning about hubris and his embrace of "responsible imperialism." Though opposed to the American invasion of the Philippines, he praised the occupation of Cuba as "liberating," and in 1898 he had welcomed the emergence of the United States as a "world power," suggesting the imperative for Britain and the United States to "confront the world as two members of one household."[144] In his discussion of the future of Asia, he envisaged a form of collective trusteeship, the new household joining in the inter-imperial mission to spread civilization. "[H]appily united in the permanent ties of a race alliance," the two powers could "pool their resources and devote their united energies to the work of the amelioration of the lot of the impoverished myriads of Asia."[145] This steroidal fantasy of global imperial development was anathema to Carnegie. But despite their disagreements about the benefits of empire, both men celebrated the utopian potential of Anglo-American union, arguing that a politically integrated "English-speaking race" would bring peace and justice to the earth.

Star Gazer: Rhodes and the English-Speaking World

Rhodes was the most controversial imperialist of the day. Born in Bishop Stortford, Hertfordshire, in 1853, he decamped to Natal in 1870, seeking to recover his deteriorating health and make his fortune. Starting with little, he proved a formidable capitalist. During the following decade, he shuttled back and forth between southern Africa, where he established a hugely profitable diamond business, and Oxford, where he studied intermittently for a degree in classics.[146] Graduating in 1881 as a wealthy man, Rhodes accumulated territory at an astonishing rate, chiefly under the auspices of the British South

---

143. Stead, *Americanization*, 437.

144. Stead, *Americanization*, 46; Stead, *RoR*, 17 (January 1898), 319.

145. Stead, *Americanization*, 213.

146. The most comprehensive biography is Robert Rotberg, with Miles Shore, *The Founder* (Oxford, 1988). On his business practices, see Robert Turrell, *Capital and Labour on the Kimberley Diamond Fields, 1871–1890* (Cambridge, 1987).

African Company. He embarked on a meteoric though ill-fated career in Cape politics, culminating in his election as Prime Minister in 1890. In January 1896, he was forced to resign for his role in the disastrous "Jameson Raid," an attempt to kindle civil unrest in the Transvaal. Initially disgraced, he was trying to rebuild his reputation when war was declared in 1899. He died in 1902 at the age of forty-eight.

Then as now, Rhodes was a lightning rod for attitudes to imperial expansion.[147] While many celebrated him as an incarnation of the expansionist spirit, a paladin heroically carving out new territories for Britain to rule, others saw him as an immoral jingo. A thoroughgoing white supremacist, he was determined to keep black Africans disenfranchised and subordinated, viewing them as a pool of cheap expendable labor. In a speech to the Cape Parliament in 1887, Rhodes made his position clear:

> we have got to treat the natives, where they are in a state of barbarism, in a different way to ourselves. We are to be lords over them. These are my politics on native affairs, and these are the politics of South Africa. Treat the natives as a subject people as long as they continue in a state of barbarism and communal tenure; be the lords over them, and let them be the subject race, and keep the liquor from them.[148]

He was the target of fierce criticism in the imperial metropole. Many liberal imperialists disdained his methods and ambitions. His "theory of civilisation is so crude and his ethical standard so low," expostulated the historian G. P. Gooch, "that he is utterly unfit to control the destinies of any country, new or old, white or black." Chesterton reviled him as a man who "invoked slaughter, violated justice, and ruined republics," all in the name of a base social Darwinism.[149] In the United States, he was both acclaimed and reviled. "It is generally conceded by the American papers," recorded the *Literary Digest*

147. On the memory of Rhodes, see Paul Maylam, *The Cult of Rhodes* (Cape Town, 2005). The most recent example is the "Rhodes Must Fall" decolonization movement that emerged first in Cape Town, then in Oxford. John Newsinger, "Why Rhodes Must Fall," *Race & Class*, 58/2 (2016), 70–78; Brian Kwoba, Rose Chantiluke, and Athinangamso Nkope (eds.), *Rhodes Must Fall* (London, 2018).

148. Speech to Cape Parliament, 23 June 1887, in Vindex [F. Verschoyle], *Cecil Rhodes* (London, 1900), 151. The speech was delivered as part of the debate over the Parliamentary Registration Bill.

149. G. P. Gooch, "Imperialism" in C. F. G. Masterman (ed.), *The Heart of Empire* (London, 1901), 362; G. K. Chesterton, "The Sultan" in Chesterton, *A Miscellany of Men* (London, 1912), 204. See also F. W. Hirst, "Imperialism and Finance" in F. W. Hirst, G. Murray, and J. L. Hammond, *Liberalism and the Empire* (London, 1900), 41–75.

following his death, that "Cecil Rhodes was a great man . . . [b]ut few, if any, call him a good man."[150] Attempting to sum up his life, an editorial in *The Nation* remarked on "the rapacity, the cruelty, the disregard of both moral and legal obligations, which his methods involved," while lamenting that he "could wrest land from the natives, he could force them into practical slavery, he could march over corpses to his goal," all cheered on by his epigones.[151] David Starr Jordan, strident anti-imperialist and eugenicist, dismissed him as a "brigand." For his fellow expansionist Roosevelt, on the other hand, Rhodes was a "great man": "He did much that was very good and his death has been a tragedy."[152]

"It is the dreamers that move the world," Rhodes observed in 1901. Incapable of seeing beyond their own lifespans, "practical men" possessed limited imaginative horizons, while the "[d]reamers and visionaries have made civilisations."[153] He was proud to see himself as such a visionary, a self-image that was endorsed by many of his critics and admirers. He was one of Chesterton's "prophets," dedicated to the proposition that "the one thing of the future was the British Empire."[154] Stead once observed that Earth was too small to contain Rhodes's monumental ambition. His dreamworld was untethered from terrestrial bounds. "'The world,' he said to me on one occasion, 'is nearly all parcelled out, and what there is left of it is being divided up, conquered, and colonised. To think of these stars,' he said, 'that you see overhead at night, these vast worlds which we can never reach. I would annex the planets if I could; I often think of that. It makes me sad to see them so clear and yet so far.'"[155] Stead was suitably awed: "Since Alexander died at Babylon, sighing for fresh worlds to conquer, has there ever been such a cry from the heart of mortal man?"[156]

We can grasp the extraordinary powers ascribed to Rhodes—and the utopian hopes invested in him—by examining some of the posthumous commentary on his life and legacy. A poem by Kipling was recited at Rhodes's funeral, anointing him a "[d]reamer devout, by vision led."[157] The *Daily Telegraph* proclaimed that "[a]t all times and under all circumstances, he was a

150. "Estimates of Cecil Rhodes," *Literary Digest*, 24/14 (1902), 453.

151. "Cecil Rhodes as a Type," *The Nation*, 3 April 1902, 264.

152. David Starr Jordan, *Imperial Democracy* (New York, 1899), 82; Roosevelt to Earl Grey, 7 April 1902, Theodore Roosevelt papers, Library of Congress.

153. Conversation with Lady Warwick, quoted in Rotberg, *Founder*, 670.

154. Chesterton, *Napoleon of Notting Hill*, 17.

155. Rhodes, *Last Will*, 190.

156. Rhodes, *Last Will*, 190.

157. Rudyard Kipling, "The View of the World," *The Times*, 9 April 1902.

Seer, which I take to be the best definition of a dreamer of dreams."[158] Henry Cust, onetime editor of the *Pall Mall Gazette*, Conservative M. P., and occasional poet, painted a reverential portrait in the *North American Review*. Rhodes, he asserted, was "England's greatest son," a genius who possessed an unrivalled capacity to make dreams come true. "There are very few among the sons of men who, born not in the list of kings and warriors and philosophers, have power within them to change profoundly the maps and minds of humanity."[159] Above all, Cust marveled, Rhodes was capable of yoking dreams to a practical agenda for their realization.

> The imagination of Rhodes was not that of a poet. He dreamed, indeed; but his dreams were not presences to be put by, they grew to purposes. His seeing, perhaps, was rather that of the mathematician. His imagination was prehensile. What he imagined clearly, he actually saw, and what he saw he touched, and in time it was. "Imagined clearly," I say; for nothing is more astonishing in the man than the deliberation and method he employed in the use of his wonderful vision. The very reality of the fancied fabric he would build brought a cold, hard sanity to choose the means by which he would approach it.[160]

Channeling Tennyson, Cust decreed that "[h]e did not dip into the future; He abode within its gates." He sought to reorder the world. "It may be a dream," Cust averred, "but Rhodes's dreams had a trick of coming true."[161]

Rhodes's dream of global order contained three nested elements: the unification of southern Africa under British rule, the consolidation of the empire through imperial federation, and the fusion of the English-speaking people. A firm believer in the principle of home rule, like Stead he thought it both possible and desirable to create vast overarching political structures that granted considerable autonomy to their constituent parts. The American Constitution provided him with a workable template. While he spent most of his adult life pursuing business opportunities and imperial expansion in Africa, Rhodes fantasized about transforming the world by harnessing the combined power

---

158. Lewis Mitchell, *The Life of the Right Honorable Cecil John Rhodes, 1853–1902* (London, 1910), I, 80–81. The first scholarly biography of Rhodes used the same phrase: Basil Williams, *Cecil Rhodes* (New York, 1921), 48.

159. Henry Cust, "Cecil Rhodes," *North American Review*, 175/548 (1902), 114, 99. Cust edited the *Pall Mall Gazette* from 1892 until 1896. On his tenure, see Robertson, *Life and Death*, 360–88.

160. Cust, "Cecil Rhodes," 101.

161. Cust, "Cecil Rhodes," 109, 108, 110.

and resources of the scattered "Anglo-Saxon race." He believed that the British were predestined to shape humanity for the better if only they recognized their sanctified responsibility. "Mr Rhodes," Stead declared, "saw in the English-speaking race the greatest instrument yet evolved for the progress and eleva-tion of mankind."[162] He was driven, so Stead liked to claim, by an overarching ideal. "And what is that ideal?" he wrote to Rhodes. "It is, in your own phrase, to colour as much of the world red as possible, to keep the English-speaking race together, not merely for the sake of vulgar, swell ambition, but because the English-speaking race represents the principles, as you have often ex-plained to me, of justice of liberty and of peace."[163] This was, Stead genuflected after Rhodes's death, "the dream—if you like to call it so—or vision which had ever been the guiding star of his life."[164] Those principles would no doubt have come as a great surprise to the countless Africans manipulated, impoverished, and brutalized by his activities. In Rhodes, the yawning gap between professed belief and squalid quotidian reality is at its starkest and most obscene.

His dream of racial supremacy had been formed early. On June 2, 1877, then aged just twenty-four, Rhodes sat down in Oxford and composed an extraor-dinary document, his "Confession of Faith."[165] It is one of the most conse-quential utopian texts of the Victorian era. Rambling, vague, and dotted with grammatical errors, it encapsulated his megalomania. He began by invoking Aristotle: "It often strikes a man to enquire what is the chief good in life." For Rhodes, the good consisted in the use of great wealth to realize a dream of racial unity that would transform humanity. "I contend that we are the finest race in the world and that the more of the world we inhabit the better it is for the human race." Imagine, he continued, how those benighted parts of the world populated by "the most despicable specimen of human beings" would profit from being "brought under Anglo-Saxon influence." Such a world would sustain an increase in the number of Anglo-Saxons, for "every acre added to our territory means in the future birth to some more of the English race who otherwise would not be brought into existence."

162. Rhodes, *Last Will*, 63.

163. Stead to Rhodes, 23 March 1901, Rhodes papers.

164. Rhodes, *Last Will*, 77.

165. The fullest printed version of the Confession is in John Flint, *Cecil Rhodes* (Boston, 1974), 248–52. An edited and annotated version is reproduced in *The Last Will and Testament of Cecil J. Rhodes*, 58–61. Here I quote from the version found in the Cecil Rhodes papers, Rhodes House Library, Oxford, MSS Afr.t.1. See also the discussion in Robert Rotberg, "Did Cecil Rhodes Really Try to Control the World?," *Journal of Imperial and Commonwealth History*, 42/3 (2014), 551–67.

We learn from having lost to cling to what we possess. We know the size of the world we know now the total extent, Africa is still lying ready for us it is our duty to take it, it is our duty to seize every opportunity of acquiring more territory and we should keep this one idea steadily before our eyes that more territory simply means more of the Anglo-Saxon race more of the best most human most honourable race the world possesses.

Above all, Rhodes contended, the fusion of the Anglo-Saxons would bring everlasting peace: "the absorption of the greater portion of the world under our rule simply means the end of all wars."[166] The "most human" of peoples would bring peace to humanity.

While Carnegie thought that political elites should direct public opinion, Rhodes went a step further, suggesting—in his most innovative contribution to racial utopian discourse—that a secret society was necessary to undertake the epic task. "The idea gleaming and dancing before ones eyes like a will-o-the-wisp at last frames itself into a plan." His model was the Society of Jesus. Its members scattered throughout the Anglo-Saxon world, such a society would spread the gospel of racial superiority, recruiting the best and the brightest of each generation to further the unionist cause. It would have two interwoven objectives: bringing the "whole uncivilized world under British rule" and the "recovery of the United States." Rhodes encouraged Stead to read *An American Politician*, an 1884 novel by the popular American writer F. Marion Crawford.[167] The reason is clear. Very loosely based on the election of Rutherford B. Hayes in 1877, the tale focuses on a politician driven by an overriding sense of duty and aided by an Anglo-American secret society.[168] Stead was smitten by the idea. In the first edition of the *Review of Reviews*, he emphasized the importance of a revolutionary vanguard, a "small nucleus of Invincible Aristoi fighting the good cause."[169]

Initially Rhodes sought the "recovery" of the United States, its reabsorption into the British Empire, a manifestation of the eighteenth-century model of imperial order, with Washington subordinate to London. His dream of a

166. Rhodes, "Confession of Faith."

167. Rhodes to Stead, ?? July 1889, Rhodes papers. Crawford was best known as a writer of ghost stories: Chris Morgan, "F. Marion Crawford" in E. F. Bleiler (ed.), *Supernatural Fiction Writers* (New York, 1985), 747–52; John Moran, *An F. Marion Crawford Companion* (New York, 1981).

168. Rhodes to Stead, ?? July 1889, Rhodes papers.

169. Stead, "To All English-Speaking Folk," 18. Milner was also keen on the idea of a secret society: Whyte, *Life*, II, 210. Rhodes asked Stead to keep the plan to himself, which he did until Rhodes gave him permission to publicize it. It was aired in the *Review of Reviews* in 1899 and in the *Last Will*: Whyte, *Life*, I, 272.

glorious racial future was tied to a historical narrative of betrayal and folly. "Owing to two or three ignorant pig-headed statesmen in the last century, at their door lies the blame. Do you ever feel mad? Do you ever feel murderous I think I do with those men." While the War of Independence had been disastrous for the British, amputating a key part of their empire, it had been equally catastrophic for the United States, which would have thrived more under the "softening and elevating influences of English rule"—"look at their government, are not the frauds that yearly come before the public view a disgrace to any country and especially theirs which is the finest in the world." He fashioned a counterfactual, suggesting that if the United States had remained part of Britain, transatlantic emigration would have been far greater during the previous century, accelerating the growth of the country. He was so proud of his unionist idea that he mused about patenting it. History would bless the man who "ultimately led to the cessation of all wars and one language throughout the world."[170] While Carnegie pondered the human capacity to extend life indefinitely, and Stead sought to commune with the dead, Rhodes dreamt of a form of earthly immortality.

George Parkin, a prominent Canadian imperialist, once claimed that Rhodes possessed "one of the exceptional and original minds of his time."[171] This was a gross exaggeration. Though bold and imaginative, Rhodes was no deep thinker. His ideas were cobbled together from a variety of sources, many of which he was exposed to during his time in Oxford.[172] Stead, as we shall see, was also a major influence. Rhodes's first serious biographer, Basil Williams, pinpointed what made him unusual. "Many . . . have held the same creed about the divinely appointed mission of the British race; but few, like Rhodes, have made it a direct spur to action throughout their lives and regarded themselves as the agents of the divine purpose in doing so." The architect Herbert Baker, who spent much time with Rhodes in the 1890s, echoed this assessment. "The secret of Rhodes's genius lay," he observed, "in his supreme gift of concentrated thought and the power of transmuting the resultant into action."[173] It was this fusion of idea and action that most impressed his

170. Rhodes, *Last Will*, 68.

171. George Parkin, *The Rhodes Scholarships* (New York, 1912), 209. At the time, Parkin was in charge of administering the Rhodes scholarship program. Two decades before, Parkin had recognized Rhodes's aim of embedding South Africa within a united empire: Parkin, *Imperial Federation*, 236.

172. On his time at Oxford, see Rotberg, *Founder*, ch. 5; George Walker, "So Much to Do,'" *Journal of Imperial and Commonwealth History*, 44/4 (2016), 697–716.

173. Williams, *Cecil Rhodes*, 51; Herbert Baker, *Cecil Rhodes, by His Architect* (London, 1934), 101.

contemporaries. The Marxist thinker H. M. Hyndman later wrote that Stead saw Rhodes as "a very necromancer of modern English Imperialism," the one person "competent above all others to realise dreams which he had persuaded himself were worthy of prompt realisation in fact."[174] Rhodes seemed to possess the rare ability to actualize radical change, to solve the thorny problem of transition that confronts all utopian dreaming.

Rhodes maintained a lifelong interest in ancient philosophy, history, and biography, scouring the annals of the past for insight and succor. He was especially taken with the fate of the Roman Empire, and the writing of Aristotle, Plato, and Thucydides. *The Meditations* of Marcus Aurelius was his favorite book. He employed a team of classicists to translate all of the references found in Gibbon's *Decline and Fall*, as well as numerous other texts, an extravagant exercise in historical bombast that filled over two hundred volumes in his personal library at Groote Schuur.[175] Winwood Reade's idiosyncratic evolutionary narrative *The Martyrdom of Man* was a further source of inspiration. "That book has made me what I am," he reportedly told Princess Catherine Radziwill.[176] Originally intending to write about the historical development of African societies, Reade ended up constructing a cosmic history—a contribution to the flowering genre of evolutionary epic—that opened with the nebular hypothesis about the birth of the universe and culminated in the posthuman emergence of a perfected species departing Earth to explore the stars.[177] Professing adherence to Darwin, he elaborated a distinctly non-Darwinian account of evolutionary change—indeed, his argument was closer to that of Robert Chambers's *Vestiges of the Natural History of Creation* than *The Descent of Man*.[178] Humanity, Reade pronounced, was "becoming more and more

174. H. M. Hyndman, *Further Reminiscences* (London, 1912), 308. Hyndman was no fan of Stead: "For myself, I never could stand the man" (307).

175. Victorian Tietze Larson, "Classics and the Acquisition and Validation of Power in Britain's 'Imperial Century' (1815–1914)," *International Journal of the Classical Tradition*, 6/2 (1999), 211. For first-hand testimony of his interest in ancient history and literature, see Sir Henry Lucy, "Cecil Rhodes," *Chambers Journal*, 9 (1919), 145; Baker, *Cecil Rhodes*, 103; Sidney Low, "Some Personal Recollections of Cecil Rhodes," *Nineteenth Century*, 51 (1902), 834.

176. Catherine Radziwill, *Cecil Rhodes* (London, 1918), 127. See also Rotberg, *Founder*, 99–100.

177. Winwood Reade, *The Martyrdom of Man* (London, 1872), ch. 4. Charles Rubin makes the case that Reade was an early transhumanist: *Eclipse of Man* (New York, 2014), 15–19.

178. For an excellent account, see Ian Hesketh, "A Good Darwinian Epic?," *Studies in the History and Philosophy of Biological and Biomedical Sciences*, 51 (2015), 44–52. For further skepticism about Rhodes's purported Darwinism, see David Paul Crook, "Historical Monkey Business," *History*, 84/276 (1999), 650–51. On Reade, see also Felix Driver, *Geography Militant*

noble, more and more divine, slowly ripening towards perfection."[179] While natural selection was operative at the early stages of human development, it was superseded by the emergence and refinement of intelligence. Humans could direct evolution for their own benefit. Once scientific naturalism had been absorbed, and the last remnants of theology shed, "human nature will be elevated, purified, and finally transformed." A terrestrial utopia beckoned. The "Earth, which is now a purgatory, will be made a paradise, not by idle prayers and supplications, but by the efforts of man himself."[180] The book met a hostile reception, chiefly because of its strident attacks on Christianity, though it later became a best-seller, inspiring a range of thinkers, including Wells and Churchill. Rhodes would no doubt have been impressed by the heroic scale of Reade's vision and his message that human evolution could be directed and perfected.

Like Stead, Rhodes was an ardent believer in the necessity of imperial federation. His second will, written in September 1877, and based in part on the "Confession of Faith," directed his executors to disburse his (then modest) wealth to further the cause. He wrote little about the specific model he had in mind, though we can at least discern its outlines. In a letter of 1888 to Charles Parnell, whose campaign for Irish Home Rule he supported, Rhodes asserted that the colonies "will have to be represented in the Imperial Parliament, where the distribution of their contributions must be decided upon." The connection he drew between the two projects was clear. "You will perhaps say that I am making the Irish question a stalking-horse for a scheme of Imperial Federation; but if so, I am at least placing Ireland in the forefront of the battle."[181] A year later, he expressed support for the model proposed by the Fair Trade League, writing to Stead that their idea of preferential duties with the colonies was "the only plan for holding us together using self-interest."[182]

Rhodes was a self-declared liberal. "The future of England must be Liberal," he wrote in 1891, in order "to fight Socialism." In a letter to the *New Statesman*

(Oxford, 2005), ch. 5. For a brilliant account of Chambers and his influence, see James Secord, *Victorian Sensation* (Chicago, 2001).

179. Reade, *Martyrdom*, 522.

180. Reade, *Martyrdom*, 444.

181. Rhodes to Charles Parnell, 19 June 1888, *Last Will*, 124–25. He donated £10,000 to the Irish Home Rule Party in 1888. Only a couple of years later, Stead, in his self-appointed role as moral avatar, helped to destroy Parnell's political career by exposing his marital infidelity.

182. Rhodes to Stead, 10 June 1891, Micr. Afr. 413, Rhodes papers. For further discussion of federation, see Rhodes to Stead, 6 July 1889, Micr. Afr. 413, Rhodes papers, and the account of his views ("a complete federal system") in Low, "Some Personal Recollections of Cecil Rhodes," 832.

penned a decade later, he characterized his position as "Liberalism *plus* Empire," in contrast to the anti-imperial tendencies he discerned in the Liberal Party.[183] Stead's militant fusion of liberal politics and imperialism clearly appealed to him. Rhodes sought out a meeting with the journalist in April 1889.[184] He had been impressed, so Stead later boasted, by the editorial line of the *Pall Mall Gazette* and Stead's personal bravery. Rhodes apparently even tried to visit him in prison following "The Maiden Tribute of Modern Babylon" scandal in 1885, subsequently attending an event at Exeter Hall that had been called to protest Stead's treatment.[185] The roles were soon reversed. Initially wary of the imperialist, Stead was enamored with Rhodes from their first meeting onward. He saw Rhodes's commitment to the spread and perfection of the "English race" as an expression of profound faith. "He is not religious in the ordinary sense," Stead wrote to Emma, his wife, after the first meeting, "but has a deeply religious conception of his duty to the world, and thinks he can best serve it by working for England."[186] Rhodes exemplified the kind of figure that Stead sought to recruit to the ecumenical civic church, his grand dreams of human perfectibility and racial unity paradigmatic instances of the imperative to "be like Christ." The meeting was a "fairy dream." After a long discussion in 1891, he wrote to Rhodes that "your idea and mine is in its essence the undertaking according to our lights to rebuild the City of God and reconstitute in the nineteenth century some modern equivalent equipped with modern appliances of the Medieval Church of the ninth century on a foundation as broad as humanity."[187] Rhodes's admission that the *Pall Mall Gazette* had informed his ideas about empire was interpreted by Stead as a form of divine intervention. "How good God is to me," he remarked. "I think that I shall be God's instrument in doing him Good."[188] Rhodes, meanwhile, saw Stead as a messenger capable of preaching his gospel of racial union and burnishing his image in the public sphere. "I am a bad writer but through my ill connected sentences you can trace the key of my ideas and you can give my ideas the literary clothing that is necessary."[189] Stead was to be amanuensis and proselyte.

After their initial meeting, the two men engaged in regular correspondence, and met whenever Rhodes was in London. One of these letters, written in the

---

183. Rhodes to Francis Schnadhorst, 23 February 1891, Rhodes to the *Spectator*, 12 October 1901; both cited in the *Last Will*, 131, 133.

184. Stead recounts their meeting in *Last Will*, 79–83. See also Whyte, *Life*, I, 269–78.

185. Rhodes, *Last Will*, 81–82.

186. Stead to Emma Stead, 4 April 1889, Whyte, *Life*, 271.

187. Rhodes, *Last Will*, 98.

188. Stead to Emma Stead, 4 April 1889, Whyte, *Life*, 268–69.

189. Rhodes to Stead, 19 August 1891 and 3 September 1891, Rhodes papers, Micr. Afr. 413.

late summer of 1891, gives a detailed insight into Rhodes's thinking at the time. Reiterating many of the ideas outlined in his "Confession of Faith," he emphasized the importance of new communications technologies and the shrinking of space: it was now essential to see the world "as a whole."[190] He restated the importance of the secret society. "Please remember the key of my idea discussed with you is a society copied from the Jesuits." Rhodes went on to praise the American Constitution as an ideal model for restructuring the British Empire—"[i]n that is Home Rule or Federation and an organisation to work this out"—although he was exercised by the trade practices of the United States, and in particular the McKinley Tariff, which had been imposed in 1890. He even suggested that Britain should declare a "commercial war" on Washington, a conflict that, after the inevitable British victory, might lead eventually to "union with America" and then "universal peace." Rhodes also returned to the loss of the American colonies.

> What an awful thought it is that if we had not lost America or if even now we could arrange with the present members of the United States Assembly and our House of Commons the peace of the world is secured for all eternity. We could hold your federal Parliament 5 years at Washington and 5 at London. The only thing sensible to carry this idea out is a secret one gradually absorbing the wealth of the world to be devoted to such an object.[191]

Within the space of three sentences, Rhodes asserted that perpetual peace could be secured by racial union, proposed a transatlantic polity with an alternating capital—demonstrating the ontological priority of race to political institutions—and contended that the only, or the best, way to create such a polity would be the formation of a secret society. This is the main piece of evidence of Rhodes's openness to formal unification between the British Empire and the United States. It is an exemplary proclamation of the racial utopian imagination.

Rhodes chided the British for failing to recognize their own greatness. It would be one of the tasks of the secret society to wake them from their long slumber, to encourage, cajole, and educate them about their consecrated fate. The "greatest people the world has ever seen," the English "do not know their strength their greatness and their destiny." If organized properly, they could assume "the sacred duty of taking the responsibility of the still uncivilised part of the world." Beyond the global civilizing mission, they would also bring about the "cessation of all wars" and the spread of one single language across

---

190. Rhodes to Stead, 19 August 1891 and 3 September 1891.
191. Rhodes to Stead, 19 August 1891 and 3 September 1891.

the world. Yet none of this would happen without dedication, planning, and ample material resources. While Carnegie speculated that union might take a century, Rhodes suggested twice that. "What a scope and what a horizon awaits at any rate for the next two centuries the best energies of the best people in the world. Perfectly feasible but needing an organization for it is impossible for one human atom to complete anything much less such an idea as this requiring the devotion of the best souls of the next 200 years."[192]

Rhodes was so impressed by Stead that in 1891 he appointed him an executor of his will. Stead spent much of the subsequent decade preaching their shared vision and molding Rhodes's public image.[193] The *Review of Reviews*, he later admitted, was dedicated to achieving their racial ambitions. "He [Rhodes] regarded it as a practical step towards the realisation of his great idea, the reunion of the English-speaking world through the agency of a central organ served in every part of the world by affiliated Helpers."[194] The encomium "To All English-Speaking Folk" that prefaced the first issue of the journal was a summa of this dream. "That was my idea as I expressed it. It was Mr Rhodes's idea also. It was 'our idea'—his idea of a secret society—broadened and made presentable to the public without in any way revealing the esoteric truth that lay behind. Mr Rhodes recognised this and eagerly welcomed it."[195] In a lengthy 1896 character sketch, Stead asserted that Rhodes was "a great man, one of the greatest men produced by our race in this century," and his overriding aim was the "extension throughout the whole world of the great principles of peace, justice, and liberty, of which the English-speaking race may be regarded as in a special sense the standard-barer of the Almighty."[196] The relationship between the two men was not always smooth. Stead excoriated Rhodes for the Jameson Raid, not least because it damaged the prospects of racial union. "I regretted that Mr Rhodes was not sent to gaol, and told him so quite frankly." Horrified by the South African war, he once again turned on his friend.[197]

192. Rhodes to Stead, 19 August 1891 and 3 September 1891. In the letter to Stead, he talked of the potential "union with America and universal peace, I mean after one hundred years."

193. Stead to Rhodes, 26 March 1891. For some early examples, see Stead, *RoR*, 1 (February 1890), 103; Stead, *RoR*, 2 (August 1890), 109–10, 128; Stead, *RoR*, 5 (May 1892), 439; Stead, *RoR*, 6 (July 1892), 5. His most extended treatments were Stead, "Character Sketch: Cecil Rhodes of Africa," *RoR*, 13 (February 1896), 116–36; Stead, "Cecil Rhodes of Africa," *RoR*, 20 (November 1899), 451–63.

194. Rhodes, *Last Will*, 99.

195. Rhodes, *Last Will*, 102.

196. Stead, "Character Sketch," *RoR*, 13 (February 1896), 116, 120.

197. Baylen, "W. T. Stead's *History of the Mystery*"; Rotberg, *Founder*, 633–36.

Disagreement over the war, and concerns about Stead's eccentricity, lead Rhodes to drop him as an executor in 1899.[198]

Rhodes died in March 1902, endowing the famous scholarship program at the University of Oxford. He hoped that it would inculcate a deep sense of kinship between elite members of his beloved Anglo-Saxon race.[199] The scholarships, Stead contended, were "for perpetuating the memory of the dreams which he dreamed."[200] The terms of the endowment were clear about Rhodes's love of the existing imperial order—it was intended to facilitate "the retention of the unity of the Empire"—while hinting at his wider Angloworld fantasy. In discussing scholarships for American citizens, Rhodes affirmed the value of "the union of the English-speaking peoples throughout the world."[201] Writing to Carnegie, Stead claimed credit for the idea. "I daresay you may discern in this provision some trace of a certain friend of yours, who has never lost an opportunity of preaching the doctrine of racial unity you have often preached so eloquently."[202] Although Stead was to play no role in managing Rhodes's huge bequest, he set out to shape his intellectual legacy.

The Grey Archangel: Americanizing Rhodes

"When Mr Rhodes died," Stead mourned, "the most conspicuous figure left in the English-speaking race since the death of Queen Victoria, disappeared. Whether loved or feared, he towered above his contemporaries." He

198. Philip Ziegler, *Legacy* (New Haven, CT, 2008), 24–25. In December 1900, Lord Esher wrote to Rhodes, commenting that "our hallucinated friend Stead—who, in spite of vagaries— is still permanently devoted to you." Esher to Rhodes, 30 December 1900, Rhodes papers. It wasn't only those close to Rhodes who distrusted Stead. In April 1901, Pollock complained to Bryce about Stead's comments in the *Daily Mail*. They were so "indiscreet" that they called into question Stead's membership of the Committee of the Anglo-American League. Pollock to Bryce, 26 April 1901, MS 120, Fol 57, Bryce papers. Pollock continued, "I will not dissimulate the fact that I have from the first disliked his being there on other grounds."

199. Anthony Kenny, *The History of the Rhodes Trust* (Oxford, 2001); Ziegler, *Legacy*.

200. Rhodes, *Last Will*, 54; W. T. Stead, "Mr Rhodes's Will and Its Genesis," *RoR*, 25 (May 1902), 479–81. The bequest was reported on widely. See, for example: *People's Journal*, 12 April 1902, 3; *Sheffield Daily Telegraph*, 7 April 1902, 6; *Yorkshire Evening Post*, 5 April 1902, 2. Rhodes's "remarkable conversation" with Stead (*RoR*, 25 [April 1902]), was discussed in the *Dundee Evening Telegraph* (10 April 1902, 4); *Hampshire Telegraph* (12 April 1902, 5).

201. Rhodes, *Last Will*, 23, 27.

202. Stead to Carnegie, 2 April 1902, Fol 88, Carnegie papers. Describing Carnegie as "one of the godfathers of Americanization," Stead tried to persuade him to endow a similar scheme in the United States. Richard Jebb observed the need for equivalent educational opportunities in the colonies: *Studies in Colonial Nationalism* (London, 1905), 298–300.

acknowledged that Rhodes attracted as much vitriol as veneration, and that they had engaged in "violent antagonism" over the war, but his sympathies were clear. "For all his faults the man was great, almost immeasurably great, when contrasted with the pigmies who pecked and twittered in his shade."[203] Stead bowed before the capacious imagination of his friend and collaborator. "Mr Rhodes was one of the rare minds whose aspirations are as wide as the world," and he would be remembered as the "first distinguished British states- man whose Imperialism was that of Race and not of Empire." Believing that Rhodes was motivated chiefly by rapacious greed, critics had repeatedly failed to grasp his "higher mystic side."[204] Rhodes amassed wealth to fight the cause of racial reunion, Stead insisted, and through this to enact peace and justice on earth.

From his days editing the *Pall Mall Gazette* through to their long conversa- tions about the future, Stead had played a significant role in shaping and refin- ing Rhodes's political views. This is most apparent in Rhodes's shifting account of the United States. In his early writings, including the "Confession of Faith," he focused on the need to integrate the British Empire. It is only after he fell into Stead's orbit that the United States—as model, inspiration, and future epicenter of the race—assumed a more substantive role. Stead's influence did not go unnoticed. Shaw went as far as to claim that Rhodes's worldview was largely distilled from Stead. "It was his expression of the meaning of England, and the influence of Anglo-American ideas, that had created in Cecil Rhodes the ambition to paint with British red as much as possible of the map of Africa."[205] Others picked up on the American dimension. In 1903 Carnegie told Stead that "it was your words I'm sure that developed him; you were his teacher."[206] Stead's son, John, felt that the role of his father had been glossed over or ignored.

My father developed Rhodes's ideas and grafted his own on them. This was one of my father's methods. When he found anyone who would work with him to forward his ideals and, as in the case of Rhodes, was in a better posi- tion to do so than he was himself, he managed to get them to work out his ideas by persuading them that they were really their own, and he let them have all the credit because it was the end only that mattered to him. This was particularly the case with Rhodes's attitude to the U.S.A. Originally Rhodes's ideas were restricted entirely to the British Empire, but father

---

203. Rhodes, *Last Will*, 51–52.
204. Rhodes, *Last Will*, 56.
205. Albert Shaw, "William T. Stead," *American Review of Reviews*, June 1912, 696.
206. Carnegie to Stead, 30 May 1903, Fol 94, Carnegie papers.

inoculated him with the idea of extending it to the whole English-speaking world, and then gave him the whole credit.[207]

There is much truth in this. At a minimum, Stead embellished Rhodes's desire for union. While Rhodes was alive, Stead was cautious about Americanizing him in public. In *The Americanization of the World*, Rhodes was portrayed as a man who "never wavered from the idea of race alliance, and the promotion in all continents and in both hemispheres of the ascendency of the English-speaking man."[208] He would have preferred the "race unified under the Union Jack," and "would, no doubt, shrink from boldly adopting the formula that, if it could not be secured in any other way than by the admission of the various parts of the British Empire as States of the American Union, it had better be brought about in that way than not at all."[209] One implication of this passage was that Rhodes was unwilling to accept American supremacy. Yet the sentence is equivocal, perhaps deliberately so, for it could also mean that although Rhodes would not accept such a scheme "boldly," he might nevertheless consent if there was no alternative. Moreover, the subsequent passage contends that he had "so intense a longing to realize the unity of the race" that he would seek ways to cooperate "in the attainment of the ideal."[210] It is striking, though, that throughout the book it is Carnegie rather than Rhodes who is painted as an unabashed advocate of racial union under American leadership. This assessment was soon to change.

In *The Last Will and Testament of Cecil John Rhodes*, published in late 1902, Stead claimed the mantle of chief interpreter of Rhodes's political vision. The book crystallized many of the arguments that he had been making about his friend in the pages of the *Review of Reviews*. The process of Americanizing Rhodes was deepened and elaborated. It is an extraordinary literary concoction, a collage of assorted wills, parts of the "Confession of Faith," extracts from their extensive correspondence, and snippets of speeches and newspaper articles, interpolated with his own commentary and recollections. The aim was to present a coherent, elevating, authoritative narrative of Rhodes's beliefs and the relationship between the two men. Placing his final will in the context of his long-held commitment to racial utopia, the emphasis was on Rhodes the visionary, the dreamer of grand dreams. Stead was portrayed as his trusted

207. Prof. John Stead to G. C. Huckaby, undated letter, reproduced in Robertson, *Life and Death of a Newspaper*, 175.

208. Stead, *Americanization*, 222. See also his encomium in *"Lest We Forget"* (London, 1901), 123–24, where he focuses on Rhodes as an avatar of empire.

209. Stead, *Americanization*, 403, 404.

210. Stead, *Americanization*, 404.

lieutenant, the guardian of his secret plans, a steadfast friend and confidant who helped to give shape to Rhodes's deeply held but inchoate ideas.

Stead insisted on his own interpretive authority. From the moment they first met, he recounted, "I felt I understood Rhodes. I, almost alone, had the key to the real Rhodes, and I felt that from that day on it was my duty and my privilege to endeavour to the best of my ability to interpret him to the world." Their ideas were so close that "after the first talk with him . . . it was never 'my ideas' or 'your ideas' but always, 'our ideas.'"[211] Adamant that Rhodes had confided in him more than in anyone else, Stead suggested that he alone had full access to Rhodes's dreamworld. Throughout *The Last Will and Testament,* he claimed credit for shaping the views of his friend and hero. "Mr Rhodes always asserted that his own ideas had been profoundly modified and moulded by the *Pall Mall Gazette.*"[212] Stead boasted that he was responsible for expanding and redirecting Rhodes's racial utopianism. Whereas Rhodes had originally been committed to the absorption of the United States into the British Empire—a position that Stead thought ridiculous—the journalist had persuaded him that the reverse was more plausible. This had occurred during one of their long meetings in 1891. "It was in this conversation, after a close and prolonged argument, that he expressed his readiness to adopt the course from which he had at first recoiled—viz., that of securing the unity of the English-speaking race by consenting to the absorption of the British Empire in the American Union if it could not be secured any other way." Rhodes, he continued, thought the end so important that he was willing to accept the "sacrifice of the monarchical features and isolated existence of the British empire." Thereafter, Rhodes was supposedly unwavering in his commitment: "the ideal of English-speaking reunion assured its natural and final place at the centre of his political aspirations."[213] Race was more important than state sovereignty. "His fatherland . . . is coterminous with the use of the tongue of his native land."

> He was devoted to the old flag, but in his ideas he was American, and in his later years he expressed to me his unhesitating readiness to accept the reunion of the race under the Stars and Stripes if it could not be obtained in any other way. Although he had no objection to the Monarchy, he unhesitatingly preferred the American to the British Constitution, and the

211. Rhodes, *Last Will,* 83, 99. According to Whyte, the book was "never very widely known and long out of print" (*Life,* 273). In *Muckraker,* Robinson suggests (implausibly) that Stead was a *naïf,* manipulated by a cunning Rhodes.

212. Rhodes, *Last Will,* 79, 80.

213. Rhodes, *Last Will,* 103, 102.

text-book which he laid down for the guidance of his noviates was a copy of the American Constitution.[214]

The Americans had taught an invaluable lesson to the world, leading Rhodes to become a "Home Ruler first and an Imperialist afterwards." He recognized that in order to survive and flourish the empire had to adopt home rule throughout its extended domain, from Ireland to Australasia.

> To be a Rhodesian, then, of the true stamp you must be a Home Ruler and something more. You must be an Imperialist, not from mere lust of dominion or pride of race, but because you believe the Empire is the best available instrument for diffusing the principles of Justice, Liberty, and Peace throughout the world. Whenever Imperialism involves the perpetration of Injustice, the suppression of Freedom, and the waging of wars other than those of self-defence, the true Rhodesian must cease to be an imperialist. But a Home Ruler and Federalist, according to the principles of the American Constitution, he can never cease to be, for Home Rule is a fundamental principle, whereas the maintenance and extension of the Empire are only means to an end, and may be changed, as Mr Rhodes was willing to change them. If, for instance, the realisation of the greater ideal of Race Unity could only be brought about by merging the British Empire in the American Republic, Mr Rhodes was prepared to advocate that radical measure.[215]

This reads like an unmediated exposition of Stead's "responsible imperialism." Although it is clear that Rhodes and Stead shared a common vision of racial supremacy, and that Stead helped mold Rhodes's views about the United States, it is less apparent whether, or to what extent, Rhodes consistently endorsed the maximalist position Stead ascribed to him. The textual evidence presented in *The Last Will and Testament*, and in the Rhodes archive, offers some support, chiefly Rhodes's long 1891 letter, though even there Rhodes refers to "your" plan for political federation. Rhodes did not mention the subject in any of his (surviving) speeches. His final will, like the earlier iteration, is much clearer on the union of the empire than on the English-speaking peoples. None of the early biographical sketches of Rhodes, written largely by people who knew or worked for him, mention the idea of formal union with the United States, though all are clear about Rhodes's admiration for the country and his fervent desire to strengthen Anglo-American relations.[216] The

214. Rhodes, *Last Will*, 52, 63.

215. Rhodes, *Last Will*, 114.

216. Gordon le Sueur, *Cecil Rhodes* (London, 1913), ch. 15, discusses Rhodes's positive attitude to the United States and imperial federation (87); Philip Jourdan, *Cecil Rhodes* (London,

subject was not mentioned in Sidney Low's 1902 overview of Rhodes's political thinking, based on several "confidential" conversations with the imperialist stretching back to 1892. Rhodes averred that "the world was made for the service of man, and more particularly of civilised, white, European men, who were most capable of utilising the crude resources of Nature for the promotion of wealth and prosperity." Low did note Rhodes's view that the British Constitution was "an absurd anachronism," and that it should be "remodelled on the lines of the American Union, with federal self-governing Colonies as the constituent States."[217] However, he did not mention any desire to see the British Empire absorbed by the United States. Presumably Stead would have replied that Rhodes refused to share his deepest dreams with such men. They were not among the invincible Aristoi.

Stead's posthumous assessment of Rhodes blended admiration and censure. "Judging him by his stature in influence, in authority and in driving force," Rhodes "belonged to the order of archangels." But, Stead admonished, "he was a grey archangel, with a crippled wing," a character flaw that "caused him to pursue a somewhat devious course in the midst of the storm-winds of race-passion and political intrigue." In particular, Rhodes "was so devoted to his ends that almost all means were to him indifferent."[218] Low had identified a similar flaw, suggesting that for Rhodes "right and wrong were to be judged by large cosmic standards, not by the rules of morality which I suppose he thought were merely conventional."[219] For Stead the disjuncture was especially problematic. The imperative to "be like Christ" meant that both the ends of human action, and the means adopted to realize them, had to be defensible, pure, unadulterated. While Stead thought that Rhodes amply fulfilled the duty to act for the good of humanity, his adoption of questionable means was a mark against him. It was both morally blameworthy and politically unwise. Rhodes's cavalier attitude, Stead implied, had led him into folly in 1895 and

---

1911), states that "[h]is greatest wish was the unification of the Empire," while noting his desire for closer relations between the Empire and the United States (73, 75–76); Howard Hensman, *Cecil Rhodes* (London, 1902), ch. 9, emphasizes his support of imperial federation; Thomas Fuller, *The Right Honourable Cecil Rhodes* (London, 1910), 236–45, endorses Stead's account of Rhodes's religion and general political views; Baker, *Cecil Rhodes*, 116–17, recalled Rhodes's support for future American imperialism in South America. However, none of them say anything about formal Anglo-American union. Williams, *Cecil Rhodes*, largely follows Stead in outlining Rhodes's views, but doesn't address the question of union.

217. Low, "Personal Recollections," 835.

218. Rhodes, *Last Will*, 139. For similar wording, see Stead, *RoR*, 21 (June 1910), 589.

219. Low, "Personal Recollections," 839.

again at the turn of the century. While damaging, these mistakes were not enough to turn Stead against Rhodes. "And yet men marvel that I loved him—and love him still."[220]

Stead was determined to locate Rhodes's life and work in a comprehensible religious frame. Both *The Americanization of the World* and *The Last Will and Testament* hailed him as an exemplar of what an ecumenical religious spirit could achieve on a global scale. While admitting that Rhodes was not a believer in any traditional form of religion, Stead presented him as a devout "man of faith," contending that the source of his religion was passionate love of country and of race, and that he believed fervently in the providential destiny of the Anglo-Saxons. Rhodes fitted Stead's ideal of a "Civic Church," its members dedicated to the service of humanity. Stead also attempted to synthesize Rhodes's professed Darwinism and his purported spirituality. A "Darwinian in Search of God," the imperialist had long expressed an evolutionary understanding of human development.

> What is the distinctive feature of that doctrine? The perfection of the species attained by the elimination of the unfit; the favourable handicapping of the fit. The most capable species survives, the least capable goes to the wall. The perfecting of the fittest species among the animals, of the races among men, and then the conferring upon the perfected species or race the title-deeds of the future; that seemed to Mr Rhodes, though his Darwinian spectacles, the way in which God is governing His world, has governed it, and will continues to govern it, so far as we can foresee the future.[221]

According to Stead, Rhodes proceeded to identify the race that seemed most likely to serve as the "divine instrument in carrying out the divine idea over the whole planet." To do so, he applied a "threefold test": which people would best universalize "Justice-Liberty-Peace"?

> "What," asked Mr Rhodes, "is the highest thing in the world? Is it not the idea of justice? I know none higher. Justice between man and man—equal, absolute, impartial, fair play and all; that surely must be the first note of a perfected society. But, secondly, there must be Liberty, for without freedom there can be no justice. Slavery in any form which denies a man a right to be himself, and to use all his faculties to their best advantage, is, and must be, unjust. And the third note of the ultimate towards which our race is

---

220. Rhodes, *Last Will*, 112.

221. Rhodes, *Last Will*, 88, 95. For Stead's own views on evolution, see *"Lest We Forget"*, 33–35. He worried about the application of Darwinism to politics.

being must surely be that of Peace, of the industrial commonwealth as opposed to military clan or fighting Empire.[222]

Rhodes was adamant that the "English-speaking race" was the preeminent agent of global justice.[223] If united, it could assume the "government of the whole world."[224] This moralized, teleological understanding of evolution—issuing in human perfection and directed by a supernatural entity—bore little relation to Darwin's own subtle account. It read more like a theologically inflected variant of Reade's purposive developmentalism.

Readers of *The Last Will and Testament* were divided over the value of Rhodes's utopian vision. Stead would have been delighted by the correspondent in the *Illustrated London News* who wrote that the volume "teaches one lesson which should abash the world": "Never were the current estimates of an eminent man's character so signally shown to need revision." Rather than a "materialist," Rhodes was revealed as an unabashed "idealist."[225] The response in the United States ranged from bafflement to outrage. "It is well-nigh the universal opinion of the American newspapers," the *Literary Digest* reported, "that Mr Rhodes's dream of world federation, as told by Mr Stead, shows that the judgement of the great south African millionaire was not well balanced."[226] Incoherent, impossible, wild, grotesque, insane: these charges and more were leveled at the plan. It is no surprise that Dos Passos avoided mentioning Rhodes in *The Anglo-Saxon Century*. Not all Americans were so dismissive. Kennedy was a great admirer, writing in *The Pan-Angles*, his 1914 manifesto for

222. Rhodes, *Last Will*, 95, 97.

223. Rhodes, *Last Will*, 97. Progress, in this account, is defined by personal and collective elevation: "We go rather to the foremost of mankind, the most cultured specimens of the civilised race, the best men, in short, of whom we have any records or knowledge since history began. What these exceptionally—it may be prematurely—evolved individuals have attained is a prophecy of what the whole phalanx of humanity may be destined to reach. They are the highwater mark of the race up till now. Progress will consist in bringing mankind up to their level" (96).

224. Rhodes, *Last Will*, 74.

225. L. F. Austin, "Our Note Book," *Illustrated London News*, 12 April 1902, 516. A writer in the *Saturday Review* (12 July 1902) noted wryly that "[i]t need not be said that there is a good deal of Mr Stead as well as of Rhodes in the volume" (52).

226. "Was Cecil Rhodes Crazy?," *Literary Digest*, 14/16 (1902), 529. The report cites views from the *Pittsburgh Chronicle Telegraph* ("wild"); *New York World* ("streak of madness"); *Baltimore News* ("nightmare"); *Hartford Courant* ("illusory and impossible"); *Detroit Journal* ("it is doubtful if anything less sane ever came from a man supposed to be in his senses"); *New York Evening Post* ("almost grotesque"); *Chicago Evening Post* ("incoherent, wild, self-contradictory"); *Pittsburgh Despatch*; and the *Baltimore Sun*.

a federal racial state, that Rhodes was an inspiration, one of those seers who "visioned the whole race without losing sight of their own local fragment." Such men saw "the need of blocking intra-race frictions to maintain our inter-race supremacy."[227] But Kennedy was an exception. In death, as in life, Rhodes polarized opinion.

Carnegie was ambivalent about the imperialist. The two men never crossed paths, though Carnegie had attempted to engineer a meeting between them in 1892.[228] Fiercely protective of the paternity of the idea of racial reunion, he resented the praise Stead lavished on Rhodes. Following Rhodes's death, Stead sent Carnegie a copy of *The Last Will and Testament*, which elicited guarded praise. Carnegie described Rhodes's 1891 letter as "the most important thing I know about him—a great forecast."[229] But he always maintained that he had outlined the case first and that Stead had then persuaded Rhodes of its merits:

> What I ask now is this "My Look Ahead" etc. for which you have created me Prophet in Excelsis—was written before Mr Rhodes rose to the true ideal of "Race Reunion." It was your words I'm sure that developed him. You were his teacher. Nor did Mr R. ever read or did you ever tell him of *The Look Ahead* which as far as I know was the first reasoned essay on the subject?[230]

Happy to grant him precedence, Stead used the pages of the *Review of Reviews* to record that it was neither Rhodes nor himself, but Carnegie, who had first argued that Britain should be subsumed into the United States. "Mr Carnegie has the prior rights."[231] A decade later, Carnegie was still fretting, querying Stead about the source of his contention that Rhodes supported federation, while reiterating the novelty of his own prediction about the "re-union of the race, the British American Union."[232] Despite this sensitivity, Carnegie was happy to quote Rhodes for support. In 1904, he praised him for rejecting a myopic form of nationalist imperialism in favor of an expansive "race imperialism." In endowing the scholarship scheme, Rhodes "saw that it was to the

227. Kennedy, *Pan-Angles*, ix (and also: 172, 190, 202–3, 220–21).

228. Carnegie to Stead, 16 May 1892, Fol 16; Stead to Carnegie, 17 May 1892, Fol 16, Carnegie papers.

229. Carnegie to Stead, 14 May 1902, Fol 90, Carnegie papers.

230. Carnegie to Stead, 30 May 1903, Fol 9, Carnegie papers. These suspicions were also raised, less directly, in an earlier letter (14 July 1902, Fol 90).

231. W. T. Stead, *RoR*, 25 (June 1901), 582.

232. Carnegie to Stead, 21 February 1911, STED 1/16, Stead papers. Carnegie reiterated his belief in the unionist prophecy in another letter to Stead, 26 July 1911, STED 1/16, Stead papers.

Republic, not to British settlements, his country had to look for the coming reunion of his race, with Britain in her rightful place as parent of it all."[233]

Stead's reputation and influence faded during the Edwardian years, though he maintained a high profile on both sides of the Atlantic. His valorization of the "English-speaking race" wobbled but never disappeared. The plan to unify with the United States, he insisted in July 1902, was "no mere fantasy of dreaming theorists."[234] It was both highly desirable and eminently feasible, if only people seized the opportunity. But he was chastened by the South African calamity. In an essay published in the *Review of Reviews* in December 1903, he cast his eye over the history of the journal, and confessed that he had overestimated the English-speaking peoples. While declaring that he still subscribed to the views expressed in "To All English-Speaking Folk," he admitted that his account was marked by a "certain note of parochialism." "The English-speaking man," he continued, was surely "a very fine fellow," but he did not possess the monopoly of "all the virtues as that with which in those days I was wont to credit him." He too could fall prey to "demoniac possession," while other peoples, it turned out, had much to commend them. Stead declared a newfound "widened faith in man."[235] Yet even as he toned down some of his more bombastic claims, Stead never lost faith in the ultimate destiny of the race. Less than a year before the *Titanic* sank, Stead welcomed the recent Anglo-American Arbitration Treaty, suggesting to Bryce that it would serve as "an admirable means of propagandism for the English-speaking world idea."[236]

Stead believed that the *Review of Reviews*, and the wider campaign for racial unity, had achieved many of its goals. Although formal union between the powers still seemed a distant prospect, relations were much closer than before. There was widespread agreement about their shared identity and common interests. "That work has been pretty effectually accomplished," he wrote in 1911. He claimed a share of credit in the transformation.[237] During the Edwardian years, Stead routinely tied his advocacy of racial union to more ambitious

233. Carnegie, *Drifting Together*, 5–6. This is a pamphlet, originally published in the *London Express*, 14 October 1904, Box 246, Carnegie papers.

234. W. T. Stead, *RoR*, 26 (July 1902), 41.

235. W. T. Stead, *RoR*, 28 (December 1903), 571.

236. Stead to Bryce, 28 June 1911, MS 140, Fol 183–84, Bryce papers. He claimed that Carnegie was keen on the idea.

237. W. T. Stead, *RoR*, 43 (January 1911), 4–5. That same year, Frederick Henry Lynch, prolific writer and active member of the American peace movement, praised the accuracy of Stead's prognostications. Writing of the "brilliancy" of *Americanization*, he thought its claims about both future world federations and Americanization were correct: "Everything is setting that way": Lynch, *The Peace Problem* (New York, 1911), 14. Carnegie wrote a preface to the volume.

(though vague) dreams of an "international" or "world" state. In 1901, he was already chafing to move on to the next step in his plan to remake the world. "The work of the Twentieth Century is the completion of the destruction of the Nationalism Militant," he proclaimed. Recognition of the unity of the "the English-speaking races" was but a preliminary step, for it would be followed by the "Realisation of the International Ideal throughout the World."[238] Though light on detail, he seemed to mean the strengthening of international governance, and in particular the creation of a system of arbitration combined with the spread of the federal idea. Racial consolidation prefigured more expansive forms of universalism. His tireless advocacy of racial union was, Stead claimed in 1907, "no Chauvinistic desire to impose the will of these groups upon the rest of the world." Rather, the English-speaking peoples "march in the van of human progress, and anything that weakens their influence retards the rate of progress of the whole body."[239] Stead died, as he had lived, committed to the belief that racial reunification would unlock the full potential of humanity.

238. W. T. Stead, "Internationalism," *RoR*, 25 (January 1901), 35, 42. He reiterated the point about success five years later: "The cause of English-speaking unity is now almost a realised ideal." Stead, *RoR*, 33 (January 1906), 3.

239. W. T. Stead, *RoR*, 36 (October 1907), 357. On his continued commitment to the racial "civilizing mission," see Stead, *RoR*, 33 (May 1906), 456.

4

Artists in Reality

H. G. WELLS AND THE NEW REPUBLIC

We are in the beginning of a new time, with such forces of organisation and unification at work in mechanical traction, in the telephone and telegraph, in a whole wonderland of novel, space-destroying appliances, and in the correlated inevitable advance in practical education, as the world has never felt before.[1]

(H. G. WELLS)

Introduction

Herbert George Wells was one of the most prominent twentieth-century public intellectuals. Born into a struggling lower middle-class family in 1866, he later studied at the Normal School of Science in South Kensington, and embarked on a brief career as a school teacher, before turning to writing.[2] His prodigious output encompassed speculative fiction, literary criticism, educational theory, scientific investigation, philosophical reflection, and social and political theorizing. During the 1890s, he wrote a succession of hugely successful "scientific romances," starting with *The Time Machine*, which captured the public imagination and established his reputation as a visionary. Over the following decade, he carved out a name for himself as a challenging political thinker, elaborating a bold account of socialism while launching a coruscating assault on the shibboleths of Victorian and Edwardian society.[3] By the outbreak of war, he was one of the most famous writers in the world.

---

1. H. G. Wells, *Anticipations* (1901; Mineola, 1999), 127.

2. For a valuable account of his life, see David C. Smith, *H. G. Wells* (New Haven, CT, 1986).

3. Studies of his political thought and activity include John Partington, *Building Cosmopolis* (Aldershot, 2003); Partington, "H. G. Wells," *Utopian Studies*, 19/3 (2008), 517–76; Lyman Tower Sargent, "The Dream Mislaid," *The Wellsian*, 10 (1987), 20–32; Emma Planinc, "Catching

Wells developed one of the most sophisticated versions of the argument for unifying the "English-speaking Peoples."[4] In the early Edwardian years, he regarded a future synthesis of Britain and its settler colonies with the United States as both inevitable and desirable, their conjoined destiny to create a New Republic that would transcend existing territorial, political, and cultural divisions. This vast polity had the potential to transfigure the human condition, forming the core of a future world-state that would bring peace and justice to the earth. Utopia was within reach.

This chapter traces Wells's shape-shifting account of the New Republic, as well as offering a novel interpretation of the philosophical foundations of his political thought, focusing in particular on his commitment to an idiosyncratic version of pragmatism. Wells's "heretical metaphysical scepticism"—and in particular his nominalism—infused his writings on society and politics, underwriting his critique of both nationalism and racial science. His ardent antinationalism helped motivate a recurrent demand for the creation of vast "synthetic" political associations, including the New Republic, while his hostility to racial theorizing distinguished him from most other unionists. Insisting on a strict distinction between the "English-speaking peoples" and "Anglo-Saxonism," Wells grounded his account of the New Republic in shared language, not racial identity, although he ended up reproducing a racialized vision of world order. I open the chapter with an account of Wells's promotion of the New Republic, before turning to his pragmatism and its political implications. I close with a discussion of Wells's conflicted attitude to imperial rule, exploring how he struggled to reconcile his early support for the continuation of the British Empire with his dream of Anglo-America.

In the Beginning of a New Time: The Larger Synthesis

As the twentieth century dawned, Wells published a series of books and articles outlining a "New Republicanism" fit for a world in flux. *Anticipations* (1901), "The Discovery of the Future" (1902), and *Mankind in the Making* (1903) constituted, he proclaimed, "a general theory of social development

---

Up with Wells," *Political Theory*, 45/5 (2017), 637–58; Richard Toye, "H. G. Wells and the New Liberalism," *Twentieth Century British History*, 19/2 (2008), 156–85; Warren Wager, *H. G. Wells and the World State* (New Haven, CT, 1961); Wager, *H. G. Wells* (Middletown, 2004).

4. Wells used "English-speaking People" and "English-speaking Peoples" interchangeably in his writings on the topic, though he employed the latter formulation more frequently. For examples of each, see H. G. Wells, *Mankind* (London, 1903), 16, 138.

and of social and political conduct."[5] In combination, they offered a methodology for delineating the shape of things to come, a set of predictions about how existing trends would reshape the world, and assorted normative arguments defending the superiority of the future order. The consummation of the English-speaking peoples stood at the very core of Wells's vision.

Anticipations established his reputation as a seer of modernity.[6] Its huge success also had practical consequences for his career, opening doors for a lower-middle-class writer, bringing him to the attention of leading thinkers and politicians, and prompting invitations to join some of the most significant campaigning organizations of the time, including the Fabian Society and the Co-efficients dining club.[7] In part, the book was a response to the limitations of fiction as a vehicle of social criticism. Wells postulated that literature was "necessarily concrete and definite; it permits of no open alternatives; its aim of illusion prevents a proper amplitude of demonstration."[8] Unimpressed by the late Victorian flourishing of utopian literary speculation, even as he benefited from the appreciative audience it had helped to create, Wells thought that most writers, including William Morris, a man he had once greatly admired, were hopelessly naïve, principally because they failed to grapple properly with the legacy of Darwin.[9] Prophetic literature had become "polemical, cautionary, or idealistic, and a mere footnote and commentary to our present discussions."[10] Modern prophecy needed to adopt the scientific method to achieve credibility. Wells outlined his case in "The Discovery of the Future," a lecture delivered in early January 1902 at the Royal Institution, and subsequently published in *Nature*.[11] It attracted wide attention. He condemned the "retrospective habit," the tendency to privilege tradition over innovation, cause over effect, the past over the future. "Yet though foresight creeps into our politics and a reference to consequence into our morality, it is still the past

5. Wells, *Mankind*, v.

6. The book was first serialized in the *Fortnightly Review* and *North American Review* between April and December 1901.

7. On Wells's fraught relationship with the Fabians, see Smith, *H. G. Wells*, ch. 4; Partington, "H. G. Wells," 522–33.

8. Wells, *Anticipations*, 1–2n.

9. Wells, *Modern Utopia*, 12.

10. Wells, *Anticipations*, 1–2n. Benjamin Kidd's *Social Evolution* (1894) was the only "serious forecast" of "things to come," though Wells was unconvinced by it. He later changed his mind about the critical functions of the novel: Wells, "The Contemporary Novel" (1912), in Wells, *An Englishman Looks at the World* (London, 1914), 148–69. On his shifting views about the purpose of literature, see Simon James, *Maps of Utopia* (Oxford, 2012), ch. 1.

11. H. G. Wells, "The Discovery of the Future," *Nature*, 65/1684 (1902), 326–31.

that dominates our lives."[12] Wells was far from alone in voicing anxiety about the burdens of history. Lord Acton, for example, had observed in 1895 that the nineteenth century was saturated with "historic ways of thought," a ubiquitous form of "historicism or historical-mindedness."[13] The "retrospective habit" offered epistemic consolation, Wells implied, because most people believed that while the past was fixed and knowable, the future lay beyond the horizon of comprehension. This was a ruinous mistake. Not only was the past far less certain than usually supposed—as geologists had recently demonstrated by drastically rewriting the history of earth—but knowledge of the future was now attainable. Indeed, Wells decreed, "along certain lines and with certain qualifications and limitations, a working knowledge of things in the future is a possible and practicable thing." Is it really, he asked,

> such an extravagant and hopeless thing to suggest that, by seeking for op-
> erating causes instead of for fossils and by criticising them as persistently
> and thoroughly as the geological record has been criticised, it may be pos-
> sible to throw a searchlight of inference forward instead of backwards and
> to attain a knowledge of coming things as clear, as universally convincing
> and infinitely more important to mankind than the clear vision of the past
> that geology has opened to us during the nineteenth century?[14]

The natural sciences had little difficulty embracing this temporal orientation. The pressing question was whether vital aspects of the human future could be foreseen. Wells rejected the possibility of predicting the course of individual lives, or of small-scale groups, arguing that only large aggregates and general "operating causes" could be grasped. The possibilities were magnificent, world-transforming, and tantalizingly close to fruition. Yet despite these sweeping claims, his catalogue of likely future changes was disappointingly vague.

> But for the nearer future, while man is still man, there are a few general
> statements that seem to grow more certain. It seems to be pretty generally
> believed to-day that our dense populations are in the opening phase of a
> process of diffusion and aeration. It seems pretty inevitable also that at least
> the mass of white population in the world will be forced some way up the

12. Wells, "Discovery of the Future," 328, 327.

13. John Acton, "Inaugural Lecture on the Study of History" in *Lectures on Modern History*, ed. J. N. Figgis and R.V. Laurence (London, 1906), 22. See also Dicey, *Introduction to the Study of the Law of the Constitution*, 14. For more on "historical-mindedness," see Bell, *Reordering the World*, ch. 5.

14. Wells, "Discovery of the Future," 329.

scale of education and personal efficiency in the next two or three decades. It is not difficult to collect reasons for supposing and such reasons have been collected, that in the near future, in a couple of hundred years as one rash optimist has written, or in a thousand or so, humanity will be definitely and consciously organising itself as a great world State, a great world State that will purge from itself much that is mean, much that is bestial, and much that makes for individual dullness and dreariness, grey mess and wretchedness in the world of to-day.[15]

Between his brief comment about the improvement of the mass of "white people" and his dream of a world-state lay intimations of the New Republic, though in the address Wells did not discuss the future polity explicitly. He was likewise unclear about how the temporal gestalt switch was to be achieved. The lecture was more a promissory note than a systematic elaboration of a futurist science.

Anticipations attempted to make good on that promise, identifying the "operative causes" that would determine the course of the new century. Proclaiming it the "first attempt to forecast the human future as a whole and to estimate the relative power of this and that great systems of influence," Wells later called *Anticipations* the "keystone to the main arch of my work," and he returned obsessively to its main themes throughout his career.[16] It was, he told the artist Cosmo Rowe, "my <u>magnum opus</u>." Wells hoped that his provocative vision might seed ideas about the necessity of radical social and political change, helping to birth the very thing it claimed to foresee. Exhorting the novelist Arnold Bennett to spread "my gospel," he confided his belief that "a real first-class boom and uproar and discussion about this book will do an infinite amount of good in the country." Wells aimed to reach a large audience, drawing the attention of "parsons and country doctors" as well as the denizens of the London literary scene.[17] He achieved his goal: the book was a best seller throughout the Angloworld, elevating him to the top rank of intellectual celebrity.[18]

Wells analyzed how assorted social, political, and technological processes were dissolving venerable patterns of power and privilege, and heralding new

---

15. Wells, "Discovery of the Future," 330–31. The lecture continues to inspire futurologists—see, for example, Martin Rees, *On the Future* (Princeton, NJ, 2018), 13–14.

16. H. G. Wells, *An Experiment in Autobiography* (1934; London, 2008), II, 643, 645.

17. Wells to Cosmo Rowe, 27 December 1901, *The Correspondence of H. G. Wells*, ed. David Smith (London, 1998), I, 390 (underlining in original); Wells to Bennett, 25 November 1901, *Arnold Bennett and H. G. Wells*, ed. Harris Wilson (Urbana, 1960), 68.

18. On its reception, see Smith, *H. G. Wells*, 92–95, 97ff.

forms of human subjectivity and political association. The English-speaking peoples were both agents and products of change. The astonishing power of new transport and communications systems—the "distinctive feature of the nineteenth century"—propelled the argument. Altering the very conditions of human existence, "[m]echanism" had triggered more than a "mere" revolution; it had catalyzed an "absolute release from the fixed condition about which human affairs circled." The reconfiguration of space and time augured a fundamental change in geopolitical ordering. Technology was "abolishing locality," dissolving traditional understandings of space, territory, and political identity.[19] As people embraced their ability to move and settle at will, territorial models of politics would be rendered irrelevant, and innovative modes of political life would emerge. "Mechanism" provided both the infrastructural means through which the world would be transformed and—in the elevation of scientific rationalism to a pervasive governing ideology—the basis for an ethos that would create new types of human and practices of rule. Parodying strains of contemporary utopianism, Chesterton painted Wells as the man who believed most fervently that "science would take charge of the future."[20]

The New Republic would be initiated by small groups of individuals, "and quite possibly in some cases wealthy men," who would challenge existing structures of political and economic power. These embryonic New Republicans—an emergent technocratic class of "efficients"—would act as a largely uncoordinated secret society, an "informal and open freemasonry," to bring about the next phase in human history. Groups would slowly coalesce, recognizing a common purpose and need for collaborative action. Sooner or later, they would form a "functional social body" composed of (among others) scientists, engineers, teachers, administrators, and managers.[21] Here Wells was channeling the obsession with "national efficiency" that gripped swathes of the Edwardian intelligentsia, fearful that the British public and state administration alike were plagued by torpor and ineptitude.[22] Rigorously planned, well-governed, and populated by highly educated individuals, the New Republic would be a beacon of hyperefficiency. However, Wells cautioned that the developmental process was beset with danger. The efficients would come into

19. Wells, *Anticipations*, 3, 44, 122, 74. For interesting commentary on Wells as a preeminent thinker of the "global industrial age," see Deudney, *Bounding Power*, chs. 8–9.

20. Chesterton, *Napoleon of Notting Hill*, 15.

21. Wells, *Anticipations*, 155, 81.

22. On "national efficiency," see G. R. Searle, *The Quest for National Efficiency* (Berkeley, 1971); Bernard Semmel, *Imperialism and Social Reform* (Cambridge, MA, 1960); Chika Tonooka, "Reverse Emulation and the Cult of Japanese Efficiency in Edwardian Britain," *Historical Journal*, 60/1 (2017), 95–119.

conflict with other social formations determined to halt their relentless march—the traditional landed aristocracy, the "helpless, superseded poor," now redundant, a social residuum he termed the "people of the Abyss," and finally "a possibly equally great number of non-productive persons living in and by social confusion."[23] The New Republicans would win out eventually, their greater organizational skills and intelligence guaranteeing victory.

Wells drew the purported mechanisms of change, as well as the end to be achieved, from debates over Anglo-American union. The cluster of associations that had emerged to promote cooperation following the Venezuela crisis represented a "preliminary sigh before the stirring of a larger movement." He scorned their activities, seeing them as principally dedicated to "entertaining travelling samples of the American leisure class in guaranteed English country houses," setting up meetings with "real titled persons"—the sarcasm drips from the page—and attending lectures by "respectable English authors."[24] But they were nevertheless a sign of things to come, a portent of synthesis.

The role assigned to human agency in this epic of world-making was unclear. Wells often argued that the New Republic would only materialize if it was willed by enough people. It required dynamic leadership, collaborative action, and careful planning. Alive to the daunting technical challenges facing humanity, and keen to grasp the possibilities they engendered, the New Republicans would be consummate "artists in reality." Their artistry combined two primary features: a desire for order, efficiency, and simplicity that was harnessed to a zealous commitment—embedded at the heart of their "ethical frame"—to construct a world-state.[25] Fusing aesthetic sensibility and political vision, they would work ceaselessly to reweave the threads of reality, transfiguring prevailing ideas about social order, political institutions, and the ends of human life. Elsewhere, however, Wells indicated that the new world would emerge regardless of human intervention, a result of socio-technical developments "with all the inevitableness and all the patience of a natural force." The "final attainment" of the Larger Synthesis appeared to be a process acting "independent of any collective or conscious will in man, as being the expression of a greater Will," and it was "working now, and may work out to its end vastly, and yet at times almost imperceptibly, as some huge secular movement in Nature," the equivalent of tectonic shifts in the earth's crust or the annihilation of mountain ranges.[26] Here we see the clash between Wells's scientific

23. Wells, *Anticipations*, 56.
24. Wells, *Anticipations*, 147.
25. Wells, *Anticipations*, 167.
26. Wells, *Anticipations*, 139, 146–47.

naturalism and the recurrent mysticism that ran through his writing. The result, however it was attained, would be a political order populated by a new
type of human, whose personality would be attuned to perpetual technological change and novel forms of living, working, and thinking.

The coming time would be an age of vast political associations. Wells identified several "spacious movements of coalescence" as possible vehicles of future
synthesis: Anglo-Saxonism, the "allied but finally very different" ideology of
British imperialism, and Pan-German, Pan-Slavic, and Pan-Latin groupings.
He also predicted that the brutality meted out by the "white" powers would
catalyze the unification of the "'Yellow' peoples'" of East Asia. Wells was skeptical about the likely success of most Pan-movements. The Pan-Slavic and the
Pan-Latin peoples were too weak and divided to form a durable polity. A Pan-
Germanic movement was feasible, not least because the Germans exhibited
remarkable technological prowess and had the most "efficient" middle classes
in Europe, but they were hamstrung by a political system at once too aristocratic and monarchical. They would fail to draw willing support for accession,
meaning that a German attempt to conquer Europe entailed war with France
to the West or Russia to the East. A more likely outcome, Wells predicted, was
a negotiated compromise between the continental powers, leading to the formation of a federal European union.[27]

For Wells, New Republican ideals would be best realized by the fusion of
the United States and the British colonial empire. "A great federation of white
English-speaking peoples," he claimed, was both likely and desirable during
the coming decades. Again stressing the significance of agency, Wells contended that the main bar to realizing the New Republic was a lack of "stimulus," a political shock that would focus minds and unleash action, although he
speculated that German naval expansion—a source of constant anxiety at the
time—and the potential emergence of an East Asian synthesis might precipitate change.[28] He rejected the argument that the very success of British settler
colonialism, populating dynamic new states across the world, corroded the
social and territorial basis for unity. Proponents of this pessimistic line had
forgotten, if they had ever realized, that the "epoch of post-road and sailing-
ship" had come to an end, and that new communications technologies
meant that planet-spanning associations were now viable.[29] However, the

27. Wells, *Anticipations*, 143, 145.

28. Wells, *Anticipations*, 146, 145–46. For a near-contemporary account of the "panic" over
German naval rearmament, see F. W. Hirst, *The Six Panics and Other Essays* (London, 1913),
59–103.

29. Wells, *Anticipations*, 127.

English-speaking peoples would not be governed from London—*Anticipations* was no hymn to lasting British predominance. Wells argued that the United States embodied the ideal of efficiency more successfully than anywhere else. It was already pulling ahead of Britain economically; political and military ascendancy would follow soon after. Consequently, the epicenter of any future union of the English-speaking peoples would be located in a new megalopolis that would sprawl between Chicago and the Atlantic. Like Carnegie, flying his patchwork ensign over Skibo, Wells mused that the New Republic would require its own elaborate iconography. The "ingenious persons" who pestered the London newspapers about arcane points of heraldry, he observed wryly, would relish the "very pleasing topic of an Anglo-American flag."[30]

Like most advocates of unity, Wells was unclear about the institutional structure of the New Republic. He referred to powers that would be possessed by the "federal government," but alternated between calling it a "federation" and "confederation."[31] Recognizing that knotty constitutional problems had to be surmounted, especially the clash between monarchical and republican models of government, he was blithely confident of success. Providential deliverance was rooted less in belief in an overmastering god—as it was for Stead—than in the transformative power of social forces then reshaping the world. He asserted that the New Republic would also resolve the vexed status of Ireland and South Africa, "two open sores of incorrigible wrong," for while they would never be happy under the incompetent administration of the British Empire, a federation of the English-speaking peoples would make it possible for them to achieve "equal fellowship," thus removing the sources of bitterness and allowing them to flourish.[32] Whatever institutional form the New Republic assumed, it would command a huge joint fleet and contain at least one hundred million "sound-bodied and educated and capable *men*." Ruling the largest empire in history, it would administer most of the existing British territories, as well as much of the Caribbean, the Americas, the Pacific, and the "larger part of black Africa."[33] Entrusted to an unprecedentedly large polity, and injected with an enervating dose of "efficiency," the civilizing mission could be enacted on a global stage.

30. Wells, *Anticipations*, 148, 148n. I discuss the significance of political symbolism, including flags, in chapter 6.

31. Wells, *Anticipations*, 148, 146; Wells, *Mankind*, 391.

32. Wells, *Anticipations*, 148–49.

33. Wells, *Anticipations*, 146. Italics in original. Oddly, and without argument, Wells also suggested that the union might in time include the Scandinavian countries. He didn't return to this point.

Adamant that his vision of the future was no idle fantasy, Wells regarded Anglo-American consolidation "not only as a possible, but as a probable, thing."[34] By the turn of the second millennium, it would be an achieved fact. However, Wells offered conflicting accounts of the political inflection of his proposals. He wrote to one correspondent that *Anticipations* was the "prospectus of a new revolutionary movement," and boasted to another that it was "designed to undermine and destroy the monarchy, monogamy, faith in God & respectability & the British Empire, all under the guise of speculation about motor cars & electrical heating."[35] Yet he informed Stead that the book was intended as "a sketch of a possible new Liberalism" that might supersede well-intentioned but obsolete strands of contemporary liberal thought, a point he also made to the young Winston Churchill.[36] Oscillation between audacious revolutionary claims and the profession of gradualism marked Wells's political thinking at the time, and it is perhaps best to read his work as trying (though often failing) to reconcile two temporal registers, a relatively modest liberal-socialist reformism aimed at influencing contemporary British debate and a hugely ambitious vision of world transformation that necessitated the dissolution of the very world he was otherwise seeking to modify. It was unclear how they could be rendered compatible.

Some race unionists saw Angloworld consolidation as the potential end of history, the apex of global political organization, while others regarded it as a transitional phase, a step on the road to a yet grander mode of political life. Wells fell squarely in the latter camp. He thought that the final stage of human political evolution—on Earth at least—would be the creation of a universal world-state, an all-encompassing synthesis of the New Republic and the other predominant powers. Birthing something greater than itself, the transatlantic polity would be self-overcoming. By the year 2000, the federation would most likely set in motion the incorporation of the European union and the "yellow state." A full-fledged universal polity would emerge only after at least another century had passed, though as he warned in "The Discovery of the Future," it might take as long as a thousand years.[37] There was no guarantee that this process would be peaceful. The synthetic associations would battle for global domination unless or until their energies could be harnessed to create a higher

---

34. Wells, *Anticipations*, 146.

35. Wells to Elizabeth Healey, 2 July 1901, and Wells to Joseph Edwards, 7 November 1901, *Correspondence*, I, 379, 383.

36. Wells to Stead, 31 October 1901, cited in Joseph Baylen, "W. T. Stead and the Early Career of H. G. Wells, 1895–1911," *Huntington Library Quarterly*, 38/1 (1974), 61; Wells to Churchill, 19 November 1901, *Correspondence*, I, 457.

37. Wells, *Anticipations*, 177; Wells, "Discovery of the Future," 331.

unity. "[T]hese syntheses or other similar synthetic conceptions, if they do not contrive to establish a rational social unity by sanely negotiated unions, will be forced to fight for physical predominance in the world."[38] Wells was tramping well-trodden ground—such visions, as we shall see in chapter 5, were essayed in science fictional narratives of the future—though he offered a more detailed analysis of the mechanism of change, and the sociopolitical foundations of such unities, than most of his contemporaries. Although Wells had initially presented *Anticipations* as a work of scientifically informed social prophecy, it ended as spirited advocacy, celebrating the virtues of the New Republic and the value of English-speaking leadership. It had more in common with his scintillating scientific romances than he cared to admit. As he confessed a few years later, "I had intended simply to work out and foretell, and before I had finished I was in a fine full blast of exhortation."[39]

Wells returned to the theme of consolidation in *Mankind in the Making*, published in 1903 as a sequel to *Anticipations*. Dedicated to "man-making," molding citizens fit for the New Republic, the book dwelt in particular on improving child-rearing practices and the design of educational regimes appropriate for the nascent technological age.[40] Wells's explicit frame of reference was the "English-speaking community," its teeming multitude of citizens "scattered under various flags and governments throughout the world." It was essential to comprehend the whole of this distributed polity, "unless our talk of co-operation, of reunion, is no more than sentimental dreaming."[41] Once again, he argued that technological and political developments were tending toward the emergence of a "new State," a "great confederation" of "republican communities" all "speaking a common language, possessing a common living body of literature and a common scientific and, in its higher stages at least, a

38. Wells, *Anticipations*, 139.

39. H. G. Wells, *The Future in America* (1906; London, 2016), 17.

40. Wells discussed the book at length with the political theorist Graham Wallas, whom he had met after the publication of *Anticipations*. Wallas's wife, Ada, wrote to Jane Wells that "Graham is in a state of real enthusiasm over H. G.'s books": 12 November 1901, GB 97, Wallas papers. As Wallas commented on Wells's work, so Wells provided input into Wallas's *Human Nature in Politics* (London, 1908). See, for example, Wallas to Wells, 11 August 1902, 17 September 1902, 8 October 1902, and 21 October 1902, Wallas papers. For Wallas's glowing view of *New Worlds for Old*, see Wallas to Wells, 10 November 1907. On their relationship, see Bell, "Pragmatic Utopianism and Race"; Martin Wiener, *Between Two Worlds* (Oxford, 1971), 77–78, 107–8. Wallas stars as Willersley in *The New Machiavelli*.

41. Wells, *Mankind*, 34, vii. It was originally serialized in the *Fortnightly Review* and *Cosmopolitan*, an American journal.

common education organisation."[42] However, his analysis was marked by spatial ambiguity. Despite opening and closing with an encomium to the English-speaking peoples, the bulk of *Mankind in the Making* refers only to Britain and the United States.[43] Canada, Australia, and New Zealand are tellingly absent. The distribution of attention is never explained, but it indicated that Wells's primary interest was in Anglo-American unification. While there were significant political obstacles to overcome, the underlying similarities between the Angloworld communities were of far greater significance.[44] "Until grave cause has been shown to the contrary," he declaimed, "there is every reason why all men who speak the same language, think the same literature and are akin in blood and spirit, and who have arrived at the great constructive conception that so many minds nowadays are reaching, should entirely disregard these old separations."[45] The territorial boundaries separating the English-speaking peoples would be transcended. It was essential, both for the scattered membership and for the wider world, to acknowledge that they were one people endowed with a common destiny, a community that "should become aware of itself collectively and should think as a whole."[46]

Carnegie played a notable but ambivalent role in Wells's writing about the New Republic. In *Anticipations*, he was cast as an exemplary American "efficient," with Wells insisting that such men were "displaying a strong disinclination to found families of functionless shareholders, and a strong disposition to contribute, by means of colleges, libraries, and splendid foundations, to the future of the whole English-speaking world."[47] Given his desire to find wealthy men to lead the New Republic, it is striking that Wells seems to have been unaware of—or to have simply ignored—Carnegie's role in initiating a transatlantic dialogue on the issue a decade earlier. After all, he fitted the model of the philanthropist dedicated to Angloworld consolidation that Wells thought might galvanize change. As we shall see, Wells was not yet finished with the puckish businessman.

Wells's prospectus of global transformation attracted its share of criticism, even from those largely sympathetic to the project it outlined. A keen admirer of the book, Churchill chided him for exaggerating the velocity and depth of change. Wells replied acidly that those born with Churchill's privilege rarely

---

42. Wells, *Mankind*, 391. For an excellent account of Wells's reckoning with the "crisis of manhood," see Bradley Deane, *Masculinity and the New Imperialism* (Cambridge, 2014), ch. 7.

43. Wells, *Mankind*, vii, 34.

44. Wells, *Mankind*, 260, 266.

45. Wells, *Mankind*, 27.

46. Wells, *Mankind*, 361.

47. Wells, *Anticipations*, 150, 151–52; see also Wells, *Mankind*, 339.

saw the world around them clearly. "I really do not think that you people who gather in great country homes realize the pace of things."[48] Stead was enthusiastic about Wells's confident predictions, welcoming them as confirmation of his own long-held beliefs. He had been one of the first to encourage Wells's early literary efforts, using the pages of the *Review of Reviews* to commend *The Time Machine* and its prodigious author. Wells acknowledged the debt he owed to the older man, once writing to Grant Richards that "I shall never cease to be grateful."[49] In a glowing long review of *Anticipations*, Stead admired Wells's attempt to "forecast the direction of the laws and forces now governing human society." Although he thought that Wells overemphasized the material determinants of historical change, thus downplaying the importance of religion, he was fulsome in his praise.

> From the day on which I read "The Time Machine" I recognized him as a man of original genius, an impression which was deepened by his subsequent stories; but I had no idea, until I read "Anticipations" month by month as they came out in the *Fortnightly*, that he was capable of taking so comprehensive a sweep and of formulating upon so many and such varied data a philosophical conception of the probable destiny of the human race.[50]

Stead likewise extolled the virtues of "The Discovery of the Future," and hailed the publication of *Mankind in the Making*.[51] Both confirmed his initial impressions of Wells's talent. Stead was quick to pinpoint the conspicuous similarities between Wells and Rhodes. The writer, like the imperialist, Stead told his readers, "thinks in continents; and there are not many such men amongst us to-day." He reiterated the point in a letter to Wells, arguing that the "idea of the gradual evolution of a New Republic so closely resembles the underlying thought of Cecil Rhodes." He requested a meeting to discuss their

48. Churchill to Wells, 17 September 1901; Wells to Churchill, 19 November 1901, *Correspondence*, I, 457. Churchill also criticized Wells's vision of rule by experts. Richard Toye argues that Churchill probably took the phrase "English-speaking peoples" from Wells: Toye, "H. G. Wells and Winston Churchill" in Steven McLean (ed.), *H. G. Wells* (Newcastle, 2008), 147–61.

49. Wells to Grant Richards, 6 November 1895, *Correspondence*, I, 249. Wells mentions Stead's own utopian work, *The Despised Sex* (1903), in passing in *Modern Utopia*, 15. See also Stead to Wells, 8 November 1897, S-456, Wells papers.

50. W. T. Stead, *RoR*, 24 (October 1901), 615.

51. W. T. Stead, *RoR*, 27 (January 1903), 52; Stead to Wells, 2 September 1903 and 20 February 1902, S-456, Wells papers.

shared ideas.[52] Wells replied cautiously. "It is very curious if I have come into a sort of agreement with the underlying ideas of Rhodes."[53] They subsequently met and engaged in occasional correspondence, though Stead was never as close to Wells as he was to Rhodes and Carnegie. This might explain the otherwise puzzling fact that he did not mention Wells's New Republican vision in his correspondence with either of them.

Wells followed the meteoric career of Rhodes with considerable interest. He was impressed by Sidney Low's posthumous sketch of the imperialist as a man of almost supernatural persuasive powers, a great talker and a bold "dreamer of dreams," albeit someone incapable of consistent or sustained reasoning.[54] Wells praised Low's account as a "first class portrait, critical, wide, concrete and vivid."[55] Elsewhere—as I discuss later—he sought to distance himself from Rhodes, chiefly by stressing the different ways in which they conceptualized Anglo-America. Yet the resemblance in aim and ambition was hard to deny. In his *Experiment in Autobiography*, written three decades later, Wells acknowledged the affinity between his early work and that of Rhodes, "a man of large conceptions and strange ignorances."

> Much the same ideas that were running through my brain round about 1900, of a great English-speaking English-thinking synthesis, leading mankind by sheer force of numbers, wealth, equipment and scope, to a progressive unity, must have been running through his brain also. He was certainly no narrow worshipper of the Union Jack, no abject devotee of the dear Queen Empress.

Wells argued that the Rhodes scholarships had been designed to corrode existing political boundaries and facilitate cooperation between peoples, signaling "a real greatness of intention, though warped by prejudices and uncritical assumptions."[56] He saw Rhodes as a fellow traveler in the attempt to think

---

52. W. T. Stead, *RoR*, 25 (October 1901), 640; Stead to Wells, 29 October 1901, S-456, Wells papers. See also the discussion in Baylen, "W. T. Stead and the Early Career of H. G. Wells," 60.

53. Wells replies (31 October 1901): Baylen, "W. T. Stead and the Early Career of H. G. Wells," 61.

54. Low, "Some Personal Recollections of Cecil Rhodes."

55. Wells to Low, 7 May 1902, *Correspondence*, I, 399–400. See also Wells to Low, 10 May 1902 and 26 May 1902, *Correspondence*, I, 401. Wells's brother, Fred, lived in South Africa—see, for example, H. G. Wells's letter to him discussing the Jameson raid, 24 January 1896, *Correspondence*, I, 258–59. The raid was, Herbert wrote, "a Capitalistic enterprise, though Jameson himself is a gallant man enough."

56. Wells, *Experiment in Autobiography*, II, 559, 760.

beyond the parochial sovereign state, to build a new world order on the crumbling ruins of the old.

Wells, too, dreamt of the stars. Whereas Rhodes looked to the heavens and yearned to colonize all he saw, Wells, possessed of a far more capacious imagination, envisaged the dispersal of humanity across the universe and its eventual transfiguration. What he had rendered in fictional form, he reiterated as social prophecy. The past century, he lectured the audience at the Royal Institution, had seen more changes in the "conditions of human life" than witnessed in the previous millennium. "Everything seems pointing to the belief that we are entering upon a progress that will go on, with an ever-widening and ever more confident stride, for ever." This "kinetic reorganisation" opened an exciting new chapter in the history of the species. "We are in the beginning of the greatest change that humanity has ever undergone." The infinite void beckoned, sparking Wells to sketch the lineaments of a posthuman future, a yet grander synthesis. "All this world is heavy with the promise of greater things, and a day will come, one day in the unending succession of days, when beings who are now latent in our thoughts and hidden in our loins, shall stand upon this earth as one stands upon a footstool and shall laugh and reach out their hands amidst the stars."[57] The New Republic was a bold first step on the road to transcendence.

Evolutionary Theory and the Transformation of Philosophy

Wells observed once that his was a "Balfourian age" characterized by profound epistemic doubt about religion, ethics, and politics. A time of both trepidation and excitement, it had, he wrote a few years later, generated an "intellectual spring unprecedented in the world's history."[58] Darwinism was the pivotal development, opening new vistas on natural history and human destiny, but a philosophical revolution was unfolding in its wake. Acknowledging that Athens represented the peak of human intellectual achievement, Wells claimed that late nineteenth-century philosophical work bore comparison.[59] Its most important expression was the "revival and restatement of nominalism under

57. Wells, "Discovery of the Future," 331. He reproduced this lyrical passage in Wells, *New Worlds for Old* (London, 1908), 241.

58. Wells, "Contemporary Novel," 160, 161–62. Wells praised Balfour's skepticism: Wells to Balfour, 26 August 1904, *Correspondence*, II, 41.

59. H. G. Wells, *First and Last Things* (1908; London, 2016), 7, 10.

the name of pragmatism."[60] He saw himself as part of the revolutionary vanguard.

During the Edwardian years, Wells forged a synthesis of evolutionary theory and pragmatist philosophy. Viewing the world as part of an unfolding evolutionary scheme, he adopted the framework developed by the eminent biologist T. H. Huxley, "Darwin's bulldog." Huxley drew on his imposing scientific authority to prescribe the form and limits of evolutionary explanation. While propagating a strict Malthusianism, arguing that natural history was a story of "ceaseless modification and the internecine struggle for existence of living things," he famously distinguished "cosmic" from "ethical" evolution.[61] The former comprised the "competition of each with all" that applied to every living thing; the latter referred to the development of human moral sentiments that repudiated the "gladiatorial theory of existence."[62] As D. G. Ritchie put it, "[W]hen these ideals have once arisen, they make social progress become something different from mere organic evolution, though, of course, such progress must, for a metaphysical theory, fall within evolution as a conception applicable to the universe as a whole."[63] In principle, the Huxleian configuration of autonomy and constraint was flexible, leaving considerable scope for human flourishing, but the conclusions he drew from it were bleak. He painted a picture of human fragility in which cosmic and ethical processes were locked in unremitting conflict.[64] Cosmic evolution—a "tenacious and powerful enemy as long as the world lasts"—was vastly more powerful than the delicate

60. Wells, "Contemporary Novel," 163. For his earliest sustained account of nominalism, see "The Rediscovery of the Unique" (1891), in Robert Philmus and David Hughes (eds.), *H. G. Wells* (Berkeley, 1975), 22–31. On historical debates over nominalism, see Wells, *The Outline of History*, ed. W. Wagar (1920; New York, 2004), II, 210–17.

61. T. H. Huxley, "Evolution and Ethics" (1893), in James Paradis and George Williams (eds.), *T. H. Huxley's "Evolution and Ethics"* (Princeton, NJ, 1989), 61. See also James Paradis, *T. H. Huxley* (Lincoln, 1979).

62. T. H. Huxley, "Prolegomena" (1894) and "Evolution and Ethics" in Paradis and Williams, *Huxley's "Evolution and Ethics"*, 62, 140.

63. David Ritchie, review of Kidd, *Social Evolution*, *International Journal of Ethics*, 5/1 (1894), 110–11. Among other things, Huxley sought to refute Herbert Spencer's naturalized evolutionary ethics, a task also pursued by Henry Sidgwick and G. E. Moore. See here Fritz Allhoff, "Evolutionary Ethics from Darwin to Moore," *History and Philosophy of the Life Sciences*, 25/1 (2003), 51–79.

64. Huxley, "Evolution and Ethics," 139. See also Hale, *Political Descent*, 206–20. For the Malthusian context, see Gregory Claeys, "The 'Survival of the Fittest' and the Origins of Social Darwinism," *Journal of the History of Ideas*, 61/2 (2000), 223–40.

ethical process, and it would eventually annihilate human progress.[65] Imagine a garden, Huxley asked his audience. If left untended, a profligate nature would soon overrun that carefully nurtured product of human cultivation, and the gardener faced a Sisyphean battle to maintain order and harmony, a battle that nature would always win in the end. Settler colonialism exhibited a similar dynamic. If a thriving colony managed to establish peace and affluence, its population would begin to increase rapidly, leading to ever-fiercer resource conflicts and the "cosmic struggle for existence." It would be undone by its own success. There was no escape from evolutionary fate. "Eden," Huxley sighed, "would have its serpent."[66]

A former student of Huxley, and an avid reader of his work, Wells adopted (while relabeling) this evolutionary framework, agreeing that the social and political world should be viewed as "aspects of one universal evolving scheme." He shared Huxley's ardent Malthusianism, declaring in *Anticipations* that "no more shattering book" than the *Essay on Population* had ever been published.[67] "Man," he wrote, "is the creature of a struggle for existence," and the key to life was "reproductive competition among individualities."[68] His early fiction experimented with these ideas, elaborating a chillingly pessimistic account of the human future. The guiding theme of *The Time Machine*, Wells informed Huxley, was evolutionary "degeneration following security."[69] He also adopted Huxley's distinction between cosmic and ethical. The process "now operating in the social body," he contended, was "essentially different from that which had differentiated species in the past and raised man to his ascendancy among the animals."[70] "Civilised man" was a combustible admixture of two elements, an "inherited factor"—the "natural man"—produced by millennia of natural selection, and an "acquired factor"—the "artificial

65. Huxley, "Evolution and Ethics," 143.

66. Huxley, "Prolegomena," 79, 78.

67. Wells, *Anticipations*, 162. See also Wells, *Mankind*, 409; Wells, *Modern Utopia*, 105, 124. For Wells's praise of Huxley, see "Huxley," *Royal College of Science Magazine*, 13 (April 1901), 211; Wells, *Mankind*, v. On Wells's education, see Smith, *H. G. Wells*, pt. I. On his writing in the context of contemporary scientific debates, see Will Tattersdill, *Science, Fiction, and the Fin-de-Siècle Periodical Press* (Cambridge, 2016); Steven McLean, *The Early Fiction of H. G. Wells* (Basingstoke, 2009).

68. Wells, *Anticipations*, 125. See also Wells, *Modern Utopia*, 95.

69. Wells to Huxley, ?? May 1895, *Correspondence*, I, 238. For discussion of the scientific context of *The Time Machine*, see James, *Maps of Utopia*, 50–64; McLean, *Early Fiction*, 11–40.

70. H. G. Wells, "Human Evolution, an Artificial Process" (1896), in Philmus and Hughes, *H. G. Wells*, 211.

man"—shaped by "tradition, suggestion, and reasoned thought."[71] Human norms and values were contingent products of historical development, neither inscribed in nor legitimated by nature. "Morality is made for man, and not man for morality."[72]

Even as Wells endorsed Huxley's bifurcated framework, he drew different political conclusions from it. Indeed, Huxley would have viewed Wells's political prescriptions as incompatible with the dictates of evolution. An exponent of classical political economy, Huxley's scientific naturalism legitimated his attacks on Spencerian laissez-faire and political radicalism alike. He eyed the swelling radical currents of the 1880s and 1890s with horror. "He needed a competitive Nature. He needed to undercut the socialist legions."[73] Huxley regarded fierce competition between individuals and states as perennial, rendering any hope of fundamental sociopolitical transformation a dangerous illusion.[74] Human nature was not malleable. Wells concurred that political philosophers must accept humans as competitive products of an ancient evolutionary process, but he rejected Huxley's fatalism, arguing that there was greater scope for autonomy—both collective and individual—than his teacher allowed. The contrast between the metaphors they employed indexes the substantive difference. Whereas Wells spoke of humanity "steering itself against the currents and winds of the universe," Huxley invoked war and combat.[75] For Wells, humans had considerable freedom of action to pursue their own ends within a spatiotemporal framework structured by evolution. With intelligent piloting, it was possible to create utopian societies "cunningly balanced against external necessities on the one hand, and the artificial factor in the individual in the other," where everyone, and indeed "every sentient creature," could be "generally happy."[76] Wells's "Modern Utopia" was characterized by universal peace and harmony, as human competition was harnessed to beneficent social ends and a program of "positive" eugenics blocked the least fit members of society from reproducing. Degeneration could be postponed

71. H. G. Wells, "The Rediscovery of the Unique" (1891), in Philmus and Hughes, *H. G. Wells*, 217.

72. H. G. Wells, "Morals and Civilisation" (1897), in Philmus and Hughes, *H. G. Wells*, 226.

73. Adrian Desmond, *Huxley* (London, 1997), II, 217.

74. Huxley, "Evolution and Ethics," 193.

75. Wells, "Human Evolution," 218; Huxley, "Prolegomena," 70, 85; Huxley, "Ethics and Evolution," 85, 141.

76. Wells, "Human Evolution," 218. For further discussion, see Wells, *New Worlds for Old*, 197–204.

indefinitely with the appropriate combination of people and policies. In contrast, Huxley had declared that such happiness was impossible.[77]

Most existing scholarship on Wells emphasizes his paramount intellectual debt to Huxley.[78] But this is only half the story. "Philosophy," Wells once observed, "correlates the sciences and keeps them subservient to the universals of life."[79] It was essential for disciplining thought and guiding action. Huxley's capacious philosophical interests included Stoicism and Buddhism, though he engaged primarily with eighteenth-century British thinkers, and especially Hume.[80] Wells rarely mentioned any of these sources, and little of Huxley's philosophical armature is found in his work. Instead, he came to regard *pragmatism* as both a reflection of and a solution to many of the conundrums of the day. Coined by Charles Peirce in 1878, the term "pragmatism" only gained wide currency after it was adopted by William James in 1898. "The pragmatic movement," James wrote later, "suddenly seems to have precipitated itself out of the air."[81] James used it to designate various tendencies in philosophy—a focus on the practical consequences of arguments, recognition that empiricism had to accommodate the lessons of Darwinism, skepticism about absolute notions of truth and value, and a critique of intellectualism and abstraction—that had recently become "conscious of themselves collectively." Pragmatists, he wrote, turn their backs on "abstraction and insufficiency, from verbal locutions, from bad *a priori* reasons, from fixed principles, closed systems, and pretended absolutes and origins," and look toward "concreteness and adequacy, towards facts, towards action and towards power." This cognitive reorientation necessitated the rejection of extant philosophical dogma, including "the pretense of finality in truth."[82] Pragmatism was soon subject to ferocious controversy, especially in the United States.[83] While less popular in Britain, where the philosophical scene was still dominated by neo-Hegelian idealism, it nevertheless began to make inroads, chiefly through the

77. Huxley, "Prolegomena," 102.

78. See, for examples, Partington, *Building Cosmopolis*; Hale, *Political Descent*, 252–300.

79. Wells, *Future in America*, 213.

80. Huxley, "Prologomena"; Huxley, "Evolution and Ethics"; Paradis, *T. H. Huxley*.

81. William James, *Pragmatism* (1907), in *Pragmatism and Other Writings*, ed. Giles Gunn (London, 2000), 1.

82. James, *Pragmatism*, 27.

83. For useful historical accounts of pragmatism, see Horace Thayer, *Meaning and Action* (Indianapolis, 1968); Christopher Hookway, "Pragmatism" in Thomas Baldwin (ed.), *The Cambridge History of Philosophy, 1870–1945* (Cambridge, 2003), 74–92. We are still missing a good transnational history of the movement.

dialectical skill and evangelical zeal of the Oxford philosopher F. C. S. Schiller, prominent then but largely forgotten today.[84]

Wells aligned himself with both James and (to a lesser extent) Schiller, proclaiming, as they had, that pragmatism was capable of transforming society, if only its lessons were absorbed.[85] (He did not engage with Peirce or John Dewey during this period.) Wells was open about his intellectual debts. In the 1930s, he informed a German philologist, Fritz Krog, that he had "assimilated Pragmatism . . . completely" during the early twentieth century, and that he had taken James "for granted."[86] In *Anticipations*, he described *The Principles of Psychology*, which he had read during the late 1890s, as "that most wonderful book," while he later stated that in the Edwardian years he had labored "under the influence" of *The Will to Believe*.[87] On hearing of his death in 1910, Wells wrote to Henry James that the philosopher had been "something big and reassuring in my background for many years," and his loss left him "baffled and helplessly distressed." Elsewhere, he anointed "that very great American" his "friend and master."[88]

Wells outlined his basic philosophical commitments in "Scepticism of the Instrument," a lecture originally delivered to the Oxford Philosophical Society, which had been established as a forum for the critique of neo-Hegelian approaches. It was published in the philosophy journal *Mind* in 1904, reprinted the following year as an appendix to *A Modern Utopia*, and incorporated and further developed in *First and Last Things*, Wells's most important philosophical text. He informed Schiller that the book was written on "sound pragmatic

---

84. Mark Porrovecchio, *F. C. S. Schiller and the Dawn of Pragmatism* (Lanham, 2011); Admir Skodo, "Eugenics and Pragmatism," *Modern Intellectual History*, 14/3 (2017), 661–87.

85. Wells mentions Schiller in "Scepticism of the Instrument," *Mind*, 13/51 (1904), 381; Wells, *First and Last Things*, 31. Although Wells was explicit about the impact of James on his work, he rarely cited sources for specific arguments. Aside from his citations of *The Will to Believe* and *The Principles of Psychology*, a heavily annotated version of which is in the Wells archive, evidence suggests that he was also familiar with *The Varieties of Religious Experience* and *Pragmatism*. In *God the Invisible King* (London, 1917), he acknowledged explicitly that his understanding of God was inspired by James.

86. Wells to Krog, 4 May 1936, in Sylvia Hardy, "H. G. Wells and William James" in McLean, *H. G. Wells*, 142–43. Hardy pioneered the pragmatist reading of Wells's views on language, though she does not cover his social and political thought.

87. Wells, *Anticipations*, 134; Wells, *The Conquest of Time* (London, 1942), 1.

88. Wells to Henry James, 31 July 1910, *Henry James and H. G. Wells*, ed. Leon Edel and Gordon Ray (London, 1958), 124; Wells, *God, the Invisible King*, 203.

lines."[89] All of his thinking, he announced at the start of *A Modern Utopia*, rested on this "heretical metaphysical scepticism."[90] Wells's pragmatism had four main components: a nominalist metaphysics; a pragmatist theory of truth (roughly, as verification through experiment); a version of James's "will to believe"; and a conception of philosophy as dedicated to elucidating and clarifying problems to facilitate (better) practice. "[M]ost of the troubles of humanity are really misunderstandings," he claimed, and in "expressing things, rendering things to each other, discussing our differences, clearing up the metaphysical conceptions upon which differences are discussed," philosophical reflection could eliminate the "confusion of purposes" besetting humanity.[91]

James respected Wells's untutored philosophical acumen. "Why can Wells," he once asked a neighbor, "without any philosophical training, write philosophy as well as the best of them?"[92] He was also clear about Wells's philosophical identity: "You're a *pragmatist!*"[93] Indeed, he regarded Wells as a leading preacher of the pragmatist gospel, blessed with extraordinary powers of persuasion. Like Tolstoy, he possessed the gift of "contagious speech," speech capable of setting a "similar mood vibrating in the reader," allowing Wells to convert them to the creed. Extolling *First and Last Things* as a "great achievement," James pronounced that it should be "used as a textbook in all the colleges of the world," and he suggested that Wells had put his "finger accurately on the true emphases and (in the main) on what seem to me the true solutions." It was worth "any 100 volumes on Metaphysics and any 200 of Ethics, of the ordinary sort."[94] In May 1906, James told John Jay Chapman, the eminent critic, that the world was on the verge of a philosophical revolution comparable to that inaugurated by Locke, and that among pragmatists leading the charge, "H. G. Wells ought to be counted in."[95] James was not alone in affirming Wells's pragmatism. In 1909, the idealist philosopher J. H. Muirhead hailed him in the pages of the *Proceedings of the Aristotelian Society* as the "latest and

---

89. Schiller to Wells, 1 March 1908, Folder S-080, Wells papers. See also Schiller to James, ?? August 1904, *The Correspondence of William James*, ed. Ignas Skrupskelis and Elizabeth Berkeley (Charlottesville, 2002), X, 622. After reading *First and Last Things*, he chided Wells for ignoring spirituality, for failing "so utterly to realise anything of the true inwardness of what I may call up-to-date spiritualism." Stead to Wells, 20 November 1908, S-456, Wells papers.

90. Wells, *Modern Utopia*, xxxi.

91. Wells, *First and Last Things*, 14.

92. J. Graham Brooks, quoted in Hardy, "H. G. Wells and William James," 131.

93. James to Wells, 4 December 1906, *Correspondence of William James*, XI, 290.

94. James to Wells, 28 November 1906, *Correspondence of William James*, XII, 126.

95. James to Chapman, 18 May 1905, *Correspondence of William James*, XI, 225.

most brilliant recruit ... to philosophy as well as to Pragmatism," while the literary critic Van Wyck Brooks argued in the first intellectual biography of the writer, that Wells was "perfectly American," not least because of his "thorough-going pragmatism." Like James, Brooks elevated him to the pragmatist pantheon: "Wells has inevitably become one of the leaders."[96] Given Wells's own proud self-identification as a pragmatist, and his recognition as such by assorted contemporary thinkers, including James and Schiller, he should be seen as one of the most prominent fin-de-siècle pragmatist thinkers, indeed as the most high-profile pragmatist political thinker of the opening two decades of the century. Recognizing him as such offers a novel understanding of the basis of his thought, as well as of the early history of pragmatism.[97] In order to grasp the character of his social and political theory, including his conception of the New Republic, it is necessary to take Wells's philosophical commitments seriously.

Metaphysical nominalism lay at the heart of Wells's pragmatism. It was a universal acid, capable of cutting through dogma and reshaping visions of reality. As he wrote in 1912,

> The essential characteristic of this great intellectual revolution amidst which we are living today, that revolution of which the revival and restatement of nominalism under the name of pragmatism is the philosophical aspect, consists in the reassertion of the importance of the individual instance as against the generalization. All our social, political, moral problems are being approached in a new spirit, in an inquiring and experimental spirit, which has small respect for abstract principles and deductive rules.[98]

He combined two claims. First, evolution had produced a human cognitive apparatus that was poorly designed to grasp the overwhelming complexity of the world. And second, that the world itself was composed of "uniques," nonidentical particulars. Classification was both "a necessary condition of the working of the mental implement" and a "departure from the objective truth of things." The human mind, on this account, only functions by "disregarding individuality and treating uniques as identically similar objects ... so as to group them under one term," and consequently, "it tends automatically to

96. John Muirhead, "Why Pluralism?," *Proceedings of the Aristotelian Society*, 9/1 (1909), 183; Van Wyck Brooks, *The World of H. G. Wells* (New York, 1915), 178.

97. On this account of "tradition," see Duncan Bell, "What Is Liberalism?," *Political Theory*, 42/6 (2014), 682–715. For an excellent account of the historiography of pragmatism, emphasizing its fragmented character, and also the "Americanization" of the doctrine, see Bruce Kuklick, "Who Owns Pragmatism?," *Modern Intellectual History*, 14/2 (2017), 565–83.

98. Wells, "Contemporary Novel," 163.

intensify the significance of that term."[99] We encounter a world of multiplicity, but our language tricks us into thinking in terms of identity and patterned regularity. Classification, generalization, intellectualism, abstraction: all were philosophically suspect. Moreover, Wells argued, as had James, that absolute truth was chimerical. "All propositions are approximations to an elusive truth."[100] Such conditional truths as were ascertainable were (fallible) products of repeated experimentation and practical verification. Even scientific "laws" were still provisional hypotheses. In Schiller's terms, "axioms" were simply "postulates" that had demonstrated their value over time.[101] Pragmatism necessitated the "abandonment of infinite assumptions" and the "extension of the experimental spirit to all human interests."[102]

This line of argument had important implications for empirical political analysis and ethics. The "uniqueness" of particulars meant that the common methodological precepts of social science, based on sweeping classifications of society, were more misleading than illuminating. In *Mankind in the Making*, for example, Wells criticized discussion of gender roles. We are told what "women" and "men" want or believe, he complained, yet there was "no such woman and no such man, but a vast variety of temperaments and dispositions, monadic, dyadic, and polymeric souls," and it was impossible to build any adequate "code" on such classifications.[103] The same was true of attempts to systematically categorize social classes, nations, and races. Wells used such arguments to intervene in debates over the nature of social science. Following the success of *Anticipations*, he was invited to join the Council of the fledgling Sociological Society, established with the intention of cementing the place of social research in the British intellectual world.[104] Wells, though, disdained the claims to scientific status made by sociologists and political economists. In a lecture delivered to the Society in January 1906, entitled "The So-Called

99. Wells, "Scepticism of the Instrument," 384, 389.

100. Wells, *First and Last Things*, 35.

101. F. C. S. Schiller, "Axioms as Postulates" in Henry Sturt (ed.), *Personal Idealism* (Oxford, 1902), 47–134. Wells praises this essay in "Scepticism of the Instrument," 381, 393.

102. Wells, *First and Last Things*, 43.

103. Wells, *Mankind*, 299.

104. The Sociological Society had been founded in 1903. For Wells's role in it, see [Lewis Mumford?], "H. G. Wells," memo, Foundations of British Sociology Archive (FBS), Keele University, GB 172 LP/11/1/2. I discuss this further in Bell, "Pragmatic Utopianism and Race." For recent accounts of Wells's utopian sociological vision, see also Ruth Levitas, "Back to the Future," *Sociological Review*, 58/4 (2010), 530–47; Krishan Kumar, "Wells and the So-called Science of Sociology" in Patrick Parrinder and Christopher Rolfe (eds.), *H. G. Wells under Revision* (Toronto, 1990), 192–217.

Science of Sociology," he drew on pragmatism to attack the legacy of Spencer and Comte, and challenge the very rationale of the new discipline.[105] Evolutionary insight and philosophical reasoning worked in harmony. Darwin, Wells averred, had demonstrated the unreliability of rigid systems of classification, revealing the "element of inexactness running through all things." The pragmatists had reinforced this picture. Wells proclaimed confidently that the "uniqueness of individuals is the objective truth," while "counting, classification, measurement, the whole fabric of mathematics, is subjective and deceitful." The physical sciences, dealing as they did with vast numbers of cases, could still construct felicitous classifications and generalizations, even if the scientists were mistaken in thinking that they exposed the unvarnished truth about the universe. Social "scientists," however, could not rely on such strategies:

> the method of classification under types, which has served so useful a purpose in . . . the subjects involving numerous but a finite number of units, has also to be abandoned in social science. We cannot put humanity into a museum or dry it for examination; our one single still living specimen is all history, all anthropology, and the fluctuating world of men. There is no satisfactory means of dividing it, and nothing else in the real world with which to compare it.[106]

It was impossible to fully isolate groups of people or trace anything but "rude general resemblances" between them. "The alleged units have as much individuality as pieces of cloud; they come, they go, they fuse, they separate." Assorted attempts had been made to circumvent this problem. Spencer, for example, disaggregated humanity into self-contained societies that "competed one with another and died and reproduced just like animals," while political economists, following Friedrich List, had "for the purposes of fiscal controversy discovered economic types." Wells expressed surprise that serious thinkers were persuaded by such blatantly deceptive arguments. Human societies were not rigidly bounded, nor were they sufficiently alike to render them functionally equivalent.[107] Nominalism entailed that common forms of reasoning about human life were faulty, especially if they were taken to reveal "absolute" truths about the world rather than providing revocable conceptual technologies for navigating it. Uniqueness ruled.

---

105. H. G. Wells, "The So-Called Science of Sociology," in Wells, *Englishman*, 197. This article was originally published in *Sociological Papers* (London, 1908), III. It was, in turn, based on an earlier article, with the same name, published in the *Independent Review*.

106. Wells, *First and Last Things*, 41; Wells, "So-Called Science," 200. See also Wells, *Experiment in Autobiography*, II, 657–58.

107. Wells, "So-Called Science," 199–201.

Wells also revised some of the bolder claims about prediction that he had made in "The Discovery of the Future." In *The Future in America*, he offered a potted history of the phases in his own "anticipatory habit," from his early forays charting the future destiny of the species to his current prognostications on the near-future of the United States. Wells admitted that his Royal Institution lecture had given an "excessive exposition and defence" of the scientific approach: "I went altogether too far in this direction." The scientific status of history and sociology was questionable.[108] Indeed, he claimed to have emerged "out of the other side" of the scientific method and into the "large temperance, the valiant inconclusiveness, the released creativeness" of philosophy. (So much for Chesteron's view of Wells as a fetishist of science.) Although it was possible to make limited forecasts, Wells continued, "the last decisions and the greatest decisions, lie in the hearts and wills of unique incalculable men."[109] His pragmatic skepticism had supplanted his earlier naïve positivism.

Wells combined (rather awkwardly) a demand for epistemic humility— "Man, thinking Man, suffers from intellectual over-confidence and a vain belief in the universal validity of reasoning"[110]—with a hugely ambitious vision of what ideas and the intellectuals who produced them could do in shaping human action. The role of the speculative writer was to educate and direct collective consciousness, identifying problems with the existing order and preparing the ground for change. While absolute truth was inaccessible, Wells argued that it was nevertheless vital to develop cogent political and moral ideals, for without them concerted human action was impossible. Human progress required adherence to beliefs that were acknowledged as "arbitrary," but which still served a valuable practical purpose—for Wells, that purpose was to bring about a socialist dawn and the eventual creation of a world-state.[111] This was the overriding ambition of his work, the function of his art. "My beliefs, my dogmas, my rules," he wrote in *First and Last Things*, "are made for my campaigning needs, like the knapsack and water bottle of a Cockney soldier invading some stupendous mountain gorge."[112] Pragmatic principles, and in particular Wells's deflationary nominalism, formed a vital part of his intellectual armory as he embarked on the campaign to build a New Republic. They did so in two main ways. First, as I explore in the next section, they

108. Wells, *Future in America*, 15.

109. Wells, *Future in America*, 15–16.

110. Wells, *First and Last Things*, 44.

111. See Bell, "Pragmatism and Prophecy," for further discussion of his pragmatist socialism.

112. Wells, *First and Last Things*, 197.

underpinned his fierce attack on nationality and race. And secondly, as I discuss in the final section, his adoption of the experimental spirit meant that he was happy to constantly revise his account of the institutional forms best fitted for realizing the world-state.

The Fluctuating World of Men: On Race and Language

Wells deplored the racial theorizing of his day, warning in 1905 of the "delirium about race and the racial struggle" shaping public debate. Two years later, in a letter to *Nature*, he rebuked "the nonsense people will talk under the influence of race mania."[113] The mania had to be confronted, for it underwrote some of the worst problems facing humanity. "I am convinced myself," he wrote in 1907,

> that there is no more evil thing in this present world than Race Prejudice; none at all. I write deliberately—it is the worst single thing in life now. It justifies and holds together more baseness, cruelty and abomination than any other sort of error in the world. Thru its body runs the black blood of coarse lust, suspicion, jealousy and persecution and all the darkest passions of the human soul.[114]

His skepticism about contemporary conceptions of race was derived, in large part, from his pragmatism.

Wells's most sustained discussion of racial theory is in chapter 10 of *A Modern Utopia*. Devotees of a pragmatist "philosophy of the unique," the inhabitants of Utopia adhered to a "science of human association" that was profoundly skeptical about the truth-value of classification and generalization. While philosophers were trained to regard generalizations as suspicious, the utopian and the statesman were taught "to mingle something very like animosity with that suspicion," because "crude classification and false generalizations" were the "curse of all organized human life." This was, of course, intended as a critique of his contemporaries, obsessed with the search for essences and "stupid generalizations" about human collectives. He argued that there were three main "aggregator ideas" molding British public debate at the time: nationality, religion, and imperialism. Despite their manifold differences, they all presupposed

---

113. Wells, *Modern Utopia*, 218, 224; Wells, "Mulattos," *Nature*, 77/149 (1907), 149.

114. H. G. Wells, "Race Prejudice," *The Independent*, 62 (1907), 382. Wells was reviewing Jean Finot's *Race Prejudice* and Sydney Olivier's *White Capital and Colored Labour*. He was impressed by the latter.

the existence of clear and tangible boundaries between those included and those excluded from the relevant group. This logic of othering had recently assumed a racialized form—the world was witnessing, Wells complained, an "extraordinary intensifications of racial definition," meaning that the "vileness, the inhumanity, the incompatibility of alien races is being steadily exaggerated."[115] The epistemic vacuum of the Balfourian age was filled by pseudoscience, as credulous (and malign) thinkers claimed the scientific and cultural authority of Darwin to burnish their ideas. Race prejudice was "shaping policies and modifying laws," and it would cause a "large proportion of the wars, hardships and cruelties the immediate future holds in store for our earth."[116] It underpinned such dangerous ideologies as Anglo-Saxonism and Pan-Germanism. Philosophy, then, was no cloistered pursuit, devoid of social significance; the fate of the world depended in part on the spread of pragmatist ideas that would counter the fetish for generalizing about racial difference and competition.[117]

Wells contended that none of the aggregator ideas could survive the skeptical gaze. Their advocates committed a variety of errors. Some assumed that there was a "best race," and regarded all others as inferior, even as "material for extermination," a view that Wells thought was popular both on the continent and in Britain. Dreaming of *Weltpolitik*, stern German professors avowed the superiority of the "Teuton," while their British equivalent, Cecil Rhodes, "affected that triumph of creative imagination," the "Anglo-Saxon race." Here we see Wells attempting to distance himself from the ur-imperialist, suggesting that despite the clear similarities between their visions of the future, their political thinking was based on very different ontological assumptions. Wells suggested that racial supremacism augured a world of death and destruction. It was a rational option for those aiming to establish a *"Welt-Apparat,"* but it would necessitate "national harrowing and reaping machines, and race-destroying fumigations."[118] The climacteric of Rhodesian politics was genocide enacted on a global scale. Even if one race did manage to predominate, Wells continued, it would then subdivide into competing factions, and conflict would begin anew. It was an invitation to perpetual war. He thought that the modern imperialist school was far more influential than the relatively marginal devotees of "scientific Welt-Politik." German, British, and Anglo-Saxon

---

115. Wells, *Modern Utopia*, 215, 216–17, 219.

116. Wells, *Modern Utopia*, 219.

117. For a later reiteration of this point, see H. G. Wells, *The Work, Wealth and Happiness of Mankind* (London, 1932), 68–69.

118. Wells, *Modern Utopia*, 229.

variations on the imperial theme coexisted with a "wider teaching" that encompassed the totality of the "white race." Proponents of each identified their own people as the chosen one, looking "with a resolute, truculent, but slightly indistinct eye to a future in which all the rest of the world will be in subjection to those elect."[119] (This was a good description of much of the Anglo-American discourse.) Wells cited Benjamin Kidd's *The Control of the Tropics* as exemplary. Kidd had argued that the "childish" peoples of the world could not be entrusted with the economic development of the untapped resources found in the tropics, and that the task should be arrogated by the advanced "white states," which would administer the territories for the benefit of humanity.[120]

Wells argued that contemporary racial theory had two main sources: philology and biology. He had criticized philology in *Anticipations*, mocking the "[u]nobservant, over-scholarly people" who "talk or write in the profoundest manner about a Teutonic race and a Keltic race." These claims were little more than "oil-lamp anthropology," possessing the same scientific credibility as Lombroso's absurd pronouncements about skull shape and criminality.[121] In *A Modern Utopia*, Wells blamed the Oxford philologist Max Müller for inspiring the misguided search for a "new political synthesis in adaptable sympathies based on linguistic affinities," a search that had spawned endless triumphalist accounts of English Teutonism, including J. R. Green's hugely popular *A Short History of the English People*.[122] Müller's work underpinned the "comparative method" propagated by Maine, Freeman, and Seeley among others, and it contributed significantly to the academic development of political science and history on both sides of the Atlantic.[123] As I noted in chapter 2, the Teutonist racial vision helped shape Carnegie's arguments for Anglo-American consolidation. Wells responded by arguing that Müller's sweeping assertions, and the library of scholarship it influenced, was based on the indefensible assumption that language "indicated kindred"—that the (purported) common language

119. Wells, *Modern Utopia*, 229–30.

120. Benjamin Kidd, *The Control of the Tropics* (London, 1898). On Kidd and his context, see David Crook, *Benjamin Kidd* (Cambridge, 1984).

121. Wells, *Anticipations*, 124, 123.

122. Wells, *Modern Utopia*, 218. For further criticism of this "pretentious rubbish," see Wells, "Race Prejudice," 383. On the arguments and influence of Müller, see Stefan Arvidsson, *Aryan Idols* (Chicago, 2006); John Davis and Angus Nichols (eds.), "Friedrich Max Müller and the Role of Philology in Victorian Thought," *Publications of the English Goethe Society*, 85/1 (2016), 67–230.

123. On the "comparative method," see Burrow, Collini, and Winch, *That Noble Science of Politics*, ch. 7; Adcock, *Liberalism and the Emergence of American Political Science*, ch. 5; Otter, "Origins of a Historical Political Science," 37–66.

of the Indo-Europeans connoted a shared "Teutonic" descent. There was no compelling evidence to support this dubious "speculative ethnology."[124]

More dangerous still, Darwin's ideas were being misappropriated. "The natural tendency of every human being towards a stupid conceit in himself and his kind, a stupid depreciation of all unlikeness, is traded upon by this bastard science."[125] Instead, Wells hailed Joseph Deniker's *The Races of Man* as an authoritative view of the best available science. Sketching an intricate cartography of the peoples of Europe, Deniker, a French anthropologist, had concluded that "race" was an unhelpful term.[126] Wells concurred, arguing that there were no distinct "pure" races in the world. Metaphysics reinforced the latest biological findings. Pragmatism demonstrated that the "mania" for race was fundamentally misguided. Races, he had written in the introduction to *A Modern Utopia*, "are no hard and fast things, no crowd of identically similar persons," but instead "massed sub-races and tribes and families each after its kind unique, and these again are clusterings of still smaller uniques and so down to each several person."[127] Wells thus embraced both methodological and ontological individualism. He reiterated his critique in *New Worlds for Old*, arguing that the socialist movement represented the "development of the collective consciousness of humanity," and that as such it necessarily transcended state boundaries and had to be "outspoken, making no truce with prejudices against race or colour." Race and nation constituted alternative "collective consciousnesses," but they were transient, parochial, and dangerous, "as vague, as fluctuating as mists or clouds; they melt, dissolve into one another; they coalesce; they split."[128] Unbounded universality would prevail.

Humanity, for Wells, was composed of a fluid mosaic of unique individuals, not homogenous groups that could be ranked and compared. Collectives were no more than the sum of their individual parts. The fetish for sweeping classification was a serious impediment to comprehension. "The natural tendency," he wrote, is to take "either an average or some quite arbitrary ideal as

124. Wells, *Modern Utopia*, 218. On the "mania for Teutonism," see Mandler, *English National Character*, 86–105.

125. Wells, *Modern Utopia*, 219.

126. Joseph Deniker, *The Races of Man* (London, 1900). Deniker was the chief librarian of the Muséum National d'Histoire Naturelle in Paris. Denying the scientific utility of "race," he coined the term "ethnic group" (*groupe ethnique*), defined as "real and palpable groupings . . . formed by virtue of community of language, religion, social institutions, etc." (3). Despite its clear relevance to Wells, he did not adopt this terminology.

127. Wells, *Modern Utopia*, 220, 23. See also *First and Last Things*, 67.

128. Wells, *New Worlds for Old*, 274.

the type, and think only of that," but it was imperative to "bear the range in mind"—"[i]t is not averages that exist, but individuals." Since all persons were "individualized," Wells denied that racial difference was inherent and "insurmountable."[129] Fomented by a toxic mixture of ignorance and poorly digested science, it was a social construct, not an ineliminable biological fact. Aware that philosophical argumentation alone was insufficient to persuade his audience, he stressed the affective value of photographic collections such as *The Living Races of Mankind*, visual archives that portrayed people from around the world in familiar situations and poses. "There are differences, no doubt, but fundamental incompatibilities—*no!*"[130]

Race wasn't the only category subjected to Wells's deflationary admonitions. The year before *A Modern Utopia* appeared, he had attacked the idea of "the People," that staple of modern democratic theory. Unless it was employed to designate the sum of the individuals in a group, the term meant nothing. Indeed, it was positively mystifying, distorting understanding of the social world and the place of humans within it. "My modest thesis," he wrote, "is that there exists nothing of the sort, that the world of men is entirely made up of the individuals that compose it." Collective action was "just the algebraic sum of all individuals action." The implications of accepting nominalism were profound, reshaping possibilities for political thought and action. Accepting that "the People" did not exist, that there were only "an enormous differentiating millions of men" going about their business, would create a political revolution.[131] Wells suggested that pragmatism dissolved conventional notions of political belonging, whether rooted in nationality, peoplehood, or race. Building a New Republican polity demanded a major cognitive and affective reorientation.

Language, not race, provided the social cement of the New Republic. Wells had long been fascinated by the nature and functions of language, asserting in *A Modern Utopia* that it was the "nourishment of the thought of man."[132] Indeed, language played a pivotal role in his understanding of human evolution and the development of the "artificial man," capable (in principle) of escaping

---

129. Wells, *Modern Utopia*, 220, 221, 222, 221.

130. Wells, *Modern Utopia*, 223, 222; H. Hutchinson, J. Gregory, and R. Lydekker, *The Living Races of Mankind* (New York, 1902). On the context of the text, and Wells's appeal to empathy, see Jane Lydon, "H. G. Wells and a Shared Humanity," *History Australia*, 12/1 (2015), 75–94. For the complexity of encounters with difference, see Qureshi, *Peoples on Parade*.

131. H. G. Wells, "Is There a People?" (1904), in Wells, *Englishman*, 245, 246, 250. See also, Wells, *First and Last Things*, 158–59.

132. Wells, *Modern Utopia*, 18.

the destruction wrought by "natural man."[133] Scolding Kidd for postulating that natural selection was still working on the "intrinsic moral qualities of man," Wells argued that the evolutionary processes "now operating in the social body" were radically different from those of the past. While the basic biological features of humanity remained the same as those found in the Paleolithic era, there had been innumerable changes in "suggestions and ideas" during the following millennia. Speech and writing were fundamental. The "artificial factor" in humanity was "modified" by two capacities, the most important of which was "suggestion"—especially the ability to follow successful examples—and the second of which was "reasoned conclusion from additions" to "individual knowledge," whether through experience or teaching.[134] Humans learnt from successes and failures, accumulating durable knowledge, both practical and theoretical. Moral norms were open to modification by human thought and speech, through complex and reversible processes of "moral education."[135] Morality was a changing set of practices and beliefs, not an absolute fixed body of doctrine established by a deity or the eternal dictates of reason.

However, the New Republic faced a major problem. The quality of written and spoken English displayed by its potential inhabitants, especially in the Colonies, was worryingly low. This hampered the growth of "racial consciousness," which depended on clear and intelligible communication, allowing for the development of a rich public culture capable of sustaining and disseminating complex ideas. The "thought of a community," Wells insisted, "is the life of that community," and if that thought was "disconnected and fragmentary," the result was weakness and division. "That does not constitute an incidental defect, but essential failure."[136] This failure had detrimental effects on its viability and sophistication. "Except for those who wish to bawl the crudest thoughts, there is no means of reaching the whole mass of these communities today." This was, he cautioned his readers, the "darkest cloud" over potential confederation.[137] Action was needed.

> We have to save, to revive this scattered, warped, tarnished and neglected language of ours, if we wish to save the future of our world. We should save not only the world of those who at present speak English, but the world of

133. For a detailed account of his views on language, stressing his debts to William James, see Sylvia Hardy, "H. G. Wells and Language" (PhD diss., University of Leicester, 1991).

134. Wells, "Human Evolution," 211, 217.

135. H. G. Wells, "The Limits of Individual Plasticity" (1895), in Philmus and Hughes, *H. G. Wells*, 39.

136. Wells, *Mankind*, 128, 390.

137. Wells, *Mankind*, 131, 132, 134.

many kindred and associated peoples who would willingly enter into our synthesis, could we make it wide enough and sane enough and noble enough for their honour.[138]

The future of both the New Republic and the World State depended on a significant improvement in the linguistic capacities—and thus the thought-worlds—of the far-flung members of the Angloworld. The answer, Wells argued in *Mankind in the Making*, lay in standardizing language, eliminating the distracting cacophony of dialects, idioms, and accents that beset communication and stunted cognitive development. The citizens of the New Republic needed to speak with "one accent, one idiom, and one intonation." This was a "necessary preliminary" to the "complete attainment of the more essential nucleus in the new Republican idea."[139] He suggested various ways that this end could be achieved. Like Carnegie and Stead, he supported the campaign for simplified spelling.[140] Moreover, he argued that much attention should be paid to the institutionalization of knowledge:

> Organized general literature would be the thinking department of the race. Once this deliberate organization of a central ganglion of interpretation and presentation began, the development of the brain and the nervous system in the social body would proceed apace. Each step would enable the next step by being wider and bolder. The general innervations of society with books and book distributing agencies would be followed by the linking up of the now almost isolated mental worlds of science, art, and political and social activity in a system of intercommunication and sympathy.[141]

The technologies that helped to make union both practical and necessary—above all the "more highly evolved" types of telegraph and phonograph—also provided the means for improving language, chiefly through the rapid dissemination of information.[142] This would help to create what he called a "Collective Mind." For Wells, then, the telegraph animated the living body of the

---

138. Wells, *Mankind*, 135.

139. Wells, *Mankind*, 136, 157. Once again, he seems to have missed a trick in not realizing Carnegie's interest in the subject: "We want an industrious committee, and we want one or two rich men" (148).

140. Wells was one of the most celebrated supporters of the cause: H. G. Paine, *Handbook of Simplified Spelling* (New York, 1920), 23. He served as Vice President of the Simplified Spelling Society. As Hardy notes, he also corresponded with the linguist C. K. Ogden, about the potential of Basic English: Hardy, "H. G. Wells and Language," 54.

141. Wells, *Mankind*, 388.

142. Wells, *Mankind*, 137.

New Republic, facilitating the flow of information around its geographically dispersed organs, while generating a form of distributed cognition, even consciousness. The discourse conjured up the vision of a cyborg imperium—a translocal fusion of humans and machines, poised to order and govern the world. In this picture, the new communications infrastructure created the very imagined community it claimed to link together across planetary distances. Wells was the cyborg theorist par excellence.

Despite his explicit rejection of racial theorizing, Wells's work presented a racialized picture of the New Republic. In part, this was because he lacked a coherent account of equality. He argued that assumptions about human equality had been discredited by Darwinism—people were more or less equal along different dimensions.[143] Some people were more intelligent, stronger, or creative than others. Talent and willpower were spread unevenly. Moreover, blanket claims about equality were incompatible with adherence to a nominalist conception of the unique. Equality, then, was not an "objective fact" but "purely a convention of conduct and intercourse," and valorizing the "false generalization" hindered the "treatment of the individual upon his merits."[144] It was better, Wells argued, to acknowledge empirical inequalities while nevertheless affirming, on instrumental grounds, an ideal of equality before the law. "In a really civilized community equality and mutual respect must be the primary assumption of all social intercourse." Such a view, he continued, should not efface the substantive differences between persons.[145] Wells's critique of equality thus acknowledged empirical variation between individuals—fitting his metaphysics and underwriting his account of the role of technocratic elites in shaping progress—while defending the social value of law. However, he did not specify how they could be reconciled, nor did he say anything about the form or distribution of such differences, leaving it unclear how the ideal of equality might constrain policies designed to recognize variation.

In addition, Wells's eugenic commitments undercut his putative antiracism. The clash was at its most stark in *Anticipations,* his most violent and racist book.[146] While clear that there were no distinct races, his proposed treatment

---

143. Wells, *Anticipations,* 163.

144. Wells, "Race Prejudice," 383. See also Wells, *Mankind,* 26.

145. Wells, "Race Prejudice," 383.

146. On fin-de-siècle eugenics, see Michael Freeden, "Eugenics and Progressive Thought," *Historical Journal,* 22/3 (1979), 645–71; Diane Paul, "Eugenics and the Left," *Journal of the History of Ideas,* 45/4 (1984), 567–90; Lucy Bland and Leslie Hall, "Eugenics in Britain" in Alison Bashford and Philippa Levine (eds.), *The Oxford Handbook of the History of Eugenics* (Oxford, 2010), 213–27.

of the "people of the abyss" disproportionately affected populations outside the Euro-Atlantic zone. "It has become apparent," he warned,

> that whole masses of human population are, as a whole, inferior in their claim upon the future to other masses, that they cannot be given opportunities or trusted with power as the superior peoples are trusted, that their characteristic weaknesses are contagious and detrimental on the civilising fabric, and that their range of incapacity tempts and demoralises the strong. To give them equality is to sink to their level, to protect and cherish them is to be swamped in their fecundity.[147]

The "efficients" of the future would have to devise policies to accommodate these facts, aiming to "check the procreation of base and servile types," even engaging in the "merciless obliteration of the weak." For example, those with transmissible diseases would be barred from having children, while capital punishment would be enforced for grave crimes. All of this necessitated a re-coding of death. The extermination of the "unfit" should be seen as a form of social hygiene, good for both society and those killed. The hard-headed citizens of the New Republic would "have little pity and less benevolence" for the swarming masses of humanity, "helpless and useless, unhappy or hatefully happy in the midst of squalid dishonour, feeble, ugly, inefficient, born of un-restrained lusts."[148] How, Wells asked, would the New Republic "treat the inferior races"—the "black," the "red," the "brown," and that "alleged termite in the woodwork, the Jew?"

> Certainly not as races at all. It will aim to establish, and it will at last, though probably only after a second century has passed, establish a world-state with a common language and a common rule. . . . It will, I have said, make the multiplication of those who fall behind a certain standard of social ef-ficiency unpleasant and difficult, and it will have cast aside by coddling laws to save adult men from themselves. It will tolerate no dark corners where the people of the abyss may fester, no vast diffused slums of peasant propri-etors, no stagnant plague-preservers. Whatever men may come into its ef-ficient citizenship it will let come—white, black, red, or brown; the effi-ciency will be the test.[149]

---

147. Wells, *Anticipations*, 163. It is not a coincidence that *Anticipations* was Wells's least prag-matist text of the era. Indeed it is arguable that his later rejection of some of the most horrific aspects of *Anticipations* was (in part) a result of his increasing engagement with pragmatist arguments.

148. Wells, *Anticipations*, 168.

149. Wells, *Anticipations*, 177. On Wells's anti-Semitism, see Bryan Cheyette, "H. G. Wells and the Jews," *Patterns of Prejudice*, 22/3 (1988), 22–35.

In principle, this argument cut across the global color line, but the eugenic eradication of the unfit would not be distributed evenly. A *minority* of "white and yellow" peoples would be joined, Wells predicted, by a *majority* "of the black and brown races."[150] Even as he denied the validity of group classification, Wells rearticulated a politics of racial domination.

In subsequent writings Wells revised his eugenic proposals, defending a more modest account of "negative eugenics" that aimed to dissuade weaker individuals from having children through the careful design of public policy.[151] Although he dropped the exterminationist violence that had capped the argument in *Anticipations*, the interlacing of race and eugenics remained. Expressing skepticism about the existence of "inferior" races, he went on to argue, contra Aristotle, that "there is no such thing as a race superior enough to have tutelage over others." But he muddied the water by asking a hypothetical question: *what if* there were "inferior" races? Would there be room for them in a utopia bound by Malthusian population constraints? His answer was stark: they would have to be "exterminated." Recent history offered several models. They could be killed in the "old Hebrew fashion," with "fire and sword," or they could be enslaved and worked to death, as the Spanish did to the Caribs. Alternatively, they could be exposed deliberately to disease, a strategy that missionaries had employed in Polynesia. Another option was "honest simple murder," as the English had committed against the Tasmanians. Finally, one might adopt a more enlightened form of cultural annihilation, establishing conditions that precipitated "race suicide," as British imperial administrators had done in Fiji. Wells concluded that the Fijian option was the least cruel. However, he maintained, it was doubtful that there was such a thing as an inferior race: even the Australian "'blackface' isn't such." Utopia nevertheless required a strategy to deal with the unfit. Public policies would be designed "without any clumsiness or race distinction." Individual fitness, not group identity, was the key.[152] But once again Wells said little about whether fitness was uniformly distributed across populations, or whether he still believed that it was concentrated (though not exclusively) in certain groups. While rejecting explicit racial discrimination, and conjuring up an imaginary world blessed by harmony and peace, Wells left open the question of how different populations

150. Wells, *Anticipations*, 158.

151. See, for example, Wells, *Mankind*, 37–40; and his comment on a paper by Francis Galton, *Sociological Papers* (London, 1905), I, 58–60. On the shift in his views on eugenics, see John Partingon, "Revising *Anticipations*," *Undying Fire*, 4 (2005), 31–44. This modified position still presupposed the appalling eugenic commitment to sort people into groups defined by their "fitness" and to judge and treat them on the basis of that classification.

152. Wells, *Modern Utopia*, 224–25.

would be affected by the eugenic order, and what kinds of policies would be required to build a future utopian state.

Despite its linguistic foundations, Wells's account was hard to differentiate from explicitly racial visions of the English-speaking peoples or Anglo-Saxondom: it drew from the same stock of images, terms, and conceptual resources. Moreover, his constant resort to charged racial markers—and in particular his tendency to classify polities as "white," "yellow," and "black"—highlighted an inability to escape the racial world-making practices shaping perceptions of society and politics. Even as he rejected racial classification, Wells reaffirmed a Eurocentric developmental account, one in which societies were assigned a place in a hierarchy crowned by the advanced ("efficient") Europeans and Americans, who took it upon themselves to help "backward" peoples realize their immanent potential. His argument was a distinctive variation on the common theme of liberal imperialism.

Given that the political entailments of Wells's argument were often hard to disentangle from the dominant racial discourse, it is unsurprising that he was sometimes interpreted as advocating the Anglo-Saxon *Weltpolitik* that he rejected explicitly. After all, Stead had seen little practical difference between the projects of Wells and Rhodes. E. Ray Lankester, an eminent zoologist and friend of Wells, declined to sign up to the younger man's dreamworld, writing in response to *Mankind in the Making* that "I don't believe that we can change the faulty nature of the Anglo-Saxon, and I don't want him to over-run the globe and eat up all the other races."[153] Reviewing *Anticipations* in *Nature*, the naturalist Frederick Headley charged Wells with endorsing the view that "Anglo-Saxonism will eventually triumph." Wells responded furiously, insisting that he had said no such thing. "I repudiated this balderdash with some asperity." Headley apologized for using the term "Anglo-Saxon," while reiterating his point about the basic structure of Wells's geopolitical forecasting.[154] Although arguments grounded in language and the "Anglo-Saxon race" were conceptually distinct, the practical implications were often hard to distinguish.

153. Lankester to Wells, 23 September 1903, cited in Smith, *H. G. Wells*, 515n19. On Lankester's influence on Wells's ideas about evolutionary degeneration, see McLean, *Early Fiction*, 11–40.

154. Frederick Headley, "The Future of the Human Race" (29 December 1904); Headley, "Fact in Sociology" (16 February 1905), in John Partington (ed.), *H. G. Wells in "Nature," 1893–1946* (Frankfurt, 2008), 203, 206–7; Wells to the Editor, ?? January 1905, *Correspondence*, II, 63–64.

Civilizer-General: The United States and Imperial Destiny

In April 1906, Wells visited the United States for the first time. Widely regarded as embodying the future, in the nineteenth century the United States was viewed as both laboratory and template for social change.[155] Wells concurred. He collected his thoughts in *The Future in America*, seeking to divine the inner essence of the country. One of his most successful books, its arguments were discussed by scholars and public intellectuals on both sides of the Atlantic. It presents a puzzle. While Wells reiterated his view that Britain and the United States were bound together by a shared history, peoplehood, and destiny, he pulled back silently from advocacy of synthetic union. "Our future is extraordinarily bound up in America's and in a sense dependent upon it," but not, he maintained, because "we dream very much of political reunions of Anglo Saxondom and the like."[156] It was as if he had never written *Anticipations* or *Mankind in the Making*. Wells seemed to have moved from impassioned prophecy-cum-endorsement of formal integration to outright rejection. Nor did the Larger Synthesis warrant discussion in *New Worlds for Old*, *First and Last Things*, and "The Great State," his other sustained pieces of sociopolitical writing during the Edwardian years.[157]

Perhaps he had simply changed his mind. This interpretation is supported by an intriguing autocritique that Wells inserted into *A Modern Utopia*. The idea of the New Republic, the narrator observes, "was pretty crude in several respects," not least because it propounded "a purely English-speaking movement," ignoring the possibility of a future synthesis of all languages. Reductive monolingualism was unsurprising from a "literary man who wrote only English." Moreover, the narrator continued, it was "colored too much by the peculiar opportunism of his time," and the author, Wells, "seemed to have more than half an eye for a prince or a millionaire of genius." (A Carnegie, perhaps?) Flawed as it was, the narrator remarked, Wells's work contained the glimmer of a better world: "the idea of a comprehensive movement of disillusioned and illuminated men behind the shams and patriotisms, the spites and personalities of the ostensible world was there."[158] It was a start.

But there is a problem with this line of interpretation. In 1914 Wells added a new preface to the English edition of *Anticipations*. Expressing pleasure at how well the book had lasted, he restated his New Republican prophecy. "The

155. On fin-de-siècle British travelers, including Wells, see Frankel, *Observing America*; Seed, "Land of the Future."

156. Wells, *Future in America*, 22.

157. H. G. Wells et al., *The Great State* (London, 1912).

158. Wells, *Modern Utopia*, 177.

whole of that chapter, the Larger Synthesis, has stood the wear of fourteen years remarkably well. For the most part it might have been written yesterday." He would change very little if he started afresh. Indeed, he claimed that the material about the New Republic and the class structure of the coming society was the "most valuable" in the book. "That conception of an open conspiracy of intellectuals and wilful people against existing institutions and existing limitations and boundaries is always with me . . . [t]hat open conspiracy will come. It is my form of political thought."[159] Listing a series of errors and miscalculations, Wells was happy to acknowledge faults with the work of his earlier self, but Anglo-American union was not among them.[160] On the eve of the First World War, then, Wells reaffirmed his account of future Anglo-American unification. How can this be squared with his commentary in *The Future in America*? The answer, I want to suggest, can be found in his views on empire and on time. In contrast with Stead, Wells's trip to the United States lead him to question his earlier advocacy. It brought home to him the substantial differences between Britain and the United States, as well as their divergent attitudes to the possession of empire. This disparity precluded any *imminent* synthesis. In the long run, however, the problems could be overcome—whether through irresistible social forces working their providential magic or by concerted human action—and the English-speaking peoples would transmute into a single political community. The synthesis was deferred, pushed deeper into the future.

Wells went in search of America's vision of the future but was underwhelmed by what he found. He argued that the key to American destiny, like that of any country or individual person, was the coherence and quality of its *will*.[161] Here the impact of James's "will to believe" on Wells's thought was clear. Wells informed his readers that he crossed the Atlantic "to find whatever consciousness or a common purpose there may be," and to ask,

> what is their Vision, their American Utopia, how much will there is shaping to attain it, how much capacity goes with the will—what, in short, there is

---

159. Wells, *Anticipations*, xiii, xiv–xv. Indeed it was. For a later iteration of the secret society idea, see Wells, *The Open Conspiracy* (New York, 1928).

160. The "stalest" section, he admitted, concerned aerial warfare. For further comments on flight, see H. G. Wells, "The Coming of Bleriot" (1909), in Wells, *Englishman*, 1–8. He expanded on the theme in *The War in the Air* (London, 1908). In the authoritative 1924 "Atlantic" edition of Wells's work, he reprinted the 1914 preface (for the sake of "amusement"), while commenting in a new note that he thought the volume remained "very largely contemporaneous." He identified chapters 2 and 3 as those of most lasting value: "Preface to Volume 4," *The Works of H. G. Wells* (London, 1924), IV, 2–3.

161. Wells, *Future in America*, 19.

in America, over and above the mere mechanical consequences of scattering multitudes of energetic Europeans athwart a vast healthy, productive and practically empty continent in the temperate zone.[162]

Wells never defined national *will* clearly, nor discussed how it could be measured, but the quest for this elusive property shadowed his visit and shaped his conclusions. Writing aboard the ocean liner *Carmania* as it hurtled across the Atlantic, he confessed that in researching the trip, he struggled to find an idea of the future animating American life.[163] The country lacked a sense of national purpose. This indictment was amply confirmed during his travels. *The Future in America* is as much a study of disenchantment as of celebration. The United States was thriving economically, and Wells was awed by the scale and tempo of change, but the social conditions, the political system, and the intellectual life of the country were all worryingly defective.

The overriding problem was that the United States promoted a hypercompetitive capitalist ethos rooted in extreme individualism and motivated by worship of wealth acquisition and private property. This drove the motor of change and threatened to undermine the grand promise of the country. Wells encountered both massive inequality and a spirited reaction against it. "Property becomes organized, consolidated, concentrated and secured. This is the fact to which America is slowly awakening at the present time." In a system of democratic equality, lacking a landed aristocracy and a disenfranchised proletariat, unchecked capitalism generated a massive concentration of wealth, a process that threatened the very foundations of society.[164] Widespread social suffering—Wells highlighted the prevalence of child labor in particular—was an inevitable consequence of fetishizing "liberty of property."[165] He picked Carnegie's hero to symbolize the degradation he witnessed. "I wish I could catch the soul of Herbert Spencer and tether it in Chicago for awhile to gather fresh evidence upon the superiority of unfettered individualistic enterprises to things managed by the state."[166] The fabled robber barons, Astor, Morgan, Rockefeller, and Carnegie, stood at the apex of this bloated system, accumulating unimaginable riches at the expense of the poor. It is little wonder that Wells sympathized with the Progressives fighting the obscene excesses of the Gilded

---

162. Wells, *Future in America*, 21.

163. Wells, *Future in America*, 21, 22–23. Wells cited assorted sources for his research, including Roosevelt, Veblen, Ostrogorsky, and the Harvard psychologist Hugo Munsterberg, author of *The Americans* (1904) (112).

164. Wells, *Future in America*, 77, 78.

165. Wells, *Future in America*, 101. See also Wells, *New Worlds for Old*, 12.

166. Wells, *Future in America*, 60.

Age, or that many leading Progressive thinkers embraced him as an inspiration and ally.[167]

Wells's portrait of Carnegie was unflattering. A "colossus of property . . . the jubilee plunger of beneficence, that rosy, gray-haired, nimble little figure, going to and fro between two continents, scattering library building as if he sowed wild oats," Carnegie

> diffuses his monument through the English-speaking lands, amid circumstances of the most flagrant publicity; the receptive learned, the philanthropic noble, bow in expectant swaths before him. He is the American fable come true; nothing seems too wild to believe of him, and he fills the European imagination with an altogether erroneous conception of the self-dissipating quality of American wealth.[168]

Carnegie was part of the problem, not a prospective ally. His exceptional philanthropy helped to mythologize the hypercapitalist class as munificent contributors to society while distracting attention from more representative figures. The industrialist reciprocated the skepticism. It is unclear when Carnegie first encountered Wells's writings, or how much of them he had read, but in a late essay, "Wages," he criticized the account of socialism offered by "that eminent authority" in *New Worlds for Old*.[169] The opportunity for collaboration had been lost.

Wells was struck by the diversity of the American population, but like the "nimble little figure," he maintained that its vibrant core was descended from British colonists. While the "typical" American was "nowhere and everywhere," Wells insisted that "he" was nevertheless an "English-speaking person, with extraordinary English traits still, in spite of much good German and Scandinavian and Irish blood he has assimilated." But Wells lacked the optimism of many other race unionists about the American ability to transform white European migrants into upstanding citizens. Dangers abounded. Some of the most despondent—and racist—passages in *The Future in America* concerned the dangers of unchecked immigration. America was foolishly admitting huge numbers of peasants from Central and Eastern Europe, and transmuting them "into a practically illiterate industrial proletariat." Uneducated, uncivilized, and poorly disciplined—*inefficient*—the teeming masses threatened social stability

---

167. On his reception by Progressives, see Bell, "Pragmatic Utopianism and Race." For the transatlantic connections between British socialists and American progressives, see Stears, *Progressives, Pluralists, and the Problems of the State*; Kloppenberg, *Uncertain Victory*.

168. Wells, *Future in America*, 89. Carnegie also appeared, in similar guise, in Wells, *New Worlds for Old*, 97; Wells, "The American Population," in Wells, *Englishman*, 311.

169. Andrew Carnegie, "Wages" in *Problems of To-day* (New York, 1908), 90–91.

and political destiny. Crowded in festering slums, they were easily manipulated by machine politicians, their sheer numbers stoking ethnic tensions and undercutting wages. The country faced an urgent choice: improve the machinery of assimilation or close the border.[170] Although Wells emphasized "efficiency" rather than "race," his arguments dovetailed with nativism, and he was hailed by supporters of immigration restriction.[171]

The social crisis precipitated by mass immigration was amplified by other vices. Horrified by the level of political corruption in the cities, Wells asked the popular socialist writer Upton Sinclair why it appeared to be so much worse in the United States than in Britain.[172] Moreover, political myopia hobbled the American system. Wells diagnosed a pathological "state-blindness"—a lack of a "sense of the state"—as a defining characteristic of American society. Despite their assertive patriotism, the typical American (male) citizen failed to recognize that "his business activities, his private employments, are constituents in a large collective process; that they affect other people and the world forever, and cannot, as he imagines, begin and end with him."[173] As the political theorist Charles Merriam glossed the idea, Wells meant that Americans lacked "political consciousness and interest expressed in political action for the commonweal."[174] This blinkered individualism simultaneously fueled the hypercompetitive capitalist economy and created the conditions of radical inequality and social dislocation that were threatening its stability. The concept was utilized frequently by scholars and public intellectuals. Garrett Droppers, an economist at the University of Chicago, wrote that Wells "in a very acute way pointed out this characteristic quality of the American mind." The young political theorist Francis Coker agreed, praising Wells for disclosing the lack of political imagination in American public life.[175] Not everyone was convinced by his sagacity. H. Perry Robinson, a correspondent for *The Times* and

170. Wells, *Future in America*, 109, 132.

171. See, for example, Joseph Auerbach, review of *Future in America*, *North American Review*, 104/608 (1907), 292–301; Frank Julian Warne, *The Immigrant Invasion* (New York, 1913), 14–15, 23–24, 195–96, 198–99, 268–70. For general context, see Lake and Reynolds, *Drawing the Global Color Line*; David C. Atkinson, *The Burden of White Supremacy* (Chapel Hill, 2017).

172. Upton Sinclair, *The Industrial Republic* (New York, 1907), 143. Deeply impressed by Wells, Sinclair dedicated the book to him and described *A Modern Utopia* as "one of the great works of our literature" (257).

173. Wells, *Future in America*, 140. He reiterated the argument in *New Worlds for Old*, 111, 245.

174. Charles Merriam, *American Political Ideas* (London, 1920), 386–87.

175. Garrett Droppers, "Sense of the State," *Journal of Political Economy*, 15/2 (1907), 112; Francis Coker, *Readings in Political Philosophy* (New York, 1914), xiii. See also Herman Finer, *Foreign Governments at Work* (Oxford, 1921), 16.

staunch advocate of an Anglo-American alliance, rejected Wells's criticism, contending that the lack of a sense of the state was what made the United States (and Britain) great in the first place.[176] For Wells, such intellectual failures damaged the quality of political life. Intelligence, and especially "intelligence inspired by constructive passion," was the "hero" of the "confused drama of human life."[177] State-blindness was an impediment to enlightenment, to recognizing both the ills of the contemporary world and how to overcome them. Although he was not explicit about the subject, the implications of Wells's argument for a future New Republic and world-state were clear. The United States was a poor candidate for leading the effort to fabricate either of them. It was not (yet) ready to engage in the epic task of building globe-spanning political associations.

Despite these problems, Wells maintained that the United States was still the best hope for humanity. Because of the "sheer virtue of its size, its free traditions, and the habit of initiative of its people," the country was and would remain indispensable, and with it the "leadership of progress must ultimately rest."[178] It was both synthesis and microcosm: a fecund synthesis of peoples and languages carving out an ever-greater role in the world and a microcosm of what may *eventually* supersede the parochial nation-state. Yet absent a fully-developed sense of the state, this would remain more an immanent potentiality than an imminent probability.

The British Empire was also an obstacle. Like many liberals and socialists, Wells was ambivalent, even conflicted, about the value and purpose of imperial rule. *Anticipations*, he had once claimed, was intended to destroy the empire.[179] Some of his best-known fictional writings can be read as imperial critique—*The War of the Worlds*, after all, opens with a blunt reminder about the genocide of the Tasmanians and later encouraged its readers to have "pity for those witless souls that suffer our dominion."[180] His other scientific romances have been read in a similar vein. Thus China Miéville interprets *The First Men in the Moon* as an anti-imperialist parable.[181] But it is a mistake to read Wells's early work as expressing a consistent rejection of empire.[182] Even

176. H. P. Robinson, *The Twentieth Century American* (New York, 1908), 89.

177. Wells, *Future in America*, 184.

178. Wells, *Future in America*, 230.

179. Wells to Healey, 2 July 1901, *Correspondence*, I, 379.

180. H. G. Wells, *The War of the Worlds* (London, 1898), 249.

181. China Miéville, "Introduction," in Wells, *The First Men in the Moon*, ed. Patrick Parrinder (London, 2005), xx–xxiv.

182. For contrasting accounts of Wells and imperialism, see Aaron Worth, "Imperial Transmissions," *Victorian Studies*, 53/1 (2010), 85; Deane, *Imperial Masculinity*, ch. 7; Paul Cantor and

in his most critical texts, he rarely escaped its magnetic pull. "I who am an Englishman," the narrator of *A Modern Utopia* declaimed, "must needs stipulate that Westminster shall still be a seat of world Empire, one of several seats if you will—where the ruling council of the world assembles."[183] In *New Worlds for Old*, Wells sketched a vision of a multilevel global polity formed by a constellation of large city-states. Maintaining peace between them, he asserted, would require "in many cases the old national form of imperial government and kindred municipalities," each united by a "common language and a common history and a common temper and race."[184] Existing empires would continue to perform a governing function in the new world order. Wells was torn between a patriotic impulse to defend the British Empire, a visionary enthusiasm for imperium as a model of postsovereign political order, and disdain for the squalid reality of imperial greed and hubris.

In the Edwardian years, Wells played an active role in public and private debates over the future of the British imperial system. The country, he wrote in 1911, was "burthened indeed, but not overwhelmed by the gigantic responsibilities of Empire."[185] He dedicated much effort to exploring those responsibilities. Most significantly, he was one of the original members of the Co-efficients. Founded in 1902 by Sidney and Beatrice Webb, it was envisaged as the "Brains Trust" for a possible new political party dedicated to improving national efficiency, though it soon became a high-powered discussion group.[186] Invitations were extended to a dozen prominent individuals, each with a particular specialization, including Leo Amery, Bertrand Russell, Harold Mackinder, Leo Maxse, William Pember Reeves, William Hewins, Lord Robert Cecil, and Lord Haldane. Sidney informed Wells that the group planned to address the "aims, policy and methods of Imperial Efficiency at home and abroad."[187] The monthly meetings of the group in 1902 and 1903, Wells recalled later, had probed the "future of this perplexing, promising and

---

Peter Hufnagel, "The Empire of the Future," *Studies in the Novel*, 38/1 (2006), 36–56; Patrick Parrinder, *Shadows of the Future* (Liverpool, 1995), 65–80; Keith Williams, "Alien Gaze" in McLean, *H. G. Wells*, 49–75.

183. Wells, *Modern Utopia*, 164.

184. Wells, *New Worlds for Old*, 323. This polity would be governed by "that great Congress to which all things are making, that permanent international Congress which will be necessary to insure the peace of the world" (324).

185. H. G. Wells, "Of the New Reign" (1911), in Wells, *Englishman*, 24–25.

186. Semmel, *Imperialism and Social Reform*, 81.

187. Webb to Wells, 12 September 1902, cited in Royden Harrison, *The Life and Times of Sidney and Beatrice Webb* (Basingstoke, 2000), 327. On Fabianism and empire, see Gregory Claeys, *Imperial Sceptics* (Cambridge, 2010), 180–98.

frustrating Empire of ours," and they played "an important part in my education."[188] Russell remarked once that he and Wells were the only non-imperialists in the group, but this was to ignore the complexity of Wells's own commitments.[189] While critical of bombastic imperialism, he was at that time no opponent of empire.

Most of the meetings of the Co-efficients addressed British imperial policy.[190] There was widespread agreement among members on the need to consolidate the settler colonial empire, though questions of imperial economic organization and defense generated substantial disagreement.[191] The group sometimes ventured further afield. In March 1903, they discussed a paper on Anglo-American relations. The minutes, penned by Amery and Mackinder, record a wide-ranging debate. They noted that although various points of potential dispute between the two countries still existed, "it was generally concluded that circumstances would ultimately bring about some form of Anglo-Saxon union," though this was not imminent. Patience was necessary. They finished by remarking that the group was split between those who supported an active policy to encourage union, and those professing greater caution.[192] Although they didn't identify which members fell into each camp, the general consensus about the future signals how widespread belief in union was at the time. Looking back from the vantage point of the 1930s, Wells recalled that during his time in the Co-efficients he still thought that the English-speaking community "might play the part of leader and mediator towards a world commonweal," and he added that this vision had been shared by Sidney Webb, Russell, Pember Reeves, and, more inchoately, Haldane and Grey. But, he continued, the "shadow of Joseph Chamberlain lay dark across the dinner-table," and agreement splintered over tariff reform and imperial federation.[193]

188. Wells, *Experiment in Autobiography*, II, 761. He later parodied it as The Pentagram Circle in *The New Machiavelli*.

189. Bertrand Russell, "H. G. Wells" in Russell, *Portraits from Memory and Other Essays* (London, 1958), 77.

190. On debates over empire in the Edwardian years, see Peter Cain, "The Economic Philosophy of Constructive Imperialism" in Cornelia Navari (ed.), *British Politics and the Spirit of the Age* (Keele, 1996), 41–65; E. H. H. Green, *The Crisis of Conservatism* (London, 1995), 59–78, 194–207; Anthony Howe, *Free Trade and Liberal England, 1846–1946* (Oxford, 1997), 191–274. On the institutional ecology of discussion, see Andrew Thompson, *Imperial Britain* (London, 2000).

191. Co-efficient Minute book, 1902 3, Assoc-17, London School of Economics and Political Science.

192. "What Should Be the Relations between Britain and the United States of America," 16 March 1903, Co-efficient Minute book, 1902–3, 3.

193. Wells, *Experiment in Autobiography*, II, 762–63.

In January 1905, Wells presented a paper to the Co-efficients addressing the question "What Part Are the Coloured Races Destined to Play in the Future Development of Civilisation?" It showcased both Wells's critique of prevailing accounts of race and his inability to escape the rhetoric and theoretical assumptions of the position he sought to repudiate. The minutes recorded an unusual amount of dissent from the assembled group. Wells opened by defining civilization as the achievement of peace, first between individuals and then between polities—a fully civilized world would be one marked by the absence of conflict. This provoked numerous objections. In particular, it was observed that many of the most civilized states had been warlike, and some of the least civilized—the "Australian black fellow," for example—were pacific. Civilization, the majority agreed, was better understood as a combination of material abundance and organizational sophistication. Wells forged on, deploying some of his standard arguments, rejecting the view that all men were equal, as expounded by liberals, Comteans, and Christians alike, and the "biologic-evolutionary" idea that there were intrinsic differences between races. Both were false. Existing inequalities, Wells maintained, could be explained by structural variables, and in principle they could be overcome. However, Wells still distinguished between "coloured" races that were clearly able to contribute to civilization on an equal basis with the "white" races, and those that might have to do so in a different manner: "even if deficient in brainpower, some of these races possess physical characteristics which might render them, either pure or interbred with higher races, the only possible basis of civilization in certain parts of the world."[194] Those places and races were left unnamed, but the image Wells conjured up was a familiar one, with the peoples of the world arranged in a hierarchy, those located at the top duty-bound to aid those below them. This was a conventional imperial cartography, albeit one fleshed out with an unorthodox account of civilization and yoked to a critique of racial science and liberal egalitarianism.

Wells was on friendly terms with some of the leading imperial ideologues of the day. His closest interlocutor on the topic was Leopold Amery. A correspondent for *The Times* during the South African War, Amery subsequently established a reputation as a dogged campaigner for army reform.[195] After flirting with Fabianism, he had drifted into the orbit of the Tory social-imperialists

194. "What Part Are the Coloured Races Destined to Play in the Future Development of Civilisation?," 18 January 1905, Co-efficient Minute book, 1904–5, 1–4.

195. Wells later noted that his satirical novel *The Autocracy of Mr Parham* (London, 1930) was an exploration of the "imagination of a modern British imperialist of the university type," and as such it might have been dedicated to Amery: *Experiment in Autobiography*, II, 501.

who followed Alfred Milner.[196] Wells cast him as Crupp in *The New Machiavelli*, a progressive Tory devoted equally to domestic improvement and to the empire. For "persons like ourselves," Amery wrote to Wells in September 1903, it made sense to "get our Imperialism independent of Tory party politics."[197] The future of the empire was too important to be left to the vicissitudes of partisan conflict. Amery later recalled that Wells had been invited to join the club nominally to represent the literary world, but actually for "original thinking on all subjects."[198] They had much in common. "Our minds certainly worked very much alike in many ways," Amery observed, "and for some years we saw a good deal of each other."[199] He marveled at Wells's extraordinary insight into future technological developments, and the sheer fertility of his imagination, although he remained suspicious of scientific rationalism. An "eighteenth century rationalist with a twentieth century technical mind," Wells lacked a real sense of historical development and placed too much emphasis on human reason in overcoming ingrained habits, and the power of tradition and custom.[200] Even in the mid-1920s, after Wells's enthusiasm for empire had waned, their views still ran parallel. "As in old coefficient days," Amery wrote to Wells in 1925, "I agree with much of the substance and method of your thinking, even when I can't follow the flights by which you reach your immediate conclusions."[201]

As Wells soon came to recognize, his dream of the New Republic chimed with the "constructive" imperialism represented by Milner and his epigones. In a self-reflective moment in *First and Last Things*, he acknowledged that the

196. For Amery's career and ideas during the Edwardian years, see David Faber, *Speaking for England* (London, 2007); William Roger Louis, *In the Name of God, Go!* (New York, 1992), 29–75. Faber describes Wells as Amery's regular "sparring partner" (311).

197. Amery to Wells, 19 September 1903, A108–1, Wells papers.

198. Leopold Amery, *My Political Life* (London, 1953), I, 225. Amery noted that Henry Newbolt, another Co-efficient, was provoked to write a historical novel, *The Old Country*, with a character modeled on Wells (226). In 1911, Amery described *The New Machiavelli* as a "bitingly faithful portrait" of the Webbs. It was "one of the nakedest books ever written but very remarkable": Diary entry, 22 January 1911, *The Leo Amery Diaries*, ed. John Barnes and David Nicholson (London, 1980), 76.

199. Amery, *My Political Life*, I, 225. On Amery's geopolitical vision(s), see Katherine Epstein, "Imperial Airs," *Journal of Imperial and Commonwealth History*, 38/4 (2010), 571–98; Richard Grayson, "Imperialism in Conservative Defence and Foreign Policy," *Journal of Imperial and Commonwealth History*, 34/4 (2006), 505–27.

200. Amery, *My Political Life*, I, 225–26.

201. Amery to Wells, 26 January 1925, A108–1, Wells papers. Amery was thanking Wells for sending him a copy of *A Year of Prophesying*.

New Republicans of *Anticipations* and *Mankind in the Making* were ruthless and overbearing. They were less a desirable ideal than an extrapolation of existing political trends.[202] "Most of the people who have written to me to call themselves New Republicans," he observed, "are I find also Imperialists and Tariff Reformers," and he admitted that of his contemporaries, those who best approximated the ideal were Milner "and the Socialist-Unionists of his group," men who were as "a type harshly constructive, inclined to an unscrupulous pose and slipping into a Kiplinesque brutality."[203] The young Winston Churchill was another devotee, and his later promotion of the "English-speaking peoples" owed much to the inspiration of Wells.[204]

Wells once wrote that "[w]e have to live in a provisional State while we dream of and work for a better one."[205] Intended as a comment on contemporary politics, this also serves as a good summary of his views about imperialism. He argued that the British Empire possessed instrumental, not intrinsic value. It was legitimate only insofar as it helped to realize a vitally important goal: the supersession of the system of states and the creation of a universal political order. If and when it stopped being useful in this sense, it would need to be replaced. As he later put it, empire was "a convenience and not a God."[206] Wells's most sustained Edwardian account of imperial reform, "Cement of Empire," was published in *Everybody's Weekly* in 1911.[207] Rejecting some of the most popular imperial reform proposals of the time, he defended an idealized liberal vision of the British Empire. His position diverged considerably from other Co-efficients. Hewins, Maxse, Amery, Milner, and Mackinder, for example, all supported Chamberlain's program of imperial tariff reform.[208] Indeed Hewins, the political economy specialist of the group, was

---

202. Wells, *First and Last Things*, 114. This part of the autocritique was also published in H. G. Wells, "My Socialism," *Contemporary Review*, 94 (1908), 175–81.

203. Wells, *First and Last Things*, 115. For Milner's views, see the papers collected in Alfred Milner, *The Nation and the Empire* (London, 1913). On Milner and his followers, see Thompson, *Wider Patriotism*; Semmel, *Imperialism and Social Reform*.

204. Toye, "H. G. Wells and Winston Churchill," 147–61.

205. Wells, *First and Last Things*, 102.

206. Wells, *Experiment in Autobiography*, II, 765.

207. It was republished as "Will the Empire Live?," in Wells, *Englishman*, 33–43.

208. On Mackinder, see Brian Blouet, "The Imperial Vision of Halford Mackinder," *Geographical Journal*, 170/4 (2004), 322–29; Gerry Kearns, *Geopolitics and Empire* (Oxford, 2009). Blouet speculates that Wells may have had some influence on Mackinder's conception of the "Heartland" thesis: "H. G. Wells and the Evolution of Some Geographic Concepts," *Area*, 9/1 (1977), 49–52.

arguably the key influence on shaping Chamberlain's views.[209] Wells proselytized an alternative imperial ideal. Sounding like a latter-day Seeley, he opined that the empire was a fortuitous product of accident and individual endeavor, rather than coherent government policy. "The normal rulers of Britain never planned it; it happened almost in spite of them."[210] It was less a vehicle of conquest than of "colonisation and diplomacy." (Given Wells's earlier acknowledgment of the fate of the Tasmanians, it is striking that he did not regard colonization as a form of violent invasion.) Echoing a common trope, he maintained that the empire was without precedent in world history. "Essentially it is an adventure of the British spirit, sanguine, discursive, and beyond comparison, insubordinate, adaptable, and originating."[211] Aligning himself with those who "desire its continuance," he launched an attack on projects for imperial preference and imperial defense, arguing that they were gravely flawed. They shared the same weakness as all plans for imperial federation: there was little that united the "incurably scattered, various and divided" parts of the empire. It faced no common foe to catalyze a sense of common purpose. The conclusion that Carnegie drew from this observation was that the empire had no viable future. Wells, by contrast, argued that if it was understood properly, and if it acted to improve the lives of its subjects, the empire could and should endure. He said little about institutional innovation, which suggests that he thought the existing governance structure was suitable. "It is to the free consent and participation of its constituent peoples that we must look for its continuance."[212]

> It is a living thing that has arisen, not a dead thing put together. Beneath the thin legal and administrative ties that hold it together lies the far more vital bond of a traditional free spontaneous activity. It has a common medium of expression in the English tongue, a unity of liberal and tolerant purpose amidst its enormous variety of localized life and colour. And it is in the developing and strengthening, the enrichment, the rendering more conscious and more purposeful, of that broad creative spirit of the British that the true cement and continuance of our Empire is to be found.[213]

---

209. For Hewins's own account, see *The Apologia of an Imperialist* (London, 1929); see also John Cunningham Wood, *British Economists and the Empire* (London, 1983), ch. 9.

210. Wells, "Will the Empire Live?," 38.

211. Wells, "Will the Empire Live?," 33, 37–38. On this trope, see Bell, *Reordering the World*, chs. 2 and 5.

212. Wells, "Will the Empire Live?," 37, 34.

213. Wells, "Will the Empire Live?," 38.

If it was to be anything, the empire had to be a civilizing force. The English language was fundamental to its resilience. Since language was an agent of civilization, the empire had to become the "medium of knowledge and thought to every intelligent person in it."[214] It could serve as a vast cyborg technology for the progressive education of humanity. Although his discussion of institutional reform was vague, Wells's commitment to liberal imperialism was clear.

However, there were serious obstacles to realizing the full potential of empire. To become "civiliser-general," it had to be governed by an enlightened administration and overseen by politicians who understood its true purpose. Instead, it was endangered by the "intellectual inertness" of those entrusted to rule, the "commonplace and dull-minded leaders."[215] This was a recurrent theme in Wells's Edwardian writings. His searing reflections on deficiencies in the British education system were inflected by a concern that schools were not producing citizens and leaders capable of pursuing the imperial mission. He lambasted the British private schools for manufacturing docile, unimaginative drones. "I submit this may be a very good training for polite servants, but it is not the way to make masters in the world."[216] The ineptitude of the imperial class even threatened the settler empire, as people in Australia, Canada, and New Zealand turned to the United States for ideas and inspiration.[217] Moreover, a successful liberal empire necessitated civilized behavior from its inhabitants. That too was lacking. In *The Future in America*, Wells deplored the racism of white Southerners in the United States, while admitting that the British were little better. Settlers in the Cape, for example, displayed the same attitude: "the dull prejudice; the readiness to take advantage of the 'boy'; the utter disrespect for colored womankind; the savage, intolerant resentment, dashed dangerously with fear, which the native arouses in him."[218] Fully achieving the potential of the British Empire required substantial change. It was threatened by the very people who shouted its virtues the loudest.

The empire, then, was worth saving. However, this created a problem for Wells, because British imperialism was a bar to union with the United States. When he was composing *Anticipations*, Washington seemed ready to embark on a policy of inexorable overseas expansion, perhaps in conjunction with the British. An era of Anglo-American inter-imperialism beckoned. Cementing

214. Wells, "Will the Empire Live?," 39.

215. Wells, "Will the Empire Live?," 39, 40–41.

216. H. G. Wells, "The Schoolmaster and the Empire" (1905), in Wells, *Englishman*, 227. *Mankind* is largely dedicated to outlining a new education ethos and syllabus to forge citizens for the New Republic.

217. Wells, *Future in America*, 42

218. Wells, *Future in America*, 169, 170.

ties between the polities would accelerate the creation of a New Republic. The hyperefficient New Republicans would properly fulfill the role of Civiliser-General, educating the world's peoples for their eventual integration into a world-state. Yet by the time Wells visited the United States, he sensed that imperial enthusiasm had cooled. The Americans were even ready to shed the Philippines "at as early a date as possible."[219] Wells recognized that future American political development would fall within continental bounds, while the British remained wedded to their imperial project. "So long as we British retain our wide and accidental sprawl of empire across the earth we cannot expect or desire the Americans to share our stresses and entanglements."[220] Given the position of the British Empire, and the current failings of the United States, it made sense to temporarily prioritize the improvement of the former over reintegration with the latter. The New Republic had to be deferred.

In Wells's Edwardian writings, we see two possible institutional foundations for the world-state. It could be built on the back of the British Empire or through Anglo-American union. Initially, Wells believed that the two models could be fused together, but it soon became apparent that this was unrealistic: they pulled in different directions. The tension could be resolved through the medium of time. *Anticipations* looked a century into the future, whereas *The Future in America* scanned a closer horizon. In the former, Wells had been sanguine that Britain and the United States were sufficiently alike to merge seamlessly together into the Larger Synthesis. The shifting technoscientific environment demanded change in the order of things, and they were best placed to dominate the emerging world. His transatlantic visit induced caution, persuading him both that American sentiment was turning away from overseas imperialism and that the ubiquity of "state-blindness" rendered the country unfit to shoulder the burden of state building on a global scale. Yet these impediments could be overcome. The unrelenting processes transforming the world would eradicate or transcend them in due course. Technoscientific progress could not be halted. Moreover, the commonalities linking the English-speaking polities were more fundamental than their differences. "[O]ur civilization," he proclaimed, "is a different thing from our Empire, a thing that reaches further into the future, that will be going on changed beyond recognition." Shared language and history meant that Americans were part "of our community, are becoming indeed the larger part of our community of

219. Wells, *Future in America*, 111. The American imperial state persisted longer than Wells thought it would: Julian Go and Anne Foster (eds.), *The American Colonial State in the Philippines* (Durham, NC, 2003).

220. Wells, *Future in America*, 22.

thought and feeling and outlook," and that this was much more "intimate than any link we have with Hindoo or Copt or Cingalese."[221] The future still belonged to the English-speaking peoples, who would eventually form the core of a world-state. In the short term, the British Empire—at least if governed properly—could continue to serve as a "civiliser-general," battling ignorance and spreading progressive institutions and values until it had completed its task. A "precursor of a world-state or nothing," the empire was a self-dissolving enterprise, preparing the way for its own eventual supersession.[222] For Wells, the English-speaking peoples remained the true vanguard of world history.

221. Wells, *Future in America*, 22–23.
222. Wells, *Experiment in Autobiography*, II, 762.

5

Machine Dreams

THE ANGLOWORLD AS SCIENCE FICTION

Of late years it has been common enough for authors to comment on the
political and social tendencies of their own days, by drawing fancy pictures of
the state of the world many generations hence, when these tendencies have
been worked out to their full development.[1]

(CHARLES OMAN)

Welcome to the Machine

Political advocacy was not confined to dry scholarly treatises, the oracular
speeches of politicians, the pages of newspapers, or the musings of wealthy
businessmen. The future of the Angloworld—and in particular Anglo-
America—was thematized widely in late nineteenth-century fiction. Arthur
Conan Doyle dedicated his 1891 novel *The White Company* to "[t]he hope of
the future, the reunion of the English speaking races."[2] He enlisted Sherlock
Holmes, who upon encountering a Mr Moulton in "The Adventures of the
Noble Bachelor," declaimed that "[i]t is always a joy to meet an American,"
because he believed resolutely that "the folly of a monarch and the blundering
of a minister in far-gone years" should not prevent "our children from being
someday citizens of the same world-wide country whose flag should be a

1. Charles Oman, "Editor's Preface," *The Reign of George the VI, 1900–1925* (London, 1899),
vii. Principally a military historian, Oman was a Fellow of All Souls Oxford; he later served as
Chichele Professor of Modern History (elected 1905) and a Conservative MP.

2. Arthur Conan Doyle, *The White Company* (London, 1891). Stead described the novel as
an important contribution to racial "reunion": *RoR*, 4 (December 1891), 637. See also Joseph
Baylen, "Sir Arthur Conan Doyle and W. T. Stead," *Albion*, 2/1 (1970), 3–16.

quartering of the Union Jack with the Stars and Stripes."[3] The composition of the Anglo-American elite was a recurrent topic in Henry James's closely observed portraits of transatlantic high society.[4] He too was enthralled by the dream of fusion, writing in October 1888 to his brother that "I can't look at the English-American world, or feel about them, anymore save as a big Anglo-Saxon total, destined to such an amount of melting together than an insistence on their difference becomes more and more idle and pedantic."[5] Poetry, and in particular the work of Tennyson, was routinely invoked by Anglo-American unionists. But it was in science fiction that we find the clearest and most elaborate accounts of the Anglo dreamworld. Such narratives offered ambitious unionists the opportunity to build imaginative worlds in which they could rehearse the sequence of events that would realize their fantasies.

Science fiction interrogates how scientific reasoning and technological progress construct human subjectivity and social order.[6] Literary historians disagree about the origins, development, and nature of the genre, with some maintaining that it can be traced back to the dawn of Western literature, others suggesting that it emerged from the intellectual ferment of early modern Europe, and still others locating its genesis in the early nineteenth century or the closing years of the Victorian age, even the nineteen-twenties, when the term was first employed self-consciously.[7] Whichever historical narrative one adopts, it is clear that the late nineteenth century witnessed the emergence of a body of work, and a mode of writing, that was grappling with an

---

3. Arthur Conan Doyle, "The Adventures of the Noble Bachelor" in Doyle, *The Adventures of Sherlock Holmes* (London, 1892), 257.

4. This topic is addressed in Priscilla Roberts, "The Geopolitics of Literature," *International History Review*, 34/1 (2012), 89–114.

5. Henry James to William James, 29 October 1888, *The Letters of Henry James*, ed. Percy Lubbock (New York, 1920), I, 143.

6. For a convincing "cultural historicist" approach to the field, see Roger Luckhurst, *Science Fiction* (Cambridge, 2005). See also John Rieder, "On Defining SF, or Not," *Science Fiction Studies*, 37/2 (2010), 191–209. For more prescriptive definitions, see Darko Suvin, *Metamorphoses of Science Fiction* (New Haven, CT, 1979); Carl Freedman, *Critical Theory and Science Fiction* (Middleton, 1990); Tom Moylan, *Scraps of an Untainted Sky* (London, 1990).

7. For conflicting accounts, see Adam Roberts, *The History of Science Fiction* (Basingstoke, 2005), chs. 1–5 (on its ancient origins); Luckhurst, *Science Fiction*, ch. 1 (on its modern ones); and George Slusser, "The Origins of Science Fiction" in David Seed (ed.), *A Companion to Science Fiction* (Oxford, 2008), 27–43. For an excellent historical overview of its modern forms, see Gerry Canavan and Eric Carl Link (eds.), *The Cambridge History of Science Fiction* (Cambridge, 2018).

unprecedented historical conjuncture. Modern science fiction was created by the combination of four developments: the rapid extension of literacy in the United States and Britain; the spread of new publishing formats that spurred formal innovation and the advent of new genres; the expansion of scientific training and technical institutions that spawned a large cohort of scientists, engineers, and teachers—the kind of technical environment in which Wells and many of his enthusiastic readers were educated. And finally, the transformation of "everyday life experience," which was, for the first time, saturated with "Mechanism." While the railway and the industrial factory provoked wonder and trepidation during the midcentury years, it was only from the 1880s that urban life came to be seen as a "machine ensemble."[8]

A popular medium of social and political thought, fin-de-siècle science fiction was interwoven with visions of racial supremacy, violent conquest, and imperial rule.[9] The genre was also utilized to explore the nature and possibilities of political orders beyond the existing system of states and empires. As Mark Mazower observes, "[S]cience allied to storytelling provided an immensely popular vehicle for articulating internationalist visions of the unification of mankind."[10] The synthesis of political divination and scientific extrapolation performed the same role for visions of Angloworld unity. Speculative fiction proved an especially fecund genre for imagining utopian racial futures. Modes of popular fiction—including romance, spy thrillers, and science fiction—"excel in inviting readers to co-create and inhabit worlds." This is in part because of their generic forms. Genres, Mark Jerng contends, serve as "fields and frames with which to organize meaning. They produce effects of truth and authority through the projection of their 'generically specific' worlds."[11] He argues that late nineteenth and early twentieth century "yellow peril" novels formed one such genre, and that their accounts of impending racial conflict embedded race into "temporal and historiographic structures of meaning-making" that shaped "anticipation and expectations of the world."[12] This argument can be generalized to the wider literature on future wars and Anglo-racial destiny.

---

8. Luckhurst, *Science Fiction*, 17–18, 29.

9. John Rieder, *Colonialism and the Emergence of Science Fiction* (Middletown, 2008); Istvan Csicsery-Ronay, "Science Fiction and Empire," *Science Fiction Studies*, 30/2 (2003), 231–45; Patricia Kerslake, *Science Fiction and Empire* (Liverpool, 2010); David Seed, "The Course of Empire," *Science Fiction Studies*, 37/2 (2010), 230–52.

10. Mazower, *Governing the World*, 26.

11. Jerng, *Racial Worldmaking*, 15, 11.

12. Jerng, *Racial Worldmaking*, 67, 207.

In contrast to high modernism's assumption that the machine was the root cause of social ills, fin-de-siècle Victorian science fiction in both the United States and Britain probed utopian machinic possibilities.[13] Technology was also read as an expression of character, individual and collective. A pivotal notion in nineteenth-century Anglo-American culture, character constituted both an explanatory category and a valorized normative ideal: an individual with a commendable character exhibited a range of virtues, almost invariably coded masculine, including self-control, self-sufficiency, perseverance, and stoicism. National (and racial) character was read in similar ways.[14] The proliferation of "mechanism" at once challenged and reinforced characterology. On the one hand, the development of technoscientific expertise was itself regarded as a manifestation of superior character. Such arguments were used to validate imperial expansion, legitimating the developmental ambitions of the civilizing mission.[15] On the other hand, new technologies threatened to corrode virtue, portending the reign of Gradgrindian materialism or the logic of dehumanization. Character, then, was expressed in how individuals and peoples negotiated the mercurial role of technoscience. A clear theme emerges in the science fictional discourse: masters of technology, not mastered by it, the "Anglo-Saxons" exhibited the necessary intellectual, material, and spiritual qualities to govern the world.

This chapter focuses on the proleptic literature of war and racial order. Writings dedicated to imagining future conflict contain some of the most elaborate attempts to envision an Anglotopian future. I identify a distinct shift in content between the 1880s and the end of the century, from a common figuration of the United States and the British Empire as antagonists to one in which they are often united in the attempt to govern the globe. I start by teasing out some of the similarities and differences between American and British narratives, before turning to Stanley Waterloo's *Armageddon*, a popular American tale of racial union in which the former colony supplants the "mother country" as the dominant partner in a mission to stabilize a chaotic world. In the remaining sections, I investigate several texts in greater detail. To examine how fantasies of imperial federation fused with Anglo-American union, I discuss Julius Vogel's *Anno Domini 2000*, a self-conscious utopian narrative penned by a one-time New Zealand Premier. Written from a settler colonial perspective—at

13. On high modernism's anti-*techne*, see Roberts, *History of Science Fiction*, chs. 8–9. Duffy, *Speed Handbook*, offers an alternative reading.

14. On the notion of character in British political culture, see Stefan Collini, *Public Moralists* (Oxford, 1991); Mandler, *English National Character*; Peter Cain, *Character, Ethics and Economics* (Abingdon, 2018).

15. Adas, *Machines as the Measure of Men*; Adas, *Dominance by Design*.

once inside and outside the metropolitan frame—it was one of the most elaborate stagings of the dream sequence that moves from colonial union to the reintegration of Britain and America. I then analyze George Griffith's *The Angel of the Revolution* and Louis Tracy's *The Final War*, two best-selling fantasies of Angloworld racial utopia published in the 1890s. Both plot the world-historical destiny of the Anglo-Saxons, although they present very different future visions, with Griffith narrating a social revolution and Tracy developing a much more conventional account of Anglo-Saxon capitalism triumphant. The chapter concludes with a reading of William Cole's *The Struggle for Empire 2236*, one of the first "space operas," which I read as an ambivalent attempt to critique the will to power underpinning the quest for racial domination.

Wars of the World

Angloworld fantasies pervaded late nineteenth-century literary culture on both sides of the Atlantic. They found their most resonant—and politically didactic—expression in the hugely popular new genre of future-war stories that flourished between the 1870s and the outbreak of the First World War.[16] These science fictional tales of future conflict nevertheless provide an illuminating map of the geopolitical anxieties and dreams of the age. The most famous of all was George Chesney's *The Battle of Dorking*, which created a sensation in 1871 and spawned numerous imitators over the following decades.[17] For Darko Suvin, the publication of Chesney's fable and Edward Bulwer-Lytton's *The Coming Race* cemented 1 May 1871 as the formative moment of British science fiction.[18] A distinguished military officer, Chesney feared that

16. For accounts of the genre, see I. F. Clarke, *Voices Prophesying War*, 2nd ed. (Oxford, 1992); Clarke, "Future-War Fiction," *Science Fiction Studies*, 24/3 (1997), 387–412; Ailise Bulfin, *Gothic Invasions* (Cardiff, 2018); Charles Gannon, *Rumors of War and Infernal Machines* (Liverpool, 2003); Seed, *Future Wars*; Antulio Echevarria, *Imagining Future War* (Westport, CT, 2007); Michael Hughes and Harry Wood, "Crimson Nightmares," *Contemporary British History*, 28/3 (2014), 294–317. For a useful general account of future-war thinking, stressing its role as a form of persuasion rather than prediction, see Lawrence Freedman, *The Future of War* (London, 2017).

17. Originally published in *Blackwood's Edinburgh Magazine*, it is anthologized in I. F. Clarke (ed.), *The Tale of the Next Great War, 1871–1914* (Syracuse, 1995), 27–74. See also Clarke, "Before and after 'The Battle of Dorking,'" *Science Fiction Studies*, 24/1 (1997), 33–46; Michael Matin, "Scrutinizing *The Battle of Dorking*," *Victorian Literature and Culture*, 39/2 (2011), 385–407. Wells cited it as an example of how not to forecast the future: Wells, *Anticipations*, 2.

18. Darko Suvin, *Victorian Science Fiction in the UK* (Boston, 1983). It was also the date that Samuel Butler delivered the manuscript of *Erewhon* to his publisher.

Britain was unprepared for the dawning era of industrial conflict, having failed to learn the brutal lessons of the American Civil War and the recent Franco-Prussian conflict. Written from the perspective of a melancholic volunteer looking back from the 1930s on a successful German invasion, it anatomized the unfolding of a calamitous British defeat.

Though not foregrounded, imperial themes percolate through Chesney's narrative and play an important role in his account of the causes and consequences of the war. British military forces throughout the world are weakened by imperial overstretch, thinned by the simultaneous need to defend Canada against an American assault, quash a rebellion in India, and battle Fenians in Ireland.[19] As such, the Americans unwittingly aid the destruction of Britain and its empire. Chesney's general ambition was clear: to stimulate demand for greater military spending and recast public attitudes to defense. "For us in England it came too late. And yet we had plenty of warnings, if only we had made use of them."[20] This pedagogical aim animated much future-war writing. "Almost overnight," I. F. Clarke argues, "fiction had replaced the tract and the pamphlet as the most efficient means of airing a nation's business in public."[21] In the 1880s and 1890s, the bulk of stories written by British authors envisaged a war between Britain and France, though by the turn of the century Germany was routinely cast as the enemy.[22] Russia too was a common foe. The genre was so popular that it spawned numerous parodies, including P. G. Wodehouse's riotous *The Swoop; or How Clarence Saved England* (1909).

Even as these speculative texts charted possible futures, they usually reproduced conventional understandings of military strategy. Despite their manifold differences, Karl von Clausewitz's *On War* and Baron de Jomini's *The Art of War*, both published in the 1830s, set the template for doctrinal debate in the

---

19. George Chesney, *The Battle of Dorking*, in Clarke (ed.), *Tale of the Next Great War*, 30–31.

20. Chesney, *Battle of Dorking*, 27.

21. Clarke, "Future-War Fiction," 391. Christian Melby rightly notes the ambiguous reception of future-war texts, the multiplicity of their aims, and the limit of their impact on public policy, as well as the ways that they often implied or celebrated a spatially extended form of Britishness: Melby, "Empire and Nation in British Future-War and Invasion-Scare Fiction, 1871–1914," *Historical Journal*, 63/2 (2020), 389–410.

22. For some representative tales, see I. F. Clarke (ed.), *The Great War with Germany, 1890–1914* (Liverpool, 1997). See also I. B. Whyte, "Anglo-German Conflict in Popular Fiction, 1870–1914" in F. Birdgham (ed.), *The First World War as a Clash of Cultures* (London, 2006), 43–100. Clarke notes that during the 1890s, both the market for future-war texts and the outlets in which they were published began to change, moving from the middle-class journals to more popular forms of mass circulation publishing ("Future-War Fiction," 404–5).

mid and late nineteenth century. It was accepted as a matter of faith that wars were settled by victory in decisive battles, a creed that underpinned an obsession with the primacy of the military offensive. The key assumption, Lawrence Freedman writes, was "that a great commander would eliminate the enemy army in battle, and in so doing deliver the enemy state up for whatever humiliation and punishment the victorious sovereign thought appropriate."[23] Despite their attempts to picture future wars and new destructive technologies, this vision of battle structured the fictional discourse. Instead, the stories differed chiefly over the imagined scale of conflict, the technoscientific means through which victory could be achieved, and the form of postwar order envisioned.

Existing scholarship on invasion texts tends to focus on technologies of violence, the accuracy of their forecasting, and the apocalyptic imagination of destruction: death rays, airships, slaughtered armies, and cities reduced to rubble.[24] The specific political projects adumbrated by the authors—and in particular the role of Anglotopian dreams—fade into the background. Yet these were didactic works, often written to advance distinctive political programs. Although transatlantic in scope, future-war narratives exhibited different national inflections. While American authors were also inspired by Chesney, their presuppositions and ideological purposes diverged from their British counterparts in revealing ways. Three main differences stand out. First, the Americans almost invariably won their wars while the British often lost (or came very close to losing) theirs. Moreover, American authors placed greater emphasis on the ability of radical new technologies to transform the conditions of both warfare and planetary life. Following Chesney's lead, British writers typically concentrated on reorienting national policy through raising the specter of weakness. Many of them focused on the European balance of power: the threat to Britain from a resurgent Germany, the old enemy France, and the hulking Russian Empire in the East. This strategy was made explicit in the preface to one of the most popular tales, William Le Queux's *The Great War in England in 1897* (1894): "In writing this book it was my endeavour to bring vividly before the public the national dangers by which we are surrounded, and the absolute necessity which lies upon England to maintain her defences

23. Freedman, *Future of War*, 8. See also Michael Howard, "Men against the Fire" in Howard, *The Lessons of History* (New Haven, CT, 1993), 97–112; Beatrice Heuser, *The Evolution of Strategy* (Cambridge, 2010), pt. III.

24. See, for example, Echevarria, *Imagining Future War*; Leo Mellor, *Reading the Ruins* (Cambridge, 2011), ch. 1; Sven Lindqvist, *A History of Bombing* (Cambridge, 2012), paras. 53–60. A notable exception is H. Bruce Franklin's classic *War Stars*, rev. ed. (Amherst, MA, 2008), chs. 1–2, though it says little about the Angloworld dimension. For a valuable survey of the scholarship, see Ailise Bulfin, "'To Arms!,'" *Literature Compass*, 12/9 (2015), 482–96.

in an adequate state of efficiency."[25] American authors seemed more concerned with triumphantly plotting the emergence of their country as a dynamic global power.[26] Finally, the relationship between the state and capitalism was imagined in different ways. Many American writers valorized the powers of capitalist enterprise, assigning a pivotal role to individual entrepreneurs, heroic business leaders, or lone geniuses (often modeled on Thomas Edison), while portraying the state and politicians as sluggish, a bar to the United States realizing its full potential rather than the primary vehicle for achieving that hallowed end. Fantasies of hypercapitalist energy were far more muted in British writings.

The American choice of enemy was also revealing. Numerous texts published during the 1880s and early 1890s portrayed a war between the United States and the British Empire, dramatizing the simmering animosity between the two countries and reflecting the deep-seated Anglophobia of large swathes of the population. Samuel Barton's *The Battle of the Swash and the Capture of Canada* (1888), arguably the first American future-war novel, was perhaps the most accomplished of these tales.[27] It looks back from 1930 on a war fought between the two powers in 1889. The legacy of the Civil War hangs heavily over the text, as the mendacious British take advantage of the tumult to derail America's ascent as a major trading state, destroying its fledgling navy and bombarding New York and other coastal cities, before salvation arrives in the form of a new weapon, an advanced torpedo boat that dethrones the Royal Navy. The government in London is forced to cede Canada and the West Indies to the United States, an act of geopolitical amputation that precipitates

25. William Le Queux, "Preface to the 9th Edition," *The Great War in England in 1897*, 11th ed. (London, 1895). In the novel, Britain is invaded by Russia and France, before Germany intervenes to help the British.

26. Susan Matarese examined 212 American utopian novels from the period. She divides representations of the United States into three categories: "moral exemplar," "benevolent superpower," and "active crusader." The first was the most popular, with a utopian America leading the world by the power of persuasion and the attractiveness of its institutions and culture. Materese, *American Foreign Policy and the Utopian Imagination* (Amherst, MA, 2010), ch. 3. Examples of each can also be found in the literary articulation of Anglo-America, though the category boundaries often blur.

27. Other examples include Samuel Reed, *The War of 1886, between the United States and Great Britain* (Cincinnati, 1882); Alvarado Fuller, *A.D. 2000* (Chicago, 1890), in which the British invade Canada (and the United States emerges victorious); Hugh Grattan Donnelly, *The Stricken Nation* (New York, 1890), in which a British naval fleet annihilates New York City; Bert Wellman, *Legal Revolution of 1902* (Chicago, 1898), in which Britain and the United States fight over Canada, with the latter (of course) emerging victorious.

the decline and fall of the Empire, as India is seized by the Russians, Australia declares independence, and Britain loses its preeminence in Europe. The novel ends with the United States regnant, occupying "the foremost position among the nations of the Earth."[28] In such stories, racial kinship was both acknowledged and superseded, the national interests of the two countries seen as divergent, their shared history more a source of acrimony than potential unity.

During the 1890s, however, the constellation of allies and enemies shifted. Many novels, both British and American, imagined the United States and the British Empire as cooperative partners, allies, or parts of a reintegrated racial-political community.[29] They supplied cultural currency to the push for rapprochement, though symptomatic differences remained, perhaps above all in the way that the relationship between the two powers was emplotted. Unlike Carnegie and Stead, many British authors were unwilling to yield leadership of the Angloworld—and hence the planet—to Washington, and the "kin across the sea" were typically cast as an enthusiastic though immature junior partner. This attitude was mirrored across the Atlantic, where in an act of familial role-reversal Britain was usually granted a supporting role alongside a newly dominant United States. This signified both a transformation in the balance of geopolitical power and an intraracial transfer of authority, with the old idea of *translatio imperii* given new science fictional form. Frank Stockton's popular *The Great War Syndicate* (1889) crystallized several of these themes. War between Britain and the United States is triggered by a dispute over fishing rights, whereupon a cabal of twenty-three "great capitalists" usurp the ineffective politicians and take charge. In an age of privatized warfare, the business leaders devise fearsome weapon systems capable of pulverizing the British, but rather than fighting their racial kin, the Americans instead demonstrate to them this newfound destructive power. Suitably apprised of their diminished status in the Anglo-American relationship, the shocked and awed British agree to serve as loyal lieutenants in "The Anglo-American Syndicate of War," an alliance that eventually pacifies the Earth.[30]

28. Samuel Barton, *The Battle of the Swash and the Capture of Canada* (New York, 1888), 126. Barton was the son of a Jacksonian New York Congressman, Samuel Barton (1785–1858).

29. There were exceptions to this trend. In 1896, for example, Charles Anson (who claimed to be a British naval officer) published *The Great Anglo-American War of 1900* (London, 1896), in which the United States defeats Britain in a war, after the Royal Navy destroys San Francisco. Some of the most popular British texts—including Le Queux's *The Great War in England 1897* and Rear-Admiral P. Colomb's *The Great War of 189-* (London, 1892)—continued to focus principally on Europe.

30. Frank Stockton, *The Great War Syndicate* (London, 1889). Stockton was a well-known author who wrote in a variety of genres. Wells mentions him positively, albeit in passing, in

Stockton's novel influenced the British author George Griffith's *The Great Pirate Syndicate*, which ends with the "long-dreamt-of ideal of an Anglo-Saxon federation."[31] Another Englishman, Geoffrey Danyers, finished his 1894 novel *Blood Is Thicker Than Water: A Political Dream* with the Americans and British "equal in the brotherhood of their race," forming "the greatest union of which history makes mention."[32] Later examples of Anglo role-switching include James Barnes's *The Unpardonable War*, where a British-American conflict of the 1920s, won by the United States as a result of a Edisonian inventor, results in an Anglo-American union dedicated to "the rule of peace, the sway of justice, and the rule of common-sense," and Roy Norton's *The Vanishing Fleets*, where access to a range of new superweapons permits the United States, intent on securing global harmony through war, to defeat Britain, Japan, and China in quick succession, before magnanimously inviting the British to aid them in realizing the President's dream of peace. Having "faith in the Anglo-Saxon race," the British and Americans sign a "defensive and offensive alliance," pledging their formidable combined power to a new commission established to maintain international order.[33] Such texts fictionalized the debates over the possible benefits of an Anglo-American union being played out in the journals and clubrooms of the North Atlantic world.

The American literature of racial union reached a crescendo of sorts in 1898. As the United States launched an imperial war against Spain, an array of texts explored the future possibilities of Angloworld domination. The "emerging faith in American technological genius," H. Bruce Franklin argues, "wedded the older faith in America's messianic destiny."[34] In Benjamin Rush Davenport's *Anglo-Saxons Onward!* the US leads a "semi-alliance" of the Anglo-Saxon nations to crush the Spanish empire and ultimately control the world, while S. W. Odell's *The Last War; or, the Triumph of the English Tongue* identified genocide as a means to racially purify the earth. In the twenty-sixth century, the highly "civilized"—all-white—"Allied Anglo-American Nations" decide,

---

Anticipations (152n). Stead recounts a conversation between Carnegie and Stockton at Skibo, in which the Scotsman claimed that the prophecies of "A Look Ahead" were coming true. "We are heading straight to the Re-United States," he informed the novelist. Stead, *Americanization*, 407.

31. George Griffith, *The Great Pirate Syndicate* (London, 1899), 264. I return to Griffith later in the chapter.

32. Geoffrey Danyers, *Blood Is Thicker Than Water* (London, 1894), 158, 159.

33. James Barnes, *The Unpardonable War* (New York, 1904), 356; Roy Norton, *The Vanishing Fleets* (New York, 1908), 339–41.

34. H. Bruce Franklin, "How America's Fictions of the Future Have Changed the World" in David Seed (ed.), *Future Wars* (Liverpool, 2012), 34. On American future-war stories, see also Thomas Clareson, *Some Kind of Paradise* (Greenwood, 1985).

more in sorrow than celebration, to engage in a "war to the end" against a dangerous racially mixed empire controlled by the Russian Czar. Fusing racial millenarianism with the pornography of violence, millions of people are slaughtered before Anglo-America triumphs, completing the conquest of the planet.[35]

Stanley Waterloo was the most famous American writer to pen a future-war narrative. Described in a *New York Times* obituary as "for thirty years one of the best known newspaper men in the United States," he published a number of successful novels, the most popular of which was *The Story of Ab* (1897), a pioneering attempt to chart the life of a prehistoric human.[36] In 1898, he released *Armageddon: A Tale of Love, War and Invention*. Like so many novels of the future, it opens with a telescopic account of geopolitical turmoil, the Spanish-American war heralding the predestined entry of the United States onto the world stage. Yet confusion reigned and the nineteenth century, we are informed, "flickered out in something like racial warfare."[37] It was as if Charles Pearson's grim predictions of global race conflict had come true. As the planet is engulfed by violence, the Americans and the British recognize their true affinities and shared interests: "the idea of an Anglo-Saxon alliance had grown and broadened." This vision had been "fostered by thinking men of both Great Britain and America," those who could "best foresee the future of races." Ultimately, though, "a tentative alliance, at least, it was evident, must come."[38] It would form the basis of a majestic racial order.

Meanwhile, an archetypal American story is unfolding on an isolated farm on the Illinois prairie. A solitary genius works feverishly on a machine that will save humanity from itself. "Dreamers make the world progress, after all. Ninety-nine out of the hundred fail. The hundredth becomes one of the world exclamation points."[39] The exclamation point in question turns out to be a

35. Benjamin Rush Davenport, *Anglo-Saxons, Onward!* (Cleveland, 1898); Samuel Odell, *The Last War; Or, the Triumph of the English Tongue* (1898; Chicago, 1939). In a later white supremacist novel, *Blood Will Tell* (1902), Davenport posits the inherent racial inferiority of black people.

36. "Stanley Waterloo Dead," *New York Times*, 12 October 1913, 15; Stanley Waterloo, *The Story of Ab* (Chicago, 1897). A "primer in eugenics and manliness for young Americans," it was also an intervention in contemporary debates about evolution: Nicholas Ruddick, *Fire in the Stone* (Middleton, 2009), 40; John Hensley, "Eugenics and Social Darwinism in Stanley Waterloo's *The Story of Ab* and Jack London's *Before Adam*," *Studies in Popular Culture*, 25/1 (2002), 1–9. On race and future war in American literature, see also Patrick B. Sharp, *Savage Perils* (Norman, 2007), ch. 1; Paul Williams, *Race, Ethnicity, and Nuclear War* (Liverpool, 2011), ch. 1.

37. Stanley Waterloo, *Armageddon* (New York, 1898), 5.

38. Waterloo, *Armageddon*, 9.

39. Waterloo, *Armageddon*, 31.

flying machine, a cigar-shaped aluminum tube able to mount a devastating array of weapons. As war looms, the Americans and British put old animosities aside, while the French, Russians, and Germans are increasingly impatient with their allotted place in the global hierarchy. Unusually for the genre, Germany plays a liminal role—though not (yet) inside the Anglo-Saxon alliance, it is imagined as a potential racial ally rather than an implacable enemy. In a more conventional act of characterization, Waterloo hymns the greatness of the Anglo-Saxons, their fecundity the main driver of global development, their glorious fate to bring civilizational light to the barbarous regions of the earth. They are, he lectures,

> groups of people who have seized upon a great part of the world, who people Northern America, though the children are apart, who have made old and ancient Australasia to blossom as the rose, who will just as surely people Africa, the lush continent so long neglected by the civilized, and enlighten Asia, as the world turns on an invisible intangible axis and brings about what men believe in and know, Night and Morning. And these made the Anglo-Saxon alliance.[40]

With painful consequences for the flow of the narrative, Waterloo then embarked on a long digression about the Panama canal, which was presented as a manifestation of the abundant virtue and technoscientific expertise of the Anglo-Saxons, whose trade and military superiority it would guarantee. "It was a magnificent exhibition of what the spirit of conquest is."[41] Infrastructural capacity was a potent expression of the will to dominate, control, and overmaster. Eventually, Waterloo remembers the main plot of the novel and returns to the imminent conflict. A formal Anglo-American Alliance is signed in anticipation of world war, the "[b]lood-relationship and self-interest" combining to promote the coalition. Past grievances are forgotten, "just as the Americans had forgotten the spirit which rose when North and South were arrayed against each other." Shared values and interests triumph, above all "the instinct of a common language, code of laws, religion and education and plan for the world's future."[42] In a rhetorical move common in the genre, Waterloo spatialized the affective connections linking Britain and the United States by suggesting that authentic American sentiment was represented by a

40. Waterloo, *Armageddon*, 91.

41. Waterloo, *Armageddon*, 123. The French began work on a canal in 1881, but the Americans took over the job in 1904. It was not completed until 1914. Julie Greene, *The Canal Builders* (London, 2009).

42. Waterloo, *Armageddon*, 140–41.

deep-seated yet dormant Anglophilia—"Below, were the real people"—and that the ubiquitous outward expressions of Anglophobia were epiphenomenal surface emotions, chiefly the product of untrustworthy politicians seeking to foment trouble and secure votes. The sense of kinship was akin to bubbling magma, waiting to burst through the earth's crust. Latent British Americophilia was likewise unleashed by the threat of conflict.[43] As was also common at such narrative junctures, Waterloo turned to Tennyson for poetic assistance, fixing on one of his less grandly metaphysical productions to give voice to British attitudes:

> Gigantic Daughter of the West
> We drink to thee across the flood,
> We know thee most, we love thee best
> For art thou not of British blood?
> Should war's mad blast again be blown,
> Permit not thou the tyrant powers
> To fight thy mother here alone
> But let thy broadsides roar with ours.
> Hands all round!
> God the tyrant's course confound!
> To our great kinsmen of the West, my friends,
> And the great name of England round and round.[44]

The ensuing war pitches the "Teutonic" races, led by the Anglo-Saxons but encompassing most Northern European states, with Japan as an ally, against a combination of the southern "Latin" races, dominated by the French and Italians (with lukewarm German support), and the "Slavs," directed by Russia. The result was entirely predictable, the Anglo-Saxon victory being decided—without much bloodshed—in a great naval battle in the Atlantic. Picturing the vast fleets from the air, Waterloo hymned the imperial sublime: "It was beautiful, but with the beauty of terror, that assembly of naked metal fighting machines lying there on the strongly heaving yet unbroken sea of blue water."[45] The enemy armada is destroyed with the help of the new "battle-ship of the

---

43. Waterloo, *Armageddon*, 160.

44. Waterloo, *Armageddon*, 140–41. This is the third verse of "Hands All Round," *The Examiner*, 7 February 1852. It can be found in a topical volume, Bliss Carman (ed.), *The World's Best Poetry, VIII* (Philadelphia, 1904), 29–30, where it is printed next to Kipling's "Recessional" in a section celebrating patriotism. It is also cited as an accurate account of Anglo-American sentiment in Doane, "Patriotism," 318.

45. Waterloo, *Armageddon*, 205.

air."[46] Sensibly recognizing where their true racial loyalties and interests lay, the Germans refuse to aid their putative allies.

At a Peace Conference in Amsterdam, the victors dictate the shape of things to come. The French, Spanish, and Portuguese empires are dissolved, their territories transferred to the more deserving Anglo-Saxons.

> We are the conquerors. Rightly or wrongly, we consider ourselves the approved of Providence in directing most of the affairs of the world, and we propose, for the present, to direct them. We do not intend to take your territory, but we do intend to establish our authority as paramount, and centuries may pass before you again acquire the position you lately held relatively, even if you develop a different growth. We believe that we are the people most adapted for the population of new lands and propose to act in accordance with this idea. We propose, for example, that the development of Africa, the new continent, to be civilized is best in our hands and we prefer that as it is gradually populated in its richer portions by the European overflow, that overflow shall not be Latin.[47]

This was a naturalized vision of Anglo-Saxon imperial order underwritten by the dynamics of social evolution. The other Western powers have forfeited the right to perform the civilizing mission, with failure in war read as a sign of their unworthiness to act as avatars of global modernity. But Waterloo was not yet finished. As a corollary of the global extension of Anglo-Saxon power, increasingly restrictive immigration controls are instituted in the United States and the British Empire to stop the further contamination of the racial stock. It was essential to protect the *Volkstaat*, upholding white supremacy through constraining freedom of movement. The story thus ends by intervening directly in the racist debates over immigration controls that permeated political discussion in the Angloworld at the time.[48] The novel is at once an index of popular anxiety and an example of a racial utopian response to it.

Waterloo's book was just one of many that reflected and helped to shape dreams of Anglo-American ascendancy. As the United States mounted its quest for great power status, American authors dropped their animosity toward Britain, instead viewing it as a friend or close ally in the mission to inaugurate the Anglo domination of the earth. Yet Britain was invariably presented as the junior partner in such endeavors, a follower rather than the

---

46. Waterloo, *Armageddon*, 152.

47. Waterloo, *Armageddon*, 242–43.

48. Lake and Reynolds, *Drawing the Global Color Line*.

natural leader, its place directing the race (and hence the world) supplanted by the economic and technoscientific dynamism of the United States. The twentieth century, they boasted, would be an Anglo-*American* century.

From Imperial Federation to Anglotopia

Literary critic Istvan Csicsery-Ronay argues that modern imperialism can be interpreted as the "steady consolidation of a universal regime of technoscience," a regime that is "hyper-global, extending beyond the limits of known space and mortality, containing an infinite variety of sublime and grotesque possibilities." Drawing on Hardt and Negri's popular account of Empire, he argues that this hegemonic position manifests a postmodern institutional form, guided by a "transglobal technocratic elite with lax ties to traditional communities."[49] It is a function of the dispersal and incessant circulation of capital after the Industrial Revolution. However, late Victorian imperial technoscientific discourse—at least in its Anglo-American expression—both assumed and propagated a different model of the future. Though often presented as embodying universal reason, the transnational vanguard it postulated was nevertheless the product of a specific (albeit spatially diffuse) political community and a singular racial imaginary. Less a postmodern form of empire than an extension of existing modernist political forms, it stretched the model of the bounded political community across space into a globe-spanning, even cosmic, cyborg order.

Imperial federation was one such model of bounded racial expansion. Like most political projects of the time, it generated its own (small) fictional literature, contributing to the swirling mass of speculative texts circulating through the Angloworld. In 1872, just as the agitation for imperial federation began to gather steam, an author writing under the pseudonym "Octogenarian" published *The British Federal Empire*.[50] George Sydenham Clarke, the British army officer whom we encountered debating Carnegie in chapter 2, penned his own narrative of future naval war in 1891. Writing under a pseudonym, he imagined a great European conflict, with Britain and France the main protagonists. Remaining neutral throughout, the United States is called on to mediate at the close of hostilities, with Britain and its "kindred nation" then assuming

49. Istvan Csicsery-Ronay, "Empire" in Mark Bould et al. (eds.), *The Routledge Companion to Science Fiction* (London, 2009), 362.

50. Octogenarian, *The British Federal Empire* (London, 1872). The story disappeared into obscurity.

a joint protectorate to govern various islands in the South Pacific.[51] The most important outcome of the war is the creation of an imperial federation—"the greatest Federation which the world has ever-known." This new polity inaugurates an age without war. Writing from the vantage point of the mid-twentieth century, the narrator declares that the future belongs "to the Anglo-Saxon people, whose alliance is the dominating factor of the present age." With the world policed by a vast Greater British naval fleet, a *"pax Anglo-Saxonica"* reigns unchallenged.[52]

Julius Vogel wrote the most interesting novel on the subject. Regarded as one of the pivotal figures in the development of the New Zealand state, he was a prominent colonial journalist and politician, twice serving as Premier (1873–57 and again in 1876), after which he was appointed the first New Zealand Agent-General in London.[53] Vogel was an ardent supporter of the imperial federation movement, arguing that without formal consolidation the British Empire would ultimately dissolve, reducing the mother-country to the status of a second-rate power and leaving the colonies at the mercy of larger predatory states.[54] *Anno Domini 2000* (1889) rendered his political ideals in fictional form.[55] The book is perhaps most notable for its bold account of gender relations. (Intriguingly, Anglo-American union was also the imaginative setting for some of the first lesbian and transgender characters in science fiction.)[56]

51. A. Nelson Seaforth [Clarke], *The Last Great Naval War* (London, 1891), 109–10.

52. Seaforth [Clarke], *Last Great Naval War*, 116. The future relationship with the United States is left unclear.

53. Raewyn Dalziel, *Julius Vogel* (Auckland, 1986).

54. Julius Vogel, "Greater or Lesser Britain," *Nineteenth Century*, 1/5 (1877), 813. See also Vogel, "The British Empire," *Nineteenth Century*, 3/3 (1878), 617–36.

55. The novel is dedicated "To the Rt. Hon Earl of Carnarvon, who, by his successful efforts to consolidate the Canadian Dominions, has greatly aided the cause of federation" (5). Cf. Henry Howard Molyneux, Fourth Earl of Carnarvon, *The Defence of the Empire*, ed. G. S. Clarke (London, 1897). On the composition and reception of *Anno Domino 2000*, see Dalziel, *Julius Vogel*, 302–4. For analysis of the text, see Dominic Alessio, "'Gender,' 'Race' and Proto-Nationalism in Julius Vogel's *Anno Domini 2000; or Woman's Destiny* (1889)," *Foundation*, 33/91 (2004), 34–54; Philip Steer, "National Pasts and Imperial Futures," *Utopian Studies*, 19/1 (2008), 49–72.

56. Gregory Casparian, *The Anglo-American Alliance* (New York, 1906). The novel centers on a passionate relationship between two women, one British, the other American; it ends with one of them undergoing sex reassignment surgery. Casparian, a former officer in the Armenian army, imagines the "fraternal union" of Britain and the United States in 1925–26 (61–62). The novel is discussed briefly in Jess Nevins, "The First Lesbian Science Fiction Novel, Published in 1906," *io9* (2011), http://io9.com/5847805/the-first-lesbian-science-fiction-novel-published-in-1906.

Vogel predicted that by the year 2000 it would be recognized universally that women were intellectually and emotionally superior to men and they would occupy almost all of the key roles in public life.[57] As a result, "[i]t has, in fact, come to be accepted that the bodily power is greater in man, and the mental power larger in woman. So to speak, woman has become the guiding, man the executive, force in the world."[58] Rather than positing a radical form of egalitarianism, Vogel reversed the valence, imagining that women were superior at roles traditionally coded male. In the novel, both the British Prime Minister and the American President are women, as are most of the main characters. While reproducing Victorian norms of masculine chivalry, this was nevertheless an audacious account of the gender order.[59]

Anno Domini 2000 is also noteworthy for its account of the emergence and functioning of Angloworld domination. In contrast to socialist visions of utopia, Vogel's novel conjured up a liberal capitalist dreamworld, a space in which the market operates productively for the benefit of everyone and basic human needs are fully satisfied. The story commences in 1915 with a secretive group of bankers intervening to halt the slide to a European war, before they lay the foundations for a rudimentary welfare state that simultaneously alleviates poverty and eliminates the grounds for social revolution.[60] This system develops over subsequent generations, and by the year 2000, the world is wealthy and largely at peace. Gradual and harmonious evolution was the key to progress,

57. Julius Vogel, *Anno Domini 2000; Or, a Woman's Destiny*, ed. R. Robinson (1889; Honolulu, 2002), 36–37, 45–47. See also the "Epilogue," 182. Vogel practiced what he preached, introducing a Woman's Suffrage Bill in 1887. On his feminist vision and its limits, see Dominic Alessio, "Promoting Paradise," *New Zealand Journal of History*, 42/1 (2008), 27; Steer, "National Pasts," 60. See also Raewyn Dalziel, "An Experiment in the Social Laboratory?" in Ian Christopher Fletcher, Phillipa Levine, and Laura Nym Mayhall (eds.), *Women's Suffrage in the British Empire* (London, 2000), 87–102.

58. Vogel, *Anno Domini 2000*, 37.

59. *Anno Domini 2000* was reviewed fairly widely. *The Athenaeum* criticized it as a "mere excuse for startling and lively statements concerning the future of the British empire" (30 March 1889, 405). Others thought it more interesting: the *Hampstead & Highgate Express* (12 October 1889, 3) commended Vogel's feminism; the *Morning Post* (17 April 1889, 2) called it a "curious book," albeit one "with a deeper meaning and purpose" than most prophetic tales; the *Glasgow Herald* (8 May 1890, 4) termed it a "striking romance"; the *Chichester Observer* (3 April 1889) deemed it "semi-socialistic."

60. Vogel, *Anno Domini 2000*, 25–33. Vogel makes this ambition explicit in the epilogue: "The writer has a strong conviction that every human being is entitled to a sufficiency of food and clothing and to decent lodging whether or not he or she is willing to or capable of work." He also expressed his hatred of "anything approaching to Communism," which would be "fatal to energy and ambition" (183).

both a constant of history and a solution to the scandal of human suffering. Sounding like Carnegie, the narrator comforts readers with the revelation that "[p]rogression, progression, always progression, has been the history of the centuries since the birth of Christ."[61] Following a line of local politicians who had authored prophetic novels or poems celebrating New Zealand—including William Pember Reeves, Alfred Domett, and George Warren Russell—Vogel extended a tradition of speculative writing that portrayed the colony as paradisiacal.[62] This was a literature of settler colonialism as the realization of utopian desire. Largely introspective, the genre said little about the place of New Zealand in the wider world, a silence that Vogel's text addressed through a double intervention in debates over imperial federation and the future of British-American relations. He envisioned a successful federal empire-state, in which "[e]ach portion of the Emperor of Britain's possessions enjoys local government, but the federal government is irresistibly strong." This was an extrapolation of his earlier writing on imperial federation, where he had argued for the development of an overarching federal structure to bind the colonial empire together.[63] At the same time, he decentered the future polity, downgrading Britain and assigning the settler colonies a far greater role than most imperial federalists allowed. Indeed, he pictured a world in which the epicenter of political authority was mobile and often opaque. "It is difficult to say which is the seat of government," he intoned, "as the Federal Parliament is held in different parts of the world and the Empire resides in many places."[64] In the novel, it is temporarily located in Melbourne. This account of political kinesis was reminiscent of Rhodes's dream of a race-empire without a permanent metropolitan core, as well as the nomadic world citizens of Wells's

61. Vogel, *Anno Domini 2000*, 35.

62. At least one hundred utopian texts related to New Zealand were published between 1778 and 1930 (the genre was most popular between 1870 and 1930). See Alessio, "Promoting Paradise," 22–23; Lyman Tower Sargent, "Utopianism and the Creation of New Zealand National Identity," *Utopian Studies*, 12/1 (2001), 1–18; Sargent, *New Zealand Utopian Literature* (Wellington, 1997); P. G. McHugh, "William Pember Reeves (1857–1932)" in Shannaugh Dorsett and Ian Hunter (eds.), *Law and Politics in British Colonial Thought* (Basingstoke, 2010), 187–208. As we saw in chapter 4, Pember Reeves was a member of the Fabians and Co-efficients alongside Wells (who had a notorious affair with his daughter, Amber Reeves).

63. Vogel, "Greater or Lesser Britain," 828–29.

64. Vogel, *Anno Domini 2000*, 39. "If a headquarters does remain, it may probably be conceded that Alexandria fulfils that position" (39). This point was a departure from his nonfictional writings, as he had firmly declared that London would always remain the seat of empire: Vogel, "The British Empire," 618.

modern utopia, and it illustrated the sense of global mobility running through speculative visions of the Angloworld, its people spread far and wide across the cyborg imperium.

In Vogel's alternate world, the British Empire was brought to the verge of ruin in 1920 by discord over Ireland. Newly wealthy and assertive, the colonies intervene to resolve the crisis: "United, they far exceeded in importance the old mother-country." London is forced reluctantly to grant Home Rule, catalyzing both the explosive growth of the Irish economy—the most successful in the world by 2000—and the federation of the Empire.[65] Reversing prevailing core-periphery dynamics, Vogel inscribes the settler colonies into the heart of the Anglo-project. This was the colonies writing back—or writing into— the metropolitan imagination. "By positioning the colonies as the means of reinvigorating the metropolis through technological and social progress," Philip Steer argues, "Vogel locates the colonial periphery as a temporal as well as a physical frontier of the Empire."[66] In Vogel's narrative the message conveyed by Macaulay's redolent "New Zealander," who voyages from the New World to gaze over the ruins of London, is circumvented, as power drains away from the old imperial center without precipitating the dissolution of the whole.[67] Decline is followed by rebirth rather than Fall. Vogel's Anglo-imperium is figured as immune to the traditional causes of degeneration, at once too large for external assault and too internally robust for corruption to corrode it from within. Imperial federation thus allows the reconciliation of *grandezza* and *libertas*—*imperium* could permanently escape the vicissitudes of historical time. Vogel can present London as partially corrupted by luxury, its inhabitants "chartered sybarites" and "luxurious to the verge of effeminacy," but rather than serving its classical role as the primary agent of decline, such hedonism is rendered harmless, even comic, because of the dispersal of political authority and economic might.[68] "The British dominions have been consolidated into the empire of United Britain; and not only is it the most powerful empire on the globe, but at present no sign is shown of any tendency to

---

65. Vogel, *Anno Domini 2000*, 38.

66. Steer, "National Pasts," 54.

67. On the "New Zealander," see my discussion in *Reordering the World*, ch. 5; Alessio, "Promoting Paradise," 34–35; Robert Dingley, "The Ruins of the Future" in Dingley and Alan Sandison (eds.) *Histories of the Future* (Basingstoke, 2000), 15–33. The future decline of the empire was fictionalized in Lang-Tung, *The Decline and Fall of the British Empire* (London, 1881); E. E. Mill, *The Decline and Fall of the British Empire* (Oxford, 1905). Both were written from the perspective of future Asian historians educating school children.

68. The quotes can be found in Vogel, *Anno Domini 2000*, 46 and 137.

weakness or decay."[69] As Vogel opens the story, the empire is in rude health. It is the most powerful polity in the world, though not yet hegemonic, for the United States, with which the empire cooperates closely, is growing in strength and confidence. By the close of the novel, an expanded British Empire reigns supreme.

Political unity was predicated on technoscientific progress. Following the wise intervention of the Prince of Wales, the citizenry is no longer distracted by having to learn useless dead languages, but are instead given an intense practical scientific training, with the result that "each person was more or less an engineer."[70] More typically American than British, this Wellsian mode of subject formation further accelerated technological progress. The novel is studded with inventions—"phonograms," force fields, aluminum air-cruisers. At one point, people are rendered immobile by a mysterious but devastating weapon that harnesses the power of electricity.[71] Portable silent "hand tele-graphs" allow journalists to stream live accounts of political debate across the polity, creating a powerful sense of instantaneity and communal identity. Vo-gel's novel exemplifies the fascination with infrastructural space, racial infor-matics, and communications systems that suffused the discourse of Anglo-world unification. It imagines the Anglo-Saxon race as a cyborg assemblage, knitted together by a dense communications network pulsating with informa-tion. The transformative potential of communications technology is rein-forced by new modes of aerial transport. Global geography is rewritten. "A journey from London to Melbourne was looked upon with as much indiffer-ence as one from London to the Continent used to be."[72] Confined to use by the government—in contrast to many American novels of the era—this air-power underwrites British military superiority over other states.[73] We are in-formed that these mighty sentinels "made easily a hundred miles an hour" across the skies of the future.[74] While it is easy to mock Vogel's lack of pro-phetic imagination about the possibilities of flight, it is worth recalling that

---

69. Vogel, *Anno Domini 2000*, 38. The federal structure incorporates Britain, Ireland, the settler colonies in Australia, Canada, and New Zealand, virtually all of southern Africa (after a Rhodesian project of massive settler colonization), and, rather more unusually, Egypt, Belgium, and the Channel Ports of France (39). Other African, Indian, and Caribbean territories are excluded, presumably on racial grounds.

70. Vogel, *Anno Domini 2000*, 58.

71. Vogel, *Anno Domini 2000*, 41, 104, 99–100.

72. Vogel, *Anno Domini 2000*, 83.

73. Vogel, *Anno Domini 2000*, 114–15.

74. Vogel, *Anno Domini 2000*, 118.

two decades later, in one of the less successful predictions in *Anticipations,* Wells rejected the viability of mass air-travel and placed his hopes in elevated train-lines connecting cities.[75]

Many advocates of imperial federation viewed it as an immense community that would dominate competitors and shape the world to its will. Others saw it as an initial step on the road to a yet grander destination: the consolidation of the whole "English-speaking race," even of humanity itself. Vogel fantasized about the predestined reunification of the federated empire and the "one re-public" across the Atlantic. While the plot here is very thin, it represents the ecstatic climax of the political energies coursing through the text. Vogel stages a dynastic dispute between the British Empire and the United States that re-sults in war.[76] The Americans launch an impetuous attack on Canada only to be swatted aside like flies, before a vast British armada is sent across the Atlan-tic to punish them. The expeditionary force captures Washington and pro-ceeds to outflank the American army in Canada. They demonstrate their abid-ing sense of kinship by refusing to massacre the brave but ineffectual American soldiers—presumably a fate reserved for the hapless "natives" that the empire continues to govern. The forlorn President is whisked aboard the advanced air-cruiser *The British Empire*, and the British celebrate "a triumph which amply redeemed the humiliation of centuries back, when the English colonies of America won their independence by force of arms."[77] The injustice of his-tory redressed, the door is opened to reuniting Anglo-America. The terms of the subsequent peace deal include a plebiscite in New England, where the inhabitants vote overwhelmingly to (re)join the British Empire, with New York anointed the new capital city of the Dominion of Canada.[78] The demo-cratic empire is extended democratically. In a mirror image of many American tales, the United States—or at least the authentic "Anglo-Saxon" element—is simultaneously reincorporated into the Angloworld and assigned a subordi-nate position within it. It has been transfigured from a powerful independent state to a region within British imperial jurisdiction. Yet there is also an impor-tant difference: in Vogel's racial dreamworld, it is neither Britain nor the United States that lead the Anglotopian community, but rather the Pacific settler colonies.

---

75. Wells, *Anticipations*, 18n. Wells was quick to admit his mistakes, as he did in the 1914 preface to the volume.

76. Vogel, *Anno Domini 2000*, 145.

77. Vogel, *Anno Domini 2000*, 161, 163.

78. Vogel, *Anno Domini 2000*, 164–65.

Even as Vogel outlined an alternative liberal vision of Anglo-futurism, he disclosed the violence and authoritarianism at its core. Inscribed in federal constitutional law is a prohibition forbidding any challenge to either the unity of the empire or the monarchy governing it. "To question even the wisdom of continuing the Empire, of preserving the succession in the imperial family, or of permitting a separation of any of the dominions was held to be rank treason; and no mercy was shown to an offender."[79] Here Vogel echoed and amplified a point he had made in his nonfictional writing on imperial unity. Criticizing those who saw the colonies as "young nations," he retorted, "From the point of view which regards the colonies and integral as inseparable parts of the Empire prognostications of the kind are little short of treasonable." He was adamant that the colonies should be barred from ever declaring independence. "If the union is desirable, it should not be open to question."[80] This speaks to the paranoia felt by many late Victorian imperialists about the durability of the political bonds linking the settler colonial system. For Vogel, only a constitutional proscription could mitigate the danger, even if it could never be eradicated.

The text is also haunted by an absent presence: there is barely any discussion of the populations ruled over by the British Empire. The chief exceptions are occasional, though revealing, comments that the only remaining political violence in the global system was the elimination of resistance in occupied Asian territories—"the guerrilla warfare that sometimes was forced on the authorities."[81] Such warfare, it is implied, was solely the fault of those who refused the benefits of British rule, thus rendering them legitimate targets for annihilation. Peace in utopia was bought at the expense of interminable violence on the periphery.

Vogel's was not the only science fictional rendering of the transition from imperial federation to global Anglo-Saxon dominion. Arthur Bennett's *Dream of an Englishman* (1893) plotted a similar course, though with less narrative verve and in a different political key. In contrast to Vogel's Angloworld liberalism, Bennett presented a Romantic Tory vision, his future commonwealth

---

79. Vogel, *Anno Domini 2000*, 87.

80. Vogel, "Greater or Lesser Britain," 813.

81. Vogel, *Anno Domini 2000*, 82. "These simultaneous 'better British' and 'better black' tropes assisted in the creation of a racialized utopian episteme that appeared to make the country's settler history distinct from that of convict/Aboriginal Australia, French/Metis/First Nation Canada, black/Boer South Africa, or rebel/black/native America": Alessio, "Promoting Paradise," 32.

predicated on stringent racial and gender exclusions.[82] He stuck fairly closely to the contours of late nineteenth-century British politics, populating his text with recognizable political figures—Forster, Chamberlain, Disraeli—while sketching an argument about the necessity of imperial union. Pouring scorn on those who rejected imperial federation as too "visionary," he charged that "the practical men have been the mistaken men in all ages, and the dreamers are the men who lead the way."[83] With unrest sweeping an empire weakened by the pernicious ideology of free trade, a conference is convened in London, "the cradle of the race that was about to dominate the world." It results in the creation of an imperial federation.[84] In this "Commonwealth of Oceana"—a title that echoed both Harrington and Froude—imperial preference supplants free trade as the governing economic policy.[85] Here Bennett offers a lightly fictionalized gloss of the plans propounded by the United Empire Trade League.[86] Rewriting the past as well as plotting the future, he complained that the cost of delay had been exorbitantly high: federating earlier might "have saved the bloody split between John Bull and Brother Jonathan in the preceding century, and kept Old England one with New until the termination of the 'course of time.'" Following the federal consolidation of the empire, the United States drops ever further behind and tries desperately to rejoin the British, Brother Jonathan indicating "that he was willing to return to the bosom of the family."[87] And so it comes to pass. This act of political transubstantiation left the world divided into three main geopolitical groupings, the United Empire of Great Britain (including the subordinate American state), the United States

82. Arthur Bennett, *The Dream of an Englishman* (London, 1893), 166, 161, 165. For his non-fictional account of imperial federation, see Bennett, "Federation Made Easy," *Imperial Federation*, 8 (1893), 320–21.

83. Bennett, *Dream*, 47. He was not the first to use the title: T. G. Lally-Tolendal, *The Dream of an Englishman* (London, 1793). Bennett's text is discussed briefly in Seed, "Land of the Future," 17.

84. Bennett, *Dream*, 127, 143, 144.

85. Harrington's utopian text was published in 1656; see James Harrington, *"The Commonwealth of Oceana" and "The System of Politics"*, ed. J. G. A. Pocock (1656; Cambridge, 1990). Froude was explicit about his debt to Harrington in his own imperial unionist text, *Oceana* (London, 1886). See here, Duncan Bell, "Republican Imperialism," *History of Political Thought*, 30/1 (2009), 166–91.

86. This was one of the organizations set up after the collapse of the Imperial Federation League in 1892. It supported a federation centered on "imperial preference," in contrast to the British Empire League (established in 1896), which was composed of free traders.

87. Bennett, *Dream*, 175.

of Europe, and the United States of South America. Over the course of the twentieth century, the latter two eventually recognize their inferiority and join the former, which is transformed into a world federation dominated by the Anglo-Saxons. Once again, the image of decline is both evoked and displaced, for "instead of the New Zealander coming to survey the ruins of St. Paul's, he came to sit within the walls of Westminster, and meet the Patagonian and the Eskimo, the Hottentot and the Celestial, and to join in their deliberations for the good of all."[88] In an abrupt switch of register, Bennett then drops into cosmic speculation.

> And some of the boldest of "the coming race" were looking out upon the stars, and wondering if there were worlds to conquer there. And the federations which their poets sang of, now, were federations of the solar system, and the union of which they dreamed embraced Orion and the Pleiades. For they were gradually discovering that the tiny planet on whose generous bosom they had built their Earthly Paradise was but an island in the ocean of infinity, and that the universe, with all its suns and stars, was one.[89]

Bennett gestures to both Edward Bulwer-Lytton's *The Coming Race*, one of the best-known science fiction texts of the era, and (as was de rigueur) Tennyson's premonitory passage in "Locksley Hall," where the narrator "dipt into the future, far as human eye could see," and hailed the "Parliament of man, the Federation of the world." As we shall see, Bennett was not the only racial unionist to project a political vision into outer space.

Murder by Machinery: On Peace through War

George Chetwynd Griffith and Louis Tracy wrote two of the most popular unionist novels of the time, their work communicating to large audiences the Anglotopian fantasies circulating through sections of the political and intellectual elite. They echoed and nourished the hunger for stories of racial salvation. While Vogel and Bennett emphasized the federation of the settler empire, with full Anglo-Saxon unification a secondary (though still vital) feature of their narratives, the balance is reversed in the work of Griffith and Tracy, as racial consolidation takes center stage. Although the two novels shared much in common—stylistically and structurally—their political messages were very different. Both posited the Anglo-Saxons as redemptive saviors of civilization, but the specific type of civilization they deemed worth saving diverged,

88. Bennett, *Dream*, 185.
89. Bennett, *Dream*, 187.

Griffith painting a socialist Anglo-future, Tracy consecrating an idealization of the existing imperial capitalist order.

Griffith's *The Angel of the Revolution* appeared in the same year as Carnegie's impassioned summons to Anglo-American union.[90] The industrialist might have approved of the utopian vision of racial peace animating the narrative, but he and his fellow plutocrats were among Griffith's main targets. When he began to write this, his first book, Griffith was a jobbing journalist working at *Pearson's Magazine*, an influential monthly periodical with a socialist flavor and a list that was to include many successful scientific romances and invasion tales. An intrepid traveler, he left home at a young age and circled the globe several times, with stints working in Australia and the United States, before settling in London. The book was an instant hit, and for a brief moment Griffith was the leading science fiction writer in the country, before he was eclipsed by Wells.[91] While popular in Britain, Griffith's work was largely ignored in the United States, chiefly because it was viewed as anti-American.[92] Channeling a host of contemporary anxieties and obsessions, above all fascination with terrorism and Anglo-Saxonism, the novel is a fast-paced fable of the technological sublime, mixing socialist politics, mannered romance, ultraviolence, and racial deliverance.

By the time Tracy published *The Final War* in 1896, he had already written several unsuccessful volumes of fiction and travelogue, based largely on his experience working in India. His panoramic novel, modeled in part on Griffith's, appeared during the protracted crisis over the Venezuela boundary. A reviewer in *The Dial*, an American literary periodical, characterized his work as "anticipatory historical fiction," an apt description of the genre as a whole.[93] Popular on both sides of the Atlantic, it was praised in the *New York Times* as a "capital story and full of action."[94] The German imperialist Karl Peters

90. George Griffith, *The Angel of the Revolution*, ed. Steven McLean (1893; London, 2012). It was originally serialized in *Pearson's Magazine* between January and October 1893.

91. Sam Moskowitz, "Critical Biography" in George Griffith, *The Raid of "Le Vengeur" and Other Stories*, ed. Moskowitz (London, 1974), 7. *Pearson's* later serialized Wells's *The War of the Worlds*. For general context, see Tattersdill, *Science, Fiction, and the Fin-de-Siècle Periodical Press*. On Wells and Griffith, see Harry Wood, "Competing Prophets," *The Wellsian*, 38 (2015), 5–23.

92. Moskowitz describes him as a "pariah" because of the perceived anti-Americanism of *The Angel of the Revolution* ("Critical Biography," 7). For an example of his views on the United States, see Griffith, "The Grave of a Nation's Honour," *Pearson's Magazine*, March 1896, 261–65, which discussed how the Monroe doctrine repressed South Americans.

93. William Morton Payne, *Dial*, 1 November 1898, 306.

94. *New York Times*, 21 November 1896, 17. Other positive reviews included the *Indianapolis Journal* (25 November 1896, 3); the *Saint Paul Globe* (17 January 1897, 10). Following his death,

thought that it exemplified the "fantastic visions" of racial conquest and domination gripping "minds" in the Angloworld at the turn of the century.[95] In a revealing interview in 1899, Tracy outlined the patriotic motivation that supplied the "germ" of the novel.[96]

> The whole world seemed to be up in arms, ready and eager to jump on Old England. All countries seemed to be snapping like fox terriers at the heels of John Bull. I thought it was time that the bull should turn and give them a taste of his horns, and let them know who was their master. For, notwithstanding the use of modern arms, you know I firmly believe in the old saying that one Englishman is worth five of any other people in the world.[97]

This passage illustrates the tenor and tone of the story. Vogel and Tracy both envisaged a future dominated by a reunified Anglo-Saxon race, but each assigned the British Empire a different part in the transition from a world of empire-states to one shaped by racial hegemony. Whereas Vogel cast imperial federation in a starring role, Tracy ignored it altogether, focusing instead on the Anglo-American axis as the constitutional vehicle for achieving planetary supremacy.

The Final War charted the "last of all wars between civilised nations"—a war, that is, between "white" states—and presents a future transatlantic union as the glorious culmination of world history.[98] Blending xenophobia with a celebratory affirmation of rigid gender and class distinctions, Tracy populated the narrative with wooden British stereotypes: preternaturally wise aristocratic politicians; omniscient and dashing military leaders; respectable, competent, slightly pompous middle-class men; rough-edged but ultimately virtuous workers, nonchalant and loyal in the face of extreme danger. Foreigners were almost invariably portrayed as inferior, even contemptible, while the female characters were usually either verging on hysteria or genuflecting before their valiant spouses and the sacred racial cause. Many of the key characters were modeled on British public figures, though all were heavily idealized. They ventriloquize his own political desire. More revealing than convincing, either as art or political program, Tracy's tale nevertheless demonstrates both

---

The Bookman described Tracy as "an able and successful novelist, whose books have enjoyed considerable popularity for the last thirty years" (28 October 1928, 27).

95. Peters, *England and the English*, 359.

96. The serial ran in *Pearson's Weekly* from 28 December 1895 to 1 August 1896.

97. "The Man Who Wrote *The Final War*," interview with Louis Tracy, *Pearson's Weekly* (20 March 1897), reprinted in George Locke, *Pearson's Weekly* (London, 1990), 115.

98. Louis Tracy, *The Final War* (London, 1896), 275. See also Tracy, "Do the Americans Really Hate Us?," *Pearson's Weekly* (12 September 1896), 1–3.

the tendency to yoke future fiction to utopian ambition and illuminates the sense of racial superiority on which it rested.

Griffith's tale of race and revolution was likewise set in the near future. Opening in 1903, most of the action unfolds in 1904, the "Year of Wonders." We meet Richard Arnold, a brilliant twenty-six-year-old "dreamer of dreams," toiling away, in poverty and alone, to unravel the mystery of heavier-than-air flight. On the verge of despair and bankruptcy, he cracks the puzzle, building a working model of an airship. Set to bring terror and then peace to the world, his invention was "to be to the twentieth century what the steam engine was to the nineteenth," appointing those who possessed it "master of a kingdom wide as the world itself."[99] *The Angel of the Revolution* was one of the best-known novels to envisage new aerial technologies as harbingers of both annihilation and perpetual peace—the *Pax Aeronautica*.[100] Flight was the quintessential technology of the coming age. Arnold and his precious plans are rescued by a mysterious stranger, Maurice Colston, who soon reveals himself to be an exiled Russian working for a secret society dedicated to the overthrow of both Tsarist despotism and the capitalist order. Committed to socialist revolution, "The Brotherhood of Freedom," widely known as "The Terrorists," strikes fear into the ruling classes of Europe. Under the guiding inspiration of the mysterious Natas, another victim of Russian brutality, it directs "the operations of the various bodies known as Nihilists, Anarchists, Socialists—in fact, all those organisations which have for their object the reform or destruction, by peaceful or violent means, of Society as it is presently constituted."[101] Tired of political oppression and economic injustice, the Brotherhood have worked assiduously to prepare the ground for worldwide revolt.

The shadow of war hangs over Europe. After professing adherence to revolutionary ideals, Arnold is inducted into the Inner Circle of the Brotherhood, and christened "Master of the Air." Work begins on constructing a full-scale version of his airship in the Outer Hebrides. The stage is set. In familiar fashion, the ensuing war pits the great powers of Europe against one another in a

99. Griffith, *Angel of the Revolution*, 25.

100. The most famous are Wells's *The War in the Air* and *The Shape of Things to Come* (London, 1933). See also Steven Mollmann, "Air-Ships and the Technological Revolution," *Science Fiction Studies*, 42/1 (2015), 20–41; Steven McLean, "Revolution as an Angel from the Sky," *Journal of Literature and Science*, 7/2 (2014), 37–61. On British views of aerial warfare, see Michael Paris, *Winged Warfare* (Manchester, 1992); Brett Holman, *The Next War in the Air* (Aldershot, 2014); David Edgerton, *England and the Aeroplane* (Basingstoke, 1991).

101. Griffith, *Angel of the Revolution*, 51. On the terror motif, see Barbara Arnett Melchiori, *Terrorism in the Late Victorian Novel* (Beckenham, 1985); Deaglán Ó Donghaile, *Blasted Literature* (Edinburgh, 2011), esp. chs. 2–4.

roiling "death-struggle." The British Empire is bound by secret treaty to the Triple Alliance (though Italy defects due to British diplomatic blunders), while the Russians are united by another secret treaty to the French. The scale of the conflict between the "Anglo-Teutonic Alliance" and the "Franco-Slavonian League" is enormous, as are the causalities, prefiguring the slaughter to come two decades later. Ten million Anglo-Teutonic soldiers and thirteen million Franco-Slavs are soon battling across the world. The latter, though, have a potent technological innovation at their disposal, a fleet of "navigable aerostats"—large armed balloons—capable of wreaking unprecedented destruction from the air. They play a critical role in the "colossal struggle which was now to be waged for the empire of the earth."[102]

Spanning fiction, history, journalism, poems, and political pamphlets, while interpolating public figures, the Angloworld intertext was dense, flexible, and shape-shifting. Like Bennett and Tracy, Griffith studded his novel with active politicians, both as homage to existing advocates of Anglo-American consolidation and to underwrite the verisimilitude of the story. Balfour serves as Prime Minister (an accurate forecast), while Morley is leader of the opposition (rather less so). Cameo appearances are made by Chamberlain, Dilke, Lord Brassey, Lord Randolph Churchill, and the Earl of Rosebery.[103] The most important role is given to Beresford, the Royal Navy Admiral whom we encountered in his debate with Mahan in chapter 2. Christened "Charlie B" by the adoring Victorian press, Beresford was the most celebrated British sailor of the day, an irascible, ambitious, publicity-hungry officer and hard-line Tory MP.[104] "That the English-speaking nations should combine to preserve the peace of the world," he later wrote in his Memoirs, "has always seemed to me a reasonable aspiration, and I have said so in both countries when opportunity served."[105] In The Final War, we first meet him repelling a French attack in the Channel. Later, he commands a British fleet with great skill and courage in the Second Battle of the Nile, a costly victory that nevertheless saves the British Empire.[106]

102. Griffith, Angel of the Revolution, 144.

103. Griffith, Angel of the Revolution, 194.

104. Beresford was promoted to Rear-Admiral in 1897, and engaged in a long-running and increasingly bitter dispute over naval policy with his superior, Admiral John ('Jackie') Fisher. On Beresford, see Geoffrey M. Bennett, Charlie B (London, 1968). For late Victorian debates about naval strategy, see Paul Kennedy, The Rise of the Anglo-German Antagonism, 1860–1914 (London, 1980); David Morgan-Owen, The Fear of Invasion (Oxford, 2017); Frei, Great Britain.

105. Charles Beresford, The Memoirs of Admiral Lord Charles Beresford (Boston, 1914), II, 398. For his debate with Mahan, see "Possibilities of an Anglo-American Reunion."

106. Griffith, Angel of the Revolution, 260–62.

Tracy's story opens in Paris in 1898 as plucky British officers uncover a Franco-German invasion plot. Determined to create mighty empires of their own, the Kaiser and the President have assembled a motley coalition (including Russia) seething with resentment at British predominance. "An army large enough to win a continent, and a navy that might sweep a dozen oceans, were ready to pounce upon the little island they all so deeply feared."[107] The defeated empire would be carved up between them: Canada to France; East Africa to Germany; Australia, New Zealand, and South Africa to be placed under the combined government of the alliance; while England and Ireland would be administered by France and Germany, with the promise of limited Home Rule in the indefinite future. Russia claimed India as a condition of its participation.[108] British politicians react to the imminent threat with patriotic stoicism, putting aside party disputes and personal animosities, as Balfour proclaims the unity of "one race, one empire, one people, one party."[109] In the opening engagement, a small force, once again under the command of Beresford, prevents an attempted invasion of the coastal town of Worthing, through a combination of technical skill and personal bravery. "The incoming tide cast up a ghastly legacy of the fight in the shape of hundreds, if not thousands, of corpses. It was in this guise, and in no other, that the army corps of France and Germany effected a landing upon British soil."[110] This complacent template, in which the British outperform their enemies in every dimension of combat, recurs throughout the book. It was made a mockery of only a few years later on the South African veldt.

The initial war in Griffith's novel is short but catastrophic. Millions are killed in a matter of weeks, fighting across the length and breadth of Europe, with conflict also taking place offstage, especially in India. The Brotherhood stand back, watching the slaughter unfold, waiting for the right moment to intervene. The British are portrayed as far less adroit than in *The Final War*. In battle after battle, at land and on sea, the brave but ineffectual British and German forces are crushed. French and Russian technological superiority precipitates the fall of Berlin and the collapse of the Triple Alliance, leaving Britain to stand alone. Driven back relentlessly, the Royal Navy loses control of the seas, the port city of Aberdeen is captured in an audacious Russian raid, and eventually southern England is invaded by a massive force of Russian, French, and Italian soldiers. The shock of the new is a frequent theme. War is now

107. Tracy, *Final War*, 14.
108. Tracy, *Final War*, 15.
109. Tracy, *Final War*, 23.
110. Tracy, *Final War*, 49.

dominated by machines. "[M]ankind stood confronted by a power that was practically irresistible, and which changed the whole aspect of warfare by land and sea."[111] The new technologies possessed by the Brotherhood—the airships and the extraordinarily powerful guns they carry—are so radical that they challenge the representational capacity of observers. With a top speed approaching two hundred miles per hour, the airships are "swift almost beyond imagination," and we are repeatedly told of the disbelief they engendered in stunned witnesses to their flight.[112] The logistics of Victorian military perception were upended.[113]

Individual courage and enterprise are supplanted by scientific creativity, infrastructural capacity, and industrial might. "[T]he personal equation had almost been eliminated from the problem of battle."[114] The rupture is at once strategic, epistemic, and moral. In his incisive 1903 short-story "The Land Ironclads," Wells probed similar themes, articulating the conflict between reason and emotion, manliness and machinery, that haunted reactions to the changing character of war.[115] Griffith was less subtle, or maybe just less troubled, viewing the development with alacrity. The Brotherhood view war in purely instrumental terms, as a means to the end of peace, rather than as possessing any inherent qualities. "To us," one of the characters remarks, "war and murder are synonymous terms, differing only as wholesale and retail."[116] They harness technology to achieve ethico-political goals. But technoscientific superiority dissolves the traditional chivalric ethos of military life and expedites the ultimate abolition of war, for it eliminates the very possibility of glory and personal recognition. Soldiering is no longer an honorable vocation. "I was born and bred a soldier," remarks General de Gallifet, a French commander. "I have seen enough of modern war, or, as I should rather call it, murder by machinery. . . . They spoke truly who prophesied that the solution of the problem of aerial navigation would make war impossible."[117] Technology had finally transcended character.

111. Griffith, *Angel of the Revolution*, 113.

112. Griffith, *Angel of the Revolution*, 197.

113. For general discussion of representation, visuality, and war, see Paul Virilio, *War and Cinema*, trans. Patrick Camiller (London, 1989); Antonie Bousquet, *The Eye of War* (Minneapolis, 2018).

114. Griffith, *Angel of the Revolution*, 294.

115. Deane, *Masculinity and the New Imperialism*, ch. 7.

116. Griffith, *Angel of the Revolution*, 349.

117. Griffith, *Angel of the Revolution*, 370.

The story takes a surprising turn when Natas confides his true intentions to one of his most trusted followers, Alan Tremayne, Lord Alanmere.[118] The narrative shifts decisively from socialist revolutionary planning to the possibility of global racial salvation. The task of pacifying the Earth was to be enacted by the mighty "Anglo-Saxon race," not a cosmopolitan phalanx of workers. Racial supremacism was presented as the guarantor of both socialist victory and perpetual peace. A wealthy aristocrat, Tremayne is a man who in his prewar career had been dedicated to one thing above all, the "Imperial Policy," a variation on the theme of imperial federation. "To this he subordinated everything else, and held as his highest, and indeed almost his only political ideal, the consolidation of Britain and her colonies into an empire commercially and politically intact and apart from the rest of the world." He had dreamt of a time when Britain and its settler colonies could be united under a "representative Imperial Parliament."[119] Natas redirects his ambition toward full-blown racial reunion, playing Stead to Tremayne's Rhodes. Square-jawed, noble, brave, and motivated by high ideals, Tremayne is an archetypal Victorian adventure hero. It goes without saying that he is a gifted orator. As war loomed, he had warned the Lords against alienating Italy. "No such speech had been heard in the House since Edmund Burke had fulminated against the miserable policy which severed America from Britain, and split the Anglo-Saxon race in two." Yet even his magnificent rhetorical powers were insufficient: "now, as then, personal feeling and class prejudice proved too strong for eloquence and logic."[120] Tremayne even looked the part, later negotiating the future of the world with the defeated generals while clad in a "dark tweed suit, with Norfolk jacket and knickerbockers, met by long shooting boots, just as though he was fresh from the moors."[121] Socialist revolution would be delivered by a man who had wandered out of a *Punch* caricature.

Seeking to persuade Tremayne to lead the revolution, Natas waxes poetic about the destiny of the Anglo-Saxons. He paints a vivid picture of Britain in ruins, and the subsequent conquest of Europe by "yellow" forces massing in

118. Natas, it turns out, had hypnotized Tremayne, the only way (it is implied) that he could have recruited the upstanding Englishman to his cause. *Pearson's* had originally published an extensive prologue detailing this hypnotism, but it was not included in the book.

119. Griffith, *Angel of the Revolution*, 147. Griffith was a great admirer of Rhodes. In a triumphalist book, *Men Who Have Made the Empire* (London, 1897), he described him as "a man who is unquestionably one of the great ones of the earth" (281), and praised his "magnificent work" in Africa. While admitting that some of Rhodes's actions were morally dubious, Griffith thought that no one saw the "greater Purpose" of empire more clearly (283).

120. Griffith, *Angel of the Revolution*, 149.

121. Griffith, *Angel of the Revolution*, 348.

the East. "There is but one power under heaven," Natas declares, "that can stand between the Western world and this destruction." The Anglo-Saxons were, after all, the "conquering race of earth, and the choicest fruit of all ages until now." United by speech and "kindred blood," and numbering nearly two hundred million, they stood on the verge of eternal greatness if only they could overcome the divisions caused by the commercial disputes and "petty jealousies" that had prohibited the emergence of "an Anglo-Saxon planet." Tremayne had the opportunity to finally realize this dream, to create a racial-political community that would "stand as a solid barrier of invincible manhood before which this impending flood of yellow barbarism should dash itself to pieces like the cloud-waves against the granite summits of the eternal hills."[122] Accepting the role, Tremayne sets to work on marshaling his forces—including a fleet of airships built by Arnold at a remote island base off the western coast of Africa—and preparing the opening moves of world revolution.

The insurrection begins in the United States. Initially Washington had remained neutral, although the corrupt administration had signed a secret treaty with the Franco-Slavonic League, meaning that when requested it would declare war on Britain, attack Canada, and dispatch a fleet to ambush the depleted Royal Navy. This nefarious behavior is attributable, Griffiths makes clear, to the capitalist hijack of the country. The government was controlled by "The Ring," a clique of rapacious millionaires, and democracy had been subverted by the shameless pursuit of profit. "Representative government in America had by this time become a complete sham."[123] This type of government did not reflect the true identity of the population. Over the years, the Brotherhood had secretly assembled a huge military force—the "Red International"—spread throughout the industrialized countries of the world, including the armies of both sides in the conflict. They were poised to spring into action on Natas's command, overthrowing their leaders and fighting under the red flag of international socialism. The North American branch composed five million, "of whom more than four millions were men in the prime of life, and nearly all of them of Anglo-Saxon blood and English speech."[124] The secret plot is foiled, and the Red International is called to arms. Workers paralyze the American state overnight. "It was not a strike for no mere trade organisation could have accomplished such a miracle. It was the force born of the accumulation of twenty years of untiring labour striking one mighty blow of which shattered the commercial fabric of a continent in a single

122. Griffith, *Angel of the Revolution*, 157.
123. Griffith, *Angel of the Revolution*, 283.
124. Griffith, *Angel of the Revolution*, 274.

instant." The government is deposed with little bloodshed. Natas appoints Tremayne the first President of the "Federation of the English-Speaking Peoples of the World," a title used interchangeably with "Anglo-Saxon Federation." "[N]ow citizens of a greater realm than the United States, and endowed with more than national duties and responsibilities," Americans are incorporated into a new globe-straddling political association.[125] Anglotopia was within reach.

Meanwhile, the Franco-Slavic forces besiege London. Famine and riots ensue. After initially rebuffing overtures from the Anglo-Saxon Federation, the British government recognizes the folly of isolation, and a choice is made to "waive the merely national idea in favour of the racial one." The King stands aside. "After all, the kinship of a race was a greater fact in the supreme hour of national disaster that the maintenance of a dynasty or the perpetuation of a particular form of government."[126] His virtuous character is demonstrated by his willingness to abdicate for the greater racial good. Britain too is subsumed into the Anglo-Saxon Federation. As Tremayne says later, "The day of states and empires, and therefore of loyalty to sovereigns, has gone by. The history of nations is the history of intrigue, quarrelling, and bloodshed, and we are determined to put a stop to warfare for good and all."[127] The primary source of obligation and political belonging was race, not state or nation or region.

In a fusion of race and technology, the *Pax Aeronautica* is maintained by those most suited to the job, the Anglo-Saxons. A naval armada that had steamed from North America soon after the revolution disgorges Red International forces onto the British mainland to fight the Franco-Slavs, and Arnold's fearsome air fleet is finally unleashed. The fighting is pitiless, the Anglo-Saxon Federation taking no prisoners. In one encounter, lasting only a few hours, three hundred thousand Russian soldiers are killed. "Then it was England against Spain; now it was Anglo-Saxondom against the world; and the conquering race of earth, armed with the most terrific powers of destruction that human wit had ever devised, was rising in its wrath, millions strong, to wipe out the stain of invasion from the sacred soil of the motherland of the Anglo-Saxon nations." Victory is ultimately declared amidst the ruins of Crystal Palace, with peace imposed on the defeated powers at a ceremony conducted in St. Paul's Cathedral. This was to be the "last battlefield of the Western nations." The cost had been exorbitant: six million soldiers and five million

125. Griffith, *Angel of the Revolution*, 284, 281, 287.
126. Griffith, *Angel of the Revolution*, 313, 310.
127. Griffith, *Angel of the Revolution*, 288.

civilians had been killed. Universal war—the "World War of 1904"—ushers in an age of "universal peace."[128]

Violence in *The Angel of the Revolution* is bifurcated and displaced. The narration of conflict is highly abstract, the astounding war-machines visiting death and destruction on anonymous undifferentiated masses arrayed on the ground. The scale of the killing is articulated chiefly through the superlatives used to catalogue it—annihilation, obliteration, butchery—and the frequent refrain that such destructive force was both unprecedented and (nearly) incapable of linguistic representation. An aerostat attack is "destructive almost beyond description," while a later battle produced an "indescribably hideous scene of slaughter."[129] Each successive encounter is pronounced the grandest, most intense, most devastating in human history, the narrative repetition dulling the horror. But a very different, though often submerged, theme snakes through the novel: the past violence inscribed on the bodies of some of the central protagonists. We are told repeatedly of the abject horrors of the Russian prison camps, and the sadism of the guards.[130] Such bodies bear the stigmata of torture. Natas's suffering at their hands is described in graphic detail. While the abstract register dominates the text, this individuated form of representation, relegated chiefly to flashbacks, is restricted to a handful of characters. What is missing is any real sense of the visceral brutality of industrial warfare, of what happens to bodies en masse when they encounter the war machine. For a book dedicated to world war, it is at once bloody and oddly bloodless.

The gender politics of *The Angel of the Revolution* was an unstable fusion—common in late Victorian socialist writings—of progressive egalitarianism and patriarchal convention. Women play a significant role in directing the course of the revolution. The Inner Council of the Brotherhood is composed of fourteen people, nine men and five women, all assigned equal status. Natasha, daughter of Natas, the eponymous Angel of the revolution, is a crack shot and later executes a traitor, but her main function in the narrative is to serve as the preternaturally beautiful love interest of Arnold, and as a moderating feminine influence of Natas's monomaniacal desire to annihilate the forces of despotism. Despite her intelligence, marshal prowess, and rank in the organization, she is prepared to submit to Arnold if he, the classic romantic knight, manages

128. Griffith, *Angel of the Revolution*, 323, 337, 293.

129. Griffith, *Angel of the Revolution*, 200, 326.

130. On the motif of revenge and the role of tortured flesh in the novel, see Sarah Cole, *At the Violet Hour* (Oxford, 2014), 101–2. David Trotter characterizes Griffith's attention to the female body as sadomasochistic: *English Novel in History*, 172.

to bring peace to the earth. "[W]hen you have made war impossible to the rivalry of nations and races, and have proclaimed peace on earth," she informs him, "then I will give myself to you, body and soul, to do with as you please, to kill or to keep alive, for then truly will you have done that which all the generations of men before you have failed to do, and it will be yours to ask and to have."[131] She willingly submits to him as her "master." Motifs of sexual purity and female innocence also run through the story. Although Griffith was more willing to grant women serious political voice than Tracy, Vogel's liberal utopia was considerably more egalitarian.

In *The Final War*, the United States likewise plays an ambivalent role. Washington's response to the unprovoked attack on Britain is initially conveyed through French eyes, with their military and political elite convinced that the President and his advisors—unaware of French plans for Canada—would choose to remain neutral, happy for the Europeans to fight among themselves.[132] The President obediently declares neutrality, but then surprises both sides by promising that the United States would absorb Canada after the war. In an echo of the financial repercussions of the American threat of war over Venezuela, Wall Street crashes and economic disaster is averted only when the great American financial institutions send huge amounts of money to the British—American capitalism saves the day.[133] The contrast with Griffith is stark. A tide of Anglophilia sweeps the country, revealing the true feelings of kinship that lay below the surface animosity. However, the American appointed to a leading role in the novel is neither a banker, a politician, nor an inventor, but rather the eponymous Admiral Mahan. He is used to voice Tracy's diagnosis of American sentiment, at one point complaining that Washington "bureaucrats" did not represent the "American nation," the vast majority of whom supported the "mother country." But Mahan's job as the midwife of Anglo-American unity is not yet complete. His fleet is initially tasked with defending American shipping in the Atlantic, though later in the novel he ignores orders and provokes a Russian attack on his ships, in doing so protecting Britain from invasion while eliminating the Tsarist threat.[134] He both symbolizes and acts as an agent of racial union.

131. Griffith, *Angel of the Revolution*, 125.

132. Tracy, *Final War*, 69–70.

133. Tracy, *Final War*, 130–32. On the economic consequences of the Venezuela threat, see Gibb, "Unmasterly Inactivity?," 23–55.

134. Tracy, *Final War*, 132, 163, chs. 18–19. For more on Mahan's views, see chapter 2. The irony was that Mahan was a notoriously poor sailor, prone to sea-sickness and viewed as an ineffective fleet officer.

Once Russia enters the war, the United States declares its wholehearted support for Britain. Speaking to a packed House of Commons, Balfour reads out a statement from the President, which climaxes with a stirring peroration on the motive power of racial identity. "The American people extend the hand of kinship and affection to the British nation, and are proud that the traditions of the great Saxon race are now to be defended and maintained by the peoples on both sides of the Atlantic." Balfour responds in kind, decreeing that the alliance between the two countries "was ordered in Heaven" and that "Nature herself called aloud for it." How strong, he boasted, "the mighty and irresistible instinct of race, of family, of mutual blood." A line had been drawn between light and darkness, progress and reaction, "the forces that have worked for selfishness, for aggrandisement, for slavery, for personal greed," and those that "work for liberty, for progress, for peace." Above all, it was a conflict between two opposing views of sociopolitical order, "an old world fighting with a new," the corrupt system of "feudalism taking its last stand against democracy." The future of the world was at stake: "It is a war of extermination; it is, in truth, the Final War."[135] In this war to end wars, the simulacra of Balfour continued, Britain and the United States were bound together, mother and son. Tracy drew on the metaphorical associations of imperial primogeniture, projecting the line of racial inheritance across the Atlantic. "America is our heir. If we passed away as an empire, in the death-throes of the fight, the splendid heritage that we have secured would descend in sacred trust to the United States, and it would henceforth be her mission to cherish, to guard, to protect it."[136] Such a characterization allowed Tracy to simultaneously embrace and demote American power, thus replicating the conventional British trope of America as junior racial collaborator.

Tracy's narrator interrupts at this point, mixing the familial metaphors. "England and America were not cousins," he declared, "they were brothers. . . . It was no alliance this. It was the reunion of one great family."[137] An editorial in *The Times* crystallized the mood. "The English-speaking race is called upon to fulfil its mission; to its hands are fully committed the future destines of mankind. The duty to which we are devoted is noble yet awe-inspiring. We are no longer fighting a national quarrel, having become the trustees of human

135. Tracy, *Final War*, 193, 195, 196.

136. Tracy, *Final War*, 196.

137. Tracy, *Final War*, 197. In an example of British wish-fulfillment at its most blatant, Tracy interjects a public exchange between the Prince of Wales and Bryant, the American Ambassador in London. Bryant proclaims, "Sir, we are all Britons. America, I assure you, is prouder to-day when she shares your peril than when in the beginning she claimed her independence" (199).

progress and civilisation."[138] Claiming the mantle of universal benefactor while rooting it in a racially exclusive vanguard, Tracy articulated the racialized cosmopolitanism that permeated Angloworld discourse. Turning back to America, he again insists on the underlying racial sympathies of its population. The war exposed Anglophobia, once thought ubiquitous, as "superficial and unreal": "deep below such fitful and transient moods there remained in the heart of the US a strong abiding love for the old country." Figured as the young, immature offspring of Britain, America reached political adulthood by aligning itself with the sagacious mother country.

> Wayward, impulsive, she might deceive herself in days of calm and prosperity. But it needed only the presence of danger, the loud, imperious call of kinship, for her to cast off her indifference and to reveal herself as she is, the western branch of the great Saxon race, the other England, one with Britain in blood, in history, in language, in feeling, in character, in destiny.[139]

British and American troops deployed together in mainland Europe start referring to themselves as "Busters" (British-US), a coinage that Tracy used repeatedly. "There was a philosophic value in the phrase. It conveyed the idea of complete unity, and at once swept aside possibilities of jealousy and differentiation."[140] The Kaiser ultimately surrenders, but only after meditating on the world-historical destiny of the English-speaking peoples. "Behind Britain was America. It was the whole race—the race that pervaded the whole world, that gave to the earth its history and to the sea its speech. Here was a power strong as that of destiny. Not all that remained of mankind could keep back the irresistible people." Posited as a quasi-Hegelian agent of reason in history, the English-speaking branch of the Anglo-Saxon race were fated to bring justice and order to the world. Their "irresistible" mission was a religious one, sacred and demanding worship.[141] They were the indispensable race-nation. Russia soon falls to internal revolt, leaving only France to face the mighty "Busters." At this point, Tracy unveils a secret superweapon, a moment that had been trailed throughout the novel. Less fanciful than many techno-fixes studding future-war novels, it turns out to be an "electric rifle," able to bewilder the French with its "demoiac rays." They are compelled to surrender in the face of the "infernal device which smote them so infallibly," the shots

138. Tracy, *Final War*, 201.

139. Tracy, *Final War*, 264, 266, 264.

140. Tracy, *Final War*, 290. In another notable interjection of reality into the narrative, Tracy offered Dr Jameson, of raid infamy, a form of redemption. In a heroic cameo, Jameson leads an unauthorized expedition to kidnap the Kaiser (ch. 37).

141. Tracy, *Final War*, 398.

representing the "last tokens of warfare between Christian races."[142] The non-Christian, barbarous world would no doubt remain a zone of brutal conflict, and as such subject to constant intervention from more advanced peoples, led by the British (with American support). The final war was not so final after all.

Both novels end with encomiums to the genius of the Anglo-Saxons, though they diverge in significant ways. *The Angel of the Revolution*, like *The Final War*, culminated with a triumphalist utopian account of the destiny of the Anglo-Saxons to enforce peace on earth. Dissolving the Brotherhood, and transferring leadership to Tremayne, Natas declares that the "empire of the earth has been given into the hands of the Anglo-Saxon race."[143] In a briefly sketched climacteric, the Islamic forces of the East are defeated in a battle on the borders of Europe. "Sultan Mohammed had accepted the terms of the Federation, and the long warfare of Cross and Crescent had ceased, as men hoped, forever."[144] Griffith's imagined geopolitical reconfiguration was also familiar. While states persist, they play a secondary role, answering to a higher power, the Anglo-Saxon Federation, which acts to police the world and to protect the West from the East. The unusual character of his prescriptions resides in their socialist content. The new "European Constitution" imposed by the Anglo-Saxon Federation contains five clauses. The first specifies the supremacy of the Anglo-Saxons. The second institutes an International Board of Arbitration and Control, albeit one under the ultimate sanction of the Federation. The third establishes new borders within Europe. So far, so conventional. The remaining two clauses dismantle the prevailing capitalist order. One of them proclaims land nationalization, extinguishing all land tenure: "the soil of each country was declared to be the sole and inalienable property of the State." The fifth clause established an extensive system of progressive taxation.[145] The legal profession, a particular irritant to Griffith, is abolished. At the moment of their world-historical triumph, the very political-economic order so closely associated with the Anglo-Saxons is dissolved.[146]

Griffith's twist necessitated an unusual conceptualization of the Anglo-Saxons. As in most such narratives, race is posited as the basic ontological category of politics. "East and west, north and south, wherever the English tongue is spoken, men must clasp hands and forget all other things save that they are brothers of blood and speech, and that the world is theirs if they

---

142. Tracy, *Final War*, 411, 428.

143. Griffith, *Angel of the Revolution*, 364.

144. Griffith, *Angel of the Revolution*, 389.

145. Griffith, *Angel of the Revolution*, 386–87.

146. Griffith later penned a sequel, *Olga Romanoff* (London, 1897). Set 125 years in the future, it charts the collapse of the racial utopia.

choose to take it." This, Natas continues, "is a work that cannot be done by any nation, but only by a whole race, which with millions of hands and a single heart devotes itself to achieve success or perishes."[147] While this sentence could have been penned by Tracy, there is a major difference. So often coded as the natural embodiment of entrepreneurial capitalism and parliamentary democracy, the Anglo-Saxons are recast by Griffith as the foundation and guarantor of a postcapitalist order. Race is unbundled from the existing institutional ecology. In most such novels, the greatness of the Anglo-Saxons is constituted, in large part, by their purported achievements and inherent characteristics, including their political institutions and economic system. Not so for Griffith, who imagines race as a substrate on which an alien, and alienating, set of institutions have been superimposed, impeding the people from realizing their true potential. Whereas most racial utopians saw political division as the main barrier to union and thence perpetual peace, for Griffith (in this novel at least) it was the superstructure of capitalism, a system that constrained and redirected the noble instincts and virtuous energy of the race, that assumed the blocking role. Politics, he reminded his readers, was a game rigged by capitalists for their own profit and at the expense of the masses. "[D]espite its splendid exterior," the social fabric "was inwardly as rotten as were the social fabrics of Rome and Byzantium on the eve of their fall."[148] No tears are shed when Westminster is reduced to rubble. The American Constitution, Natas declares as he literally rips it to shreds, is not worth saving. "For a hundred and fifty years this has been boasted as the bulwark of liberty, and used as the instrument of social and commercial oppression. The Republic of America has been governed, not by patriots and statesmen, but by millionaires and their hired political puppets. It is therefore a fraud and a sham, and deserves no longer to exist!" (No doubt Carnegie would have been unimpressed.) Griffith says little about what made the Anglo-Saxons great, but he repeatedly invokes two values: conquest and freedom. They are, he avers, a colonizing race, their superiority demonstrated by imperial success. They were also the "race which for a thousand years had stood in the forefront of the battle for freedom."[149] While putatively antithetical, these values were often reconciled in the contemporary imperial imaginary: conquest was seen as both an expression of freedom (only a truly free race being capable of doing it properly) and as a necessary step to securing freedom for others less fortunate (through the agency of the civilizing mission).

147. Griffith, *Angel of the Revolution*, 158.
148. Griffith, *Angel of the Revolution*, 281.
149. Griffith, *Angel of the Revolution*, 285.

Tracy scripted a more conventional ending. The final chapter, "The Destiny of the Race," reveals the full scope of his racial utopianism. Tennyson's "Parliament of Man" is once again summoned to provide mood-music, with Tracy decreeing the British-American alliance as the "consummation of the poet's dream." Like Griffith, he suggests the creation of an International Court of Arbitration.[150] But Tracy's ultimate aims were far grander. He interpolated the rise of the Anglo-Saxons—in a manner that resonated with Freeman's sweeping racial history—into a teleological account of humanity, arguing that the world had seen only three "preponderating races," each of which represented a "cosmic force" guiding progress.[151] The first emerged in Greece, home of art, where humans initially glimpsed "the perfect life of man." The Greeks, he asserted, "gave to mankind its implements, its faith, its yearnings, its strength: and doing so exhausted itself," before the sacred flame was passed to the Romans, men of action and strenuous builders of empire, whose destiny it was to "found the great doctrines of jurisdiction, to give Law to the nations." Finally, after a millennium and more, it was now the time of the "Saxons," "the third overwhelming dynasty that the world has known," who represented a powerful new force in the world: "Art and Law had had their day: there followed the dominance of science."[152] Technoscientific mastery was the key to Saxon destiny. This epistemic transformation heralded a political one, as the empire of the future would not be defined by traditional forms of conquest and rule, but would instead be of a "subtler, a more enduring, a more resistless kind." Reproducing a standard social Darwinian trope, Tracy hailed the inherent superiority of the "Saxon."

> For the message that science gave the world was that race alone would conquer in the struggle for existence which showed greatest adaptability, which could easiest accommodate itself to the boundless variations of earth's wayward moods. It was the cruel law of the survival of the fittest.[153]

To "such a race," he boasted, "the earth lay open, offering its dominion."[154] Superiority was defined by the adaptability of character, individual and collective, and the capacity to harness the forces of nature for human ends. Here was a prime example of the braiding of technoscientific mastery, moral virtue, and political destiny. The "Saxons" proved their suitability to rule, and were provided

---

150. Tracy, *Final War*, 458, 442–43.

151. See, for example, Freeman, *Comparative Politics*, esp. ch. 2.

152. Tracy, *Final War*, 459, 461.

153. Tracy, *Final War*, 462.

154. Tracy, *Final War*, 462–63.

with the tools to enact it, through unparalleled comprehension and control of the natural world. Evolution was both the cause and the justification of racial paramountcy. "This, then, is the mission of the Saxon race—slowly but surely to map itself over the earth, to absorb the nations, to bring to pass that wonderful world of a dream united in a single family and speaking a common speech."[155] The Parliament of Man would be built by a united Anglo-America.

Argosies of Magic Sails: The Nemesis of Cosmic Empire

Though Cecil Rhodes dreamt of the stars, he left it to others to chart the relationship between cosmic exploration and earthly imperium. In sub-Tennysonian vein, Bennett hinted at a future beyond the earth, while in *The War of the Worlds* (1898), Wells inverted the colonial gaze by portraying humanity prostrate before a conquering alien species.[156] William Cole's *The Struggle for Empire: A Story of the Year 2236* (1900), one of the most ambitious prophetic novels of the era, questioned millenarian imaginings of the Anglo future by projecting the pathologies of imperial domination into outer space.[157] While it quickly disappeared into literary oblivion, it has recently been rediscovered as a key Victorian science fiction text, indeed as the first "space opera."[158] My interest, though, resides less in its account of space travel than in its characterization and critique of the Anglo-Saxon imperial impulse. It was a dystopian double to racial utopian celebration.

155. Tracy, *Final War*, 463. Tracy wrote numerous books, some written in collaboration with the more talented M. P. Shiel. His output included other future-war stories, such as *The Lost Provinces* (London, 1898) and *The Invaders* (London, 1901). The latter sees the Germans joining the French to invade a Britain distracted by the South African war.

156. Wells, *War of the Worlds*. His other future-war stories include "The Land Ironclads," *Strand Magazine*, 23/156 (1903), 751–69; *The War in the Air* (London, 1908); and *The World Set Free* (London, 1914). On ambiguities in the story, see Peter Fitting, "Estranged Invaders" in Patrick Parrinder (ed.), *Learning from Other Worlds* (Durham, NC, 2001), 127–45.

157. Little is known about Cole. Born in 1869, he was educated at Eton and Oxford, and wrote four novels between 1899 and 1908: Richard Bleiler, "Introduction" in Kate MacDonald (ed.), *Political Future Fiction* (London, 2013), 107–32.

158. Positive reviews included the *Morning Post* (20 September 1900); *The Outlook* (24 March 1900, 25). An excellent scholarly edition can be found in MacDonald, *Political Future Fiction*, I. I use this text in what follows. Bleiler identifies it as the first "space opera" ("Introduction," 107). Elsewhere, he laments its "bewildering" lack of reception as "one of the great missed opportunities of the genre": *Science Fiction* (Kent, 1990), 107, 148. However, he doesn't identify the critical political purpose of the volume. It is also reprinted in George Locke (ed.), *Sources of Science Fiction* (London, 1998).

The opening passage summons the image of a thriving imperial metropolis. "The sun rose in unrivalled splendour over the immense city of London, the superb capital, not only of England, but of the world, the Solar System, and the stars."[159] No longer simply the nodal point in the web of nineteenth-century planetary capitalism, Britain was the epicenter of a galactic empire, "for the Anglo-Saxon race long ago absorbed the whole of the globe."[160] Their rise to preeminence, we are informed in a familiar plotline, began in the late nineteenth century when the states of the world assembled for an apocalyptic battle, with the British Empire, the United States, and Germany arrayed against the combined forces of France, Russia, Austria, Turkey, and Italy. "The earth was shaken by the convulsion."[161] The Anglo-Saxons had divided the spoils between them, with "England" assuming control of Turkey, most of the Russian Empire in Asia, and strategically significant parts of France, Italy, and Spain. Germany claimed large chunks of France, Italy, and mainland Russia. This planetary land grab was followed by further geopolitical branching and intra-"Teutonic" division, the most significant element of which involved the reunification of Britain and the United States, creating a single polity that subsequently entered into "a federal union with all the Teutonic States of Europe."[162] Whereas this kind of geopolitical chess-game was a staple of many future-war novels, for Cole it was only a brief prologue to a far more ambitious story. There followed a period—time unspecified—in which the other peoples of the Western world slowly dissolve or weaken. The "French race," for example, "gradually died out," their country "absorbed by the Federal Union," as too were Spain and Italy, while the Russian and Ottoman Empires shrank into insignificance, until finally "the Anglo-Saxon race was dominant."[163] The rest of humanity is ignored, presumably because it is assumed that they would be ruled over by the Anglo-Saxon empire. The "world" of civilization, progress, and moral concern was not coterminous with the universal.

Over the following centuries, science and technology come to dominate education in the Angloworld, creating—as in Vogel's tale and Wells's yearning—a new breed of techno-efficient citizen, until the moment when humanity is ready to set sail for the stars. The result is a cosmic reenactment of the history of Western settler colonialism.

159. Cole, *Struggle for Empire*, 134.
160. Cole, *Struggle for Empire*, 136.
161. Cole, *Struggle for Empire*, 136.
162. Cole, *Struggle for Empire*, 136.
163. Cole, *Struggle for Empire*, 136.

They had found Mars, Mercury, and Venus uninhabited, and only waiting to be taken possession of. The others were inhabited, but the natives were quite harmless. A virgin soil that hardly required any cultivation, a salubrious climate, trees laden with the most luscious fruits, myriads of animals, and vast mineral wealth spread quite a fever for emigration. Hundreds of thousands of pioneers, adventurers, and scientists rushed into the deep unknown, and reached their destination in safety.[164]

The settler project was based on a strict division of labor. In a resonant echo of Wells's bifurcation of the Eloi and the Morlocks, Cole's Earth is split between "those who had great brain power and those who had very little. The former did all the commanding and organizing, the latter did the menial work."[165] But whereas Wells extrapolated class divisions into the deep future, applying evolutionary logic to the conflict between labor and capital, Cole presents a more explicitly racialized account, with the "brains" drawn from the Anglo-Saxons and the "menial" laborers from the rest of humanity.

In both Vogel's and Tracy's fables of technoscientific progress, material development and moral virtue are presented as mutually reinforcing. In contrast, Cole sets them in opposition: the tension between *techne* and morality gives the novel its critical purchase. In a key passage, he paints a picture of an Anglo-governed planet consumed by what Hobson, in his analysis of *Imperialism*, written in the same year as Cole's novel, termed the "earth-hunger" of the Europeans and Americans.

The human race, in its greediness, ate up the earth, appropriating every acre of ground, and then it inundated the planetary system. The same was the case with the intellectual giants of the age; their curiosity was insatiable, their ambition boundless, and their greed all-devouring. The planetary world which had been opened to their researches did not content them for long.[166]

Cole thus attributes to an anthropomorphic Anglo-Saxondom a set of limitless appetites—it inundates, appropriates, and devours. Propelled by a voracious ambition to conquer and exploit, this was colonization figured as pure will to power, an urge to scour space for extractable value and the luster of domination. "There was present everywhere an intense fever for acquisition; men burned with a desire to plunder in these new regions."

164. Cole, *Struggle for Empire*, 138.
165. Cole, *Struggle for Empire*, 138.
166. Cole, *Struggle for Empire*, 138; Hobson, *Imperialism*, 13.

Dim accounts had been handed down from generation to generation of a certain great man named Napoleon Bonaparte who once nearly conquered the world. Now there were thousands of Bonapartes endowed with colossal intellect, vast energy, and boundless ambition, each burning to wrest for himself a world from the great Unknown. Provinces and countries were not even thought of; they desired to rule over a planet, a system, a universe.[167]

Rapacity was combined with an assault on the natural order. "And so the Anglo-Saxon race went on wresting fresh secrets from Nature every day. . . . To know at that time meant to possess."[168] Futuristic technoscience was the epistemic foundation and the primary modality of space colonization, a power/knowledge nexus put at the service of boundless human avarice. This distinguished it from earthly precursors. Scientists, not hardy conquistadors, led the charge for cosmic loot and Lebensraum, their technical skills harnessed to projects of exploitation, unbundled from a moral framework that might constrain their ambition. "Exulting in their might, the gray-haired scientists steered their vessels through the dark depths of space, while they ransacked worlds for treasures and luxuries." In a nod to then common practices of impe- rial display, in which "exotic" peoples, plants, and animals were shipped around the world to titillate metropolitan populations, Cole pictures the fascination with space artifacts and organisms. "Rare and beautiful plants were uprooted, and strange animals were captured and stowed away in the interior of the ships, and finally deposited in London or the other great cities of the world."[169] He articulates a vision of human reason extricated from its moral grounding, an anxiety common at the time and which the ensuing decades did so much to bear out. This line of thought found its bleakest and most sophisticated expression half a century later in Adorno and Horkheimer's *Dialectic of Enlightenment*.[170]

In a reiteration of the classical imperial narrative, *hubris* spawned *nemesis*. The human colonists meet an equally aggressive civilization based on Sirius.[171] Following a dispute over property rights on the mineral-rich planet of Iosia, Earth sends a vast battlefleet (flying the Union Jack) to punish the upstart

167. Cole, *Struggle for Empire*, 138.

168. Cole, *Struggle for Empire*, 140.

169. Cole, *Struggle for Empire*, 140. On late Victorian spectacular display, see Peter Hoffen- berg, *An Empire on Display* (Berkeley, 2001); Qureshi, *Peoples on Parade*.

170. Theodor Adorno and Max Horkheimer, *Dialectic of Enlightenment*, ed. G. S. Noerr, trans. E. Jephcott (1947; Stanford, 2002). See also Langdon Winner, *Autonomous Technology* (Cam- bridge, MA, 1978).

171. Wells's "Modern Utopia" was located on a planet beyond Sirius: Wells, *Modern Utopia*, 15, 168.

Sirians in an act of cosmic gunboat diplomacy. Cole portrays the citizens of Earth as having mixed feelings about the venture, with some yearning for the glories of military victory, while many others "secretly wished that the national ambition had been more restrained, and that they had been contented with their own planet, and not crossed the oceans of space in search of fresh lands and fresh enemies."[172] Here Cole stages the contemporary debate about whether imperial consolidation or further territorial expansion was the best strategy to pursue. Strikingly, and despite the fact that we are never presented with a picture of individual Sirians or their civilization, Cole's protagonists are assigned basic moral equality in the conflict—their motivations are assumed to be the same as those of humanity.[173] The inhabitants of Earth are confronted with the consequences of their greed as the battlefleet is destroyed by the sophisticated Sirians, who then fight their way to Earth, bombarding it with cataclysmic effect. London, the "most splendid city of the Universe," is annihilated: "When day dawned it was but a shapeless heap of smoking ruins."[174] This was an instance of urbicide, the fascination with pulverized cities that pervades late Victorian science fiction and provides ghostly intimations of the wars of the twentieth century. There are also clear echoes of the New Zealander, but rather than a postcollapse visitation from the New World, we are presented with an alien intelligence hastening decline and fall.[175]

Unlike Griffith's tale of the apocalypse, Cole's novel is conspicuously graphic in its portrayal of violence. Suvin once dismissed *The Struggle for Empire* as "perfunctory, bloodthirsty, and socially idiotic."[176] This is only partly correct: while the social description is stilted and unimaginative, the depiction of violence—its undoubted bloodthirstiness—serves to challenge Anglo-Saxon hubris. There is little glory in Cole's portrait of the visceral, claustrophobic war in space, nor much room for individual honor and skill. While the Anglo-Saxons (of course) act with great courage, the battle scenes are marked by carnage and bodily suffering. After one exchange, for example,

172. Cole, *Struggle for Empire*, 198.

173. Dominic Alessio suggests that an earlier New Zealand work, *The Great Romance* (1881), was the first novel to treat aliens in a sympathetic manner. Alessio, "Document in the History of Science-Fiction," *Science Fiction Studies*, 20/3 (1993), 305–40.

174. Cole, *Struggle for Empire*, 189.

175. Cole, *Struggle for Empire*, 181. At one point, Cole invokes God as an arbiter of interstellar affairs, though this theme isn't well integrated into the narrative (176, 179).

176. Suvin, *Victorian Science Fiction*, 79.

[m]any of the vessels bore on their exteriors the ghastly traces of the collision. Arms, legs, strips of skin, and heads, often so burnt and bruised as to
be hardly recognisable, were hanging on to the torpedo-nets or wedged up
between the rods and wires. These were quickly removed, and the blood
was washed away from the windows and the other parts of the hulls where
it had been splashed.[177]

After another engagement, Cole writes that the crew of the targeted spaceships
"twisted their bodies into every conceivable form. They writhed on the floor
like snakes, they clutched at the guns and levers, and then they fell back dead,
the blood streaming from their mouths and nostrils."[178] Even as the discussion of alien fleets and space battle defamiliarizes the reader, projecting us
beyond the limited temporal and spatial horizons of the quotidian, the de-
scriptions of the vulnerability of human flesh refamiliarizes, bringing us face-
to-face with the elemental logic of battle and its bloody cost. Cole likewise
refuses the romance of masculine chivalry, the soldier as virtuous agent of
destruction capable of shaping the battlescape through bravery, skill, and force
of character. The power of these depictions of colonial ultraviolence thus resides in their articulation of visibility, for while description of this kind could
be found in accounts of European and American conflict against nameless
black and brown bodies, it was very rarely projected onto "Anglo-Saxons." This
act of transference carried a strong affective charge, illustrating the human
price of colonialism and rendering concrete the usual mystifying abstractions
utilized to talk about the consequences of war. Violence, then, can serve both
as a form of titillation—as was widespread in the invasion literature—and as
a potential source of critique. In Cole's tale, it is the cause of sorrow and regret,
not glorious memorialization. "Many of us who have lived through the terrible
events of the year 2236 and the five succeeding years," the narrator intones,
"often wished that we had been contented with our own planet, and limited
our ambition to a more humble sphere. We still exist, but it will be many years
before we recover from the effects of that awful struggle."[179]

Nevertheless, the scope of Cole's critique is limited. He emphasizes the
dangers of colonial overexpansion and (implicitly) the lack of sufficient preparation for war, not the underlying structures of race, power, or empire. Warning against arrogance and the intoxication of power, he was calling for a pru-
dential imperial strategy, not the revolutionary transformation portended in

177. Cole, *Struggle for Empire*, 158. Bleiler notes that Cole's depictions of battle are "probably
the most gruesome and most powerful prepared up to modern times": Bleiler, *Science Fiction*, 147.
178. Cole, *Struggle for Empire*, 166.
179. Cole, *Struggle for Empire*, 139.

The Angel of the Revolution. In painting a picture of unremitting imperial violence, the text produces a surplus of meaning that might serve as the basis for a more thoroughgoing critique, but its potential is undercut by the reproduction of conventional didactic tropes of the military science fiction genre. Even as Cole criticizes settler expansion and the perilous divorce of morality and progress, he also makes the case for the dangers of geostrategic myopia. Complacency and moral laxity condemned the Anglo-Saxons to defeat.

> The strategy employed by the Sirian Admiral-in-Chief was exquisite. Day by day he kept on destroying and hemming in the Anglo-Saxons, driving them exactly where he wanted them to go. Oh, why had they been so slack in their preparations? Such was the lamentation uttered by hundreds of captains when they began to recognise their own powerlessness to turn away those terrible fleets.[180]

The trope of proleptic lamentation was threaded through *The Battle of Dorking* and its array of imitators, those powerful "admonitory essays in preparedness."[181] Here it helps to structure the narrative arc of the novel, though it is rarely placed center stage. It was a recurring theme in Cole's work. In a later more conventional novel, *The Death Trap* (1907), for example, German forces invade a militarily weak Britain before they are defeated—though only after much bloodshed—and the Kaiser is forced to hand over his prized colonies. The ultimate winner, though, is the United States, which emerges as the dominant global power.[182]

There is no heroic redeemer in *The Story of Empire*. The scientists are depicted as intellectually brilliant but morally bankrupt, the military as brave though largely ineffective, humanity itself as having forfeited virtue in pursuit of material progress. Earth is saved at the last minute by a scientist, Dr Tarrant, who invents a weapon—the mysterious "Electro-Ednogen" machine— capable of destroying the Sirian warships with ease. In this sense, the novel reprises the common superweapon-as-savior theme.[183] Yet unlike the heroic Edisonian genius who populated so many American invasion stories, or Tracy's archetypal self-effacing British engineer, here the redeemer of Earth is portrayed in deeply unflattering terms, as a man driven chiefly by vainglory,

---

180. Cole, *Struggle for Empire*, 181.

181. The phrase is from Clarke, "Future-War Fiction," 391.

182. It is anthologized in I. F. Clarke (ed.), *British Future Fiction, 1700–1914*, VII (London, 2000). Bleiler speculates plausibly that Cole was the "R. W. Cole" who published several nonfiction pieces on deficiencies in British military education (and preparation) in the *Saturday Review* ("Introduction," 123).

183. See especially, Franklin, *War Stars*, ch. 1.

greed, and sexual desire. Demanding vast wealth and ludicrous titles, he only puts his technology at the disposal of the embattled population upon receipt of a written contract promising him a huge chunk of the spoils of war.

> The Admiral-in-Chief went to a telephone and transmitted a few orders, while James Tarrant's eyes gleamed with a strange bright light.
>
> "Now about the reward," continued the Admiral. "In the name of our Empire, I promise that what you ask for will be granted. That is—"
>
> "That in case of success I have the title of Prince of Kairet, and have the supreme government of one of their planets if we conquer them, together with the absolute disposal of its revenues."
>
> "We agree," said the Admiral, and the other officers bowed their assent.[184]

Tarrant embodies the very dualism between morality and technoscience that provoked the war. The story closes with him feted by vast crowds in London, a new bride on his arm, garlanded with lavish epithets and honors, "Prince of Kairet, Duke of England, Admiral of the Fleet, Field-Marshal of the Anglo-Saxon Empire."[185]

In Cole's narrative, then, the classical logic of decline and fall—the hubris that causes nemesis—is circumvented by the timely intervention of a technological fix. Empire is given a second chance, but only at the expense of the divorce of morality and science. *The Struggle for Empire* is not a full-blown critique of imperialism or settler colonization, but rather of their excess. And this excess, Cole warns, is underpinned by a combination of complacency and, more importantly, the unbundling of morality and *techne*. Learning how to avoid these pitfalls, he implies, can help establish a more effective and durable form of colonial order. There was hope for the Anglo-Saxons yet.

---

184. Cole, *Struggle for Empire*, 190. Earlier, he had expressed an ambition to "make myself Master of the Universe" (146).

185. Cole, *Struggle for Empire*, 197.

6

Beyond the Sovereign State

ISOPOLITAN CITIZENSHIP AND RACE PATRIOTISM

States, however, constitute only one among many types of political entities. As soon as any body of men have been grouped under a common political name, that name may acquire emotional associations as well as intellectually analysable meaning.[1]

(GRAHAM WALLAS)

Introduction

Citizenship and patriotism have long and intricate conceptual histories. Both were the subject of ferocious debate in the late nineteenth century, as questions of racial difference, imperial domination, and gender equality recast arguments about the meaning of political community.[2] Challenging the isomorphic relationship between the territorial state, sovereignty, and political obligation, many unionists promoted the idea of common ("isopolitan") citizenship, an innovative form of membership that encompassed the totality of the "English-speaking people." This was often fused with a commitment to "race patriotism," a reengineered account of loyalty and affective signification that identified race as a privileged site of political devotion, even love. These

1. Wallas, *Human Nature and Politics*, 81–82.

2. For useful historical accounts of the concepts, see Mary Dietz, "Patriotism" and Michael Walzer, "Citizenship" in Terence Ball, James Farr, and Russell Hanson (eds.), *Political Innovation and Conceptual Change* (Cambridge, 1989), 177–93, 211–20; Maurizio Viroli, *For Love of Country* (Oxford, 1995); J. G. A Pocock, "The Ideal of Citizenship since Classical Times" in Ronald Beiner (ed.), *Theorizing Citizenship* (Albany, 1995), 29–52; Ayelet Shachar et al. (eds.), *Oxford Handbook of Citizenship* (Oxford, 2017), pt. II.

conceptual moves played an integral role in attempts to forge a sense of "strong political peoplehood," demarcating a group bound by a shared identity, a bundle of common rights and obligations, and a durable claim on the allegiance of its members.[3]

This chapter explores efforts to rethink the meaning of political belonging. The opening section delineates various models of citizenship found in Anglo-world debate, focusing in particular on isopolitanism. I then examine the most authoritative account of isopolity, propounded by the famed legal theorist Albert Venn Dicey, before surveying other articulations of the idea, including those of Carnegie, Stead, and Wells. The penultimate section analyzes race patriotism. Just as citizenship was rearticulated as a form of identification with the Anglo-Saxon or English race, so too was patriotic regard: individuals owed allegiance to a nested set of communities, including their country and their race. I conclude with a discussion of political symbolism, showing how race unionists designed rituals and markers of identity—from flags to public holidays—that evoked and glorified Anglo-America.

Remaking Citizenship: Race, Empire, Isopolity

Late nineteenth-century debates over citizenship centered on the meaning of political community and the distribution of political rights. In the United States, two enduring and acrimonious disputes—over the status of African-Americans and women—dovetailed with two more recent ones. All of them were racialized. Organized campaigning for female suffrage had emerged first in the 1840s, gathering momentum through the following decades, until a rich transatlantic suffrage network flourished, encompassing activists in Britain and the United States.[4] In the infamous *Dred Scott* decision of 1857, the Supreme Court ruled that African-Americans, whether free or enslaved, were excluded from the ambit of the Constitution and were thus ineligible for citizenship. Although this judgment was overturned by the Fourteenth Amendment in 1868, a decision reinforced by the consolidation of male suffrage in the Fifteenth Amendment of 1870, the systemic racist oppression of the Jim Crow

---

3. For a compelling analysis of political peoplehood, see Rogers Smith, *Stories of Peoplehood* (Cambridge, 2003), ch. 1; Smith, *Political Peoplehood* (Chicago, 2015).

4. Sara Graham, *Woman Suffrage and the New Democracy* (New Haven, CT, 1997); Kevin Corder and Christina Wolbrecht, *Counting Women's Ballots* (Cambridge, 2016); Sophia van Wingerden, *The Women's Suffrage Movement in Britain, 1866–1928* (Basingstoke, 1999); Patricia Harrison, *Collecting Links* (Westport, CT, 2000).

regime soon undermined legislative decree.[5] Voter intimidation, education and property tests, lynching and other forms of terrorist violence: all were utilized to practically disenfranchise black citizens.[6] Despite increasing resistance, the United States remained a patriarchal *Herrenvolk* democracy. During the late nineteenth century, immigration restriction and colonial expansion were added to the febrile mix. Fears about racial contamination catalyzed efforts to limit, even eliminate, immigration from East Asia as well as Southern and Eastern Europe.[7]

The imperial wars of the 1890s posed another charged question. Should inhabitants of newly occupied territories be granted citizenship? Most political thinkers opposed the extension of political rights to those they deemed backward, worrying that the Anglo-Saxon character of the American state was under threat. The new citizens would corrupt the racial-political community. Abbott Lawrence Lowell exemplified this position. In an 1899 essay, he acknowledged that the ideal of equality was central to American political thought and institutions, but argued that it had two main senses, incorporating civic and political rights. Since the abolition of slavery, the former were justifiably accepted as universal in scope, yet political rights were "quite a different matter," and should be granted only to those who could utilize them properly. "The art of self-government is one of the most difficult to learn," he opined, "for it requires a perpetual self-restraint on the part of the whole people, which is not really attained until it has become unconscious." The Anglo-Saxons had internalized the doctrine through centuries of living under the stern discipline of law. It had become habitual. But few others had achieved this monumental feat, and the United States had been vindicated in excluding the Chinese from naturalization. He also thought that it was reasonable to severely curtail the political rights of African-Americans, for they had yet to learn the appropriate

5. On the legal dimensions of African-American emancipation, see Alexander Tsesis, *We Shall Overcome* (New Haven, CT, 2008); Michael Klarman, *From Jim Crow to Civil Rights* (Oxford, 2004), chs. 1–2.

6. Eric Foner, *Reconstruction* (New York, 1988); Gary Gerstle, *American Crucible* (Princeton, NJ, 2001), chs. 1–2; Rogers Smith, *Civic Ideals* (New Haven, CT, 1997); Gregory Carter, "Race and Citizenship" in Ronald Bayor (ed.), *Oxford Handbook of American Immigration and Ethnicity* (Oxford, 2016), 166–82. On the split between African-American activists and the white feminist movement, see Faye Dudden, *Fighting Chance* (Oxford, 2011).

7. Desmond King, *Making Americans* (Cambridge, MA, 2000); Beth Lew-Williams, *The Chinese Must Go* (Cambridge, MA, 2018); Matthew F. Jacobson, *Whiteness of a Different Color* (Cambridge, MA, 1999); David Roediger, "Whiteness and Race" in Bayor, *Oxford Handbook of American Immigration and Ethnicity*, 197–212.

lessons. The inhabitants of the Philippines were likewise far from ready.[8] As Daniel Immerwahr puts it, the governing elite faced a trilemma—they could uphold only two of white supremacy, imperialism, and republican equality.[9] They chose to sacrifice republicanism on the altar of racism and expansion. In 1901, the Supreme Court formalized this view, ruling in the "insular cases" that the Constitution did not extend to territories captured in the Spanish-American war.[10]

Rarely adhering to traditional "national" citizenship norms, British conceptions of political membership have encompassed multiple forms and levels of belonging.[11] Public policy and political theory have often struggled to accommodate variations in local practice. Debates over empire and citizenship differed significantly from those in the United States. Whereas most American imperialists were loath to grant political membership to conquered and subjugated territories, their British equivalents were among the most fervent advocates of rescaling citizenship, though they did so in a way that was determined by the color line. Reflecting the complexity of the imperial system, various models of belonging were propounded. At the turn of the twentieth century, there was no single legal citizenship status in either Britain or its empire. All those born in territories ruled over by the monarch were classified as "British subjects," a category derived from a feudal conception of allegiance to the Crown. As the political philosopher Ernest Barker put it in 1906,

> The idea of a personal tie to a personal monarch has served to bind, not only conquered populations to their conqueror, but distant colonies to their mother country. It is an idea essentially feudal, as the word allegiance of itself indicates: it is the idea which underlies the British Empire

8. A. Lawrence Lowell, "The Colonial Expansion of the United States," *Atlantic Monthly*, 83 (January 1899), 150, 152, 151.

9. Immerwahr, *How to Hide an Empire*, ch. 5.

10. Bartholomew Sparrow, *The Insular Cases and the Emergence of American Empire* (Lawrence, 2006); Juan Torruella, "Ruling America's Colonies," *Yale Law & Policy Review*, 32/1 (2013), 57–95. As Sparrow notes, the decision split the Court, which ruled by a majority of 5–4 in most cases.

11. Rieko Karatani, *Defining British Citizenship* (London, 2003), chs. 1–3. On British debate, see also Brad Beaven and John Griffiths, "Creating the Exemplary Citizen," *Contemporary British History*, 22/2 (2008), 203–25; Michael Freeden, "Civil Society and the Good Citizen" in Jose Harris (ed.), *Civil Society in British History* (Oxford, 2003); Julia Stapleton, "Citizenship versus Patriotism in Twentieth Century England," *Historical Journal*, 48/1 (2005), 151–78. For a sweeping comparative perspective on imperial citizenship, see Joseph Fradera, *The Imperial Nation*, trans. Ruth Mackay (Princeton, NJ, 2018).

today. Common allegiance to the Crown, not common citizenship issuing in the election of a common parliament, is the basis on which it
rests.[12]

Substantive differences in rights and obligations between and within the diverse territories, often demarcated by claims about "civilization," supervened
on this basic status.

Even though it lacked legislative warrant, the vocabulary of citizenship permeated imperial ideology. The journalist William Monypenny's suggestion
that Britain and its settler colonies were already linked by a gossamer-thin
thread, a "common throne and a common citizenship," would have struck
many of his contemporaries as uncontroversial.[13] The idea of citizenship was
often employed in this nonjuridical sense, to designate a particular ethos or
model of belonging rather than a status enshrined in law.[14] Sometimes it was
used to label an existing condition, while at other times it was aspirational,
identifying a normatively desirable form of membership. Milner offered the
most influential articulation of the former. In a speech in 1906, he affirmed that
Britain and its settler colonies were coequal members of a single political community. "Their peoples are not foreigners to us, or to one another, but fellow
citizens. . . . One throne, one flag, one citizenship."[15] Admitting that subject,
not citizen, was the correct legal category, he maintained that there was a
higher sense of citizenship defined by loyalty to the (white colonial) empire.
"[M]en exist, and happily in increasing numbers, who are conscious of such
membership, who mean something definite when they say that the empire is
their 'country,' the State to which they feel themselves to belong, and to which
their highest allegiance is due." Traditional legal conceptions of citizenship
were obsolete because they failed to capture this new reality. "The existence,
the growth, the potency of this sentiment is a momentous fact, though legal
and juridical notions may not have expanded to correspond with it, and no

12. Ernest Barker, *The Political Thought of Plato and Aristotle* (London, 1906), 298. The constitutional structure of empire was discussed authoritatively in Sir William Anson, *The Law and
Custom of the Constitution* (Oxford, 1892), II, 206–71; Alpheus Todd, *Parliamentary Government
in the British Colonies* (London, 1880).

13. William Monypenny, "The Imperial Ideal" in Charles Goldman (ed.), *The Empire and the
Century* (London, 1905), 22. For a valuable analysis of imperial debates, see Daniel Gorman,
Imperial Citizenship (Manchester, 2006).

14. Citizenship only entered law in 1948 with the passing of the British Nationality Act. The
Act designated members of the Dominions "British Commonwealth Citizens." This was distin-
guished from the "Colonies and United Kingdom Citizenship" assigned to individuals in the
Dependencies. The designations were changed again in the 1981 British Nationality Act.

15. Speech, Manchester, 14 December 1906, in Milner, *Nation and Empire* (London, 1913), 141.

word has yet been coined to describe membership of the body-politic towards which that loyalty is felt."[16] The contours of this model of imperial citizenship were demarcated by the practice of racial categorization. Graham Wallas ventriloquized the standard view when he observed that "'citizenship' as applied to five-sixths of the inhabitants of the empire would be misleading."[17] It embraced only the white population.

Turn-of-the-century metropolitan British arguments over citizenship were in essence about whether, or to what extent, the status of subjecthood should be supplanted, modified, or replaced. The main dispute was over which specific account of multilevel political membership—which configuration of universalism and particularity—should prevail.[18] Four rival models can be discerned: *imperial-statist, institutional-imperial, racial-imperial*, and *racial-isopolitan*. Although sometimes blurred, they entailed different conceptualizations of the *content* of citizenship (the bundle of rights and obligations specified) and its *scope* (how and where lines of inclusion were drawn).

Imperial-statist citizenship posited that citizenship should be coextensive with state boundaries. This was a conventional view of its scope. Defenders of this model sought to cultivate a bifocal form of political belonging: an individual was simultaneously a citizen of a state and a member (subject) of an overarching imperial structure. Even though citizenship was confined to individual polities, loyalty to the empire was often postulated as an integral element of *good* citizenship. To be a virtuous Australian citizen demanded loyalty to both Australia and the British Empire.[19] But only some states were deemed sufficiently "civilised" to implement a system of citizenship. Indians or Fijians, for example, were not (yet) citizens, though at some unspecified

16. Milner, "Introduction" in Milner, *Nation and Empire*, xii. On Milner's thought, see Thompson, *Wider Patriotism*. Imperial citizenship was a key theme in the writings of Lionel Curtis and the other members of the Round Table group. See here Gorman, *Imperial Citizenship*; Deborah Lavin, *From Empire to International Commonwealth* (Oxford, 1995); Jeanne Morefield, *Empires without Imperialism* (Oxford, 2014), ch. 3.

17. Wallas, *Human Nature and Politics*, 81.

18. I leave aside the issue of indigenous rights, which barely figured in the metropolitan discourse over the Angloworld, a fact that itself speaks volumes about the exclusionary role of racialized argument. See Julie Evans et al., *Equal Subjects, Unequal Rights* (Manchester, 2003); Coel Kirkby, "The Politics and Practice of 'Native' Enfranchisement in Canada and the Cape Colony, c.1880–1900" (PhD diss., University of Cambridge, 2013).

19. For examples of Australian debates over empire citizenship, see James Walter and Margaret MacLeod, *The Citizens' Bargain* (Sydney, 2002), pt. I. On the Canadian case, see Peter Price, "Naturalising Subjects, Creating Citizens," *Journal of Imperial and Commonwealth History*, 45/1 (2017), 1–21.

point in the future they might achieve this hallowed standing. Writing in 1902, Herbert Samuel claimed that "no one disputes the desirability of raising the colonists from the status of subjects to that of citizens of the empire," though few were willing to say when this would occur.[20] Versions of the imperial-statist view dominated metropolitan political debate.

Institutional-imperial citizenship specified that citizenship should be an entitlement of all members of the British Empire, where this typically meant all those born within territories where the monarch was sovereign. It drew on the Roman precedent of the Edict of Caracalla (212 CE) that had granted citizenship to all "free men" living in the empire. In essence, this was an argument for redescribing subjecthood in the evocative language of citizenship. On this account, the boundaries of imperial citizenship tracked the shifting jurisdictional reach of the British Empire. Broad in scope, it was thin in content. Imperial citizenship in this sense typically meant a limited form of equality before the law. Sketching one variant of the argument, James Bryce insisted that it was essential to distinguish between the public and private dimensions of citizenship. Private citizen rights included those relating to property ownership and marriage, while public rights (including suffrage) authorized participation in government. "[T]he really essential point seems to me to be that we should dwell upon the fact that the citizenship which gives a man or woman full private rights, entitling him to be treated everywhere in the British Empire as equal in respect of all private rights to all his fellow subjects, is the basis of our whole imperial conception."[21] This minimalist view was compatible with a more extensive local register of rights and duties. Political rights, Bryce asserted, were "a completely different matter." Participation in government, whether though suffrage or eligibility to stand for public office, should be calibrated to local circumstances and depended "to a large extent upon local laws."[22] Different categories of "citizen" should be treated differently. Elsewhere, he was clear about the reason for exclusion: "[the] native population

---

20. Herbert Samuel, *Liberalism* (London, 1902), 336. Though principally talking about the settler colonies, Samuel included Jamaica and Singapore in his list of examples. On conflicting views about India and imperial citizenship, and how the ideal fed into anticolonialism, see Mark Frost, "Imperial Citizenship or Else," *Journal of Imperial and Commonwealth History*, 48/5 (2018), 845–73.

21. James Bryce, in E. B. Sargent (ed.), *British Citizenship* (London, 1912), 28.

22. Sargent, *British Citizenship*, 27 and 28; James Bryce, "Some Difficulties in Colonial Government Encountered by Great Britain and How They Have Been Met," *Annals of the American Academy of Political and Social Science*, 30 (1907), 19. He once again stressed the existence of "absolutely equal civil rights" (20). Dylan Lino observes that Bryce was unusual in arguing that the ambit of the constitution stopped at the boundaries of the United Kingdom (because its

is not qualified by its racial characteristics and by its state of education and enlightenment to work self-governing institutions." A version of the stratified model was enacted in the British Nationality and Status of Aliens Act of 1914, which encoded in law both the inclusive civil minimalism and the provisions for variable treatment.[23]

Racial-imperial citizenship explicitly utilized racial criteria to identify people considered suitable for citizenship status within the Empire. Whereas the institutional-imperial account drained the content of citizenship by reducing it to a thin notion of subjecthood, the racial-imperial one preserved a full-fledged notion of citizenship by narrowing its scope, rendering it far more exclusive. The differentiation was usually achieved by distinguishing between the populations of the settler colonies and the dependent empire (in particular India), with only the members of the former deemed capable of citizenship. The latter would have to make do with a more basic empire-spanning subjecthood. Institutional diversity was parasitic on racial difference, which both explained and justified the proposed legal-institutional variation. The "white" settler colonies were thought sufficiently "civilised" to be granted formal political equality with the "mother country." As Hobhouse wrote in 1914, the "despotic principle" of imperial domination "tends now to coincide with the colour line," as the settler colonies had been granted a large degree of self-government.[24] Lord Plunket, a former Governor of New Zealand, adumbrated a racial-imperial account of membership. "In my view," he wrote in 1912,

> full British citizenship, good for any and every part of the empire, and entitled to recognition by foreign states, cannot be given to British subjects of colour, though their present position by some system of give and take, might be, and most certainly ought to be, improved. I should give full British citizenship to all born under the British flag and of pure white stock.[25]

---

scope was determined by representation in Parliament). Lino, "Albert Venn Dicey and the Constitutional Theory of Empire," *Oxford Journal of Legal Studies*, 36/4 (2016), 759.

23. The 1914 Act stated, "Nothing in this Act shall take away or abridge any power vested in, or exercisable by, the Legislature or Government of any British Possession, or affect the operation of any law at present in force which has been passed in exercise of such a power, or prevent any such Legislature or Government from treating differently different classes of British subjects."

24. Leonard Hobhouse, "The Growth of the State" in Hobhouse, *Liberalism and Other Writings*, ed. James Meadowcroft (Cambridge, 1914), 148.

25. William Plunket, Fifth Baron Plunket, in Sargent, *British Citizenship*, 11.

This notion of citizenship assumed an increasingly prominent role during the Edwardian era.[26] Indeed Lowell, recently appointed President of Harvard, claimed that in 1908 common citizenship already bound the "Anglo-Saxon" members of the British Empire.[27]

Racial-isopolitan citizenship was grounded in racial identity. It pervaded the discourse of Anglo-American union. The concept of isopolity, or "common citizenship" as the late Victorians also called it, had a long though intermittent history. In the ancient Greek and Roman worlds, *isopoliteia* (ἰσοπολιτεία) was a practice in which independent states reciprocally granted citizenship rights to members of other independent states, usually via treaty arrangements, to establish a form of political union.[28] It was a specific constitutional variant of a wider set of kinship-based practices that bound together autonomous political communities.[29] Although discussed by ancient historians, isopolity was absent from the major philosophical writings of the time. For Sheldon Wolin, it signals an attempt to break down "rigid" conceptions of citizenship, though he maintains rather tendentiously that its failure to "attain theoretical embodiment" in philosophical treatises means that it "lay outside the meaning of 'the political.'"[30] Scholars of the ancient world often distinguish—in a way not always found clearly or consistently in either the original texts or in the nineteenth century—between *isopoliteia* and *sympoliteia*.[31] The latter identifies the practice of merging two or more political communities to create a confederation or federation. A late Victorian textbook defined *isopoliteia*, by contrast, as "[e]quality of rights between different communities or states;

26. Gorman, *Imperial Citizenship*.

27. A. Lawrence Lowell, *The Government of England* (1908; London, 1914), II, 432.

28. J. O. Larsen, *Greek Federal States* (Oxford, 1968), 202–7. The standard scholarly reference is Wilfried Gawantka, *Isopolitie* (Munich, 1975).

29. Sue Elwyn, "Interstate Kinship and Roman Foreign Policy," *Transactions of the American Philological Association*, 123 (1993), 261–86. For examples, see Hans Becke and Peter Funke (eds.), *Federalism in Greek Antiquity* (Cambridge, 2015), 103, 105, 219.

30. Sheldon Wolin, *Politics and Vision*, rev. ed. (Princeton, NJ, 2004), 67. The concept is also mentioned, though in different senses, in Smith, *Political Peoplehood*, 26; Peter Riesenberg, *Citizenship in the Western Tradition* (Chapel Hill, 1994), 52; Andrew Linklater, *Violence and Civilization in the Western States-System* (Cambridge, 2017), 54, 77.

31. Mason Hammond, "Germania Patria," *Harvard Studies in Classical Philology*, 60 (1951), 147–74. It is worth noting that in the ancient texts, including Polybius, the two concepts were often used interchangeably (Larsen, *Greek Federal States*). On the looseness of the ancient terminology (and the overly neat distinctions drawn by modern scholars), see Adrià Piñol Villanueva, "Halicarnassus—Salmakis," *Klio*, 99/1 (2017), 26–50.

reciprocity of rights."[32] This captured both its range of usage and its conceptual breadth.

While the concept largely disappeared from view in the early modern era, it was rediscovered during the nineteenth century by historians working on the ancient world. In the 1880s and 1890s, isopolity was redeployed in arguments about how best to unify Anglo-America. It was modified in three main ways. First, a wider set of rights and duties was prescribed. In the ancient model, isopolity typically involved reciprocal arrangements concerning property-ownership and intermarriage, whereas in the nineteenth century it was often stretched to encompass the full set of modern civil and political rights, including extensive (though rarely universal) suffrage. Second, the format of the association was transformed. In ancient usage, isopolity was usually the product of an asymmetrical relationship: powerful polities granted citizenship rights to weaker ones, usually in recognition of their support in war.[33] The nineteenth-century view encoded a stronger notion of reciprocity. Supporters of Anglo-isopolity argued that it could only succeed because the British Empire and the United States were both powerful, and neither would dominate the isopolitan community. (The relationship between Britain and its settler colonies was closer to the ancient precedents, though it differed insofar as the colonies were formally subordinate to Britain rather than just materially weaker.) Finally, isopolity was racialized: its scope was explicitly defined in terms of racial identity. There are at least two ways that citizenship can be conceptualized in this manner. It can be conferred exclusively on persons ascribed a particular racial identity. Plunket's argument exemplifies this strategy. Alternatively, members of states that have been racialized in a particular manner can be assigned citizenship, on the assumption that most of them will exhibit the appropriate racial characteristics. The former is an individuated account, the latter a collective one. Arguments for racial isopolity were typically of the second kind: isopolity was justified as a practice that bound together white "Anglo-Saxon" states.

Isopolitanism creates a single space in which citizens of all incorporated polities are free to move across borders and engage fully in civil and political life.[34] Unlike the racial-institutional model of citizenship, the racial isopolitan

---

32. Henry Bradley and James Bradley (eds.), *A New English Dictionary on Historical Principles* (Oxford, 1901), V, 1045.

33. Elwyn, "Interstate Kinship and Roman Foreign Policy," 265, 267.

34. Lorenzo Veracini insightfully utilizes the concept of isopolitanism to theorize the mode of belonging central to all settler colonialism. I am using it in a narrower constitutional sense. On his account, for example, the United States and Israel constitute an isopolity, whereas on mine they do not. However, his notion of an "isopolitan sensibility" is a useful way of

variant traversed the boundaries of empire, incorporating the rapidly expanding population of the United States, while excluding hundreds of millions of British subjects. Anglo isopolity spanned two conceptually distinct versions. In the first, it imagined a political relationship forged between several fully independent Anglo-Saxon states. This connoted the eventual dissolution of the imperial bond between Britain and its settler colonies, because it could only work if all the participant communities were politically equal. This post-colonial position was advocated (as we shall see) by Freeman and Carnegie. The other variant glossed over questions of legal-political hierarchy, stipulating that it was possible to create an integrated system of isopolitan citizenship comprising an imperial polity, its settler colonies, and at least one very large independent state. This position was endorsed by Dicey and Bryce. There was a further disagreement over the ultimate purpose of isopolity. For some, including Bryce, Dicey, and Freeman, isopolity was a preferable alternative to the sympolitan integration of Anglo-America or the Angloworld as a whole, while for others, including Carnegie, Stead, and Wells, it was an integral element of full political union.

Dicey on Isopolitan Citizenship

Albert Venn Dicey was one of the most eminent legal scholars in the English-speaking world.[35] Vinerian Professor of the Laws of England at Oxford from 1882 to 1909, he was a staunch liberal, a fervent opponent of Irish Home Rule, and an enthusiastic imperialist. He was also the most authoritative proponent of racial isopolitanism.[36] In April 1897, Dicey published an article in the

---

conceptualizing the desire to unite colonial spaces even in the absence of common citizenship: "Isopolitics, Deep Colonizing, Settler Colonialism," *Interventions*, 13/2 (2011), 177–78. In another recent usage, Paul Magnette conceptualizes European Union citizenship in isopolitan terms: "How Can One Be a European?," *European Law Journal*, 13/5 (2007), 664–79.

35. On Dicey's career and ideas, see Richard Cosgrove, *The Rule of Law* (London, 1980); Julia Stapleton, "Dicey and His Legacy," *History of Political Thought*, 16/2 (1995) 234–55; Mark Walters, "Dicey on Writing *The Law of the Constitution*," *Oxford Journal of Legal Studies*, 32/1 (2012), 21–49; James Kirkby, "A. V. Dicey and English Constitutionalism," *History of European Ideas*, 45/1 (2019), 33–46.

36. On the entanglement of his ideas about law and empire see Lino, "Albert Venn Dicey"; Dylan Lino, "The Rule of Law and the Rule of Empire," *Modern Law Review*, 81/5 (2018), 739–64; Thomas Poole, *Reason of State* (Cambridge, 2015), 197–206. On his account of Irish Home Rule, see Christopher Harvie, "Ideology and Home Rule," *English Historical Review*, 91/359 (1976), 298–314; Hugh Tulloch, "A. V. Dicey and the Irish Question," *Irish Jurist*, 15/1 (1980), 137–65.

Contemporary Review arguing for the extension of "common civil and political rights throughout the whole of the English-speaking people." He maintained that the creation of a racial "isopolity" would secure the union of Britain and the United States.[37]

It is not clear why Dicey decided to employ the conceptual apparatus of isopolity. After centuries of neglect, the idea had reemerged in nineteenth-century historical writing, and he may have encountered it in various contexts. The two most likely sources were the original classical texts and the burgeoning scholarship on the ancient world. The most famous account was in the *Histories* of Polybius (16.26.9), where in book 16 we find the following passage describing the Athenian grant of isopolitan rights to their much weaker Rhodian allies:

> As soon as this despatch had been read, the people, influenced both by its contents and by their warm feelings towards Attalus, were prepared to vote for the war: and when the Rhodians also entered and argued at great length to the same effect, the Athenians at once decreed the war against Philip. They gave the Rhodians also a magnificent reception, honored their state with a crown of valour, and voted all Rhodians equal rights of citizenship at Athens.[38]

But Dicey may have drawn the idea from modern scholarship. Isopolity was discussed, for example, in Barthold Georg Niebuhr's *History of Rome* (1828–42), the most influential work of ancient history published during the century.[39] He defined the concept in a chapter entitled "On the Rights of Isopolity and Municipium."

> Isopolity was a relation entered into by treaty between two *perfectly equal and independent cities*, mutually securing all those privileges to their citizens, which a resident alien could not exercise at all, or only through the

37. Dicey, "Common Citizenship for the English Race," 457–76. The essay was reproduced in *Living Age*, 6/14 (1897), 691–705. Anderson, *Race and Rapprochement*, 123, conflates arguments for a defensive alliance between the United States and the British Empire with advocacy of common citizenship, and in doing so misattributes the former position to Dicey.

38. Polybius, *The Histories of Polybius*, trans. from the text of F. Hultsch by E. Shuckburgh (London, 1889), II, 193.

39. The first two volumes of the *Römische Geschichte* were published in 1812. The first English translation appeared in 1827, but it was superseded by the superior translation of the second edition (1847–51). On the diffuse British reception of Niebuhr's ideas, and their role in legitimating imperialism, see Maike Oergel, "Germania and Great(er) Britain," *Angermion*, 5/1 (2012), 91–118.

mediation of a guardian; the right of intermarriage, of purchasing landed property, of making contracts of every kind, of suing and being sued in person, of being exempted from imposts where citizens were so; and also of partaking in sacrifices and festivals.[40]

Niebuhr glossed over the power inequalities at the core of ancient grants of isopolity and implied that political rights were excluded from the practice. The ambiguity that plagued conceptions of isopolity in later decades can be traced in part to his account of the topic. While other scholars challenged aspects of this argument, no consensus on the exact meaning emerged. Given Niebuhr's scholarly influence, it comes as little surprise that a variety of celebrated British works also mention isopolity, including Connop Thirlwall's *A History of Greece* and (very briefly) Thomas Arnold's *History of Rome*.[41] John Kemble, one of the most significant proponents of "Anglo-Saxonist" interpretations of British history, used the term in *The Saxons in England*, though only in passing. In a chapter on the origins of Anglo-Saxon towns, he sketched how the municipal governance structures within the Roman Empire had persisted through time. "The constitution of a provincial city of the empire, in the days when the republic still possessed virtue and principle, was of this description, at all events from the period of the Social, Marsic or Italian war, when the cities of Italy wrested isopolity, or at least isotely, from Rome."[42] Having studied at Göttingen with Jacob Grimm, Kemble would have been well acquainted with the latest German historical research.

The other most frequent usage of the term "isopolity" was in histories of international law. In 1893, the British legal scholar Thomas Walker stated that "Greek care for the stranger appeared at its best in treaties for the mutual administration of justice to the sojourning foreigner, and in international conventions for the establishment of mixed tribunals or even for the grant of isopolity."[43] In his 1901 discussion of ancient Greek political life in *A Treatise on Public International Law*, the American historian and diplomat Hannis

---

40. Barthold Georg Niebuhr, *The History of Rome*, trans. Julius Hare and Connop Thirlwall (Cambridge, 1832), II, 51. Italics added. He was less clear in defining sympolity (see, e.g., 51, 59, 587).

41. Connop Thirlwall, *A History of Greece* (London, 1839), VI, 50; Thomas Arnold, *History of Rome* (London, 1840), II, 224. Arnold challenged Niebuhr's account of the Roman grant of isopolity to Samnium. Thirlwall was one of the translators of Niebuhr.

42. John Kemble, *The Saxons in England* (London, 1849), II, 270. "Isotely" was the practice of granting a limited range of rights to noncitizens.

43. Thomas Walker, *The Science of International Law* (London, 1893), 214. Walker was a Fellow of Peterhouse, Cambridge.

Taylor repeated Walker's account almost verbatim, asserting that isopolity involved the grant of civic rights to foreign individuals or communities. "The most notable feature of this liberal policy was that part of it embodied in international conventions providing for the mutual administration of justice to resident foreigners, for the establishment of mixed tribunals, or even for the grant of isopolity."[44] The most detailed discussion was found in Coleman Phillipson's *International Law and Customs of the Greeks and Romans*, published to acclaim in 1911.[45] He defined isopolity as the grant—sometimes unilateral, sometimes established through treaty—of private rights of citizenship, principally intermarriage and the right to hold property. Rejecting Niebhur's contention that political rights were formally excluded from isopolitan citizenship, he noted that the original decrees were couched in very general terms, speaking only "of the participation in all things divine and human," and that such a "comprehensive concession" invariably included at least some political rights.[46] He also distinguished isopolity from sympolity, an "enlargement of reciprocal isopolity" that is "practically a federal union of States with interchange of full civic and probably full political rights."[47] As these examples attest, both the content and the scope of isopolitan citizenship were disputed. In particular, there was disagreement over the extent to which political rights were integral to the ancient practice, and if so what kind, and whether rough parity between the members was a prerequisite for the grant of citizenship

44. Hannis Taylor, *A Treatise on International Public Law* (Chicago, 1901), 12. This largely repeated the analysis in Thomas Walker, *A History of the Law of Nations* (Cambridge, 1899), I, 40.

45. Coleman Phillipson, *International Law and Customs of the Greeks and Romans* (London, 1911), I, 141–45. Phillipson was a prolific British barrister and legal academic. See also Henry Brougham Leech, *An Essay on Ancient International Law* (Dublin, 1877), 71 (Leech was a British Barrister, and Fellow of Clare College, Cambridge); Amos Hershey, "The History of International Relations during Antiquity and the Middle Ages," *American Journal of International Law*, 5/4 (1911), 915–16 (Hershey was a Professor of Political Science at Indiana University). William S. Ferguson, *Greek Imperialism* (New York, 1913), 31–32, draws a clear distinction between isopolity ("reciprocity of citizenship," granting nonpolitical rights) and sympolity ("joint citizenship," encompassing full political rights). Ferguson was a Professor of Ancient History at Harvard.

46. Phillipson, *International Law*, I, 141–42.

47. Phillipson, *International Law*, I, 144. The concept could be used for other purposes. Adolf von Harnack, Professor of Church History in Berlin, utilized it to describe the status of the Jewish diaspora within the Roman Empire, in his influential *The Mission and Expansion of Christianity in the First Three Centuries*, trans. James Moffatt (London, 1908), I, 14.

rights. This uncertainty was reflected in debate over the possibility of Anglo-racial citizenship.

Dicey's justification of isopolity developed many of the themes he had outlined in his *Lectures Introductory to the Study of the Law of the Constitution*, perhaps above all the centrality of the "rule of law" as a guarantor of political freedom and stability.[48] It was marked by his habitual caution, his reverence for evolutionary change, and his affirmation of what he thought of as the signal British virtues of prudence and sensitivity to circumstance. He opened the essay by rejecting one possible interpretation of his argument, insisting that isopolity did not entail full political union.[49] He was adamant that he was not promoting sympolity. Throughout his constitutional writings, Dicey was critical of federalism, viewing it as a form of government that was fundamentally unstable. "Federal government means weak government."[50] Amplified by his suspicion of radical constitutional engineering, this belief underpinned his deep skepticism of imperial federation. In the eighth edition of the *Introduction*, published in 1915, he applauded the honorable ambition of the federalists while scorning their cherished project as a "delusion."[51] Isopolity, by contrast, was a workable policy.

Dicey was keen to play down the difficulty of implementation, asserting that isopolity was rooted in the accumulated historical experience of the Anglo-Saxons and that enacting it would require no great constitutional upheaval, only the passing of an Act of Parliament and an Act of Congress. "There would, for the foundation of a common citizenship, be no need for any revolution even of a legal kind in the Constitution either of England or of the United States."[52] Underwriting its historical continuity, there was an important precedent for the policy. "The political status . . . of an American citizen would be exactly the same as that of his grandfather, who, before 1776, was an inhabitant of Massachusetts, but a subject of the British Crown." He would be able to vote in national elections, serve as an MP, Prime Minister, or Member of the House of Lords, just as the British isopolitan citizen would be able to stand for all

48. Dicey, *Lectures Introductory to the Study of the Law of the Constitution*.

49. Dicey, "Common Citizenship," 457.

50. Dicey, *Introduction to the Study of the Law of the Constitution*, 97. "My belief in Federalism as a general form of government for the whole civilized world has never been very strong," he wrote in 1915, "and it is weakened by the experience of the last twenty or thirty years. The complete failure of the American Union to give adequate legal protection to the Blacks, has made a very strong impression on my mind." Dicey to Agnes Fry, 25 November 1915, *Memorials of Albert Venn Dicey*, ed. Robert Rait (London, 1925), 247.

51. Dicey, *Introduction to the Study of the Law of the Constitution*, xcix.

52. Dicey, "Common Citizenship," 459.

American offices, bar the presidency, which was subject to a birthplace clause.[53] For Dicey, progress demanded a return to the moment before the "English people" was split asunder by an inept government in London. Creating an isopolity would represent a welcome form of historical course correction.

Dicey's argument for isopolity was shot through with ambiguity. Oscillating between a planet-straddling account of the "English-speaking peoples" and the specific focus on transatlantic politics, its geographical referent was unstable. Dicey also refrained from examining in any detail the constitutional implications of a form of citizenship that incorporated both independent states and settler colonies. Moreover, while explicit that there was no *necessary* connection between isopolity and sympolity, he implied that the former smoothed the path to the latter. European historical experience was instructive. Precipitating state formation, isopolitan citizenship had acted as a powerful catalyst for the consolidation of the German principalities.

> In this matter much instruction may be derived from the annals of Germany; for in Germany isopolity preceded in practice, if not in theory, the development of political unity, and nothing has conduced more to German well-being, and ultimately to German greatness, than the ease with which the subjects of one German State passed into the public employment of any other.[54]

In preparing the essay, Dicey discussed the history and theory of isopolity with his close friend Bryce. In early 1897, he enquired about the citizenship practices of the Holy Roman Empire. "[W]as there not, both in theory + in reality a common German citizenship, i.e. was there anything to prevent a Hanoverian or a Saxon from entering the public service of Prussia?"[55] And if so, did it occur without naturalization? The careers of Heinrich Stein and Gerhard von Scharnhorst suggested to Dicey that this was the case. He required a swift response. "I should be very glad if you could send me a short answer to my questions as I want to make a reference to Germany in a lecture on Friday as to the possibility of 'A Common citizenship for both branches of the English people.'[56] The lecture was delivered in Cambridge in February 1897. Bryce confirmed what Dicey suspected, that in practice at least there had been a form

53. Dicey, "Common Citizenship," 462.

54. Dicey, "Common Citizenship," 458.

55. Dicey to Bryce, 23 February 1897, MS 2, Fol 236, Bryce papers.

56. Dicey to Bryce, 23 February 1897, MS 2, Fol 236, Bryce papers. The lecture, delivered on 26 February 1897, was noted briefly in *The Nation*, 64 (1897), 198.

of common citizenship in Germany, and as such "citizenship can exist without national unity."[57] Even as isopolitanism provided the grounds for a limited form of transatlantic union, it prompted the question of how far integration might proceed.

For Dicey, institutions were effective only insofar as they conformed with existing cultural norms. Isopolity was a constitutional technology that supervened on, and would help to reproduce, a powerful sense of collective (racial) identity. Institutionalizing affect, it would legally codify an underlying sentiment. "I assume that the desire for some sort of unity does exist, and my contention is that, given such a desire, there is no legal difficulty in giving effect to it."[58] Isopolity did not entail the imposition of an alien set of laws and institutions on the common law structures of the Angloworld. There existed a powerful bond of shared values, sentiments, and beliefs throughout the English-speaking lands, indissolubly linking the "English constitutional Monarchy and the English Federal Republic."[59] In Dicey's choice of terminology—one that was unlikely to win many American converts—we can discern another reason why he downplayed the radicalism of the idea: the American constitution was a modified version of the British one, adapted to new circumstances. This familiar historical argument had been sketched most prominently in Bryce's anglicized account of American institutions in *The American Commonwealth*.[60]

Dicey catalogued some of the interests and values purportedly connecting Britain to the United States. First, they venerated political freedom, as demonstrated by their refusal to institute conscription and stoke militarism. "The two English-speaking nations, in the first place, stand apart from that admiration for military power which prevails throughout Continental Europe."[61] Second, they shared—and shared an admiration for—the same kind of political virtues. In a laudatory passage, he compared the unlikely bedfellows of Canning and Lincoln, declaring them united in their "unwavering steadfastness of purpose, in their absolute belief in the cause of which they were the defenders, in their abhorrence of violence, in their endless patience, in their trust in law, in their supreme clemency which, though it may at moments seem to be weakness is in reality only another form of prudence and of justice."[62]

57. Dicey to Bryce, 26 February 1897, MS 2, Fol 238, Bryce papers.

58. Dicey, "Common Citizenship," 459.

59. Dicey, "Common Citizenship," 468.

60. James Bryce, *The American Commonwealth*, 3 vols. (London, 1888). I discuss the historical narratives underlying unionist claims in chapter 2.

61. Dicey, "Common Citizenship," 468.

62. Dicey, "Common Citizenship," 471.

Moreover, and vitally, the two polities were bound by shared economic and geopolitical interests.

Above all, the Anglo-Saxons were knitted together by a rich legal culture. Throughout his writings, Dicey championed the centrality of the common law to the development, stability, and splendor of the British political community, a legacy shared by the United States and the other settler colonies. His work played a fundamental role in constructing the "great tradition" of constitutional scholarship that emerged during the late nineteenth century, a tradition in which the United States and Britain were celebrated as distinctive bearers of a superior civilization.[63] In outlining the legal basis for isopolity, he dropped into lyrical mode:

> When at some distant period thinkers sum up the results of English as they now sum up the results of Grecian or of Roman civilisation, they will, we may anticipate, hold that its main permanent effect has been the diffusion throughout the whole world of the law of England, together with those notions of freedom, of justice, and of equity to which English law gives embodiment.[64]

For Dicey, the law was both the reason why Britain and the United States should be united and the primary instrument through which this could be achieved. The geographical reach and deep historical roots of the common law demonstrated the "essential unity of the whole English race." Because they were immersed in this legal culture and understood its profound implications, lawyers were best placed to argue for common citizenship. The existence of a shared legal system made isopolity a simple extension of underlying legal norms and values: "Common citizenship is the logical, one might almost say the necessary result of the inheritance of a common law."[65] It would be the consummation of the venerable tradition.

Dicey adduced three other reasons to support isopolitanism. First, both countries were powerful actors on the world stage, so neither would regard an isopolity as enacting a dependent relationship. (Again, he failed to address the inequality between Britain and its settler colonies.) Second, slavery had been abolished in the United States, opening the way for British participation. And finally, the historical memories of Anglo-American conflict had faded, meaning that plans for union would gain a more receptive hearing than in the

---

63. Anthony Brundage and Richard Cosgrove, *The Great Tradition* (Palo Alto, 2007).

64. Dicey, "Common Citizenship," 469.

65. Dicey, "Common Citizenship," 469, 470.

past.[66] Despite his caution, a radical ambition could occasionally be glimpsed behind the cool legal formulations of Dicey's prose.

> The creation of a common English citizenship would of itself intensify throughout the whole English race that sentiment of national unity, the increase of which is, in one form or another, suggesting plans for binding closer together England and her colonies; and a common citizenship would be no small advantage if it did no more than emphasize the feeling that the two branches of the English people were bound together by the feeling of common nationality.[67]

He can be read as suggesting (whether intentionally or not) that the creation of an isopolity would open the door to future political union—this was the lesson taught by modern German history. An underlying sense of *nationhood* was already perceptible.

Time was of the essence. At a moment of intense racist paranoia about the dangers of mass migration in the United States and the British settler colonies, Dicey avowed that some forms of "white" immigration were essential for the successful reproduction of the racial-political order. "Before opinion or law has fixed a definite bar against free emigration, it would be well to ensure to every member of the English people the right to free settlement in every English-speaking land," he wrote.[68] Although the published text was not explicit about the target of this argument, it referred chiefly to Chinese immigration into Australia. Dicey endorsed the racialized immigration controls being proposed there and elsewhere in the Angloworld. Bryce was once again a sounding board. In 1901 Dicey wrote to him,

> There is a terrible danger that as we cannot talk of human equality with [the] same confidence with wh. the best men of the 18th & the earlier 19th Century spoke of it, & as we are compelled to attach more importance than they did to race, we may come to give up faith in the truth of wh. I think they had a firm hold, that the qualities wh. races have in common are at least as important as, (I should say more important than) the characteristics in wh. they differ. then the whole matter is complicated to my mind by the growth of an idea, wh. I think may be true that race[s] with different ideals and different moralities had best live a-part. I cannot myself feel at all sure that the cry for a "White Australia" is not at bottom a sound one.[69]

66. Dicey, "Common Citizenship," 473.
67. Dicey, "Common Citizenship," 465.
68. Dicey, "Common Citizenship," 466.
69. Dicey to Bryce, 25 December 1901, MS 3, Fol 7, Bryce papers.

He reiterated the point in 1902: "Greatly against my will + what one may call one's natural prejudices, I am coming to the conclusion that the Australians are probably right in excluding the Chinese, or in wishing to do so."[70] But Dicey was adamant that fear of Asian immigration should not impede free movement for white citizens around the Angloworld. Racial isopolitanism provided a fitting institutional answer. He returned to the theme in the *Introduction to the Study of the Law of the Constitution*, arguing that "it may turn out difficult, or even impossible, to establish throughout the Empire that equal citizenship of all British subjects which exists in the United Kingdom and which Englishmen in the middle of the nineteenth century hoped to see established throughout the length and breadth of the Empire."[71] Immigration barriers were necessary to preserve the racial composition of the settler world. Dicey sought to remap political space by altering the meaning of borders and sovereignty. He figured the state as a racialized and differentially accessible entity: permeable to Anglo-isopolitans, restricted to everyone else. On this account, racial identity determined the scope of political membership.

The essay received a mixed reaction. A writer in the Tory *Saturday Review* charged that Dicey exhibited "consummate ignorance of the true feelings of the great majority of Americans towards England."[72] In the *American Review of Reviews*, Albert Shaw objected that the role of the monarchy marked an irreconcilable difference between British and American forms of government, rendering "hopelessly unattainable any such scheme of inter-citizenship between England and the United States."[73] Others offered praise. The American journalist Richard T. Colburn thought Dicey's idea "very hospitable" though ultimately unworkable.[74] Concurring with his main argument, Stead nevertheless fulminated against Dicey's choice of terminology, writing that he "uses a word that is almost enough to ruin it from the popular point of view. The fearsome word is 'isopolity.'" Although Dicey "seems rather fond of his invention," Stead huffed, it was "enough to label any proposal isopolitan to prejudice it seriously in the public mind."[75] Writing to Bryce, Dicey remarked

---

70. Dicey to Bryce, 16 May 1902, MS 3, Fol 16, Bryce papers.

71. Dicey, *Introduction to the Study of the Law of the Constitution*, 8th ed., liv.

72. "Reviews and Magazines," *Saturday Review of Politics, Literature, Science and Art*, 10 November 1897, 394.

73. Albert Shaw, "Progress of the World," *American Review of Reviews*, 15 (June 1897), 654. Shaw had earlier seemed more open to the idea: Shaw, "An American View of Home Rule and Federation," *Contemporary Review*, 62 (1893), 315–18.

74. Richard Colburn, "Improvident Civilization," *Proceedings of the American Association for the Advancement of Science*, 46 (1897), 403.

75. Stead, *RoR*, 25 (April 1897), 370. See also Stead, *RoR*, 24 (July 1901), 94.

that his argument had been lauded in *The Speaker*, though the reviewer had described it as a dream. Dicey was unperturbed. "Yet it is a dream wh. under slightly different circumstances might easily have been turned into a reality."[76] Changing geopolitical circumstances soon led him to modify his prognosis.

Spending the year 1898 at Harvard Law School, Dicey had a ringside seat for the swirling debate over American imperial policy.[77] In late November, he confided in his diary that American imperial expansion—"extending American possessions abroad and taking a part in European politics"—promised little benefit and many risks. A few days later, he noted that the "wisest course" for Washington was to avoid absorbing the Philippines.[78] Yet Dicey was convinced that a moment of opportunity had arrived. The consequence of war with Spain, he wrote to Bryce in May, "is to make an *entente cordiale* if not an actual alliance between England + the U.S. imperative," and such a development "may save Anglo-Saxon principles of law & liberty if nothing else will."[79] Ever cautious, Dicey worried that British hostility to the United States ran deeper than was apparent. "Between ourselves I do not think the feeling in favour of the U.S. nearly so strong in England as is generally supposed."[80] Talk was cheap. This skepticism about the political efficacy of sentiment prompted Dicey to criticize the naïve rhetoric permeating debate over racial union. In September 1898, he confessed to Charles W. Eliot, the long-serving President of Harvard, that "I cannot get rid of the conviction that sentiment which has a close connection with sensitiveness is an uncertain foundation on which to base national policy." He worried about "the fallacies of personification," the ascription of emotional states, including "benevolence sympathy & the like," to human collectives. A viable racial union had to be based on common identity *and* joint interests.

---

76. Dicey to Bryce, 7 May 1897, MS Bryce 2, Fol 244. Cf. *The Speaker*, 15 (April 1897), 385–87. For a later positive appraisal, from a law professor at the University of California, see Orrin McMurray, "Inter-Citizenship," *Yale Law Journal*, 27/3 (1918), 299–316.

77. Dicey, *Memorials*, ch. 10. He was impressed by what he found: Dicey, "The Teaching of English Law at Harvard," *Harvard Law Review*, 13/5 (1900), 422–40. See also the discussion in Richard Cosgrove, "A. V. Dicey at the Harvard Law School, 1898," *Harvard Library Bulletin*, 26 (1978), 325–35.

78. Diary of A. V. Dicey, 17–20 November 1898 and 24–25 November 1898, cited in Dicey, *Memorials*, 166, 168.

79. Dicey to Bryce, 12 May 1898, MS 2, Fol 259, Bryce papers. See also Dicey to Bryce, 2 May 1898, MS 2, Fol 256.

80. Dicey to Bryce, 12 May 1898, MS 2, Fol 260–61, Bryce papers. This was in the context of accepting an invitation to the Anglo-American Dinner on 3 June 1898.

No one can rejoice more keenly than I do at the good feeling at present existing, but I want us to recognise that if it is to be permanent we must base it on permanent causes. To these I can trust. I believe for instance that the whole English people on both sides of the Atlantic & in every part of the world have at last, though rather slowly caught hold of the idea that the Anglo Saxon race & Anglo-Saxon ideals of justice & the like are destined to rule the world, & that this splendid future can be wrecked only by a quarrel between the two branches of the English race. This belief is to my mind based on the most undoubted facts & if it can once pervade the whole English people, will make war between England & America an absolute impossibility.[81]

At once giving legal expression to sentiment and securing common interests, a system of isopolitan citizenship would institutionalize union by establishing a solid though limited constitutional foundation. Dicey restated his case in the October 1898 edition of the *Atlantic Monthly*. He opened by admitting that his previous advocacy had achieved little. "The proposal fell flat. It was inopportune." But the situation had changed in the intervening months, as Britain sided openly with the United States in the Spanish-American war, and now "[a]ll the world is talking of the close ties which bind together all the divisions of the English people."[82] Thinkers on both sides of the Atlantic emphasized the commonalities between the two powers, searching for the best way to secure permanent cooperation. He reaffirmed his commitment to isopolity, "a perfectly sound and reasonable suggestion." The future of the race looked bright, if only the moment could be seized. "We perceive that the English-speaking peoples are destined in a century or two to become the dominant power throughout the civilized world. Their future supremacy is nearly as certain as any future event can be." While present geopolitical and economic conditions precluded any formal alliance, it was both feasible and highly desirable to sign an Anglo-American arbitration treaty and foster a "moral alliance." This would encourage further development. "[I]t is impossible to forgo the dream, or the hope, or, if we look to the distant future, the expectation that a growing sense of essential unity may ultimately give birth to some scheme of common citizenship."[83]

81. Dicey to Eliot, 20 September 1898, UAI 5.150, Box 36, Charles W. Eliot papers, Harvard University Archives. I thank Prof. Mark Walters for drawing this document to my attention.

82. A. V. Dicey, "England and America," *Atlantic Monthly*, 82 (October 1898), 441. The article was commended in *The Nation*, 67 (1898), 262 and the *New York Times*, 3 October 1898.

83. Dicey, "England and America," 442, 441, 445.

Dwelling Together in Unity:
Isopolitan Citizenship and Beyond

Dicey was not the first to call for an Anglo-American isopolity. Versions of the argument (though not the terminology) circulated in late eighteenth-century deliberations over American independence, and the idea echoed, albeit very faintly, through the nineteenth century. In September 1853, the poet Arthur Clough used the concept in a letter to Charles Eliot Norton.

> The old classical system by which closer ties of relationship between this country and that, than between this and some third, seems no bad one. Between America and England, between the British North American colonies in particular the United States, one would be glad if there could exist some isopolity: that a man might be a citizen in which he pleased, and change about as he chooses.[84]

Others employed the language of citizenship to indicate the deep bonds of racial identity. In *Greater Britain*, Dilke argued that the United States and Britain were conjoined by a shared racial heritage: "That which raises us above the provincialism of citizenship of little England is our citizenship of the greater 'Saxondom' which includes all that is best and wisest in the world."[85]

During the 1880s, the idea of common citizenship took on a new lease of life. Among others, Freeman expressed support for the idea. In a coruscating attack, he charged advocates of imperial federation with failing to heed the wisdom of the Greeks, who had perfected a template for establishing new colonies. The profound difference between ancient and modern forms of governance was instantiated in their contrasting conceptions of political obligation. In the Hellenic world, it was centered on the city. "The Greek was before all things a citizen." The modern European notion of personal allegiance, a type of feudal fealty that bound individuals to the sovereign, was alien to them: "The Greek would have regarded himself degraded by the name of 'subject.'"[86] The difference between subjecthood and citizenship shaped their respective forms of colonization, for "while the active duties of the citizen of a commonwealth can hardly be discharged beyond the territories of that commonwealth, the duties of the subject of . . . a personal master, are as binding on one part of the earth's surface as on another." The Greeks planted free cities populated by

---

84. Clough to Norton, 23 September 1853, Clough, *The Poems and Prose Remains of Arthur Hugh Clough* (London, 1869), I, 212.

85. Dilke, *Greater Britain*, II, 155–56.

86. Freeman, "Greater Greece," 18, 23; Freeman, "Imperial Federation" (1885), Appendix in Freeman, *Greater Greece and Greater Britain*, 142.

free citizens.[87] Modern European colonists, including the British, remained bound to their "mother land" by formal and subordinate ties of political allegiance.[88] The connections between metropole and colony were the "brightest facts of Greek or Phoenician political life," while those of the modern colonial system were "among the darkest."[89]

Aside from identifying some conceptual problems with schemes for imperial federation—notably the impossibility of creating a proper federal structure between communities that were not formally independent—Freeman also worried about a glaring anomaly: the majority of the "English-speaking people" were excluded. "It is the most curious illustration of the modern theory of colonization, the substitution of mere personal allegiance for nationality in the higher sense, that any mind could take in for a moment the thought of a federation of the English-speaking people of which the United States should not form a part."[90] This failure to comprehend the meaning of "higher nationality" was catastrophic. After all, he declared on an American lecture tour, the United States was not a foreign country, but rather "England with a difference."[91] His priorities were clear. "The sentiment is possibly unpatriotic," Freeman wrote, "but I cannot help looking on such a friendly union of the English and English-speaking folk as an immeasurably higher object than the maintenance of any so-called British Empire."[92] Because of the differential size of the two polities, Freeman thought that a British-American federation was impossible, but he also claimed that the wondrous power of electricity meant that the political vision of the ancients could be replicated on a global scale. "Geographical distance, political separation, fierce rivalry, cruel warfare, never snapped the enduring tie which bound every Greek to every other Greek. So the Englishman of Britain, of America, of Africa, of Australia, should be each to his distant brother as were the Greek of Massalia, the Greek of Kyrênê, and the Greek of Chersôn."[93] Isopolitan citizenship was an essential element of racial destiny. "I have often dreamed," he wrote, "that something like the Greek συμπολιτεία, a power in the citizens in each country of taking

87. Freeman, "Greater Greece," 29. Freeman was one of the main authorities on federal systems of government: Freeman, *History of Federal Government* (London, 1863). On Freeman's ideas about imperial federation and race, see Duncan Bell, "Alter Orbis" in Conlin and Bremner, *Making History*, 217–35.

88. Freeman, "Greater Greece," 23, 30, 27.

89. Freeman, "Imperial Federation," 121.

90. Freeman, *Greater Greece and Greater Britain*, 140, 141.

91. Freeman, *Some Impressions*, 10. The tour lasted from October 1881 to April 1882.

92. Freeman, "Imperial Federation," 143.

93. Freeman, *Some Impressions*, 24.

up the citizenship of the other at pleasure, might not be beyond hope; but I have never ventured to dream of more than that." Reiterating the point in a letter to Goldwin Smith in August 1888, he looked forward to a future when inhabitants of Britain, the United States, and the settler colonies, could take up "citizenship at pleasure" in each polity.[94]

Freeman viewed the chances of success as slim, for as long as there were only two independent "English" nations—the United States and Britain— building an effective system of common citizenship was unlikely. The two countries would be rivals, jostling for position and unwilling to cooperate fully. The answer lay in granting independence to the settler colonies. Creating a cluster of independent polities would establish the foundations for "something like an abiding political alliance" between the members of the English-speaking world.[95] For Freeman, then, the dissolution of the colonial empire was a necessary condition for achieving the more important goal of racial unity. His attack on the imperial federalists for failing to recognize the true significance and spatial scope of Anglo-Saxondom resonated widely. A similar line was adopted, for example, by the influential Canadian journalist John Redpath Dougall, who argued that federalist plans ignored the true "unity of the Anglo-Saxon race." He called instead for a "pan-Saxon alliance" rooted in common citizenship, "so that a man, by simply transferring his domicile, would enter on all the rights of citizenship in his new home."[96] As with Dicey, the suggestion was that this would recreate the status that pertained in the years before American independence.

Bryce was also an advocate of isopolity. Although skeptical of radical plans for political union, he searched for ways to deepen connections and foster cooperation between the two countries. At the height of the Venezuela crisis, he wrote an article seeking to diffuse tension between London and Washington, while expressing hope for their future relations.

> The average Englishman likes America far better than any foreign nation; he admires the "go," as he calls it, of your people, and is soon at home among you. In fact, he does not regard you as a foreign nation. . . . The

---

94. Freeman, "Imperial Federation," 142; Freeman to Smith, 19 August 1888, Freeman, *Life and Letters*, II, 384. Smith was open to the idea. In his critical response to Carnegie, he argued that "[m]utual privilege in respect to naturalization laws might not be impracticable." Smith, "Anglo-Saxon Union," 171.

95. Freeman, *Greater Greece and Greater Britain*, 142.

96. John Dougall, "An Anglo-Saxon Alliance," *Contemporary Review*, 48 (1885), 700, 703, 704. Born in Scotland, Dougall was the editor and founder of the popular daily newspaper *The Montreal Witness*, and a leader of the temperance movement.

educated and thoughtful Englishman has looked upon your Republic as the champion of freedom and peace, has held you to be our natural ally, and has even indulged the hope of a permanent alliance with you, under which the citizens of each country should have the rights of citizenship in the other and be aided by the consuls and protected by the fleets of the other all over the world.[97]

Two years later, he argued that a defensive alliance was implausible, while listing practical steps that could be taken to capitalize on the increasing transatlantic amity. An arbitration treaty was one such option. So too was "recognition of common citizenship, securing to the citizens of each, in the country of the other, certain rights not enjoyed by other foreigners."[98] Like Freeman and Dicey, both close friends, he regarded this option as much more feasible than grander schemes for sympolitan unification.

Carnegie, Stead, and Wells all promoted common citizenship as a constitutive part of their unionist dreams. Stead used the pages of the *Review of Reviews* to advocate "one common citizenship for all the English-speaking lands," while *The Americanization of the World* contained an extended discussion of Dicey's proposal, an idea "strongly supported in other quarters." He regarded it as one of several strategies that could secure union, though, as we have seen, Stead deplored the terminology adopted by the famed legal thinker.[99] In *Triumphant Democracy*, Carnegie argued that one of the defining glories of the United States was that it remade "*subjects* (insulting word)" into citizens, thus elevating and ennobling them.[100] He promoted common citizenship throughout his writings on racial union. "A Look Ahead" drew a parallel between empire past and racial union future. "Until a little more than a hundred years ago the English-speaking race dwelt together in unity, the American being as much a citizen of Britain as the Englishman, Scotsman, Welshman, or Irishman." Such a situation could and should be replicated. "[M]y belief," Carnegie wrote, was that "the future is certainly to see a reunion of the separated parts and once again a common citizenship."[101] A decade later, he foresaw "the coming of the day of common citizenship within the wide and ever-expanding boundaries of our race."[102]

97. Bryce, "British Feeling on the Venezuela Question," 151.

98. James Bryce, "The Essential Unity of England and America," *Atlantic Monthly*, 82 (July 1898), 29.

99. W. T. Stead, *RoR*, 9 (February 1894), 190; Stead, *RoR*, 23 (February 1901), 142; Stead, *Americanization*, 423–25.

100. Carnegie, *Triumphant Democracy*, 18. Italics in original.

101. Carnegie, *Reunion*, 3, 9. He called it "a common British-American citizenship" (10).

102. Andrew Carnegie, *The Empire of Business* (New York, 1902), 186.

Wells embraced proposals for common citizenship, viewing their popularity among his contemporaries as part of the intellectual flux that marked the end of the century. He thought that expansive poststatist models of political membership were vital for securing the "larger synthesis" of the English-speaking peoples. By the close of the twentieth century, he predicted in *Anticipations*, the New Republic would have a "practically homogenous citizenship" of at least one hundred million "sound-bodied and educated and capable men."[103] Most likely referring to Dicey, he praised a recent "interesting proposal" for "interchangeable citizenship," meaning that members of various English-speaking polities could claim political rights in all the designated units. Given the rising skepticism about traditional ways of ordering social and political life, he thought that many similar plans would be formulated in the coming years.[104] *Mankind in the Making* did not mention common citizenship explicitly, though it was implied by Wells's analysis and endorsement of the New Republic. However, discussion of the topic was absent from his other Edwardian writings on the "English-speaking peoples," as his support for formal unification dropped away.

While most calls for isopolity emanated from British intellectuals, it is striking that the most detailed case for the policy was made by the American lawyer John Randolph Dos Passos in *The Anglo-Saxon Century and the Unification of the English-speaking People*.

> I propose the establishment of a common, interchangeable, citizenship between all English-speaking Nations and Colonies by the abrogation of the naturalisation laws of the United States and the British Empire, so that the citizens of each can, at will, upon landing in the other's territory, become citizens of any of the countries dominated by these Governments.[105]

In order to build a "permanent and indissoluble" union between Britain and the United States, Dos Passos recommended free trade, currency standardization, the creation of an arbitration court, and the incorporation of Canada into the United States.[106] Skeptical about establishing a single transatlantic state, he maintained that his project provided legal and political recognition for underlying racial-cultural affinities and interests. At the heart of his

---

103. Wells, *Anticipations*, 146.

104. Wells, *Anticipations*, 148.

105. Dos Passos, *Anglo-Saxon Century*, ix. The book was published originally in 1902, and sold out quickly, necessitating a 2nd edition (vii). A skilled lawyer, Dos Passos's *Treatise on the Law of Stockbrokers and Stock Exchanges* (1882) was a standard work. He was a key figure in the development of the modern trust company.

106. Dos Passos, *Anglo-Saxon Century*, ix.

argument—"the crucial point of my subject"—was citizenship.[107] "By a single stroke of parliamentary and constitutional legislation the individuals composing the Anglo-Saxon race would enjoy common political rights, and, in fact and deed, become members of the same political family."[108]

Dos Passos was clear about the appropriate designation and intellectual pedigree of his proposal. "This may be called common or reciprocal citizenship. The Greeks termed it 'Isopolity.'" The new legislation would create a racial space in which citizens were able to move freely within a single order of rights and responsibilities, not having to worry about the jurisdictional limits of the territorial state. "An Englishman under the American flag would be an American; an American under the English flag would be an Englishman. A citizen of Great Britain visiting the United States would, upon landing, become *eo instanti* a citizen of the United States, *pro hac vice*, pending the duration of the visit." Two types of rights would be granted. The first were civil: an "Isopolite" would enjoy the same property rights as a "native-born citizen," including "buying, selling, trading in, or disposing of the same by will," as well as identical commercial rights and privileges. The second were political: the isopolite would be entitled to vote in all federal, state, and local elections, as well as having an obligation to pay taxes, perform jury service, and (if necessary) be conscripted by the military.[109] Dos Passos argued that isopolitan status should be voluntary. "The volition to embrace temporarily or permanently a citizenship in any other English-speaking country would rest with each individual."[110]

Dos Passos appealed to various precedents. Noting that isopolity was "very ancient," he argued that "[s]omething like it existed in the Grecian states, which, in establishing a federal union among themselves, interchanged civic rights." Citing Niebuhr's *History of Rome*, he maintained that it was forged between independent and equal polities.[111] Sympoly, by contrast, involved "the protection which a larger or stronger state gave to a smaller or weaker

107. Dos Passos, *Anglo-Saxon Century*, 179. Dos Passos's account was praised in "Contemporary Literature," *Westminster Review*, 160 (1903), 587–88. A review of the book in the *Yale Law Review* observed, "Most thinking men are probably to-day agreed that Anglo-Saxon unity in some form and degree is a fact which a not distant future has in store. The logic of events is clearly pointing in that direction." In [S. W. E.], "Review of Dos Passos, *Anglo-Saxon Century*," 105.

108. Dos Passos, *Anglo-Saxon Century*, 180.

109. Dos Passos, *Anglo-Saxon Century*, 182, 181.

110. Dos Passos, *Anglo-Saxon Century*, 180.

111. Dos Passos, *Anglo-Saxon Century*, 185. Dos Passos cited Dicken's 1894 edition of Mommsen's *History of Rome*, I, 88, 51. Using Niebuhr's *Lecture on the History of Rome*, he also asserted that isopolity existed "in some essential features" among the Romans.

one," and as such it institutionalized a connection based on unequal relations.[112] The result was a bifurcated political system, with the citizens of the stronger power possessing a wider range of rights than the members of the weaker one. The chief benefit for the latter was the security provided by close association with the former. Turning to Niebuhr's *Lectures on Ethnography and Geography*, Dos Passos once again compared sympolity and isopolity: "Isopolite states . . . generally stood to each other in a relation of perfect equality, and were quite independent in their transactions with foreign countries."[113] In this unconventional account, isopolity pertained between two equal states and involved symmetrical reciprocity, whereas sympolity had little to do with federalism, as most scholars insisted, but instead crystallized an unequal relationship between a strong and a weak polity. Dos Passos also hailed Freeman, Bryce, and Dicey as eminent contemporary advocates of common citizenship.[114] He concurred with them that enacting isopolity would not require major constitutional changes in either Britain or the United States. Nor did he see it as equivalent to (or a species of) military alliance. Yet despite its modest constitutional character, he thought that the new regime would have profound and lasting effects. Echoing Dicey's conceptual language, he argued that isopolity "would practically make the English-speaking people, so far as the outside world is concerned, one nation, inspired by one great, noble purpose."[115] In addition to expanding the scope of the community, it would also animate, even transform, the behavior and beliefs of its members, at once restoring the "office of a citizen to its high and elevated sphere" and serving to "elevate and enlighten all the citizens," ultimately infusing "the manners, morals and legislation of all the countries involved."[116] Constitutional design could remake Anglo-America, setting it on course to fulfill its destined role of world leadership.

Fractal Loyalty and Love: On Race Patriotism

Most British and American thinkers regarded patriotism as a political virtue, essential for a healthy and flourishing community, though they also recognized that it could morph into illegitimate aggression and jingoism. (At the time, nationalism and patriotism were rarely delineated conceptually.) In 1902,

---

112. Dos Passos, *Anglo-Saxon Century*, 184–85.
113. Dos Passos, *Anglo-Saxon Century*, 186.
114. Dos Passos, *Anglo-Saxon Century*, 56, 113, 170, 188–89, 209, 211–13.
115. Dos Passos, *Anglo-Saxon Century*, 188, 189.
116. Dos Passos, *Anglo-Saxon Century*, 200, 202.

W. H. Kent observed that "[p]atriotism and Imperialism, with all their various derivatives, hold a strangely conspicuous place in the language of current English politics."[117] They were often conjoined. Just as citizenship was rescaled to fit imperial structures, so too was patriotism. Since the British Empire sprawled across the world, it was often asserted that the compass of patriotism stretched (or should stretch) far beyond state boundaries. The true patriot owed allegiance to the empire as a whole, not (or not only) to any particular polity within it. Moreover, the languages of citizenship and patriotism often blurred together. In the introduction to a collection of classic statements on the subject, George Frisbie Hoar, Senator for Massachusetts, could define patriotism simply as "good citizenship."[118] Many British imperialists submitted that good citizenship necessitated imperial patriotism.[119] Both citizenship and patriotism were thought necessary for a functioning empire or possible Anglo-American union. Mutable and disputed, the concepts were arrayed in various configurations and utilized for diverse purposes.

As with the nested model of citizenship, most advocates of imperial patriotism did not regard it as incompatible with local iterations. Writing during the First World War, the distinguished American historian George Louis Beer recounted that during the late nineteenth century the ambition to secure British colonial union grew perceptibly, and many people "unconsciously and consciously, transferred their ultimate dedication from the local community to the world-wide state of which it constituted merely a member." Political parochialism expanded into a form of "imperial patriotism" which was viewed as "entirely consistent with colonial nationalism."[120] Milner exemplified this shift, repeatedly distinguishing between "wider" and "local" forms of patriotism while insisting that they were necessarily connected.[121] In a speech in

---

117. W. H. Kent, "Patriotism or Imperialism?," *Westminster Review*, 157 (1902), 126. Kent went on to argue that they should be seen as antithetical. On the variety of British debate, see J. H. Grainger, *Patriotisms* (London, 1986).

118. George Hoar, "Love of Country" in Hoar, *The Book of Patriotism* (Boston, 1902), xiii.

119. See, for example, Charles Dilke, *The British Empire* (London, 1899), 139.

120. George Louis Beer, *The English-Speaking Peoples* (London, 1917), 176. On the growing sense of national consciousness and patriotism in the colonies, see Richard Jebb, *Studies in Colonial Nationalism* (London, 1905). While in favor of closer economic connection between Britain and the colonies, Jebb argued that it should be on the basis of "alliance," not "federation." Very critical of the United States, he did not advocate racial union. As one reviewer put it, "[N]o dream of Anglo-Saxon dominion is suggested": Willard Hotchkiss, review of Jebb, *Annals of the American Academy of Political and Social Science*, 219 (1905), 429.

121. Milner, Speech, Cape Colony, 20 April 1900, *Nation and Empire*, 19–20.

Vancouver in 1908, he implored his audience to affirm both Canadian and imperial patriotism, the one reinforcing the other.[122]

Such arguments did not go unchallenged. Critics of the imperial wars of the 1890s saw patriotism as both cause and curse. The British liberal thinker J. M. Robertson sketched one of the most vigorous rejoinders, arguing in *Patriotism and Empire* that patriotism was the manifestation of a gratuitous worship of size and military capacity. "The mere proof of the possession of superior power," he charged, "is held to have in it something ethically ennobling; and the banal pride in it, dubbed 'patriotism,' passes for an incontestable virtue." In the modern world, as in the ancient, patriotism sanctioned political violence and militarism. It meant love of *more* country. War, imperial aggression, and patriotism all sprang from the same underlying psychological dispositions: malice, passion, and pride. "Here is our ethical problem."[123] The American anti-imperial campaigner William Garrison was also clear where blame resided. "We have too long been in fetters to the fetish of patriotism, not unnaturally, because in the Civil War patriotism was on the side of truth and liberty," he wrote in 1898. "But as an unreasoning sentiment nothing can be more pernicious or more calculated to enslave the mind."[124] Carl Schurz, esteemed American politician and journalist, drew on republican arguments to make a similar point. Spawning a "strange moral and political color-blindness," war created "false ideals of patriotism and civic virtue."[125]

Those keen to defend patriotism sought to distinguish legitimate from illegitimate modalities, though there was little agreement on where to draw the line. The Cambridge archaeologist Charles Waldstein did so by differentiating chauvinism and patriotism.

> Chauvinism can in no sense be called an outcome, or even a modification, of patriotism. They are two distinct, if not opposed, ideas, the following of either of which points to characters and temperaments as different as the

122. Milner, Speech, Vancouver, 9 October 1908, *Nation and Empire*, 302–10.

123. John Robertson, *Patriotism and Empire*, 2nd ed. (London, 1900), 25, 71. Robertson drew on the American sociologist Franklin Giddings's idea of "consciousness of kind" to make this argument (5–6). For other criticisms, see Gooch, "Imperialism," 311. The philosopher D. G. Ritchie, Robertson's bête noire, called for "the ideals of a new and wider patriotism." Ritchie, "The Moral Problems of War," *International Journal of Ethics*, 11/4 (1901), 504–5. I discuss both Ritchie and Giddings in chapter 7.

124. William Garrison, "War and Imperialism Fatal to Self-Government," *Advocate of Peace*, 60/9 (1898), 212.

125. Carl Schurz, "Militarism and Democracy," *Annals of the Academy of Political and Social Science*, 13/12 (1899), 100. I return to Garrison and Schurz in chapter 7.

generous are from the covetous. Patriotism is a positive attitude of the soul; Chauvinism is a negative tendency or passion. Patriotism is the love of and devotion to the fatherland, to the wider or the more restricted home, and to the common interests and aspirations and ideals of these. Chauvinism marks an attitude antagonistic to all persons, interests and ideas, not within this wider or narrower father land or home. . . . While the patriot who loves his people and his country is therefore likely to be tolerant, even generous and affectionate, toward the stranger, the Chauvinist is likely to direct the burning fire of his animosity even toward special spheres and groupings within his own country.[126]

Advocates of imperial patriotism denied that they were encouraging aggression. Milner asserted that contemplation of the vast imperial system, and recognition of the heroic efforts of those who had established it, induced gratitude and a "spirit of humble admiration."[127] It was neither a bombastic nor a belligerent sentiment. Writing in his popular *Lectures on Law and Public Opinion in England during the Nineteenth Century*, delivered originally at Harvard, Dicey contended that imperialism generated "a form of patriotism which has a high absolute worth of its own, and is both excited and justified by the lessons of history." "Any man," he wrote later, "may feel pride in an imperial patriotism grounded on the legitimate belief that the Empire built up by England furthers the prosperity and the happiness of the whole body of British subjects."[128]

Patriotism was also refashioned in explicitly racial terms. *Race patriotism* was defined as love of—and loyalty to—the race, not (or not only) the state or empire. There were strong and weak variants. The former viewed race as the primary object of loyalty and belonging, trumping the claims of individual states. The more common weaker form identified race as an important source of loyalty and belonging, without assigning it priority. It posited a *fractal* vision of political belonging in which loyalty was owed and given to communities nested within one another. An individual could be at once a proud patriot of a region, a state, an empire, a race. As Sinclair Kennedy put it in *The Pan-Angles*,

Among the Britannic Pan-Angles is now growing a further patriotism for the ideal of a Britannic whole of which each of the six nations would be a

126. Waldstein, "English-speaking Brotherhood," 225–26.

127. Milner, Speech at the Guildhall, 23 April 1907, *Nation and Empire*, 172–73.

128. A. V. Dicey, *Lectures on the Relation between Law and Public Opinion in England during the Nineteenth Century* (London, 1905), 454–5; Dicey, *Introduction to the Study of the Law of the Constitution*, 8th ed., xcviii.

part. Throughout the Pan-Angle world let us add to these patriotisms for our dreamed-of Britannic whole and for our United States a still larger patriotism for our English-speaking civilization, our Pan-Angle lands.[129]

There were two main spatial inflections of the idea. One of them, *Imperial race patriotism*, focused on the members of "the race" living within the British Empire. The other, more expansive conception—*race patriotism simpliciter*—encompassed all members of the designated race, giving equal attention to those within the empire and the United States. Milner's "Credo," published after his death in 1925, was the most famous encapsulation of the former.

> I am a Nationalist and not a cosmopolitan. . . . I am a British (indeed primarily an English) Nationalist. If I am also an Imperialist, it is because the destiny of the English race, owing to its insular position and long supremacy at sea, has been to strike roots in different parts of the world. . . . My patriotism knows no geographical, but only racial limits. I am an imperialist and not a Little Englander because I am a British Race Patriot. . . . It is not the soil of England, dear as it is to me, but the speech, the tradition, the spiritual heritage, the principles, the aspirations of the British race.[130]

The expansive form of race patriotism was a common theme in debates over Anglo-America. The deconstruction of traditional forms of state-centric patriotism was justified in various ways: it affirmed parochial forms of attachment that impeded new and more capacious types of political order; it stoked jingoism in Britain; it limited the imaginative horizons of individuals; it obfuscated the cardinal importance of racial identity.[131] Another prominent

---

129. Kennedy, *Pan-Angles*, 207.

130. Alfred Milner, "Credo," *The Times*, 25 July 1925. On the significance of imperial race patriotism, see John C. Mitcham, *Race and Imperial Defence in the British World, 1870–1914* (Cambridge, 2016), ch. 2. A. G. Hopkins notes that "race patriotism" was a "much-advertised concept" in the settler colonies: "Globalisation and Decolonisation," *Journal of Imperial and Commonwealth History*, 45/5 (2017), 735. The tension between the two positions is usefully elaborated in Lake, "British World or New World?," 36–50, though she contrasts "British race patriotism" with "Anglo-Saxonism," whereas I would suggest that the latter was also the subject of claims about the proper scope of race patriotism.

131. Today, political theorists often distinguish between patriotism and nationalism, as well as between forms of patriot regard, often following Jürgen Habermas's influential account of "constitutional patriotism." For relevant discussion, see Habermas, "The European Nation-State" in Habermas, *The Inclusion of the Other*, trans. Jeremy J. Shapiro (Cambridge, 1996), ch. 5; Margaret Moore, "Defending Community" in Duncan Bell (ed.), *Ethics and World Politics* (Oxford, 2010), 130–45; Margaret Canovan, "Patriotism Is Not Enough," *British Journal of Political Science*, 30/3 (2000), 413–32; Jan-Werner Müller, *Constitutional Patriotism* (Princeton, NJ,

concern was that American patriotism had long fed the flames of Anglophobia. As Goldwin Smith put it in 1890, "[A] generation at least will probably pass . . . before Americans who read no annals but their own will cease, historically at least, to identify patriotism with hostility to Great Britain."[132] Doane, the high-profile Bishop of Albany, argued that authentic patriotism expressed "the highest civic virtue and the noblest earthly motive," but that it had often been distorted by xenophobia. "Of all so-called patriotic hatreds the attempt to foster American hatred of England is the most unpardonable and the most unnatural."[133]

The concept of race patriotism was most commonly associated with Balfour, who argued for variations on the theme from the 1880s onward. One of his best-known statements of the creed came in a speech delivered in Toronto at the height of the Venezuela crisis. Appalled by the deteriorating situation, he warned that conflict with the United States "carries with it something of the unnatural horror of a civil war," and it would involve the dreadful prospect of fighting "our own flesh and blood."

> I feel, so far as I can speak for my countrymen, that our pride in the race to which we belong is a pride which includes every English-speaking community in the world. We have a domestic patriotism as Scotchmen, or as Englishmen, or as Irishmen, or what you will. We have an imperial patriotism as citizens of the British Empire. But surely, in addition to that, we also have an Anglo-Saxon patriotism which embraces within its ample folds the whole of that great race which has done so much in every branch of human effort, and above all in that branch of human effort which has produced free institutions and free communities.

Declaring himself "an idealist and a dreamer," he aimed to make war between the Anglo-Saxons impossible. "I look forward with confidence to the time when our ideals will have become real and our dreams will be embodied in actual political fact."[134] Outlining a fractal account of patriotism in which loyalty was owed to groups at different geographical scales, he embraced the

---

2007); Cécile Laborde, "From Constitutional to Civic Patriotism," *British Journal of Political Science*, 32/4 (2002), 591–612.

132. Goldwin Smith, "The Hatred of England," *North American Review*, 150/402 (1890), 554.

133. Doane, "Patriotism," 314, 310. For discussions of misleading historical education, see George Burton Adams, *The British Empire and a League of Peace* (London, 1919).

134. Arthur Balfour, Speech at Manchester, 1896, in Balfour, *Mind of Arthur James Balfour*, 2–3. On "Anglo-Saxon patriotism," see also "Mr Balfour on Foreign Affairs," *The Times*, 16 January 1896, 10. For a useful analysis of his views, see Tomes, *Balfour and Foreign Policy*, chs. 2–4. I also discuss Balfour's unionism in this book's introduction.

"subordinate" patriotism that the Scottish displayed to Scotland.[135] This sub-state model of loyalty was embedded within British patriotism, which in turn was a component of a wider imperial patriotism. A yet more expansive "Anglo-Saxon patriotism" incorporated the United States. In an address in Wales in 1909, he sang the praise of the "great English-speaking community," while maintaining that "the local and the larger patriotism work together for a common end."[136] There was no conflict between the different scales. At the widest geographical expanse, he identified a thin form of "Western" patriotism.[137]

Balfour was not the only high-profile politician to retool patriotism. At a speech in Toronto in 1887, Joseph Chamberlain made a similar point.

> But I should think that our patriotism was dwarfed and stunted if it did not embrace the Greater Britain beyond the seas—(*loud cheers*)—if it did not include the young and vigorous nations carrying throughout the globe the knowledge of the English tongue and the English love of liberty and law; and, gentlemen, with these feelings I refuse to think or speak of the United States of America as a foreign nation (*Applause*). We are all of the same blood. I refuse to make any distinction between the interests of Englishmen in England, in Canada, and in the United States.[138]

Although Chamberlain never pulled back from seeing Britain and the United States as members of the same racial community, his views on patriotism were inconsistent. In an address on the subject delivered at the University of Edinburgh in 1897, he adumbrated a more traditional statist conception of political loyalty, specifying an admixture of territory and historical experience, not racial identity or even empire, as its source and principal object. "It is the clear duty of Patriotism, not dwelling over much on details, to consider in its broadest aspects this question of the expansion of the Empire in which we seem to be fulfilling the manifest destiny of our race."[139] Empire was an expression of patriotism, not the space for its instantiation. This was the patriotic analogue of the statist-imperial vision of citizenship.

It was Balfour's formulation that attracted the most attention. Writing in 1900, Beresford asserted that he had "well expressed this unity of principles

---

135. Arthur Balfour, speech 20 September 1896, reproduced in Barnard Alderson, *Arthur James Balfour, His Life and Work* (London, 1903), 275–76.

136. Arthur Balfour, "Race and Nationality," *Transactions of the Honourable Society of Cymmrodorion, Session 1908–9* (London, 1909), 241, 242.

137. Tomes, *Balfour and Foreign Policy*, 38–39.

138. Chamberlain, "Mild Sovereignty of the Queen," 7. This passage was cited positively in Kennedy, *Pan-Angles*, 176.

139. Joseph Chamberlain, *Patriotism* (London, 1897), 57.

which is so powerful a lever in bringing the component parts of the race into touch."[140] Mahan was likewise convinced. Arguing that the clamor for rapprochement was based on racial affinity, he claimed that in order to designate "the disposition underlying such a tendency," Balfour had coined a resonant slogan that captured a vital phenomenon. "The phrase is so pregnant of solution for the problems of the future, as conceived by the writer, that he hopes to see it obtain the currency due to the value of the idea which it formulates."[141] Mahan followed his own advice. In *The Problem of Asia and Its Effect upon International Politics*, published in 1900, he described "race patriotism" as something that "in our epoch, is tending to bind peoples into larger groups than the existing nationalities."[142] Underpinning burgeoning attempts to forge continent-straddling "pan" political associations, it was one of the most significant features of contemporary world politics.

Race patriotism was mobilized by supporters of American expansion. Richard Olney, who had served as Secretary of State in the Cleveland administration, was adamant about the connection, observing in a widely discussed speech at Harvard in early 1898,

> There is a patriotism of race as well as of country—and the Anglo-American is as little likely to be indifferent to the one as the other. Family quarrels there have been heretofore and doubtless will be again, and the two peoples, at the safe distance which the broad Atlantic interposes, take with each other liberties of speech which only the fondest and dearest relatives indulge in. Nevertheless, that they would be found standing together against any alien foe by whom either was menaced by destruction or irreparable calamity, it is not permissible to doubt. Nothing less could be expected of the close community between them in origin, speech, thought, literature, institutions, ideals—in the kind and degree of civilization enjoyed by both. In that same community, and in that cooperation in good works that should result from it, lies, it is not too much to say, the best hope for the future not only for the two kindred peoples but of the human race itself. [143]

140. Beresford, "Future of the Anglo-Saxon Race," 809.

141. Mahan, "Twentieth Century Outlook," 531; Mahan to Col. Sterling, 13 February 1896 [Reel 2], Mahan papers. For a further mention of Balfour, see also G. S. Clarke, "England and America," *Living Age*, 10/9 (1898), 693. The article appeared originally in *The Nineteenth Century*.

142. Alfred Mahan, *The Problem of Asia and Its Effect upon International Politics* (Boston, 1900), 67.

143. Richard Olney, "International Isolation of the United States," *Atlantic Monthly*, 81 (May 1898), 588.

In Britain, race patriotism was frequently cited as a reason to support American imperial endeavors. Thus an anonymous contributor to the Tory *Quarterly Review* could argue in 1898 that "whereas Germany and Russia are as oil and vinegar blended, the feeling of race-patriotism gives a far deeper, a far more real foundation to the long-wished-for, ardently desired Anglo-Saxon understanding."[144] Inter-imperial coordination beckoned.

Like isopolitan citizenship, race patriotism could be utilized as either an alternative to deep political integration or as a necessary component of it. Balfour was convinced that racial kinship was a more fundamental bond than any treaty or alliance. "[O]ur relations with your great Republic," he wrote to Carnegie in 1903, "should be based on that foundation of mutual comprehension, affection, and esteem which forms stronger links than the most formal treaties. This, at all events, has been through all my political life my most fondly cherished hope."[145] Conan Doyle articulated a similar view. In a letter to Stead in 1898, he sought to clarify his position on racial reunion. Rejecting full political integration, he had meant instead "a restoration of racial patriotism, a reunion of sympathies, an earnest endeavour to clear away prejudices and to see things from a common point of view." Once only a distant prospect, this dream was now a "bright beacon in sight of either nation." He finished on a cautionary note, perhaps aimed at curbing Stead's enthusiasm: the "danger now is that we go too fast."[146]

Carnegie, Stead, Wells, and Rhodes, on the other hand, viewed racial patriotism as a constitutive element of deeper union. It was the form of patriotism appropriate for a new overarching polity. In "A Look Ahead," Carnegie argued for the redefinition of patriotism. He contended that being a citizen of a large state expanded the imaginative horizons of its inhabitants. "Every state should aim to be great and powerful, and noble in the exercise of its power, because power in the State, nobly exercised, is the strongest influence in creating good and patriotic citizens." Citizens were both reflections and expressions of the greatness of their political community. "A small and petty political unity tends to breed small and petty men of all classes; dealing with great affairs broadens and elevates the character."[147] Such accounts, common in the literature on Anglo-America, implied that geographical scale shaped, even

144. "The United States and Spain," *Quarterly Review*, 188 (1898), 239.

145. Balfour to Carnegie, 30 January 1903, Fol 94, Carnegie papers.

146. Conan Doyle to Stead, 30 May 1898, STED 1/22, Stead papers. In the same letter, he also modified his earlier racial classification: "But let it be Anglo-Celtic and not Anglo-Saxon reunion, please."

147. Carnegie, *Reunion*, 18. Carnegie was a friend of Balfour, and praised his support for racial union: Carnegie to Stead, 16 May 1892, STED 1/16, Stead papers.

determined, the political consciousness and behavior of citizens. Carnegie's second argument concerned the mutable boundaries of identity and affect. While great states both necessitated and reproduced dynamic citizens, patriotism itself was not integrally bound to the traditional sovereign state. History taught that it was "ever expansive." As communications technologies shattered traditional understandings of time and space, so the scope of political love and loyalty grew.

> Centuries ago the people of Perugia and Assisi, fifteen miles apart, were deadly enemies, attacked each other, and played at making war and treaties. Even St Francis was wounded in one of these campaigns. The patriotism of the Perugian and the Assisian could not embrace an area so great as fifteen miles. To-day patriotism stretches over hundreds of miles—in some cases thousands of miles—and does not lose but gain in intensity as it covers a wider area. There is more to be patriotic about. The patriotism of to-day which melts when pushed beyond the shores of the island of Britain may safely be trusted to partake in the near future of the expansive quality. It will soon grow and cover the doings of the race wherever situated, beyond the bounds of the old home.[148]

The cyborg apparatus of the modern world transfigured political belonging. The influence of Freeman was once again apparent, and Carnegie praised his vision of a "wider and nobler patriotism"—the ability to prioritize race above state or empire.[149] Racial patriotism ran through Carnegie's subsequent writings on reunion. In his essay "Labour," for example, he welcomed "a future charged with this potent race patriotism which seems to be dawning upon us."[150]

Race patriotism was also a central theme in Carnegie's critique of American imperialism. In 1899, he argued that treaties and defense pacts were temporary and fragile, whereas the "patriotism of race lies deeper and is not disturbed by waves upon the surface."[151] The previous year, he had written in an unpublished manuscript that "there is a race patriotism, as well as a national patriotism, and it is unusually strong among English-speaking people."[152] Such patriotism did not require conjoint military action or the occupation of distant lands. Moreover, it was compatible with love of country. "There is coming

148. Carnegie, *Reunion*, 22–23.

149. Carnegie, *Reunion*, 22.

150. Carnegie, *Empire of Business*, 183.

151. Carnegie, "Americanism versus Imperialism," 5–6.

152. Andrew Carnegie, "Anglo-American Alliance. A Look Today" [hand written: "And a Look Ahead"] 1898, Box 251, Carnegie papers.

soon—we see its dawn already—the patriotism of Race, our English-speaking Race, not to supplant but to supplement, extend and dignify the narrower patriotism of country."[153] After the disastrous wars in East Asia and southern Africa, he remained committed to this fractal conception. In a July 1903 letter to Balfour, he emphasized the heady strength of race patriotism, while once again affirming that it was compatible with national patriotism. American political experience was illustrative: "as the Virginian of to-day supplements State Patriotism by the wider Patriotism of the Union, so are the American and the Briton some day to cherish Patriotism of the whole Race."[154] This was a telling example, with Britain reduced to the equivalent of a state within the federal structure. Carnegie veered between two different claims about race patriotism. Sometimes he talked as if it was an established fact, deeply ingrained in the population of the Angloworld ("unusually strong among English-speaking people"), while at other times he adopted the future tense, seeing it as an emergent property nourished by new communications technologies.

For Stead, common citizenship was essential for any viable project to build a "United States of the English-speaking World." In a long character sketch published in the *Review of Reviews* in 1891, he applauded Balfour for viewing closer relations between Britain and the United States as "the greatest of all objects," and suggested that he was committed to reuniting the race in such an "elastic" manner that it could "accommodate Republic plus Monarchy."[155] He quoted Balfour's Toronto speech in the *Review of Reviews* and later in *The Americanization of the World*, praising its "wise" and "eloquent" words and its fractal account of patriotic attachment.[156] Stead also commended the steadfast race patriotism of his fellow unionists. "There is no American so enthusiastic and so delighted at the progress made by the conception of race-patriotism than Mr. Carnegie," he pronounced in 1898.[157]

Wells had a much more conflicted view. He regularly assailed the patriotic impulse, construing it as an atavistic hangover and an obstacle to the dissolution of the modern sovereign state. *Mankind in the Making* castigated traditional

153. Carnegie, response to a toast, 1901, Box 251, Carnegie papers. The Toast was to "this union of the Chambers of Commerce of the commercial capitals of the old and new worlds" (3).

154. Carnegie to Balfour, 23 July 1903, Fol 97; Balfour to Carnegie, 26 July 1903, Fol 98, Carnegie papers. In his reply, Balfour wrote, "I have no wish, public or private, nearer my heart than that of securing and preserving genuinely good relations with the U.S.A., whom I do not in any sense regard as a foreign community."

155. W. T. Stead, *RoR*, 4 (November 1891), 468.

156. W. T. Stead, *RoR*, 17 (June 1898), 603; Stead, *Americanization*, 16.

157. W. T. Stead, *RoR*, 17 (June 1898), 612. See also Stead, *Americanization*, 223, 436.

conceptions of political loyalty: "Much that passes for patriotism is no more than a generalized jealousy gorgeously clad."[158] Wells was equally dismissive of "patriots of nationality" and "patriots of empire"—the former tried to convince people that the "miscellany of European squatters in the Transvaal are one nation and those in Cape Colony another," while those professing the latter "would have me . . . hail as my fellow-subjects and collaborators in man-making a host of Tamil-speaking, Tamil-thinking Dravidians, while separating me from every English-speaking, English-thinking person."[159] Both positions were untenable. Yet even as he criticized accounts of the *intrinsic* value of state-patriotic loyalty he offered an *instrumental* defense of other kinds of political belonging. The New Republic would be marked by a form of provisional iden-tification. "In his inmost soul there must be no loyalty or submission to any king or colour, save only if it conduces to the service of the future of the race." Just as kingship is "a secondary and debateable thing" to the New Republican, "so are the loyalties of nationality, and all our local and party adhesions."[160] Elsewhere Wells stressed the durability of patriotic sentiment. In *New Worlds for Old*, he argued that in a future socialist state patriotism would have to evolve, adapting to new circumstances, but that it would not "starve under Socialist conditions." In particular, people would express a powerful sense of "civic patriotism," a passionate attachment to their city that would be embed-ded within the husk of older forms of political association that were still ca-pable of generating affection and loyalty. Maintaining peace and stability be-tween the city-polities of the future, "there will still be in many cases the old national form of imperial government," bound by a "common language and a common history and a common temper and race."[161] Modern conditions meant that patriotism had to be recalibrated, not eliminated.

Race patriotism was occasionally stretched even further. It could be figured as a step on the road to the universal. Howard Angus Kennedy, a Canadian journalist and historian, outlined this vision in the preface to "The Story of Empire," a popular book series that he edited.

> There is room in a single breast for patriotism of every dimension. We love our own town, our own village, more than any other; we are glad to meet men who hail from the same country. Scotsman stands by Scotsman, Irish-man by Irishman, Welshman by Welshman, even Manxman by Manxman, all the world over. This is patriotism. It is a greater patriotism which creates

158. Wells, *Mankind*, 26.
159. Wells, *Mankind*, 27.
160. Wells, *Mankind*, 26.
161. Wells, *New Worlds for Old*, 322.

a sense of common citizenship in every British heart; and a greater patriotism still which in England declines to call an American a foreigner, and in America refuses to be childishly stirred up against the sister Empire. In the future an international patriotism will flourish, to the confusion of strife-makers and the great content of the peace-loving mass of mankind, whose essential oneness is already a commonplace of science and religion.[162]

Kennedy unwittingly articulated the tension that ran through such accounts. "Till we can have the greater patriotism let us cultivate the less," he suggested. This injunction pointed to support for the very parochial kind of patriotism that impeded the emergence of the universal form he sought. It was self-defeating. The most capacious accounts saw patriotism as a dynamic and ever-expanding mode of political belonging that could ultimately encompass the whole of humanity. Hosmer evoked such a future: "great indeed will be the statesman of the future who shall reconstitute the family bond, conciliate the members into an equal brotherhood, found the vaster union which must be the next great step forward in the universal fraternity of man, when patriotism may be merged into a love that will take in all humanity."[163] Wells predicted that eventually individual racial-political unities would be dissolved into a species-embracing universalism. Carnegie likewise hinted at a utopian transformation of political belonging. "[I]n the dim future," he dreamt,

> it might even come that the pride of the citizen in the race as a whole would exceed that which he had in any part thereof; as the citizen of the Republic to-day is prouder of being an American than he is of being a native of any State of the Union. This is a far look ahead, no doubt, but patriotism is an expansive quality, and men to-day are as patriotic in regard to an entire continent as the ancients were about their respective cities and provinces. The time is coming when even race patriotism will give place to the citizenship of the world.[164]

Political Symbolism and the Racial Mythscape

Carnegie's oscillation between present and future tense, between descriptive accuracy and ethico-political aspiration, indexed the instability of visions of political belonging beyond state borders. Graham Wallas offered one of the more sophisticated challenges to the idea. His pioneering *Human Nature and*

---

162. Howard Angus Kennedy, "Prologue" in Walter Besant, *The Rise of the Empire* (London, 1897), xiv. Besant's volume appeared in the series. The preface is dated 1897.

163. Hosmer, "American Evolution," 36.

164. Carnegie, "Imperial Federation," 506.

Politics, written in dialogue with Wells, issued in skepticism that patriotic attachment could be stretched across the empire. "But if the task of state building in Europe during the nineteenth century was difficult, still more difficult is the task before the English statesmen of the twentieth century of creating an imperial patriotism."[165] The main problem was that the purported content of imperial patriotism was very thin, consisting chiefly of vague admonitions about how the remit of liberty had been extended throughout the imperial system. "But political freedom, even in its noblest form, is a negative quality, and the word is apt to bear different meanings in Bengal and Rhodesia and Australia."[166] While communications technologies had abolished geographical constraints, it was still an open question how far political loyalty could stretch. Even if achievable, capacious forms of political attachment would not result from "our sense and muscles" but instead "our powers of imagination and sympathy," for the state was created, maintained, and reproduced through human creativity—it was "an entity of the mind, a symbol, a personification, or an abstraction."[167] The imperialists struggled to excite imaginative sympathy.

> The modern English imperialists tried for some time to apply the idea of national homogeneity to the facts of the British Empire. From the publication of Seeley's *Expansion of England* in 1883 to the Peace of Vereeniging in 1902 they strove to believe in the existence of a "Blood," an "island Race," consisting of homogenous English-speaking individuals, among whom were to be reckoned not only the whole population of the United Kingdom, but all the reasonably white inhabitants of our colonies and dependencies; while they thought of the other inhabitants of the Empire as "the white man's burden"—the necessary material for the exercise of the white man's virtues.[168]

But homogeneity was more phantasm than fact. It had to be created, not discovered. Wallas argued that imperial "idealists" had "persuaded themselves that it would come peacefully and inevitably as a result of the reading of imperial poems and the summoning of an imperial Council," while the more hardheaded "Bismarckian realists," such as Milner, thought it might be forged on the battlefields of southern Africa.[169] Neither strategy was credible. In a

165. Wallas, *Human Nature and Politics*, 80.

166. Wallas, *Human Nature and Politics*, 81.

167. Wallas, *Human Nature and Politics*, 273–74. Contrast this with Dicey's admonitions against personification.

168. Wallas, *Human Nature and Politics*, 280–81.

169. Wallas, *Human Nature and Politics*, 281.

nominalist vein, similar to that adumbrated by Wells, Wallas rejected the notion of homogenous groups, arguing that valorizing the idea threatened the world with destruction. He offered a counterintuitive Darwinian alternative, contending that evolution taught that humanity should be seen as a single biological group, which provided the foundation for a universalistic love of humanity. The "intellectual tragedy" of the nineteenth century was that the opposite lesson had been extracted from Darwin: "the discovery of organic evolution, instead of stimulating such a general love of humanity, seemed to show that it was forever impossible."[170]

Wallas was arguing against the grain. During the previous century, nationalist movements had fashioned endless symbols and stories of collective identity across the Euro-American world. Crafting a resonant symbolic order to inculcate a sense of shared national belonging and common destiny was widely acknowledged as an essential feature of state building. At the heart of such projects was the formation and dissemination of mythical narratives about the communal past, its present condition, and its possible future. Myths of this kind are radically simplified stories that ascribe fixed and coherent meanings to selected events, people, and places. Myths in complex modern societies are not reducible to the varieties of sacred myth anatomized by anthropologists, though they often possess similar structural properties—"stories of origins and foundings, stories of the exploits of culture heroes, stories of rebirth or renewal, and eschatological stories."[171] Easily intelligible and transmissible, they help to constitute or bolster particular visions of self, society, and world. We can refer to the totality of myths within any given collective as the communal "mythscape."[172] This is the discursive space in which myths are shaped, circulated, and contested. The "governing" myths of a community—those that help determine its predominant self-understandings—are always challenged by, and supervene on, a variety of "subaltern" myths. The specific forms assumed by mythscapes are always the result of power: struggles over the meaning of the past comprise a core dimension of modern politics.

Imperial federalists narrated and fêted the unity of Britain and its settler colonies, developing an iconography of Greater Britain centered on the glories of colonization, the authoritative legacy of the common law and the ancient constitution, and the sacred freedoms of the English, all wrapped in the Union

---

170. Wallas, *Human Nature and Politics*, 287.

171. Christopher Flood, *Political Myths* (London, 1996), 41.

172. I expand on this argument in Duncan Bell, "Mythscapes," *British Journal of Sociology*, 54/1 (2003), 63–81; Bell, "Agonistic Democracy and the Politics of Memory," *Constellations*, 15/1 (2008), 148–66.

Jack and watched over by a virtuous monarch.[173] Proponents of Anglo-America likewise recognized the importance of political symbolism and myth construction. I am not suggesting that they were autonomous rational actors instrumentally manipulating words, images, and symbols to secure some pre-given end. They believed, or at least professed to believe, in the stories they told and the pictures they painted. But the more reflective among them were conscious of the need to persuade, cajole, and convince a wider audience of the veracity of their claims, and they deliberated about the best rhetorical strategies and argumentative moves to do so. They sought to build a case for strong political peoplehood—for an encompassing racial-political community—with the discursive materials at hand.

Although they drew on some of the same rhetorical strategies, tropes, and images as the imperial federalists, race unionists faced an even stiffer challenge because they had to overcome the inconvenient fact that the United States had waged a war of independence against British rule and that Anglophobia was a prominent feature of American political culture throughout the nineteenth century. Reframing points of contention, they emphasized the enduring bases of unity.[174] Stead, in particular, was cognizant of the value of political mythologizing. "The difficulty of expressing in symbol or by word the substantial unity of the English-speaking race has often perplexed those who recognise the unity beneath all its multifarious political organisations," he remarked in 1896.[175] He utilized the *Review of Reviews* to float assorted schemes of his own and to publicize the ideas of others. Race unionists attempted to animate or amplify an existing mythic substrate—the unity of "the race"—that purportedly bound the two countries, while also seeking to create new symbols and rituals of belonging. They aimed to flesh out a coherent picture of a shared past and a glorious destiny.

Anglo-American relations were a staple topic for cartoonists on both sides of the Atlantic. A multivalent visual repertoire at once reflected and helped to

173. Duncan Bell, "The Idea of a Patriot Queen," *Journal of Imperial and Commonwealth History*, 34/1 (2006), 1–19. On the use of American exemplars by imperial thinkers, see also Patrick Kirkwood, "Alexander Hamilton and the Early Republic in Edwardian Imperial Thought," *Britain and the World*, 12/1 (2019), 28–50.

174. In chapter 2 I explored some of the historical narratives that were employed to make the case for unity. A further example is the interest of Anglo-Saxonists in mythologizing the *Mayflower* and the "Pilgrim fathers" as founding figures of a transatlantic people. For a brief discussion, see Martha Vandrei, "The Pilgrim's Progress," *History Today*, 70/5 (2020), 58–71. Stead cited the *Mayflower* as seeding English liberty across the Atlantic: *Americanization*, 3, 26, 189.

175. Stead, *RoR*, 13 (June 1896), 486.

bolster the assorted positions under discussion. The representations of rap-prochement and inter-imperialism gave rise to what Stephen Tuffnell terms a "visual culture of hybrid, transnational symbolism." Traditional images and motifs of Britain and the United States were juxtaposed or blended together to affirm their newfound sense of commonality. Britannia and Columbia, John Bull and Uncle Sam: icons of national identity were increasingly placed to-gether in the same frame, signifying cooperation and shared racial past and purpose.[176] Such images were countered by those portraying long-standing animosities between Britain and the United States. American Anglophobia and (to a lesser extent) British anti-Americanism generated contrasting visual vocabularies.[177]

Literature played at least three roles in the unionist discourse. First, as I explored in chapter 5, novels and short stories were used to map possible Anglo-futures. These texts served as pointed commentaries on the present and as sketches of alternative racial orders, often saturated with utopian desire. (Dystopian doubles performed a premonitory function, warning of dangers, of paths not taken, of the deleterious consequences of inaction.) Second, the canon of English literature was postulated as a core element of the Anglo cul-ture that unionists sought to unite politically. An inheritance of the race, a reservoir of shared images and phrases, as well as an object of reverence, liter-ary genius had helped to make the English-speaking peoples. Shakespeare was the most frequently cited figure in this strategy of literary annexation. "What more potent influence can be conceived in this respect [political union] than the mighty Shakespeare?" asked Dos Passos. Stead concurred: "[W]e all owe allegiance to Shakespeare if to no other man of woman born."[178] The King James Bible was also enlisted to the cause. "As I have implied more than once," the Liberal Prime Minister Herbert Asquith observed in 1911, the "English Bible" belonged to the totality of the English-speaking world. Reflecting on this fact strengthened the case for an Anglo-American arbitration treaty, as conflict be-tween the English-speaking people would refute the dictates of the New Testa-ment, a system of morality that suffused the distributed community.[179] At the

---

176. Stephen Tuffnell, "'The International Siamese Twins'" in Richard Scully and Andrekos Varnava (eds.), *Comic Empires* (Manchester, 2020). On visual representations of American imperialism, see also Bonnie Miller, "The Image Makers' Arsenal in the Age of War and Empire," *Journal of American Studies*, 45/1 (2011), 53–75.

177. Tuffnell, "'International Siamese Twins.'"

178. Dos Passos, *Anglo-Saxon Century*, 139; Stead, *Americanization*, 149.

179. Herbert Asquith, "The English Bible" in Asquith, *Occasional Addresses, 1893–1916* (Lon-don, 1918), 134. This was an address delivered at the Bible Tercentenary Meeting at the Albert Hall, 20 March 1911.

same meeting a message was read on behalf of President Taft. "Carlyle long ago declared that all English-speaking peoples were one in being subject of King Shakespeare," Stead commented in the *Review of Reviews*, but "it has been reserved for President Taft to 'go one better' . . . and to claim the Bible as the true Bond of Union between the British and American peoples." "This Book of Books," he recorded Taft as saying,

> has not only reigned supreme in England for three centuries, but has bound together, as nothing else could, two great Anglo-Saxon nations, one in blood, in speech, and in common religious life. Our laws, our literature and our social life owe whatever excellence they possess largely to the influence of this our chief classic, acknowledged as such equally on both sides of the sea. Americans must, therefore, with unfeigned satisfaction join in thanksgiving to the God of the Bible, Who has thus bound together the Old and the New world by so precious a tie.[180]

Poets were a frequent source of inspiration. Stead acclaimed Lowell as the master poet of the race. Kipling was seen as an avatar of union, his words capable of inspiring loyalty and political veneration. In the May 1899 edition of the *North American Review*, the eminent American novelist and literary critic W. D. Howells asked "what is the poetry first in the heart and mind" of that year? Kipling, possibly "the most famous man in the world," stood out, his work at once mirroring and channeling the spirit of the age.

> It is none the less a prodigious thing to utter one's age, or one's day, as Mr Kipling has uttered his, to sound the dominant of its scale so that it shall be felt in the nerves vibrating to the limit of our race, which is our world. The prodigy is none the less because this dominant is the note of race-patriotism. . . . It is a mighty and a lusty note, full of faith and hope; and it is the note which makes Kipling famous wherever an Anglo-Saxon word is spoken or an Anglo-Saxon shot is fired.[181]

Stead applauded Kipling's poem "The Song of the English," recommending the "laureate of the Empire" as an ideal candidate to compose a "song of the whole English-speaking race" for use in schools.[182] But not everyone was so keen to elevate him to chief versifier of racial unity. "Our state is militant and aggressive," Wells cautioned in 1897, "and Mr Kipling is its poet." In *A Modern Utopia*, he claimed that ardent imperialists expressed "Kiplinesque brutality,"

---

180. W. T. Stead recorded it in *RoR*, 43 (April 1911), 321–22.
181. William Howells, "The New Poetry," *North American Review*, 168/510 (1899), 582, 583.
182. W. T. Stead, *RoR*, 7 (May 1893), 507.

and described him as a man "whose want of intellectual deliberation is only equalled by his poetic power."[183] But it was Tennyson, as we have seen, who was interpolated most frequently into the Angloworld intertext. His reverberating phrase "the Parliament of Man, the Federation of the World" was so popular that in 1907 Ramsay MacDonald complained it had "become threadbare by constant use on platforms."[184] The ritual incantation encoded a tension: was the federation that of the Angloworld or humanity? The vagueness was part of its evocative power.

Effective forms of national identification require the inculcation of shared beliefs and habits. This is "banal nationalism," the sedimented everyday forms of representation, attachment, and performance that build and reproduce a sense of collective belonging. Examples range from international sporting events, through the design and use of flags, coinage and uniforms, to patterns of vernacular speech, the construction of school curricula and writing of textbooks, to the unreflective distinctions drawn between "domestic" and "foreign" news.[185] Race unionists were alive to this crucial dimension of politics. Some maintained that "the race" required its own flag. "I foresee great scope for the ingenious persons who write so abundantly to the London evening papers upon etymological points, issues of heraldry, and the correct Union Jack," wrote Wells sardonically, "in the very pleasing topic of a possible Anglo-American flag."[186] As we have seen, Carnegie proudly flew his hybrid Union Jack / Stars and Stripes from a turret at Skibo, a simple but effective representation of union. Other markers were discussed. Drawing on Mommsen's account of Roman strategies of political unification, Dos Passos emphasized the importance of a common coinage.[187] In 1896, Stead reported that Lord Grey had sent him a sketch of an escutcheon "of the English-speaking Race," a marker of unity that could be worn on uniforms and sported by those committed to Anglo-America.[188]

An annual date to celebrate racial unity was also debated. Stead reasoned that the Fourth of July was ideal. In 1898, he attacked "Little Englanders" who refused to honor it, lamenting their inability to "stretch their conceptions of England so far as to include the whole English-speaking race." Insular and myopic, they were mere "parish politicians" who should spend more time

---

183. Wells, "Morals and Civilisation," 214; Wells, *Modern Utopia*, 115, 228.

184. Ramsey MacDonald, *Labour and the Empire* (London, 1907), 36. I discuss Tennyson in the book's introduction.

185. Michael Billig, *Banal Nationalism* (London, 1995).

186. Wells, *Anticipations*, 148n.

187. Dos Passos, *Anglo-Saxon Century*, 206.

188. W. T. Stead, *RoR*, 13 (June 1896), 486. Stead also mentions it in *Americanization*, 421.

traveling the world, "to breathe for a moment the larger air of that informal aggregation of free nations all round the world which we name when we drink the health of all English-speaking peoples."[189] The adoption of Independence Day was a further expression of his desire to Americanize British institutions and cultural life. He returned to the theme in 1909.

> [T]he proper day for the celebration of the unity of the English-speaking race is July 4th. The Declaration of American Independence was the charter of that colonial liberty which has alone made Great Britain and Empire Day possible. George Washington is recognised to-day as the greatest Englishman of the eighteenth century who rendered the greatest service to England of any of her sons. For it was he who defeated the Jingoes of the eighteenth century, and Jingoism then, as now, was the deadliest enemy of the Empire.[190]

Walter Besant thought that St. George's Day was the best option.[191] While Stead approved of the aim, he remained agnostic about the choice of date. "All our liberties, and the institutions which are even more distinctive of the English-speaking race than their literature, spring from the famous submission of King John to his barons at Runnymede," he commented. The specific date was a mere detail—the vital thing was to select a day for celebration, when "English-speaking folk shall be reminded of the unity of their race, the splendour of its history, and the magnificence of its future."[192] The American historian William Roscoe Thayer argued in the *North American Review* for the twelfth of February, birthday of Lincoln and Darwin. He envisaged "a day of international festival, a sort of Pan-Anglo-Saxon reunion," when the far-flung members of the race came together to "reaffirm their racial principles, to feel the thrill of common hopes and common emotions, and to realise in the most convincing way that blood is thicker than water." Lincoln represented the Anglo-Saxon genius for government, manifested in political liberty and law, while Darwin embodied the fearless search for Truth that distinguished the race.[193] In *The Americanization of the World*, Stead once again endorsed the

---

189. W. T. Stead, *RoR*, 26 (June 1898), 600.

190. W. T. Stead, *RoR*, 234 (June 1909), 490. See also *RoR*, 39 (March 1909), 212, on the importance of erecting statues to Washington and Lincoln in London.

191. Walter Besant, "A Plea for St. George's Day," *Cornhill Magazine*, 2/10 (1897), 435–47.

192. W. T. Stead, *RoR*, 15 (April 1897), 346.

193. William Thayer, "The Centennial of Lincoln and Darwin," *North American Review*, 188/632 (1908), 21. Principally a historian of Italy, Thayer was affiliated with Harvard, and served as President of the American Historical Association in 1918–19. Stead praised the idea: *RoR*, 38 (August 1908), 148.

Fourth of July as the "fete day of the race," although he admitted that British public opinion might balk at the idea. Noting that Shakespeare's birthday and the anniversary of Magna Carta had also been suggested, he proposed that September the Third might serve as "Reunion Day." It was the date on which the British government had recognized American Independence and Cromwell had opened his Parliament.[194]

Sport has long been a source of symbolic power and a significant element of public diplomacy. Stead proposed that sporting competition might help to consolidate Anglo-America and the wider English-speaking people. "No one who remembers the important part which the Isthmian Games played in ancient Greece," he remarked, "will be disposed to deny the political importance of athletics and of sport generally as a means of promoting a sense of unity among the English-speaking peoples of the world." Indeed, sport had already worked its magic in helping to fuse together the disparate territories of the Australian federation, having done more to establish the lived reality of Australian national life than the complex political discussions that surrounded federation.[195] But sport also had the potential to cause or deepen tensions. Various incidents bedeviled the 1908 London Olympics, leading to animosity between the British and American teams and a flurry of negative publicity on both sides of the Atlantic, though Balfour and Roosevelt endeavored to smooth over the problems in the name of intraracial harmony.[196] This was a stark reminder about the Janus-faced character of competition. A decade later, Stead was still hunting for ways to consolidate the racial mythscape. We find him in 1910 endorsing the plan of Sir Harry Brittain, Tory politician and journalist, to commemorate a century of peace between Britain and the United States.[197] The following year he suggested to Bryce, then serving as British Ambassador in Washington, that a monument to George Washington be constructed in London. Such a monument, especially if endowed by public subscription from around the empire, "would be an admirable means of propagandism for the English-speaking world idea."[198] Such propaganda was

194. Stead, *Americanization*, 419–20. He reprinted the text of the Declaration of Independence (33–39), encouraging his readers to absorb its wisdom.

195. Stead, *Americanization*, 334. On "race patriotism" and cricket, see Jared Van Duinen, *The British World and an Australian National Identity* (Basingstoke, 2017), 3–4, 6, 21–22.

196. J. Simon Rofe and Alan Tomlinson, "Strenuous Competition on the Field of Play, Diplomacy off It," *Journal of the Gilded Age and Progressive Era*, 15/1 (2016), 60–79.

197. Whyte, *Life of Stead*, II, 226. In 1902, Brittain had established the Pilgrims Society to promote the Anglo-American cause. See here Bowman, *Pilgrims Society and Public Diplomacy*.

198. Stead to Bryce, 28 June 1911, MS Bryce 140, Fol 183–84.

essential to index the underlying unity of the race and to project it to the forefront of political consciousness.

All of these proposals were intended to either craft or reinforce the racial mythscape, inculcating a sense of shared identity between the British and Americans. They were predicated on the idea that the foundations for political unity existed already, but that they had been obscured by a combination of ignorance, mendacity, and an unduly narrow understanding of patriotism. It was essential to expose them to the light, to nourish them through speech, text, and image, and to extend them by developing new rituals of racial identification.

7

A Messenger of Peace to the World

RACIAL UTOPIANISM AND
THE ABOLITION OF WAR

To all intents and purposes war would by degree die out from the face of the earth—it would become impossible. The armed camp, which burdens the Old World, enslaves the nations, and impedes progress, would disappear. If you had the Anglo-Saxon race, acting on common ground, they could determine the balance of power for a fully peopled earth. Such a moral force would be irresistible, and argument would take the place of war, in the settlement of international disputes.[1]

(SIR GEORGE GREY)

Prologue: On Democratic Peace

The dream of perpetual peace has fascinated Western thinkers for centuries. Professed by the Duc de Sully, the Abbe Saint Pierre, Kant, and Bentham, and satirized by Leibniz and Voltaire, the project to eliminate war has been viewed as both a viable goal and a naive fantasy.[2] While a stream of peace plans were issued during the long eighteenth century, it was only in the subsequent hundred years that an array of institutions and social movements emerged to try

1. George Grey, "The Federation of the English-speaking People," *Contemporary Review*, 66 (1894), 207.

2. Daniele Archibugi, "Models of International Organization in Perpetual Peace Projects," *Review of International Studies*, 18/4 (1992), 295–317; Béla Kapossy, Isaac Nakhimovsky, and Richard Whatmore (eds.), *Commerce and Peace in the Enlightenment* (Cambridge, 2017); Esref Aksu, *Early Notions of Global Governance* (Cardiff, 2009). For a recent iteration, see Alex Bellamy, *World Peace (And How We Can Achieve It)* (Oxford, 2019).

and realize it.[3] Peace campaigns sprang up throughout the North Atlantic world to advocate disarmament, arbitration, and the limitation of warfare. The boldest activists believed that permanent universal peace was attainable. Others, more modest in their aims, sought to regulate conflict, eliminating its worst excesses while admitting that organized violence would remain an integral feature of the human condition. Questions of war and peace percolated through the discourse of Anglo-America, with some of the most ambitious proponents of union claiming that it could abolish war once and forever.

Today, establishing interstate peace is most commonly associated with the globalization of representative democracy. A world of democracies, we are told, would be a world free from the evil of war. The end of history is figured as the terminal point—the ultimate telos—of liberal democratic capitalism. Scholarly arguments have played an important performative role in elaborating and spreading this vision. Rooted at the very heart of the discipline of International Relations (IR), where it offers "as close as anything we have to an empirical law," the "democratic peace thesis" has filtered from the academy into the wider world, exerting a deep influence on practical politics from the 1990s to the present. It has been propagated by governments, NGOs, think tanks, and a phalanx of international organizations.[4] Political philosophers frequently invoke the idea to bolster the ethico-political case for global reform. John Rawls, for example, argued that the thesis underpinned his account of the "Law of Peoples as a realistic utopia."[5]

The idea of *pax democratica* is usually traced to Immanuel Kant's 1795 essay "Perpetual Peace: A Philosophical Sketch," an interpretation cemented by Michael Doyle's influential writings in the 1980s.[6] Other notable figures have also

---

3. Michael Howard, *The Invention of Peace* (London, 2000); Sandi Cooper, *Patriotic Pacifism* (Oxford, 1991); Winter, *Dreams of Peace and Freedom*, ch. 1.

4. Jack Levy, "Domestic Politics and War," *Journal of Interdisciplinary History*, 18/4 (1988), 661–62. On the performative dimensions of the peace thesis, see Christopher Hobson et al., "Between the Theory and Practice of Democratic Peace," *International Relations*, 25/2 (2011), 147–85; Piki Ish-Shalom, *Democratic Peace* (Ann Arbor, 2013); Ido Oren, "The Subjectivity of the Democratic Peace," *International Security*, 20/2 (1995), 147–84.

5. John Rawls, *The Law of Peoples* (Cambridge MA, 1999), 46. For a cosmopolitan critique, see Daniele Archibugi, "From Peace between Democracies to Global Democracy" in Archibugi, Mathias Koenig-Archibugi, and Raffaele Marchetti (eds.), *Global Democracy* (Cambridge, 2012), 254–73. Christopher Kutz, *On War and Democracy* (Princeton, NJ, 2016), observes that the democratic peace has become "a comforting mainstay of political thought," chiefly in the United States (1–2).

6. Immanuel Kant, "Perpetual Peace" (1795), in Kant, *Political Writings*, 2nd ed., ed. Hans Reiss (Cambridge, 1991), 93–130; Michael Doyle, "Kant, Liberal Legacies, and Foreign Affairs,"

been hailed as progenitors, including Thomas Paine and Jeremy Bentham.[7] This mythopoeic history conceals as much as it reveals: the intellectual history of perpetual peace is both more complex and more problematic than the enlightenment fable allows. The conventional narrative encodes problems of canonicity and periodization. Focusing on select figures from the canon misses much of the contextual specificity of arguments about eradicating war, drawing attention away from the extensive debate over the subject while exaggerating the influence of a handful of thinkers and texts. Concentrating on the late eighteenth century, meanwhile, effaces or ignores the febrile discourse about popular politics and violence that accompanied the uneven spread of democratic regimes during the nineteenth and twentieth centuries. It misses, that is, the dual victory of democracy as political institution and normative ideal. Long predicted, that world-historical process catalyzed a transvaluation of democratic shibboleths. At the end of the nineteenth century, as purportedly democratic states engaged in a frenzy of imperial violence, many observers began to question the pacific character of democracy. Other routes to peace were explored.

In this chapter, I locate Anglotopian visions of universal peace in the context of fin-de-siècle debates about democracy, empire, race, and war. I contend that the most ambitious projects for Anglo-American synthesis promoted the idea of a global racial peace—the abolition of war through the unification of Britain and the United States. Recognizing the character and significance of such arguments requires a reappraisal of the genealogy of modern peace discourse. After delineating several popular visions of peace that circulated during the nineteenth century, I introduce the "democratic war thesis" and the "democratic empire thesis." The former posited that democratic political structures caused or exacerbated inter-state conflict, while the latter suggested that vast empires could cooperatively govern the world and eradicate war. The remainder of the chapter anatomizes the racial peace thesis, which was propounded, albeit in different forms, by Carnegie, Rhodes, Stead, and Wells, many of the

---

Philosophy & Public Affairs, 12/3–4 (1983), 205–35 and 323–353; Doyle, "Liberalism and World Politics," *American Political Science Review*, 80/4 (1986), 1151–69. The popularity of Kant's argument has waxed and waned: Eric Easley, *The War over "Perpetual Peace"* (Basingstoke, 2005). For a critique of Doyle's reading of Kant, see Georg Cavallar, "Kantian Perspectives on Democratic Peace," *Review of International Studies*, 27/2 (2001), 229–48.

7. Thomas Walker, "The Forgotten Prophet," *International Studies Quarterly*, 44/1 (2000), 51–72; Tomas Baum, "A Quest for Inspiration in the Liberal Peace Paradigm," *European Journal of International Relations*, 14/3 (2008), 431–53. See also Stefano Recchia and Nadia Urbinati, "Giuseppe Mazzini's International Political Thought," in Recchia and Urbinati (eds.), *A Cosmopolitanism of Nations* (Princeton, NJ, 2009), 1–31.

science fiction writers discussed in chapter 5, and an array of other unionist political thinkers. This was the utopian core of the Anglo-racial dreamworld.

Defeating the Engineries of Death: Variations on a Pacific Theme

The nineteenth century saw the flowering of peace movements on both sides of the Atlantic, though their growth was patchy, and their reach and impact often limited.[8] We can distinguish four strands of peace argument circulating in British and American political discourse. Two distinct (ideal-typical) liberal internationalist positions took shape: *structural-liberal* and *radical-liberal*. *Socialism* offered a distinct alternative.[9] *Republican* ideas, meanwhile, were especially prominent in the United States. Often interwoven or blurred in practice, these positions nevertheless differed in their diagnoses of the principal causes of war and in their prescriptions for how to achieve peace.

Liberals of all stripes emphasized the importance of commerce as a solvent of war. Many eighteenth-century thinkers, including David Hume and Adam Smith, had characterized international trade as a Janus-faced phenomenon, capable of securing prosperity and stability while also precipitating spirals of competition. Hume, for example, observed that states tended to "look upon their neighbours with a suspicious eye, to consider all trading states as their rivals, and to suppose that it is impossible for any of them to flourish, but at their expense." "Jealousy of trade," as he termed it, was omnipresent.[10] Others were more optimistic. "[I]f commerce were permitted to act to the universal extent it is capable of," Thomas Paine announced in *The Rights of Man*, "it would extirpate the system of war, and produce a revolution in the uncivilized state of governments."[11] A quarter of a century later, the Swiss-French liberal

---

8. On the transnational circuits of the peace movement, see Michael Howard, *War and the Liberal Conscience* (New York, 2008), ch. 2; Cooper, *Patriotic Pacifism*; W. H. van der Linden, *The International Peace Movement, 1815–1874* (Amsterdam, 1987); Mazower, *Governing the World*, 3–154.

9. I have adapted the typology used by Laity, who distinguishes liberal, radical, and socialist arguments: *British Peace Movement*, 9–10. However, this terminology can be misleading, for most radicals were self-professed liberals.

10. David Hume, "Of the Jealousy of Trade" (1758), in Hume, *Essays, Moral, Political, and Literary*, ed. Eugene Miller (Indianapolis, 1985), 328. For the late eighteenth-century context, see Istvan Hont, *Jealousy of Trade* (Cambridge, MA, 2005); Isaac Nakhimovsky, *The Closed Commercial State* (Princeton, NJ, 2011); Kapossy, Nakhimovsky, and Whatmore, *Commerce and Peace in the Enlightenment*.

11. Thomas Paine, *The Rights of Man*, ed. H. Bonner (1791; London, 1906), 189.

thinker Benjamin Constant embedded the argument in a narrative of civilizational progress. "We have finally reached the age of commerce," he decreed, "an age which must necessarily replace that of war, as the age of war was bound to precede it." Adopting the stadial conception of socioeconomic development made famous by his Scottish teachers, Constant relegated war to a passing phase of human history. "The former is all savage impulse, the latter civilized calculation. It is clear that the more the commercial tendency prevails, the weaker must the tendency to war become."[12] Such arguments suggested that the intensification of trade would lock states into mutually beneficial patterns of exchange. This was combined with a more general supposition that the development of commercial societies would prompt a fundamental shift in domestic norms and institutions, spawning a new sociopolitical order predisposed to peaceful interaction. This belief coursed through the British peace movement, shaping liberal internationalist visions. The argument was promulgated in its most unabashed form by Richard Cobden and his epigones. Free trade, he wrote in 1835, was the "grand panacea" that would "serve to inoculate with the healthy and saving taste for civilization all the nations of the world."[13] The beneficent effects of commercial society were encoded in the technical idiom of classical political economy. As John Stuart Mill argued in *Principles of Political Economy*, the most influential midcentury text on the subject, it is "commerce which is rapidly rendering war obsolete."[14] They were likewise central to many feminist accounts of international peace.[15]

In the closing decades of the century, legal discourse assumed an increasingly important role in both the fissiparous peace movement and liberal internationalist ideology. While debate over the law of nations stretched back deep into European history, it was only in the second half of the nineteenth century that international law emerged as a codified body of thought buttressed by an institutional apparatus encompassing specialized training, an active transnational professoriate, the dissemination of textbooks and scholarly journals,

---

12. Benjamin Constant, "The Spirit of Conquest" (1814), in Constant, *Political Writings*, ed. Biancamaria Fontana (Cambridge, 1988), 53.

13. Richard Cobden, "England, Ireland, and America" (1835), in Cobden, *Political Writings* (London, 1867), I, 45. On American debates about Cobden and free trade, see Marc-William Palen, *The 'Conspiracy' of Free Trade* (Cambridge, 2016).

14. John Stuart Mill, *Principles of Political Economy* (1848), in *Collected Works*, ed. J. Robson (Toronto, 1965), III, 594. Mill also thought that settler colonialism had pacifying effects: Duncan Bell, "John Stuart Mill on Colonies," *Political Theory*, 38/1 (2010), 34–64.

15. Marc-William Palen, "British Free Trade and the International Feminist Vision for Peace, c.1846–1946" in David Thackeray, Andrew Thompson, and Richard Toye (eds.), *Imagining Britain's Economic Future, c.1800–1975* (Basingstoke, 2018), 115–33.

and the formation of professional associations, above all the Institut de Droit International, founded in Ghent in 1873. International law at once reflected and prescribed the spatial division of humanity, formalizing a hierarchical world order.[16] Seeking to expand the scope of legally binding norms and propel human progress, a newly emboldened group of international lawyers regarded themselves as a vanguard that could help to tame a perilous international system. Striking an uneasy balance between particularism and universalism, they synthesized a belief in the moral value of nationality with a commitment to expanding international cooperation, mirroring the dominant liberal sensibility of the period. International lawyers and the peace movement converged on the importance of arbitration as a mechanism for limiting the frequency of war.

Liberal arguments were typically predicated on a stratified vision of world order: claims about "peace" usually designated a condition pertaining between states characterized as "civilized."[17] The rest of the world was excluded for the foreseeable future. Adherents of such arguments rarely saw any tension between support for imperial rule and claims about the advent of international peace and stability.[18] Universalism was conditioned and delimited by a racialized conception of the world. Yet even as they concurred about the significance of commercial society, international law, and civilizational development, liberals were divided over a plethora of issues, including the causes of war and the most effective institutional response to it. Those propounding *structural-liberal* arguments identified the failure of political and economic cooperation between states as the principal cause of war. Emphasizing the dangers of economic protectionism and unrestrained realpolitik, they advocated free trade and the codification of international law as the most apposite policy responses.[19] They viewed the quality or condition of domestic norms and institutions

16. Martti Koskenniemi, *The Gentle Civiliser of Nations* (Cambridge, 2001), 11–166; Francis Boyle, *Foundations of World Order* (Durham, NC, 1999), 7; Casper Sylvest, "International Law in Nineteenth-Century Britain," *British Yearbook of International Law* (Oxford, 2005), 9–70; Benjamin Coates, *Legalist Empire* (Oxford, 2016). On international legal debates about peace, see Hippler and Vec, *Paradoxes of Peace in Nineteenth Century Europe*, pt. I.

17. I explore this idea further in Bell, *Reordering the World*, ch. 2. On "peace" as a legal category, see Jens Bartelson, *War in International Thought* (Cambridge, 2018), ch. 4; David Kennedy, *Of Law and War* (Princeton, NJ, 2006).

18. On divisions over empire in the British peace movement, see Martin Ceadel, *The Origins of War Prevention* (Oxford, 1996), 112–15; Laity, *British Peace Movement*, 81.

19. On nineteenth-century ideas about realpolitik, see John Bew, *Realpolitik* (Oxford, 2015), pts. I and II; Duncan Kelly, "August Ludwig von Rochau and *Realpolitik* as Historical Political Theory," *Global Intellectual History*, 3/3 (2018), 301–30.

as of (relatively) marginal significance for comprehending or reforming international order. Gladstone propounded a theologically inflected variant of structural-liberalism, stressing the importance of diplomacy, trade, the Concert of Europe, and regulatory arbitration.[20] In the closing years of the Victorian era, Henry Sidgwick developed a cautious internationalism grounded in structural-liberal claims.[21] During the following decade, Norman Angell sketched a more elaborate version. War, he argued in his best-selling *The Great Illusion*, belonged

> to a stage of development out of which we have passed; that the commerce and industry of a people no longer depend upon the expansion of its political frontiers; that a nation's political and economic frontiers do not now necessarily coincide; that military power is socially and economically futile, and can have no relation to the prosperity of the people exercising it; that it is impossible for one nation to seize by force the wealth or trade of another—to enrich itself by subjugating, or imposing its will by force on another; that, in short, war, even when victorious, can no longer achieve those aims for which people strive.[22]

In neo-Blochian vein, Angell concluded that "complex financial interdependence" made war economically irrational. The expansion of a system of commercial societies had furnished the material basis for peace. But he closed on a guarded note, cautioning that war remained a threat until this new economic truth was universally acknowledged. A policy of mass education about the prohibitive costs of violence was necessary to spread the gospel of interdependence.

Radical-liberal arguments identified free trade and international law as necessary but insufficient responses to the pathologies of the existing system. They combined coruscating attacks on economic protectionism with a thoroughgoing diagnostic critique of the structures, norms, and institutions of domestic politics. The principal causes of war, they suggested, were to be

20. Martin Ceadel, "Gladstone and the Liberal Theory of International Relations" in Peter Ghosh and Lawrence Goldman (eds.), *Politics and Culture in Victorian Britain* (Oxford, 2006), 74–94.

21. Duncan Bell and Casper Sylvest, "International Society in Victorian Political Thought," *Modern Intellectual History*, 3/2 (2006), 207–38.

22. Norman Angell, *The Great Illusion* (London, 1910), x. On the ambiguity of the text, see Martin Ceadel, "The Founding Text of International Relations?," *Review of International Studies*, 37/4 (2011), 1671–93. See also Lucian Ashworth, *Creating International Studies* (Aldershot, 1999). For a similar argument about the economic irrationality of war, from a key figure in the British peace movement, see H. S. Perris, *Pax Britannica* (London, 1913).

found in the internal ordering of states. Regime type both explained the prevalence of violence and offered a way to escape its lethal embrace. Blaming the political, military, and economic elites for the perpetuation of militarism and state aggression, they argued that since war was fought in the interests of a privileged minority, substantive domestic reform would dampen the frequency of conflict. The road to peace started with the elimination of hereditary privilege combined with increased participation in political life. This argument had been crystallized by Paine in his dissection of the belligerent character of politics "on the old system."[23] It echoed loudly down through the nineteenth century. Cobden was clear where blame could be assigned and redemption found: "The middle and industrious classes of England can have no interest apart from the preservation of peace. The honours, the fame, the emoluments of war belong not to them; the battle plain is the harvest field of the aristocracy, watered with the blood of the people."[24] Such arguments were reiterated, in one form or another, in the writings of James and John Stuart Mill, Spencer, Hobson, Hobhouse, and Bertrand Russell. It was in advocacy of the radical-liberal position that the lineaments of a democratic peace thesis can be discerned, for it was asserted that interstate aggression would diminish as "the people" assumed a more substantive political role. In the language of contemporary IR theory, nineteenth-century arguments linking democracy and peace were invariably *monadic* in form, stipulating that democracies were more peaceful than any other kind of regime. The *dyadic* formulation of the democratic peace thesis so familiar today—the empirical observation that democracies do not fight one another—emerged only in the mid-twentieth century.

Yet even as those adopting radical liberal positions agreed on the significance of regime type, they diverged over which factors to emphasize in explaining the distressing frequency of conflict, and over the best response to adopt. The main point of contention was the nature of capitalism. Some of them, Spencer most ardently, thought that the most convincing answer was political: the best way to secure peace was to forge a limited, even minimalist, state. Unleashing the unruly forces of capitalism would bring an end to war. Others, progressives and new liberals especially, argued that aspects of capitalism—and in particular finance—helped to fuel conflict. It was cause, not cure. Hobson presented the most famous version of this argument in his

23. Paine, *Rights of Man*, 143ff. For Paine on international politics, see Robert Lamb, "The Liberal Cosmopolitanism of Thomas Paine," *Journal of Politics*, 76/3 (2014), 636–48.

24. Cobden, "England, Ireland, and America," 42–43.

theory of underdevelopment.[25] They differed from more radical socialists in believing that the answer was the reform of capitalism rather than its abolition. The structure of commercial society could be modified to limit war and address questions of social and political inequality.

Socialists maintained that capitalism was the principal cause of war.[26] Although in Britain and the United States they never came close to matching the numbers or influence of liberals, they offered some of the most trenchant and sophisticated accounts of war. Socialists were divided between reformers and revolutionaries. Revolutionaries, including Marx, Luxemburg, Lenin, and Trotsky, postulated a necessary connection between (imperial) war and capitalism, and they were largely dismissive of European peace movements, viewing them as misguided in their diagnoses of the problem and far too conservative in their preferred solutions.[27] Proper socialists, Lenin averred, "understand the inevitable connection between wars and the class struggle within a country; we understand that wars cannot be abolished unless classes are abolished and socialism is created; we also differ in that we regard civil wars, i.e. wars waged by an oppressed class against the oppressor class . . . as fully legitimate, progressive and necessary."[28] Universal peace, on this account, could only be achieved through the violent supersession of the capitalist order. While acknowledging that actually existing capitalism was prone to violence, reformists, such as Eduard Bernstein and Karl Kautsky, denied the inevitability of capitalist war, maintaining that fundamental political and social restructuring could mitigate the problem. Short of an anticapitalist revolution, many socialists in the years before the First World War espoused a general strike against military mobilization, a dream of transnational solidarity that

25. Hobson, *Imperialism*. For a discussion of this line of argument, see Claeys, *Imperial Sceptics*, ch. 3.

26. Much of the most innovative socialist thought emanated from Germany. See here Roger Chickering, *Imperial Germany and a World without War* (Princeton, NJ, 1975).

27. See, for example, Rosa Luxemburg, "Peace Utopias," *Labour Monthly*, July 1911, 421–28. For the British context, see Martin Shaw, "Marxism, War and Peace in Britain, 1895–1945" in Richard Taylor and Nigel Young (eds.), *Campaigns for Peace* (Manchester, 1987), 49–72. British socialists were divided over the legitimacy of empire. H. M. Hyndman, for example, was broadly supportive of British imperialism and naval expansion. For the broad range of views, see Claeys, *Imperial Sceptics*, 124–234; Matthew Johnson, *Militarism and the British Left, 1902–1914* (Basingstoke, 2013). Socialists were also willing to adopt less radical strategies, including arbitration: William Morris and E. Belford Bax, *Socialism* (London, 1893), 284–85.

28. Vladimir Lenin, *Socialism and War*, in Lenin, *Collected Works*, ed. Julian Katzer (1915; Moscow, 1964), XXI, 299.

died in the trenches alongside those who were supposed to enact it.[29] The reformist alternative blurred into the radical-liberalism (or liberal socialism) of thinkers such as Hobson and Hobhouse.

For most of the nineteenth century, the peace movement in the United States was far smaller and less prominent than its British counterpart.[30] It only gained significant momentum, resources, and members during the 1890s, in opposition to war in the Philippines and the imperial turn in American foreign policy. The American campaign, like the British, was dominated by a moderate form of legalism that emphasized international codification and regulatory arbitration.[31] But American arguments were also shaped by another tradition—echoes of which could be found in British radicalism—that offered a *republican* critique of the morally and politically corrosive effects of war, imperialism, and extended foreign commitments. Such activities defied the prophetic words of George Washington's Farewell Address. "Why forego the advantages of so peculiar a situation?" he had pleaded. "Why quit our own to stand upon foreign ground? Why, by interweaving our destiny with that of any part of Europe, entangle our peace and prosperity in the toils of European ambition, rivalship, interest, humor or caprice?"[32] Republican skepticism of standing armies, foreign alliances, military interventions, and extra-continental imperialism was braided through nineteenth-century American political debate, and it shaped both the substance and rhetoric of the criticisms leveled against imperial war during the 1890s. The peace campaigner William Lloyd Garrison, son of a famous abolitionist father, was dismayed. "I despair for the republic," he complained in 1898, for "the example of previous republics, wrecked on this rock of foreign empire" issued in a clear warning.[33] Conquest eroded political virtue. "Imperial rule abroad necessitates imperial rule at home. . . . War is incompatible with free government. It is the handmaid of despotism."[34]

29. Ceadel, *Semi-Detached Idealists*, 173; Douglas Newton, *British Labour, European Socialism, and the Struggle for Peace, 1889–1914* (Oxford, 1985); Cooper, *Patriotic Pacifism*; Kenneth Waltz, *Man, the State, and War* (New York, 1959), 128–29.

30. On the American peace movement, see Charles DeBenedetti, *The Peace Reform in American History* (Bloomington, 1980); Patterson, *Towards a Warless World*.

31. Patterson, *Towards a Warless World*, 13; Reid, "Peace and Law"; Wertheim, "League of Nations."

32. George Washington, *Washington's Farewell Address* (New York, 1906), 27.

33. Garrison, "War and Imperialism," 211.

34. Garrison, "War and Imperialism," 208 and 210. The republican tradition also contained the resources for justifying imperialism: Bell, *Reordering the World*, chs. 4, 12. On the use of ancient Rome in republican arguments over empire, see Kristofer Allerfeldt, "Rome, Race, and

The prominent journalist and politician Carl Schurz likewise emphasized the dangers that imperialism heralded for a democratic republic. Lambasting the hypocrisy of governments that proclaimed their desire for peace while arming themselves for cataclysmic war, he contended that modern technoscience amplified long-standing aggressive habits.

> Thus the very advances in the sciences and arts which constitute one part of our modern civilization are pressed into the service of efforts to perfect the engineries of death, devastation and oppression, which are to make brute force in our days more and more terrible and destructive, and to render the weak more and more helpless as against the strong. It looks as if most civilized powers, although constantly speaking of peace, were preparing for a gigantic killing-and-demolishing match such as the most barbarous ages have hardly ever witnessed, and this at the expense of incalculable sacrifice to their peoples.[35]

Schurz warned that encroaching militarism endangered American democracy, counterposing the "true democratic spirit" against that venerable republican fear, a system of "great standing armies."[36] It was, he argued, possible "to demoralize the constitutional system and to infuse a dangerous element of arbitrary power into the government without making it a monarchy in form and nature." Constitutionalism was threatened by "warlike experiments."[37] The hazard was especially acute in a democratic state, because passions could be unleashed by the very prospect of war. Stable politics required the taming of affect and the rule of "calm reasoning," but, he warned, "nothing is more calculated" to destabilize such a system than "martial excitements which stir the blood." The clamor for war produced "a strange moral and political color-blindness" among citizens that threatened to undermine the existing order.[38] Instead of mimicking the European powers, and especially Britain, Schurz pleaded for the United States to hold fast to its traditions, maintaining a small

---

the Republic," *Journal of the Gilded Age and Progressive Era*, 7/3 (2008), 297–323. On the debate over the war, see Hilfrich, *Debating American Exceptionalism*.

35. Schurz, "Militarism and Democracy," 77. On Schurz, see, Hans Trefousse, *Carl Schurz*, 2nd ed. (New York, 1998).

36. Schurz, "Militarism and Democracy," 82, 90. Fear of standing armies was a common theme. For another example, see William Jennings Bryan, "Imperialism" (1900), in *Speeches of William Jennings Bryan* (New York, 1909), II, 27–29: "it is ever a menace to a republican form of government" (27).

37. Schurz, "Militarism and Democracy," 98.

38. Schurz, "Militarism and Democracy," 98, 99, 100.

(preferably citizen) army, abjuring foreign entanglements, and recognizing the injustice and moral corruption of imperial rule.

Republican anti-imperialism was frequently mobilized to shore up white racial supremacy.[39] David Starr Jordan, Stanford scientist and prominent anti-imperial campaigner, launched a searing attack on militarism while fretting about the danger that imperialism posed to Anglo-Saxon purity. Standing armies, he wrote in a critique of the American assault on the Philippines, contain "the seeds of decay," for as "militarism grows democracy must die."[40] But democratic rule was no universal political ideal, for self-government could only be attained among biologically superior peoples. Starr asserted that his fellow citizens faced an unpalatable choice if they continued to pursue foreign empire. Either they could incorporate the Philippines into the American body politic, instigating its contamination by an "inferior" race, or they could govern the conquered territory as an external entity, which required an elaborate colonial bureaucracy that would stoke militarism.[41]

Although liberal and republican peace arguments overlapped, there were some notable differences between them. Their theoretical emphases, conceptual framing, and historical references varied. Moreover, they adopted contrasting political vocabularies. Republicans expressly invoked the republican character of the country, a designation that carried a powerful affective charge, conjuring up a redolent blend of memory, myth, and history. Their claims were embedded in a historical metanarrative that fused the story of ancient republicanism with the modern evolution of the United States. Liberals of most stripes assigned commercial society a central role in their analysis of historical development, as well as their accounts of the causes of and cures for violence, while republicans placed great discursive weight on the dangers that warfare, imperial expansion, and moral corruption posed to political virtue.

The prevalence of interstate and imperial violence undercut the optimism of free trade propagandists. The growth of commercial societies had failed to establish a peaceful world. "The Reign of Peace has not come," observed the

---

39. On how racist arguments were employed by imperialists and their critics, see Hilfrich, *Debating American Exceptionalism*, ch. 3.

40. David Jordan, *The Question of the Philippines* (Palo Alto, 1899), 42.

41. Jordan's work highlights the intellectual fluidly of political traditions, as he drew on republican themes, Cobdenite economics, progressivism, and Galton's eugenics to make his idiosyncratic case for peace. See also James Abrahamson, "David Starr Jordan and American Anti-Militarism," *Pacific Northwest Quarterly*, 67/2 (1976), 76–87. On "peace eugenics," see Paul Crook, *Darwinism, War and History* (Cambridge, 1994), 119–24. The constitutional issue was addressed by the Supreme Court in the so-called Insular Cases in 1901.

historian W. E. H. Lecky in a critical discussion of Cobdenite ideology.[42] Hume had been validated. Democracy too had proved a disappointment. As Britain and the United States embarked on imperial wars, many thinkers lost confidence in the rationality of democratic publics. The brittle and easily manipulated social psychology of the masses was often cited as an insidious threat to progress and peace. The latest scientific theories were cited as authoritative evidence, with Gustave Le Bon's *The Crowd* wielding a powerful influence.[43] In Britain, the menace was often characterized as "jingoism," an aggressive nationalistic disposition that could afflict people across the political spectrum, but to which the working classes—easily stirred by the mass media—were thought to be especially susceptible.[44] Such arguments fed into, and drew sustenance from, the questioning of democracy's promise that was so popular among late nineteenth-century political thinkers. Maine offered a morbid summa: "We are propelled by an irresistible force on a definite path towards an unavoidable end—towards Democracy—as towards Death."[45]

The nature of democracy—and in particular its limits—was a core concern of the nascent discipline of political science.[46] In 1901, Woodrow Wilson, then teaching at Princeton, opened an essay by noting that it was "no longer possible to mistake the reaction against democracy. The nineteenth century was above all others a century of democracy; and yet the world is no more convinced of the benefits of democracy as a form of government at its end than it was at its beginning."[47] Wallas registered the ambivalence in *Human Nature*

42. W. E. H. Lecky, *The Empire* (London, 1893), 12.

43. Gustave Le Bon, *The Crowd* (London, 1896). See, more generally, Richard Bellamy, "The Advent of the Masses and the Making of the Theory of Democracy" in Terence Ball and Bellamy (eds.), *The Cambridge History of Twentieth Century Political Thought* (Cambridge, 2003), 70–103; Claeys, *Dystopia*, 18–57; Jaap van Ginneken, *Crowds, Psychology, and Politics, 1871–1899* (Cambridge, 1992).

44. J. A. Hobson, *The Psychology of Jingoism* (London, 1901).

45. Henry Maine, *Popular Government* (London, 1885), 174. For further discussion, see Burrow, Collini, and Winch, *That Noble Science of Politics*; Ella Dzelzainis and Ruth Livesey (eds.), *The American Experiment and the Idea of Democracy in British Culture, 1776–1914* (Aldershot, 2013).

46. John Gunnell, *Imagining the American Polity* (Philadelphia, 2004); Adcock, *Liberalism and the Emergence of American Political Science*; Blatt, *Race and the Making of American Political Science*.

47. Woodrow Wilson, "Democracy and Efficiency," *Atlantic Monthly*, 87 (March 1901), 289. Wilson himself wrote little about democracy and foreign affairs until the First World War, and even then his views were ambiguous, though he clearly held to some version of the monadic account of democratic peace. As John Thompson notes, he was not an advocate of extensive democracy promotion, chiefly because he thought democracy was only suitable for societies

in Politics: "in the very nations which have most wholeheartedly acquired representative democracy, politicians and political students seem puzzled and disappointed by their experience of it."[48] The refutation of the idea that democracies were peaceful was a source of pained disappointment.

In 1904, Hobhouse wrote *Democracy and Reaction* in response to the crisis of democratic faith. "Both the friends and enemies of democracy," he observed, had once "inclined to the belief that when the people came into power there would be a time of rapid and radical domestic change combined in all probability with peace abroad—for where was the interest of the masses in any war?"[49] Such hopes had been dashed: the record of reform was poor; aggression and militarism abounded. "Aggrandisement, war, compulsory enlistment, lavish expenditure, Protection, arbitrary government, class legislation, follow naturally one upon the other."[50] Hobhouse concluded his grim analysis by penning an epitaph for democratic optimism: "the conclusion that democracies would not be warlike—if stated as a universal rule—must certainly rank among the shattered illusions" of the age.[51] Reviewing Hobhouse's book, Morley proffered a similarly downbeat assessment.

> The effect has been indeed a surprise to those who made sure that, if you only gave the workingman votes and secured a sufficiently cheap press, England might be trusted to beat her swords into ploughshares and her spears into pruninghooks. Reformers had overlooked the truth set out by Tocqueville when he said "Nations are like men; they are still prouder of what flatters their passions, than of what serves their interest." The idea of empire intervened because the circumstances of empire changed.[52]

The imperial violence of the closing years of the century muted optimism about the pacific potential of democracy. The Reform Act of 1886 extended

---

with appropriate social conditions and "character" (an argument ultimately derived from Burke). Thompson, "Woodrow Wilson" in Michael Cox, Timothy Lynch, and Nicholas Bouchet (eds.), *US Foreign Policy and Democracy Promotion* (Routledge, 2013), 53–69.

48. Wallas, *Human Nature and Politics*, 2.

49. Leonard Hobhouse, *Democracy and Reaction*, ed. Peter Clarke (1904; Brighton, 1972), 49–50.

50. Hobhouse, *Democracy and Reaction*, 55.

51. Hobhouse, *Democracy and Reaction*, 142.

52. Morley, "Democracy and Reaction," 273. The passage is loosely derived from de Tocqueville's *Recollections*. For a contemporaneous rendering, see *The Recollections of Alexis de Tocqueville*, ed. Comte de Tocqueville, trans. Alexander Teixeira de Mattos (New York, 1896), 360: "For nations are like men, they love still more that which flatters their passions than that which serves their interests."

the franchise to the bulk of the British adult male population, yet it seemed to make little difference to the bellicosity of the country. The United States, once seen as a beacon of democracy by liberals, appeared keen to follow the British example by constructing a large navy and a globe-straddling empire. On both sides of the Atlantic, celebratory accounts of democracy were shadowed by skepticism and anxiety. Few rejected democracy entirely, but many were nervous, even fearful, about the changes it portended. The reality of democratic life was far less inspiring than the confident proclamations of the philosophers, political economists, and peace campaigners had once led people to believe.

Pax Anglo-Saxonia? Democracy, War, Empire

Even as the cherished hope that democracy would end war faded, debate over the character of organized violence continued to rage. The military and geopolitical lessons of the American Civil War and the Franco-German War spawned new warnings, new hopes, and new fantasies about conflicts to come. This was reinforced by the fabrication of technologies that promised to revolutionize battle. Machine guns, the telegraph, steamships, submarines, bicycles, automobiles, the airplane: all were fodder for the imaginative extrapolations of military futurology. Questions about the frequency, scale, and brutality of industrial war filtered into both recondite debate and popular culture.

Military professionals were stubbornly unmoved by visions of perpetual peace or the democratic mitigation of political violence. In 1898, Jean de Bloch's sprawling multivolume analysis of the changing meaning of war was distilled into a single-volume English text, *Is War Now Impossible?*, with a long introductory interview conducted by Stead. Bloch argued that war had been transformed by technology, the advantage switching from offense to defense. Daring military operations, culminating in a decisive battle, would be replaced by prolonged attritional violence. Future wars would be settled by famine rather than combat, "not the slaying of men, but the bankruptcy of nations and the break-up of the whole social organization."[53] The implication (as Angell later restated) was that war had been rendered irrational. The book attracted much attention, not least from members of the peace movement, but it was roundly dismissed by British military commentators, as it had been elsewhere in Europe. Bloch was criticized for relying on an outdated understanding of strategy and technology, and for paying insufficient attention to the moral dimensions of conflict, especially the significance of ethos, character, and

---

53. Jean de Bloch, *Is War Now Impossible?* (London, 1899), xvii. See also Bloch, "The Wars of the Future," *Contemporary Review*, 80/429 (1901), 305–32.

martial spirit.[54] Although they saw war as an ineliminable feature of human existence, military intellectuals recognized that social and political changes could not
be ignored. Many worried that an energized democratic public would interfere
with the traditional business of war preparation and planning. The more creative
among them sought to take advantage of the new political dispensation, adapting
their communicative strategies to the age of mass politics. One of the most effective ways of doing so was through the fictional rendition of future wars. A striking
number of the invasion novels I discussed in chapter 5 were produced by serving
or retired military officers.[55] Even as they blamed the vagaries of democratic politics for many of the strategic and geopolitical failures they warned about, the financial and rhetorical success of such novels depended on a willing democratic
public to disseminate their ideas and potentially act on them.

The debates over future war contained many strands, some innovative,
others long established. The "empire peace thesis" was an example of the latter,
the "democratic war thesis" the former. Positing a strong causal connection
between the franchise and interstate violence, democratic war arguments came
in weak and strong versions. Inverting the monadic democratic peace argument, the strong form suggested that representative democracies were prone
to violence. They were intrinsically bellicose. The weaker (and more common)
variant contended that democracies offered new channels for the expression of
violence: wars would assume a distinct democratic modality. Democratic
norms and structures neither eliminated war nor dampened its frequency.

In an 1871 lecture to the Peace Society, Seeley hinted at the strong argument,
contending that hope in the possibility of democratic peace had largely disappeared. He opened by stressing the persistence of violence.

> Half a century ago it might have been thought that war was merely the guilty
> game of kings and aristocracies, and that the introduction of popular govern-
> ment would make it obsolete: but I think we have seen enough to convince
> us that peoples can quarrel as well as kings; that scarcely any cause of war
> which operated in monarchical Europe will cease to operate in the popular
> Europe of the future.[56]

---

54. On his reception in British military circles, see Michael Welch, "The Centenary of the
British Publication of Jean de Bloch's *Is War Now Impossible?* (1899–1999)," *War in History*, 7/3
(2000), 273–94; T. H. E. Travers, "Technology, Tactics, and Morale," *Journal of Modern History*,
51/2 (1979), 264–86; Freedman, *Future of War*, ch. 2.

55. Michael A. Matin, "The Creativity of War Planners," *ELH: English Literary History*, 78/4
(2011), 801–31.

56. John Seeley, "The United States of Europe," *Macmillan's Magazine*, 23 (1871), 438. Seeley
rejected the idea that war could be abolished as hopelessly utopian: Seeley, "The Impartial Study
of Politics," *Contemporary Review*, 54 (1888), 57.

Moreover, he continued, wars between democracies had the potential to be *more* destructive than older forms of political violence. These "wars of the peoples," he predicted, "will be far more gigantic, more wasteful of blood and suffering, than ever were the wars of the kings."[57] The scale and brutality of democratic war would be unprecedented. Thirty years later, Wells propounded the strong thesis in *Anticipations*, arguing that representative democracy was particularly susceptible to spasms of violence. Unless checked, its rapid spread was likely to result in spirals of destruction, as democratic politicians fueled anxiety about external threats, nurturing "enmity between people and people" to retain power. The fate of democracy was grim. "[T]he phases of the democratic sequence are simple and sure," he averred with characteristic assurance.

> Nearer, and ever nearer, the politicians of the coming times will force one another towards the verge, not because they want to go over it, not because anyone wants to go over it, but because they are, by their very nature, compelled to go that way, because to go in any other direction is to break up and lose power. . . . [T]he final development of the democratic system, so far as intrinsic forces go, will be, not the rule of the boss, nor the rule of the trust, nor the rule of the newspaper; no rule, indeed, but international rivalry, international competition, international exasperation and hostility, and at last—irresistible and overwhelming—the definite establishment of the rule of that most stern and educational of all masters—*War*.[58]

The logic of electoral competition, amplified by the enveloping mediocrity of the political elite, meant that war was an inescapable outcome of democratic politics.

This argument was derived from Wells's abiding skepticism about the form that democracy had assumed. He dismissed as a distorting myth the idea that the nineteenth century had witnessed the noble "sovereign people" usurping power from traditional elites—this was little more than a comforting story peddled by "eloquent persons." The truth was rather less elevating. Democratic development was a product of "the decline of the old ruling classes in the face of the quasi-natural growth of mechanism and industrialism," combined with the "unpreparedness and want of organization in the new intelligent elements of the State." While filling a vacuum created by technoscientific progress, democracy in its current format was incapable of surviving and thriving in a complex sociopolitical environment, for it prohibited the embrace of expertise

57. Seeley, "United States of Europe," 438.
58. Wells, *Anticipations*, 95.

and knowledge.[59] Modern politics was characterized by a glaring epistemic failure. Now brandishing the keys to power, the uneducated masses could not defuse the inherent conflictual dynamics of the state system; indeed their ignorance and susceptibility to irrational passions only exacerbated the situation. Without realizing it, the governing class and the people worked in tandem to reproduce the existing pattern of political order. It could not last: "this grey confusion that is Democracy must pass away inevitably by its own inherent conditions, as the twilight passes, as the embryonic confusion of the cocoon creature passes, into the higher stage, into the higher organism, the world-state of the coming years."[60] Wells thought that war could be eliminated, but only through the collaborative action of a nascent class of "efficients" who would remodel society from within, heralding the emergence of ever-larger political combinations, including (above all) the English-speaking New Republic. Neither government nor conventional social movements would redeem the world, because such change could only be effected by a "mass of power and intelligence altogether outside the official state systems of today." Constituting a "new social Hercules," this advance guard would strangle "the serpents of war and national animosity in his cradle."[61]

Rebuking the blood-thirstiness of his compatriots, William James adopted a version of the weaker argument in his germinal essay "The Moral Equivalent of War." Leveling his fire at the Panglossian advocates of democracy, James argued that democratic politics simply channeled the truculent habits of the people in a new direction. He singled out the volatility of "public opinion," a live issue in the aftermath of the wars in South Africa and the Philippines. "Our ancestors have bred pugnacity into our bone and marrow, and thousands of years won't breed it out of us. The popular imagination fairly fattens on the thought of wars. Let public opinion once reach a certain fighting pitch, and no ruler can withstand it."[62] This was a common line of argument in British and American anti-imperial circles. E. L. Godkin, long-serving editor of *The Nation*, tendered another critique of democratic passion. Initially an advocate of a Millian form of democracy, he became increasingly disenchanted as the press and public clamored for war against Spain. The people, it turned out, were not

---

59. Wells, *Anticipations*, 86–87.

60. Wells, *Anticipations*, 99. I discuss this argument further in chapter 4.

61. Wells, *Anticipations*, 147.

62. William James, "The Moral Equivalent of War" (1906), in James, *Writings, 1902–1910* (New York, 1987), 283. James finishes the essay by approvingly citing Wells's account of the unintended benefits of military institutions. On James's views about imperial expansion, see Alexander Livingston, *Damn Great Empires!* (Oxford, 2016).

as rational and pacific as once predicted, while their elected leaders routinely fomented aggression for political advantage. According to Godkin, the jingo believed that "if a nation is to be great it must, like Rome, be 'imperial'; that is, must reign over a large number of communities of one sort or other as 'war lord,' and do them good, and elevate them, not in their own way, but in yours."[63] In a republican vein, he warned that the swing to imperialism signaled the end of the American dream. Democracy had the potential to corrupt both the institutions and ideals of the republic.

In 1915, Du Bois outlined an innovative imperial variant of the democratic war argument. He argued that the principal cause of the unfolding global conflagration was to be found not in obscure Balkan squabbles but in intra-European imperial competition. This competition, moreover, had been molded and directed by the growth of democratic politics within European societies. No longer able to exploit their workers in the traditional manner, capitalists had formed a racialized alliance with labor and looked outward to territories inhabited by the "darker nations of the world" for new spaces and populations to exploit. The remarkable burst of imperial expansion in the late nineteenth century, above all in Africa, was thus integrally related to the extension of the franchise to the working classes. "The present world war is, then, the result of jealousies engendered by the recent rise of armed national associations of labor and capital whose aim is the exploitation of the wealth of the world mainly outside the European circle of nations."[64] Like James, Du Bois did not reject democracy, only its perverted expressions. The answer to the abject failings of modern politics was the development of a better, more truly egalitarian, form of democratic politics, one that was not distorted by the color line.

The empire peace thesis, on the other hand, conjectured that war could be diminished, even eliminated, in a world managed by great empires. There were two main variants. The *inter-imperial* form claimed that global stability was best secured by a system of imperial coordination, in which the dominant powers in the system maintained order by limiting the number of autonomous polities, through both formal and informal modalities of rule. *Hegemonic imperial* arguments, in contrast, postulated that one dominant empire was necessary to secure peace and stability. Unsurprisingly, British thinkers typically

63. Edwin Godkin, "Imperialism," *The Nation*, 65 (1897), 511. See also the discussion in Myles Beaupre, "What Are the Philippines Going to Do to Us?," *Journal of American Studies*, 46/3 (2012), 711–27.

64. W. E. B. Du Bois, "The African Roots of War" (1915), in *Writings by W. E. B Du Bois in Periodicals Edited by Others*, ed. Herbert Aptheker (New York, 1982), II, 99, 100. Published originally in the *Atlantic Monthly* (May 1915).

assigned their own empire this imposing role, boasting of its unique combination of strategic capacity and political virtue. Arguments for imperial peace had internal and external dimensions. Empires, it was claimed, had the capacity to impose and uphold peace on territories within their jurisdiction. They facilitated the pacification of previously (or potentially) warring peoples, acting as a regulator of established (or incipient) patterns of violence.[65] The larger the empire, the more of the earth it could pacify. Due to their size, economic strength, and military capabilities, empires could also exert a pacifying influence outside their territory. They could either balance other polities, upholding a peaceful equilibrium between great powers, or (in the hegemonic variant of the argument) they could dominate the system by outmatching opponents, deterring violence, or intervening to bring conflicts to an end.

Bombastic imperial peace arguments studded the celebratory literature on the British Empire. In a high-profile Edwardian survey, the journalist, author, and businessman Charles Goldman wrote that the "true" imperialist, "so far from seeking war, seeks a security for peace by remedying the weakness and isolation which are the primary causes of war."[66] The trend of the time was toward larger political units. In his chapter, W. F. Monypenny, a leader writer for *The Times*, heralded the arrival of "imperator pacificus"—the mythic figure for "whom the Middle Ages longed." Unlike its Roman predecessor, the British Empire would not ensure stability "by holding the nations of the world in its iron grip," but rather through deploying its overwhelming strength with altruistic intent, "leaving full scope for the free play of the multitudinous forces of humanity in all of their legitimate fields of action." Another contributor, the journalist and author J. L. Garvin, hymned the world-historical teleology of the imperial order: "The final consolidation of the British empire would be by far the greatest step ever taken towards the ultimate integration of mankind."[67]

The imperial peace argument could be found in unexpected places. Hobson outlined a version of the inter-imperial form in *Imperialism*, a book best known for its radical-liberal analysis of the nefarious alliance between finance capital

65. This was at odds with the reality of imperial rule. On how the British Empire fostered and policed violence, see Mark Doyle, *Communal Violence in the British Empire* (London, 2017); Kim Wagner, "Savage Warfare," *History Workshop Journal*, 85/1 (2018), 217–37. For further discussion of the language of the imperial peace, see Ali Parchami, *Hegemonic Peace and Empire* (London, 2009), chs. 4, 5.

66. Charles Goldman, "Introduction" in Goldman (ed.), *The Empire and Century* (London, 1905), xviii.

67. Monypenny, "Imperial Ideal," 25; James Garvin, "The Maintenance of the Empire" in Goldman, *Empire and Century*, 25, 124.

and the governing elite. Elaborating the benefits of a system of federal empires ruling the "uncivilised" spaces of the earth, he envisaged a Pan-Anglo-Saxon polity taking its place alongside Pan-Teutonic, Pan-Slavic, and Pan-Latin entities, each "related by ties of common blood, language, and institutions." Future world order would be dominated by massive federal polities, each based on linguistic or racial identity. "Christendom thus laid out in a few great federal empires, each with a retinue of uncivilized dependencies, seems to me the most legitimate development of present tendencies and one which would offer the best hope of permanent peace on an assured basis of inter-Imperialism."[68] Agglomerating imperial power offered the best hope for universal peace.

Herbert Samuel, political thinker and senior liberal politician, made a case—reminiscent of Wells's—for inter-imperialism, tying it explicitly to a utopian dream of global unity. "If the growth of great empires disturbs for a time the general tranquility," he argued in *Liberalism*, "their existence, once established, is the surest guarantee of a lasting general peace."

> When Europe was divided into hundreds of petty principalities it was the scene of constant turmoil, from which the formation of large centralized states alone could rescue it. In the same way, many of those who look forward to a distant future in which the harmony, perhaps the federation, of nations will inaugurate a permanent reign of peace, see in the gradual substitution of a few world-empires for an infinite number of independent and mutually hostile polities, a step towards this ultimate goal. . . . The argument must not, of course, be pushed too far; it should not lead men to ignore genuine sentiments of nationality or be used to justify the conquest of progressive, liberty-loving peoples; but the fact remains that the present control of one-half of the land-area of the earth by four powers, England, Russia, the United States, and France, renders an ideal of ultimate unity less utopian; and viewed in this light, the maintenance of the British empire may be counted a service to the true interests of mankind.[69]

This argument prefigured later concerns over the "security dilemma" in international relations. The dilemma arises when two or more states coexisting in a condition of anarchy—lacking a global political authority to regulate their interactions—are drawn into a conflictual posture despite their (potentially)

---

68. Hobson, *Imperialism*, 332. Lenin picked out this passage for critique (and comparison with Kautsky's writing), deriding it as the expression of "the cant of English parsons": Lenin, *Imperialism, the Highest Stage of Capitalism* (1916; London, 1996), 122.

69. Herbert Samuel, *Liberalism* (London, 1902), 322–23.

nonaggressive intent.[70] In a condition of uncertainty, governments are compelled to engage in actions that can inadvertently generate further insecurity. The greater the number of sovereign units populating the system, the higher the probability of conflict. This logic pointed to the need for overarching political associations, perhaps even a world-state. It was frequently utilized to buttress the imperial peace. "Not many things are more evil than a frontier," Samuel warned, "and the fewer frontiers there are to divide the human family the more possible its eventual unity becomes." Empires performed a dual progressive function. First, by dissolving frontiers—through conquest if necessary—they reduced the number of units in the system, hastening the reunification of humanity. And second, as a civilizing force, empire could accelerate the growth of the cosmopolitan sentiments necessary to sustain a universal order. Allowing for the development of a "new and a better freedom," empire was thus a "civilizing and pacifying force, helpful to the progress of mankind."[71] A "cosmopolitan and humanitarian" spirit impelled liberals to embrace the imperial mission.[72]

Another variant of the argument specified that it was only "democratic empires"—empires ruled by democratic states—that were potential agents of universal peace. Combining huge economic and military resources with the moral legitimacy bestowed by popular government, they were both able and obligated to govern the rest of the world. In one sense, this was but the latest iteration of the venerable Western imperial argument about the rights and duties of "civilized" powers to bring progress to the "barbarian" places of the earth.[73] But it was inflected with two distinctly fin-de-siècle concerns: physical scale and democratic participation. Democratic-empire arguments embodied the common belief that one of the main tendencies of the age was the emergence of a small number of massive omnicompetent political units, created either through federation or conquest (or both). Moreover, while such arguments often focused attention on democracy as a system of government, they almost invariably associated it with Britain and the United States. As such, democratic peace arguments were usually assertions of Anglo-American supremacy.

70. Ken Booth and Nicholas Wheeler, *The Security Dilemma* (Basingstoke, 2007). The dilemma was named by John Herz in the early years of the Cold War: "Idealist Internationalism and the Security Dilemma," *World Politics*, 2/2 (1950), 157–80.

71. Samuel, *Liberalism*, 325.

72. Samuel, *Liberalism*, 332, 335.

73. For a succinct summary of justificatory arguments, see Tully, "Lineages of Contemporary Imperialism."

Throughout his long career, Stead promoted both the British Empire and an Anglo-American federal union as solutions to the problem of war. He emphasized internal and external pacification. During the 1880s and 1890s, he was, as he later wrote, "enamoured of the idea that the British Imperial power was the instrument for maintaining peace among races which would otherwise have been cursed by internecine warfare, and of putting down the horrors of slavery and of other barbarous works in vast regions." The empire had an unmatched ability to pacify and civilize, aiding subject peoples on the road to eventual freedom and inclusion in a universal political order dedicated to peace and justice. "The maintenance of the Roman peace throughout the 300 millions of India by an army which was much fewer in numbers than the force maintained in a small European country seemed to me an end for which it was worthwhile to make many sacrifices."[74] At the heart of Stead's vision of imperial Pax was the heavy metal of the Royal Navy. In 1884, he launched an energetic campaign to increase spending on the fleet.[75] Although "The Truth about the Navy" struck many contemporaries as incompatible with his support of the peace movement, Stead managed to reconcile the two, even if only to his own satisfaction. Since maritime supremacy and economic success required a massive fleet, and since the empire was an agent for good, it followed for Stead that British naval capacity was a vital interest for humanity. Moreover, a strong navy was essential for maintaining untrammeled connections between the scattered elements of the "English-speaking race." National security, imperial consolidation, racial unity, economic development, and liberal internationalism were conveniently synchronized. It was a commonplace that the British Empire had successfully replicated the "Roman peace." Stead went further, suggesting that the ancient template had been superseded by the "English-speaking peace," an irenic space of stability and progressive order that was slowly being stretched over the face of the earth.[76]

The eminent British idealist philosopher D. G. Ritchie offered perhaps the most sophisticated argument for a democratic variant of imperial peace.

74. Stead, "Great Pacifist," 610.

75. Whyte, *Life*, I, 105–6, 145–59. See also his extensive correspondence with Admiral "Jackie" Fisher, a key figure in the naval agitation: STED 1/27, Stead papers. For Fisher's appreciation of Stead, see *Memoirs, by Admiral of the Fleet, Lord Fisher* (London, 1919), "Cromwell and Martin Luther rolled into one" (264). Stead, like Fisher, was scornful of Beresford (293), whom we met in chapters 1 and 5. In *The Six Panics and Other Essays*, ch. 4, F. W. Hirst attacked Stead for fueling the naval panic of 1884. Stead reprised his ultranavalism in the dreadnought debates of 1908: Ceadel, *Semi-Detached Idealists*, 166.

76. W. T. Stead, *RoR*, 3 (March 1891), 216. For a contemporary critique of the Roman peace idea, see Reinsch, *World Politics*, 12–13.

Ritchie turned to Kant for inspiration, though the lesson he drew from him had nothing to do with democracy or republican institutions. Instead Richie emphasized the signal importance of political autonomy. "Kant saw quite clearly," he expostulated, "that there is only one way in which war between independent nations can be prevented; and that is by the nations ceasing to be independent." The fewer the units in the system, the lower the probability of conflict. The "prevention of war within great areas" would follow from the absorption of small states by large ones, either through coercion or voluntary union. Ritchie argued that while federation—"the greatest political invention of modern times"—was an effective solvent of sovereignty, insofar as it eliminated the anarchic international state of nature, it was radically incomplete. Democratic empires, ideally acting in concert, were required to rule the backward populations of the earth.

> A federation of civilized nations may be possible, when they are all constitutionally governed; but there may also remain large parts of the earth unfit for constitutional government. Tropical lands are apt to become black anarchies or white tyrannies; and in the interest of black and white alike the controlling hand of governments influenced by the ideas of temperate and civilized countries is absolutely necessary. . . . This is a federation of the world, which is not an altogether visionary ideal. The "European Concert," international congresses of all kinds, existing federal institutions—these are the germs out of which may grow the diminution, the mitigation, and, possibly, the cessation of wars.[77]

The idea that federal political structures were the solution to balancing autonomy and authority within imperial systems was a recurrent theme in political argument. Yet federalism was only thought appropriate for advanced "civilised" polities. Rule by the "enlightened" was usually prescribed for the "non-civilised," barbarian zones—those populated by non-"white" peoples. The democratic-empire thesis was a specific institutional variation on this general white supremacist theme.

Idealist philosophers disagreed over the best way to bring about peace and justice.[78] While Ritchie endorsed a federal version of the imperial peace, his esteemed teacher T. H. Green had earlier rejected the idea. Admitting that

---

77. David G. Ritchie, "War and Peace," *International Journal of Ethics*, 11/2 (1901), 157, 152, 157–58. For his commitment to federations (including of the "English-speaking peoples"), see Robert Latta, "Memoir" in David G. Ritchie, *Philosophical Studies*, ed. Latta (London, 1905), 48–52.

78. For the wide spectrum of idealist views on empire and international politics, see David Boucher, "British Idealism, the State and International Relations," *Journal of the History of Ideas*,

projects "of perpetual peace, to be logical, must be projects of all-embracing empire," Green argued that a world of independent nations expressing particularistic sentiments was more realistic and also more fulfilling. If they were properly constituted and directed toward the common good, not only would "the occasions of conflict between nations disappear," those nations would by virtue of the same development acquire a more altruistic "organ of expression and action" for dealing with each other.[79] In other words, Green suggested a radical-liberal answer to the problem, focusing on regime type as the key variable.

While common in Britain, democratic peace arguments could also be found in the United States. The eminent Columbia University sociologist Franklin Giddings propounded an elaborate version. While he did not endorse full union with Britain, Giddings called for a resolute "friendly alliance" between the two imperial powers.[80] He argued that war could only be abolished by drastically reducing the number of independent political units, and that this entailed the absorption of smaller states by "democratic empires," above all the United States and Britain. Rejecting Nietzsche's fetishization of power and the facile servility of Tolstoy, he claimed that "[u]nless the whole course of history is meaningless for the future, there is to be no cessation of war . . . until vast empires embrace all nations." But not all imperial forms would suffice, because if they were centralizing and despotic—or if they embraced socialism—they would "end in degeneration."[81] Democratic empires, by contrast, upheld the value of individual liberty and tolerated local and ethnic differences, and as such they provided an effective foundation for perpetual peace.[82] Balancing universalism and particularism in a fruitful equilibrium, the grateful subject populations would recognize the beneficence of their overlords and social evolution could be channeled in a pacific direction. "Only when the democratic empire has compassed the uttermost parts of the world," he concluded, "will there be that perfect understanding among men

---

55/4 (1994), 671–94; Boucher, "'Sane' and 'Insane' Imperialism," *History of European Ideas*, 44/8 (2018), 1189–204; Jeanne Morefield, *Covenants without Swords* (Princeton, NJ, 2005).

79. T. H. Green, "The Right of the State over the Individual in War" (1886), in Green, *Lectures on the Principles of Political Obligation*, ed. Paul Harris and John Murrow (Cambridge, 1986), 134.

80. Franklin Giddings, *Democracy and Empire* (London, 1900), 279.

81. Giddings, *Democracy and Empire*, 357.

82. Despite his claim about tolerance, Giddings was adamant that progressive democracies required ethnically homogenous populations, and he supported strict immigration controls. See, for example, his lecture notes in Box 3, Giddings papers, Butler Library, Columbia University.

which is necessary for the growth of moral kinship. Only in the spiritual brotherhood of that secular republic, created by blood and iron not less than by thought and love, will the kingdom of heaven be established on earth."[83]

This account was derived from Gidding's evolutionary social theory. He posited that there was an underlying principle animating social development: "Integration and differentiation may, and normally do, proceed together."[84] This principle was reflected in his defense of empire and the particular "democratic" form that he prescribed. Giddings argued that a federal structure would allow for distinct semiautonomous communities, each "homogenous in nearly every respect—in blood, in traditions, in beliefs, in interests," to flourish within an overarching constitutional structure that would regulate and coordinate the whole.[85] Protecting the homogeneity of its constituent parts was vital, because durable forms of human association, including political communities, were a product of a particular "mental state," which Giddings referred to as "consciousness of kind." A strong sense of such consciousness, based on intersubjective recognition, was essential for a flourishing, dynamic society.[86] The role of imperial government was not to impose a single identity or regime type on its subjects, but was strictly limited to external defense, the suppression of conflict between its principal units, and the maintenance of a limited empire-wide legal system that guaranteed "protection of life and property" in each community. It was possible to balance heterogeneity and homogeneity. Britain furnished the model for such an empire, translating the idea to "wonderful perfection," while the United States was "destined to create" another variant.[87] Naturalizing imperialism, Giddings contended that this destiny was inscribed in the evolutionary process as part of "cosmic law," and that rejecting it was as pointless as offering "opposition to the trade-wind or the storm."[88] He also tackled the thorny question of consent. Surely those subjected to coercive power had to affirm the authority of such an order? Giddings rejected this conception of democratic legitimacy, arguing that consent should be understood retrospectively, from the perspective of a fully developed rational agent. He moved quickly from the example of childrearing to that of governing subject peoples. "Approval," Giddings argued, could only be "given or withheld after full experience of the nature, objects, and excellence of

83. Giddings, *Democracy and Empire*, 357.

84. Giddings, *Democracy and Empire*, 352.

85. Giddings, *Democracy and Empire*, 11.

86. Franklin Giddings, *The Principles of Sociology* (London, 1896), 17; Giddings, "The Concepts and Methods of Sociology," *American Journal of Sociology*, 10/2 (1904), 167–76.

87. Giddings, *Democracy and Empire*, 11, 12.

88. Giddings, *Democracy and Empire*, 270, 279.

government, and after the attainment of full maturity to understand and interpret it."

> [I]f a barbarian people is compelled to accept the authority of a state more advanced in civilization, the test of the rightfulness or wrongfulness of this imposition of authority is to be found not at all in any assent or resistance at the moment when the government begins, but only in the degree of probability that, after full experience of what government can do to raise the subject population to a higher place of life, a free and rational consent will be given by those who have come to understand all that has been done.[89]

Giddings precluded the very possibility of legitimate critique by those subject to imperial rule, effacing their political agency in the present while deferring any possible evaluative judgment to some unspecified future point.

Imperial peace arguments did not go unchallenged. Some imperialists rejected the search for peace and system stability, insisting on the essential generative functions of war. Reinsch, for example, argued that competing national imperialisms were preferable to a static imperial hegemony because they drove political dynamism and human progress: "we are still very far distant from a millennium of peace."[90] But criticism also emanated from those disturbed by imperial aggression. Robertson charged that visions of a "peace-making imperial life" depended on perpetual conflict. "Without barbarian territory to steal and militant barbarians to shoot, the fabric of tinfoil glory passes away as a peepshow. Blessed are the powder-and-shot peacemakers, for they shall always go on inheriting more earth."[91] In an analysis of justificatory arguments for empire, Hobson singled out Giddings for critical attention, while in *Imperialism* he derided his "curious doctrine" of retrospective legitimation.[92] Gooch painted Giddings as an egregious example of those proclaiming that expansion was a law of nature.[93] Robertson also accused Ritchie of utilizing faulty consequentialist reasoning to encourage endless foreign conquest in the

---

89. Giddings, *Democracy and Empire*, 265.

90. Reinsch, *World Politics*, 360.

91. Robertson, *Patriotism and Empire*, 54. Robertson was taking aim at the arguments of the poet and editor William Henley. For a discussion of Henley, see Karma Nabulsi, *Traditions of War* (Oxford, 1999), 117, 121, 123.

92. J. A. Hobson, "The Scientific Basis of Imperialism," *Political Science Quarterly*, 17/3 (1902), 462, 470, 473; Hobson, *Imperialism*, 211n. See also the critique in William Salter, review of Giddings, *Democracy and Empire*, *International Journal of Ethics*, 11/1 (1900), 124–25.

93. Gooch, "Imperialism," 312, 329.

name of peace. Echoing the republican critique, he castigated such arguments for undercutting the very foundations of democracy.

> When, then, a democracy or a quasi-democracy proceeds to coerce another self-governing community on the plea of advancing civilization, it is giving the lie to its own fundamental principle, and the professed democrats who justify such coercion are men forsworn. And the sequel is historically so sure that we may call it a law of political evolution. The principle of democracy, negated at its source, suffers paralysis; and the ruling community comes to be ruled by the brute force it had created and sanctioned.[94]

Ritchie was unpersuaded. In reply, he restated the argument that peace could only be secured by the dissolution of smaller polities and the pursuit of an active imperial policy.

> Nations are to one another in the same position as individuals who have no state over them (e.g., persons of different nationalities shipwrecked on a desert island). War is therefore inevitable in some cases, where the threat of war, as a means of enforcing claims, proves ineffectual: and war must remain the ultimate court of appeal (the appeal to God, as John Locke calls it) except in so far as nations cease to be absolutely sovereign and independent and become absorbed in larger political organisms with legal tribunals and sufficient police or soldiery to enforce their decisions. Everything that helps towards the ideal of a federation of the world (not in a mere sentimental sense but in the stricter political sense of the term "federation") or of greater portions of it, seems to me a genuine movement for durable peace. Peace and order within a nation have only been secured by the reign of law, which means the strict enforcement of law. All government rests on public opinion; but all government involves the potential use of force. The peace of mankind cannot be rested on vague sentiment (more or less consciously anarchical) but requires regulated force as its ultimate safeguard.[95]

In an account of the "ethics of internationalism" published in 1906, Hobson challenged Ritchie while silently rejecting his own earlier argument about the pacific character of "inter-imperialism." He argued that although the peoples of the world were becoming interdependent, and consequently lacked good

---

94. John Robertson, "The Moral Problems of War," *International Journal of Ethics*, 11/3 (1901), 284.

95. David Ritchie, "The Moral Problems of War," *International Journal of Ethics*, 11/4 (1901), 495–96.

reasons for embarking on war, nefarious elites continued to propagate a Hobbesian vision of states as autonomous self-interested units. "The apparent oppositions of interest between nations . . . are not oppositions between the interests of people conceived as a whole; they are oppositions of class interests within the nation."[96] While critical of the Cobdenite line that commerce would eliminate war—on the grounds that it had failed to take account of the role of class interests in generating conflict—Hobson reserved his greatest ire for the "new imperialists" who dreamt that empires would establish perpetual peace. The result was deeply reactionary: "a few gigantic empires dividing the earth between them, coterminous with one another, powerful, definite and rich, will form a new sort of equilibrium of forces—fear, not gain, and not love, is designated as the ultimate peacemaker." Singling out Ritchie, one of the "great ethical teachers in England of recent years," Hobson stressed that such a vision was anathema to internationalism because it was based on a flawed social ontology and eradicated individual and national liberty.[97] Instead, he outlined a more subtle variant of the monadic radical-liberal argument.

> [T]he conception of a real republic, by which is meant an effective democracy, is essential to the achievement of peaceable relations between the nations of the world; not of course the mere form of a republic, not a form in which the power of the people is usurped by bosses and formally registered by the vote of the people, but a real republic in which the people themselves, the several units, express themselves with freedom and equality in the determination of their own affairs.[98]

The crude simulacra of democracy existing at the time provided a cloak of legitimacy for the continued rule of war-mongering elites. Only in an *authentic* democracy, free from the distorting effects of class power, would the people recognize that peaceful cooperation was in their interest. In order to salvage the democratic peace argument from the cauldron of imperial aggression, it was necessary to recode the meaning of popular politics, demarcating its aberrant and ideal forms. Democracy could be remodeled by drawing a distinction between form and content. In the United States, Progressive thinkers argued that democracy, if scoured of the monopolistic economic elites that threatened to undermine its emancipatory potential, remained an answer to the problem

---

96. Hobson, "Ethics of Internationalism," 28. I discuss this article briefly in Bell, "On J. A. Hobson's 'The Ethics of Internationalism,'" *Ethics*, 125/1 (2014), 120–22.

97. Hobson, "Ethics of Internationalism," 23, 27.

98. Hobson, "Ethics of Internationalism," 28.

of war.[99] In Britain, the recombinant task was shouldered, among many others, by a group of pluralist writers, including Hobhouse and G. D. H. Cole.[100]

The Anglotopian Dream: Ending the Murder of Men by Men

The rapprochement between Britain and the United States has long puzzled political scientists. In one of the most persuasive analyses, Srdjan Vucetic argues that patterns of Anglo-American cooperation originated in the creation of a "racial peace" between the two powers. The rapprochement was, he contends, "established on the basis of race, or, more specifically, because American and British elites succeeded in framing their community as a single Anglo-Saxon brotherhood." Democracy played only a derivate role: "the Anglo-American elites indeed understood each other as fellow democrats, but their antecedent ontology was always race, not regime type."[101] The process that Vucetic identifies was an *intra-racial peace project*—the realization of a security community *between* the "Anglo" powers. But the discourse of the time also contained a far more ambitious claim. The primary utopian dream was that the union of Britain and the United States would bring peace to the earth. War would be abolished once and for all. Although not all unionists preached such an agenda, it was a remarkably common theme, straddling experiments in fiction writing and the more conventional literature of political analysis and prescription.

Such arguments were not confined to the musings of detached observers of the political scene or those lacking experience of government. In 1894, a year after Carnegie published "A Look Ahead," the elderly colonial administrator Sir George Grey argued that perpetual peace would follow invariably from racial reunification. While an Arbitration Council would be an important first step, he thought that a full federation of the Anglo-Saxon peoples was likely to emerge in time, and that it would shape the destiny of humanity. In an unusual move, Grey also emphasized the importance of women in securing peace. "The influence of woman . . . will tend, probably as much as any other cause, to make nations unwilling to plunge into scenes of bloodshed and useless destruction of life and property."[102] Women, he implied, were by nature

---

99. John Thompson, *Reformers and War* (Cambridge, 1987), 91–103.

100. Leonie Holthaus, *Pluralist Democracy in International Relations* (Basingstoke, 2018).

101. Srdjan Vucetic, "A Racialized Peace?," *Foreign Policy Analysis*, 7/4 (2011), 403–4; Vucetic, *Anglosphere*.

102. Grey, "Federation of the English-speaking Race," 207.

more pacific than men. As with Stead and Wells, Grey thought that a racial polity would inaugurate the political millennium, "that last great federation, the brotherhood of man, which Tennyson and Burns have sung to us."[103] In response, Stead hailed Grey as the "Nestor of Colonial statesmen."[104]

Some serving politicians floated visions of racial peace. In a speech in 1899, Chamberlain, at the time Secretary of State for the Colonies, proclaimed that the "union—the alliance, if you please—the understanding between these two great nations is indeed a guarantee for the peace of the world."[105] Highlighting once again that institutional minimalism did not exclude racial utopia, Balfour regularly hymned the pacifying power of Anglo-America. In 1911, he observed that it is "predestined that in the world's history" Britain and the United States "should carry out, not by any formal alliances, not by parchments and treaties, but by something far deeper than those mere external and formal symbols, the ideals and aims in regard to self-government, order, liberty and individuals." He concluded by enunciating the core ambition running through the racial dreamworld: "we are for peace, peace, peace above all!"[106] Like so many others, he thought that arbitration was the key to unlocking it. While an Anglo-American treaty would secure peace between the two English-speaking powers, it would also signal "the beginning of a new era."

> It will be the first attempt to reach that view of a common bond between all civilised nations which shall prevent these barbarous survivals being still used among us; and if that prophecy—not too sanguine, as I hope—be fulfilled, then you . . . may surely look back upon this day . . . as one of the most significant epochs in the progress of civilization.[107]

Balfour was happy to admit to idealism, but he insisted that it was grounded in reality. He invoked the common distinction between modes of utopianism, one useless, the other essential. The former was alienated from social reality, and thus incapable of motivating change; the latter worked with the grain of history to help transform the world. "It is not a fantastic representation of what might be if the world only were constructed on different lines from what it is. Such dreams are useless. The vision that I am calling up before you is based on

103. Grey, "Federation of the English-speaking Race," 209. For more on his views about federal Anglo-Saxon union—the "solitary idea" that "sufficed to keep his heart warm" (196)—see James Milne, *The Romance of a Pro-consul*, 2nd ed. (London, 1899), ch. 18.

104. Stead, *Americanization*, 434.

105. Chamberlain, Speech at Leicester, 30 November 1899, *The Times*, 1 December 1897, 7.

106. Wilfrid M. Short, "Foreword," in Balfour, *Mind of Arthur James Balfour*, 4.

107. Arthur Balfour, Speech at the Guildhall, City of London, 28 April 1911, in Short, *Mind of Arthur James Balfour*, 8.

the realities of history and the realities of the past, the realities of the present, and the common burden thrown upon the two great nations in the future."[108] This echoed his friend Carnegie's ruminations on the value of social dreaming.

Most proponents of racial peace spent little time discussing how Anglo-America would abolish war, though we can discern two (often interwoven) lines of argument. One focused on brute geopolitical power: their combined military and industrial resources would be so overwhelming that no other polities would seek to challenge it or each other. The other focused on moral suasion: the example set by Anglo-America—especially in more utopian renderings of its development—would impress other peoples so much that they would seek to imitate it. "It should be no ambition of ours to dominate the world," Stead warned, "save by the influence of idea and the force of our example."[109] These claims were underwritten by an argument about legitimacy: Anglo-America could and should claim a privileged role due to its unique political virtues. Beresford, for example, wrote of his own plan for a defensive alliance that "[g]eographically, and by virtue of character and numbers, such an alliance would be irresistible in promoting peace. Who can doubt that the heavy sword which the united Anglo-Saxon race could throw into the balance would constitute them the arbiters between contending nations?" Their unique military strength meant they could transcend the quotidian dynamics of interstate politics. He then adduced a normative claim about the responsibility bestowed by racial superiority. "And what race has ever shown itself more fitted to such power, so honestly likely to wield it with honour and justice?"[110] Standing outside of history, the Anglo-Saxons could occupy an Archimedean point, monitoring, regulating, and shaping the behavior of other peoples and polities.

As justificatory arguments varied, so too did institutional prescriptions for realizing the Anglo dreamworld. The two most popular themes were international arbitration and naval supremacy. As I argued in chapter 2, arbitration came in both regulatory and revisionary forms. Advocates of the former thought that the creation of a system of arbitration, starting with a treaty between the United States and Britain, was vital for restricting interstate conflict. Exponents of the revisionary position argued that arbitration was only a preliminary step to a fundamental restructuring of global order. In 1885, John

---

108. Arthur Balfour, Speech to the Pilgrims Club, 28 June 1911, in Balfour, *Mind of Arthur James Balfour*, 10.

109. Stead, *Americanization*, 437.

110. Charles Beresford, "The Anglo-American Entente," *Pall Mall Magazine* 18 (1899), 382.

Dougall, a prominent Canadian journalist, contended that the fusion of the Anglo-Saxon peoples—a "pan-Saxon alliance"—was "not only desirable, but possibly a necessity." His institutional proposals were fairly modest: isopolitan citizenship and the creation of a transatlantic arbitration council. The alliance could and should "impose righteousness and peace" on the earth. Critics would most likely view this "as equivalent to annexing all of the world," and Dougall conceded that "to some extent it would virtually be," but such an alliance would "be a grand step towards the goal which visionaries set before them of a federation of man which would settle all differences by arbitration." He prophesied that the alliance would serve as "a messenger of peace to the world."[111]

It was widely assumed that naval supremacy both explained the global expansion of British power during the previous three centuries and underwrote future Anglo-American dominion. Such arguments drew on a long tradition of thought that stressed the exceptional qualities of the British Empire, as maritime, commercial, Protestant, and free.[112] The valorization of naval power had been given resonant intellectual justification with the publication of Mahan's *The Influence of Sea Power upon History*, a text that was celebrated in Britain as proof of a venerable conviction, and which was utilized by politicians in the United States, Roosevelt above all, to make the case for expanding the Navy. Command of the sea was figured as the key to Angloworld union. An anonymous article by "Nauticus" in the *Fortnightly Review* in 1894 made the case clearly. The world could "place its confidence in the integrity and fairness of the Anglo-Saxon race," the author declaimed, but to secure peace and disarmament "it seems necessary that some superior power should be created." A unified Anglo-polity would be "a supreme sea-Power of the world," determining the fate of humanity.

> It is not merely that the combined navies would be strong. Far more weighty are the considerations that the British Empire and the United States share between them nearly all the work of providing other countries with the food, raw material and manufactures which those countries cannot provide at home, and of carrying the ocean-borne trade of the world. Why should not your combined navies declare war, refuse henceforth to acknowledge the right of any civilized Power to close her port or the ports of another Power by blockading or otherwise? Surely that would sound the knell of war.[113]

111. Dougall, "An Anglo-Saxon Alliance," 700, 704, 700.
112. David Armitage, *The Ideological Origins of the British Empire* (Cambridge, 2000).
113. Nauticus, "The United Anglo-Saxon Will," *Fortnightly Review*, 72 (1894), 392.

The immense expanse of the world's oceans was central to the Anglotopian imagination, but so too were the depths below and (increasingly) the skies above. An incessant flow of merchant ships, protected by the American and British fleet(s), generated the wealth and global influence necessary to maintain geo-economic superiority. Buried deep beneath the surface was a rapidly expanding system of telegraph cables, thousands of miles of wire encased in gutta percha carrying electrical messages around the scattered outposts of the racial polity. This was the infrastructural foundation of a cyborg order. Such arguments were increasingly supplemented, or even supplanted, by accounts of the future role of airpower, with new vehicles—often modeled on naval vessels—allowing vast oceans to be traversed at unprecedented speed. Science fictional narratives, of the kind I explored in chapter 5, served as thought experiments for reimagining the spatial dimensions of Anglo-American power.

Proclaiming that the "day of small States appears to have passed," Dicey asserted that large empires were necessary in a world transformed.[114] He thought that his proposal for isopolitan citizenship between Britain and the United States had pacific implications. The "great common interest" of the two countries, he wrote, was the "maintenance of peace." His argument cited both the internal and external dimensions of the racial peace. The British and Americans already performed a valuable service by pacifying their own extensive territories. "The enforcement of the *pax Britannica* throughout the British Empire and the maintenance of civilised order throughout the length and breadth of the United States—and this without recourse to conscription—is the main service which the Anglo-Saxon race renders to civilisation." But internal pacification was only a foundation for the initiation of a wider project. A future alliance between the powers "would permanently secure the peace of a large portion of the world."[115] Echoing the oceanic geopolitics of Mahan, Dicey's argument for peace-through-isopoly was grounded in a claim that the British and Americans would "assert an effective command of the seas."[116] He was also a long-standing proponent of an arbitration treaty between the two countries.[117]

Carnegie was convinced that the synthesis of the English-speaking peoples would spark an unprecedented era of peace. "The new nation," he remarked in

114. Dicey, *Lectures on the Relation between Law and Public Opinion*, 453.

115. Dicey, "Common Citizenship," 467.

116. Dicey, "Common Citizenship," 467. For more on the imperial Pax, see Dicey, *Lectures*, 453ff.

117. Dicey, "Common Citizenship," 473–74; Dicey to Bryce, 23 March 1911, MS 3, Fol 86–77, Bryce papers.

"A Look Ahead," would dominate the world and "banish from the earth its greatest stain—the murder of men by men."[118] The transition would be peaceful because a unified Anglo-America was unassailable: "such a giant among pigmies would never need to exert its power, but only to intimate its wishes and decisions." Global disarmament would invariably follow as no other states would need to maintain a navy or standing army.[119] In a racialized account of unipolarity, Carnegie reasoned that a united Anglo polity would deter competition. Troubling as he found it, the unashamed bellicosity of the British and Americans did little to dampen his confidence that they would eventually bring peace to the world. All of history was pushing in that direction. Even as war raged in South Africa and the Philippines, Carnegie remained hopeful. "When the tempest howls it is in vain that a still small voice is lifted," he wrote to Stead in August 1900. "We must bear the blast, knowing that the day of peace will soon return, when brutal passions will be forgotten and the voice of reason, progress and civilisation will be heard. That day is not as far off as people imagine."[120] All is well since all grows better.

Goldwin Smith doubted the plausibility of Carnegie's proposal, warning that it might cause the very thing it sought to eradicate. The "consciousness of irresistible power," he argued, "is more apt to incline to aggression than to the enforcement of peace, while the jealousy which such combination would excite could hardly fail to lead to counter-combination and call the rest of the world to arms."[121] He lodged two objections. Absent viable checks and balances, an immense Anglo-American union would be unable to exercise the self-restraint necessary to fulfill the role Carnegie assigned it. Smith also invoked the relentless logic of realpolitik, predicting that a budding Anglo-American power would provoke counterbalancing from other states. It would restage the traditional dynamics of European geopolitics on a global scale. Rather than assuring a *pax Anglo-Saxonia*, union could ignite an arms race and renewed conflict.[122]

Although Carnegie regarded the "British-American" union as the most desirable form of supranational organization, he was willing to explore other institutional routes to peace. As I discussed in chapter 2, he had long advocated arbitration, arguing that Anglo-America should take the lead in molding the

118. Carnegie, "A Look Ahead," 12–13. For his mentors' views on war, see Paul Schuurman, "Herbert Spencer and the Paradox of War," *Intellectual History Review*, 26/4 (2016), 519–35.

119. Carnegie, "A Look Ahead," 13.

120. Carnegie to Stead, 22 August 1900, Fol 77, Carnegie papers.

121. Smith, "Anglo-Saxon Union," 172.

122. On different understandings of the idea, see Richard Little, *The Balance of Power in International Relations* (Cambridge, 2007).

burgeoning system of international law. Combining racial romanticism with Panglossian legalism, Carnegie (of course) remained optimistic. "[T]he tide," he wrote in 1905, "has set in as never before for peaceful arbitration instead of barbarous war."[123] During the Edwardian years, he toyed with the idea of a "League of Peace," an alliance of the great powers—including but not limited to Britain and the United States—that would address the vexed issue of enforcement. As he wrote in a letter to *The World* in May 1905, "What we need is an alliance of nations strong enough to enforce a peaceful settlement of international disputes in the future. France, Great Britain, America, and Germany could do this."[124] He fused the two ideas together in his widely publicized Rectorial Address at St. Andrews that same year, claiming that a "reign of peace through arbitration" could be underwritten by the military and economic power of the League.[125] He emphasized this connection in one of his numerous attempts to convince Roosevelt of the merits of arbitration. "One cannot think over the subject of war," he wrote to the President in 1906, "without coming to the 'League of Peace' idea as the easiest and best solution."[126] Rather than an alternative to empire, Carnegie posited a form of inter-imperial governance as guarantor of universal peace.

Carnegie's attempts at persuasion failed. "I believe in peace," Roosevelt replied, "but I believe that as things are at present, the cause not only of peace but of what is greater than peace, justice, is favoured by having those nations which really stand at the head of civilisation show, not merely by words but by action, that they ask peace in the name of justice and not from any weakness."[127] Mahan was scathing about both the message and the messenger. "Personally," he had informed one of his British military correspondents in 1896, "I think that while peace throughout the world is to be prayed for, I consider no greater misfortune could well happen than that the civilised nations should abandon their preparations for war and take to arbitration." For both Roosevelt and Mahan, the national interest took priority over nebulous claims about international law or morality. In attempting to recruit Roosevelt, Carnegie reverted to his Anglotopian dream. "I often picture our English-speaking race as some day to be so powerful as to be able to give the world what the Scotch call in the churches, an *'in-tim-a-tion'*—that an appeal to arms would

123. Carnegie to the *Daily News*, 22 August 1905, Fol 119, Carnegie papers.

124. Carnegie to *The World*, 31 May 1905, Fol 117, Carnegie papers.

125. Carnegie, *A Rectorial Address* (1905), 10. See also Carnegie, "War as the Mother of Valor and Civilization," *Advocate of Peace*, 72/4 (1910), 82–83.

126. Carnegie to Roosevelt, 27 August 1906, Fol 132, Carnegie papers.

127. Roosevelt to Carnegie, 6 August 1906, Fol 132, Carnegie papers; Mahan to Col. Sterling, 13 February 1896, Reel 2, Mahan papers.

be highly distasteful to that power (our race), which by raising its arm could compel peace."[128] All versions of arbitration were plagued by the question of implementation.[129] The 1899 Hague Conference that led to the establishment of the Court of Arbitration included no mechanism to enforce its decisions. This allowed states to endorse it while guaranteeing that the new legal body would invariably fail to realize the aims of its supporters. Whereas Stead answered the enforcement dilemma by confining the arbitration process to a limited subset of cases, thus redrawing the criteria for justiciability, Carnegie insisted that the threat of concerted military action would motivate compliance.

Despite its multinational composition, Carnegie's League of Peace was not a distinct alternative to his Anglotopian dream, for it would be dominated by the English-speaking states. Moreover, like his account of Anglo-American union, it was inflected by his belief in the ontological primacy of race. In one of the early iterations of the idea, he argued that it was essential to ally (not unify) with Germany, given their shared Teutonic origins. In 1904, he wrote to Frederic Harrison, the leading positivist thinker, outlining his views on relations between the English-speaking world and that "kindred people." In light of the abiding racial connection, and because German industrial growth would soon far surpass that of Britain, Carnegie thought it wise to "seek friendship and alliance." They could work together to police the international system. "I'm a great believer in race—a Race Imperialist."[130]

During the Edwardian years, Carnegie bombarded leading politicians on both sides of the Atlantic with assorted peace plans. The unrelenting barrage elicited polite responses but little action. Carnegie was unperturbed, convinced that history was tending toward peace and human unity. His plans were regularly seen as utopian, even by friends and admirers. Following his St. Andrews address, Andrew Dickson White, eminent scholar and diplomat, gently punctured this optimism. "I share your horror of war," White wrote, "and, like you, repudiate the dictum that it is a training school of the virtues."

128. Carnegie to Roosevelt, 27 August 1906, Fol 132, Carnegie papers. "The police supervision of backward states is another question, which does not appeal to me as being quite ripe, while the cause of arbitration is." For further advocacy of the League of Peace, see Carnegie to Roosevelt, 14 February 1907, Fol 139; Carnegie to Morley, 5 September 1906, Fol 133, Carnegie papers.

129. See, for the relevant texts of the Hague conferences, James Scott Brown (ed.), *Texts of the Peace Conferences at the Hague, 1899 and 1907* (Boston, 1908). Brown discusses the limited scope of arbitration in his commentary. See also Jacques Dumas, "Sanctions of International Arbitration," *American Journal of International Law*, 5/4 (1911), 934–57.

130. Carnegie to Frederic Harrison, 3 October 1904, Fol 107, Carnegie papers.

But he was not persuaded by Carnegie's argument. War was an expression of "what the theologians call the 'old Adam' in men or what a philosopher like Immanuel Kant characterizes as the 'radical evil in human nature.'" It could not be banished. "I see no ground for opining that the human race will ever become perfectly just, perfectly benevolent, or perfectly faithful to obligations," and in the coming centuries war was likely to remain a feature of international politics. Echoing Smith's worries, White suggested that a League of Peace may prove counterproductive: creating an "armed league to conquer peace by means of the sword" was playing with fire.[131] Moncure Conway, Hegelian abolitionist theologian, likewise warned Carnegie about the dangers of yoking imperial powers together.

> I quite agree with you that Great Britain, France and the United States could in combination enforce arbitration on all other nations,—that is, on the nations signatory to the Hague Conventions. I fear, however, that they would have to agree together to countenance each other in the exploitation and devouring of the small and helpless peoples and tribes. . . . [W]e are now in the situation of ancient Rome, which, according to Livy, had to conquer the whole world in self-defense. Wherever a country makes a conquest and annexes territory, the acquisition must be surrounded by a Monroe Doctrine. England has carried its empire around the world at the cost of fighting every race and securing the hostility of the majority of mankind.[132]

Like Smith, Conway was skeptical about the benign intentions of imperialists and the ability of a hegemonic stabilizer to refrain from aggressive expansion. The history of empire, and of the British Empire in particular, was an inglorious one: unrestrained power would invariably be abused. Carnegie made little effort to address such fears.

Fusing a belief that technoscience could transform political circumstances with the theological imperative to seek worldly redemption, Stead was among the most ambitious racial utopians. His cyborg vision rested on the potentiality of the electrical current, which had, he argued in 1890, "re-energised the world." The annihilation of time and space meant that it was now possible to

---

131. White to Carnegie, 29 November 1905, Fol 122, Carnegie papers.

132. Conway to Carnegie, 11 December 1905, Fol 122, Carnegie papers. Conway had first encountered Carnegie in 1888, and remained an admirer. See Daniel Conway, *Autobiography* (New York, 1904), II, 426–27. On Conway and his milieu, see Lloyd D. Easton, *Hegel's First American Followers* (Athens, 1966).

unify humanity, and electricity was "destined" to help abolish war.[133] An English-speaking federal polity was the principal institutional vehicle for enacting universality and securing perpetual peace, eliminating the horrific possibility of conflict between the two wings of the race and possessing so much military and economic power that it could police the earth. The "greatest of all World-Powers," it would be "supreme on sea and unassailable on land, permanently delivered from all fear of hostile attack, and capable of wielding irresistible influence in all parts of this planet."[134] If "England and America were one," he predicted in *The Americanization of the World*, "they would be able to maintain the peace of the world and general disarmament."[135]

Like other racial utopians, Stead divined both danger and hope in techno-scientific progress. Less than a year before he died on the *Titanic*, we find him charting yet another route through the future. He envisioned the "Coming World State," or "Empire of Peace," a new political combination that would reshape battle in the air and at sea. The initial step would be an arbitration treaty. Anglo-America could then harness nascent technologies to govern the world.

> For the aeroplane and the submarine will in a year or two reduce the world to anarchy unless some substitute is found by which authority can be enforced without arms. Fortunately the English-speaking world under the Stars and Stripes and the Union Jack has in its possession of the granaries and cattle ranches of the world a means of persuasion more potent than Dreadnoughts. A World-State or Empire of Peace which could lay any lawless State under an interdict which deprived it of all supplies of money, food-stuffs, or raw materials from any part of their territories, would be more efficacious in bringing it to reason than the excommunication of Pope Hildebrand.[136]

The colossal agricultural resources of the English-speaking peoples, combined with their overwhelming naval superiority, provided a formidable means of deterring, or if necessary annihilating, those willing to disturb the project of racial peace.

Rhodes—or at least Stead's Americanized Rhodes—was likewise convinced that the Anglo-Saxon race could establish peace on earth. In his long

133. W. T. Stead, *RoR*, 1 (March 1890), 230.

134. Stead, *Americanization*, 13, 396.

135. Stead, *Americanization*, 409.

136. W. T. Stead, *RoR*, 44 (July 1911), 35. Hildebrand—Gregory VII—was Pope between 1073 and 1085.

1891 letter to Stead, he prophesized that union with the United States would mean "universal peace" within a century, although he said nothing about the mechanisms that would bring this about.[137] In *The Americanization of the World*, Stead quoted Rhodes boasting, soon before his death, about the pacifying capacity of the Anglo-Saxons. Rhodes had "inveighed, as is his wont, against the madness of the monarch which had wrecked the fairest prospect of international peace which had ever dawned upon the world." The Revolution was a tragedy not only for the British Empire and the Anglo-Saxons but for humanity. Stead proceeded to ventriloquize Rhodes, who supposedly told him that "[i]f only we had held together . . . there would have been no need for another cannon to be cast in the whole world." The Federation of the English-speaking people, he continued, "would be strong enough in its command of all the material resources of the planet to compel the decision of all international quarrels by a more rational method than that of war."[138] Due to their overwhelming power, peace could be instituted without resort to violence. As one of Rhodes's admirers wrote in a posthumous homily, "Rhodes wanted peace and the power to enforce it. To his idea [*sic*] the understanding of the Anglo-Saxon race meant the necessary peace of the world."[139]

Racial utopians disagreed about the role of violence in fashioning a peaceful world. For many, including Carnegie and Stead, the transition could be peaceful, though it ultimately depended on the threat of violence. Their utopianism encompassed the mechanisms and the telos of transformation. Others, like Wells, argued that war would be necessary to secure peace. Fascinated by political violence, Wells wrote perceptively about military affairs, and he has a claim to being one of the most innovative theorists of war in the early twentieth century.[140] Throughout his career, he scorned the view that peace could be established without purgative violence. Writing in the shadow of Hitler, Stalin, and Mussolini, Wells summarized his long-held position. "I remain persuaded that there will have to be a last conflict to inaugurate the peace of mankind," he cautioned. "Rather than a war between sovereign governments, however, it is far more likely to be a war to suppress these wherever they are found." The obdurate remnants of sovereign power would have to be extinguished. "Peace will have to be kept—forcibly. For ages." The Darwinian logic was clear. "The distinction people draw between moral and physical force is

---

137. Rhodes, *Last Will*, 66.

138. Stead, *Americanization*, 403–4.

139. Cust, "Cecil Rhodes," 113.

140. Freedman, *Future of War*, 18–21; T. H. E. Travers, "Future Warfare" in Brian Bond and Ian Roy (eds.), *War and Society* (London, 1975), 67–87.

flimsy and unsound. Life is conflict and the only way to universal peace is through the defeat and obliteration of every minor organization of force."[141] Peace projects should not assume the underlying goodness of human nature or depend on political institutions to channel it in an altruistic direction, nor could they reliably cite the power of rationality to neutralize aggression. These were the obsolete hopes of pre-Darwinian utopianism. Modern utopian politics had to be fitted to, and made compatible with, the competitive character of humanity. Violence was needed to pacify reactionary elements of the global population, those still committed to nationalism and other parochial forms of communal loyalty.[142] Wars were necessary to end war, but once resistance had been extirpated, peace and justice would reign. This was a notably darker picture of the future than that sketched by Carnegie and Stead.

For much of Western history, war has been conceptualized as what Jens Bartelson terms an *ontogenetic* activity—a productive, generative force in human affairs, constructing identities and interests through the test of organized violence. As such, it is a sense-making activity, a "primordial force that imposes structure on a world that would otherwise be too chaotic to be accessible to understanding."[143] The fin de siècle was a key moment of transition in the meaning of war, as this traditional understanding was increasingly challenged by those who saw political violence as a senseless, destructive activity that should be tamed or, if possible, eliminated entirely. The debates over Anglotopian peace straddle this epochal fault line. For many of its adherents, including Wells and most of the science fiction writers, the ontogenetic understanding echoed loudly, and they saw violence as the road to ultimate peace. For others, including Carnegie and Stead, while military power might be useful in motivating disarmament and monitoring compliance, perpetual peace was achievable without recourse to violence. A new age was dawning.

Mixing hard-edged pessimism with visionary idealism, Wells predicted in *Anticipations* that the English-speaking New Republic would maintain—and enforce—the peace of the world. The institutional logic of his argument was straightforward. A small number of political syntheses would develop in different parts of the world, with the New Republic emerging as the largest and most powerful. A universal polity, a world-state, would develop from the fusion of these regional-racial composites. It would be dominated by the ideas,

141. Wells, *Experiment in Autobiography*, II, 668.
142. Wells, *Experiment in Autobiography*, II, 678.
143. Bartelson, *War in International Thought*, 16.

norms, and values of the English-speaking peoples. Through this process of state-formation, the "final peace of the world may be assured forever."[144] Although the New Republic faded from view in his later Edwardian writings— for reasons that I discussed in chapter 4—he restated the basic social theory of perpetual peace in a variety of texts. The pacific world of *A Modern Utopia*, most significantly, was produced by coagulation of synthetic communities built from the fusion of smaller ones.[145]

Wells, as we have seen, endorsed the democratic war argument. He worried that both the "gray" people and the political elites were prone to militarism, though he thought that the former, if properly educated, would eventually endorse synthesis. Invested in the reproduction and ideological stabilization of existing hierarchies, it was the politicians who blocked progress.

> In spite of all the pageant of modern war, synthesis is in the trend of the world. To aid and develop it, could be made the open and secure policy of any great modern empire now. Modern war, modern international hostility, is, I believe, possible only through the stupid illiteracy of the mass of men and the conceit and intellectual indolence of rulers and those who feed the public mind. Were the will of the mass of men lit and conscious, I am firmly convinced it would now burn steadily for synthesis and peace.[146]

World peace was possible if enough people willed it. Historical developments were pointing in that very direction, though complacency would be fatal. In *New Worlds for Old*, Wells opined that a "permanent international Congress" was necessary to regulate interaction between the new polities that would invariably flower over the coming decades, though he mentioned it only in passing and said nothing about its constitutional form. Such an institution was "necessary to insure the peace of the world." This, he continued, was "my own dream of the order that may emerge from the confusion of distrusts and tentative and dangerous absurdities, those reactions of fear and old traditional attitudes and racial misconceptions which one speaks of as international relations today."[147] The New Republic had been supplanted by something

---

144. Wells, *Anticipations*, 146.

145. Wells, *Modern Utopia*, 36. In *First and Last Things*, meanwhile, he had written—in quasi-Spencerian terms—about the pivotal role war played in history. "Through war and military organisation, and through war and military organisation only," he argued, "has it become possible to conceive of peace" (141).

146. Wells, *Modern Utopia*, 232.

147. Wells, *New Worlds for Old*, 324.

approximating Carnegie's ideal. From Anglo-American synthesis through visions of the world-state, Wells searched for ways to transcend the prevailing order of nations, states, and empires. Laced through this shape-shifting pattern of argument were two core commitments. The first was that perpetual peace was a live possibility, a condition realizable through skillful institutional engineering and the transvaluation of existing norms and belief systems. The second was that the process would be long and bloody. Peace was only possible for those willing to pass through the valley of death.

Both Carnegie and Stead adopted and adapted the radical liberal diagnosis of war, though they differed in the implications they drew from it. Carnegie was a more conventional apostle, contending that the venal behavior of traditional political and military elites was the principal cause of war. His solution took several interlocking forms. First, it was essential to establish a system of arbitration. Moreover, the pacifying power of the demos needed to be harnessed, an argument that bolstered his preference for American democracy over British monarchy. While Stead likewise blamed the frequency of war on entrenched elites, he was not as bold as Carnegie in his support for democratic restructuring, expressing considerable skepticism about the political rationality and benign intent of the people, especially in the wake of the South African debacle. Both also thought that the pulsating dynamism of commercial society would help to tame violence. Carnegie, proud disciple of Spencer, was adamant that capitalism was a solvent of war. His arguments were reinforced by republican concerns about the moral corruption fermented by imperial conquest. Stead was more worried than Carnegie about the political consequences of socioeconomic inequality, though he stopped short of advocating radical domestic social reform. His attention was focused chiefly on arbitration, the deterrent effects of naval power, and the police functions of a new Anglo-American superstate. In this as so much else, Wells's ideas traversed and extended beyond conventional traditions and conceptual schemes. Unlike Stead and Carnegie, he placed little weight on the ability of law to constrain the behavior of peoples or political institutions, and he did not regard arbitration as either a panacea or an important institutional step to Anglo-American union. He dismissed the pacifying effects of free trade. Nor did he align neatly with his fellow socialists, as he rejected the explanatory priority of capitalism. For Wells, the combination of new Janus-faced technological changes, competitive human nature, and the perverse logic of democratic politics were the chief causes of war in the industrial age. Democracy was part of the problem, not a solution to it. Perpetual peace would only come through the development of a new political union, a world-state built on the foundations of Anglo-American synthesis.

A Peace Such as the World Had Ever Known

Claims about geopolitical positioning, the pacifying power of moral suasion, and the unique virtues of the Anglo-Saxons, pervaded science fiction portrayals of the Angloworld. Furnishing maps of future worlds, speculative novelists often imagined that the union of Britain and the United States would issue in perpetual peace. These literary texts were typically instantiations of the peace-through-war idiom, fictionalizing the arguments of social prophets like Wells. Many of them added an extra ingredient to the Angloworld discursive repertoire, a technological *novum*—a weapon, a mode of transport, a medium of communication—that guaranteed victory in war and underwrote dreams of peace.

Bennett's Tory utopian romance, *The Dream of an Englishman*, culminated in an Anglo-American alliance (of an unspecified kind) overseeing the abolition of war and poverty, with peoples and states willingly joining it until the whole "*common wealth*" of the earth is united. It would ultimately guarantee the harmony of the galaxy.[148] In Tracy's *The Final War*, the reunion of Britain and the United States catalyzed the pacification of the international system. "In this last mad eruption, the evil genius of war had exhausted itself and humanity had cast it forth as a noisome thing to be tolerated no more. The Saxon race, for a moment, held the world in fear. But it was only to give to the nations abiding rest, to soothe ambition, to repair injustice, to mete out to all freedom before the law of justice."[149] Unassailable military might guaranteed peace enforcement, while racial-political virtue prohibited the misuse of such power. "So peace ruled: not that sullen silence which harbours in its breast poisonous passions, but a peace such as the world had ever known, deep, eternal, and serene."[150] Tracy ended his fable by proclaiming that the Anglo-Saxons were destined "to order and rule the world, to give it peace and freedom, to bestow upon it peace and happiness."[151] Acting on behalf of humanity, the "purpose" of the race was

> not one of empire, of ravage, of possession: rather a holy and religious purpose that had for its aim the union of the world in one eternal bond of peace. It was the dream of philosophy, the message of science, the yearning of art. In its beneficent light the earth would bloom into a new beauty. It

148. Bennett, *Dream*, 185–86. Italics in original.
149. Tracy, *Final War*, 458.
150. Tracy, *Final War*, 458.
151. Tracy, *Final War*, 464.

was a mission that no brute force or savage hate could stay on its triumphant course.[152]

The Anglo-Saxons were destined to bring about the political millennium. "This vision—far off, it may be—already dawns; and in the glory of its celestial light is the peace of nations."[153]

Combining racial unionism and the socialist critique of capitalism, Griffith's *The Angel of Revolution* outlined one of the most striking utopian programs. Different modalities of political violence stud the text. The story opens with a foreboding sense of an imminent European conflict.[154] But the key moment is the deployment of a superweapon assemblage—an air fleet sporting an unprecedentedly destructive artillery system—that transforms the terms of human association. "Mankind," we are told portentously, "stood confronted by a power that was practically irresistible, and which changed the whole aspect of warfare by land and sea." The new weapon "revolutionised the world," rendering "war impossible."[155] Initiative, valor, and glory no longer played a determinate role, for war had mutated into anonymous, mechanized slaughter. "In the new warfare people will not be merely killed, they will be annihilated."[156] Hegemonic stability was underwritten by technological ingenuity.

Griffith's text suggests that only through cleansing violence might the world be made afresh. The hero, with the aid of his plucky accomplices, must "fight his way through universal war to that peace." Later in the story, one of the characters pinpointed the genocidal logic that runs through the narrative: "if war can be cured by nothing but war, we will wage it to the point of extermination."[157] (We had to destroy the village in order to save it.) Griffith's political theory of war echoes the diagnostic arguments of both radical liberals and socialists. Rather than identifying a will to violence at the core of the human condition, whether rooted in original sin or biological endowment, he implies that ordinary people are capable of living together peacefully. Political violence is a product of malign capitalist elites and their pawns acting against the interests of humanity as a whole. "The peoples of the world would be good enough friends if their rulers and politicians let them."[158] All they need is an

152. Tracy, *Final War*, 398.

153. Tracy, *Final War*, 464.

154. Griffith, *Angel of the Revolution*, 30–31.

155. Griffith, *Angel of the Revolution*, 113, 130.

156. Griffith, *Angel of the Revolution*, 219.

157. Griffith, *Angel of the Revolution*, 162, 349.

158. Griffith, *Angel of the Revolution*, 349.

agent willing and able to depose those elites and govern on their behalf. The Anglo-Saxons alone possess the necessary virtue. Command of the skies is at once a sign and symbol of technological modernity, and thus an index of racial superiority. Existing modes of warfare depended on the existence of either a large standing army—a formation subject to enduring fears about political corruption—or a powerful Navy. The air fleet supersedes both, though it is closer in ideological inflection to the naval template, given its technocratic form, lack of territorial concentration, and ability to traverse planetary spaces. Griffith concludes the tale with the victorious Anglo-Saxons enforcing world peace through superior military technoscience. "[T]he fate of Humanity would be fixed for centuries to come."[159]

While Anglotopian peace was a common theme in the genre, it was not universal. Cole and Vogel concluded their novels on more ambiguous notes. Vogel's utopia, set in and around the year 2000, is marked by peace, though the condition is fragile and requires an army of nearly three million men to maintain it. "Two other empires and one republic alone approach it in power, and a cordial understanding exists between them to repress war to the utmost extent possible. They constitute the police of the world."[160] War has been tamed, not eliminated, and the empire remains vigilant for its recrudescence. "Happily in our day war is a remote contingency," the Emperor recounts, "but it is never impossible. We preserve peace by being prepared for war."[161] The "utmost extent," however, does not encompass counterinsurgency operations, which remain necessary to suppress resistance to the British Empire in Africa and Asia.[162] Vogel's narrative does not conclude with a discussion of racial peace, as was the norm, but rather with a long account of succession to the imperial throne. He emphasized one of the core messages of the book, that women were capable of playing an equal role in public life. The future Anglo-Saxon polity is presented as a eutopian space, its happiness and prosperity unrivaled in human history, and Vogel implies that this is a world where peace is enforced by the consolidated Anglo-Saxon empire, but he stops short of announcing the final eradication of war.

Cole's novel climaxes with brutal violence. Fresh from their fortuitous victory over the alien Sirians, the Anglo-Saxons exact a merciless revenge.

Then the Anglo-Saxon fleet formed into line with exultation, and the order was given to bombard the capital of Kairet. What followed was but a

159. Griffith, *Angel of the Revolution*, 310.
160. Vogel, *Anno Domini 2000*, 39, 58.
161. Vogel, *Anno Domini 2000*, 53.
162. Vogel, *Anno Domini 2000*, 82.

counterpart of what had previously happened at London. Drawn up in long lines, the ships hovered among the clouds, and crossed and recrossed over the terrified city, raining down death and destruction, while the lightning flashed and the thunder rolled through the air. It lasted for hours, and then the fleets withdrew from the smoking ruins and sent an envoy to demand the surrender of all the fortresses, dockyards, and important cities, and informing the Government of what had happened to their own fleet at the earth.[163]

After this initial demand is rejected, the Anglo-Saxon fleet attacks cities and towns across the planet. The Sirians eventually surrender unconditionally, and the Anglo-Saxon battlefleet expels them from their homeland. Reparations are demanded and soldiers are posted to the Sirian colonies, distant outposts of a galaxy-spanning military occupation force. Peace was finally declared between the "two great Powers of the Universe."[164] Like Wells's *War of the Worlds*, Cole leaves open the possibility of further conflict against the aliens.

The American literature of racial reunion was likewise saturated with utopian themes. Global peace was both the aim and the achievement of Stockton's "Great War Syndicate," while Waterloo's *Armageddon* urges the pacific implications of military technoscience.[165] In the first part of the novel, he stressed the importance of controlling the oceans. "The water owners must be the world's owners," we are told in Mahanian terms. "No more may the greatest of struggles be upon the land. No longer lies Armageddon—where the nations battle—in the vale of Esdraelon. It lies where the sea-fields give deep soundings."[166] The completion of the Panama Canal, a glorious "pathway for mankind," allows the American and British fleets easy access to the blue planet. An age of peace and prosperity beckoned. "Because of it bread shall be plentiful throughout the world. Famine shall cease to threaten any branch of mankind."[167] When war erupts, the telegraph comes into its own, facilitating instantaneous communication between the leaders of the Anglo-American alliance: "Warm were the Atlantic cables."[168] The chief instrument of peace was a new aerial weapon system, "The Valkyr." With the development of such destructive technologies the world reached a threshold: species-annihilation

163. Cole, *Struggle for Empire*, 195.

164. Cole, *Struggle for Empire*, 196.

165. Stockton, *Great War Syndicate*; Waterloo, *Armageddon*. For further examples, see Matarese, *American Foreign Policy and the Utopian Imagination*, ch. 3.

166. Waterloo, *Armageddon*, 136.

167. Waterloo, *Armageddon*, 133–34.

168. Waterloo, *Armageddon*, 141.

had become a real possibility. The inventor, David Appleton, opines that "[c]ivilization has reached a point where war is suicide."[169] With the genie released, it was essential for responsible powers to harness the new destructive capabilities for the end of peace.

> To have a world at peace there must be massed in the controlling nations such power of destruction as may not be even questioned. So we shall build our appliances of destruction, calling to our aid every discovery and achievement of science. When there are but chances about war, when it means death to all, to the vast majority of all who engage in it, there will be peace.[170]

Some American racial providentialists saw the Anglo-Saxons as God's instrument for eradicating human conflict. Fiske concluded *American Political Ideas from the Standpoint of Universal History* with a forecast that the development of the "English race" would precipitate the consolidation of humanity and the end of war. The only way to secure perpetual peace was by concentrating military power in the most peaceful communities, above all Britain and the United States. Federalism, he continued, offered the ultimate institutional solution to the problem of war, containing the "seeds of permanent peace between nations," for it allowed the creation of ever-larger groupings, eliminating the possibility of interpolity strife while maintaining a significant element of political autonomy. Citing Tennyson, he concluded by sketching the emergence of the Parliament of Man.

> Thus we may foresee in general outline how, through the gradual concentration of the preponderance of physical power into the hands of the most pacific communities, the wretched business of warfare must finally become obsolete all over the globe. The element of distance is now fast becoming eliminated from political problems, and the history of human progress politically will continue in the future to be what it has been in the past,—the history of the successive union of groups of men into larger and more complex aggregates.[171]

Strong promoted arbitration as a vehicle for enacting divine will. The Creator, he argued in 1898, "is committed to international arbitration, because he is pledged to ultimate peace." Abbott, his fellow social gospel campaigner,

---

169. Waterloo, *Armageddon*, 258
170. Waterloo, *Armageddon*, 259.
171. Fiske, *American Political Ideas*, 151–52.

made an explicit case for conjoining arbitration and Anglo-American unity. He sketched the terms of an alliance:

> first, absolute reciprocity of trade; second, a tribunal to which should be referred for settlement, as a matter of course, all questions arising between the two nations, as now all questions arising between the various States of this Union are referred to the Supreme Court of the United States; third, a mutual pledge that an assault on one should be regarded as an assault on both, so that as towards other nations these two would be united as the various States of this Union stand united toward all other States.

The scope of the alliance was broad, including Canada and Australasia; over time he envisaged it expanding to include "such provinces in Asia and Africa as are under British domination and administration." This behemoth would act as a magnet. "It would gradually draw into itself other peoples of like minds though of foreign race, such as, in the far East, the people of Japan," and in doing so it would create a "new confederation based on principles and ideas not on tradition, and bounded by the possibilities of human development not by geographical lines." Giving "a new significance to the motto E Pluribus Unum," the end result would be a macrocosmic variant of the United States, the creation of a new "United States of the World" in which the old country would be a "component part." The new racial polity would "surpass all that present imagination can conceive or present hope anticipate."[172] This was a vision of race as utopian destiny.

In 1899, Albion Tourgée—soldier, diplomat, and judge—anointed the "Anglo-Saxons" the "peacemakers of the twentieth century." A celebrated campaigner for racial equality and civil rights in the United States, Tourgée was also a keen advocate of global Anglo-Saxon domination. He argued that it was pointless to define the Anglo-Saxons in terms of their common origins or language. Instead they were bound by a "common aim and purpose," as the "nations, actual and embryonic, which have derived their institutions, customs, laws in short, their civilisation, from the common law of England and the religious and political ideals which have been shaped by the genius and experience of English-speaking peoples."[173] The main ideals were political: the subservience of the state to the individual and government by popular consent. They were conjoined by this "common ethical quality": "not unity of origin, but identity of aspiration." He reiterated the widespread trope that closer union

172. Abbott, "Basis of an Anglo-American Understanding," 521.

173. Albion Tourgée, "The Twentieth Century Peacemakers," *Contemporary Review*, 75 (1899), 887, 888. On his life and work, see Mark Elliott, *Color-Blind Justice* (Oxford, 2006).

was both desirable and necessary. For Tourgée, the world faced a decision: follow the path of the Anglo-Saxons or that of continental despotism.[174] The choice between freedom and tyranny was particularly relevant for the "unde-veloped world": the "semi-civilised" peoples could either be ruled by the be-nevolent Anglo-Saxons, who aimed to bring them up to a standard of civiliza-tion where they could govern themselves, or the militaristic continental states, who would simply exploit them. Given the general bellicosity of the contend-ers for global domination, it was essential that the British and American peoples combine. No opponents could match their unified power. The Anglo-Saxons, he concluded, "are the peacemakers of the twentieth century, the pro-tectors of the world's liberty, of free economic development, and of the weak nationalities of the earth."[175]

Others were less optimistic that peace could be secured without resort to prolonged violence. Like Reinsch, H. H. Powers, a historian and political com-mentator based at Cornell University, maintained that evolutionary progress, in human affairs as with the rest of the natural world, was defined by the relent-less and often brutal "substitution of the more efficient for the less efficient forms of life."[176] As regrettable as this might be, the process stood outside of the moral order. "It is as useless to speculate about the ethics of this universal competition as to speculate about the ethics of gravitation. So far as we can see, the process is non-ethical, altogether transcending the limits of moral obligation."[177] These were immutable laws of human development. It followed, he claimed, that like "every phase of the struggle for existence, race competi-tion is constructive," producing increasingly efficient groups and generating a "progressive consolidation of groups looking towards an ultimate synthesis." Contra racial utopians such as Wells, this did not mean that ever-larger politi-cal units would coalesce until finally the world itself fell under the sway of a sovereign power that would guarantee peace. While Powers argued that every-one would welcome the Tennysonian "parliament of man, a federation of the world," he maintained that it was not within reach—indeed it was "impossible under the existing conditions of social progress."[178] One day "social instincts" might be recoded, allowing people to create new political syntheses, but in the meantime, territorial consolidation would remain a product of coercion and imperial war. Powers embraced this purifying fate.

174. Tourgée, "Twentieth Century Peacemakers," 889, 897.

175. Tourgée, "Twentieth Century Peacemakers," 903.

176. H. H. Powers, "The Ethics of Expansion," *International Journal of Ethics*, 10/3 (1900), 288–306.

177. Powers, "Ethics of Expansion," 288–89.

178. Powers, "Ethics of Expansion," 293.

We are confronted, therefore, with an ultimate synthesis of humanity, perhaps not far remote as such things go, the main lines of which we can already trace. Like every adjustment effected by nature, it will be based, not upon the equality but upon the inequality of its component parts. Some race, more virile and constructive than the rest, will get the ascendency. Other races, though nominally independent, will take their cue from this, recognizing at first by vehement denials and then by sullen acquiescence a hegemony which will at last pass over into automatic and even enthusiastic allegiance as time brings its inevitable adaptations. In attaining this result the weak races of the temperate zones seem destined to extinction, those of the tropics to subjection. What else should or can be the fate of inferiority?[179]

Racial conflict, then, was preferable to sterile attempts to craft new international institutions. Indeed, the search for peaceful union was counterproductive. "It is scarcely too much to say that a peaceful federation of mankind at the present juncture would be a misfortune, over-burdening the delicate selective agencies working within organized society with the gross, heavy work which should be done by the powerful enginery of race conflict."[180] Eyeing the international scene, Powers warned that European federation would be a threat to Anglo-Saxon dominance. The British and Americans had the upper hand. It was essential that they, the dominant race, act together to reinforce their position. "Of all possible combinations looking toward world dominion, this is the only one likely to secure a bloodless supremacy. From beginning to end it is most nearly identical with universal interests, unless indeed the civilization itself prove deficient in capacity for growth and adaptation, and on this point we may take our chances."[181] Though Powers said nothing about possible institutional arrangements for cooperation, the general thrust of his argument was clear. The Anglo-Saxons had to unify to survive and thrive in a hypercompetitive world marked by unforgiving racial competition. Acting in concert, they could maintain domination, and eventually, initially by force but then by moral exemplarity, they could inaugurate a new phase in human development. The "social instincts" could be superseded. Peace would reign.

179. Powers, "Ethics of Expansion," 293.

180. Powers, "Ethics of Expansion," 297.

181. Powers, "Ethics of Expansion," 304. See also Powers, "The War as a Suggestion of Manifest Destiny," *Annals of the American Academy of Political and Social Science*, 12/2 (1898), 173–92. For a later version of the argument for Anglo-American cooperation under conditions of race competition, see Powers, *America among the Nations* (New York, 1917).

Although the racial peace discourse was at its most intense in the years straddling the new century, it did not evaporate during the Edwardian era. Indeed, it was reiterated on both sides of the Atlantic and in the other outposts of the Angloworld. Stead and Carnegie continued to beat the drum. Dos Passos was also optimistic. In *The Anglo-Saxon Century and the Unification of the English-speaking People*, he argued that racial union would lead invariably to the "elimination of war and the advancement of civilisation," because "power lodged in the proper hands hurts no one."[182] In a quasi-Hegelian vein, the workings of reason in history offered proof.

> History, in all its stages, conjectural, traditional, and authentic, discloses with almost painful clearness that there are underlying forces governing the progress of the human race, which are made manifest in successive ages only by their results, and with which conscious volition seems to have but little to do. . . . If I am right in what I have said of the Anglo-Saxon race in its two great branches, the inference becomes clear. To that race primarily belongs in a preponderating degree the future of mankind, because it has proved its title to its guardianship.[183]

Five years later, the expatriate British novelist and journalist H. Perry Robinson asserted, without much in the way of argument, that "[t]he ultimate domination of the world by the Anglo-Saxon (let us call him so) seems to be reasonably assured; and no less assured is it that at some time wars will cease." All that remained was the issue of political will. "The question for both Englishmen and Americans to ask themselves is whether, recognising the responsibility that already rests upon it, the Anglo-Saxon race dare or can for conscience' sake—hang back and postpone the advent of Universal Peace, which it is in its power to bring about—to-day, no matter what the motives of jealousy, or self-interest, or of self-distrust may be than retrain it."[184] A year later, following a visit from the United States Navy to Australia, we find G. H. Reid, a leading Australian politician, proclaiming that "[p]eace could have no better champions. Humanity could have no better allies. Their united power is the

---

182. Dos Passos, *Anglo-Saxon Century*, vii, xiii.

183. Dos Passos, *Anglo-Saxon Century*, 47.

184. Robinson, *Twentieth Century American*, 19. Born in Britain, Robinson spent much of the 1890s living and working in the United States. In 1900, he returned to Britain to work for *The Times*. During the First World War, he was selected by the government as one of five official journalists, a service for which he was knighted in 1920.

best guaranty the world has ever had of a new reign of justice, liberty and progress in all parts of the globe."[185]

On the eve of the First World War, the Swedish libertarian thinker August Schvan assigned the Anglo-Saxons the primary role in bringing peace to the earth. They could combine their naval forces to pacify the Atlantic and Pacific, before turning their benevolent attention to the rest of the planet. They were uniquely placed to do so because of their combination of military might and moral legitimacy. "Whatever their failings in the past, the Anglo-Saxon peoples to-day stand out in unison as upholders of this fundamental doctrine which alone can guarantee the greatest amount of happiness to the greatest number." It was only through such action that war could be eliminated. "It is the primary condition for a successful Anglo-Saxon combine on which the satisfactory solution of peace and disarmament hangs."[186] Writing in the same year, the British journalist and historian J. Ellis Barker was still making the case for racial peace.

> The greatest interest of the Anglo-Saxon nations is peace, security, and the restriction of armaments. These blessings can scarcely be obtained by the federation of the world, dreamt of by the late Mr Stead, or by the federation of Europe, as proposed by other dreamers, but only by the federation of the Anglo-Saxon nations. Experience shows that the world can only be at peace if it is controlled by one nation. It will be at peace only when the *pax Romana* has been replaced by the *pax Britannica*, by the peace of the Anglo-Saxons, when the military Great Powers have, owing to the growth of the Anglo-Saxon nations, become militarily small Powers. The world must either become Anglo-Saxon or fall a prey to militarism.[187]

While racial reunion was desirable on "ideal grounds," it was also eminently practical. Both countries shared the same interests and strategic vulnerabilities. Following Mahan, he argued that it was essential for the "Anglo-Saxons"

185. G. H. Reid, "An After-Glance at the Visit of the American Fleet to Australia," *North American Review*, 189/640 (1909), 404–9. Reid was a former Premier of New South Wales and the fourth Prime Minister of Australia.

186. August Schvan, "Anglo-Saxon Co-operation and Peace," *North American Review*, 198/697 (1913), 812, 819. Schvan's proto-Nozickian views are discussed in Barbara Goodwin, "Taxation in Utopia," *Utopian Studies*, 19/2 (2008), 313–31. He later supported a world state.

187. James Barker, "An Anglo-American Reunion" (1913), in Barker, *The Great Problems of British Statesmanship* (London, 1917), 426. Note his (mis)characterization of Stead. A historian of modern Germany, Barker had also written *Great and Greater Britain* (London, 1909). Dedicated to Chamberlain, it advocated imperial federation (on a model of imperial preference) and emphasized the need for military and naval efficiency.

to control the seas, especially in the absence of standing armies. He addressed an old objection by insisting that their democratic systems rendered them more similar than was usually thought. "The argument that they cannot combine because one is a monarchy and the other a republic is a fallacious one. Both are democracies. They differ only in outward form, but not in the essence and the spirit, of their government." Indeed, he continued, Britain was ruled by a hereditary president, the United States by an elected king.[188] While principally interested in securing a defensive alliance between Britain and the United States, he left open the possibility of deeper integration in the future.

The onset of war dulled but did not extinguish the appetite for racial utopia. The conflict provoked a major reconsideration of the potential mechanisms for establishing international peace.[189] Prior to 1914, internationalists were generally averse to creating powerful international organizations.[190] Such skepticism in part explains the hopes invested in regulatory visions of arbitration. Even the most radical Anglotopians tended to focus their energies on formalizing connections between elements of the Angloworld, and in particular the United States and Britain, though, as we have seen, some of the most prominent, including Wells, Carnegie, and Stead, regarded this as the prologue to an eventual world-state. As the war dragged on, the idea of a multilateral League or Union gained support. While it ultimately resulted in a pallid League of Nations, the shift in international thought was indelible.[191]

As plans for a postwar international organization circulated, Anglotopian visions continued to emerge. In 1915, Kennedy predicted that racial federation

188. Barker, "An Anglo-American Reunion," 426–27.

189. On how the war led to a redefinition of peace, see William Mulligan, *The Great War for Peace* (New Haven, CT, 2014). For debates about postwar order, see also George Egerton, *Great Britain and the Creation of the League of Nations* (Chapel Hill, 1978); Patrick Cohrs, *The Unfinished Peace after World War I* (Cambridge, 2006), ch. 2; Duncan Kelly, *Reconstruction* (Oxford, forth.).

190. On this skepticism about international organizations, see Sylvest, *British Liberal Internationalism*; Ceadel, "Gladstone and a Liberal Theory of International Relations." There were, of course, exceptions, but they remained marginal. For example, Frederic Seebohm, *On International Reform* (London, 1871), called for an international police force.

191. For a survey of contemporary views, locating them in the long history of peace projects, see Lord Phillimore, *Schemes for Maintaining General Peace* (London, 1920), pts IV and V. For examples, see Leonard Woolf, *International Government* (London, 1916); Woolf (ed.), *The Framework of a Lasting Peace* (London, 1917); A. L. Lowell, *A League to Enforce Peace* (Cambridge, MA, 1916); J. A. Hobson, *Towards International Government* (London, 1915); G. Lowes Dickinson, *The War and the Way Out* (London, 1915); James Bryce, *Proposals for the Prevention of Future Wars* (London, 1917).

would help to secure peace between and beyond the "Pan-Angles," a distributed people composing the (white) populations of the United States, Australia, Canada, Great Britain, Newfoundland, New Zealand, and South Africa. It
would do so by dampening the security dilemma. While the English-speaking
peoples had been at peace for nearly a century, he worried that "frictions are
bound to arise," given the lethal combination of sovereignty and international
competition.[192] Racial homogeneity and shared history were insufficient to
guarantee intraracial peace. Political institutions were needed to bind them
together, harnessing their collective power while eliminating possible causes
of conflict. "If for us is coming the great millennium, so sweetly dreamed of by
so many, it will not come sooner by perpetuating opportunities for discord."[193]
His argument for a "common government" of the "Pan-Angles" encompassed
two distinct senses of peace. First, a federation would ensure peace between
the scattered members of the "race," and second, a huge unified polity could
help to bring about—in some unspecified manner—a global racial peace.
Barker too was unperturbed by the course of the war, reiterating in 1917 his
claim that Anglo-American union was the best, and perhaps the only, way of
bringing peace to the blasted earth.

> The hope to secure the peace of the world by arbitration treaties or by some
> great international organisation such as a federation or a great league of
> nations, may prove an illusion. All attempts to eliminate war by mutual
> agreement among states have failed since the time when the Greek states
> created their Amphyctionic Council. All endeavours to link together the
> satisfied and the land-hungry nations and to combine them for the defence
> of the territorial status quo may prove futile. The peace of the world can
> most easily be maintained not by creating an artificial and unnatural part-
> nership between nations of different, and perhaps irreconcilable, aims and
> interests, a partnership which will break down at the first opportunity, but
> by creating a permanent partnership between freedom-loving and peace-
> loving Anglo-Saxon nations which in addition have the advantage of be-
> longing to the same race, of speaking the same language, of having the same
> ideals, the same laws, and the same traditions. A British-American union
> devised for the protection of their possessions against attack should be the

192. Kennedy, *Pan-Angles*, 121.

193. Kennedy, *Pan-Angles*, 129. A *New York Times* review of the book (15 November 1914)
noted how the war had changed the geopolitical equation, but concluded that "[i]t may come
about that the United States and the six nations embraced in Great Britain may form a federal
union to care for their common interests."

most powerful instrument imaginable not only for protecting the future peace of the Anglo-Saxons but also for protecting the peace of the world.[194]

He was swimming against a swelling tide. While the dream of racial peace never disappeared entirely, it was articulated far less frequently in subsequent decades. It had firmly captured the attention of Anglo-American unionists during the closing years of the Victorian age, but as the twentieth century unfolded in a frenzy of political violence it was supplanted by competing visions of conflict management and global governance.

194. Barker, "Anglo-American Reunion," 432. He added this passage as a postscript to the original 1913 essay.

8

Conclusion

UNVEILING THE SPHINX

There lies before the people of Great Britain a choice of two alternatives. If they decide to merge the existence of the British Empire in the United States of the English-speaking World, they may continue for all time to be an integral part of the greatest of all World-Powers, supreme on sea and unassailable on land, permanently delivered from all fear of hostile attack, and capable of wielding irresistible influence in all parts of this planet.[1]

(W. T. STEAD)

I believe in the Prince of Peace. I believe that War is Murder. I believe that armies and navies are at bottom the tinsel and braggadocio of oppression and wrong; and I believe that the wicked conquest of weaker and darker nations by nations white and stronger but foreshadows the death of that strength.[2]

(W. E. B. DU BOIS)

Futures Past / Past Futures

Dreamworlds of Race has explored the discourse of Anglo-American (re)union that flared at the end of the nineteenth century. Seeking to uncover its conceptual presuppositions, theoretical claims, rhetorical strategies, and political goals, I have read the boldest articulations of the idea as a form of racial utopianism. Unionists, including Carnegie, Rhodes, Stead, and Wells, sought to recast the territorial configuration of world politics, integrating or coordinating the principal homelands of the "Anglo-Saxon race" or "English-speaking

1. Stead, *Americanization*, 396.
2. W. E. B. Du Bois, "Credo" (1904), *Writings*, I, 229. Published originally in *The Independent*, October 1904.

357

peoples." They were motivated by a shared set of concerns: the respective trajectories of the British Empire and the United States, threats from strategic
competitors old and new, the advent of mass democratic politics, the revolutionary potential of communications technologies, the future of war and
peace. Despite many points of convergence, they differed significantly over a
broad range issues, including how best to apprehend the racial community,
the degree to which dreams should be institutionalized, and the ultimate ends
of union.

The story of my four main protagonists fizzled out without them ever combining their remarkable resources or public profiles to agitate for union.
Rhodes died young, his final Will enunciating his imperialism and desire for
strengthened relations with the United States, but stopping short of promoting integration. Carnegie went to his grave committed to the dream, but during the Edwardian years he was increasingly preoccupied with philanthropy
and the travails of the peace movement, and he never lavished funding on
specific projects for racial reunion. Stead too remained resolute, but his reputation declined during the opening decade of the twentieth century, not least
because of his very public commitment to spiritualism—he became as much
a source of satire as influence or authority. Although Wells never entirely lost
faith in the superiority of his beloved English-speaking peoples, his interest in
a synthetic New Republic faded, and by the end of the First World War he was
calling for an omnicompetent League of Nations that would augur the "death
knell" of all empires.[3] Superseded in his plans by a new model of global
governance, Wells came to think of empire as an obsolete relic in an emergent
cosmopolitical order. He promoted variations on the theme of a world-state
until his death in 1946.

Although it peaked in the years straddling the turn of the twentieth century,
the discourse of Anglo-American union never disappeared. Writing in the *Political Science Quarterly* in 1915, the American historian R. L. Schulyer claimed
that "the conception of Britannic-American unity has taken hold of too many
minds to be pronounced a mere fancy or a delusion."[4] So it proved. The
popularity of unionism has waxed and waned over the last century, its form
and terminology mutating, even as a powerful thread of continuity runs
through its various iterations. While the language of "Anglo-Saxonism" was

3. H. G. Wells, "The Death Knell of Empires," *Current History*, 8/2 (1918), 353–54. For a
polemical attack on Wells's anti-imperialism, and much else besides, see Henry Arthur Jones,
My Dear Wells (New York, 1921), v–vi, 52, 99, 228–29, 257, 269. On Wells's shifting views about
empire, see also Partington, *Building Cosmopolis*, chs. 4, 6; Bell, "Founding the World State."

4. R. L. Schuyler, review of Kennedy, *The Pan-Angles*, *Political Science Quarterly*, 30/3 (1915),
525.

(largely) supplanted by the "English-speaking peoples" and more recently the "Anglosphere," visions of racial-political unity continued to inspire support, sometimes pitched in competition with alternative world-ordering projects—federalist, imperial, democratic—but more often merging with them. Fin-de-siècle unionist ideas were absorbed into discourses of Western unification or schemes for unions of democracies, with their early advocates conscripted as honored precursors. During the Second World War, for example, Rhodes was recruited as a progenitor of Clarence Streit's Union Now movement, which backed the federal unification of the Atlantic democracies.[5] Policy proposals forged when Victoria sat on the throne continued to attract new adherents. Thus in 1940 American war planners briefly considered the possibility of Anglo-American (re)unification.[6] Proposals for racial isopolitan citizenship have been floated at various junctures. Churchill professed his support for the idea during the war years.[7] The dream of union also continued to stir speculative fantasies. In 1930, Churchill published a short story in which the South won the Civil War. The Confederate victory split the United States asunder, resulting eventually (after the voluntary abolition of slavery) in the fusion of the two distinct territories with Britain to create an "English Speaking Association" that prevents the First World War.[8]

The twentieth century ended as it had begun: with celebration of the world-historical role of the Angloworld. Some recent arguments extol it as the prime mover of modernity. Niall Ferguson eulogizes the impact of "Anglobalization," understood as the "history of globalization as it was promoted by Great Britain and her colonies."[9] He assures us that spreading capitalist institutions and liberal politics around the world, by force if necessary, has brought incalculable

5. "Father of Union Now," *Scribner's Commentary*, June 1941, 81. The movement started with Clarence Streit, *Union Now* (New York, 1939). On Streit, see Rosenboim, *Emergence of Globalism*, 114–21; Bell, *Reordering*, ch. 8. The political scientist George Catlin offered an alternative vision to Streit, focusing on Anglo-American union and grounded in an account of the cultural unity of "Anglo-Saxony." For a discussion, see Daniel Gorman, "George Catlin, the Science of Politics, and Anglo-American Union," *Modern Intellectual History*, 15/1 (2018), 123–52.

6. Stephen Wertheim, *Tomorrow, the World* (Cambridge, MA, 2020), ch. 2.

7. Richard Toye, *Churchill's Empire* (Basingstoke, 2010), 240–41. On the highly critical African-American reaction to Churchill's post-Second World War calls for an Anglo-American alliance, see Clive Webb, "Reluctant Partners," *Journal of Transatlantic Studies*, 14/4 (2016), 350–64.

8. Winston Churchill, "If Lee Had Not Won the Battle of Gettysburg" (1930), *Wisconsin Magazine of History*, 44/4 (1961), 250. On counterfactual narratives, see Catherine Gallagher, *Telling It Like It Wasn't* (Chicago, 2018).

9. Niall Ferguson, *Empire* (London, 2003), xxiv.

benefits to humanity. Planet-spanning associations once again fired the imagination, unleashing expressions of excitement, hope, skepticism, and horror. The idea of the "Anglosphere" gained popularity in the late 1990s and continues to attract support, albeit limited, in the countries it claims to embrace.[10] Moreover, the campaign to extricate Britain from the European Union spawned a reheated variant of imperial federation, with the emergence of a project to integrate Canada, Australia, New Zealand, and the United Kingdom (CANZUK).[11] Its boosters see this as a venture that fits neatly under a broad Anglosphere canopy, the United States and CANZUK constituting the two branches of a gigantic economic and geopolitical bloc. Contemporary unionists share much in common with their predecessors, not least a belief in the fundamental unity of the English colonial diaspora and the superiority of its political, economic, and cultural institutions, but they usually lack the support base, the full integrationist agenda, and the utopian ambitions of earlier iterations. Mark Mazower is correct to suggest that "[t]he idea of governing the world is becoming yesterday's dream."[12]

Rather than tracking these Angloworld fantasies across the twentieth century and beyond, this concluding chapter steers a different course, reflecting on some of the ways that time and history have underpinned visions of Anglo-America. The discourse of racial union was usually predicated on a specific account of both space and historical temporality. The chosen people—whether designated Aryan, Teutonic, Anglo-Saxon, or English-speaking—was imagined as superior to all others, their greatness ordained by their unique historical trajectory and extant racial characteristics. They had been, and remained, the pioneers of human progress. This historical story produced a stratified global geography: the vanguard of modern humanity was concentrated in specific places, chiefly Britain and its past and present settler colonies in North America and the South Pacific. In teleological fashion, it was often asserted that the United States constituted, or would soon constitute, the apex of this historical arc. The discourses that I analyze in the following pages disrupt and reorient these spatiotemporal assumptions, positing alternative conceptions of past, present, and future.

10. For an example, see James Bennett, *The Anglosphere Challenge* (Lanham, 2004). On the idea, see Vucetic, *Anglosphere*; Michael Kenny and Nick Pearce, *Shadows of Empire* (Cambridge, 2018); Andrew Mycock and Ben Wellings (eds.), *The Anglosphere* (Oxford, 2020).

11. Bell and Vucetic, "Brexit, CANZUK, and the Legacy of Empire"; Bell, "Anglospheres" in Mycock and Wellings, *The Anglosphere*, 38–55.

12. Mazower, *Governing the World*, 427. For a discussion of maximalist exceptions, who see CANZUK as a nascent polity, see Bell and Vucetic, "Brexit."

I turn first to a popular body of speculative fiction published during the late twentieth century and into the new millennium, focusing especially on the "neo-Victorian" reworking of Anglo-America. "Steampunk" writing in particular redefined, revised, or subverted many of the foundational myths and historiographical claims that pervade the racial utopian discourse. This transtemporal staging exemplifies how, as Tom Gunning puts it, the "two ends of the Twentieth Century hail each other like long lost twins."[13] The second half of the chapter returns to the fin de siècle. *Dreamworlds of Race* has anatomized a specific articulation of transnational white supremacism. The final words in the book are given to some of those excluded from its ambit. The tradition of political thinking that Robert Gooding-Williams's terms "Afro-modern" addresses the "political and social organization of white supremacy, the nature and effects of racial ideologies, and the possibilities of black emancipation."[14] Although Afro-modern writers prior to the First World War rarely addressed the prospect of Anglo-American union, they had much to say about Anglo-Saxonist ideology and its pernicious effects, and many of them, including Du Bois and Scholes, illuminated and rebutted justifications of racial superiority. I conclude by discussing some of their ideas about race and empire. While the steampunk literature renarrates the history of Anglo-modernity by erasing the primacy of the United States, Afro-modernists sought to destabilize the historical validation of racial domination, clearing the ground for imagining alternative futures.

Ghosts of Empire: Steampunk Geopolitics

[H]istory was malleable, time a fiction.[15]

(JOHN CROWLEY)

Fin-de-siècle speculative writers imagined a plethora of competing and contrasting future worlds. The dreams of Anglo-American union that I have examined contributed to this feverish interrogation of "futurity." While the prophetic timelines adopted by the authors varied, many of those thinking the future predicted (or hoped) that the main building blocks of Anglo-America would be in place by the end of the twentieth century. Theirs was a millennial

---

13. Tom Gunning, "Re-Newing Old Technologies" in David Thorburn and Henry Jenkins (eds.), *Rethinking Media Change* (Cambridge, MA, 2003), 51. On the "dialectical relationship" between the nineteenth century and the present, see also Clayton, *Charles Dickens in Cyberspace*; Aris Mousoutzanis, *Fin-de-Siècle Fictions, 1890s–1990s* (Basingstoke, 2014).

14. Robert Gooding-Williams, *In the Shadow of Du Bois* (Cambridge, MA, 2009), 3.

15. John Crowley, *The Great Work of Time* (1989; New York, 1991), 66.

project in both its ambition and its timing. Carnegie thought that one hundred years was a feasible horizon for full integration, while Rhodes mused about "union with America and universal peace, I mean after one hundred years." By then, the imperial federation of Vogel's *Anno Domini 2000* had been firmly established for several decades, and the New England states were on the brink of reincorporation into the British Empire. Wells predicted that the synthetic New Republic would be fully operational by the year 2000.[16]

Turning to the end of the twentieth century, we find a world that would have struck them as both familiar and utterly alien. They were correct to predict that Britain would be overtaken by the United States, and they would have applauded the so-called "special relationship," even if its loosely institutionalized form would have disappointed the more ambitious among them. They would also have recognized assorted projects for redrawing the geopolitical landscape. Contemporary Anglo-unionists, their lineal heirs, are still promoting the integration of the Angloworld. Some of the most influential of them have followed in the footsteps of their Victorian predecessors by utilizing the narrative possibilities of science fiction. The American businessman and writer James Bennett borrowed the term "Anglosphere," which he subsequently helped to popularize, from a science fiction novel, Neal Stephenson's *The Diamond Age*.[17] More recently he has sketched a vision of the future, "A Day in the Life of the Union 2036," in making his case for CANZUK.[18] During the 1990s, Andrew Roberts, a devotee of the Anglosphere, penned a dystopian novel set in 2045 to warn against the purported totalitarian dangers of European integration.[19] The eminent poet and historian Robert Conquest described his proposed "Anglosphere Alliance"—an earlier variant of which was endorsed by Margaret Thatcher in 1999—as a "work of political and cultural science fiction."[20] This was no throwaway remark. A member of the British Interplanetary Society since the 1940s, Conquest had a long-standing interest

16. Carnegie to Balfour, 1903 [n.d.], Fol 97, Carnegie papers; Rhodes to Stead, 19 August 1891, Rhodes papers; Vogel, *Anno Domini 2000*; Wells, *Anticipations*, ch. 8.

17. Bennett, *Anglosphere Challenge*. He acknowledges the debt in "The Anglosphere as the Big Somewhere," *Quadrant Online*, 27 September 2018.

18. James Bennett, *A Time for Audacity* (Washington, DC, 2016).

19. Andrew Roberts, *The Aachen Memorandum* (London, 1995). See also Roberts, "I Lay Claim to the Title 'Nostradamus of the Right,'" *Daily Telegraph*, 22 April 2004. Roberts has also advocated CANZUK.

20. Robert Conquest, "An Anglosphere in the Neosphere (A Political Exercise)" in Conquest, *The Dragons of Expectation* (New York, 2005), 222. See also Margaret Thatcher, "The Language of Liberty," Speech to the English-Speaking Union, 7 December 1999, https://www.margaretthatcher.org/document/108386.

in science fiction.[21] While many Anglosphere boosters do not engage in such genre-hopping exercises, it is striking that several of the leading advocates of the idea have drawn inspiration, concepts, and narrative techniques from speculative literature. As with their fin-de-siècle predecessors, they see the line between fiction and fact, theoretical argumentation and literary elaboration, as at once permeable and politically generative. They are attentive to the motive force of the imagination, and of speculative world-building, as a perspicacious mode of persuasion.

Proponents of the Anglosphere were not the only ones reprising earlier speculative imaginaries. During the late twentieth century, a substantial body of "neo-Victorian" writing scoured the nineteenth century for creative (even ethico-political) inspiration, and fabricated counterfactual worlds in which the British Empire retained a predominant role. This discourse—which falls under the capacious umbrella of "steampunk"—has staged an intriguing confrontation with the imperial legacies of the Victorian age. Kate Mitchell argues that neo-Victorian writings can be seen as "memory-texts," performances of the past that actively shape our vision of it.[22] In the following pages, I discuss some of the most popular of these memory-texts, focusing in particular on how they configure Anglo-America. Most contributors to fin-de-siècle (re)-unionist debate sought to decenter Britain, imagining the country either as a junior partner in a future racial union or subsuming it within an expanding United States. It was a commonplace that Britain would cede its leadership of the Angloworld: the future was Anglo-*American*. The neo-Victorians, by contrast, repeatedly demote the United States to the margins, confining it to geopolitical irrelevance. This constitutes a deliberate erasure, a spatiotemporal rupture that carves the Anglo from Anglo-America and rewrites the trajectory of the modern world. Excising (maybe exorcising) the long-predicted rise to global supremacy of the United States offers a way of picturing alternatives to our present—it is an *un-American* vision of Anglo-modernity—as well as illuminating the historical choices and moments that produced our current reality.

Steampunk is best defined, according to Jess Nevins, as a "spectrum of constitutive tropes and motifs rather than a coherent and discrete literary subgenre."[23] Claiming Wells as a key source of inspiration, steampunk writers celebrate their debts to and immersion in Victorian history and aesthetics.

---

21. Early in his career he published a science fiction novel, *A World of Difference* (1955), as well as co-editing several science fiction anthologies with Kinglsey Amis.

22. Kate Mitchell, *History and Cultural Memory in Neo-Victorian Fiction* (Basingstoke, 2010).

23. Jess Nevins, "Prescriptivists vs. Descriptivists," *Science Fiction Studies*, 38/3 (2011), 517.

Now encompassing a wide array of geographic and historical locations, as well as music, art, and design, it has morphed into a vibrant subculture.[24] Literary scholars and cultural theorists have been drawn to steampunk because of its willingness to collapse the boundaries between historical fact and speculative fiction. Indeed, it is often seen as exemplifying a postmodernist conception of temporality, with history treated as a palimpsest, "not linear, but layered, recursive, branching, conjectural, and algorithmic."[25] The relationship between past, present, and future is enthusiastically reengineered, with arresting juxtapositions and consciously anachronistic world-building disclosing the elusive nature of historical time, the importance of contingency, and the vexed nature of representation. Rather than a project of archaeological discovery and mimetic reproduction, history becomes a source of creative insight and perceptual disruption. But steampunk has other valences. It forms, Elizabeth Ho argues, "a highly visible, highly aestheticized code for confronting empire again and anew; it is a site within which the memory of empire and its surrounding discourses and strategies of representation can be replayed and played out."[26] Whether intentionally or not, it is a way of thinking with and against the ghosts of empire.

It is sometimes claimed that steampunk was formulated originally as a critique of Victorian social and political norms. In this vein, Christine Ferguson suggests that its trailblazers adopted the "framework of alternative history to explicitly condemn nineteenth- and twentieth century systems of power and domination. Fantastical in plot and ontology, their socio-political targets are nonetheless unmistakable and relatively unambiguous."[27] However, there are no intrinsic steampunk normative commitments: much of it is politically nebulous, and both white supremacists and postcolonial writers have sought

24. Rachel A. Bowser and Brian Croxall (eds.), *Like Clockwork* (Minneapolis, 2016); Claire Nally, *Steampunk* (London, 2019); Jess Nevins, "Introduction" in Ann and Jeff VanderMeer (eds.), *Steampunk* (San Francisco, 2008), 1–12. Note that my claims about steampunk are limited to a set of prominent texts, not the genre as a whole. Recent steampunk writers, in particular, have moved beyond the British Empire to encompass a wide range of historical and geographical references.

25. Roger Whitson, *Steampunk and Nineteenth-Century Digital Humanities* (Abingdon, 2016), 191. On steampunk conceptions of history, see also Margaret Rose, "Extraordinary Pasts," *Journal of the Fantastic in the Arts*, 20/3 (2009), 319–33; Patrick Jagoda, "Clacking Control Societies," *Neo-Victorian Studies*, 3/1 (2010), 46–71; Steffen Hantke, "Difference Engines and Other Infernal Devices," *Extrapolation*, 40/3 (1999), 244–54; Shannon Lee Dawdy, "Clockpunk Anthropology and the Ruins of Modernity," *Current Anthropology*, 51/6 (2010), 761–93.

26. Elizabeth Ho, *Neo-Victorianism and the Memory of Empire* (London, 2011), 5.

27. Christine Ferguson, "Surface Tensions," *Neo-Victorian Studies*, 4/2 (2011), 73.

to harness its imagery and ambitions for their own purposes.[28] Some steam-punk authors do regard the genre as providing a platform for sociopolitical critique. The aim behind the politically engaged strands of the genre is cap-tured in the title of an interview with novelist Paul Di Filippo: "Democratising the Past to Improve the Future." "At its best," he maintains, "steampunk fiction promotes understanding of the roots of our current global scene, and offers lateral insights as to how we could improve retroactively on some of the choices we made, all unknowing, in the path of technological development."[29] It offers the possibility of rethinking time and history, tracing alternative paths through the modern world and into the present.

In 1971, Michael Moorcock, a leading British "new wave" science fiction writer, published *The Warlord of the Air*, a novel that is often read as a founda-tional steampunk text.[30] With playful wit and political punch, he crafted a counterfactual twentieth century in which the British Empire, knitted together by a fleet of magnificent airships, continues to rule the waves. Subtitled "A Scientific Romance," the resonance with fin-de-siècle science fiction is pal-pable and deliberate. "Probably been reading a bit too much H. G. Wells, eh?" asks one of the characters.[31] The world of 1973 is dominated by immense empires, the British controlling much of the planet, the Russians and Japanese administering the bulk of China, while the Americans, an empire in denial, claim the title of "Greater American Commonwealth" for their territories in Cuba, Panama, the Philippines, Vietnam, Korea, Taiwan, and Hawaii. British officials boast that their ostensibly liberal imperial order guarantees global peace and stability. "You could give me a brief outline of history since 1902,"

28. For some of the critiques, as well as a discussion of how postcolonial forms of steampunk have sought to overcome them, see Diana Pho, "Punking the Other" in Bowser and Croxall, *Like Clockwork*, 127–52.

29. Lisa Yaszek, "Democratising the Past to Improve the Future," *Neo-Victorian Studies*, 3/1 (2010), 190. Democratization is achieved (supposedly) by "[r]emoving technology from the exclusive hands of scientists and researchers and autocrats" (190).

30. Michael Moorcock, *The Warlord of the Air* (1971; London, 2013). It is "the genre's incep-tive text": Ferguson, "Surface Tensions," 73.

31. Moorcock, *Warlord*, 65. Wells makes two other appearances (182, 214–15). Reflecting on the book two decades later, Moorcock professed his admiration for Wells, while acknowledging that his own anarchism underwrote a different set of commitments. He preferred the politics of Kropotkin, "that most kindly of anarchist intellectuals." Moorcock, "Dear Reader" (1993), *Warlord*, 12. Moorcock was clear that the text was (in part) an "homage" to Edwardian adventure literature (13). During the 1970s, he assembled the first anthology of future-war narratives: Moorcock (ed.), *England Invaded* (London, 1977). On Moorcock, see Colin Greenland, *Entropy Exhibition* (London, 1983).

the time-traveling Bengal Lancer Oswald Bastable suggests to the pointedly named Major Enoch Powell, a British military officer assigned to look after him. "He shrugged. 'Nothing much has happened really. Seventy Years of glorious peace, all in all. Damned dull,'" comes the reply. For Bastable, the *Pax Britannica* appears, initially at least, as a glorious "vision of Utopia," a world at peace overseen by a benevolent British imperium.[32] "How those Victorians would have loved to see all this," Powell muses: "[a]ll their ideals and dreams realized so fully."[33] But nemesis awaits. A motley group of revolutionaries, led by the Anglo-Chinese warlord General O. T. Shaw, and including Vladimir Ilyitch Ulianov, a lightly fictionalized Lenin, launches a campaign of violent resistance against the imperial powers, sparking worldwide revolt. Written as the war in Vietnam raged, the novel stages, then undercuts, the familiar fantasy of empire as a guarantor of peace, stability, and progress.

The Difference Engine, published in 1990, remains the best-known steampunk text. Written by William Gibson and Bruce Sterling, the novel imagines a nineteenth-century world shaped by an explosive information revolution. The discoveries of Charles Babbage—above all his Analytical Engine—galvanize rebellion at home and geopolitical expansion abroad. In the 1820s, the "Industrial Radicals," headed by Lord Byron, overthrow the traditional landed aristocracy, survive a coup by Wellington, and repress a violent Luddite insurgency, before establishing a government ideologically committed to scientific rationalism, social progress, and meritocratic rule. In a picture Wells would have appreciated, the midcentury imperial state is headed by the "Industrial Lords": Babbage, Brunel, Darwin, Engels, Galton, and Huxley among them. Following the death of Byron, Brunel becomes Prime Minister, his position threatened briefly by the sinister Galton, an arch-eugenicist who endorses the "systematic breeding of the human species," before the menace is neutralized by Oliphant, a syphilitic secret agent.[34] This is no shiny utopia. Although the governing elite has been replaced, the class structure below remains largely intact, and the ruthless "Industrial Rads" have constructed a totalizing surveillance system—an all-seeing "Eye"—utilizing the computational power of the Central Statistical Bureau.[35] Social inequality, poverty, and suffering are

---

32. Moorcock, *Warlord*, 76.

33. Moorcock, *Warlord*, 88, 74, 73, 76.

34. William Gibson and Bruce Sterling, *The Difference Engine* (1990; London, 2011), 341. The novel adopts several themes and characters from Disraeli's *Sybil, or the Two Nations* (1845).

35. Gibson and Sterling, *Difference Engine*, 310. See also Catherine Siemann, "The Steampunk City in Crisis" in Bowser and Croxall, *Like Clockwork*, 51–70; Herbert Sussman, "Cyberpunk Meets Charles Babbage," *Victorian Studies*, 38/1 (1994), 1–23; Nicholas Spencer, "Rethinking Ambivalence," *Contemporary Literature*, 40/3 (1999), 403–29.

ubiquitous. As with late nineteenth-century tales of future war, the novel re-writes both the geography and the historical trajectory of global order. London continues to rule over a planet-straddling empire, though there are some no-table differences. It is Britain that "opens" Japan to Western "civilisation," the Irish famine is averted, and the United States is divided into fragile cantons: the Confederate States, French Mexico, the Republics of California and Texas. Karl Marx oversees a communard revolutionary state in New York City.[36] The novel culminates with intimations of a posthuman future, as an artificial intel-ligence system originally designed by Ada Lovelace, rogue mathematical ge-nius, comes to consciousness—an eye that "at last must see itself"[37]—in 1991. Britain is reinscribed as the principal agent of an imperial world ordering proj-ect and (possibly) as the terminal hegemonic human power. The emergent technoscientific system portends the true end of history.

These two novels present contrasting visions of Anglo-modernity. In Moor-cock's tale, the United States never rose to global dominance, and it is normal-ized as a second-rank power, albeit one that seems unwilling to admit to its own imperial ambitions or form. Gibson and Sterling, by contrast, decompose the United States, fracturing it into competing polities that become the site for great power interference and intervention, a playground for a European impe-rial great game. In both cases, it is the British who benefit from this historical rerouting, the speculative world-building premised on the longevity of their imperial supremacy.

The dissolution of the United States finds its most extreme manifestation in another popular steampunk novel, S. M. Stirling's *The Peshawar Lancers*, which appeared in 2002. It is set largely in the year 2025, as King-Emperor John II rules over half of humanity. But this is empire with a difference. In Octo-ber 1878, a volley of comets had devastated the Northern hemisphere, killing millions in firestorms and tsunamis. Cold and famine claim tens of millions more in the following years, until Prime Minister Disraeli lead an "exodus" of the surviving British elite to northern India. Ninety percent of the British population was wiped out, with an even higher proportion of Americans suf-fering the same fate. Following this cataclysmic "Fall"—an appellation reso-nant with both biblical and historical meanings—the empire was gradually rebuilt, with India at its core and the Cape and Australia comprising its other main zones. The transplanted British population slowly absorbed and re-worked Indian culture, their language, dress, and religion all assuming new

36. Gibson and Sterling, *Difference Engine*, 303–4.
37. Gibson and Sterling, *Difference Engine*, 383.

hybrid forms. The "Angrezi Raj" emerged, a new Anglo empire born from the ruins of the old.

Throughout Stirling's novel, British imperial power is valorized: its ability to survive and eventually thrive—albeit in radically modified form—is figured as a marker of fortitude, skill, and audacity. The characterization recalls the celebratory adventure tales of the late Victorian empire, with the story following the exploits of an archetypal square-jawed hero, Athelstane King, a man who could have escaped from the pages of a Rider Haggard novel. He ventriloquizes the commonplaces of nineteenth-century imperial ideology. At one point he recounts the dream of imperial peace. "The Gods knew the Empire had its faults, but what was it *for*, if not the Imperial peace that held half mankind in order under the rule of law."[38] The geopolitical maneuverings mirror fin-de-siècle invasion literature, with British power challenged by the belligerent Russians and "Dai-Nippon," an empire originating in Japan but headquartered in Peking. Across the twentieth century, the new-old empire fights off assorted rebellions and slowly develops an industrial civilization, as what was once Europe and the United States descend deeper into "barbarism," with nomadic bands of cannibals roving across the shattered cities and denuded landscape. Efforts to "re-colonise" them meet with limited success. Britain, with a population of six and a half million, becomes a "Crown Colony" lacking representation in the Imperial Parliament in Delhi. The political dissolution of America is absolute: "The Empire claimed the whole of the North American continent."[39] In practice, we are informed, this meant that the Angrezi Raj exerted control over a handful of tenuous ports and trading posts, as most of the continent was empty. Sterling annihilates the United States, terminating both its population and its sociopolitical existence. The spatial shift of the imperial center to Asia is reminiscent of Vogel's reformatting of British imperial power in *Anno Domini 2000*, although in *The Peshawar Lancers* London is no gleaming center of opulent depravity, but rather an eviscerated shell, as if waiting for the "New Zealander" to sketch it.

The future is also a site for neo-Victorian appropriation. A baroque, wildly imaginative mediation on the revolutionary implications of nanotech, Stephenson's *The Diamond Age* dissolves the boundaries between human and machine.[40] It is set in an uncanny geopolitical terrain, at once familiar and

38. S. M. Stirling, *The Peshawar Lancers* (New York, 2002), 314.

39. Stirling, *Peshawar Lancers*, 471.

40. Neil Stephenson, *The Diamond Age: Or, A Young Lady's Illustrated Primer* (1995; London, 2011). For readings of the novel, see Stefania Forlini, "Technology and Morality," *Neo-Victorian Studies*, 3/1 (2010), 72–98; Peter Brigg, "The Future of the Past Viewed from the Present," *Extrapolation*, 40/2 (1999), 116–24. *The Diamond Age* has generated criticisms similar to those

alien, a possible future haunted by the ghosts of empires past. The story unfolds in and around twenty-second-century Shanghai. The proliferation of
nanotech has eliminated traditional forms of territoriality, and humanity is
divided between "phyles" bound by religious beliefs, political ideologies, ethnicity, or lifestyle choice, rather than traditional sovereign states. The members
of the "neo-Morrisite" phyle, for example, are dedicated to the production of
beautiful artifacts. "New Atlantis," "Nippon," and "Han" dominate the new
world order, though the New Atlanteans, due to their control of nanotech
infrastructure, are the most powerful phyle. They are committed to a "neo-
Victorian" ideology that seeks to replicate Victorian manners and mores, an
orientation motivated in part by the belief that moral relativism contributed
to social collapse at the end of the twentieth century. (The "Anglosphere" is
mentioned in passing in a description of New Atlantis.)[41] "Some cultures
were simply better than others," intones one of their leaders. "This was not a
subjective value judgment, merely an observation that some cultures thrived
and expanded while others failed."[42] The neo-Victorians live by this conviction, just as their forebears supposedly did. While Stephenson's picture of
future geopolitics has been interpreted as the "conquest of geography over
history," the past—and in particular nineteenth-century imperialism—is omnipresent. The center of gravity for world history has moved East, upending
the nineteenth-century narrative of the westward directionality of civilization,
but rather than the Chinese or Japanese being the main beneficiaries, it is the
descendants of the western states, intent on exploiting and subordinating the
Han and Nipponese in a nanotech rerun of the Opium Wars. Stephenson
eradicates the Angloworld from the map of the world, though its deterritorial-
ized heir furnishes the ideological and technological basis for a postsovereign
phyle.[43] Once again the imperial past is decentered, only to be rearticulated
in a different form.

There are also some direct connections between late twentieth-century
speculative fiction and the literature of racial union. Part metaphysical reflection on temporality, part adventure story, John Crowley's *The Great Work of
Time* appeared as the Cold War fizzled out. It utilizes Rhodes's utopic *Last Will
and Testament* as raw material for rewriting the twentieth century. In an

---

leveled at cyberpunk, notably for its depiction of China: Greta Aiyu Niu, "Techno-Orientalism,
Nanotechnology, Posthumans, and Post-Posthumanism," *MELUS*, 33/4 (2008), 73–96; Michael
Longan and Tim Oakes, "Geography's Conquest of History in *The Diamond Age*" in Rob Kitchin
and James Kneal (eds.), *Lost in Space* (London, 2002), 39–56.

41. Stephenson, *Diamond Age*, 410.

42. Stephenson, *Diamond Age*, 20–21.

43. Ho, *Neo-Victorianism*, 156–57.

"Afterword," Crowley acknowledges his debt to the historical work of Jan Morris, crediting her with opening up "a world more fantastical than any he could himself invent."[44] The book opens in Wellsian mode with a reclusive mathematical genius inventing a time machine, which is soon hijacked by a secret society of British imperialists, the mysterious Otherhood. "[S]ort of Jesuits of the Empire," these time-traveling avatars are the proud upholders of Rhodes's vanguardist dream.[45] "The stories you have heard are true. Cecil Rhodes, at his death, left his entire fortune, and its increase, to found and continue a secret society, which should, by whatever means possible, preserve and extend the British Empire."[46] The Otherhood uses the machine to interfere repeatedly in history. Composed of "men and women who by some means could insert themselves into the stream of the past, and with their foreknowledge alter it, and thus alter the future of that past, the future in which they themselves had their original being," they halt the First and Second Worlds Wars and bring peace to the world. But there is a heavy cost to be paid.

Dennis Winterset, a thrusting young officer in the Colonial Service, is recruited to the Society.[47] Sir Geoffrey Davenant, a senior Otherhood Fellow, informs him that Rhodes often talked of his cosmic ambitions. "He wanted the world for England. And more. 'The moon, too,' he used to say. 'I often think of the Moon.'"[48] In this parallel world—or series of branching, parallel worlds—Rhodes's original vision of racial purity has been superseded. As one Fellow comments, "The most disagreeable thing about old Rhodes and the empire of his day was its racialism, of course. Absolutely unworkable, too. Nothing more impossible to sustain than a world order based on some race's inherent superiority."[49] Yet all is not well among the imperial time-lords. They are permitted to travel back no further than 1893, when (in the initial part

---

44. Crowley, *Great Work*, 135. He cites Morris's *Pax Britannica* (1968) and *Farewell the Trumpets* (1978), as well as Gertrude Millin's *Cecil Rhodes* (1933). The latter was also a source for Hannah Arendt's discussion of Rhodes in *The Origins of Totalitarianism*.

45. The quote is from Crowley, *Great Work*, 63.

46. Crowley, *Great Work*, 25, 26, 27.

47. Crowley paints a perfect miniportrait of Winterset, "exactly the sort of man who was chosen, or who chose himself, to serve the Empire in those years—a respectable second at Oxford, a cricketer more steady than showy, a reserved, sensible, presentable lad with sound principles and few beliefs": Crowley, *Great Work*, 13.

48. Crowley, *Great Work*, 64. This captures his ambition. "I would annex the planets if I could; I often think of that. It makes me sad to see them so clear and yet so far." Rhodes, *Last Will*, 190.

49. Crowley, *Great Work*, 66.

of the story) Rhodes died, but something appears to have gone wrong.[50] Winterset is ordered to return to the "Original Situation" and kill Rhodes to stop him changing his bequest to endow scholarships in Oxford, thereby dissolving the Society by aborting its creation. "[W]e must send our agents down along the defiles of time and intercept our own grandfather there, at the very moment when he is about to turn away from the work of generating us."[51] Winterset meets Rhodes in a simulacrum of Groote Schuur. At one point, he later recalls, "Rhodes contended—no one disputed him—that if we (he meant the Empire, of course) had not lost America, the peace of the world could have been secured forever. 'Forever,' he said. 'Perpetual Peace.' And his pale opaque eyes were moist."[52] The United States plays a double role in *The Great Work of Time*. It recedes into the background in the world where Rhodes's Will reached fruition, subordinate once more to the British Empire triumphant, while in the "real" history that Crowley interweaves with the parallel worlds, a chastened, time-stranded Winterer informs us, from the late twentieth century, that "we are all Americans now, aren't we."[53] The counterfactual British-centric world is replaced with something closer to the truth of Anglo-American relations.

These texts also explore the meaning and possible implications of utopian politics. In *The Warlord of the Air*, the imperial dream is exposed as a sham, its benefits accruing principally to the dominant powers and its continuation dependent on the violent repression of dissent and resistance. But General Shaw's alternative egalitarian order also leads to mass killing. The global rebellion, animated by Ulianov's catechism that utopian ends justify violent means, culminates with the atomic incineration of Hiroshima.[54] Even though the latter model of society might be preferable to the former, and Moorcock's anti-imperial sympathies are clear, neither is bloodless. Indeed, the ambiguous ending of the novel leaves the question of utopian desire unresolved. Toward the end of *The Great Work of Time*, Davenent, by then "President *pro tem*" of the Otherhood, travels far into the future to discover what the imperial missionaries have wrought. He is confronted by a scene of metaphysical horror, a world wracked by ontological instability, its form ruptured by each alteration of the past—beings, buildings, whole cities flicker in and out of existence. This transmogrifying zone is inhabited by various species, including orphic Angels

50. Crowley, *Great Work*, 61–62.
51. Crowley, *Great Work*, 73.
52. Crowley, *Great Work*, 117.
53. Crowley, *Great Work*, 1.
54. Moorcock, *Warlord*, ch. 7.

who feel exquisite pain from the changes rippling across time, "like the snap of a whip infinitely long." The imperial ambition to create global peace and stability had catalyzed its antithesis. "It was true: this is what they had striven for: a world of perfect hierarchies, of no change forever. God, how they must have longed for it!"[55] An Angel asks Davenant to put them out of their misery, intimating a final decline and fall, the terminal dissolution—and unintended consummation—of the dreams of empire embodied in the Society and Rhodes's Will. As the flux intensifies, so ultimately the world will "sicken and fail." "I shall tell you what I see at the end of all your wishings," said the Angel.

> At the far end of the last changed world, after there is nothing left that can change. There is then only a forest, growing in the sea. . . . The sea is still and the forest is thick; it grows upward from the black bottom, and its topmost branches reach into the sunlight, which penetrates a little into the warm upper waters. That's all. There is nothing else anywhere forever. Your wishes have come true: the Empire is quiet. There is not, nor will there be, change anymore; never will one thing be confused again with another, higher for lower, better for lesser, master for servant. Perpetual Peace.[56]

There is a powerful echo of Wells's Time Traveller here, glimpsing the world thirty million years in the future, the heat death of the sun slowly eliminating life on earth. "Overhead it was a deep Indian red and starless, and southeastward it grew brighter to a glowing scarlet where, cut by the horizon, lay the huge hull of the sun, red and motionless."[57] Yet there is also an important difference. For Crowley, the end of the world is marked by stasis, while for Wells natural selection is still playing out: change is occurring even as life is extinguished. What unites them is the final eradication of a form of life. Davenant grants the request to "put out this world like a light" by stopping Winterset from assassinating Rhodes, collapsing the branching universe back into our own singular history—a world in which Perpetual Peace remains utopian fantasy and the United States a dominant power.

By destabilizing linear renderings of time and space, these neo-Victorian memory-texts challenge two of the constitutive assumptions underpinning the imperial and racial ideologies of the period they reimagine. The unionists often postulated a conception of history that saw racial formations as the chief agents of sociopolitical development, and identified the "English race" as the motor of civilizational progress. But many of them, and especially those

55. Crowley, *Great Work*, 101–2.
56. Crowley, *Great Work*, 102.
57. H. G. Wells, *The Time Machine* (1895; London, 2005), 82.

committed to Teutonism, also made a spatial claim: history moved in a westward direction, its key point of departure located either thousands of years ago in the Indo-Ayran spaces of Asia or, more proximately, in the medieval forest clearings of Germany. In the modern era, Britain had been the principal home for the race, nourishing its development and spreading it across the world through commerce and colonization. In a continuation of the long history of westward movement, the United States was beginning to assume the leadership role. It would drive the further development of humanity. Scrambling this framing of human history, the steampunk texts I have discussed recode the spatiotemporal coordinates of industrial modernity, though without transcending or rejecting them.

Peoples Irreverent toward Time: Afro-modernism contra White Supremacy

Yet here we are.[58]

(COLSON WHITEHEAD)

Dreams of Anglo-unionism were bounded by the global color line. The understanding of race as a biocultural assemblage—whether couched in the language of Anglo-Saxonism, the English-speaking-people, or the English race—almost always precluded the incorporation of those not racialized white. The late nineteenth century witnessed the spread of transnational visions of white supremacism, the intensification of antiblack racism under the Jim Crow regime of terror, and the extension of imperial conquest and control by European powers and the United States. These conjoined developments prompted widespread reflection on, and growing resistance to, what Du Bois termed the "religion of whiteness."[59] Intellectuals and activists mobilized to fight injustice and challenge the ideological architecture of racial domination. People, texts, and ideas circulated through the fragile communications networks of what Marina Bilbija calls the "Black Anglosphere," a globe-straddling zone of contact and intellectual exchange that incorporated the Black Atlantic while extending beyond it to encompass thinkers throughout the United States and the British Empire.[60] At once a space of resistance and a

---

58. Colson Whitehead, *The Underground Railroad* (2016; London, 2017), 341.

59. Du Bois, "The Souls of White Folk," in *Writings*, II, 26.

60. Bilbija, *Worlds of Color*, unpublished manuscript (2019). "The conditions of possibility for the Black Anglosphere were the material medium of the periodical and the shared linguistic medium of English" (ch. 4). Cf. Paul Gilroy, *The Black Atlantic* (London, 1993).

manifestation of the power dynamics perpetuating racial hierarchies, the Black Anglosphere was shaped by the technological infrastructure that aided domination while offering a vital transoceanic communications network for activists and thinkers to challenge the unjust system. A primary goal of late nineteenth-century Afro-modern thinkers was the excavation and critique of racial ideologies used to legitimate the subordination of peoples of color. The writer, editor, and activist T. Thomas Fortune, founder of the short-lived Afro-American League, was among the most high-profile critics of racial ideology, penning fierce attacks on white supremacy and charting the political economy of racial violence.[61] In her classic *A Voice from the South: By a Black Woman of the South*, the philosopher and campaigner Anna Julia Cooper made the case for the importance of African-American women in the project of racial emancipation, contending that they possessed special epistemic insight into the nature of oppression and could thus play a vital role in confronting it.[62] John Edward Bruce, who wrote under the pen-name "Bruce Grit," was one of the most prominent black journalists of the time. Two years before Josiah Strong published *Our Country*, his extended love poem to the Anglo-Saxons, Bruce delivered a speech in Washington entitled "Is This Our Country?" He scorned the idea that black Americans could or should claim membership. "Our Country! Oh, what a mockery, what a farce! What a delusion! What a lie!" Until equal rights and equal treatment were secured, the country would continue to belong to others. "It will never be our country until every living being of every race and nationality within its vast borders is secure in his or her civil and political rights." There was little room for optimism.[63] He was also scathing about the "White Man's Burden." Such an encumbrance, Bruce declaimed in 1910, is "largely of his own making," and if only he would "attend strictly to his own business and permit other people to attend to theirs, his burden would not be so large and so heavy." But the white man "has an obsession," Bruce continued, "which leads him to believe that God has called him to assist Him in ruling

---

61. For a valuable collection of his writings, see Shawn Leigh Alexander (ed.), *T. Thomas Fortune, the Afro-American Agitator* (Gainesville, 2008). On Fortune's thought, see Tommy Curry, "The Fortune of Wells," *Transactions of the Charles S. Peirce Society*, 48/4 (2012), 456–82; Emma Lou Thornbrough, *T. Thomas Fortune* (Chicago, 1972).

62. Anna Cooper, *A Voice from the South* (Xenia, 1892). On her political thinking, see Joy James, *The Talented Tenth* (Abingdon, 1997), ch. 2; Vivian M. May, *Anna Julia Cooper, Visionary Black Feminist* (Abingdon, 2007).

63. John Bruce, "Is This Our Country?" (1883), in *The Selected Writings of John Edward Bruce*, ed. Peter Gilbert (New York, 1971), 23, 24. For a pessimistic assessment of race relations in the United States, see Bruce, "The Negro and His Future" (c.1900), in *Selected Writings*, 59–60. On Bruce, see Ralph Crowder, *John Edward Bruce* (New York, 2004).

and governing other peoples and is so filled with this conceit that he imagines that races alien to his own know nothing of civilization or the science of government."[64] According to Bruce, each race/nation had a God-given destiny to fulfill, and it was a form of blasphemy to interfere with it. A time of reckoning was long overdue.

Bruce's argument highlights one of the central themes in fin-de-siècle Afro-modern thought: the reclamation and celebration of black historical experience. As white racial utopians contended that the past offered definitive evidence of Anglo-Saxon superiority, authors across the Black Anglo-sphere sought to recover and disseminate a counter-history, one that acknowledged and elevated the contributions made by black peoples over time and into the present. They emphasized the essential role that historical narratives played in legitimating political orders.[65] In *The Souls of Black Folk*, Du Bois wrote,

> The silently growing assumption of this age is that the probation of races is past, and that the backward races of to-day are of proven inefficiency and not worth saving. Such an assumption is the arrogance of peoples irreverent towards Time and ignorant of the deeds of men. A thousand years ago such an assumption, easily possible, would have made it difficult for the Teuton to prove his right to life. Two thousand years ago such dogmatism, readily welcome, would have scouted the idea of blond races ever leading civilization.[66]

Du Bois recognized the power of historical narration, the ideological functions performed, implicitly and explicitly, by the way that the past development of humanity was framed and taught. The dominant plotlines of the age, scholarly and popular alike, simultaneously elevated the role of the "blond races" in explaining the progressive development of humanity and denigrated the historical experience of everyone else, and especially Africans and their descendants. He argued that the past of the African continent—written out of world history by Hegel and other European thinkers—and the ongoing story of the African diaspora needed restoration. Autobiographical reflection was a popular medium: Alexander Crummell, Frederick Douglass, Ida B. Wells, and Du Bois, among others, shared their own life experiences as messages of resistance

---

64. Bruce, "The White Man's Burden" (c.1910), in *Selected Writings*, 97–98.

65. For a valuable account of the role of history in legitimation narratives, see Nomi Claire Lazar, *Out of Joint* (New Haven, CT, 2019).

66. Du Bois, *The Souls of Black Folk*, 196.

and hope.[67] It also underwrote a sustained effort to insert peoples of color into the record of human progress. Black historiography flourished.[68] Remapping the past would expose both the world-historical importance of specific black societies and the partial and contingent success of those professing the religion of whiteness. It would destabilize, through relativizing, claims about historical destiny and necessity. Such concerns also animated Du Bois's call for the development of a sociology of race. Existing social theories were "woefully unorganized," and had failed to grapple properly with the nature of historical change. In particular, "the meaning of 'swift' and 'slow' in human doing, and the limits of human perfectibility," remained "veiled, unanswered sphinxes on the shores of science."[69] This explained why scholars had ignored the many precedents that existed for purportedly unique "Aryan" ideas and institutions.[70] Once the sphinxes had been unveiled, the record of human achievement and advance would demonstrate that the white supremacist boast of universal superiority was false.

A common line of argument among those building counter-discourses of world history was that the Egyptians were black and that they had seeded Western civilization. First articulated in the late eighteenth century, this was a recurrent theme in the critical historiography wielded against racial supremacy, because it identified a revered society that contradicted assertions about the inherent backwardness of Africans and their comparative insignificance in world history. The title of the last book published by the black nationalist pioneer Martin Delany crystallized the historical and geographical scope of this work: *The Principia of Ethnology: The Origin of Races and Color, with an Archaeological Compendium of Ethiopian and Egyptian Civilization.*[71] Bruce suggested that the arrogant profession of Anglo-Saxon superiority was laced with irony, for rather than emerging from Germanic forests, the political institutions claimed by whites as their own progeny were inherited from the "black

67. V. P. Franklin, *Living Our Stories, Telling Our Truths* (Oxford, 1996).

68. Stephen Hall, *A Faithful Account of the Race* (Chapel Hill, 2009); Ralph Crowder, *John Edward Bruce*, ch. 5; Robin D. G. Kelley, "'But a Local Phase of a World Problem,'" *Journal of American History*, 86/3 (1999), 1045–77.

69. Du Bois, *Souls*, 196.

70. Du Bois, "Laboratory in Sociology at Atlanta University," in *Writings*, I, 158.

71. Delany, *The Principia of Ethnology* (Philadelphia, 1879). On Delany, see Robert S. Levine, *Martin Delany, Frederick Douglass, and the Politics of Representative Identity* (Chapel Hill, 1997). For an acute reading of his political vision, see Tommie Shelby, "Two Conceptions of Black Nationalism," *Political Theory*, 31/5 (2003), 664–92. On the "classical" age of black nationalism, see Wilson Moses, *The Golden Age of Black Nationalism, 1850–1925* (Oxford, 1978); Dean Robinson, *Black Nationalism in American Politics and Thought* (Cambridge, 2001), ch. 1.

race," because the central pillar of modern "civil government and jurisprudence" originated in Egypt. "Jethro, a black man, and father in law of Moses, conceived and introduced into Egypt through Moses, the Law-giver of Israel, the system of courts now in vogue in all the civilized countries of the world."[72] This attempt at historical recuperation portended its own form of utopianism. "[W]hether from virile barbarians or noble savages or stately Ethiopians," Wilson Moses argues, the proponents of "Egyptomorphic Afrocentrism" worked out "a historiography of progress" that furnished a "utopian teleology in African American thought, which advanced the idea of an unstoppable progress toward a racially enlightened and egalitarian society in the future."[73] Exposing the thread linking past, present, and future, counter-histories could serve as the foundation for a range of alternative utopian imaginaries.

Afro-modern writers frequently utilized speculative fiction as a medium of political critique, vindication, and desire. Just as a counter-canon of history and social science emerged to challenge the claims of white supremacy, so a range of stories imagined futures beyond racial domination. Du Bois was far from alone in recombining genres and using fantastical plots to critique the present and sketch other forms of life.[74] W. Andrew Shepard suggests that any discussion of Afrofuturism should start with Delany, the author of (arguably) the first work of African-American speculative fiction, *Blake, or the Huts of America*, an extraordinary novel that "gestures towards a utopian possibility in pan-Africanism that is congruent with Delany's political tracts."[75] The story follows a black man born in Cuba, then enslaved in the United States, who escapes and travels through the American South and Canada, meticulously

---

72. Bruce, "White Man's Burden," 97–98. On Egypt in nineteenth-century African-American thought, see Moses, *Afrotopia*. For general context, see Scott Trafton, *Egypt Land* (Durham, NC, 2004). On the complexity of African-American attitudes to Africa, see Michelle Mitchell, "'The Black Man's Burden,'" *International Review of Social History*, 44/4 (1999), 7–99; Jeannette Jones, "'The Negro's Peculiar Work,'" *Journal of American Studies*, 52/2 (2018), 1–28.

73. Moses, *Afrotopia*, 238, 15. Afrocentrism, he argues, could also be utilised to bolster a retrotopian narrative of decline, a "utopianism of the past, based on the belief that African Americans were much less than their ancestors had been, but . . . would achieve all the benefits of first-class American citizenship" (237). Rather than reject or transcend racial thinking, black scholars sought to remake it in a less exclusionary fashion: Mia Bay, *The White Image in the Black Mind* (Oxford, 2000), chs. 1–3.

74. See especially W. E. B. Du Bois, "The Comet," a short story (in part inspired by Wells) that was published in *Darkwater* (New York, 1920), 253–74. It is reproduced in Sheree R. Thomas's pioneering anthology, *Dark Matter* (New York, 2000), 5–19.

75. Andrew Shepard, "Afrofuturism in the Nineteenth and Twentieth Centuries" in Canavan and Link (eds.), *The Cambridge History of Science Fiction*, 101.

cataloguing the depredations of racial domination while building a transnational organization to fight slavery.[76]

African-American speculative fiction flourished in the closing years of the century.[77] The best-known of these texts is Sutton Grigg's *Imperium in Imperio*, published in 1899.[78] A Baptist pastor who sold the book door to door, Griggs explored racial injustice, miscegenation, and the meaning of black empowerment through fictionalizing some of the key debates over political strategy gripping African-American intellectuals and activists. Running through the story is a searing critique of the hypocrisy of "Anglo-Saxon" Americans who preached the glory of liberty while upholding a system that denied it to millions of their fellow citizens. Griggs also set out to challenge the "fear of combinations"—of large-scale collective action—that he thought inhibited African-American efforts to fight injustice.[79] Mirroring the fascination with secret societies found in Rhodes, Stead, Wells, and other Anglo-racial unionists, *Imperium in Imperio* imagines an underground society of African-Americans, with roots stretching back to the Revolutionary era, who create a clandestine self-governing polity in Texas—"one of the most remarkable and at the same time one of the most important things connected with modern civilization."[80] The aim of the Imperium was to "unite all Negroes in a body to do that which the United States government says it cannot do—to secure protection for their lives and the full enjoyment of all rights and privileges due American citizens."[81] One of the two main characters, Belton Piedmont,

76. Martin Delany, *Blake, or the Huts of America*, ed. Jerome McGann (1859, 1861–62; Cambridge, MA: Harvard University Press, 2017); Shepard, "Afrofuturism," 102; Brit Rusert, "Delany's Comet," *American Quarterly*, 65/4 (2013), 799–829. Initially serialized in magazine form, it was first published as a book in 1970.

77. Examples include Frances Harper, *Iola Leroy* (1892)—possibly the first Afrofuturist text written by a woman—and Edward Johnson, *Light ahead for the Negro* (1904): Shepard, "Afrofuturism." See also Mark Bould, "Revolutionary African-American SF before Black Power SF," *Extrapolation*, 51/1 (2010), 53–81.

78. Sutton Griggs, *Imperium in Imperio* (1899; New York, 2003). Cornel West describes it as the "first major political novel written by an African American" ("Introduction," xvi). See also Moses, *Golden Age*, ch. 9; Caroline Levander, "Sutton Griggs and the Borderlands of Empire," *American Literary History*, 22/1 (2010), 57–84; Liza Yaszek, "The Bannekerade" in Isiah Lavender III (ed.), *Black and Brown Planets* (Jackson, 2014), 15–30; Gruesser, *Empire Abroad*, ch. 2; and more generally, Finnie Coleman, *Sutton E. Griggs and the Struggle against White Supremacy* (Knoxville, 2007).

79. Griggs, *Imperium*, 45, 47.

80. Griggs, *Imperium*, 130.

81. Griggs, *Imperium*, 125.

professes his undying loyalty to and love for the "negro race," a variant of race patriotism that provided an alternative to claims of Anglo-Saxon racial belonging.[82] The story culminates with the Imperium on the verge of declaring war against the United States. Thematizing various currents of thought percolating through African-American debate, while offering a prefigurative vision of a future politics grounded in racial pride and solidarity, Griggs emphasizes the need for concerted planning and social coordination as a prerequisite of effective resistance. The utopian edge of the novel is furnished by the idea that African-Americans could secretly create a nation of millions and establish a self-governing political association in the face of Jim Crow, though it can also be read as a warning against employing violence where peaceful means are available.

While the steampunk novels I discussed in the last section dethrone the United States from geopolitical ascendency, none of them present a thoroughgoing challenge to the racial ideologies that sustained imperial politics during the nineteenth century. Some of the most powerful attempts to do so have emerged from within the African-American literary tradition. Colson Whitehead's recent masterpiece, *The Underground Railroad*, evokes steampunk themes and tropes while moving beyond them (it has been labeled the first "Afro-punk" engagement with slavery).[83] Set in roughly the same period as *The Difference Engine*, it follows the tortuous journey of Cora, a slave girl running for freedom across the blasted landscape of American racial violence, as she moves through different iterations of domination in a literalized version of the underground railroad that aided fugitives. Whitehead's spare narrative offers a phenomenology of racial-imperial whiteness, an indictment of its assumptions, articulations, and consequences. The "American spirit," the slave-catcher Ridgeway informs Cora, was "one that called us from the Old World to the New, to conquer and build and civilize. And destroy that what needs to be destroyed. To lift up the lesser races. If not lift up, subjugate. And if not subjugate, exterminate. Our destiny by divine prescription—the American imperative."[84] The black intellectual Elijah Lander levels an alternative judgment on the providential dream of whiteness. "The white race believes—believes with all its heart—that it is their right to take the land. To kill Indians. Make war. Enslave their brothers. This nation shouldn't exist, if there is any

---

82. Griggs, *Imperium*, 153.

83. Whitehead, *Underground Railroad*. Matt Sandler describes it as the first "Afro-punk novel of slavery": "A Clanking Ride to an Uncertain Freedom," *Los Angeles Review of Books*, 10 September 2016.

84. Whitehead, *Underground Railroad*, 266.

justice in the world, for its foundations are murder, theft, and cruelty. Yet here we are."[85] At once looking backward and forward, an act of remembrance and a monitory warning, the novel can be read as an exemplary "critical dystopia," a text that paints a picture of abjection and horror while offering glimpses of hope for a better future.[86]

Running through much of Du Bois's writing as the twentieth century dawned, and as visions of Anglo-Saxon unification proliferated, was a meditation on the "flood of white Americanism."[87] Like many of his contemporaries, he was adamant that the Atlantic slave trade was at the root of continuing racial prejudice and violence.[88] Du Bois stood out not only because of his intellectual stature, but because he offered a sophisticated account of the interlacing of "whiteness" and global politics, returning frequently to the transversal character of the color line.[89] In 1906, he explained that the "tendency of the great nations of the day is territorial, political and economic expansion," which had invariably "brought them into contact with darker peoples," as a consequence of which the "Negro problem in America is but a local phase of

85. Whitehead, *Underground Railroad*, 341.

86. On *The Underground Railroad* as critical dystopia, see Mathias Thaler, "Bleak Dreams, Not Nightmares," *Constellations*, 26/4(2019), 607–22. For the original concept, see Moylan, *Scraps of the Untainted Sky*.

87. The expression is from Du Bois, *Souls*, 7. On his intellectual formation, see also Shamoon Zamir, *Dark Voices* (Chicago, 1995); Barrington S. Edwards, "W. E. B. Du Bois between Worlds," *Du Bois Review*, 3/2 (2006), 395–424; Gooding-Williams, *In the Shadow of Du Bois*; Stephanie Shaw, *W. E. B. Du Bois and* The Souls of Black Folk (Chapel Hill, 2013). On his early career, see David Levering Lewis, *W. E. B. Du Bois* (New York, 1993), I. Other illuminating accounts of his political thought (and legacy) include Lawrie Balfour, *Democracy's Reconstruction* (New York, 2006); Adolph Reed Jr., *W. E. B. Du Bois and American Political Thought* (Oxford, 1997); Melvin Rogers, "The People, Rhetoric, and Affect," *American Political Science Review*, 106/1 (2012), 188–203.

88. W. E. B. Du Bois, "The Development of a People" (1904), in *Writings*, I, 209–13. This was originally published in the *International Journal of Ethics* (April 1904).

89. W. E. B. Du Bois, "The Present Outlook for the Dark Races of Mankind" (1900), *Writings*, I, 78 (published originally in the Philadelphia *Church Review*, October 1900). See also Du Bois, *Souls*, 3, 14, 33; Du Bois, "Race Friction between Black and White" (1908), in *Writings*, I, 389 (published originally in the May 1908 edition of the *American Journal of Sociology*). As Paul Taylor observes, despite the continuing popularity of this formulation, Du Bois rejected the idea of a *single* invariant "problem": "W. E. B. Du Bois," *Philosophy Compass*, 5/11 (2010), 905. For black internationalisms, see Keisha N. Blain, Christopher Cameron, and Ashley D. Farmer (eds.), *New Perspectives on the Black Intellectual Tradition* (Chicago, 2018), pt. I; Keisha N. Blain, *Set the World on Fire* (Philadelphia, 2018); Getachew, *Worldmaking after Empire*; Inés Valdez, *Transnational Cosmopolitanism* (Cambridge, 2019), chs. 3–5.

a world problem." Or to put it another way: "The policy of expansion, then, simply means world problems of the Color Line."[90] Although *The Souls of Black Folk* focused chiefly on domestic politics, the shadow of empire hangs over the text, intruding at various points. One of the reasons Du Bois rejected Booker T. Washington's ameliorative program was that a refusal to advocate political equality for African-Americans "practically accepts the alleged inferiority of the Negro races," and that as such it had deleterious *global* implications.[91] He also argued that American imperialism in the Caribbean, Hawaii, and the Philippines negated arguments for black emigration as it demonstrated that nowhere was safe from the grip of white supremacy.[92] Imperial expansion was anathema to human progress, while boasts about the gift of civilization masked a plethora of sins. "War, murder, slavery, extermination, and debauchery,—this has again and again been the result of carrying civilization and the blessed gospel to the isles of the sea and the heathen without the law."[93]

The British Empire played an ambivalent role in nineteenth-century Afro-modern thought. The charge sheet against it was damning: Britain had dominated the Atlantic slave trade, it was widely thought to have supported the Southern states during the Civil War, its settlers had dispossessed and exterminated indigenous populations across the world, its colonists maintained regimes of racial discrimination and violence, and its thinkers provided some of the most popular rationales for white supremacism. Despite this catalogue of infamy, Afro-modern attitudes to the country were conflicted. Britain was often damned for its past and present sins even as it was compared favorably to other European empires and the states of the American South. The visibility of Ida B. Wells's transatlantic antilynching campaign demonstrated to some that, despite its own complicity, Britain offered a welcome space for articulating claims against the worsening American apartheid order.[94] In the opening years of the century, Du Bois argued that despite the manifest harms inflicted by the British in India and its African territories, they were nevertheless considerably better at addressing the problem of the color line than other Western

90. W. E. B. Du Bois, "The Color Line Belts the World" (1906), in *Writings*, I, 330. Published originally in *Collier's Weekly* (October 1906).

91. Du Bois, *Souls*, 40.

92. Du Bois, *Souls*, 42.

93. Du Bois, *Souls*, 122.

94. On her travels in Britain, see Sarah Silkey, *Black Woman Reformer* (Athens, 2015). On her life, see Mia Bay, *To Tell the Truth Freely* (New York, 2009). Edward Wilmot Blyden was also an Anglophile: Teshale Tibebu, *Edward Wilmot Blyden and the Racial Nationalist Imagination* (Rochester, 2012).

powers. "Say what you will of England's rapacity and injustice, (and much can be said) the plain fact remains that no other European nation—and America least of all—has governed its alien subjects with half the wisdom and justice that England has." In 1900, he hoped for a British victory in South Africa, arguing that it would represent "a step towards the solution of the greater Negro problem." He also praised British rule in Egypt. Our "brown cousins" had been "rescued from war and rapine, slavery and centuries of misrule," he contended, and they were "to-day enjoying stable government under England and rapid industrial advancement."[95] Du Bois accepted at face value the exculpatory claims made to legitimate the unique properties and policies of the British Empire. But in drawing a firm line between the actions and attitudes of the British and Americans, he implicitly rejected the unionist contention that Anglo-America was a single entity. Rather than a transatlantic polity grounded in a shared racial identity, Du Bois imagined a stratified and divided space in which campaigners could mobilize support in one part to fight racial domination in another. However, as the twentieth century wore on, Du Bois rejected British exceptionalism. The British Empire, he came to think, was a paradigmatic expression of European aggression, designed to subjugate and exploit the "darker nations" of the world.[96]

Du Bois contended that the "religion of whiteness" would not survive its own evident intellectual and political failings. Intimations of its end could be divined in the Japanese defeat of the Russians in 1905, an episode that "marked an epoch": "The magic of the word 'white' is already broken, and the Color Line in civilization has been crossed in modern times as it was in the great past."[97] For centuries "the white races have had the hegemony of civilization—so far so that 'white' and 'civilized' have become synonymous in everyday speech." Invoking the recuperative historical narrative about the African origins of Western civilization, Du Bois lamented that "men have forgotten where civilization started."[98] His prewar analysis of whiteness culminated

95. Du Bois, "Present Outlook," 73–74.

96. See, for example, Du Bois, "African Roots of War."

97. Du Bois, "Color Line Belts the World," 330. He continued, "The awakening of the yellow races is certain" (330). Defenders of the empire were likewise impressed by the magnitude of the event. "Well do I remember," the British classicist and imperial thinker Alfred Zimmern wrote later, "the impression made upon my mind when . . . I read of the first great victory of the Japanese over the Russians. I went into my class and told them I was going to lay aside Greek history for that morning, 'because', I said, 'I feel I must speak to you about the most important historical event which has happened, or is likely to happen, in our lifetime, the victory of a non-white people over a white people.'" Zimmern, The Third British Empire (Oxford, 1926), 82.

98. Du Bois, "Color Line Belts the World," 330.

in "The Souls of White Folk," published in 1910, which targeted those who "have become painfully conscious of their whiteness," the ever-growing number "in whose minds the paleness of their bodily skins is fraught with tremendous and eternal significance."[99] They were true believers in racial religion.

> The discovery of personal whiteness among the world's peoples is a very modern thing—a nineteenth and twentieth century matter, indeed. The ancient world would have laughed at such a distinction. The middle ages regarded it with mild curiosity, and even up to the eighteenth century we were hammering our national mannikins into one great Universal Man with fine frenzy which ignored color and race as well as birth. Today we have changed all that, and the world, in sudden emotional conversion, has discovered that it is white, and, by that token, wonderful.[100]

As absurd, even comedic, as it was, this "extraordinary dictum" had grave consequences for political life throughout the world. "That nations are coming to believe it is manifest daily." It was also a catastrophe for those infected with it. "I sit and see the souls of the White Folk daily shrivelling and dying in the fierce flame of this new fanaticism."[101]

Du Bois argued that the best social science of the day had wholly discredited the idea of race as a distinctive entity. This was the most important lesson taught by the 1911 Universal Races Congress in London. The meeting reinforced his long-standing view that "the problem of race is a world problem," and that it was exacerbated by new communications and transport technologies: "the question of contact between differing masses and groups of men" was "daily made critical by the physical shrinking of the world in our day."[102] But the meeting also highlighted that arguments about racial superiority were fallacious.

99. Du Bois, "Souls of White Folk," in *Writings*, II, 25. An updated and extended version of the essay was later published in *Darkwater*.

100. Du Bois, "Souls of White Folk," in *Writings*, II 25.

101. Du Bois, "Souls of White Folk," in *Writings*, II, 26, 27.

102. W. E. B. Du Bois, "Coming of the Lesser Folk," in *Writings*, II, 45. Originally published in the *New York Post* (August 1911). For analysis of the event, see Paul Rich, "'The Baptism of a New Era,'" *Ethnic and Racial Studies*, 7/4 (1984), 534–50; Susan Pennybacker, "The Universal Races Congress, London Political Culture, and Imperial Dissent, 1900–1939," *Radical History Review*, 92 (2005), 103–17; Jonathan Schneer, "Anti-imperial London" in Gretchen Holbrook Gerzina (ed.), *Black Victorians / Black Victoriana* (New Brunswick, 2003), 175–86; Kyle T. Mays, "Transnational Progressivism," *American Indian Quarterly*, 37/3 (2013), 243–61.

To realize the full meaning of the statements made by these men one must not forget the racial philosophy upon which America has long been nursed. The central idea of that philosophy has been that there are vast and, for all practical purposes, unbridgeable differences between the races of men, the whites representing the higher noble stock, the blacks the lower meaner race.[103]

Du Bois conceded that substantive differences existed between human populations—above all levels of "civilization" defined broadly in terms of industrial and educational development—while maintaining that variation was caused by social and cultural factors and did not correspond to "physical characteristics." Nor were those differences so deeply ingrained that they would take an age to overcome; such work could be done in a matter of decades.[104] Though it formed only a part of the effort to fight racial injustice, a combination of history, sociology, and science could be harnessed to dissolve the intellectual rationale for white supremacy.

Although Britain was home to a far smaller community of writers of color, the stirrings of concerted resistance to systematic racial injustice could be discerned by the final decade of the century. In the early 1890s, the creation of the Society for the Recognition of the Brotherhood of Man, and the tireless activism and writing of campaigners such as Celestine Edwards and Ida Wells, challenged the "hegemonic racialism of the metropolitan culture."[105] The Indian nationalist intellectual and political leader Dadabhai Naoroji used his platform as an MP in Westminster to continue his attack on the egregious injustices of British imperial rule, resulting in *Poverty and Un-British Rule in India* in 1901.[106] Home to various publications, and a stopping-off point for activists from around the world, London was an important nodal point in the networks of the Black Anglosphere. In 1900, the Pan-African Conference, organized by the Trinidadian barrister Henry Sylvester Williams, drew thirty-seven

103. W. E. B. Du Bois, "The First Universal Races Congress" (1911), in *Writings*, II, 48. See also Du Bois, "Scientific Reasons against Race Antagonism" (1914), in *Writings*, II, 92–94 (*Boston Globe*, 19 July 1914). For Du Bois's famous earlier account of race, see *The Conservation of Races* (Washington, DC, 1897).

104. Du Bois, "First Universal Races Congress," in *Writings*, II, 49.

105. Lorimer, *Science, Race Relations and Resistance*, 285.

106. Dadabhai Naoroji, *Poverty and Un-British Rule in India in 1901* (London, 1901). See also the discussion of Shyamji Krishnavarma and (later) Shapurji Saklatvala in Priyamvada Gopal, *Insurgent Empire* (London, 2019), ch. 5.

delegates to London to discuss the fate of Africa and the African diaspora.[107] Its most visible result was the proclamation, drafted by Du Bois, that the problem of the twentieth century would be the problem of the color line.[108] Although it made little impression on wider society or white intellectual elites at the time, it helped seed the later development of pan-Africanism.[109]

Theophilus Scholes produced one of the most sustained fin-de-siècle accounts of white supremacy.[110] Born in Jamaica, Scholes moved to Britain in 1884, training first as a Baptist missionary in London and then as a doctor in Edinburgh. He had long dreamt of spreading Christian teaching in Africa, and during the 1880s he spent several years in the Congo Free State—prior to the worst atrocities perpetrated by the regime of Leopold II—followed by a shorter stint in Nigeria, before settling in London in 1896, where he wrote a sequence of books about imperial affairs.[111] Scholes forged a substantial reputation across the Black Anglosphere, his influence stretching from early twentieth-century Pan-African circles through to Jomo Kenyatta in the 1930s.[112] His two-volume magnum opus, *Glimpses of the Ages*, made a notable mark. Bruce, author of the first account of Scholes, wrote in *The Voice* that "[e]very Negro who thinks" should read it, while Du Bois introduced the readers of *Horizon* to Scholes's work in 1907 and drew on some of his historical arguments when discussing ancient Egypt.[113] Gustav Spiller, Secretary of the 1911 Universal Races Congress, praised the "two excellent volumes" in the proceedings of the event.[114] As late as 1942, Alain Locke and Bernhard Stern

107. Sherwood, *Origins of Pan-Africanism*; Adi, *Pan-Africanism*, 19–22. Sylvester had formed the African Association in 1897.

108. Du Bois, "To the Nations of the World," in *Writings*, I, 10–11.

109. Lorimer, *Science, Race Relations and Resistance*, ch. 7.

110. There is little scholarship on Scholes. For a valuable account of his life and activities, see Kim Blake, "T. E. S. Scholes," *Race & Class*, 49/1 (2007), 62–80. The most detailed discussion of his ideas can be found in Wigmoore Francis, "White Negroes, Black Hebrews, and the Anti-Imperialist Narratives of Theophilus Scholes," *Journal of Caribbean History*, 46/1 (2012), 33–60; Francis, "Nineteenth- and Early-Twentieth-Century Perspectives on Women in the Discourses of Radical Black Caribbean Men," *Small Axe*, 7/1 (2003), 116–39. He is mentioned briefly in Jeffrey Green, *Black Edwardians* (Abingdon, 1998), 241–43; Stephen Howe, *Afrocentrism* (London, 1999), 44–45.

111. David Killingray suggests that he had lost his faith by the turn of the century: "The Black Atlantic Missionary Movement and Africa, 1780s–1920s," *Journal of Religion in Africa* 31/3 (2003), 20.

112. Blake, "Scholes," 78; Imanuel Geiss, *The Pan-African Movement* (London, 1974), 108, 110.

113. John Bruce, "Dr. Theophilus E. S. Scholes, M.D.," *The Voice*, 4/2 (March 1907), 115; Geiss, *Pan-African Movement*, 215.

114. Gustav Spiller (ed.), *Inter-racial Problems* (London, 1911), 31.

excerpted Scholes's work in *When Peoples Meet*, their anthology of literature on "racial contact."[115] Scholes discussed many of the figures who populate the pages of *Dreamworlds of Race*—Bryce, Chamberlain, Freeman, Froude, Mommsen, Stead, and Rhodes, as well as Douglass, Du Bois, Blyden, Delany, Fortune, and Washington. He offers a valuable counterpoint to the articulation of the white racial dreamworld. Of particular interest for my purposes is that Scholes outlined a distinctive argument about Anglo-American relations and the dangers of racial union.

In *The British Empire and Alliances*, published in 1899, Scholes warned that racial injustice was threatening the viability of the empire.[116] Written as a broadly sympathetic internal critique, the book charged that Britain was failing to live up to its professed commitments. He opened by expressing skepticism about the feasibility of alliances with other major powers. The most obvious candidate was the United States—"the other great branch of the Anglo-Saxon race"—but even though the improved relations between the two countries was "a most gratifying augury," the power of "material interests" outweighed that of racial affinity. While blood may be thicker than water, material interest was thicker than blood.[117] But what if circumstances changed? Shifting into speculative mode, Scholes imagined a future conflict in which France allied with Russia to fight Britain and the United States, with the latter emerging victorious. Even under such conditions an alliance would fail because the two states would jostle for supremacy. Alliances only worked when they were asymmetrical, binding weaker states to stronger ones, whereas there was rough parity between Britain and the United States.[118]

The main impediment to British success was located within the empire. In order to succeed in an increasingly dangerous international environment, it was necessary to induce a sense of common interest and destiny in its scattered peoples, but fruitful "cooperation" was impossible so long as the imperial government presided over institutionalized racial discrimination.[119] The main

---

115. Alain Locke and Bernhard Stern (eds.), *When Peoples Meet* (New York, 1942). See Locke, "When Peoples Meet" (1942), in *Works of Alain Locke*, ed. Charles Molesworth (Oxford, 2012), 365–66. Locke had known Scholes since they met in Oxford prior to the First World War: Leonard Harris and Charles Molesworth, *Alain L. Locke* (Chicago, 2009), 67.

116. Scholes, *British Empire*, ch. 1.

117. Scholes, *British Empire*, 9, 10. On the "masculinist ethos" pervading the work of Scholes (and others), see Francis, "Nineteenth- and Early-Twentieth-Century Perspectives," 130–39.

118. Scholes, *British Empire*, 404. Addressing many core topics in foreign and imperial policy, as well as the structures of racial domination, *British Empire* should be added to the body of texts studied by those excavating the history of international thought in the Atlantic world.

119. Scholes, *British Empire*, 257–58.

theme of the book was the gross injustice of "Colour Prejudice," which constituted "that sum of human vanity, that most transparent, yet most revered
and popular of all human follies." It was a "peculiar fever to which the Anglo-
Saxon race is specially susceptible," though it afflicted Americans more deeply
than the British. Racial injustice was "bad enough" in India and southern Africa, he acknowledged, but in Britain itself it was "comparatively mild." It was
realized principally in the "political aspects" of the empire: the lack of self-
determination and equal treatment granted to subjects. Possessing "capacities
of consolidation and assimilation," Britain, the "wealthiest and most peaceful
of all nations," was still redeemable.[120] Rather than calling for the dissolution
of the empire, Scholes demanded that it live up to its promise by instituting a
policy of "internal adjustment," removing discriminatory barriers and ensuring
equality between subjects.[121] The United States, on the other hand, had forfeited the chance to become the "custodian" of world peace in an orgy of racial
prejudice, violence, and hatred.[122] The cancer of "color prejudice" had metas-
tasized through society.

Scholes carefully delineated the ideological justifications of white supremacy before unleashing a barrage of counterarguments. He contended that one
of the chief "modes of operation" through which racial domination was reproduced was "the association of all great achievements with the white skin, and
the white skin with everything great," combined with the equation of "everything that is contemptible with skins that are not white, and skins that are not
white with everything that it contemptible."[123] This message had been promulgated by numerous American and British scholars. He paid particular attention to Freeman. Targeting the racist comments about African-Americans
found in *Some Impressions of the United States*, Scholes labeled him a "pedant
and a dilettante," a man who had "in a frenzy of morbid rage" launched a "savage and cowardly attack" on innocent people. In doing so, Scholes contended,
Freeman "presents the spectacle of a man glorying in his own shame."[124] He
also made a more general point about the nature of historical imagination and
its ethico-political entailments. As was typical of those who sought to ground
racial superiority in appeals to the past, Freeman had embraced a "toxic use of

120. Scholes, *British Empire*, 394, 391, 395. Despite his critique of "colour prejudice," Scholes
was broadly positive in his appraisal of European civilisation, describing it as the "trustee and
guardian for the rest of mankind" (12).

121. Scholes, *British Empire*, 386–87.

122. Scholes, *British Empire*, 6.

123. Scholes, *British Empire*, 398.

124. Scholes, *British Empire*, 276, 283. He also challenged Froude's vicious racism about the
West Indies (267–72).

history," an intellectual strategy that "produces that state of mind which exaggerates the achievements of progressive races, and particularly his own, whilst it holds races that are less progressive in contemptuous disregard, and even loathing." In particular, Freeman was guilty of the "radical delusion" that "intellectual attainments and moral virtues, are attributes not of the mind but of the skin."[125] Such claims were based on a fundamental misunderstanding of historical dynamics. Scholes opined that if scholars adopted an appropriately capacious view of world history, they would recognize that all peoples rose and fell, undergoing periods of progressive development before they eventually declined. Drawing on Afrocentric vindicationist arguments, he maintained that the "spark" of Europe was found in Egypt and consequently that "the corner-stone of the world's civilisation was laid by the Negro."[126] In failing to acknowledge these pivotal aspects of world history, Freeman was demonstrating his profound limitations as a historian and adherent of the comparative method.

Scholes's thought over the following decade is a study in furious disillusion. While *The British Empire and Alliances* was critical of British conduct, it argued that unjust policies could be altered without too much difficulty. Britain remained the indispensable empire-state. But the experience of war in South Africa and its aftermath, combined with the increasing "colour prejudice" of metropolitan discourse, smothered Scholes's optimism and changed his attitude to the imperial order. As with Du Bois, his judgment of the British Empire hardened. Chamberlain—the "Nestor of Imperialism"—symbolized the betrayal of the imperial promise.[127] Scholes also came to think that the malign influence of the United States was spreading across the Atlantic. In particular, he argued that British efforts to secure an alliance with Washington were one of the chief causes of the increasing racial injustice percolating through the empire. Rather than a cause for celebration, as he had once seen it, rapprochement was strengthening the hold of white supremacy. This theme was central to his next attempt to grapple with the nature and future of empire.

Glimpses of the Ages was published in two volumes, the first in 1905, the second following in 1908.[128] Over nearly one thousand pages, Scholes ranged across time and space, as well as disciplinary borders, to unravel the racial

125. Scholes, *British Empire*, 277, 283.

126. Scholes, *British Empire*, 277–78, 282.

127. "Bartholomew Smith" [Scholes], *Chamberlain and Chamberlainism* (London, 1903); Scholes, *Glimpses of the Ages* (London, 1908), II, ch. 17.

128. In the second volume, he suggested that he planned six volumes in total (the third would be on "Afro-Americans"), though these did not come to fruition.

ideologies that legitimated imperial power and the subjection of much of the world to the "white race." His ambition was to undermine the conjoint claims, which he took to be pervasive in the United States and (increasingly) Britain, that the "white race" was inherently superior, the "coloured races" irremediably inferior. Part of his task was to refute ethnologists, such as Augustus Keane, who claimed that differences in physiology between peoples mapped onto variations in cognitive capacity. Elaborating on some of the arguments he had sketched in *The British Empire*, Scholes also challenged the conception of time, and vision of world history, that underpinned racial ideology. The belief that the "white race" had long been in the vanguard of progress was a central pillar of imperial legitimation strategies. If history demonstrated what biology was supposed to confirm—that white people were best fitted to rule—then the ideal of "cooperation as equals" was a hopeless illusion, and the relationship between the "white races" and the rest of humanity would be a "relation of perpetual wardship."[129] The color line would fix global hierarchy in perpetuity. The opening chapters of the first volume of *Glimpses* refuted claims about biological variation, arguing that the best contemporary science proved that there was no substantive difference in the moral or mental capacities of peoples.[130] He pointed to the growing list of eminent black thinkers in the United States as evidence that progress was possible even under extremely hostile conditions—among others, he singled out Du Bois and Fortune. Moreover, he continued, the great black leaders of recent times—Douglass, Blyden, L'Ouverture, and Washington—were the equal of any historical figure.[131] A proper grasp of history, meanwhile, showed that the "white race" had often lagged behind the most advanced societies, indeed they had frequently sunk into barbarism, while "coloured" peoples created monuments to civilization and drove the progress of the world. He reiterated, at considerably greater length, his earlier argument that the black Egyptians were the "educators of modern Europe."[132]

Like Du Bois, Scholes offered an alternative understanding of historical temporality, one that refused to ordain the "white races" as the chosen people(s) of the earth. He did so by attacking the inevitability of sociopolitical progress.

---

129. Scholes, *Glimpses*, I, 3, 4.

130. Scholes, *Glimpses*, I, 5–165.

131. Scholes, *Glimpses*, ch. 24. He also discussed a critical British review of Du Bois's *Souls* (179–80).

132. Scholes, *Glimpses*, I, 173–74, 235 (and ch. 20). William H. Ferris offered another account of the route from Egypt through to the West in *The African Abroad* (New Haven, CT, 1913). For an analysis of his arguments, see Tommy Curry, *The Philosophical Treatise of William H. Ferris* (Lanham, 2016).

Rather than following a linear trajectory, the "movement" of history was characterized by persistent "oscillation."[133] Contrary to popular belief, the present era was one of "retrogression," not upward development. While he acknowledged some welcome changes—including the common desire for peace, manifested in support for international arbitration—there were far more signs of declension, most notably the prevalence of imperial war and the spread of racial injustice. Those who hailed the extension of the franchise invariably overlooked "the refusal of equal rights in the British empire" and "the preventing of equal rights" in the United States.[134] Democracy was rigged as a white man's game. The deplorable condition of contemporary sociopolitical life was the product of a moral and epistemic failure: a refusal to accept the basic equality of all humans. The white race "announces the right to possess the inheritances of those coloured races and the duty to shape their destiny." Science, scholarship, literature, law: all were wielded to justify racial supremacy. The likely result of the "backward oscillation" would be widespread social upheaval, the subjugated of the earth rising to challenge their oppressors.[135]

To give conceptual shape to these claims, Scholes proposed a theory of social development in which racial difference was assigned a subordinate role. He distinguished races, nations/peoples, and tribes. Race was the "largest or primary division of mankind, classified according to the colour of the skin, the colour and structure of the hair of the head, according to the features, and according to language." On this account there were three races: "Caucasic, Mongolic, and Ethiopic." Nations or peoples—he used the terms interchangeably—were groups of individuals, "whether they be of the same race or different races, whether they speak the same or different languages," that were ruled by a particular government. Finally, a tribe was "one or more savage clans having a common name, a common dialect, a common government, and a common territory." The key difference between races, on the one hand, and peoples and tribes on the other, was that the latter were organic wholes, possessing a "corporeal or corporate form," whereas the former lacked both properties. Nations and tribes were both "communities," an "organic, conscious, and intelligent unit, which thinks, feels, plans, and executes," and thus possessed a "personality," whereas races were "impersonal," a mere "boundary, a combination of qualities, devoid of personality."[136] It followed that the units of socio-historical

133. Scholes, *Glimpses*, I, viii.

134. Scholes, *Glimpses*, I, ix, x. Scholes also reminded his readers that, "as an outcome of British colonisation, the aboriginal peoples have been practically destroyed" (2).

135. Scholes, *Glimpses*, II, 1, I, 3–4, xv.

136. Scholes, *Glimpses*, I, 283–84, 292, 284. He was clear about the analogy with individual persons: "a community is but an individual magnified" (I, 292). He also argued that units,

development were communities rather than races. Among other things, it was possible to attribute characteristics, such as industrious, weak, strong, and rich, to communities, but it would be "meaningless" to apply them to races. Scholes also clarified his usage of "white race(s)." When using the term, he meant those communities dominated by Caucasians. "This phrase, according to the definitions just given, should be Caucasian peoples or nations, white section of the Aryan race, white section of the Indo-European, the Indo-Germanic, or of the Japhetic race."[137] It principally referred to the states of the Euro-American world.

Scholes went on to argue that individual units, whether natural or artificial persons, typically passed through three phases of life: juvenescence, adolescence, and senility (or immaturity, maturity, and decay).[138] World history pulsated with multiple communities coexisting at different phases of corporate life. Civilization—defined chiefly in terms of technoscientific advance—was unevenly distributed across time and space. It was not, and had never been, the possession of any one community, let alone a single race. Those, like Freeman, who claimed that a privileged race determined the course of history misunderstood both past and present. They confused a part for the whole. Scholes hypothesized that there were two principal mechanisms through which communities developed civilization. Some of them, including ancient Peru, China, and Egypt, managed it *spontaneously*, without following other "models." Others were *imitative*, copying or building on the achievements of previous communities. Western civilization was an example of the latter.[139] After all, the "Negro Egyptians were the chief originators of European civilisation."[140] The mythology of white supremacy was based on an historical illusion.

Scholes spent much of the second volume of *Glimpses* excoriating the racial injustices of the imperial powers, Britain above all. He reprised his attack on Chamberlain, and lambasted Froude's racist commentary on the Caribbean. Lyman Abbott, whom I discussed in chapter 2, was held up as an example of

---

though they displayed many qualities, could be represented by their guiding characteristic (the Italian love of art, the British mastery of commerce, etc.). Debates over personification continue to this day. See, for example, Alexander Wendt, "The State as Person in International Theory," *Review of International Studies*, 30/2 (2004), 289–316, and, for a contrasting view, Sean Fleming, *Leviathan on a Leash* (Princeton, NJ, 2020).

137. Scholes, *Glimpses*, I, 284–85. His earlier ascriptions of success and achievement to races was thus only "metaphorical" (292).

138. Scholes, *Glimpses*, I, 294.

139. Scholes, *Glimpses*, I, ch. 27.

140. Scholes, *Glimpses*, I, 338, 384.

a prominent Christian willing to endorse imperial violence to spread the gospel in Africa.[141] Stead was dismissed as a "complacent and enthusiastic expounder and admirer" of Rhodes's poisonous creed. Rhodes himself was figured as one of the embodiments of British imperial injustice. Scholes cited a passage from Stead's glowing 1902 portrait in the *Review of Reviews*, but rather than celebrating Rhodes's proclamations as those of a visionary genius, Scholes distilled from them a "Rhodesian law of the hurling of the 'unfit' to the wall." This law was enacted in a sequence: "friendship at first, then subjection, then subjugation, and then repression, or, to put it in one word, force, is the way by which the coloured races are brought into the British Empire."[142] Once snared, they were promised a form of equality that was then habitually denied in practice. As chief instigator of an act forcing "coloured" labor into the brutal diamond mines, Rhodes practiced what he preached, but the law that he embodied was widely held and routinely enforced—indeed, it had come to define British imperial policy.[143] The intensification of racial domination was proof that the leading "civilization" had entered a degenerate phase. "Race ascendency," Scholes declared, was "intrinsically immoral." Despite widespread belief in progress, there was a "prevailing poverty in the realm of morals," expressed chiefly in the continued growth of "colour prejudice."[144] Neither technoscientific capacity nor geopolitical power were markers of virtue; indeed, if misused, as they had been by the imperial states, they undermined claims to both political legitimacy and moral exemplarity.

The tragedy was that things could have been otherwise. Scholes still held that British imperial policy, and British attitudes to "coloured" populations, had been less prejudiced until a shift began in the early 1880s. There had been "opportunity" for hard-working and talented individuals to make something of themselves. (Once again, he can be charged with painting a nostalgic portrait of midcentury imperial dynamics.) That era had closed and it was now the "characteristic conceit of the Anglo-Saxon" to believe that "the power to rule began with himself, and must end with himself."[145] This deplorable shift had three causes. The first was that the British Empire was increasingly intent on exploiting its subjects in the interests of the "white race"—this was symbolized above all by Chamberlain's pronouncements and policies. Although vague on the timing and sources of this shift, Scholes implied that it was

141. Scholes, *Glimpses*, II, 197, 45.

142. Scholes, *Glimpses*, II, 15, 91. See here Rhodes, *Last Will*, 95 (I discuss this passage in chapter 3).

143. Scholes, *Glimpses*, II, 361.

144. Scholes, *Glimpses*, II, 252, 182.

145. Scholes, *Glimpses*, II, 269, 277.

generated by increased international competition and the need to produce greater economic resources. The other causes were located within the Anglo-world. In both instances, the British elite had bowed to pressure. Some of this emanated from its settler periphery. The "mother country," argued Scholes, had "surrendered its juster native policy" to the demands of its colonists, principally those in South Africa.[146] The tail was now wagging the dog.

The third reason for the shift in racial attitudes and policy was the attempt to build an "Anglo-American friendship."[147] In the past, Scholes claimed, the policies of London and Washington had diverged significantly, but in order to secure a closer relationship, the British government had reneged on its earlier commitments. "The attitude of the United States has been unjust, the attitude of England has been comparatively just, but, as in the case of South Africa, England surrendered her juster position for the unjust position of America."[148] Scholes was adamant about the connection though unclear about the mechanisms. He referenced Chamberlain's May 1898 speech—delivered, he noted, at a time when union was "being vociferously boomed"—as proof.[149] He also identified Bryce's 1902 Romanes lecture, "The Relations of the Advanced and the Backward Races of Mankind," as an example of the careless racism infecting British discourse. Opining on the issue of interracial marriage in the United States, Bryce had maintained that "the mixture of races very dissimilar, and especially of European whites and blacks, tends rather to lower rather than improve the stock," though he then qualified his argument by adding that the "data are imperfect." For Scholes, this sloppiness represented a "moral crime." Bryce, by then serving as British Ambassador to United States, was a "philosophic historian" and an "eminent statesman," and his view on such a freighted topic was likely to have "great influence."[150] The explanation for his extraordinary lapse was clear: "the theory of Anglo-American friendship."

> Thereby, as the friendship of the Euro-American would be more useful to England than the friendship of the Afro-American would be, abandoning her former position with respect to the nature of the dispute that exists between the two American sections, England takes the side of the stronger

---

146. Scholes, *Glimpses*, II, 299.

147. Scholes, *Glimpses*, II, 299–300, 285.

148. Scholes, *Glimpses*, II, 300.

149. Scholes, *Glimpses*, II, 300–301. I discuss the speech briefly in the Introduction.

150. Scholes, *Glimpses*, II, 310, 309. See James Bryce, *The Relations of the Advanced and the Backward Races of Mankind* (Oxford, 1902), 35.

against the weaker. Thus is Anglo-American friendship a cause of England's change of policy towards the colored races.[151]

Britain was willing to drop its ostensible commitment to progressive racial development in order to accommodate those who oversaw a segregated Jim Crow society. Du Bois's religion of whiteness trumped any residual belief in equality or fairness. Scholes argued that the shift in British attitudes portended doom for the empire, causing its "devitalization" and the thorough demoralization of those subjects who had once believed in it. (The autobiographical sting here is manifest.) Scholes quoted a passage from *The Narrative of Frederick Douglass* in which the sumptuous house and hospitality of a wealthy plantation owner, Colonel Edward Lloyd, is compared with the wretched condition of his slaves. For Scholes, the stark contrast between foreground and background was echoed in the British Empire. While the imperial elite presented a positive face to the world, its "coloured" subjects suffered "their poverty, their oppression, their degradation, their humiliation, and their vilification."[152] Britain had cast its lot with the settler colonial regimes and with the United States. The "abandonment of a great principle by England" was the "price that is paid" for trying to build Anglo-America.[153]

Not everyone, then, welcomed the rapprochement of Britain and the United States or celebrated the supposed world-historical destiny of the "English race." Two among the countless many excluded from the compass of white supremacism, Du Bois and Scholes reflected on its reach and power, and sought to undermine its intellectual and political foundations. They recognized, as did the proponents of Anglotopia, the vital importance of history in shaping visions of a world to come. To battle the pernicious ideological scaffolding of white supremacy effectively, it was essential to challenge both its contemporary manifestations and its legitimating historical narratives. A better future could only be achieved by reclaiming the past.

151. Scholes, *Glimpses*, II, 311, 312.

152. Scholes, *Glimpses*, II, 323–27, 328. The discussion can be found in Frederick Douglass, *The Narrative of Frederick Douglass* (Boston, 1845), ch. 3.

153. Scholes, *Glimpses*, II, 423.

BIBLIOGRAPHY

Manuscript Sources

James Bryce papers, Bodleian Library, University of Oxford

Andrew Carnegie papers, Library of Congress, Washington

Co-efficients Dining Club papers, LSE Library Archives and Special Collections

Foundations of British Sociology Archive, Keele University

Franklin Giddings papers, Rare Book & Manuscript Library, Columbia University

E. A. Freeman papers, John Rylands Library, University of Manchester

Alfred Thayer Mahan papers, Library of Congress, Washington

Cecil Rhodes papers, Rhodes House Library, University of Oxford

Royal Commonwealth Society papers, University of Cambridge Library

John Robert Seeley papers, University of London Library

W. T. Stead papers, Churchill Archives Centre, Churchill College, Cambridge

Clarence Streit papers, Library of Congress, Washington

Graham Wallace papers, LSE Archives and Special Collections

H. G. Wells papers, Rare Book and Manuscript Library, University of Illinois at Urbana-Champaign

Printed Primary Sources

[Anon.], "Bishop Doane on the War," *New York Times*, 16 November 1898, 6.

[Anon.], "Captain Mahan on Imperial Federation," *The Nation*, 22 May 1902, 400–401.

[Anon.], "Cecil Rhodes as a Type," *The Nation*, 3 April 1902, 264–65.

[Anon.], "Contemporary Literature: Sociology, Politics and Jurisprudence," *Westminster Review*, 160 (1903), 585–89.

[Anon.], "Estimates of Cecil Rhodes," *Literary Digest*, 24/14 (1902), 453–54.

[Anon.], "Father of Union Now," *Scribner's Commentary*, June 1941, 81.

[Anon.], "The Federation of the British Empire: Thoughts for the Queen's Jubilee on Imperial Federation," *Westminster Review*, 128 (1887), 484–94.

[Anon.], "Gladstone's Ghost Talks with Stead," *New York Times*, 1 November 1909, 4.

[Anon.], "Mr Carnegie Defends Spelling Reform Plan," *New York Times*, 25 March 1906, 4.

[Anon.], "Mr. Carnegie's Greatest Gift," *The Nation*, 91 (1910), 597.

[Anon.], "Our Australian Possessions," *London Quarterly Review*, 1/2 (1853), 517–57.

[Anon.], review of Frederic Whyte, *A Modern Knight-Errant*, *Saturday Review*, 12 December 1925, 405.

[Anon.], "Reviews and Magazines," *Saturday Review of Politics, Literature, Science and Art*, 10 November 1897, 393–95.

[Anon.], "Stanley Waterloo Dead: Veteran Editor and Author a Victim of Pneumonia," *New York Times*, 12 October 1913, 15.

[Anon.], "The United States and Spain," *Quarterly Review*, 188 (1898), 216–43.

[Anon.], "Was Cecil Rhodes Crazy?," *Literary Digest*, 24/16 (1902), 529–30.

Abbott, Lyman, *The Rights of Man: A Twentieth Century Problem* (Boston: Houghton Mifflin, 1902).

———, "The Basis of an Anglo-American Understanding," *North American Review*, 166/498 (1898), 513–21.

———, *The Evolution of Christianity* (Boston: Houghton, Mifflin, 1892).

Acton, John Emerich Edward Dalberg, "Inaugural Lecture on the Study of History" in *Lectures on Modern History*, ed. J. N. Figgis and R. V. Laurence (London: Macmillan, 1906), 1–30.

———, review of James Bryce, *American Commonwealth*, *English Historical Review*, 4/14 (1889), 388–96.

Adams, George Burton, *The British Empire and a League of Peace: Suggesting the Purpose and Form of an Alliance of the English-speaking Peoples* (London: G. P. Putnam, 1919).

———, "A Century of Anglo-Saxon Expansion," *Atlantic Monthly*, 79 (April 1897), 528–38.

Adorno, Theodor, and Max Horkheimer, *Dialectic of Enlightenment: Philosophical Fragments*, ed. G. S. Noerr, trans. E. Jephcott (1947; Stanford: Stanford University Press, 2002).

Alderson, Barnard, *Andrew Carnegie: The Man and His Work* (New York: Doubleday, 1902).

———, *Arthur James Balfour, His Life and Work* (London: Grant Richards, 1903).

Alger, R. A., "America's Attitude toward England," *North American Review*, 170/520 (1900), 332–34.

Angell, Norman, *The Political Conditions of Allied Success: A Plea for the Protective Union of the Democracies* (New York: Putnam, 1918).

———, *The Great Illusion: A Study of the Relation of Military Power in Nations to Their Economic and Social Advantage* (London: G. P. Putnam's, 1910).

Anglo-American Committee, *An American Response to Expressions of English Sympathy* (New York: Anglo-American Committee, 1899).

Anson, Charles, *The Great Anglo-American War of 1900* (London: Stanford, 1896).

Anson, William, *The Law and Custom of the Constitution*, 3 vols. (Oxford: Clarendon, 1886–1892).

Anthony, Edwyn, "Mr Andrew Carnegie and the Re-union of the English-speaking Race," *Westminster Review*, 163/6 (1905), 636–42.

Arnold, Thomas, *History of Rome*, 3 vols. (London: T. Fellowes, 1838–42).

Asquith, Herbert H., "The English Bible" (1911), in Asquith, *Occasional Addresses, 1893–1916* (London: Macmillan, 1918), 127–36.

Auerbach, Joseph, review of Wells, *Future in America*, *North American Review*, 104/608 (1907), 292–301.

Austin, Louis F., "Our Note Book," *Illustrated London News*, 12 April 1902, 516.

Baker, Herbert, *Cecil Rhodes, by His Architect* (London: Oxford University Press, 1934).

Balfour, Arthur J., *The Mind of Arthur James Balfour; Selections from His Non-Political Writings, Speeches, and Addresses, 1878–1917*, ed. Wilfrid Short (New York: George Dorran, 1918).

————, "Race and Nationality," *Transactions of the Honourable Society of Cymmrodorion, Session 1908–9* (London, 1909), 237–42.

Barker, Ernest, *Political Thought in England, 1848–1914* (London: Butterworth, 1915).

————, *The Political Thought of Plato and Aristotle* (London: Methuen, 1906).

Barker, James Ellis, "An Anglo-American Reunion" (1913), in Barker, *The Great Problems of British Statesmanship* (London: Macmillan, 1917), 398–431.

————, *Great and Greater Britain: The Problems of Motherland and Empire* (London: Smith, 1909).

Barnes, James, *The Unpardonable War* (New York: Macmillan, 1904).

Barton, Samuel, *The Battle of the Swash and the Capture of Canada* (New York: Charles Dillingham, 1888).

Beer, George Louis, *The English-Speaking Peoples: Their Future Relations and Joint International Obligations* (London: Macmillan, 1917).

Bellamy, Edward, *Looking Backward 2000–1887*, ed. Matthew Beaumont (1888; Oxford: Oxford University Press, 2009).

Bennett, Arthur, *The Dream of an Englishman* (London: Simpkin, 1893).

————, "Federation Made Easy," *Imperial Federation*, 8 (1893), 320–21.

Bérard, Victor, *British Imperialism and Commercial Supremacy*, trans. H. W. Foskett (London: Longman's, Green, 1906).

Beresford, Charles, *The Memoirs of Admiral Lord Charles Beresford*, 2 vols. (Boston: Little, Brown, 1914).

————, "The Future of the Anglo-Saxon Race," *North American Review*, 171/529 (1900), 802–10.

————, "The Anglo-American Entente," *Pall Mall Magazine*, 18 (1899), 379–83.

————, *The Break-up of China* (New York: Harper, 1899).

————, "China and the Great Powers," *North American Review*, 168/510 (1899), 53–58.

Besant, Walter, *Autobiography of Walter Besant* (New York: Dodd, 1902).

————, "Object of Atlantic Union," *New York Times*, 4 June 1900.

————, "A Plea for St. George's Day," *Cornhill Magazine*, 2/10 (1897), 435–47.

————, *The Rise of the Empire* (London: Horace Marshall, 1897).

————, "The Future of the Anglo-Saxon Race," *North American Review*, 163/477 (1896), 129–43.

Bloch, Jean de, "The Wars of the Future," *Contemporary Review*, 80 (1901), 305–32.

————, *Is War Now Impossible? Being an Abridgement of "The War of the Future in Its Technical, Economic and Political Relations," with a Prefatory Conversation with the Author by W. T. Stead* (London: Grant Richards, 1899).

Boutmy, Gaston, *The English People: A Study of Their Political Psychology*, trans. E. English (London: G. P. Putnam, 1904).

Bradley, Henry, and James Murray (eds.), *A New English Dictionary on Historical Principles: Founded Mainly on the Materials Collected by the Philological Society* (Oxford: Clarendon Press, 1901).

Brooks, Van Wyck, *The World of H. G. Wells* (New York: Haskell, 1915).

Brougham Leech, Henry, *An Essay on Ancient International Law* (Dublin: Ponsonby & Murphy, 1877).

Brown, James Scott (ed.), *Texts of the Peace Conferences at the Hague, 1899 and 1907* (Boston: Ginn, 1908).

Bruce, John Edward, "The White Man's Burden" (c.1910), in *The Selected Writings of John Edward Bruce*, ed. Peter Gilbert (New York: Arno, 1971), 97–99.

————, "Dr. Theophilus E. S. Scholes, M.D.," *The Voice*, 4/2 (March 1907), 115.

————, "The Negro and His Future" (c.1900), in *Selected Writings*, 59–60.

————, "Is This Our Country?" (1883), in *Selected Writings*, 23–25.

Bryan, William Jennings, *Bryan on Imperialism: Speeches, Newspaper Articles, and Interviews* (Chicago: Bentley & Company, 1900).

————, "Imperialism" (1900), in *Speeches of William Jennings Bryan* (New York: Funk & Wagnalls, 1909), II, 17–49.

Bryce, James, *Proposals for the Prevention of Future Wars* (London: G. Allen & Unwin, 1917).

————, "The Influence of National Character and Historical Environment on the Development of the Common Law," *Journal of the Society of Comparative Legislation*, 8/2 (1907), 203–16.

————, "Some Difficulties in Colonial Government Encountered by Great Britain and How They Have Been Met," *Annals of the American Academy of Political and Social Science*, 30 (1907), 16–23.

————, "Arbitration with Great Britain: Public Felling in England on the Subject of a Treaty," *Advocate of Peace*, 66/4 (1904), 64–65.

————, *The Relations of the Advanced and the Backward Races of Mankind* (Oxford: Clarendon, 1902).

————, "Some Reflections on the State of Cuba," *North American Review*, 174/545 (1902), 445–56.

————, "The Essential Unity of England and America," *Atlantic Monthly*, 82 (July 1898), 22–29.

————, "British Feeling on the Venezuela Question," *North American Review*, 162/471 (1896), 145–53.

————, "Political Organisation in the United States and England," *North American Review*, 156/434 (1893), 105–18.

————, "Edward Augustus Freeman," *English Historical Review*, 7/27 (1892), 497–509.

————, "An Age of Discontent," *Contemporary Review*, 59 (1891), 14–29.

————, "Thoughts on the Negro Problem," *North American Review*, 153/421 (1891), 641–60.

————, *The American Commonwealth*, 3 vols. (London: Macmillan, 1888).

————, "The Predictions of Hamilton and de Tocqueville," *Johns Hopkins Studies in Historical and Political Science*, 5th ser. 9 (1887), 5–57.

Butler, Samuel, *Erewhon*, ed. Peter Mudford (1872; London: Penguin, 1970).

Carman, Bliss (ed.), *The World's Best Poetry, VIII: National Spirit* (Philadelphia: Morris, 1904).

Carnegie, Andrew, "Confession of Religious Faith," in Carnegie, *Miscellaneous Writings of Andrew Carnegie*, ed. Burton Hendrick, 2 vols. (New York: Doubleday, 1933), II.

————, *The Autobiography of Andrew Carnegie* (1920; London: Penguin, 2006).

————, "Labour" in Carnegie, *The Empire of Business* (New York: Doubleday, 1917), 233–65.

————, *Address to the Fourth American Peace Congress, St. Louis, May 1913* (New York: Redfield, 1913).

————, *A Rectorial Address Delivered to the Students in the University of Aberdeen, 6th June, 1912* (New York: Redfield, 1912).

————, *Britain and Her Offspring* (London: Wertheimer, 1911).

————, "The Moral Issue Involved in War," *Advocate of Peace*, 73/2 (1911), 34–36.

————, *Speech by Andrew Carnegie at the Annual Meeting of the Peace Society in the Guildhall, London, May 24th, 1910* (London: The Peace Society, 1910).

——, "War as the Mother of Valor and Civilization," *Advocate of Peace*, 72/4 (1910), 82–83.

——, "The Path to Peace," *Advocate of Peace*, 71/8 (1909), 184–85.

——, "The Wrong Path," *Advocate of Peace*, 71/5 (1909), 103.

——, *The Wrong Path; A Speech Delivered at the Annual Meeting of the New York Peace Society, on April 21st, 1909* (New York: Peace Society, 1909).

——, "Wages" in *Problems of To-day: Wealth, Labor, Socialism* (New York: Doubleday, 1908), 85–97.

——, *The Negro in America; An Address Delivered before the Philosophical Institution of Edinburgh, 16th October 1907* (Inverness: Carruthers, 1907).

——, *A League of Peace; A Rectorial Address Delivered to the Students in the University of St. Andrews, 17th October, 1905* (Boston: Ginn, 1906).

——, *Drifting Together: Will the United States and Canada Unite?* (New York: The World's Work Press, 1904).

——, *The Empire of Business* (New York: Doubleday, 1902).

——, "The Opportunity of the United States," *North American Review*, 174/546 (1902), 606–12.

——, *A Rectorial Address Delivered to the Students in the University of St. Andrews, 22nd October, 1902* (Edinburgh: Constable, 1902).

——, *Three Busy Weeks: Dr Carnegie at Perth, Edinburgh, Greenock, Falkirk, Stirling, Hawarden, Liverpool, St. Andrews, Dundee*, ed. Andrew S. Cunningham (Dunfermline: Clark & Sons, 1902).

——, "Americanism versus Imperialism: II," *North American Review*, 168/508 (1899), 362–72.

——, "Americanism versus Imperialism," *North American Review*, 168/506 (1899), 1–13.

——, "The South African Question," *North American Review*, 169/517 (1899), 798–804.

——, "Distant Possessions: The Parting of the Ways," *North American Review*, 167/501 (1898), 239–48.

——, "The Venezuelan Question," *North American Review*, 162/471 (1896), 129–44.

——, "A Look Ahead," *North American Review*, 156/439 (1893), 685–710.

——, *The Reunion of Britain and America: A Look Ahead* (Edinburgh: Andrew Elliott, 1893).

——, "Imperial Federation: An American View," *Nineteenth Century*, 30 (1891), 490–508.

——, "Do Americans Really Hate England?," *North American Review*, 150/403 (1890), 753–58.

——, "The Gospel of Wealth" (1889), reprinted in Carnegie, *The Autobiography of Andrew Carnegie*, 323–36.

——, "Democracy in England," *North American Review*, 142/350 (1886), 74–80.

——, *Triumphant Democracy, or, Fifty Years' March of the Republic* (New York: Scribner's & Sons, 1886).

——, *An American Four in Hand in Britain* (New York: Scribner's, 1883).

——, *Round the World* (New York: Scribner's, 1883).

——, "As Others See Us," *Fortnightly Review*, 31/182 (1882), 157–65.

Casparian, Gregory, *The Anglo-American Alliance: A Serio-Comic Romance and Forecast of the Future* (New York: Mayflower, 1906).

Chamberlain, Joseph, "Speech at Leicester (30 November)," *The Times*, 1 December 1899, 7.

——, "Recent Developments of Policy in the United States," *Scribner's Magazine*, 24 (1898), 674–82.

——, "The Mild Sovereignty of the Queen" (30 December 1887), in Chamberlain, *Foreign and Colonial Speeches* (London: Routledge, 1897), 3–14.

——, *Patriotism: Address Delivered to the Students of the University of Glasgow, on November 3rd, 1897, on the Occasion of His Installation as Lord Rector* (London: Constable, 1897).

——, "The True Conception of Empire" (31 March 1897), in Chamberlain, *Foreign and Colonial Speeches*, 241–49.

Chapman, Frederick William, "The Changed Significance of 'Anglo-Saxon,'" *Education*, 20 (1900), 368–69.

Chesney, George, *The Battle of Dorking* (1871), in Clarke, *Tale of the Next Great War*, 27–73.

Chesterton, G. K., "The Great Shipwreck as Analogy," *Illustrated London News*, 11 May 1912, in Chesterton, *Collected Works* (San Francisco: Ignatius Press, 1988), XXIX, 288–91.

——, "The Sultan" in Chesterton, *A Miscellany of Men* (London: Methuen, 1912), 202–8.

——, *The Napoleon of Notting Hill* (London: Bodley, 1904).

Clark, John Spencer, *The Life and Letters of John Fiske* (Boston: Houghton Mifflin, 1917).

Clarke, George Sydenham, "Imperial Responsibilities a National Gain," *North American Review*, 168/507 (1899), 129–41.

——, "England and America: Is an Anglo-American Alliance Possible?," *Living Age*, 10/9 (1898), 691–99.

——, "A Naval Union with Great Britain: A Reply to Mr. Andrew Carnegie," *North American Review*, 158/448 (1894), 353–65.

——, [pseud. A. Nelson Seaforth], *The Last Great Naval War: An Historical Retrospect* (London: Cassell, 1891).

Clough, Arthur, *The Poems and Prose Remains of Arthur Hugh Clough*, 2 vols. (London: Macmillan, 1869).

Coates, James (ed.), *Has W. T. Stead Returned?: A Symposium* (London: Fowler, 1913).

Cobden, Richard, "England, Ireland, and America" (1835), in Cobden, *Political Writings* (London: William Ridgway, 1867), I, 1–154.

Coker, Francis, *Readings in Political Philosophy* (London: Macmillan, 1914).

Colburn, Richard T., "Improvident Civilization," *Proceedings of the American Association for the Advancement of Science*, 46 (1897), 395–448.

Cole, William Robert, *The Struggle for Empire: A Story of the Year 2236* (1900), in *Political Future Fiction*, ed. R. Bleiler (London: Pickering & Chatto, 2013), I, 133–99.

Colomb, Philip Howard, *The Great War of 189-* (London: Heinemann, 1892).

Conant, Charles, "The Economic Basis of Imperialism," *North American Review*, 167/502 (1898), 326–40.

Constant, Benjamin, "The Spirit of Conquest" (1814), in *Political Writings*, ed. Biancamaria Fontana (Cambridge: Cambridge University Press, 1988), 51–165.

Conway, Daniel, *Autobiography: Memories and Experiences of Moncure Daniel Conway* (New York: Houghton, Mifflin, 1904).

Cooper, Anna Julia, *A Voice from the South: By a Black Woman of the South* (Xenia, OH: Aldine, 1892).

Cust, Henry, "Cecil Rhodes," *North American Review*, 175/548 (1902), 99–114.

Danyers, Geoffrey, *Blood Is Thicker Than Water: A Political Dream* (London: Tower, 1894).

Davenport, Benjamin Rush, *Blood Will Tell: The Strange Story of a Son of Ham* (Cleveland: Caxton, 1902).

————, *Anglo-Saxons, Onward! A Romance of the Future* (Cleveland: Hubbell, 1898).

Davis, Andrew McFarland, "John Fiske," *Proceedings of the American Academy of Arts and Sciences*, 37/23 (1902), 665–72.

Delany, Martin, *The Principia of Ethnology: The Origin of Races and Color, with an Archaeological Compendium of Ethiopian and Egyptian Civilization* (Philadelphia: Harper & Brother, 1879).

————, *Blake, or the Huts of America*, ed. Jerome McGann (1861; Cambridge, MA: Harvard University Press, 2017).

Demolins, Edmond, *Anglo-Saxon Superiority: To What It Is Due*, trans. Louis Bert Lavigne (London: Leadenhall, 1898).

Deniker, Joseph, *The Races of Man: An Outline of Anthropology and Ethnography* (London: Walter Scott, 1900).

De Winton, Frances W., "Address," *Proceedings of the Royal Geographical Society*, 11 (1889), 613–22.

Dicey, Albert Venn, *Memorials of Albert Venn Dicey, Being Chiefly Letters and Diaries*, ed. Robert S. Rait (London: Macmillan, 1925).

————, *Introduction to the Study of the Law of the Constitution*, 8th ed. (1885; London, 1915).

————, *Lectures on the Relation between Law and Public Opinion in England during the Nineteenth Century* (London: Macmillan, 1905).

————, "The Teaching of English Law at Harvard," *Harvard Law Review*, 13/5 (1900), 422–40.

————, "England and America," *Atlantic Monthly*, 82 (October 1898), 441–45.

————, "A Common Citizenship for the English Race," *Contemporary Review*, 71 (1897), 457–76.

————, *Lectures Introductory to the Study of the Law of the Constitution* (London: Macmillan, 1885).

Dickinson, G. Lowes, *The War and the Way Out* (London: Chancery Lane Press, 1915).

Dilke, Charles W., "America and England in the East," *North American Review*, 169/515 (1899), 558–63.

————, *The British Empire* (London: Chatto & Windus, 1899).

————, "An Anglo-American Alliance," *Pall Mall Magazine*, 16/65 (1898), 37–38.

————, *Problems of Greater Britain* (London: Macmillan, 1890).

————, *Greater Britain, a Record of Travel in English-Speaking Countries during 1866 and 1867*, 2 vols. (London: Macmillan, 1868).

Doane, William C., "Patriotism: Its Defects, Its Dangers and Its Duties," *North American Review*, 166/496 (1898), 310–23.

Donnelly, Hugh Grattan, *The Stricken Nation* (New York: C. T. Baker, 1890).

Dos Passos, John Roderigo, *The Anglo-Saxon Century and the Unification of the English-speaking People*, 2nd ed. (New York: Putnam, 1903).

Dougall, John D., "An Anglo-Saxon Alliance," *Contemporary Review*, 48 (1885), 693–707.

Douglass, Frederick, *The Narrative of Frederick Douglass* (Boston: Anti-Slavery Office, 1845).

Doyle, Arthur Conan, "The Adventures of the Noble Bachelor" in Doyle, *The Adventures of Sherlock Holmes* (London: George Newnes, 1892), 235–60.

————, *The White Company* (London: George Newnes, 1891).

Droppers, Garrett, "Sense of the State," *Journal of Political Economy*, 15/2 (1907), 109–12.

Du Bois, W. E. B., "The Comet" in Du Bois, *Darkwater: Voices from within the Veil* (New York: Harcourt, Brace & Howe, 1920), 253–74.

————, "The African Roots of War" (1915), in *Writings by W. E. B Du Bois in Periodicals Edited by Others*, ed. Herbert Aptheker (New York: Kraus-Thompson, 1982), II, 98–105.

———, "Scientific Reasons against Race Antagonism" (1914), in *Writings*, II, 92–94.

———, "Coming of the Lesser Folk" (1911), in *Writings*, II, 43–47.

———, "The First Universal Races Congress" (1911), in *Writings*, II, 48–51.

———, "The Souls of White Folk" (1910), in *Writings*, II, 25–29.

———, "Race Friction between Black and White" (1908), in *Writings*, I, 386–90.

———, "The Color Line Belts the World" (1906), in *Writings*, I, 330–31.

———, "Credo" (1904), in *Writings*, I, 229–30.

———, "The Development of a People" (1904), in *Writings*, I, 203–15.

———, "The Laboratory in Sociology at Atlanta University" (1903), in *Writings*, I, 158–60.

———, *The Souls of Black Folk* (1903; New York: Penguin, 2018).

———, "The Present Outlook for the Dark Races of Mankind" (1900), in *Writings*, I, 73–82.

———, "To the Nations of the World" (1900), in W. E. B. Du Bois Papers (MS 312), Special Collections and University Archives, University of Massachusetts Amherst Libraries.

———, *The Conservation of Races* (Washington, DC: American Negro Academy, 1897).

Dumas, Jacques, "Sanctions of International Arbitration," *American Journal of International Law*, 5/4 (1911), 934–57.

Duras, Victor H., *Universal Peace* (New York: Broadway, 1908).

Egerton, Hugh E., *Federations and Unions within the British Empire* (Oxford: Oxford University Press, 1911).

Ferguson, William S., *Greek Imperialism* (New York: Houghton Mifflin, 1913).

Fernald, James, *The Imperial Republic* (New York: Funk & Wagnalls, 1898).

Ferris, William H., *The African Abroad or, His Evolution in Western Civilization: Tracing His Development under Caucasian Milieu* (New Haven, CT: Tuttle, Taylor, 1913).

Finer, Herman, *Foreign Governments at Work* (Oxford: Oxford University Press, 1921).

Finlay, Robert, "International Arbitration," *North American Review*, 179/576 (1904), 659–70.

Fisher, Herbert A. L., *James Bryce* (London: Macmillan, 1927).

———, *Political Unions* (Oxford: Oxford University Press, 1911).

Fisher, John, *Memoirs, by Admiral of the Fleet, Lord Fisher* (London: Hodder & Stoughton, 1919).

Fiske, John, "Edward Augustus Freeman" (1893), in Fiske, *A Century of Science and Other Essays* (Boston: Houghton Mifflin, 1899), 265–85.

———, *The Discovery of America*, 2 vols. (Boston: Houghton Mifflin, 1892).

———, *The Critical Period of American History, 1783–1789* (Boston: Houghton Mifflin, 1888).

———, *American Political Ideas Viewed from the Standpoint of Universal History* (Boston: Houghton Mifflin, 1885).

———, "Manifest Destiny," *Harper's Magazine* (March 1885), 578–89.

———, *Outlines of Cosmic Philosophy, Based on the Doctrine of Evolution, with Criticisms on the Positive Philosophy* (Boston: James Osgood, 1874).

Foote, G. W., "Social Dreams," *Progress*, 6 (1886), 189–94.

Freeman, Edward A., *The Life and Letters of Edward A. Freeman*, ed. W. R. W. Stephens, 2 vols. (London: Macmillan, 1895).

———, "The Physical and Political Bases of National Unity" in Arthur Silva White (ed.), *Britannic Confederation* (London: Royal Scottish Geographical Society, 1892), 33–56.

———, "George Washington, the Expander of England" in Freeman, *Greater Greece and Greater Britain* (London: Macmillan, 1886), 62–103.

———, "Imperial Federation" (1885), Appendix in Freeman, *Greater Greece and Greater Britain*, 104–43.

———, *Some Impressions of the United States* (London: Longmans, Green and Co, 1883).

———, "An Introduction to American Institutional History," *Johns Hopkins University Studies in Historical and Political Science*, 1/1 (1882), 13–39.

———, *Lectures to American Audiences* (Philadelphia: Porter, 1882).

———, *Comparative Politics: Six Lectures Read before the Royal Institution in January and February 1873* (London: Macmillan, 1873).

———, *History of Federal Government: From the Foundation of the Achaian League to the Disruption of the United States* (London: Macmillan, 1863).

Froude, James Anthony, *Oceana, or England and Her Colonies* (London: Longman, 1886).

Fuller, Alvarado M., *A.D. 2000* (Chicago: Laird & Lee, 1890).

Fuller, Thomas, *The Right Honourable Cecil Rhodes: A Monograph and Reminiscence* (London: Longman's, 1910).

Garrison, William Lloyd, "War and Imperialism Fatal to Self-Government," *Advocate of Peace*, 60/9 (1898), 208–12.

Garvin, James L., "The Maintenance of the Empire: A Study in the Economics of Power" in Goldman, *The Empire and Century*, 61–80.

Giddings, Franklin Henry, "The Concepts and Methods of Sociology," *American Journal of Sociology*, 10/2 (1904), 161–76.

———, *Democracy and Empire* (London: Macmillan, 1900).

———, *The Principles of Sociology: An Analysis of the Phenomena of Association and of Social Organization* (London: Macmillan, 1896).

Gladstone, William E., "Kin Beyond Sea," *North American Review*, 127/264 (1878), 179–212.

Godkin, Edwin Lawrence, "Imperialism," *The Nation*, 65 (1897), 511–14.

Goldman, Charles Sydney (ed.), *The Empire and Century: A Series of Essays on Imperial Problems and Possibilities by Various Authors* (London: John Murray, 1905).

Gooch, George Peabody, review of *The Hindrances of Good Citizenship*, *International Journal of Ethics*, 21/1 (1910), 110–12.

———, "Imperialism" in C. F. G. Masterman (ed.), *The Heart of Empire* (London: Unwin, 1901), 308–94.

Green, Thomas Hill, "The Right of the State over the Individual in War" (1886), in Green, *Lectures on the Principles of Political Obligation*, ed. Paul Harris and John Murrow (Cambridge: Cambridge University Press, 1986), 130–35.

Greenslet, Ferris, *James Russell Lowell, His Life and Work* (Boston: Houghton, Mifflin, 1905).

Grey, Henry, Earl Grey, "How Shall We Retain the Colonies?," *Nineteenth Century*, 5 (1879), 935–54.

Grey, Sir George, "The Federation of the English-speaking People: A Talk with Sir George Grey," *Contemporary Review*, 66 (1894), 192–209.

Griffith, George, *The Great Pirate Syndicate* (London: F. V. White, 1899).

———, *Men Who Have Made the Empire* (London: Pearson, 1897).

———, *Olga Romanoff: Or, the Syren of the Skies: A Sequel to "The Angel of the Revolution"* (London: Simpkin, Marshall, 1897).

———, "The Grave of a Nation's Honour," *Pearson's Magazine* (March 1896), 261–65.

————, *The Angel of the Revolution: A Tale of the Coming Terror*, ed. Steven McLean (1893; London: Victorian Secrets, 2012).

Griggs, Sutton, *Imperium in Imperio* (1899; New York: Modern Classics, 2003).

Hale, Edward Everett, *James Russell Lowell* (Boston: Small, Maynard, 1899).

Hammond, J. L., "Colonial and Foreign Policy" in F. W. Hirst, Gilbert Murray, and Hammond, *Liberalism and the Empire* (London, 1900), 161–62.

Hankins, Franklin, "Race as a Factor in Political Theory" in Charles Merriam and Harry Elmer Barnes (eds.), *A History of Political Theories, Recent Times* (New York: Macmillan, 1924), 508–48.

Harnack, Adolf von, *The Mission and Expansion of Christianity in the First Three Centuries*, trans. James Moffatt, 2 vols. (London: Williams & Norgate, 1908).

Harper, Edith K., *Stead, the Man: Personal Reminiscences* (London: William Rider, 1918).

Harrington, James, *"The Commonwealth of Oceana" and "The System of Politics"*, ed. J. G. A. Pocock (1656; Cambridge: Cambridge University Press, 1990).

Harrison, Benjamin, "Musings upon Current Topics, II," *North American Review*, 172/532 (1901), 354–58.

————, "The Status of Annexed Territory and of Its Free Civilized Inhabitants," *North American Review*, 172/530 (1901), 1–22.

Hay, William D., *Three Hundred Years Hence* (London: Newman and Co., 1881).

Hazeltine, Mayo, "The United States and Great Britain: A Reply to Mr. David A. Wells," *North American Review*, 162/474 (1896), 594–606.

Hensman, Howard, *Cecil Rhodes: A Study of a Career* (London: Blackwood, 1902).

Hershey, Amos S., "The History of International Relations during Antiquity and the Middle Ages," *American Journal of International Law*, 5/4 (1911), 901–33.

Hewins, William Albert Samuel, *The Apologia of an Imperialist: Forty Years of Empire Policy* (London: Constable, 1929).

Hirst, Francis Wrigley, *The Six Panics and Other Essays* (London: Methuen, 1913).

————, "Imperialism and Finance" in F. W. Hirst, G. Murray, and J. L. Hammond, *Liberalism and the Empire* (London: R. Brimley Johnson, 1900), 41–75.

Hoar, George F., "Love of Country" in Hoar, *The Book of Patriotism* (Boston: Hall & Locke, 1902), xiii–xx.

Hobhouse, Leonard T., *Liberalism and Other Writings*, ed. J. Meadowcroft (1911; Cambridge: Cambridge University Press, 1994).

————, "The Growth of the State" in Hobhouse, *Liberalism and Other Writings*, 136–51.

————, *Social Evolution and Political Theory* (New York: Columbia University Press, 1911).

————, *Democracy and Reaction*, ed. Peter Clarke (1904; Brighton: Harvester, 1972).

Hobson, John Atkinson, *Towards International Government* (London: G. Allen & Unwin, 1915).

————, *Canada To-day* (London: Fisher Unwin, 1906).

————, "The Ethics of Internationalism," *International Journal of Ethics*, 17/1 (1906), 16–28.

————, *Imperialism: A Study*, ed. Philip Siegelman (1902; Ann Arbor: University of Michigan Press, 1997).

————, "The Scientific Basis of Imperialism," *Political Science Quarterly*, 17/3 (1902), 460–89.

————, *The Psychology of Jingoism* (London: Grant Richards, 1901).

———, "Edward Bellamy and the Utopian Romance," *The Humanitarian*, 13 (1898), 179–89.

Horwill, Herbert, "W. T. Stead," *The Nation*, 17 March 1926, 292.

Hosmer, James K., "The American Evolution: Dependence, Independence, Interdependence," *Atlantic Monthly*, 82 (July 1898), 29–36.

———, *A Short History of Anglo-Saxon Freedom: The Polity of the English-speaking Race* (New York: Scribner's, 1890).

Hotchkiss, Willard, review of Jebb, *Studies in Colonial Nationalism*, *Annals of the American Academy of Political and Social Science*, 219 (1905), 427–29.

Howells, William D., "The New Poetry," *North American Review*, 168/510 (1899), 581–92.

Hume, David, "Of the Jealousy of Trade" (1758), in Hume, *Essays, Moral, Political, and Literary*, ed. Eugene Miller (Indianapolis: Liberty Fund, 1985), 327–32.

Hutchinson, H. N., J. W. Gregory, and R. Lydekker, *The Living Races of Mankind* (New York: Appleton, 1902).

Huxley, Thomas Henry, "Prolegomena to *Ethics and Evolution*" (1894), in *T. H. Huxley's "Evolution and Ethics"*, ed. James Paradis and George Williams (Princeton, NJ: Princeton University Press, 1989), 59–103.

———, "Evolution and Ethics" (1893), in *Huxley's "Evolution and Ethics"*, 104–45.

———, "The Struggle for Existence in Human Society: A Programme," *Popular Science Monthly*, 32/4 (1888), 161–80.

———, *Hume* (London: Macmillan, 1879).

Hyndman, Henry Mayers, *Further Reminiscences* (London: MacMillan, 1912).

Jackson, Frederick Turner, "The Significance of the Frontier in American History" (1893), in J. M. Faragher (ed.), *Rereading Frederick Jackson Turner* (New Haven, CT: Yale University Press, 1998), 31–60.

James, Henry, *The Letters of Henry James*, ed. Percy Lubbock (New York: Charles Scribner's, 1920).

James, William, *The Correspondence of William James*, 12 vols., ed. Ignas Skrupskelis and Elizabeth Berkeley (Charlottesville: University Press of Virginia, 2002–2004).

———, *Pragmatism* (1907), in *Pragmatism and Other Writings*, ed. Giles Gunn (London: Penguin, 2000).

———, "The Moral Equivalent of War" (1906), in James, *Writings, 1902–1910* (New York: Penguin, 1987), 274–86.

Jebb, Richard, *Studies in Colonial Nationalism* (London: Edward Arnold, 1905).

Jevons, H. Stanley, "The Development of an International Parliament," *Contemporary Review*, 92 (1907), 305–26.

Jeyes, Samuel, *Mr. Chamberlain, His Life and Public Career* (London: Sands, 1903).

Jones, Henry Arthur, *My Dear Wells: A Manual for the Haters of England; Being a Series of Letters Addressed to Mr. H. G. Wells* (New York: E. P. Dutton, 1921).

Jordan, David Starr, *Imperial Democracy* (New York: Appleton, 1899).

———, *The Question of the Philippines, An Address Delivered before the Graduate Club of Leland Stanford Junior University on February 14th 1899* (Palo Alto: Valentine, 1899).

Jourdan, Philip, *Cecil Rhodes: His Private Life, by His Private Secretary* (London: John Lane, 1911).

Kant, Immanuel, "Perpetual Peace: A Philosophical Sketch" (1795), in Kant, *Political Writings*, 2nd ed., ed. Hans Reiss (Cambridge: Cambridge University Press, 1991), 93–130.

Kaufmann, Moritz, *Utopias, or Schemes of Social Improvement, from Thomas More to Karl Marx* (London: Kegan Paul, 1879).

Kayser, Harriett, *Bishop Potter, the People's Friend* (New York: Whittaker, 1910).

Kemble, John M., *The Saxons in England: A History of the English Commonwealth till the Period of the Norman Conquest*, 2 vols. (London: Longman, Brown, Green & Longmans, 1849).

Kennedy, Howard Angus, "Prologue," in Besant, *The Rise of the Empire* (1897), vii–xiv.

Kennedy, Sinclair, *The Pan-Angles: A Consideration of the Federation of the Seven English-Speaking Nations* (London: Longman's, 1915).

Kent, W. H., "Patriotism or Imperialism?," *Westminster Review*, 157 (1902), 126–38.

Kidd, Benjamin, *The Control of the Tropics* (London: Macmillan, 1898).

———, *Social Evolution* (London: Macmillan, 1894).

Kipling, Rudyard, "The View of the World," *The Times*, 9 April 1902.

———, "The White Man's Burden: The United States and the Philippine Islands," *McClure's Magazine*, 12 (1899), 290–91.

Lally-Tolendal, Trophime-Gérard, *The Dream of an Englishman, Faithful to His King and Country* (London: P. Elmsly, 1793).

Lang-Tung [pseud.], *The Decline and Fall of the British Empire: Being a History of England between the Years 1840–1981* (London: F. V. White, 1881).

Latta, Robert, "Memoir" in David G. Ritchie, *Philosophical Studies*, ed. Latta (London: Macmillan, 1905), 1–65.

Lecky, W. E. H., *The Empire: Its Value and Its Growth* (London: Longman's, 1893).

Leech, H. J. (ed.), *The Public Letters of the Rt. Hon. John Bright* (London: Sampson, 1895).

Lenin, Vladimir Ilyich, *Imperialism, the Highest Stage of Capitalism* (1916; London: Pluto, 1996).

———, *Socialism and War* (1915), in Lenin, *Collected Works*, ed. Julian Katzer (Moscow: Progress, 1964), XXI, 295–388.

Le Bon, Gustave, *The Crowd, A Study of the Popular Mind* (London: E. Benn, 1896).

Le Queux, William, "Preface to the 9th Edition," *The Great War in England in 1897*, 11th ed. (London: Tower, 1895).

Le Sueur, Gordon, *Cecil Rhodes: The Man and His Work* (London: Murray, 1913).

Little, J. Stanley, *Progress of British Empire in the Century* (London: Chambers, 1903).

Lodge, Henry C., "England, Venezuela, and the Monroe Doctrine," *North American Review*, 160/463 (1895), 651–58.

Lord, Eleanor, "International Arbitration," *Annals of the American Academy of Political and Social Science*, 2 (1892), 39–55.

Lovett, Robert Morss, "A Nonconformist Journalist," *New Republic*, 16 December 1925, 115.

Low, Sidney, "Some Personal Recollections of Cecil Rhodes," *Nineteenth Century and After*, 51 (1902), 828–40.

Lowell, A. Lawrence, *A League to Enforce Peace* (Boston: World Peace Foundation, 1915).

———, *The Government of England* (1908; London: Macmillan, 1914).

———, "The Colonial Expansion of the United States," *Atlantic Monthly*, 83 (January 1899), 145–54.

———, review, Hosmer, *Annals of the American Academy of Political and Social Science*, 1/1 (1891), 492–95.

Lowell, James Russell, *American Ideas for English Readers* (London: Cupples, 1902).

Lucy, Henry, "Cecil Rhodes: Some Personal Reminisces," *Chambers Journal*, 9 (1919), 145.

Luxemburg, Rosa, "Peace Utopias," *Labour Monthly*, July 1911, 421–28.

Lynch, Frederick Henry, *The Peace Problem: The Task of the Twentieth Century* (New York: Fleming H. Revell Company, 1911).

MacDonald, Ramsey, *Labour and the Empire* (London: George Allen, 1907).

Macnie, John, *The Diothas; or, A Far Look Ahead* (New York: Putnam's, 1883).

Mahan, Alfred T., *The Letters and Papers of Alfred Thayer Mahan*, ed. Robert Seager and Doris Maguire, 3 vols. (Annapolis, MD: Naval Institute Press, 1975).

———, "Motives to Imperial Federation" (1902), in Mahan, *Retrospect & Prospect: Studies in International Relations Naval and Political* (Boston: Little, Brown, 1902), 89–138.

———, "The Influence of the South African War upon the Prestige of the British Empire" (1901), in Mahan, *Retrospect & Prospect*, 57–88.

———, *The Problem of Asia and Its Effect upon International Politics* (Boston: Little, Brown, 1900).

———, "The Peace Conference and the Moral Aspect of War," *North American Review*, 169/515 (1899), 433–47.

———, "A Twentieth Century Outlook," *Harper's*, 95/508 (1897), 521–33.

———, *The Influence of Sea Power on History, 1660–1783* (London: Marston & Low, 1890).

———, "The United States Looking Outward," *Atlantic Monthly*, 66 (December 1890), 816–24.

Mahan, Alfred T., and Charles Beresford, "Possibilities of an Anglo-American Reunion," *North American Review*, 159/456 (1894), 551–73.

Maine, Henry S., *Popular Government* (London: John Murray, 1885).

———, *Ancient Law* (London: Dent, 1861).

Matthews, Brander, *Americanisms and Briticisms, with Other Essays on Other Isms* (New York: Harper, 1892).

McMurray, Orrin, "Inter-Citizenship: A Basis for World Peace," *Yale Law Journal*, 27/3 (1918), 299–316.

Mead, Edwin, "The United States as a World Power," *Advocate of Peace*, 75/3 (1913), 57–62.

Merriam, Charles, *American Political Ideas: Studies in the Development of American Political Thought, 1865–1917* (London: Macmillan, 1920).

Mill, Elliot Evan, *The Decline and Fall of the British Empire: A Brief Account of Those Causes Which Resulted in the Destruction of Our Late Ally, together with a Comparison between the British and Roman Empires; Appointed for Use in the National Schools of Japan* (Oxford: Alden, 1905).

Mill, John Stuart, *Autobiography* (1873), in *The Collected Works of John Stuart Mill*, ed. John Robson (Toronto: University of Toronto Press, 1981), I.

———, *On Liberty* (1859), in *The Collected Works of John Stuart Mill*, ed. John Robson (Toronto: University of Toronto Press, 1977), XVIII.

———, *Principles of Political Economy* (1848), in *The Collected Works of John Stuart Mill*, ed. John Robson (Toronto: University of Toronto Press, 1965), III.

Milne, James, *The Romance of a Pro-consul: Being the Personal Life and Memoirs of the Right Hon. Sir George Grey*, 2nd ed. (London: Chatto & Windus, 1899).

Milner, Alfred, "Credo," *The Times*, 25 July 1925.

———, *The Nation and the Empire* (London: Constable, 1913).

Mitchell, Lewis, *The Life of the Right Honorable Cecil John Rhodes, 1853–1902* (London: Kennerley, 1910).

Molyneux, Henry Howard, Fourth Earl of Carnarvon, *The Defence of the Empire: A Selection from the Letters and Speeches of Henry Howard Molyneux, Fourth Earl of Carnarvon*, ed. G. S. Clarke (London: John Murray, 1897).

Monypenny, William F., "The Imperial Ideal" in Goldman, *The Empire and Century*, 5–28.

Moore, George Edward, *Principia Ethica* (Cambridge: Cambridge University Press, 1903).

More, Thomas, *Utopia*, ed. George Logan and Robert Adams (1516; Cambridge: Cambridge University Press, 1988).

Morley, John, *Recollections* (London: Macmillan, 1917).

———, "Democracy and Reaction" (1904), in Morley, *Critical Miscellanies* (London: Macmillan, 1908), IV, 267–328.

———, "Arbitration with America," *Nineteenth Century*, 40 (1896), 320–37.

———, "The Expansion of England," *Macmillan's Magazine*, 49 (1884), 241–58.

Morris, William, *News from Nowhere and Other Writings*, ed. Clive Wilmer (London: Penguin, 1993).

Morris, William, and E. Belford Bax, *Socialism, Its Growth and Outcome* (London: Swan Sonnenschein, 1893).

Muirhead, John Henry, "Why Pluralism?," *Proceedings of the Aristotelian Society*, 9/1 (1909), 183–225.

———, "What Imperialism Means" (1900), in David Boucher (ed.), *The British Idealists* (Cambridge: Cambridge University Press, 1997), 237–52.

Naoroji, Dadabhai, *Poverty and Un-British Rule in India in 1901* (London: Sonnenschein, 1901).

Nauticus [pseud.], "The United Anglo-Saxon Will," *Fortnightly Review*, 72 (1894), 391–97.

Niebuhr, Barthold Georg, *The History of Rome*, trans. Julius Hare and Connop Thirlwall (Cambridge: Cambridge University Press, 1832).

Norton, Roy, *The Vanishing Fleets* (New York: Appleton, 1908).

Octogenarian [pseud.], *The British Federal Empire; How It Was Founded, A Speech Delivered in a Certain Year of the Twentieth Century, in a Certain City of the Empire* (London: C. H. Clarke, 1872).

Odell, Samuel, *The Last War; Or, the Triumph of the English Tongue* (1898; Chicago: Kerr, 1939).

Oliver, Frederick S., *Alexander Hamilton: An Essay on American Union* (London: Macmillan, 1906).

Olney, Richard, "International Isolation of the United States," *Atlantic Monthly*, 81 (May 1898), 577–89.

Oman, Charles, "Editor's Preface," *The Reign of George the VI. 1900–1925: A Forecast Written in the Year 1763* (London: Rivington's, 1899).

Paine, H. G., *Handbook of Simplified Spelling* (New York: Simplified Spelling Board, 1920).

Paine, Thomas, *The Rights of Man*, ed. H. Bonner (1791; London: Watts, 1906).

Parkes, Henry, "Australia and the Imperial Connection," *Nineteenth Century*, 15 (1884), 867–72.

Parkin, George, *The Rhodes Scholarships* (New York: Houghton Mifflin, 1912).

———, *Imperial Federation: The Problem of National Unity* (London: Macmillan, 1892).

Pearson, Charles, *National Life and Character: A Forecast* (London: Macmillan, 1893).

Perris, Henry S., *Pax Britannica: A Study of the History of British Pacification* (London: Macmillan, 1913).

Peters, Karl, *England and the English* (London: Hurst & Blackett, 1904).

Phillimore, Walter, Lord Phillimore, *Schemes for Maintaining General Peace* (London: H. M. Stationary Office, 1920).

Phillipson, Coleman, *International Law and Customs of the Greeks and Romans*, 2 vols. (London: MacMillan, 1911).

Poley, Arthur, *The Federal Systems of the United States and the British Empire: Their Origin, Nature and Development* (Boston: Pitman, 1913).

Pollock, Frederick, "The Monroe Doctrine," *Nineteenth Century and After*, 52/308 (1902), 533–53.

Polybius, *The Histories of Polybius*, trans. E. Shuckburgh (London: Macmillan, 1889).

Potter, Henry Codman, "National Bigness or Greatness: Which?," *North American Review*, 168/509 (1899), 433–44.

Powers, H. H., *America among the Nations* (New York: Macmillan, 1917).

———, "The Ethics of Expansion," *International Journal of Ethics*, 10/3 (1900), 288–306.

———, "The War as a Suggestion of Manifest Destiny," *Annals of the American Academy of Political and Social Science*, 12/2 (1898), 173–92.

Radziwill, Catherine, *Cecil Rhodes: Man and Empire-Maker* (London: Cassell, 1918).

Raymond, E. T., "W. T. Stead" in Raymond, *Portraits of the Nineties* (London: Fisher Unwin, 1921), 179.

Reade, Winwood, *The Martyrdom of Man* (London: Trubner, 1872).

Reed, Samuel, *The War of 1886, between the United States and Great Britain* (Cincinnati: Robert Clare, 1882).

Rees, William Lee, *The Life and Times of Sir George Grey*, 2 vols. (London: Hutchinson, 1892).

Reid, G. H., "An After-Glance at the Visit of the American Fleet to Australia," *North American Review*, 189/640 (1909), 404–9.

Reinsch, Paul S., *Public International Unions: Their Work and Organization* (London: Ginn, 1911).

———, *World Politics at the End of the Nineteenth Century* (New York: Macmillan, 1900).

Rhodes, Cecil, *The Last Will and Testament of Cecil J. Rhodes*, ed. W. T. Stead (London: Review of Reviews, 1902).

———, Speech to Cape Parliament, 23 June 1887, in Vindex [F. Verschoyle], *Cecil Rhodes, His Political Life and Speeches, 1881–1900* (London: Chapman, 1900), 151–66.

Richter, Eugen, *Pictures of the Socialistic Future*, trans. Henry Wright (London: Sonnenschein, 1893).

Ritchie, David George, "The Moral Problems of War—A Reply to Mr J. M. Robertson," *International Journal of Ethics*, 11/4 (1901), 493–505.

———, "War and Peace," *International Journal of Ethics*, 11/2 (1901), 137–58.

———, review of Kidd, *Social Evolution*, *International Journal of Ethics*, 5/1 (1894), 107–20.

———, *Darwinism and Politics* (London: Sonnenschein, 1889).

Robertson, John Mackinnon, "The Moral Problems of War," *International Journal of Ethics*, 11/3 (1901), 273–90.

———, *Patriotism and Empire*, 2nd ed. (London: Grant Richards, 1900).

Robinson, H. P., *The Twentieth Century American: Being a Comparative Study of the Peoples of the Two Great Anglo-Saxon Nations* (New York: Chautauqua, 1908).

Roosevelt, Theodore, *The Naval War of 1812, or the History of the United States Navy during the Last War with Great Britain* (New York: Putnam's, 1900).

————, *The Winning of the West*, 4 vols. (New York: Putnam's, 1889).

Salter, William, review of Giddings, *Democracy and Empire, International Journal of Ethics*, 11/1 (1900), 123–28.

Samuel, Herbert, *Liberalism: An Attempt to State the Principles and Proposals of Contemporary Liberalism in England* (London: Grant Richard, 1902).

Sargent, Edmund Beale (ed.), *British Citizenship: A Discussion* (London: Royal Colonial Institute, 1912).

Schiller, Ferdinand Canning Scott, "Axioms as Postulates" in Henry Sturt (ed.), *Personal Idealism* (Oxford: Oxford University Press, 1902), 47–134.

Scholes, T. E. S., *Glimpses of the Ages, or the 'Superior' and 'Inferior' Races, So-called, Discussed in the Light of Science and History*, 2 vols. (London: John Long, 1905, 1908).

————, "Bartholomew Smith" [Scholes], *Chamberlain and Chamberlainism* (London: John Long, 1903).

————, *The British Empire and Alliances; or, Britain's Duty to Her Colonies and Subject Races* (London: Elliott Stock, 1899).

Schurz, Carl, "Militarism and Democracy," *Annals of the American Academy of Political and Social Science*, 13/12 (1899), 77–103.

Schuyler, R. L., review of Sinclair Kennedy, *The Pan-Angles, Political Science Quarterly*, 30/3 (1915), 525–26.

Schvan, August, "Anglo-Saxon Co-operation and Peace," *North American Review*, 198/697 (1913), 808–22.

Scudder, Horace Elisha, *James Russell Lowell: A Biography*, 2 vols. (Boston: Houghton, Mifflin, 1901).

Seebohm, Frederic, *On International Reform* (London: Longman's, 1871).

Seeley, John Robert, "The Impartial Study of Politics: Inaugural Address to the Cardiff Society for the Impartial Discussion of Politics and Other Questions, October 18th 1886," *Contemporary Review*, 54 (1888), 52–65.

————, "The United States of Europe," *Macmillan's Magazine*, 23 (1871), 436–48.

Shaw, Albert, review of Whyte, *Life and Letters of W. T. Stead, American Historical Review*, 32/1 (1926), 112–15.

————, "William T. Stead," *American Review of Reviews* (June 1912), 689–98.

————, "Progress of the World," *American Review of Reviews*, 15 (June 1897), 654.

————, "An American View of Home Rule and Federation," *Contemporary Review*, 62 (1892), 305–18.

Sidgwick, Henry, *The Development of European Polity*, ed. Eleanor Sidgwick (London: Macmillan, 1903).

Sinclair, Upton, *The Industrial Republic: A Study of the America of Ten Years Hence* (New York: Doubleday, 1907).

Slater, William M., review of Giddings, *Democracy and Empire, International Journal of Ethics*, 11/1 (1900), 124–26.

Slosson, Edwin, *Six Major Prophets* (New York: Little, Brown, 1917).

Smith, Goldwin, "Anglo-Saxon Union: A Response to Mr. Carnegie," *North American Review*, 157/441 (1893), 170–85.

————, *Canada and the Canadian Question* (London: Macmillan, 1891).

———, "The Hatred of England," *North American Review*, 150/402 (1890), 547–62.

———, "Prophets of Unrest," *The Forum*, 14/8 (1889), 599–614.

———, "The Expansion of England," *Contemporary Review*, 45 (1884), 524–40.

Spencer, Herbert, *An Autobiography*, 2 vols. (New York: Appleton, 1904).

———, "Imperialism and Slavery" in Spencer, *Facts and Comments* (New York: Appleton, 1902), 157–71.

———, "Re-Barbarization" in Spencer, *Facts and Comments*, 172–89.

———, "The Proper Sphere of Government" (1843), in Spencer, *The Man Versus the State* (Indianapolis: Liberty Fund, 1982), 181–264.

Spiller, Gustav, *Papers on Inter-racial Problems: Communicated to the First Universal Races Congress, Held at the University of London, July 26–29, 1911* (London: King & Son 1911).

Stead, Estelle, *My Father, Personal & Spiritual Reminisces* (London: Heinemann, 1913).

Stead, William Thomas, "The Great Pacifist: An Autobiographical Character Sketch," *Review of Reviews for Australasia*, 6 (1912), 609–20.

———, *How I Know That the Dead Return* (Boston: Ball, 1909).

———, *In Our Midst: The Letters of Callicrates to Dione, Queen of the Xanthians, Concerning England and the English, Anno Domini 1902* (London: Review of Reviews, 1903).

———, *The Americanization of the World* (London: Review of Reviews, 1902).

———, "Mr Rhodes's Will and Its Genesis," *Review of Reviews*, 25 (May 1902), 479–81.

———, *"Lest We Forget": A Keepsake from the Nineteenth Century* (London: Review of Reviews, 1901).

———, *Shall I Slay My Brother Boer? An Appeal to the Conscience of Britain* (London: Review of Reviews, 1899).

———, *The United States of Europe on the Eve of the Parliament of Peace* (London: William Clowes, 1899).

———, *Satan's Invisible World Displayed, Or, Despairing Democracy; A Study of Greater New York* (London: Review of Reviews, 1898).

———, *Always Arbitrate before You Fight: An Appeal to English-Speaking Folk* (London: Review of Reviews, 1896).

———, "Character Sketch: Cecil Rhodes of Africa," *Review of Reviews*, 13 (February 1896), 113–36.

———, "Character Sketch: President Cleveland," *Review of Reviews*, 18 (January 1896), 17–33.

———, "Jingoism in America," *Contemporary Review*, 68 (1895), 334–47.

———, *If Christ Came to Chicago! A Plea for the Union of All Who Love in the Service of All Who Suffer* (London: Review of Reviews, 1894).

———, "The Civic Church" in J. H. Barrows (ed.), *The World's Parliament of Religions* (London: Review of Reviews, 1893), II, 1209–15.

———, *From the Old World to the New; A Christmas Story of the World's Fair, 1893* (London: Review of Reviews, 1893).

———, "Character Sketch: Sir Charles Dilke," *Review of Reviews*, 6 (August 1892), 127–41.

———, "Character Sketch: Arthur Balfour," *Review of Reviews*, 4 (November 1891), 457–69.

———, "James Russell Lowell: His Message, and How It Helped Me," *Review of Reviews*, 4 (August 1891), 235–47.

———, "Looking Forward," *Review of Reviews*, 1 (March 1890), 230.

————, "To All English-speaking Folk," *Review of Reviews*, 1 (January 1890), 15–20.

————, "The Future of Journalism," *Contemporary Review*, 50 (1886), 663–79.

————, "Government by Journalism," *Contemporary Review*, 49 (1886), 653–74.

————, "Programme 1885," *Pall Mall Gazette*, 1 January 1885, 1.

————, "The English beyond the Sea," *Pall Mall Gazette*, 4 October 1884, 1.

————, "The Old and the New," *Pall Mall Gazette*, 1 January 1884, 1.

————, "The Gospel According to the *Pall Mall Gazette*" (1880), reproduced in Whyte, *The Life of W. T. Stead*, II, 321–28.

Stein, Robert, "Anglo-French-German Alliance—a Guarantee of Peace," *Advocate of Peace*, 67/7 (1905), 147–51.

Stevenson, Adlai, "Bryan or McKinley? The Present Duty of American Citizens," *North American Review*, 171/527 (1900), 433–516.

Stewart, Herbert L., "The Alleged Egotism in the Demand for Personal Immortality," *Biblical World*, 51/1 (1918), 19–30.

Stockton, Frank, *The Great War Syndicate* (London: Longman's, 1889).

Streator, Martin Lyman, *The Anglo-American Alliance in Prophecy, or the Promises to the Fathers* (London: Werner, 1900).

Streit, Clarence, *Union Now: A Proposal for a Federal Union of the Democracies of the North Atlantic* (New York: Harper, 1939).

Strong, Josiah, "Tendencies toward the Unity of the World," *Advocate of Peace*, 65/10 (1903), 178–79.

————, *Expansion under New World Conditions* (New York: Baker, 1900).

————, "Promoting Arbitration," *Advocate of Peace*, 60/9 (1898), 212–13.

————, *The New Era, or the Coming Kingdom* (New York: Baker & Taylor, 1893).

————, *Our Country: Its Possible Future and Its Present Crisis* (New York: Baker & Taylor, 1885).

Stubbs, William, *The Constitutional History of England, in Its Origin and Development*, 3 vols. (Oxford: Clarendon Press, 1874–78).

[S. W. E.], review of Dos Passos, *Anglo-Saxon Century*, *Yale Law Journal*, 13/2 (1903), 105–6.

Sydenham-Clarke, George, "A Naval Union with Great Britain: A Reply to Mr. Andrew Carnegie," *North American Review*, 158/448 (1894), 353–65.

Taylor, Charles Carlisle, *The Life of Admiral Mahan* (New York: George H. Doran Company, 1920).

Taylor, Hannis, *A Treatise on International Public Law* (Chicago: Callaghan, 1901).

————, "England's Colonial Empire," *North American Review*, 162/475 (1896), 682–97.

Tennyson, Alfred, *Poems of Tennyson* (Oxford: Oxford University Press, 1910).

Thayer, William Roscoe, "The Centennial of Lincoln and Darwin," *North American Review*, 188/632 (1908), 21–25.

Thirlwall, Connop, *A History of Greece*, 8 vols. (London: Longman, 1835–47).

Tocqueville, Alexis H. C. M. C. de, *The Recollections of Alexis de Tocqueville*, ed. Comte de Tocqueville, trans. Alexander Teixeira de Mattos (New York: Macmillan, 1896).

————, *Democracy in America*, ed. Henry Reeve, 2 vols. (London: Longman, Green, 1839).

Todd, Alpheus, *Parliamentary Government in the British Colonies* (London: Longman's, 1880).

Tourgée, Albion, "The Twentieth Century Peacemakers," *Contemporary Review*, 75 (1899), 886–908.

Tracy, Louis, *The Invaders: A Story of Britain in Peril* (London: Pearson, 1901).

———, *The Lost Provinces: A Sequel to "An American Emperor"* (London: Pearson, 1898).

———, "The Man Who Wrote *The Final War*," *Pearson's Weekly* (20 March 1897), reprinted in George Locke, *Pearson's Weekly: A Checklist of Fiction 1890–1939* (London: Ferret, 1990), 115–16.

———, "Do the Americans Really Hate Us?," *Pearson's Weekly* (12 September 1896), 1–3.

———, *The Final War* (London: Putnam's, 1896).

Trueblood, Benjamin F., *The Federation of the World* (Boston: Houghton, Miffin & Company, 1899).

———, "A Proposed Anglo-American War Alliance," *Advocate of Peace*, 56/5 (1894), 101–4.

Turner, Alfred, *Stead the Man: Personal Reminisces, by Edith Harper* (London: William Rider, 1918).

Vogel, Julius, *Anno Domini 2000; Or, a Woman's Destiny*, ed. R. Robinson (1889; Honolulu: University of Hawaii Press, 2002).

———, "The British Empire—Mr. Lowe and Lord Blachford," *Nineteenth Century*, 3 (1878), 617–36.

———, "Greater or Lesser Britain," *Nineteenth Century*, 1/5 (1877), 809–31.

Waldstein, Charles, "The English-speaking Brotherhood," *North American Review*, 167/501 (1898), 223–38.

Walker, Thomas A., *A History of the Law of Nations* (Cambridge: Cambridge University Press, 1899).

———, *The Science of International Law* (London: C. J. Clay, 1893).

Wallas, Graham, *Human Nature and Politics* (London: Constable, 1908).

Warne, Frank Julian, *The Immigrant Invasion* (New York: Frank Mead, 1913).

Washington, George, *Washington's Farewell Address, Webster's First Bunker Hill Oration, and Other Patriotic Selections* (New York: Maynard, Merrill, 1906).

Waterloo, Stanley, *Armageddon: A Tale of Love, War, and Invention* (New York: Rand, McNally, 1898).

———, *The Story of Ab: A Tale of the Time of the Caveman* (Chicago: Way & Williams, 1897).

Wellman, Bert, *Legal Revolution of 1902* (Chicago: C. H. Kerr & Co., 1898).

Wells, David, "Great Britain and the United States: Their True Relations," *North American Review*, 162/473 (1896), 385–405.

Wells, Herbert George, *The Correspondence of H. G. Wells*, ed. David Smith, 4 vols. (London: Pickering & Chatto, 1998).

———, *The Conquest of Time* (London: Prometheus, 1942).

———, *An Experiment in Autobiography*, 2 vols. (1934; London: Faber, 2008).

———, *The Shape of Things to Come* (London: Hutchinson, 1933).

———, *The Work, Wealth and Happiness of Mankind* (London: Heinemann, 1932).

———, *The Autocracy of Mr Parham* (London: Heinemann, 1930).

———, *The Open Conspiracy: Blueprints for a World Revolution* (New York: Doubleday, 1928).

———, "Preface to Volume 4" in *The Works of H. G. Wells* (London, 1924), IV, 2–3.

———, *The Outline of History*, ed. W. Warren Wagar, 2 vols. (1920; New York: Barnes & Noble, 2004).

———, "The Death Knell of Empires," *Current History*, 8/2 (1918), 353–54.

———, *God the Invisible King* (London: Cassell, 1917).

———, *An Englishman Looks at the World* (London: Cassell & Co, 1914).

———, *The World Set Free* (London: MacMillan, 1914).

———, "Cement of Empire," *Everybody's Weekly*, 1/1 (1911), 33–41.

———, "The Contemporary Novel" (1911), in Wells, *An Englishman Looks at the World*, 148–69.

———, *The New Machiavelli*, ed. Simon James (1911; London: Penguin, 2005).

———, "Of the New Reign" (1911), in Wells, *An Englishman Looks at the World*, 22–32.

———, "Will the Empire Live?" (1911), in Wells, *An Englishman Looks at the World*, 33–43.

———, *First and Last Things: A Confession of Faith and Rule of Life* (1908; London: Read, 2016).

———, "My Socialism," *Contemporary Review*, 94 (1908), 175–81.

———, *New Worlds for Old* (London: Macmillan, 1908).

———, *The War in the Air* (London: Bell, 1908).

———, "Mulattos," *Nature*, 77/1990 (1907), 149.

———, "Race Prejudice," *The Independent*, 62 (1907), 381–84.

———, "The So-Called Science of Sociology" (1907), in Wells, *An Englishman Looks at the World*, 192–206.

———, *The Future in America: A Search after Realities* (1906; London: Read, 2016).

———, *A Modern Utopia*, ed. Gregory Claeys (1905; London: Penguin, 2005).

———, "The Schoolmaster and the Empire" (1905), in Wells, *An Englishman Looks at the World*, 218–29.

———, "Is There a People?" (1904), in Wells, *An Englishman Looks at the World*, 245–50.

———, "Scepticism of the Instrument," *Mind*, 13/51 (1904), 379–93.

———, "The Land Ironclads," *Strand Magazine*, 23/156 (1903), 751–69.

———, *Mankind in the Making* (London: Chapman, 1903).

———, "The Discovery of the Future," *Nature*, 65/1684 (1902), 326–33.

———, *Anticipations of the Reaction of Mechanical and Scientific Progress upon Human Life and Thought* (1901; Mineola, NY: Dover, 1999).

———, *The First Men in the Moon*, ed. Patrick Parrinder (1901; London: Penguin, 2005).

———, "Huxley," *Royal College of Science Magazine*, 13 (April 1901), 209–11.

———, "On Comparative Theology" (1898), in Philmus and Hughes, *H. G. Wells*, 40–46.

———, *The War of the Worlds* (London: Heinemann, 1898).

———, "Morals and Civilisation" (1897), in Philmus and Hughes, *H. G. Wells*, 220–28.

———, "Human Evolution, an Artificial Process" (1896), in Philmus and Hughes, *H. G. Wells*, 211–19.

———, "The Limits of Individual Plasticity" (1895), in Philmus and Hughes, *H. G. Wells*, 36–39.

———, *The Time Machine* (1895; London, 2005).

———, "The Rediscovery of the Unique" (1891), in Philmus and Hughes, *H. G. Wells*, 22–31.

Wells, Herbert George, et al., *The Great State: Essays in Construction* (London: Macmillan, 1912).

Westlake, John, "International Arbitration," *International Journal of Ethics*, 7/1 (1896), 1–20.

White, Andrew Dickinson, *The Autobiography of Andrew Dickinson White*, 2 vols. (London: Macmillan, 1905).

White, Arthur Silva, "British Unity," *Scottish Geographical Magazine*, 12 (1896), 391–414.

———, "An Anglo-American Alliance," *North American Review*, 158/449 (1894), 484–93.

———, "The Position of Geography in the Cycle of the Sciences," *Geographical Journal*, 2/2 (1893), 178–79.

———(ed.), *Britannic Confederation: A Series of Papers* (London: George Philip, 1892).

Whitman, Sidney, "W. T. Stead" in Whitman, *Things I Remember: The Recollections of a Political Writer in the Capitals of Europe* (New York: Frederick Stokes, 1916), 236–37.

Whyte, Frederick, *The Life of W. T. Stead*, 2 vols. (London: Jonathan Cape, 1925).

Williams, Basil, *Cecil Rhodes* (New York: Henry Holt, 1921).

Wilson, A. J., *An Open Letter to Mr W. T. Stead on His Friendship for Cecil J. Rhodes* (London: J. Paterson, 1902).

Wilson, Woodrow, "Democracy and Efficiency," *Atlantic Monthly*, 87 (March 1901), 289–99.

Woolf, Leonard (ed.), *The Framework of a Lasting Peace* (London: G. Allen & Unwin, 1917).

———, *International Government* (London: G. Allen & Unwin, 1916).

Yarros, Victor, "Theoretical and Practical Nietzscheism," *American Journal of Sociology*, 6/5 (1901), 682–94.

Zimmern, Alfred, *The Third British Empire* (Oxford: Oxford University Press, 1926).

Secondary Sources

Abrahamson, James, "David Starr Jordan and American Anti-Militarism," *Pacific Northwest Quarterly*, 67/2 (1976), 76–87.

Abravanel, Genevieve, *Americanizing Britain: The Rise of Modernism in the Age of the Entertainment Empire* (Oxford: Oxford University Press, 2012).

Adams, Bluford, "World Conquerors or a Dying People? Racial Theory, Regional Anxiety, and the Brahmin Anglo-Saxonists," *Journal of the Gilded Age and Progressive Era*, 8/2 (2009), 189–215.

Adams, Iestyn, *Brothers across the Ocean: British Foreign Policy and the Origins of the Anglo-American 'Special Relationship'* (London: Tauris, 2005).

Adas, Michael, *Dominance by Design: Technological Imperatives and America's Civilizing Mission* (Cambridge, MA: Harvard University Press, 2006).

———, *Machines as the Measure of Men: Science, Technology, and Ideologies of Western Dominance* (Ithaca, NY: Cornell University Press, 1999).

Adcock, Robert, *Liberalism and the Emergence of American Political Science: A Transatlantic Tale* (Oxford: Oxford University Press, 2014).

Adcock, Robert, Mark Bevir, and Shannon Stimson (eds.), *Modern Political Science: Anglo-American Exchanges since 1880* (Princeton, NJ: Princeton University Press, 2007).

Adi, Hakim, *Pan-Africanism: A History* (London: Bloomsbury, 2018).

Aksu, Esref, *Early Notions of Global Governance: Selected Eighteenth-Century Proposals for 'Perpetual Peace'* (Cardiff: University of Wales Press, 2009).

Alessio, Dominic, "Promoting Paradise: Utopianism and National Identity in New Zealand, 1870–1930," *New Zealand Journal of History*, 42/1 (2008), 22–23.

———, "'Gender,' 'Race' and Proto-Nationalism in Julius Vogel's *Anno Domini 2000; or Woman's Destiny* (1889)," *Foundation*, 33/91 (2004), 36–54.

———, "Document in the History of Science-Fiction: *The Great Romance*, by The Inhabitant," *Science Fiction Studies*, 20/3 (1993), 305–40.

Alexander, Shawn Leigh (ed.), *T. Thomas Fortune, the Afro-American Agitator* (Gainesville: University of Florida Press, 2008).

Allen, Harry C., *Great Britain and the United States: A History of Anglo-American Relations* (New York: St. Martin's, 1954).

Allerfeldt, Kristofer, "Rome, Race, and the Republic: Progressive America and the Fall of the Roman Empire, 1890–1920," *Journal of the Gilded Age and Progressive Era*, 7/3 (2008), 297–323.

Allhoff, Fritz, "Evolutionary Ethics from Darwin to Moore," *History and Philosophy of the Life Sciences*, 25/1 (2003), 51–79.

Amery, Leopold, *My Political Life, Volume 1: England before the Storm, 1896–1914* (London: Hutchinson, 1953).

Anderson, Benedict, *Imagined Communities: Reflections on the Origin and Spread of Nationalism*, new ed. (London: Verso, 2006).

Anderson, Stuart, *Race and Rapprochement: Anglo-Saxonism and Anglo-American Relations, 1895–1904* (Rutherford, NJ: Fairleigh Dickinson University Press, 1981).

———, "Racial Anglo-Saxonism and American Response to the Boer War," *Diplomatic History*, 2/3 (1978), 219–36.

Archibugi, Daniele, "From Peace between Democracies to Global Democracy" in Archibugi, Mathias Koenig-Archibugi, and Raffaele Marchetti (eds.), et al. (eds.), *Global Democracy: Normative and Empirical Perspectives* (Cambridge: Cambridge University Press, 2012), 254–73.

———, "Models of International Organization in Perpetual Peace Projects," *Review of International Studies*, 18/4 (1992), 295–317.

Armitage, David, *The Ideological Origins of the British Empire* (Cambridge: Cambridge University Press, 2000).

Arscott Caroline, and Claire Pettit (eds.), *Victorians Decoded: Art and Telegraphy* (London: Courthauld, 2016).

Arvidsson, Stefan, *Aryan Idols: Indo-European Mythology as Ideology and Science* (Chicago: University of Chicago Press, 2006).

Ashworth, Lucian, *Creating International Studies: Angell, Mitrany and the Liberal Tradition* (Aldershot: Ashgate, 1999).

Atkinson, David C., *The Burden of White Supremacy: Containing Asian Migration in the British Empire and the United States* (Chapel Hill: University of North Carolina Press, 2017).

Aydin, Cemil, *The Politics of Anti-Westernism in Asia: Visions of World Order in Pan-Islamic and Pan-Asian Thought* (New York: Columbia University Press, 2007).

Baker, Lee, *From Savage to Negro: Anthropology and the Construction of Race, 1896–1954* (Berkeley: University of California Press, 1998).

Balfour, Lawrie, *Democracy's Reconstruction: Thinking Politically with W. E. B. Du Bois* (New York: Oxford University Press, 2006).

Ball, Terence, James Farr, and Russell Hanson (eds.), *Political Innovation and Conceptual Change* (Cambridge: Cambridge University Press, 1989).

Barnes, John, and David Nicholson (eds.), *The Leo Amery Diaries, Vol 1: 1896–1929* (London: Hutchinson, 1980).

Bartelson, Jens, *War in International Thought* (Cambridge: Cambridge University Press, 2018).

Baum, Tomas, "A Quest for Inspiration in the Liberal Peace Paradigm: Back to Bentham?," *European Journal of International Relations*, 14/3 (2008), 431–53.

Bay, Mia, *To Tell the Truth Freely: The Life of Ida B. Wells* (New York: Hill & Wang, 2009).

——, *The White Image in the Black Mind: African-American Ideas about White People, 1830–1925* (Oxford: Oxford University Press, 2000).

Baylen, Joseph, "W. T. Stead as Publisher and Editor of the *Review of Reviews*," *Victorian Periodicals Review*, 12/2 (1979), 70–83.

——, "W. T. Stead and the Early Career of H. G. Wells, 1895–1911," *Huntington Library Quarterly*, 38/1 (1974), 53–79.

——, "Sir Arthur Conan Doyle and W. T. Stead: The Novelist and the Journalist," *Albion*, 2/1 (1970), 3–16.

——, "A Victorian's 'Crusade' in Chicago, 1893–94," *Journal of American History*, 51/3 (1964), 418–34.

——, "W. T. Stead's *History of the Mystery* and the Jameson Raid," *Journal of British Studies*, 4/1 (1964), 104–32.

——, "W. T. Stead and the Irony of Idealism," *Canadian Historical Review*, 40/4 (1959), 304–14.

Beaumont, Matthew, *Utopia Ltd.: Ideologies of Social Dreaming in England, 1870–1900*, 2nd ed. (Edinburgh: Haymarket, 2009).

Beaupre, Myles, "What Are the Philippines Going to Do to Us? E. L. Godkin on Democracy, Empire and Anti-imperialism," *Journal of American Studies*, 46/3 (2012), 711–27.

Beaven, Brad, and John Griffiths, "Creating the Exemplary Citizen: The Changing Notion of Citizenship in Britain 1870–1939," *Contemporary British History*, 22/2 (2008), 203–25.

Beck, Hans, and Peter Funke (eds.), *Federalism in Greek Antiquity* (Cambridge: Cambridge University Press, 2015).

Bederman, Gail, *Manliness and Civilization: A Cultural History of Gender and Race in the United States, 1880–1917* (Chicago: University of Chicago Press, 1995).

Beiner, Ronald (ed.), *Theorizing Citizenship* (Albany: State University of New York Press, 1995).

Beisner, Robert, *Twelve against Empire: The Anti-Imperialists 1898–1900* (New York: McGraw Hill, 1968).

Bélanger, Damien-Claude, *Prejudice and Pride: Canadian Intellectuals Confront the United States, 1891–1945* (Toronto: University of Toronto Press, 2011).

Belich, James, *Replenishing the Earth: The Settler Revolution and the Rise of the Angloworld* (Oxford: Oxford University Press, 2009).

Bell, Duncan, "Cyborg Imperium, c.1900" in Anne Chapman and Natalie Hume (eds.), *Coding and Representation from the Nineteenth Century to the Present: Scrambled Messages* (London: Routledge, forth.).

——, "Anglospheres: Empire Redivivus?" in Mycock and Wellings, *The Anglosphere*, 38–55.

——(ed.), *Empire, Race and Global Justice* (Cambridge: Cambridge University Press, 2019).

——, "Pragmatic Utopianism and Race: H. G. Wells as Social Scientist," *Modern Intellectual History*, 16/3 (2019), 863–95.

———, "Founding the World State: H. G. Wells on Empire and the English-Speaking Peoples," *International Studies Quarterly*, 62/4 (2018), 867–79.

———, "Pragmatism and Prophecy: H. G. Wells on the Metaphysics of Socialism," *American Political Science Review*, 112/2 (2018), 409–22.

———, "Empire" in Mark Bevir (ed.), *Historicism in the Victorian Human Sciences* (Cambridge: Cambridge University Press, 2017), 211–36.

———, *Reordering the World: Essays on Liberalism and Empire* (Princeton, NJ: Princeton University Press, 2016).

———, "Before the Democratic Peace: Racial Utopianism, Empire, and the Abolition of War," *European Journal of International Relations*, 20/3 (2014), 647–70.

———, "Beyond the Sovereign State: Isopolitan Citizenship, Race, and Anglo-American Union," *Political Studies*, 62/2 (2014), 418–34.

———, "On J. A. Hobson's 'The Ethics of Internationalism,'" *Ethics*, 125/1 (2014), 120–22.

———, "What Is Liberalism?," *Political Theory*, 42/6 (2014), 682–715.

———, "The Project for a New Anglo Century: Race, Space, and Global Order" in Katzenstein, *Anglo-America and Its Discontents*, 33–56.

———, "John Stuart Mill on Colonies," *Political Theory*, 38/1 (2010), 34–64.

———, "Republican Imperialism: J. A. Froude and the Virtue of Empire," *History of Political Thought*, 30/1 (2009), 166–91.

———, "Agonistic Democracy and the Politics of Memory," *Constellations*, 15/1 (2008), 148–66.

———, *The Idea of Greater Britain: Empire and the Future of World Order, 1860–1900* (Princeton, NJ: Princeton University Press, 2007).

———, "The Victorian Idea of a Global State" in Bell (ed.), *Victorian Visions of Global Order: Empire and International Relations in Nineteenth Century British Political Thought* (Cambridge: Cambridge University Press, 2007), 159–85.

———, "The Idea of a Patriot Queen: The Monarchy, the Constitution, and the Iconographic Order of Greater Britain, 1860–1900," *Journal of Imperial and Commonwealth History*, 34/1 (2006), 1–19.

———, "Mythscapes: Memory, Mythology, and National Identity," *British Journal of Sociology*, 54/1 (2003), 63–81.

Bell, Duncan, and Caspar Sylvest, "International Society in Victorian Political Thought: T. H. Green, Herbert Spencer, and Henry Sidgwick," *Modern Intellectual History*, 3/2 (2006), 207–38.

Bell, Duncan, and Srdjan Vucetic, "Brexit, CANZUK, and the Legacy of Empire," *British Journal of Politics and International Relations*, 21/2 (2019), 367–82.

Bell, Morag, "Edinburgh and Empire: Geographical Science and Citizenship for a 'New Age,' c.1900," *Scottish Geographical Magazine*, 111/3 (1995), 139–49.

Bellamy, Alex, *World Peace (And How We Can Achieve It)* (Oxford: Oxford University Press, 2019).

Bellamy, Richard, "The Advent of the Masses and the Making of the Theory of Democracy" in Bellamy and Terence Ball, *The Cambridge History of Twentieth Century Political Thought* (Cambridge: Cambridge University Press, 2003), 70–103.

Bennett, Geoffrey M., *Charlie B: A Biography of Admiral Lord Beresford of Metemmeh and Curraghmore* (London: Dawnay, 1968).

Bennett, James, "The Anglosphere as the Big Somewhere," *Quadrant Online*, 27 September 2018, https://quadrant.org.au/magazine/2018/10/anglosphere-big-somewhere/.

——, *A Time for Audacity: How Brexit Has Created the CANZUK Option* (Washington, DC: Pole to Pole, 2016).

——, *The Anglosphere Challenge: Why the English-Speaking Nations Will Lead the Way in the Twenty-First Century* (Lanham: Rowman & Littlefield, 2004).

Bergholz, Max, "Thinking the Nation," *American Historical Review*, 123/2 (2018), 518–28.

Berman, Milton, *John Fiske: The Evolution of a Popularizer* (Cambridge, MA: Harvard University Press, 1961).

Bethencourt, Francisco, *Racisms: From the Crusades to the Twentieth Century* (Princeton, NJ: Princeton University Press, 2013).

Bew, John, *Realpolitik: A History* (Oxford: Oxford University Press, 2015).

Bilbija, Marina, "Worlds of Color: Black Print Networks and the Making of the English-Speaking World," unpublished manuscript (2019).

Billig, Michael, *Banal Nationalism* (London: Sage Publications, 1995).

Blain, Keisha N., *Set the World on Fire: Black Nationalist Women and the Global Struggle for Freedom* (Philadelphia: University of Pennsylvania Press, 2018).

Blain, Keisha N., Christopher Cameron, and Ashley D. Farmer (eds.), *New Perspectives on the Black Intellectual Tradition* (Evanston, IL: Northwestern University Press, 2018).

Blake, Kim, "T. E. S. Scholes: The Unknown Pan Africanist," *Race & Class*, 49/1 (2007), 62–80.

Blake, Nelson, "The Olney-Pauncefote Treaty of 1897," *American Historical Review*, 50/2 (1945), 228–43.

Bland, Lucy, and Leslie Hall, "Eugenics in Britain: The View from the Metropole" in Alison Bashford and Philippa Levine (eds.), *The Oxford Handbook of the History of Eugenics* (Oxford: Oxford University Press, 2010), 213–27.

Blatt, Jessica, *Race and the Making of American Political Science* (Philadelphia: University of Pennsylvania Press, 2018).

Bleiler, Everett Franklin (ed.), *Supernatural Fiction Writers* (New York: Scribner's, 1985).

Bleiler, Richard, "Introduction" in Kate MacDonald (ed.), *Political Future Fiction: Speculative and Counter-Factual Politics in Edwardian Fiction, Vol. 1: The Empire of the Future* (London: Pickering & Chatto, 2013), 107–32.

——, *Science Fiction: The Early Years* (Kent, OH: Kent State University Press, 1990).

Bloch, Ernst, *The Principle of Hope*, 3 vols. (1954–59; Cambridge MA: MIT Press, 1986).

Blouet, Brian, "The Imperial Vision of Halford Mackinder," *Geographical Journal*, 170/4 (2004), 322–29.

——, "H. G. Wells and the Evolution of Some Geographic Concepts," *Area*, 9/1 (1977), 49–54.

Boege, Fred W., "Sir Walter Besant: Novelist," *Nineteenth Century Fiction*, 10 (1956), 249–80; 11 (1956), 32–60.

Bönker, Dirk, *Militarism in a Global Age: Naval Ambitions in Germany and the United States before World War I* (Ithaca, NY: Cornell University Press, 2012).

Booth, Ken, and Nicholas J. Wheeler, *The Security Dilemma: Fear, Cooperation and Trust in World Politics* (Basingstoke: Macmillan, 2007).

Bosco, Andrea, *The Round Table Movement and the Fall of the "Second" British Empire (1909–1919)* (Newcastle: Cambridge Scholars, 2017).

Boucher, David, Boucher, "'Sane' and 'Insane' Imperialism: British Idealism, New Liberalism and Liberal Imperialism," *History of European Ideas*, 44/8 (2018), 1189–204.

———, "British Idealism, the State and International Relations," *Journal of the History of Ideas*, 55/4 (1994), 671–94.

Bould, Mark, "Revolutionary African-American SF before Black Power SF," *Extrapolation*, 51/1 (2010), 53–81.

Bousquet, Antonie, *The Eye of War: Military Perception from the Telescope to the Drone* (Minneapolis: University of Minnesota Press, 2018).

Bowman, Stephen, *The Pilgrims Society and Public Diplomacy, 1895–1945* (Edinburgh: Edinburgh University Press, 2018).

Bowser, Rachel A., and Brian Croxall (eds.), *Like Clockwork: Steampunk Pasts, Presents, and Futures* (Minneapolis: University of Minnesota Press, 2016).

Boyes, Aaron, "Towards the 'Federated States of North America': The Advocacy for Political Union between Canada and the United States, 1885–1896," PhD diss., University of Ottawa, 2016.

Boyle, Francis, *Foundations of World Order: The Legalist Approach to International Relations* (Durham, NC: Duke University Press, 1999).

Boyle, Thomas, "The Venezuela Crisis and the Liberal Opposition, 1895–6," *Journal of Modern History*, 50/3 (1978), 1185–212.

Brake, Laurel, Ed King, Roger Luckhurst, and James Mussell (eds.), *W. T. Stead: Newspaper Revolutionary* (Chicago: University of Chicago Press, 2013).

Brandon, Ruth, *The Spiritualists: The Passion for the Occult in the Nineteenth and Twentieth Centuries* (New York: Knopf, 1983).

Brantlinger, Patrick, *Taming Cannibals: Race and the Victorians* (Ithaca, NY: Cornell University Press, 2011).

———, "Kipling's 'The White Man's Burden' and Its Afterlives," *English Literature in Transition, 1880–1920*, 50/2 (2007), 172–91.

———, *Dark Vanishings: Discourse on the Extinction of Primitive Races* (Ithaca, NY: Cornell University Press, 2003).

Brigg, Peter, "The Future of the Past Viewed from the Present: Neal Stephenson's *The Diamond Age*," *Extrapolation*, 40/2 (1999), 116–24.

Brown, Ira, *Lyman Abbott, Christian Evolutionist: A Study in Religious Liberalism* (Cambridge, MA: Harvard University Press, 1953).

Brown, Nicola, Carolyn Burdett, and Pamela Thurschwell (eds.), *The Victorian Supernatural* (Cambridge: Cambridge University Press, 2004).

Brown, Stewart, *W. T. Stead* (Oxford: Oxford University Press, 2019).

———, "W. T. Stead and the Civic Church, 1886–1895: The Visions behind 'If Christ Came to Chicago!,'" *Journal of Ecclesiastical History*, 66/2 (2015), 320–39.

———, "W. T. Stead, the 'New Journalism,' and the 'New Church' in Late Victorian and Edwardian Britain" in Stewart Brown, Frances Knight, and John Morgan-Guy (eds.), *Religion, Identity, and Conflict in Britain: From the Restoration to the Twentieth Century* (Abingdon: Routledge, 2013), 213–32.

Brundage, Anthony, and Richard Cosgrove, *The Great Tradition: Constitutional History and National Identity in Britain and the United States, 1870–1960* (Palo Alto: Stanford University Press, 2007).

Bueltmann, Tanja, David Gleeson, and Donald MacRaild, "Invisible Diaspora? English Ethnicity in the United States before 1920," *Journal of American Ethnic History*, 33/4 (2014), 5–30.

Bueltmann, Tanja, and Donald M. MacRaild, "Globalizing St George: English Associations in the Anglo-World to the 1930s," *Journal of Global History*, 7/1 (2012), 79–105.

Bulfin, Ailise, *Gothic Invasions: Imperialism, War, and Fin-de-Siecle Popular Fiction, 1890–1914* (Cardiff: University of Wales Press, 2018).

———, "'To Arms!' Invasion Narratives and Late-Victorian Literature," *Literature Compass*, 12/9 (2015), 482–96.

Burk, Kathleen, *The Lion and the Eagle: The Interaction of the British and American Empires 1783–1972* (London: Bloomsbury, 2018).

———, *Old World, New World: Great Britain and America from the Beginning* (London: Grove Press, 2009).

Burrow, John, "Some British Views on the United States Constitution" in R. C. Simmons (ed.), *The United States Constitution: The First 200 Years* (Manchester: Manchester University Press, 1989), 116–38.

———, *A Liberal Descent: Victorian Historians and the English Past* (Cambridge: Cambridge University Press, 1981).

———, *Evolution and Society: A Study in Victorian Social Theory* (Cambridge: Cambridge University Press, 1966).

Burrow, John, Stefan Collini, and Donald Winch, *That Noble Science of Politics: A Study in Nineteenth-Century Intellectual History* (Cambridge: Cambridge University Press, 1983).

Burton, Antoinette, and Isabel Hofmeyr, "The Spine of Empire? Books and the Making of an Imperial Commons" in Burton and Hofmeyr (eds.), *Ten Books That Shaped the British Empire* (Durham, NC: Duke University Press, 2014), 1–28.

Burton, David H., "Theodore Roosevelt and His English Correspondents: A Special Relationship of Friends," *Transactions of the American Philosophical Society*, 63/2 (1973), 3–70.

Butler, Leslie, *Critical Americans: Victorian Intellectuals and Transatlantic Liberal Reform* (Chapel Hill: University of North Carolina Press, 2009).

Buzan, Barry, and George Lawson, *The Global Transformation: History, Modernity and the Making of International Relations* (Cambridge: Cambridge University Press, 2015).

Cain, Peter, *Character, Ethics and Economics: British Debates on Empire, 1860–1914* (Abingdon: Routledge, 2018).

———, "Radicalism, Gladstone, and the Liberal Critique of Disraelian 'Imperialism'" in Bell, *Victorian Visions of Global Order*, 215–38.

———, "The Economic Philosophy of Constructive Imperialism" in Cornelia Navari (ed.), *British Politics and the Spirit of the Age: Political Concepts in Action* (Keele: Keele University Press, 1996), 41–65.

Campbell, A. E., *Great Britain and the United States, 1895–1903* (London: Longman's, 1960).

Campbell, Duncan A., *Unlikely Allies: Britain, America and the Victorian Origins of the Special Relationship* (London: Continuum, 2007).

Canavan, Gerry, and Eric Carl Link (eds.), *The Cambridge History of Science Fiction* (Cambridge: Cambridge University Press, 2018).

Canovan, Margaret, "Patriotism Is Not Enough," *British Journal of Political Science*, 30/3 (2000), 413–32.

Cantor, Paul, and Peter Hufnagel, "The Empire of the Future: Imperialism and Modernism in H. G. Wells," *Studies in the Novel*, 38/1 (2006), 36–56.

Carroll, Siobhan, *An Empire of Air and Water: Uncolonizable Space in the British Imagination, 1750–1850* (Philadelphia: University of Pennsylvania Press, 2015).

Carter, Gregory T., "Race and Citizenship" in Ronald Bayor (ed.), *Oxford Handbook of American Immigration and Ethnicity* (Oxford: Oxford University Press, 2016), 166–82.

Case, Holly, *The Age of Questions: Or, A First Attempt at an Aggregate History of the Eastern, Social, Woman, American, Jewish, Polish, Bullion, Tuberculosis, and Many Other Questions over the Nineteenth Century, and Beyond* (Princeton, NJ: Princeton University Press, 2018).

Cavallar, Georg, "Kantian Perspectives on Democratic Peace: Alternatives to Doyle," *Review of International Studies*, 27/2 (2001), 229–48.

Ceadel, Martin, "The Founding Text of International Relations? Norman Angell's Seminal yet Flawed *The Great Illusion* (1909–1938)," *Review of International Studies*, 37/4 (2011), 1671–93.

——, *Living the Great Illusion: Norman Angell, 1872–1967* (Oxford: Oxford University Press, 2009).

——, "Cobden and Peace" in Anthony Howe and Simon Morgan (eds.), *Re-thinking Nineteenth Century Liberalism: Richard Cobden Bicentenary Essays* (Aldershot: Ashgate, 2006), 189–208.

——, "Gladstone and the Liberal Theory of International Relations" in Peter Ghosh and Lawrence Goldman (eds.), *Politics and Culture in Victorian Britain: Essays in Memory of Colin Matthew* (Oxford: Oxford University Press, 2006), 74–94.

——, *Semi-Detached Idealists: The British Peace Movement and International Relations, 1854–1945* (Oxford: Oxford University Press, 2000).

——, *The Origins of War Prevention: The British Peace Movement and International Relations, 1730–1854* (Oxford: Oxford University Press, 1996).

Cheng, Seymour C.Y., *Schemes for the Federation of the British Empire* (New York: Columbia University Press, 1931).

Cheyette, Bryan, "H. G. Wells and the Jews: Antisemitism, Socialism, and English Culture," *Patterns of Prejudice*, 22/3 (1988), 22–35.

Chickering, Roger, *Imperial Germany and a World without War: The Peace Movement and German Society, 1892–1914* (Princeton, NJ: Princeton University Press, 1975).

Churchill, Winston, "If Lee Had Not Won the Battle of Gettysburg," *Wisconsin Magazine of History*, 44/4 (1961), 243–51.

Claeys, Gregory, *Dystopia: A Natural History* (Oxford: Oxford University Press, 2016).

——, "News from Somewhere: Enhanced Sociability and the Composite Definition of Utopia and Dystopia," *History*, 98/330 (2013), 145–73.

——, *Imperial Sceptics: British Critics of Empire, 1850–1930* (Cambridge: Cambridge University Press, 2010).

——, "The Reshaping of the Utopian Genre in Britain, c.1870–1900" in Claeys (ed.), *Late Victorian Utopianism: A Prospectus* (London: Pickering & Chatto, 2009), I, ix–xxx.

———, "The 'Survival of the Fittest' and the Origins of Social Darwinism," *Journal of the History of Ideas*, 6/2 (2000), 223–40.

Clareson, Thomas, *Some Kind of Paradise: The Emergence of American Science Fiction* (Greenwood: Praeger, 1985).

Clark, Michael D., "The Empire of the Dead and the Empire of the Living: John Fiske and the Spatialization of Tradition," *American Studies*, 38/3 (1997), 91–107.

Clarke, Ignatius Frederick (ed.), *British Future Fiction, 1700–1914, Vol. VII: Disasters-to-Come* (London: Pickering & Chatto, 2000).

———, "Before and after 'The Battle of Dorking,'" *Science Fiction Studies*, 24/1 (1997), 33–46.

———, "Future-War Fiction: The First Main Phase, 1871–1900," *Science Fiction Studies*, 24/3 (1997), 387–412.

———(ed.), *The Great War with Germany, 1890–1914: Fictions and Fantasies of the War-to-Come* (Liverpool: Liverpool University Press, 1997).

———(ed.), *The Tale of the Next Great War, 1871–1914* (Syracuse: Syracuse University Press, 1995).

———, *Voices Prophesying War: Future Wars, 1763–3749*, 2nd ed. (Oxford: Oxford University Press, 1992).

Clarke, Peter, "The English-Speaking Peoples before Churchill," *Britain and the World*, 4/2 (2011), 199–231.

Coates, Benjamin, *Legalist Empire: International Law and American Foreign Relations in the Early Twentieth Century* (Oxford: Oxford University Press, 2016).

Cohrs, Patrick, *The Unfinished Peace after World War I: America, Britain and the Stabilisation of Europe, 1919–1932* (Cambridge: Cambridge University Press, 2006).

Cole, Sarah, *Inventing Tomorrow: H. G. Wells and the Twentieth Century* (New York: Columbia University Press, 2019).

———, *At the Violet Hour: Modernism and Violence in England and Ireland* (Oxford: Oxford University Press, 2014).

Coleman, Finnie, *Sutton E. Griggs and the Struggle against White Supremacy* (Knoxville: University of Tennessee Press, 2007).

Collini, Stefan, *Public Moralists: Political Thought and Intellectual Life in Britain, 1850–1930* (Oxford: Clarendon, 1991).

Conquest, Robert, "An Anglosphere in the Neosphere (A Political Exercise)" in Conquest, *The Dragons of Expectation: Reality and Delusion in the Course of History* (New York: W. W. Norton, 2005), 221–32.

Conlin, Jon, "The Consolations of Amero-Teutonism" in Conlin and Alex Bremner (eds.), *Making History: Edward Augustus Freeman and Victorian Cultural Politics* (Oxford: Oxford University Press, 2015), 101–18.

Conrad, Sebastian, and Dominic Sachsenmaier (eds.), *Competing Visions of World Order* (Basingstoke: Palgrave, 2007).

Cooper, Dana, *Informal Ambassadors: American Women, Transatlantic Marriages, and Anglo-American Relations, 1865–1945* (Kent, OH: Kent State University Press, 2014).

Cooper, Sandi E., *Patriotic Pacifism: Waging War on War in Europe, 1815–1914* (Oxford: Oxford University Press, 1991).

Corder, Kevin, and Christina Wolbrecht, *Counting Women's Ballots: Female Voters from Suffrage through the New Deal* (Cambridge: Cambridge University Press, 2016).

Cosgrove, Richard A., *The Rule of Law: Albert Venn Dicey, Victorian Jurist* (London: Macmillan, 1980).

———, "A. V. Dicey at the Harvard Law School, 1898: A Study in the Anglo-American Legal Community," *Harvard Library Bulletin*, 26 (1978), 325–35.

Crapol, Edward, *America for Americans: Economic Nationalism and Anglophobia in the Late Nineteenth Century* (Westport, CT: Greenwood, 1973).

Crofton, Sarah, "'Julia Says': The Spirit-Writing and Editorial Mediumship of W. T. Stead," *19: Interdisciplinary Studies in the Long Nineteenth Century*, 16 (2013), 1–15.

Crook, Paul, "Historical Monkey Business: The Myth of a Darwinized British Imperial Discourse," *History*, 84/276 (1999), 633–57.

———, *Darwinism, War and History: The Debate over the Biology of War from the "Origins of Species" to the First World War* (Cambridge: Cambridge University Press, 1994).

———, *Benjamin Kidd: Portrait of a Social Darwinist* (Cambridge: Cambridge University Press, 1984).

Crowder, Ralph, *John Edward Bruce: Politician, Journalist, and Self-Trained Historian of the African Diaspora* (New York: New York University Press, 2004).

Crowley, John, *The Great Work of Time* (1989; New York: Bantam, 1991).

Csicsery-Ronay, Istvan, "Empire" in Mark Bould, Andrew Butler, Adam Roberts, and Sherryl Vint (eds.), *The Routledge Companion to Science Fiction* (London: Routledge, 2009), 363–72.

———, "Science Fiction and Empire," *Science Fiction Studies*, 30/2 (2003), 231–45.

Cullinane, Michael Patrick, *Theodore Roosevelt's Ghost: The History and Memory of an American Icon* (Baton Rouge: Louisiana State University Press, 2017).

———, "Imperial 'Character': How Race and Civilization Shaped Theodore Roosevelt's Imperialism" in Hans Krabbendam and John M. Thompson (eds.), *America's Transatlantic Turn: Theodore Roosevelt and the "Discovery" of Europe* (New York: Palgrave Macmillan, 2012), 31–47.

———, *Liberty and American Anti-Imperialism: 1898–1909* (Basingstoke: Palgrave, 2012).

Curry, Tommy (ed.), *The Philosophical Treatise of William H. Ferris: Selected Readings from The African Abroad or, His Evolution in Western Civilization* (Lanham: Rowman & Littlefield, 2016).

———, "The Fortune of Wells: Ida B. Wells-Barnett's Use of T. Thomas Fortune's Philosophy of Social Agitation as a Prolegomenon to Militant Civil Rights Activism," *Transactions of the Charles S. Peirce Society*, 48/4 (2012), 456–82.

Dalziel, Raewyn, "An Experiment in the Social Laboratory? Suffrage, National Identity, and Mythologies of Race in New Zealand in the 1890s" in Ian Christopher Fletcher, Phillipa Levine, and Laura Nym Mayhall (eds.), *Women's Suffrage in the British Empire: Citizenship, Nation, and Race* (London: Routledge, 2000), 87–102.

———, *Julius Vogel: Business Politician* (Auckland: Oxford University Press, 1986).

Davis, John, and Angus Nichols (eds.), "Friedrich Max Müller and the Role of Philology in Victorian Thought," *Publications of the English Goethe Society*, 85/1 (2016), 67–230.

Dawdy, Shannon Lee, "Clockpunk Anthropology and the Ruins of Modernity," *Current Anthropology*, 51/6 (2010), 761–93.

Deane, Bradley, *Masculinity and the New Imperialism: Rewriting Manhood in British Popular Literature, 1870–1914* (Cambridge: Cambridge University Press, 2014).

DeBenedetti, Charles, *The Peace Reform in American History* (Bloomington: Indiana University Press, 1980).

Desmond, Adrian, *Huxley: Evolution's High Priest*, 2 vols. (London: Michael Joseph, 1997).

Deudney, Daniel, *Bounding Power: Republican Security Theory from the Polis to the Global Village* (Princeton, NJ: Princeton University Press, 2007).

Devereux, Cecily, "'The Maiden Tribute' and the Rise of the White Slave in the Nineteenth Century: The Making of an Imperial Construct," *Victorian Review*, 26/2 (2000), 1–23.

DeVine, Christine, *Nineteenth-Century British Travelers in the New World* (Farnham: Ashgate, 2013).

Dietz, Mary, "Patriotism" in Ball, Farr, and Hanson, *Political Innovation and Conceptual Change*, 177–93.

Dingley, Robert, "The Ruins of the Future: Macaulay's New Zealander and the Spirit of the Age" in Dingley and Alan Sandison (eds.), *Histories of the Future: Studies in Fact, Fantasy and Science Fiction* (Basingstoke: Palgrave, 2000), 15–33.

Donovan, Stephen, "Congo Utopia," *English Studies in Africa*, 59/1 (2016), 63–75.

Doyle, Mark, *Communal Violence in the British Empire: Disturbing the Pax* (London: Bloomsbury, 2017).

Doyle, Michael, "Liberalism and World Politics," *American Political Science Review*, 80/4 (1986), 1151–69.

———, "Kant, Liberal Legacies, and Foreign Affairs, Part 2," *Philosophy & Public Affairs*, 12/4 (1983), 323–53.

———, "Kant, Liberal Legacies, and Foreign Affairs," *Philosophy & Public Affairs*, 12/3 (1983), 205–35.

Driver, Felix, *Geography Militant: Cultures of Exploration and Empire* (Oxford: Blackwell, 2005).

Dudden, Faye, *Fighting Chance: The Struggle over Woman Suffrage and Black Suffrage in Reconstruction America* (Oxford: Oxford University Press, 2011).

Duffy, Enda, *The Speed Handbook: Velocity, Pleasure, Modernism* (Durham, NC: Duke University Press, 2009).

Dugdale, Blanche, *Arthur James Balfour*, 2 vols. (London: Hutchinson, 1936).

Dyer, Thomas G., *Theodore Roosevelt and the Idea of Race* (Baton Rouge: Louisiana State University Press, 1980).

Dzelzainis Ella, and Ruth Livesey (eds.), *The American Experiment and the Idea of Democracy in British Culture, 1776–1914* (Aldershot: Ashgate, 2013).

Earle, Edward Mead, "H. G. Wells, British Patriot in Search of a World State," *World Politics*, 2/2 (1950), 181–208.

Easley, Eric, *The War over "Perpetual Peace": An Exploration into the History of a Foundational International Relations Text* (Basingstoke: Palgrave, 2005).

Easterling, Keller, *Extrastatecraft: The Power of Infrastructure Space* (London: Verso, 2014).

Easton, Lloyd D., *Hegel's First American Followers: The Ohio Hegelians: John B. Stallo, Peter Kaufmann, Moncure Conway and August Willich, with Key Writings* (Athens: Ohio University Press, 1966).

Echevarria, Antullio G., II, *Imagining Future War: The West's Technological Revolution and Visions of Wars to Come, 1880–1914* (Westport, CT: Praeger, 2007).

Edel, Leon, and Gordon Ray (eds.), *Henry James and H. G. Wells* (London: Hart-Davis, 1958).

Edgerton, David, *England and the Aeroplane: An Essay on a Militant and Technological Nation* (Basingstoke: Macmillan, 1991).

Edwards, Barrington S., "W. E. B. Du Bois between Worlds: Berlin, Empirical Social Research, and the Race Question," *Du Bois Review*, 3/2 (2006), 395–424.

Edwards, Wendy, "Forging an Ideology for American Missions: Josiah Strong and Manifest Destiny" in Wilbert Shenk (ed.), *North American Foreign Missions, 1810–1914* (Grand Rapids, MI: Eerdmans, 2004), 163–91.

Egerton, George, *Great Britain and the Creation of the League of Nations: Strategy, Politics, and International Organization, 1914–1919* (Chapel Hill: University of North Carolina Press, 1978).

Eisenstadt, A. S., *Carnegie's Model Republic:* Triumphant Democracy *and the British-American Relationship* (Albany: State University of New York Press, 2007).

Eliot, Simon, "'His Generation Read Histories': Walter Besant, Chatto and Windus and 'All Sorts and Conditions of Men,'" *Publishing History*, 21/1 (1987), 25–67.

Elliott, Mark, *Color-Blind Justice: Albion Tourgée and the Quest for Racial Equality from the Civil War to Plessy v. Ferguson* (Oxford: Oxford University Press, 2006).

Elwyn, Sue, "Interstate Kinship and Roman Foreign Policy," *Transactions of the American Philological Association*, 123 (1993), 261–86.

Epstein, Katherine, "Imperial Airs: Leo Amery, Air Power and Empire, 1873–1945," *Journal of Imperial and Commonwealth History*, 38/4 (2010), 571–98.

Evans, Julie, Patricia Grimshaw, David Philips, and Shurlee Swain, *Equal Subjects, Unequal Rights: Indigenous People in British Settler Colonies, 1830–1910* (Manchester: Manchester University Press, 2003).

Faber, David, *Speaking for England: Leo, Julian and John Amery* (London: Simon & Schuster, 2007).

Fair, John, "F. S. Oliver, Alexander Hamilton, and the 'American Plan' for Resolving Britain's Constitutional Crises, 1903–1921," *Twentieth Century British History*, 10/1 (1999), 1–26.

Ferguson, Christine, "Surface Tensions: Steampunk, Subculture, and the Ideology of Style," *Neo-Victorian Studies*, 4/2 (2011), 66–90.

Ferguson, Niall, *Colossus: The Rise and Fall of the American Empire* (London: Penguin, 2004).

———, *Empire: How Britain Made the Modern World* (London: Penguin, 2003).

Fitting, Peter, "Estranged Invaders: *The War of the Worlds*" in Patrick Parrinder (ed.), *Learning from Other Worlds: Estrangement, Cognition, and the Politics of Science Fiction* (Durham, NC: Duke University Press, 2001), 127–45.

Fleming, Sean, *Leviathan on a Leash: A Political Theory of State Responsibility* (Princeton, NJ: Princeton University Press, 2020).

Flint, John, *Cecil Rhodes* (Boston: Little, Brown, 1974).

Flood, Christopher, *Political Myths* (London: Routledge, 1996).

Foner, Eric, *Reconstruction: America's Unfinished Revolution, 1863–1877* (New York: Harper & Row, 1988).

Forlini, Stefania, "Technology and Morality: The Stuff of Steampunk," *Neo-Victorian Studies*, 3/1 (2010), 72–98.

Fradera, Joseph, *The Imperial Nation: Citizens and Subjects in the British, French, Spanish, and American Empires*, trans. Ruth Mackay (Princeton, NJ: Princeton University Press, 2018).

Francis, Wigmoore, "White Negroes, Black Hebrews, and the Anti-Imperialist Narratives of Theophilus Scholes," *Journal of Caribbean History*, 46/1 (2012), 33–60.

———, "Nineteenth- and Early-Twentieth-Century Perspectives on Women in the Discourses of Radical Black Caribbean Men," *Small Axe*, 7/1 (2003), 116–39.

Frankel, Robert, *Observing America: The Commentary of British Visitors to the United States, 1890–1950* (Madison: University of Wisconsin Press, 2007).

Franklin, H. Bruce, "How America's Fictions of the Future Have Changed the World" in David Seed (ed.), *Future Wars: The Anticipations and the Fears* (Liverpool: Liverpool University Press, 2012).

———, *War Stars: The Superweapon and the American Imagination*, rev. ed. (Amherst: University of Massachusetts Press, 1998).

Franklin, V. P., *Living Our Stories, Telling Our Truths: Autobiography and the Making of the African-American Intellectual Tradition* (Oxford: Oxford University Press, 1996).

Frantzen, Allen, and John Niles (eds.), *Anglo-Saxonism and the Construction of Social Identity* (Gainesville: University Press of Florida, 1997).

Fredrickson, George, *Racism: A Short History* (Princeton, NJ: Princeton University Press, 2002).

Freeden, Michael, "Civil Society and the Good Citizen" in Jose Harris (ed.), *Civil Society in British History: Ideas, Identities, Institutions* (Oxford: Oxford University Press, 2003), 275–92.

———, "Eugenics and Progressive Thought: A Study in Ideological Affinity," *Historical Journal*, 22/3 (1979), 645–71.

Freedman, Carl, *Critical Theory and Science Fiction* (Middleton: Wesleyan University Press, 1990).

Freedman, Lawrence, *The Future of War: A History* (London: Penguin, 2017).

Frei, Gabriela, *Great Britain, International Law, and the Evolution of Maritime Strategic Thought, 1865–1914* (Oxford: Oxford University Press, 2020).

Frost, Mark, "Imperial Citizenship or Else: Liberal Ideals and the India Unmaking of Empire, 1890–1919," *Journal of Imperial and Commonwealth History*, 48/5 (2018), 845–73.

Gallagher, Catherine, *Telling It Like It Wasn't: The Counterfactual Imagination in History and Fiction* (Chicago: University of Chicago Press, 2018).

Gannon, Charles, *Rumors of War and Infernal Machines: Technomilitary Agenda-Setting in American and British Speculative Fiction* (Liverpool: Liverpool University Press, 2003).

Garvin, Joseph L., and Julian Amery, *The Life of Joseph Chamberlain, Vol. 3, 1895–1900, Empire and World Policy* (London: Macmillan, 1932).

Gatewood, Willard, *Black Americans and the White Man's Burden, 1898–1903* (Urbana: University of Illinois Press, 1975).

Gawantka, Wilfried, *Isopolitie: Ein Beitrag zur Geschichte der Zwischenstaatlichen Beziehungen in der Griechischen Antike* (Munich: Beck, 1975).

Geiss, Imanuel, *The Pan-African Movement* (London: Methuen, 1974).

Geoghegan, Vincent, *Ernst Bloch* (London: Routledge 1996).

Gerlach, Murney, *British Liberalism and the United States: Political and Social Thought in the Late Victorian Age* (Basingstoke: Palgrave, 2001).

Gerstle, Gary, *American Crucible: Race and Nation in the Twentieth Century* (Princeton, NJ: Princeton University Press, 2001).

———, "Theodore Roosevelt and the Divided Character of American Nationalism," *Journal of American History*, 86/3 (1999), 1280–307.

Getachew, Adom, *Worldmaking after Empire: The Rise and Fall of Self-Determination* (Princeton, NJ: Princeton University Press, 2019).

Geuss, Raymond, *Reality and Its Dreams* (Cambridge, MA: Harvard University Press, 2016).

Gibb, Paul, "Unmasterly Inactivity? Sir Julian Pauncefote, Lord Salisbury, and the Venezuela Dispute," *Diplomacy & Statecraft*, 16/1 (2005), 23–55.

Gibson, William, and Bruce Sterling, *The Difference Engine* (1990; London: Gollancz, 2011).

Giles, Paul, *Atlantic Republic: The American Tradition in English Literature* (Oxford: Oxford University Press, 2009).

Gilroy, Paul, *Postcolonial Melancholia* (New York: Columbia University Press, 2006).

———, *Against Race: Imagining Political Culture beyond the Color Line* (Cambridge, MA: Harvard University Press, 2002).

———, *The Black Atlantic: Modernity and Double Consciousness* (London: Verso, 1993).

Ginneken, Jaap van, *Crowds, Psychology, and Politics, 1871–1899* (Cambridge: Cambridge University Press, 1992).

Go, Julian, *Patterns of Empire: The British and American Empires, 1688 to Present* (Cambridge: Cambridge University Press, 2012).

Go, Julian, and Anne Foster (eds.), *The American Colonial State in the Philippines: Global Perspectives* (Durham, NC: Duke University Press, 2003).

Gooch, John, "Sir George Clarke's Career at the Committee of Imperial Defence, 1904–1907," *Historical Journal*, 18/3 (1975), 555–69.

Gooday, Graeme, "Electrical Futures Past," *Endeavour*, 29/4 (2005), 150–55.

Gooding-Williams, Robert, *In the Shadow of Du Bois: Afro-Modern Political Thought in America* (Cambridge, MA: Harvard University Press, 2009).

Goodwin, Barbara, "Taxation in Utopia," *Utopian Studies*, 19/2 (2008), 313–31.

Goodwyn, Helena, "Margaret Harkness, W. T. Stead, and the Transatlantic Social Gospel Network" in Lisa Robertson and Flore Janssen (eds.), *Authorship and Activism: Margaret Harkness and Writing Social Engagement, 1880–1921* (Manchester: Manchester University Press, 2018).

———, "A 'New' Journalist: The Americanization of W. T. Stead," *Journal of Victorian Culture*, 23/3 (2018), 405–20.

Gopal, Priyamvada, *Insurgent Empire: Anticolonial Resistance and British Dissent* (London: Verso, 2019).

Gorman, Daniel, "George Catlin, the Science of Politics, and Anglo-American Union," *Modern Intellectual History*, 15/1 (2018), 123–52.

———, *Imperial Citizenship: Empire and the Question of Belonging* (Manchester: Manchester University Press, 2006).

Graham, Sara Hunter, *Woman Suffrage and the New Democracy* (New Haven, CT: Yale University Press, 1997).

Grainger, J. H., *Patriotisms: Britain, 1900–1939* (London: Routledge, 1986).

Grandin, Greg, *The End of the Myth: From the Frontier to the Border Wall in the Mind of America* (New York: Metropolitan Books, 2019).

Gray, Chris Hables, Heidi J. Figueroa, and Steven Menor (eds.), *The Cyborg Handbook* (London: Routledge, 1995).

Graybar, Lloyd, *Albert Shaw of the Review of Reviews: An Intellectual Biography* (Lexington: University Press of Kentucky, 1974).

Grayson, Richard, "Imperialism in Conservative Defence and Foreign Policy: Leo Amery and the Chamberlains, 1903–39," *Journal of Imperial and Commonwealth History*, 34/4 (2006), 505–27.

Green, Ewen Henry Harvey, *The Crisis of Conservatism: The Politics, Economics and Ideology of the Conservative Party 1880–1914* (London: Routledge, 1995).

Green, Jeffrey, *Black Edwardians: Black People in Britain 1901–1914* (Abingdon: Routledge, 1998).

Greene, Julie, *The Canal Builders: Making America's Empire at the Panama Canal* (London: Penguin, 2009).

Greenland, Colin, *Entropy Exhibition: Michael Moorcock and the British "New Wave" in Science Fiction* (London: Routledge, 1983).

Gruesser, John Cullen, *The Empire Abroad and the Empire at Home: African American Literature and the Era of Overseas Expansion* (Athens: University of Georgia Press, 2012).

Guglielmo, Thomas, *White on Arrival: Italians, Race, Color, and Power in Chicago, 1890–1945* (Oxford: Oxford University Press, 2000).

Gunnell, John, *Imagining the American Polity: Political Science and the Discourse of Democracy* (Philadelphia: Penn State University Press, 2004).

Gunning, Tom, "Re-Newing Old Technologies" in David Thorburn and Henry Jenkins (eds.), *Rethinking Media Change: The Aesthetics of Transition* (Cambridge, MA: MIT Press, 2003), 39–60.

Guyatt, Nicholas, *Providence and the Invention of the United States, 1607–1876* (Cambridge: Cambridge University Press, 2007).

Habermas, Jürgen, "The European Nation-State: On the Past and Future of Sovereignty and Citizenship" in Habermas, *The Inclusion of the Other: Studies in Political Theory*, trans. Jeremy J. Shapiro (Cambridge: Polity Press, 1996), 105–28.

Haglund, David, *The US "Culture Wars" and the Anglo-American Special Relationship* (New York: Palgrave, 2019).

Hale, Piers, *Political Descent: Malthus, Mutualism, and the Politics of Evolution in Victorian England* (Chicago: Chicago University Press, 2014).

Hall, Stephen, *A Faithful Account of the Race: African American Historical Writing in Nineteenth-Century America* (Chapel Hill: University of North Carolina Press, 2009).

Hammond, Mason, "Germania Patria," *Harvard Studies in Classical Philology*, 60 (1951), 147–74.

Hantke, Steffen, "Difference Engines and Other Infernal Devices: History according to Steampunk," *Extrapolation*, 40/3 (1999), 244–54.

Haraway, Donna, "A Cyborg Manifesto: Science, Technology, and Socialist-Feminism in the Late Twentieth Century" in Haraway, *Simians, Cyborgs, and Women: The Reinvention of Nature* (London: Routledge, 1991), 149–81.

Hardy, Sylvia, "H. G. Wells and William James: A Pragmatic Approach" in McLean, *H. G. Wells*, 130–46.

———, "H. G. Wells and Language," PhD diss., University of Leicester, 1991.

Harris, Leonard, and Charles Molesworth, *Alain L. Locke: The Biography of a Philosopher* (Chicago: University of Chicago Press, 2009).

Harrison, Patricia, *Collecting Links: The British and American Woman Suffrage Movements, 1900–1914* (Westport, CT: Greenwood Press, 2000).

Harrison, Royden, *The Life and Times of Sidney and Beatrice Webb: 1858–1905* (Basingstoke: Palgrave, 2000).

Harvie, Christopher, "Ideology and Home Rule: James Bryce, A. V. Dicey and Ireland, 1880–1887," *English Historical Review*, 91/359 (1976), 298–314.

Hayles, N. Katherine, "Unfinished Work: From Cyborg to Cognisphere," *Theory Culture Society*, 23/7 (2006), 159–66.

——, *How We Became Posthuman: Virtual Bodies in Cybernetics, Literature, and Informatics* (Chicago: University of Chicago Press, 1999).

Headrick, Daniel, *Power over Peoples: Technology, Environments, and Western Imperialism, 1400 to the Present* (Princeton, NJ: Princeton University Press, 2010).

——, *The Tools of Empire: Technology and European Imperialism in the Nineteenth Century* (Oxford: Oxford University Press, 1981).

Henderson, Eroll, "The Revolution Will Not Be Theorised: Du Bois, Locke, and the Howard School's Challenge to White Supremacist IR Theory," *Millennium*, 45/3 (2017), 492–510.

Hensley, John, "Eugenics and Social Darwinism in Stanley Waterloo's *The Story of Ab* and Jack London's *Before Adam*," *Studies in Popular Culture*, 25/1 (2002), 1–9.

Herrick, F. H., "Gladstone and the Concept of the 'English-Speaking Peoples,'" *Journal of British Studies*, 12/1 (1972), 150–56.

Herring, George, *From Colony to Superpower: U.S. Foreign Relations since 1776* (Oxford: Oxford University Press, 2008).

Herz, John, "Idealist Internationalism and the Security Dilemma," *World Politics*, 2/2 (1950), 157–80.

Hesketh, Ian, "A Good Darwinian Epic? Winwood Reade and the Making of a Late Victorian Evolutionary Epic," *Studies in the History and Philosophy of Biological and Biomedical Sciences*, 51 (2015), 44–52.

Heuser, Beatrice, *The Evolution of Strategy: Thinking War from Antiquity to the Present* (Cambridge: Cambridge University Press, 2010).

Hilfrich, Fabian, *Debating American Exceptionalism: Empire and Democracy in the Wake of the Spanish-American War* (Basingstoke: Palgrave Macmillan, 2012).

Hippler, Thomas, and Miloš Vec (eds.), *Paradoxes of Peace in Nineteenth Century Europe* (Oxford: Oxford University Press, 2015).

Ho, Elizabeth, *Neo-Victorianism and the Memory of Empire* (London: Bloomsbury, 2011).

Hobson, Christopher, Tony Smith, John Owen, Anna Geis, and Piki Ish-Shalom, "Roundtable: Between the Theory and Practice of Democratic Peace," *International Relations*, 25/2 (2011), 147–85.

Hobson, John M., *The Eurocentric Conception of World Politics: Western International Theory, 1760–2010* (Cambridge: Cambridge University Press, 2012).

Hoffenberg, Peter, *An Empire on Display: English, Indian, and Australian Exhibitions from the Crystal Palace to the Great War* (Berkeley: University of California Press, 2001).

Hoganson, Kristin, *Fighting for American Manhood: How Gender Politics Provoked the Spanish-American and Philippine-American Wars* (New Haven, CT: Yale University Press, 1998).

Holman, Brett, *The Next War in the Air: Britain's Fear of the Bomber, 1908–1941* (Aldershot: Ashgate, 2014).

Holthaus, Leonie, *Pluralist Democracy in International Relations: L. T. Hobhouse, G. D. H. Cole, and David Mitrany* (Basingstoke: Palgrave, 2018).

Hont, Istvan, *Jealousy of Trade: International Competition and the Nation-State in Historical Perspective* (Cambridge, MA: Harvard University Press, 2005).

Hookway, Christopher, "Pragmatism" in Thomas Baldwin (ed.), *The Cambridge History of Philosophy, 1870–1945* (Cambridge: Cambridge University Press, 2003), 74–92.

Hopkins, A. G., *American Empire: A Global History* (Princeton, NJ: Princeton University Press, 2018).

———, "Globalisation and Decolonisation," *Journal of Imperial and Commonwealth History*, 45/5 (2017), 729–45.

Horsman, Reginald, *Race and Manifest Destiny: The Origins of American Racial Anglo-Saxonism* (Cambridge, MA: Harvard University Press, 1986).

Howard, Michael, *War and the Liberal Conscience* (New York: Columbia University Press, 2008).

———, *The Invention of Peace: Reflections on War and International Order* (London: Yale University Press, 2000).

———, "Men against the Fire: The Doctrine of the Offensive in 1914" in Howard, *The Lessons of History* (New Haven, CT: Yale University Press, 1993), 97–112.

Howe, Anthony, *Free Trade and Liberal England, 1846–1946* (Oxford: Clarendon, 1997).

Howe, Stephen, *Afrocentrism: Mythical Pasts and Imagined Homes* (London: Verso, 1999).

Hughes, Michael, and Harry Wood, "Crimson Nightmares: Tales of Invasion and Fears of Revolution in Early Twentieth-Century Britain," *Contemporary British History*, 28/3 (2014), 294–317.

Humphrey, R. A. "Anglo-American Rivalries and the Venezuela Crisis of 1895," *Transactions of the Royal Historical Society*, 17 (1967), 131–64.

Hunt, Tristram, "Foreword," W. Sydney Robinson, *Muckraker: The Scandalous Life and Times of W. T. Stead: Britain's First Investigative Journalist* (London: Robson, 2013), xi.

Immerwahr, Daniel, *How to Hide an Empire: A Short History of the Greater United States* (New York: Penguin, 2019).

Ions, Edmund, *James Bryce and American Democracy, 1870–1922* (London: Macmillan, 1968).

Ish-Shalom, Piki, *Democratic Peace: A Political Biography* (Ann Arbor: University of Michigan Press, 2013).

Jacobson, Matthew F., *Whiteness of a Different Color: European Immigrants and the Alchemy of Race* (Cambridge, MA: Harvard University Press, 1999).

Jagoda, Patrick, "Clacking Control Societies: Steampunk, History, and the Difference Engine of Escape," *Neo-Victorian Studies*, 3/1 (2010), 46–71.

James, Joy, *The Talented Tenth: Black Leaders and American Intellectuals* (Abingdon: Routledge, 1997).

James, Simon, *Maps of Utopia: H. G. Wells, Modernity and the End of Culture* (Oxford: Oxford University Press, 2012).

Jameson, Frederic, *Archaeologies of the Future: The Desire Called Utopia and Other Science Fictions* (London: Verso, 2007).

Jerng, Mark C., *Racial Worldmaking: The Power of Popular Fiction* (New York: Fordham University Press, 2017).

Johnson, Matthew, *Militarism and the British Left, 1902–1914* (Basingstoke: Palgrave, 2013).

Jones, Jeannette Eileen, "'The Negro's Peculiar Work': Jim Crow and Black Discourses on US Empire, Race, and the African Question, 1877–1900," *Journal of American Studies*, 52/2 (2018), 1–28.

Kahan, Paul, *The Homestead Strike: Labor, Violence, and American Industry* (London: Routledge, 2014).

Kapossy, Béla, Isaac Nakhimovsky, and Richard Whatmore (eds.), *Commerce and Peace in the Enlightenment* (Cambridge: Cambridge University Press, 2017).

Karatani, Rieko, *Defining British Citizenship: Empire, Commonwealth and Modern Britain* (London: Frank Cass, 2003).

Katzenstein, Peter (ed.), *Anglo-America and Its Discontents* (London: Routledge, 2012).

Kearns, Gerry, *Geopolitics and Empire: The Legacy of Halford Mackinder* (Oxford: Oxford University Press, 2009).

Kelley, Robin D. G., "'But a Local Phase of a World Problem': Black History's Global Vision," *Journal of American History*, 86/3 (1999), 1045–77.

Kelly, Duncan, *Reconstruction: The First World War and the Origins of Modern Politics* (Oxford: Oxford University Press, forth.).

———, "August Ludwig von Rochau and *Realpolitik* as Historical Political Theory," *Global Intellectual History*, 3/3 (2018), 301–30.

Kendle, John, *The Round Table Movement and Imperial Union* (Toronto: University of Toronto Press, 1975).

Kennedy, David, *Of Law and War* (Princeton, NJ: Princeton University Press, 2006).

Kennedy, Paul, *The Parliament of Man: The Past, Present, and Future of the United Nations* (New York: Random House, 2006).

———, *The Rise of the Anglo-German Antagonism, 1860–1914* (London: Allen & Unwin, 1980).

Kenny, Anthony, *The History of the Rhodes Trust* (Oxford: Oxford University Press, 2001).

Kenny, Michael, and Nick Pearce, *Shadows of Empire: The Anglosphere in British Politics* (Cambridge: Polity, 2018).

Kern, Stephen, *The Culture of Time and Space, 1880–1918* (Cambridge, MA: Harvard University Press, 1983).

Kerslake, Patricia, *Science Fiction and Empire* (Liverpool: Liverpool University Press, 2010).

Ketabgian, Tamara, *The Lives of Machines: The Industrial Imaginary in Victorian Literature and Culture* (Ann Arbor: University of Michigan Press, 2011).

Killingray, David, "The Black Atlantic Missionary Movement and Africa, 1780s–1920s," *Journal of Religion in Africa*, 31/3 (2003), 3–31.

King, Desmond, *Making Americans: Immigration, Race, and the Origins of the Diverse Democracy* (Cambridge, MA: Harvard University Press, 2000).

Kirkby, Coel, "The Politics and Practice of 'Native' Enfranchisement in Canada and the Cape Colony, c.1880–1900," PhD diss., University of Cambridge, 2013.

Kirkby, James, "A. V. Dicey and English Constitutionalism," *History of European Ideas*, 45/1 (2019), 33–46.

Kirkwood, Patrick, "Alexander Hamilton and the Early Republic in Edwardian Imperial Thought," *Britain and the World*, 12/1 (2019), 28–50.

———, "'Lord Cromer's Shadow': Political Anglo-Saxonism and the Egyptian Protectorate as a Model in the American Philippines," *Journal of World History*, 27/1 (2016), 1–26.

Klarman, Michael, *From Jim Crow to Civil Rights: The Supreme Court and the Struggle for Racial Equality* (Oxford: Oxford University Press, 2004).

Klein, Kerwin Lee, *Frontiers of Historical Imagination: Narrating the European Conquest of Native America, 1890–1990* (Berkeley: University of California Press, 1997).

Kloppenberg, James T., *Uncertain Victory: Social Democracy and Progressivism in European and American Thought, 1870–1920* (Oxford: Oxford University Press, 1986).

Kohn, Edward, *This Kindred People: Canadian-American Relations and the Anglo-Saxon Idea, 1895–1903* (Montreal: McGill-Queen's University Press, 2004).

Koselleck, Reinhart, "The Temporalization of Utopia" in Koselleck, *The Practice of Conceptual History: Timing History, Spacing Concepts*, trans. Todd Samuel Presener (Stanford: Stanford University Press, 2002), 84–99.

Koskenniemi, Martti, *The Gentle Civiliser of Nations: The Rise and Fall of International Law 1870–1960* (Cambridge: Cambridge University Press, 2001).

Kramer, Paul A., "Empires, Exceptions, and Anglo-Saxons: Race and Rule between the British and United States Empires, 1880–1910," *Journal of American History*, 88/4 (2002), 1315–53.

Kuklick, Bruce, "Who Owns Pragmatism?," *Modern Intellectual History*, 14/2 (2017), 565–83.

———, *The Rise of American Philosophy: Cambridge Massachusetts, 1860–1930* (New Haven, CT: Yale University Press, 1977).

Kumar, Krishan, "Wells and the So-called Science of Sociology" in Patrick Parrinder and Christopher Rolfe (eds.), *H. G. Wells under Revision* (Toronto: Susquehanna University Press, 1990), 192–217.

Kupchan, Charles, *How Enemies Become Friends: The Sources of Stable Peace* (Princeton, NJ: Princeton University Press, 2010).

Kutz, Christopher, *On War and Democracy* (Princeton, NJ: Princeton University Press, 2016).

Kwoba, Brian, Rose Chantiluke, and Athinangamso Nkope (eds.), *Rhodes Must Fall: The Struggle to Decolonise the Racist Heart of Empire* (London: Zed, 2018).

Laborde, Cécile, "From Constitutional to Civic Patriotism," *British Journal of Political Science*, 32/4 (2002), 591–612.

Laity, Paul, *The British Peace Movement, 1870–1914* (Oxford: Clarendon Press, 2001).

Lake, Marilyn, *Progressive New World: How Settler Colonialism and Transpacific Exchange Shaped American Reform* (Cambridge, MA: Harvard University Press, 2019).

———, "British World or New World? Anglo-Saxonism and Australian Engagement with America," *History Australia*, 10/3 (2013), 36–50.

Lake, Marilyn, and Henry Reynolds, *Drawing the Global Colour Line: White Men's Countries and the International Challenge of Racial Equality* (Cambridge: Cambridge University Press, 2008).

Lamb, Robert, "The Liberal Cosmopolitanism of Thomas Paine," *Journal of Politics*, 76/3 (2014), 636–48.

Larsen, J. A. O., *Greek Federal States: Their Institutions and History* (Oxford: Clarendon Press, 1968).

Larson, Victoria Tietze, "Classics and the Acquisition and Validation of Power in Britain's 'Imperial Century' (1815–1914)," *International Journal of the Classical Tradition*, 6/2 (1999), 185–225.

Lavin, Deborah, *From Empire to International Commonwealth: A Biography of Lionel Curtis* (Oxford: Clarendon, 1995).

Lazar, Nomi Claire, *Out of Joint: Power, Crisis, and the Rhetoric of Time* (New Haven, CT: Yale University Press, 2019).

Lessoff, Alan, "Progress before Modernization: Foreign Interpretations of American Development in James Bryce's Generation," *American Nineteenth Century History*, 1/2 (2000), 69–96.

Lester, Alan, and Fae Dussart, *Colonization and the Origins of Humanitarian Governance: Protecting Aborigines across the Nineteenth-Century British Empire* (Cambridge: Cambridge University Press, 2014).

Levander, Caroline, "Sutton Griggs and the Borderlands of Empire," *American Literary History*, 22/1 (2010), 57–84.

Levine, Robert S., *Martin Delany, Frederick Douglass, and the Politics of Representative Identity* (Chapel Hill: University of North Carolina Press, 1997).

Levitas, Ruth, "Back to the Future: Wells, Sociology, Utopia and Method," *Sociological Review*, 58/4 (2010), 530–47.

———, "The Imaginary Reconstitution of Society" in Moylan and Baccolini (eds.), *Utopia-Method-Vision: The Use Value of Social Dreaming* (Oxford: Peter Lang, 2007), 53–54.

———, *The Concept of Utopia* (Syracuse: Syracuse University Press, 1990).

Levy, Jack S., "Domestic Politics and War," *Journal of Interdisciplinary History*, 18/4 (1988), 653–73.

Lewis, David Levering, *W. E. B. Du Bois: Biography of a Race, 1868–1919* (New York: Henry Holt, 1993).

Lew-Williams, Beth, *The Chinese Must Go: Violence, Exclusion, and the Making of the Alien in America* (Cambridge, MA: Harvard University Press, 2018).

Linden, Wim H. van der, *The International Peace Movement, 1815–1874* (Amsterdam: Tilleul, 1987).

Lindqvist, Sven, *A History of Bombing* (Cambridge: Granta, 2012).

Linklater, Andrew, *Violence and Civilization in the Western States-System* (Cambridge: Cambridge University Press, 2017).

Lino, Dylan, "The Rule of Law and the Rule of Empire: A. V. Dicey in Imperial Context," *Modern Law Review*, 81/5 (2018), 739–64.

———, "Albert Venn Dicey and the Constitutional Theory of Empire," *Oxford Journal of Legal Studies*, 36/4 (2016), 751–80.

Little, Richard, *The Balance of Power in International Relations: Metaphors, Myths and Models* (Cambridge: Cambridge University Press, 2007).

Livingston, Alexander, *Damn Great Empires! William James and the Politics of Pragmatism* (Oxford: Oxford University Press, 2016).

Locke, Alain, "When Peoples Meet" (1942), in *Works of Alain Locke*, ed. Charles Molesworth (Oxford: Oxford University Press, 2012), 365–66.

Locke, Alain, and Bernhard Stern (eds.), *When Peoples Meet: A Study in Race and Culture Contacts* (New York: Committee on Workshops, Progressive Education Association, 1942).

Locke, George (ed.), *Sources of Science Fiction: Future War Novels of the 1890s* (London: Routledge, 1998).

——, *Pearson's Weekly: A Checklist of Fiction, 1890–1939* (London: Ferret Fantasy, 1990).

Long, David, and Brian Schmidt (eds.), *Imperialism and Internationalism in the Discipline of International Relations* (Albany: State University of New York Press, 2005).

Longan, Michael, and Tim Oakes, "Geography's Conquest of History in *The Diamond Age*" in Rob Kitchin and James Kneal (eds.), *Lost in Space: Geographies of Science Fiction* (London: Bloomsbury, 2002), 39–56.

Lorimer, Douglas, *Science, Race Relations and Resistance: Britain, 1870–1914* (Manchester: Manchester University Press, 2013).

Louis, William Roger, *In the Name of God, Go! Leo Amery and the British Empire in the Age of Churchill* (New York: Norton, 1992).

Lovric-Pernak, Kristina, "Aim: Peace—Sanction: War: International Arbitration and the Problem of Enforcement" in Thomas Hippler and Milos Vec (eds.), *Paradoxes of Peace in Nineteenth Century Europe* (Oxford: Oxford University Press, 2015), 62–74.

Luckhurst, Roger, *Science Fiction* (Cambridge: Polity, 2005).

——, *The Invention of Telepathy, 1870–1901* (Oxford: Oxford University Press, 2002).

Lukacs, John, *A New Republic: A History of the United States in the Twentieth Century* (New Haven, CT: Yale University Press, 2004).

Lydon, Jane, "H. G. Wells and a Shared Humanity: Photography, Humanitarianism and Empire," *History Australia*, 12/1 (2015), 75–94.

Magee, Gary B., and Andrew S. Thompson, *Empire and Globalisation: Networks of People, Goods and Capital in the British World, c.1850–1914* (Cambridge: Cambridge University Press, 2010).

Magnette, Paul, "How Can One Be a European? Reflections on the Pillars of European Civic Identity," *European Law Journal*, 13/5 (2007), 664–79.

Mandler, Peter, *The English National Character: The History of an Idea from Edmund Burke to Tony Blair* (New Haven, CT: Yale University Press, 2006).

Mann, Abigail, and Kathleen Rogers, "Objects and Objectivity: Harriet Martineau as Nineteenth-Century Cyborg," *Prose Studies*, 33/3 (2011), 241–56.

Manuel, Frank, and Fritzie Manuel, *Utopian Thought in the Western World* (Cambridge, MA: Harvard University Press, 1979).

Marks, George (ed.), *The Black Press Views American Imperialism* (New York: Arno, 1971).

Marsh, Peter, *Joseph Chamberlain: Entrepreneur in Politics* (New Haven, CT: Yale University Press, 1994).

Martin, Ged, "Empire Federalism and Imperial Parliamentary Union, 1820–1870," *Historical Journal*, 16/1 (1973), 65–92.

Marvin, Carolyn, *When Old Technologies Were New: Thinking about Electric Communication in the Late Nineteenth Century* (Oxford: Oxford University Press, 1988).

Matarese, Susan M., *American Foreign Policy and the Utopian Imagination* (Amherst: University of Massachusetts Press, 2010).

Matin, A. Michael, "The Creativity of War Planners: Armed Forces Professionals and the Pre-1914 British Invasion-Scare Genre," *ELH: English Literary History*, 78/4 (2011), 801–31.

——, "Scrutinizing *The Battle of Dorking*: The Royal United Services Institution and the Mid-Victorian Invasion Controversy," *Victorian Literature and Culture*, 39/2 (2011), 385–407.

Matthew, H. C. G., *Gladstone, 1809–1898* (Oxford: Oxford University Press, 1997).

May, Vivian M., *Anna Julia Cooper, Visionary Black Feminist: A Critical Introduction* (Abingdon: Routledge, 2007).

Mayers, David, *Dissenting Voices in America's Rise to Power* (Cambridge: Cambridge University Press, 2007).

Maylam, Paul, *The Cult of Rhodes: Remembering an Imperialist in Africa* (Cape Town: David Philip, 2005).

Mays, Kyle T., "Transnational Progressivism: African Americans, Native Americans, and the Universal Races Congress of 1911," *American Indian Quarterly*, 37/3 (2013), 243–61.

Mazower, Mark, *Governing the World: The History of an Idea* (London: Penguin, 2012).

McHugh, Paul G., "William Pember Reeves (1857–1932): Lawyer-Politician, Historian and 'Rough Architect' of the New Zealand State" in Shannaugh Dorsett and Ian Hunter (eds.), *Law and Politics in British Colonial Thought: Transpositions of Empire* (Basingstoke: Palgrave, 2010), 187–208.

McLean, Steven, "Revolution as an Angel from the Sky: George Griffith's Aeronautical Speculation," *Journal of Literature and Science*, 7/2 (2014), 37–61.

———, *The Early Fiction of H. G. Wells* (Basingstoke: Palgrave, 2009).

———(ed.), *H. G Wells: Interdisciplinary Essays* (Newcastle: Cambridge Scholars Publishing, 2008).

Meadowcroft, James, *Conceptualising the State: Innovation and Dispute in British Political Thought 1880–1914* (Oxford: Oxford University Press, 1995).

Melby, Christian, "Empire and Nation in British Future-War and Invasion-Scare Fiction, 1871–1914," *Historical Journal*, 63/2 (2020), 389–410.

Melchiori, Barbara Arnett, *Terrorism in the Late Victorian Novel* (Beckenham: Croom Helm, 1985).

Mellor, Leo, *Reading the Ruins: Modernism, Bombsites and British Culture* (Cambridge: Cambridge University Press, 2011).

Meyer, Paul R., "The Fear of Cultural Decline: Josiah Strong's Thoughts about Reform and Expansion," *Church History*, 42/3 (1973), 396–405.

Miéville, China, "Introduction," in Wells, *The First Men in the Moon*, ed. Patrick Parrinder (London: Penguin, 2005), xx–xxiv.

Miller, Bonnie, "The Image Makers' Arsenal in the Age of War and Empire: A Cartoon Essay, Featuring the Work of Charles Bartholomew (of the *Minneapolis Journal*) and Albert Wilbur (of the *Denver Post*)," *Journal of American Studies*, 45/1 (2011), 53–75.

Miller, Brook, *America and the British Imaginary in Turn-of-the-Twentieth-Century Literature* (Basingstoke: Palgrave, 2010).

Milne, David, *Worldmaking: The Art and Science of American Diplomacy* (New York: Farrar, Straus and Giroux, 2015).

Mitcham, John C., *Race and Imperial Defence in the British World, 1870–1914* (Cambridge, 2016).

Mitchell, Kate, *History and Cultural Memory in Neo-Victorian Fiction: Victorian Afterimages* (Basingstoke: Palgrave, 2010).

Mitchell, Michelle, "'The Black Man's Burden': African Americans, Imperialism and Notions of Racial Manhood, 1890–1910," *International Review of Social History*, 44/4 (1999), 7–99.

Mollmann, Steven, "Air-Ships and the Technological Revolution: Detached Violence in George Griffith and H. G. Wells," *Science Fiction Studies*, 42/1 (2015), 20–41.

Moore, Margaret, "Defending Community: Nationalism, Patriotism, and Culture" in Duncan Bell (ed.), *Ethics and World Politics* (Oxford: Oxford University Press, 2010), 130–45.

Moorcock, Michael, *The Warlord of the Air* (1971; London: Titan, 2013).

——(ed.), *England Invaded: A Collection of Fantasy Fiction* (London: W. H. Allen, 1977).

Moran, John (ed.), *An F. Marion Crawford Companion* (New York: Greenwood Press, 1981).

Morefield, Jeanne, *Empires without Imperialism: Anglo-American Decline and the Politics of Deflection* (Oxford: Oxford University Press, 2014).

——, *Covenants without Swords: Idealist Liberalism and the Spirit of Empire* (Princeton, NJ: Princeton University Press, 2005).

Morgan, Cecilia, *Building Better Britains? Settler Societies in the British World, 1783–1920* (Toronto: University of Toronto Press, 2016).

Morgan, Chris, "F. Marion Crawford" in E. F. Bleiler (ed.), *Supernatural Fiction Writers* (New York: Scribner's, 1985), 747–52.

Morgan-Owen, David, *The Fear of Invasion: Strategy, Politics, and British War Planning, 1880–1914* (Oxford: Oxford University Press, 2017).

Morus, Iwan Rhys, "No Mere Dream: Material Culture and Electrical Imagination in Late Victorian Britain," *Centaurus*, 57/3 (2015), 173–91.

——, "'The Nervous System of Britain': Space, Time and the Electric Telegraph in the Victorian Age," *British Journal for the History of Science*, 33/4 (2000), 455–75.

Moses, Wilson, *Afrotopia: The Roots of African American Popular History* (Cambridge: Cambridge University Press, 1998).

——, *The Golden Age of Black Nationalism, 1850–1925* (Oxford: Oxford University Press, 1978).

Moskowitz, Sam, "Critical Biography" in George Griffith, *The Raid of "Le Vengeur" and Other Stories*, ed. Moskowitz (London: Ferrett Fantasy, 1974).

Mousoutzanis, Aris, *Fin-de-Siècle Fictions, 1890s–1990s: Apocalypse, Technoscience, Empire* (Basingstoke: Palgrave, 2014).

Moylan, Tom, *Scraps of an Untainted Sky: Science Fiction, Utopia, Dystopia* (London: Perseus, 1990).

Mulanax, Richard, *The Boer War in American Politics and Diplomacy* (Lanham: University Press of America, 1994).

Muller, Dorothea, "Josiah Strong and American Nationalism: A Revaluation," *Journal of American History*, 53/3 (1966), 487–503.

Müller, Jan-Werner, *Constitutional Patriotism* (Princeton, NJ: Princeton University Press, 2007).

Mulligan, William, *The Great War for Peace* (New Haven, CT: Yale University Press, 2014).

Mulvey, Christopher, *Transatlantic Manners: Social Patterns in Nineteenth-Century Anglo-American Travel Literature* (Cambridge: Cambridge University Press, 1990).

Mutch, Deborah, "Are We Christians?': W. T. Stead, Keir Hardie and the Boer War" in Brake, Luckhurst, Mussell, and King, *W. T. Stead*, 133–48.

Muri, Allison, *The Enlightenment Cyborg: A History of Communications and Control in the Human Machine, 1660–1830* (Toronto: University of Toronto Press, 2007).

Murphy, Gretchen, *Shadowing the White Man's Burden: U.S. Imperialism and the Problem of the Color Line* (New York: New York University Press, 2010).

Mycock, Andrew, and Ben Wellings (eds.), *The Anglosphere: Continuity, Dissonance and Location* (Oxford: Oxford University Press, 2020).

Nabulsi, Karma, *Traditions of War: Occupation, Resistance and the Law* (Oxford: Oxford University Press, 1999).

Nakhimovsky, Isaac, *The Closed Commercial State: Perpetual Peace and Commercial Society from Rousseau to Fichte* (Princeton, NJ: Princeton University Press, 2011).

Nally, Claire, *Steampunk: Gender, Subculture and the Neo-Victorian* (London: Bloomsbury, 2019).

Nasaw, David, *Andrew Carnegie* (London: Penguin, 2006).

Neill, Anna, "The Made Man and the 'Minor' Novel: Erewhon, ANT, and Empire," *Victorian Studies*, 60/1 (2017), 53–73.

Nevins, Jess, "The First Lesbian Science Fiction Novel, Published in 1906," *io9* (10 July 2011), http://io9.com/5847805/the-first-lesbian-science-fiction-novel-published-in-1906.

———, "Prescriptivists vs. Descriptivists: Defining Steampunk," *Science Fiction Studies*, 38/3 (2011), 513–18.

———, "Introduction: The 19th Century Roots of Steampunk" in Ann VanderMeer and Jeff VanderMeer (eds.), *Steampunk* (San Francisco, 2008), 1–12.

Newsinger, John, "Why Rhodes Must Fall," *Race & Class*, 58/2 (2016), 70–78.

Newton, Douglas J., *British Labour, European Socialism, and the Struggle for Peace, 1889–1914* (Oxford: Oxford University Press, 1985).

Nicholls, David, *The Lost Prime Minister: A Life of Sir Charles Dilke* (London: Hambledon, 1995).

Nimcocks, Walter, *Milner's Young Men: The "Kindergarten" in Edwardian Imperial Affairs* (Durham, NC: Duke University Press, 1968).

Niu, Greta Aiyu, "Techno-Orientalism, Nanotechnology, Posthumans, and Post-Posthumanism in Neal Stephenson's and Linda Nagata's Science Fiction," *MELUS*, 33/4 (2008), 73–96.

Novick, Peter, *That Noble Dream: The "Objectivity Question" and the American Historical Profession* (Cambridge: Cambridge University Press, 1988).

Ó Donghaile, Deaglán, *Blasted Literature: Victorian Political Fiction and the Shock of Modernism* (Edinburgh: Edinburgh University Press, 2011).

Oergel, Maike, "Germania and Great(er) Britain: German Scholarship and the Legitimization of the British Empire," *Angermion: Yearbook for Anglo-German Literary Criticism, Intellectual History and Cultural Transfer*, 5/1 (2012), 91–118.

Ogren, Christine, "Complexities of Efficiency Reform: The Case of Simplified Spelling, 1876–1921," *History of Education*, 57/3 (2017), 333–68.

Oldstone-Moore, Christopher, *Hugh Price Hughes: Founder of a New Methodism, Conscience of a New Nonconformity* (Cardiff: University of Wales Press, 1999).

Oren, Ido, "The Subjectivity of the Democratic Peace," *International Security*, 20/2 (1995), 147–84.

Otis, Laura, *Networking: Communicating with Bodies and Machines in the Nineteenth Century* (Ann Arbor: University of Michigan Press, 2011).

———, "The Other End of the Wire: Uncertainties of Organic and Telegraphic Communication," *Configurations*, 9/2 (2001), 181–206.

Otter, Sandra Den, "The Origins of a Historical Political Science in Late Victorian and Edwardian Britain" in Adcock, Bevir, and Stimson, *Modern Political Science*, 66–96.

Palen, Marc-William, "British Free Trade and the International Feminist Vision for Peace, c.1846–1946" in David Thackeray, Andrew Thompson, and Richard Toye (eds.), *Imagining*

Britain's Economic Future, c.1800–1975: Trade, Consumerism and Global Markets (Basingstoke: Palgrave, 2018), 115–33.

———, *The 'Conspiracy' of Free Trade: The Anglo-American Struggle over Empire and Economic Globalization, 1846–1896* (Cambridge: Cambridge University Press, 2016).

———, "Foreign Relations in the Gilded Age: A British Free-Trade Conspiracy?," *Diplomatic History*, 37/2 (2013), 217–47.

Paradis, James, "*Evolution and Ethics* in Its Victorian Context" in Paradis and George C. Williams (eds.), *Evolution and Ethics: T. H. Huxley's Evolution and Ethics Essays in Its Victorian and Sociological Context* (Princeton, NJ: Princeton University Press, 1989), 1–56.

———, *T. H. Huxley: Man's Place in Nature* (Lincoln: University of Nebraska Press, 1979).

Parchami, Ali, *Hegemonic Peace and Empire: The Pax Romana, Britannica and Americana* (London: Routledge, 2009).

Paris, Michael, *Winged Warfare: Literature and Theory of Aerial Warfare in Britain, 1859–1917* (Manchester: Manchester University Press, 1992).

Parrinder, Patrick, *Shadows of the Future: H. G. Wells, Science Fiction and Prophecy* (Liverpool: Liverpool University Press, 1995).

Partington, John (ed.), *H. G. Wells in "Nature," 1893–1946: A Reception Reader* (Frankfurt: Peter Lang, 2008).

———, "H. G. Wells: A Political Life," *Utopian Studies*, 19/3 (2008), 517–76.

———, "Revising *Anticipations*: Wells on Race and Class, 1901 to 1905," *Undying Fire*, 4 (2005), 31–44.

———, *Building Cosmopolis: The Political Thought of H. G. Wells* (Aldershot: Ashgate, 2003).

———, "H. G. Wells and the World State: A Liberal Cosmopolitan in a Totalitarian Age," *International Relations*, 17/2 (2003), 233–46.

Patterson, David S., *Towards a Warless World: The Travail of the American Peace Movement, 1887–1914* (Bloomington: Indiana University Press, 1976).

———, "Andrew Carnegie's Quest for World Peace," *Proceedings of the American Philosophical Society*, 114/5 (1970), 371–83.

Paul, Diane, "Eugenics and the Left," *Journal of the History of Ideas*, 45/4 (1984), 567–90.

Payne, William Morton, "Recent Fiction," *The Dial*, 1 November 1898, 301–6.

Pennybacker, Susan, "The Universal Races Congress, London Political Culture, and Imperial Dissent, 1900–1939," *Radical History Review*, 92 (2005), 103–17.

Perkins, Bradford, *The Great Rapprochement: England and the United States, 1895–1914* (New York: Atheneum, 1968).

Perras, Arne, *Carl Peters and German Imperialism, 1856–1918* (Oxford: Oxford University Press, 2004).

Phillips, Paul, *The Controversialist: An Intellectual Life of Goldwin Smith* (Westport, CT: Praeger, 2002).

Philmus, Robert, and David Hughes (eds.), *H. G. Wells: Early Writings in Science & Science Fiction* (Berkeley: University of California Press, 1975).

Pho, Diana, "Punking the Other: On the Performance of Racial and National Identities in Steampunk" in Bowser and Croxall, *Like Clockwork*, 127–52.

Pickering, Andrew, "Cyborg History and the WWII Regime," *Perspectives on Science*, 3/1 (1995), 1–45.

Planinc, Emma, "Catching Up with Wells: The Political Theory of H. G. Wells's Science Fiction," *Political Theory*, 45/5 (2017), 637–58.

Pocock, J. G. A. "The Ideal of Citizenship since Classical Times" in Ronald Beiner (ed.), *Theorizing Citizenship* (Albany: SUNY Press, 1995), 29–52.

Poole, Thomas, *Reason of State: Law, Prerogative and Empire* (Cambridge: Cambridge University Press, 2015).

Porrovecchio, Mark, *F. C. S. Schiller and the Dawn of Pragmatism: The Rhetoric of a Philosophical Rebel* (Lanham: Lexington, 2011).

Potter, Simon, "W. T. Stead, Imperial Federation, and the South African War" in Brake et al., *W. T. Stead*, 115–32.

Preston, Andrew, *Sword of the Spirit, Shield of Faith: Religion in American War and Diplomacy* (New York: Random House, 2012).

Prévost, Stéphanie, "W. T. Stead and the Eastern Question (1875–1911); or, How to Rouse England and Why?," *19: Interdisciplinary Studies in the Long Nineteenth Century*, 16 (2013), 1–28.

Price, Peter, "Naturalising Subjects, Creating Citizens: Naturalisation Law and the Conditioning of 'Citizenship' in Canada, 1881–1914," *Journal of Imperial and Commonwealth History*, 45/1 (2017), 1–21.

Prochaska, Frank, *Eminent Victorians on American Democracy: The View from Albion* (Oxford: Oxford University Press, 2011).

Qureshi, Sadiah, *Peoples on Parade: Exhibitions, Empire and Anthropology in Nineteenth-Century Britain* (Chicago: University of Chicago Press, 2012).

Rabinich, Anson, *The Human Motor: Energy, Fatigue, and the Origins of Modernity* (Berkeley: University of California Press, 1992).

Rawls, John, *The Law of Peoples: With "The Idea of Public Reason Revisited"* (Cambridge, MA: Harvard University Press, 1999).

Recchia, Stefano, and Nadia Urbinati, "Giuseppe Mazzini's International Political Thought" in Stefano Recchia and Nadia Urbinat (eds.), *A Cosmopolitanism of Nations: Giuseppe Mazzini's Writings on Democracy, Nation Building, and International Relations* (Princeton, NJ: Princeton University Press, 2009), 1–31.

Reed, Adolph, Jr., *W. E. B. Du Bois and American Political Thought: Fabianism and the Color Line* (Oxford: Oxford University Press, 1997).

Reed, James E., "American Foreign Policy, the Politics of Missions, and Josiah Strong, 1890–1900," *Church History*, 41/2 (1972), 230–45.

Rees, Martin, *On the Future: Prospects for Humanity* (Princeton, NJ: Princeton University Press, 2018).

Reid, Cecilie, "Peace and Law: Peace Activism and International Arbitration, 1895–1907," *Peace & Change*, 29/3 (2004), 521–48.

Ricard, Serge (ed.), *A Companion to Theodore Roosevelt* (Chichester: Wiley-Blackwell, 2011).

Rich, Paul, *Race and Empire in British Politics* (Cambridge: Cambridge University Press, 1990).

———, "'The Baptism of a New Era': The 1911 Universal Races Congress and the Liberal Ideology of Race," *Ethnic and Racial Studies*, 7/4 (1984), 534–50.

Rieder, John, "On Defining SF, or Not: Genre Theory, SF, and History," *Science Fiction Studies*, 37/2 (2010), 191–209.

———, *Colonialism and the Emergence of Science Fiction* (Middletown: Wesleyan University Press, 2008).

Riesenberg, Peter, *Citizenship in the Western Tradition: Plato to Rousseau* (Chapel Hill: University of North Carolina Press, 1994).

Riskin, Jessica (ed.), *The Restless Clock: A History of the Centuries-Long Argument over What Makes Living Things Tick* (Chicago: University of Chicago Press, 2016).

———, *Genesis Redux: Essays in the History and Philosophy of Artificial Life* (Chicago: University of Chicago Press, 2007).

Roberts, Adam, *The History of Science Fiction* (Basingstoke: Palgrave, 2005).

Roberts, Andrew, "I Lay Claim to the Title 'Nostradamus of the Right,'" *Daily Telegraph*, 22 April 2004.

———, *The Aachen Memorandum* (London: Weidenfeld & Nicholson, 1995).

Roberts, Priscilla, "The Geopolitics of Literature: The Shifting International Theme in the Works of Henry James," *International History Review*, 34/1 (2012), 89–114.

———, "World War I and Anglo-American Relations: The Role of Philip Kerr and *The Round Table*," *Round Table*, 95/383 (2006), 113–39.

Robertson, Michael, *The Last Utopians: Four Late Nineteenth-Century Visionaries and Their Legacy* (Princeton, NJ: Princeton University Press, 2018).

Robertson-Scott, John William, *The Life and Death of a Newspaper* (London: Methuen, 1952).

Robinson, Dean, *Black Nationalism in American Politics and Thought* (Cambridge: Cambridge University Press, 2001).

Rodgers, Daniel, *Atlantic Crossings: Social Politics in a Progressive Age* (Cambridge, MA: Harvard University Press, 1998).

Roediger, David, "Whiteness and Race" in Bayor, *Oxford Handbook of American Immigration and Ethnicity*, 197–212.

Roemer, Kenneth M., "Paradise Transformed: Varieties of Nineteenth-Century Utopias" in Gregory Claeys (ed.), *The Cambridge Companion to Science Fiction* (Cambridge: Cambridge University Press, 2010), 79–106.

———, *The Obsolete Necessity: America in Utopian Writings* (Kent, OH: Kent State University Press, 1976).

Rofe, J. Simon, and Alan Tomlinson, "Strenuous Competition on the Field of Play, Diplomacy off It: The 1908 London Olympics, Theodore Roosevelt and Arthur Balfour, and Transatlantic Relations," *Journal of the Gilded Age and Progressive Era*, 15/1 (2016), 60–79.

Rogers, Gayle, "Restaging the Disaster: Dos Passos and National Literatures after the Spanish-American War," *Journal of Modern Literature*, 36/2 (2013), 61–79.

Rogers, Melvin, "The People, Rhetoric, and Affect: On the Political Force of Du Bois's *The Souls of Black Folk*," *American Political Science Review*, 106/1 (2012), 188–203.

Rosa, Hartmut, *Social Acceleration: A New Theory of Modernity*, trans. Jonathan Trejo-Mathys (New York: Columbia University Press, 2009).

Rose, Margaret, "Extraordinary Pasts: Steampunk as a Mode of Historical Representation," *Journal of the Fantastic in the Arts*, 20/3 (2009), 319–33.

Rosenboim, Or, *The Emergence of Globalism: Visions of World Order in Britain and the United States, 1939–1950* (Princeton, NJ: Princeton University Press, 2017).

Ross, Dorothy, *The Origins of American Social Science* (Cambridge: Cambridge University Press, 1992).

Rotberg, Robert, "Did Cecil Rhodes Really Try to Control the World?," *Journal of Imperial and Commonwealth History*, 42/3 (2014), 551–67.

———, with Miles Shore, *The Founder: Cecil Rhodes and the Pursuit of Power* (Oxford: Oxford University Press, 1988).

Rubin, Charles, *Eclipse of Man: Human Extinction and the Meaning of Progress* (New York: Encounter, 2014).

Ruddick, Nicholas, *Fire in the Stone: Prehistoric Fiction from Charles Darwin to Jean M. Auel* (Middleton: Wesleyan University Press, 2009).

Ruotsila, Markku, "Lord Sydenham of Combe's World Jewish Conspiracy," *Patterns of Prejudice*, 34/3 (2000), 47–64.

Rusert, Brit, "Delany's Comet: Fugitive Science and the Speculative Imaginary of Emancipation," *American Quarterly*, 65/4 (2013), 799–829.

Russell, Bertrand, *Portraits from Memory and Other Essays* (London: Allen & Unwin, 1958).

Sandler, Matt, "A Clanking Ride to an Uncertain Freedom," *Los Angeles Review of Books*, 10 September 2016.

Sargent, Lyman Tower, "Utopianism and the Creation of New Zealand National Identity," *Utopian Studies*, 12/1 (2001), 1–18.

———, *New Zealand Utopian Literature: An Annotated Bibliography* (Wellington: Stout Centre, 1997).

———, "The Three Faces of Utopianism Revisited," *Utopian Studies*, 5/1 (1994), 1–37.

———, "The Dream Mislaid: The Political Theory of H. G. Wells," *The Wellsian*, 10 (1987), 20–32.

Saum, Lewis, "John Fiske and the West," *Huntington Library Quarterly*, 48/1 (1985), 47–68.

Saveth, Edward N., *American Historians and European Immigrants, 1875–1925* (New York: Columbia University Press, 1948).

Schake, Kori, *Safe Passage: The Transition from British to American Hegemony* (Cambridge, MA: Harvard University Press, 2017).

Scheureman, William, *Liberal Democracy and the Social Acceleration of Time* (Baltimore: Johns Hopkins University Press, 2004).

Schmidt, Brian, "Paul S. Reinsch and the Study of Imperialism and Internationalism" in Long and Schmidt, *Imperialism and Internationalism in the Discipline of International Relations*, 43–69.

Schneer, Jonathan, "Anti-imperial London: The Pan-African Conference of 1900" in Gretchen Holbrook Gerzina (ed.), *Black Victorians / Black Victoriana* (New Brunswick: Rutgers University Press, 2003), 175–186.

Schumacher, Frank, "Lessons of Empire: The United States, the Quest for Colonial Expertise and the British Example, 1898–1917" in Ursula Lehmkuhl and Gustav Schmidt (eds.), *From Enmity to Friendship: Anglo-American Relations in the 19th and 20th Century* (Augsburg: Wissner, 2005), 71–98.

Schuurman, Paul, "Herbert Spencer and the Paradox of War," *Intellectual History Review*, 26/4 (2016), 519–35.

Schwarz, Bill, *The White Man's World: Memories of Empire* (Oxford: Oxford University Press, 2011).

Seager, Robert, *Alfred Thayer Mahan: The Man and His Letters* (Annapolis: Naval Academy Press, 1977).

Searle, Geoffrey Russell, *The Quest for National Efficiency: A Study in British Politics and Political Thought, 1899–1914* (Berkeley: University of California Press, 1971).

Secord, James, *Victorian Sensation: The Extraordinary Publication, Reception, and Secret Authorship of* Vestiges of the Natural History of Creation (Chicago: University of Chicago Press, 2001).

Seed, David, "The Land of the Future: British Accounts of the USA at the Turn of the Nineteenth Century," *European Journal of American Studies*, 11/2 (2016), 1–24.

———, "The Course of Empire: A Survey of the Imperial Theme in Early Anglophone Science Fiction," *Science Fiction Studies*, 37/2 (2010), 230–52.

Semmel, Bernard, *Liberalism and Naval Strategy: Ideology, Interest, and Sea Power during the Pax Britannica* (London: Allen & Unwin, 1986).

———, *Imperialism and Social Reform: English Social-Imperial Thought, 1895–1914* (Cambridge, MA: Harvard University Press, 1960).

Sera-Shriar, Efram (ed.), *Historicizing Humans: Deep Time, Revolution and Race in Nineteenth-Century British Sciences* (Pittsburgh: University of Pittsburgh Press, 2018).

———, *The Making of British Anthropology, 1813–1871* (London: Pickering & Chatto, 2013).

Sexton, Jay, *The Monroe Doctrine: Empire and Nation in Nineteenth Century America* (New York: Hill & Wang, 2012).

Shachar, Ayelet, Rainer Bauboeck, Irene Bloemraad, and Maarten Vink (eds.), *Oxford Handbook of Citizenship* (Oxford: Oxford University Press, 2017).

Shannon, Richard, *Gladstone and the Bulgarian Agitation 1876* (London: Thomas Nelson, 1963).

Sharp, Patrick B., *Savage Perils: Racial Frontiers of Nuclear Apocalypse in American Culture* (Norman: University of Oklahoma Press, 2007).

Shaw, Martin, "Marxism, War and Peace in Britain, 1895–1945" in Richard Taylor and Nigel Young (eds.), *Campaigns for Peace: Peace Movements in Britain in the Twentieth Century* (Manchester: Manchester University Press, 1987), 49–72.

Shaw, Stephanie, *W. E. B. Du Bois and* The Souls of Black Folk (Chapel Hill: University of North Carolina Press, 2013).

Shelby, Tommie, "Two Conceptions of Black Nationalism: Martin Delany on the Meaning of Black Political Solidarity," *Political Theory*, 31/5 (2003), 664–92.

Shepard, Andrew W., "Afrofuturism in the Nineteenth and Twentieth Centuries" in Canavan and Link, *The Cambridge History of Science Fiction*, 101–19.

Sherwood, Marika, *The Origins of Pan-Africanism: Henry Sylvester Williams and the African Diaspora* (Abingdon: Routledge, 2010).

Shilliam, Robbie, "What about Marcus Garvey? Race and the Transformation of Sovereignty Debate," *Review of International Studies*, 32/3 (2006), 379–400.

Siemann, Catherine, "The Steampunk City in Crisis" in Bowser and Croxall, *Like Clockwork*, 51–70.

Silkey, Sarah, *Black Woman Reformer: Ida B. Wells, Lynching, and Transatlantic Activism* (Athens: University of Georgia Press, 2015).

Skinner, Quentin, "On the Slogans of Republican Political Theory," *European Journal of Political Theory*, 9/1 (2010), 95–102.

Skodo, Admir, "Eugenics and Pragmatism: F. C. S. Schiller's Philosophical Politics," *Modern Intellectual History*, 14/3 (2015), 661–87.

Slusser, George, "The Origins of Science Fiction" in David Seed (ed.), *A Companion to Science Fiction* (Oxford: Blackwell, 2008), 27–43.

Smith, David, *H. G. Wells: Desperately Mortal* (New Haven, CT: Yale University Press, 1986).

Smith, Gary Love, "When Stead Came to Chicago: The 'Social Gospel Novel' and the Chicago Civic Federation," *American Presbyterians*, 68/3 (1990), 193–205.

Smith, Rogers M., *Political Peoplehood: The Roles of Values, Interests, and Identities* (Chicago: University of Chicago Press, 2015).

——, *Stories of Peoplehood: The Politics and Morals of Political Membership* (Cambridge: Cambridge University Press, 2003).

——, *Civic Ideals: Conflicting Visions of Citizenship in U.S. History* (New Haven, CT: Yale University Press, 1997).

Sneider, Allison, *Suffragists in an Imperial Age: U.S. Expansionism and the Woman Question* (Oxford: Oxford University Press, 2008).

Sparrow, Bartholomew, *The Insular Cases and the Emergence of American Empire* (Lawrence: University Press of Kansas, 2006).

Spencer, Nicholas, "Rethinking Ambivalence: Technopolitics and the Luddites in William Gibson and Bruce Sterling's *The Difference Engine*," *Contemporary Literature*, 40/3 (1999), 403–29.

Stapleton, Julia, "Citizenship versus Patriotism in Twentieth Century England," *Historical Journal*, 48/1 (2005), 151–78.

——, "Dicey and His Legacy," *History of Political Thought*, 16/2 (1995) 234–55.

Stears, Marc, *Progressives, Pluralists, and the Problems of the State: Ideologies of Reform in the United States and Britain, 1909–1926* (Oxford: Oxford University Press, 2002).

Steer, Philip, "National Pasts and Imperial Futures: Temporality, Economics, and Empire in William Morris's *News from Nowhere* (1890) and Julius Vogel's *Anno Domini 2000* (1889)," *Utopian Studies*, 19/1 (2008), 49–72.

Steinberg, Oded, *Race, Nation, History: Anglo-German Thought in the Victorian Era* (Philadelphia: University of Pennsylvania Press, 2019).

Stephanson, Anders, *Manifest Destiny: American Expansion and the Empire of Right* (New York: Hill & Wang, 1995).

Stephenson, Neil, *The Diamond Age: Or, A Young Lady's Illustrated Primer* (1995; London: Penguin, 2011).

Stirling, S. M., *The Peshawar Lancers* (New York: Ace, 2002).

Stocking, George, *Race, Culture and Evolution: Essays in the History of Anthropology* (New York: Free Press, 1968).

Stott, Annette, "A Material Response to Spiritual Crisis: Alexander Ross's Anglo-Israelist Monument of 1898–1899," *Journal of the American Academy of Religion*, 87/1 (2019), 225–59.

Strath, Bo, "Perpetual Peace as Irony, as Utopia, and as Politics" in Hippler and Vec, *Paradoxes of Peace in Nineteenth Century Europe*, 261–83.

Sumida, Jon Tetsuro, *Inventing Grand Strategy and Teaching Command: The Classic Works of Alfred Thayer Mahan Reconsidered* (Baltimore: John Hopkins University Press, 1997).

Sussman, Herbert, *Victorian Technology: Invention, Innovation, and the Rise of the Machine* (Westport, CT: Praeger, 2009).

———, "Machine Dreams: The Culture of Technology," *Victorian Literature and Culture*, 28/1 (2000), 197–204.

———, "Cyberpunk Meets Charles Babbage: 'The Difference Engine' as Alternative Victorian History," *Victorian Studies*, 38/1 (1994), 1–23.

Suvin, Darko, *Victorian Science Fiction in the UK: The Discourse of Power and Knowledge* (Boston: GK Hall, 1983).

———, *Metamorphoses of Science Fiction: On the Poetics and History of a Literary Genre* (New Haven, CT: Yale University Press, 1979).

Sylvest, Casper, *British Liberal Internationalism, 1880–1930: Making Progress?* (Manchester: Manchester University Press, 2009).

———, "International Law in Nineteenth-Century Britain," *British Yearbook of International Law* (Oxford: Oxford University Press, 2005), 9–70.

Tal, Nimrod, "Putting Out the 'Embers of This Resentment': Anglo-American Relations and the Rewriting of the British Response to the American Civil War, 1914–1925," *Journal of the Civil War Era*, 8/1 (2014), 87–110.

Tattersdill, Will, *Science, Fiction, and the Fin-de-Siècle Periodical Press* (Cambridge: Cambridge University Press, 2016).

Taylor, Paul, "W. E. B. Du Bois," *Philosophy Compass*, 5/11 (2010), 904–15.

Thaler, Mathias, "Bleak Dreams, Not Nightmares: Critical Dystopias and the Necessity of Melancholic Hope," *Constellations*, 26/4 (2019), 607–22.

Thatcher, Margaret, "The Language of Liberty," Speech to the English-Speaking Union, 7 December 1999, https://www.margaretthatcher.org/document/108386.

Thayer, Horace, *Meaning and Action: A Critical History of Pragmatism* (Indianapolis: Bobbs-Merrill, 1968).

Thomas, Katie-Louise, "Racial Alliance and Postal Networks in Conan Doyle's 'A Study in Scarlet,'" *Journal of Colonialism and Colonial History*, 2/1 (2001), 9–23.

Thomas, Sheree R. (ed.), *Dark Matter: A Century of Speculative Fiction from the African Diaspora* (New York: Grand Central, 2000).

Thompson, Andrew, *Imperial Britain: The Empire in British Politics, 1880–1932* (London: Routledge, 2000).

Thompson, J. Lee, *A Wider Patriotism: Alfred Milner and the British Empire* (London: Pickering & Chatto, 2007).

Thompson, John, "Woodrow Wilson" in Michael Cox, Timothy Lynch, and Nicolas Bouchet (eds.), *US Foreign Policy and Democracy Promotion* (London: Routledge, 2013), 53–69.

———, *Reformers and War: American Progressive Publicists and the First World War* (Cambridge: Cambridge University Press, 1987).

Thornbrough, Emma Lou, *T. Thomas Fortune: Militant Journalist* (Chicago: University of Chicago Press, 1972).

Tibebu, Teshale, *Edward Wilmot Blyden and the Racial Nationalist Imagination* (Rochester: Boydell and Brewer, 2012).

Tilchin, William, *Theodore Roosevelt and the British Empire: A Study in Presidential Statecraft* (New York: St. Martin's, 1997).

Tomes, Jason, *Balfour and Foreign Policy: The International Thought of a Conservative Statesman* (Cambridge: Cambridge University Press, 1997).

Tompkins, E. Berkeley, *Anti-Imperialism in the United States: The Great Debate, 1890–1920* (Philadelphia: University of Pennsylvania Press, 1970).

Tonooka, Chika, "Reverse Emulation and the Cult of Japanese Efficiency in Edwardian Britain," *Historical Journal*, 60/1 (2017), 95–119.

Torruella, Juan, "Ruling America's Colonies: The Insular Cases," *Yale Law & Policy Review*, 32/1 (2013), 57–95.

Toye, Richard, *Churchill's Empire: The World That Made Him and the World He Made* (Basingstoke: Palgrave, 2010).

———, "H. G. Wells and Winston Churchill: A Reassessment" in McLean, *H. G. Wells*, 147–61.

———, "H. G. Wells and the New Liberalism," *Twentieth Century British History*, 19/2 (2008), 156–85.

Trafton, Scott, *Egypt Land: Race and Nineteenth-Century American Egyptomania* (Durham, NC: Duke University Press, 2004).

Travers, T. H. E., "Technology, Tactics, and Morale: Jean de Bloch, the Boer War, and British Military Theory, 1900–1914," *Journal of Modern History*, 51/2 (1979), 264–86.

———, "Future Warfare: H. G. Wells and British Military Theory" in Brian Bond and Ian Roy (eds.), *War and Society: A Yearbook of Military History* (London: Croom Helm, 1975), 67–87.

Trefousse, Hans L., *Carl Schurz: A Biography*, 2nd ed. (New York: Fordham University Press, 1998).

Tregenza, John, *Professor of Democracy: The Life of Charles Henry Pearson* (Cambridge: Cambridge University Press, 1968).

Trotter, David, *The English Novel in History, 1895–1920* (Oxford: Oxford University Press, 1993).

Tsesis, Alexander, *We Shall Overcome: A History of Civil Rights and the Law* (New Haven, CT: Yale University Press, 2008).

Tuffnell, Stephen, "'The International Siamese Twins': The Visual Imagery of Anglo-American Inter-Imperialism" in Richard Scully and Andrekos Varnava (eds.), *Comic Empires: The Imperialism of Cartoons, Caricature, and Satirical Art* (Manchester: Manchester University Press, forth.).

———, "Anglo-American Inter-Imperialism: US Expansion and the British World, c.1865–1914," *Britain and the World*, 7/2 (2014), 174–95.

———, "'Uncle Sam Is to Be Sacrificed': Anglophobia in Late Nineteenth-Century Politics and Culture," *American Nineteenth Century History*, 12/1 (2011), 77–99.

Tulloch, Hugh, *James Bryce's American Commonwealth: The Anglo-American Background* (London: Boydell, 1988).

———, "A. V. Dicey and the Irish Question: 1870–1920," *Irish Jurist*, 15/1 (1980), 137–65.

———, "Changing British Attitudes towards the United States in the 1880s," *Historical Journal*, 20/4 (1977), 825–40.

Tully, James, "Lineages of Contemporary Imperialism" in Duncan Kelly (ed.), *Lineages of Empire: The Historical Roots of British Imperial Thought* (Oxford: Oxford University Press, 2009), 3–31.

Turrell, Robert, *Capital and Labour on the Kimberley Diamond Fields, 1871–1890* (Cambridge: Cambridge University Press, 1987).

Tuveson, Ernest, *Redeemer Nation: The Idea of America's Millennial Role* (Chicago: University of Chicago Press, 1968).

Tyrrell, Ian, and Jay Sexton (eds.), *Empire's Twin: U.S. Anti-Imperialism from the Founding Era to the Age of Terrorism* (Ithaca, NY: Cornell University Press, 2015).

United States Department of State, *Papers Relating to the Foreign Relations of the United States* (Washington, DC: Government Printing Office 1895), I, 542–45.

Valdez, Inés, *Transnational Cosmopolitanism: Kant, Du Bois, and Justice as a Political Craft* (Cambridge: Cambridge University Press, 2019).

Vandrei, Martha, "The Pilgrim's Progress," *History Today*, 70/5 (2020), 58–71.

Van Duinen, Jared, *The British World and an Australian National Identity: Anglo-Australian Cricket, 1860–1901* (Basingstoke: Palgrave Macmillan, 2017).

Van Wingerden, Sophia A., *The Women's Suffrage Movement in Britain, 1866–1928* (Basingstoke: Palgrave MacMillan, 1999).

Veracini, Lorenzo, "Isopolitics, Deep Colonizing, Settler Colonialism," *Interventions*, 13/2 (2011), 171–89.

Vermeir, Koen, "RoboCop Dissected: Man-Machine and Mind-Body in the Enlightenment," *Technology and Culture*, 49/4 (2008), 1036–44.

Villanueva, Adrià Piñol, "Halicarnassus—Salmakis: A pre-Classical *sympoliteia?*," *Klio*, 99/1 (2017), 26–50.

Virilio, Paul, *War and Cinema: The Logistics of Perception*, trans. Patrick Camiller (London: Verso, 1989).

Viroli, Maurizio, *For Love of Country: An Essay on Patriotism and Nationalism* (Oxford: Clarendon Press, 1995).

Vitalis, Robert, *White World Order, Black Power Politics: The Birth of American International Relations* (Ithaca, NY: Cornell University Press, 2015).

Vucetic, Srdjan, *The Anglosphere: A Genealogy of a Racialized Identity in International Relations* (Palo Alto: Stanford University Press, 2011).

———, "A Racialized Peace? How Britain and the US Made Their Relationship Special," *Foreign Policy Analysis*, 7/4 (2011), 403–22.

Wager, Warren, *H. G. Wells: Traversing Time* (Middletown: Wesleyan University Press, 2004).

———, *H. G. Wells and the World State* (New Haven, CT: Yale University Press, 1961).

Wagner, Kim, "Savage Warfare: Violence and the Rule of Colonial Difference in Early British Counterinsurgency," *History Workshop Journal*, 85/1 (2018), 217–37.

Waligore, Joseph, "The Christian Deist Writings of Benjamin Franklin," *Pennsylvania Magazine of History and Biography*, 140/1 (2016), 7–29.

Walker, George, "'So Much to Do': Oxford and the Wills of Cecil Rhodes," *Journal of Imperial and Commonwealth History*, 44/4 (2016), 697–716.

Walker, Thomas, "The Forgotten Prophet: Thomas Paine's Cosmopolitanism and International Relations Theory," *International Studies Quarterly*, 44/1 (2000), 51–72.

Walkowitz, Judith, *City of Dreadful Delight: Narratives of Sexual Danger in Late-Victorian London* (Chicago: University of Chicago Press, 1992).

Wallace, Elisabeth, *Goldwin Smith, Victorian Liberal* (Toronto: University of Toronto Press, 1957).

Walter, James, and Margaret MacLeod, *The Citizens' Bargain: A Documentary History of Australian views since 1890* (Sydney: UNSW Press, 2002).

Walters, Mark, "Dicey on Writing *The Law of the Constitution*," *Oxford Journal of Legal Studies*, 32/1 (2012), 21–49.

Waltz, Kenneth, *Man, the State, and War: A Theoretical Analysis* (New York: Columbia University Press, 1959).

Walzer, Michael, "Citizenship" in Ball, Farr, and Hanson, *Political Innovation and Conceptual Change*, 211–20.

Webb, Clive, "Reluctant Partners: African Americans and the Origins of the Special Relationship," *Journal of Transatlantic Studies*, 14/4 (2016), 350–64.

Weber, Peter, "The Pacifism of Andrew Carnegie and Edwin Ginn: The Emergence of a Philanthropic Internationalism," *Global Society*, 29/4 (2015), 530–50.

Wegner, Philip, *Imaginary Communities: Utopia, the Nation, and the Spatial Histories of Modernity* (Berkeley: University of California Press, 2002).

Weiner, Joel, *The Americanization of the British Press, 1830s–1914: Speed in the Age of Transatlantic Journalism* (Basingstoke: Palgrave, 2011).

Welch, Michael, "The Centenary of the British Publication of Jean de Bloch's *Is War Now Impossible?* (1899–1999)," *War in History*, 7/3 (2000), 273–94.

Wendt, Alexander, "The State as Person in International Theory," *Review of International Studies*, 30/2 (2004), 289–316.

Wertheim, Stephen, *Tomorrow, the World* (Cambridge, MA: Harvard University Press, 2020).

———, "The League of Nations: Retreat from International Law?," *Journal of Global History*, 7/2 (2012), 210–32.

Wetzel, Benjamin, "Onward Christian Soldiers: Lyman Abbott's Justification of the Spanish-American War," *Journal of Church and State*, 54/3 (2011), 406–25.

White, John, "Andrew Carnegie and Herbert Spencer: A Special Relationship," *Journal of American Studies*, 13/1 (1979), 57–71.

Whitehead, Colson, *The Underground Railroad* (2016; London: Doubleday, 2017).

Whitson, Roger, *Steampunk and Nineteenth-Century Digital Humanities: Literary Retrofuturisms, Media Archaeologies, Alternate Histories* (Abingdon: Routledge, 2016).

Whyte, Ian Boyd, "Anglo-German Conflict in Popular Fiction, 1870–1914" in F. Birdgham (ed.), *The First World War as a Clash of Cultures* (London: Boydell & Brewer, 2006), 43–100.

Wiener, Martin, *Between Two Worlds: The Political Thought of Graham Wallas* (Oxford: Oxford University Press, 1971).

Williams, Keith, "Alien Gaze: Postcolonial Vision in *The War of the Worlds*" in McLean, *H. G. Wells*, 49–75.

Williams, Paul, *Race, Ethnicity, and Nuclear War: Representations of Nuclear Weapons and Post-Apocalyptic Worlds* (Liverpool: Liverpool University Press, 2011).

Williams, William Appleman, "The Frontier Thesis and American Foreign Policy," *Pacific Historical Review*, 24/4 (1955), 379–95.

Wilson, Ann Marie, "In the Name of God, Civilization, and Humanity: The United States and the Armenian Massacres of the 1890s," *Le Mouvement Social*, 227 (2009), 27–44.

Wilson, Harris (ed.), *Arnold Bennett and H. G. Wells* (Urbana: Illinois University Press, 1960).

Wilson, Keith (ed.), *The International Impact of the Boer War* (Durham: Acumen, 2001).

Winner, Langdon, *Autonomous Technology: Technics-out-of-Control as a Theme in Political Thought* (Cambridge, MA: MIT Press, 1978).

Winter, Jay, *Dreams of Peace and Freedom: Utopian Moments in the Twentieth Century* (New Haven, CT: Yale University Press, 2006).

Wolin, Sheldon, *Politics and Vision: Continuity and Innovation in Western Political Thought*, rev. ed. (Princeton, NJ: Princeton University Press, 2004).

Wood, Harry, "Competing Prophets: H. G. Wells, George Griffith, and Visions of Future War, 1893–1914," *The Wellsian*, 38 (2015), 5–23.

Wood, John Cunningham, *British Economists and the Empire* (London: Croom Helm, 1983).

Wooley, Wesley, *Alternatives to Anarchy: American Supranationalism since World War II* (Bloomington: Indiana University Press, 1988).

Worth, Aaron, *Imperial Media: Colonial Networks and Information Technologies in the British Literary Imagination, 1857–1918* (Columbus: Ohio State University Press, 2014).

———, "Imperial Transmissions: H. G. Wells, 1897–1901," *Victorian Studies*, 53/1 (2010), 65–89.

Yaszek, Lisa, "The Bannekerade" in Isiah Lavender III (ed.), *Black and Brown Planets: The Politics of Race in Science Fiction* (Jackson: University Press of Mississippi, 2014), 15–30.

———, "Democratising the Past to Improve the Future: An Interview with Steampunk Godfather Paul di Filippo," *Neo-Victorian Studies*, 3/1 (2010), 189–95.

Younis, Musab, "'United by Blood': Race and Transnationalism during the Belle Époque," *Nations and Nationalism*, 23/3 (2017), 484–504.

Zack, Naomi (ed.), *The Oxford Handbook of the Philosophy of Race* (Oxford: Oxford University Press, 2016).

Zamir, Shamoon, *Dark Voices: W. E. B. Du Bois and American Thought, 1888–1903* (Chicago: University of Chicago Press, 1995).

Ziegler, Philip, *Legacy: Cecil Rhodes, the Rhodes Trust and Rhodes Scholarships* (New Haven, CT: Yale University Press, 2008).

Zimmerman, Jonathan, "Simplified Spelling and the Cult of Efficiency in the 'Progressive' Era," *Journal of the Gilded Age and the Progressive Era*, 9/3 (2010), 366–94.

Zimmermann, Warren, *First Great Triumph: How Five Americans Made Their Country a World Power* (New York: Farrar, Strauss & Giroux, 2002).

INDEX

Abbott, Lyman, 10, 16, 33, 91–92, 391–392

Aberdeen, 231

Acton, John Emerich Dalberg, Lord Acton, 58, 155

Adams, George Burton, 10

Adams, Herbert Baxter, 26, 60, 61

Adorno, Theodor, 246; *Dialectic of Enlightenment*, 246

Afro-American League, 374

African-Americans, 30, 35, 53n53, 79–80, 123, 252–254, 359n7, 375–384

Afrocentric reading of Egypt, 32, 376–377, 388, 391

Afromodern, political tradition, 361, 373–394

Alaskan boundary dispute, 12

Albany, New York, 284

American Civil War, 56–57, 207–208, 210, 281, 315, 359, 382

American Political Science Association, 116

The American Review of Reviews, 116, 270

American Revolution, 56–57, 64–65, 86, 128

Amery, Leopold, 194, 195, 196–197, 198

Anderson, Benedict, 37

Anderson, Stuart, 262n37

Angell, Norman, 307, 315; *The Great Illusion*, 307

Anglo-American Committee, 11, 12–13

Anglo-American League, 11

Anglo-American Union, 10–11

Anglophobia, 9–10, 50–51, 57, 66, 214–215

Anglosphere, term, 359, 362, 369

Angloworld, term, 1–2. *See also* Anglosphere, term

Anthony, Edwyn, 97

Anti-Semitism, 85n149

Arbitration: international, 13–16, 71–72, 73–88, 91–92, 98–99, 103, 109, 118–119, 128, 150–151, 242, 272, 276–277, 302, 306–307, 309n27, 310, 330–331, 332–339, 343, 348–349, 354; regulatory, conception of, 73–74, 307, 310, 354, 390; revisionary, conception of, 73–74, 118

Aristotle, 133, 136

Armenian massacres, 90

Arnold, Matthew, 44

Arnold, Thomas, 263; *History of Rome*, 263

Aron, Raymond, 7

Asquith, Herbert, 295–296

Astor, John Jacob, 190

The Atlantic Monthly, 272

Atlantic Union, 11

The Australasian Review of Reviews, 116

Australia, 2, 9, 17, 30, 37, 52, 122, 163, 200, 211, 227, 231, 256, 269–270, 274, 349, 353, 355, 360, 367; cricket, 299; Immigration Restriction Act (1901), 30, 299; "White Australia" policy, 30, 269–270

Austria, 244

Azikiwe, Nnamdi, 7

Babbage, Charles, 39, 366

Baker, Herbert, 135

Balfour, A. J., 14–16, 97, 128, 166, 230, 231, 238, 284–286, 287, 289, 299, 331–332; race patriotism, concept of, 284–286; racial union, view of, 14–16

Banal nationalism, idea of, 297–298

A NOTE ON THE TYPE

This book has been composed in Arno, an Old-style serif typeface in the classic Venetian tradition, designed by Robert Slimbach at Adobe.